TESTING THE SOCIAL SAFETY NET

TESTING THE SOCIAL SAFETY NET

The Impact of Changes in
Support Programs during the
Reagan Administration

Martha R. Burt
Karen J. Pittman

The Changing Domestic Priorities Series

John L. Palmer and Isabel V. Sawhill, Editors

THE URBAN INSTITUTE PRESS · WASHINGTON, D.C.

Copyright © 1985
THE URBAN INSTITUTE
2100 M Street, N.W.
Washington, D.C. 20037

Library of Congress Cataloging in Publication Data

Burt, Martha R.
  Testing the social safety net.

  (The Changing domestic priorities series)
  Includes bibliographical references.
  1. United States—Social policy. 2. Child welfare—
United States. 3. Mentally ill—Services for—United
States. 4. Aged—Services for—United States. 5. United
States—Politics and government—1981-
I. Pittman, Karen J., 1952-   . II. Title. III. Series.
HV95.B87   1985   361.6'1'0973   85-20878
ISBN 0-87766-392-0 (pbk.)

Printed in the United States of America
9 8 7 6 5 4 3 2

AMERICA'S CHILDREN: WHO CARES?
Growing Needs and Declining Assistance in the Reagan Era (1985),
Madeleine H. Kimmich

TESTING THE SOCIAL SAFETY NET
The Impact of Changes in Support Programs during the Reagan Administration
(1985),
Martha R. Burt and Karen J. Pittman

Conference Volumes

THE SOCIAL CONTRACT REVISITED
Aims and Outcomes of President Reagan's Social Welfare Policy (1984), edited
by D. Lee Bawden

NATURAL RESOURCES AND THE ENVIRONMENT
The Reagan Approach (1984), edited by Paul R. Portney

FEDERAL BUDGET POLICY IN THE 1980s (1984), edited by
Gregory B. Mills and John L. Palmer

THE REAGAN REGULATORY STRATEGY
An Assessment (1984), edited by George C. Eads and Michael Fix

THE LEGACY OF REAGANOMICS
Prospects for Long-term Growth (1984), edited by Charles R. Hulten and Isabel
V. Sawhill

THE REAGAN PRESIDENCY AND THE GOVERNING OF AMERICA
(1984), edited by Lester M. Salamon and Michael S. Lund

Advisory Board of the
Changing Domestic Priorities Project

CONTENTS

TABLES

THE CHANGING DOMESTIC PRIORITIES SERIES

Listed below are the titles available, or soon to be available, in the Changing Domestic Priorities Series

Books

THE REAGAN EXPERIMENT
An Examination of Economic and Social Policies under the Reagan Administration (1982), John L. Palmer and Isabel V. Sawhill, editors

HOUSING ASSISTANCE FOR OLDER AMERICANS
The Reagan Prescription (1982), James P. Zais, Raymond J. Struyk, and Thomas Thibodeau

MEDICAID IN THE REAGAN ERA
Federal Policy and State Choices (1982), Randall R. Bovbjerg and John Holahan

WAGE INFLATION
Prospects for Deceleration (1983), Wayne Vroman

OLDER AMERICANS IN THE REAGAN ERA
Impacts of Federal Policy Changes (1983), James R. Storey

FEDERAL HOUSING POLICY AT PRESIDENT REAGAN'S MIDTERM
(1983), Raymond J. Struyk, Neil Mayer, and John A. Tuccillo

STATE AND LOCAL FISCAL RELATIONS IN THE EARLY 1980s
(1983), Steven D. Gold

THE DEFICIT DILEMMA
Budget Policy in the Reagan Era (1983), Gregory B. Mills and John L. Palmer

HOUSING FINANCE
A Changing System in the Reagan Era (1983), John A. Tuccillo with John L. Goodman, Jr.

PUBLIC OPINION DURING THE REAGAN ADMINISTRATION
National Issues, Private Concerns (1983), John L. Goodman, Jr.

RELIEF OR REFORM?
Reagan's Regulatory Dilemma (1984), George C. Eads and Michael Fix

THE REAGAN RECORD
An Assessment of America's Changing Domestic Priorities (1984), John L. Palmer and Isabel V. Sawhill, editors (Ballinger Publishing Co.)

ECONOMIC POLICY IN THE REAGAN YEARS
(1984), Charles F. Stone and Isabel V. Sawhill

URBAN HOUSING IN THE 1980s
Markets and Policies (1984), Margery Austin Turner and Raymond J. Struyk

MAKING TAX CHOICES
(1985), Joseph J. Minarik

FOREWORD

This book is part of The Urban Institute's Changing Domestic Priorities project. The project is examining changes that are occurring in the nation's domestic policies under the Reagan administration and is analyzing the effects of those changes on people, places, and institutions.

When President Reagan took office, he recognized that some individuals had a legitimate claim on public support. These were the "truly needy," people whose poor health, poverty, disability, or dependency (in the case of children) was so extreme, and their resources so limited, that government had an obligation to protect them. The "social safety net," as the president termed it, was to remain intact for such individuals.

This book examines the effects of changes made during the first Reagan administration on the well-being of selected needy groups in our society. It is one of several books and papers in the Changing Domestic Priorities project that focuses on how various groups, such as minorities, children, families headed by women, and the elderly, have fared under the Reagan administration.

To test whether the social safety net indeed remained in place, Martha R. Burt and Karen J. Pittman look at three populations—abused, neglected, and dependent children; the chronically mentally ill; and the low-income elderly—people who are considered needy and vulnerable by almost anyone's definition. Each population has in the past been the beneficiary of an array of federal programs, many of which were the target of administration changes in the early 1980s. The authors' intent is to trace the effects of federal changes through state and local governments to service delivery agencies and needy people themselves. The book assembles an extensive amount of empirical information describing the characteristics and needs of the populations studied, the pre-Reagan history of federal involvement in programs directed toward

xv

helping them, and the changes enacted in these programs during the Reagan administration. Detailed information collected by the researchers in on-site visits to four geographically, economically, and politically diverse urban areas enables them to document the direct impact of recent changes on each population at the service delivery level.

The results of this assessment are discussed in the context of the administration's strong commitment to returning responsibility to the state or local level as well as the nonprofit sector and to increasing governmental efficiency. The question is raised whether, for the three populations studied, greater local commitment, more efficient program operation, or other factors have maintained an effective safety net or whether the shift away from federal involvement coupled with reduced federal financial resources has adversely affected the overall welfare of each group. The study concludes that these three populations have not been equally protected across the four jurisdictions investigated and that, in general, the necessity to serve more people with fewer resources has resulted in reduced local ability to maintain service levels.

In light of continued pressures on the federal budget and ongoing administration proposals to cut social welfare spending further, these results are instructive. As the debate goes on about the appropriate role of the federal government in providing a social safety net for the nation's most vulnerable citizens, both the local adjustments to, and the human costs of, federal retrenchment that are revealed in this volume should be carefully considered.

John L. Palmer
Isabel V. Sawhill
Editors
Changing Domestic Priorities Series

ACKNOWLEDGMENTS

Many people contributed to the success of this study. We thank Janet C. Gornick, Josephine Hobson, Madeleine H. Kimmich, and Sherry Sanborne for their assistance with data collection and agency contacts during our site visits to the four cities involved in the study. Terri Murray provided exceptional technical assistance in typing the manuscript. Agency and budget staff in all participating cities answered questions, organized meetings, provided agency records and updated material as new budgets were finalized, filled in the blanks, and generally were extremely cooperative. The manuscript reviewers contributed thoughtful and provocative comments and advice, most of which have been incorporated in the book.

The authors' own division of labor resulted in Karen Pittman having major responsibility for assembling the material and writing chapters 1, 2, 7 and 8; Martha Burt assembled the data for and wrote the remaining chapters. Both authors are jointly responsible for the introduction.

The support of the Ford Foundation and the John D. and Catherine T. MacArthur Foundation is gratefully acknowledged.

ABOUT THE AUTHORS

Martha R. Burt, director of the Social Services Research program, a part of the Human Resources Policy Center at The Urban Institute, received her Ph.D. in sociology from the University of Wisconsin in 1972. Burt's work at the Institute has covered many aspects of the social service needs of vulnerable populations. She has focused on issues such as teenage childbearing and parenting, child and adult protective services, housing and day programming needs of disabled adults, emergency food and shelter programs, service needs of the elderly, and service needs of sexual assault victims. Her publications include *Private Crisis, Public Cost: Policy Perspectives on Teenage Childbearing*, numerous articles and reports, and congressional testimony.

Karen J. Pittman is currently the director of the Adolescent Pregnancy Prevention Clearinghouse at the Children's Defense Fund in Washington, D.C., and is a Ph.D candidate in sociology at the University of Chicago. Pittman was a research associate at The Urban Institute from 1980 to 1984. Her research focuses on children, minorities, the poor, and the institutions that assist them. Her publications include *Black and White Children in America: Key Facts* and *Preventing Children Having Children*. Her work has appeared in the journal *Family Planning Perspectives*.

INTRODUCTION

The Reagan administration came into office with a plan to reduce the role of the federal government as overseer and provider for America's families and communities. Philosophically, the plan diverged from all administrations since President Franklin D. Roosevelt's New Deal of the 1930s in questioning the responsibility of government to promote general social welfare and assuage economic inequities. Its goals have been to reduce domestic spending sharply, to shift administrative, financial, and policymaking responsibility for most social programs to lower levels of government, and to ensure that the remaining federally supported programs serve only those clearly incapable of sustaining themselves without assistance. In enunciating these goals, the Reagan administration "took sides" on two important issues about the appropriate role of government in general, and the federal government in particular. The administration expressed a clear preference for private action over public action, and for local responsibility and control over federal responsibility and control.

According to administration views, if government removed itself from interference in social welfare issues, the private sector—including individuals, nonprofit agencies, and businesses—would be free to act in the best interests of needy citizens. Government was viewed as retaining some residual responsiblity to protect needy individuals, but the administration never clearly defined who deserved to receive this protection, nor did it specify how much and what kinds of protection should remain within the scope of federal responsibility.

The administration's preference for giving responsibility for social welfare programs to the private sector complements its preference for having local actors, either private or public, determine service priorities and raise the resources to meet them at the local level. Federal action was seen as overly prescriptive, controlling, demanding, and as insensitive to local circumstances, resources, and values. Local control was perceived as being better able to target resources on those most in need and apply local priorities in the distribution of those resources. President Reagan never addressed the issue of horizontal fairness—whether individuals with identical needs but living in different localities would enjoy equivalent levels of support and assistance. Yet a primary argument for federal control over social welfare programs has long been that the nation as a whole has a responsibility to its neediest individuals and that the national government must act to assure that localities provide at least minimum levels of help to those in need.

The Reagan administration has at least partially achieved its goals of reducing spending for domestic social welfare programs and of returning control to local and state governments. The question, of course, is "at whose expense?" Have private individuals, charitable organizations, and businesses stepped in to provide supports for the needy? Have state and local governments protected from deprivation and want those who cannot help themselves? Have the needy been protected uniformly across jurisdictions or have local decisions resulted in levels of support demonstrably more uneven than before the federal government withdrew a significant amount of resources from social welfare programs? In this volume we attempt to answer these questions.

The work reported here is part of the much larger Changing Domestic Priorities (CDP) project at The Urban Institute that assesses the impact of the first Reagan administration on many aspects of social policy and practice. In this book we draw on material from the larger study and refer to other publications stemming from it when they provide more extensive treatment of particular complex issues than would be appropriate for our purposes. The special characteristic of our work is its focus on *needy populations* rather than on government programs. Individuals may be eligible for and receive assistance from a large range of programs and services. Our goal was to assess the cumulative impact of numerous program changes on the well-being of certain groups of needy people.

Focus on the Truly Needy

The Reagan administration set out to contain what it believed to be a slack and billowing "social safety net." The administration maintained that while some people receiving federal government benefits needed and deserved them, some significant amount of government assistance went to people who did not truly need it. Mistargeting, mismanagement, inefficiency, fraud, and abuse were blamed for absorbing unnecessarily large portions of available resources. Martin Anderson, assistant to President Reagan for policy development during 1981 and 1982, describes the Reagan administration as "concerned about ensuring that people who cannot help themselves receive help."[1] He adds,

> When we call a program ineffective, we usually mean that the program does not work very well in achieving what we believe are essentially legitimate goals. Reagan's basic objective was to reform existing social welfare programs so that they could more effectively achieve their original goals. (p. 18)
> The objective is not to eliminate the programs. (p. 25)
> The objective is not to dump the programs on the states and localities, forcing them to raise taxes to whatever extent they can in order to continue programs.
> The objective is to improve the operation of those social welfare programs, and to reduce their costs, by returning responsibility and resources to a level of government more appropriate for these programs. (p. 25)[2]

With all the effort directed at changing programs perceived by the administration as inappropriate, has the social safety net held strong for those whom most people consider deserving of its protection?

For the purposes of this study we have assumed that being without financial resources and being unable to live or work independently by reason of age or disability qualifies a person as truly needy, especially when coupled with the absence of someone else who can fulfill a caretaker role.

This criterion encompasses more people than we had the resources to include in this study, so some further narrowing of focus was imperative. After careful consideration of the many possibilities, we decided that we should include one group from each of the broad categories of the young, the old, and the disabled. In our society, each of these broad categories of people is perceived as less able and more vulnerable than "normal adults." Within each broad category we looked for a clearly definable subcategory that was both highly vulnerable and traditionally the recipient of some form of government assistance to reduce their vulnerability. The final choices were (1) abused, neglected, and dependent children, (2) the chronically mentally ill, and (3) the low-income elderly. These three populations can be considered needy and deserving of assistance by most people's definition. We explored the effects of Reagan administration policy and program changes on the well-being of these selected groups.

The first population—abused, neglected, and dependent children—is children whose parent(s) chronically fail to provide them with the minimal

---

1. Martin Anderson, "The Objectives of the Reagan Administration's Social Welfare Policy," in D.L. Bawden, ed., *The Social Contract Revisited* (Washington, D.C.: Urban Institute Press, 1984), p. 17.
2. Anderson, "*The Objectives.*"

necessities of life (neglected children), children whose parents actively abuse them physically (abused children), or children who have been removed from parental custody (dependent children). Our culture perceives all children as vulnerable, but they are not expected to provide for their own welfare; their parents are expected to take care of them. When parents fail or refuse to support their own children or actively abuse them, those children usually have no recourse to anyone but government for protection. They are among the most vulnerable of individuals because they have neither the maturity nor the skills to protect themselves, and they have lost their natural protectors—a caring parent or parents.

The population of abused, neglected, and dependent children includes many poor children, but is not limited to the poor. Children in poverty, another subgroup of the larger category of the young, are the subject of another publication in the Changing Domestic Priorities series.[3]

The second population—the chronically mentally ill—is defined as adults wholly or partially unable to maintain "normal" levels of productivity and self-sufficiency. A vast number of disabling conditions exist, from those that constitute mere annoyances to those that completely incapacitate their victims. We selected chronically mentally ill adults as our second population because the condition is seriously disabling, affects a sizable number of people directly and a much larger number of family members indirectly, and is often mis-understood.

The chronically mentally ill suffer from a disability that often leaves them unable to tolerate the stresses of normal work and family life, unable to care for themselves or to act in their own best interests, and sometimes unable to maintain contact with reality. Under the best of circumstances their condition can be stabilized enough to enable them to live peacefully in the community, but stress and uncertainty may result in repeated short- or long-term hospitalization. Many have no network of family or friends on whom to rely for care, and many have only an erratic work history, or no work history at all. Their disability renders them vulnerable; frequently isolation means they have no one to support them; and government programs, if available, are often their only resource.

Our third population is the low-income elderly. Our society generally perceives the elderly as less capacitated than their younger cohorts, regardless of their true state of competence. Many elderly people remain healthy and active, and a large proportion also has financial security. Among the elderly,

---

3. Madeleine H. Kimmich, *America's Children: Who Cares? Growing Needs and Declining Assistance in the Reagan Era* (Washington, D.C.: Urban Institute Press, 1985).

those with low incomes are more vulnerable to disruptions and reductions in their quality of life from many causes.

People in this group have usually earned all they are going to earn in their lifetimes and frequently live on fixed incomes just barely adequate to meet their regular expenses. Many have chronic illnesses or disabilities that restrict their activities or that partially or totally incapacitate them. While many have existing family and support networks, others live alone or far from family members. The older they are, the more likely they are to be isolated, incapacitated, and poor. Any extraordinary circumstance, and even some predictable ones, are likely to strain their resources beyond their capacity. Serious illnesses or injuries, winter heating bills, rising property taxes, or simply increasing disability due to various conditions accompanying advancing age pose major threats to the well-being of the low-income elderly.

We selected these populations because, in addition to meeting our criteria for defining people with important claims on government for protection and support, they meet several other criteria. They contain sizable numbers of individuals in need of assistance. They all have complex service needs that under existing institutional arrangements cannot be met without drawing on multiple sources of funding and often multiple service providers. Because of these complex needs (needs for housing, income assistance, health and social services), small changes in benefits and services from individual programs can have large cumulative impacts. Finally, all have been targets of important federal programs that the Reagan administration has changed in significant ways.

Approach

The guiding question in this volume is, "what has happened to services for these three populations?" Answering this question inevitably leads to discussions of changes in the funding, administration, and regulation of the many federal programs that serve these populations. The focus of the book, however, is on changes in the levels, types, and adequacy of supportive services available to these populations, not on changes in programs. The provision of comparable or consistent services is at the heart of the Reagan promise to maintain government support for highly vulnerable groups. As Martin Anderson articulates the administration's goals, *more effective programs* pursuing the same goals was the objective.[4]

---

4. Anderson, "*The Objectives*," pp. 18, 25.

How could services for the truly needy have remained intact in the face of federal cuts in program budgets and policy changes affecting eligibility, services covered, and maximum allowable costs? Several possible adjustments could have occurred, either separately or in combination, that would have left services for the three selected populations at levels comparable to those existing before Reagan took office.

First, federal cuts and regulatory changes may not have affected these populations, although policy changes may have reduced services to other populations. Second, states and localities could have raised local revenues to replace federal cuts directed toward these groups. Third, states and localities could have shifted their priorities so that the reduced level of funding was targeted more specifically on services for these populations (albeit other populations would then experience disproportional cuts in service). Fourth, states and localities may have offset reduced funding by increased administrative efficiency and service coordination. Fifth, states and localities may have shifted clients to open-ended federal programs when categorical federal funds were cut. Thus services would continue and the federal coffers would continue to pay for them, despite the federal intent to reduce its commitment to financing these programs. Sixth, the nonprofit sector may have filled the gap left by loss of federal support.

This sort of shifting, setting priorities, and belt tightening is very much in line with the Reagan administration's goals to reduce domestic spending overall and to transfer responsibility for domestic social programs to states, localities, and the private sector. If public and private agencies in states and localities have taken enough of these actions to protect services for the truly needy, we would conclude that the administration's faith in the "new federalism" was sound, and that its domestic policies were successful.

At a different level of action, support for needy populations could have been maintained, or even improved, by fundamental redesign or reform of programs at the federal level. Observers have long criticized the ability of public programs to meet the needs of the three populations under study here. For example, years of dissatisfaction with child welfare services, excessive use of foster care, and low frequency of adoption had culminated in the Adoption Assistance and Child Welfare Act of 1980 just before Reagan assumed the presidency. Deinstitutionalization of the chronically mentally ill had proved unsuccessful from the point of view of the individual welfare of former mental patients because communities did not have programs to make stable community residence feasible. Families were experiencing great strain in caring for their poor and frail elderly members; many elderly had lost family members and had no one to take care of them; and resources to provide health care and social supports were severely strained. The Reagan administration, in its avowed desire to improve program effectiveness, might have undertaken a thorough review and overhaul of critical programs for these populations in an effort to better achieve the program goals of helping people who cannot help themselves. In subsequent chapters we look at the extent to which this happened.

Certainly the pre-Reagan mix of services was not optimal. It is possible that budgetary pressures could force agencies to redesign their services in ways that constitute absolute improvements over previous arrangements. However, we would judge that offering fewer services, in the face of stable or increased need, indicates an actual reduction in the level of commitment to protect the truly needy. The ultimate test of success lies in documenting actual changes in services to the populations under study and determining whether programs have been able to maintain or increase their assistance to needy individuals in accordance with program goals.

Documenting changes in services requires an understanding of the needs of the populations being studied. Next, a thorough knowledge is required of the programs that cumulatively serve these populations, including the changes these programs have undergone during the Reagan years. Most important, information is needed from the local level on changes in services—changes in numbers of clients served, in the quality, quantity, coordination, or timeliness of the services, and in the relation between public and private funders and service providers.

Documenting changes in federally funded, regulated, or administered programs is a formidable task. Documenting changes in services to specific populations supported by those programs is nearly impossible. We must move from the black and white of budgets and numbers served to the grayness of impressions, conjectures, and waiting lists. Clinicians, practitioners, and case workers—those providing or coordinating the services for the elderly, the mentally ill, and the children coming into the child welfare system—seldom have time to document the changes they are trying to handle. Nonetheless, it is with them that the story lies. This volume, therefore, presents a combination of impressions and numbers.

Methodology

Since service delivery occurs at the local level, we went to four cities and their surrounding counties in order to gather data on the impact of federal changes. The choice of cities was constrained by several factors. Primary among these was a large research effort under way at The Urban Institute— the Changing Domestic Priorities project—to trace the impact of Reagan administration policies and actions, of which this study is a small part. The project involved a sample of eighteen states, so the cities chosen for this volume had to be in those states. This condition meant that researchers at the city level would have a great deal of state-level data available from other components of the project. In addition, several other project components would also use city-based data, so the cities had to meet the research needs of a variety of people. Cities had to be geographically diverse. A variety of different fiscal conditions and governmental philosophies was desirable. Based on these considerations, the four cities chosen were San Diego, Richmond, Detroit, and Boston.

These four cities (or, more accurately, urban areas because their respective surrounding counties are included in the data) differed substantially in their economic structure and condition.[5] Boston's economy is expanding and is driven by high-technology manufacturing and financial, medical, and educational services. Detroit is heavily dependent upon manufacturing, and particularly automobile manufacturing. It suffers disproportionately from cyclical downturns and is, in addition, experiencing longer-term problems due to foreign competition. Richmond's economy is stable and diversified, with state and local government the largest employer and the Phillip Morris Company the largest private employer. San Diego has experienced explosive growth, driven both by military installations and defense contractors and by high-technology manufacturing, particularly in the electronics and biomedical industries.

The long-term fiscal situation of local governments in the areas has reflected the condition of their local economies, institutional constraints, and political cultures. San Diego and Boston have been constrained by state limitations on local revenue raising (Propositions 13 and $2 \frac{1}{2}$, respectively). San Diego's political culture might best be termed as aggressively conservative with a preference for market-oriented solutions and a small governmental role (except for environmental and amenity issues). Boston's spending levels, until constrained by Proposition $2 \frac{1}{2}$—which placed severe limits on use of the property tax—have been characterized by traditional northeastern liberalism. Detroit's fiscal situation has been seriously affected by the decline of the automobile industry since the late 1970s. The duration and severity of the resulting revenue shortfalls have mitigated Detroit's traditional union-oriented liberalism and propensity for high levels of public spending. Richmond, a consolidated city-county, perceives itself as constrained from increasing its tax rates and thus its spending because of tax competition with surrounding

---

5. This paragraph and the next one are taken from Harold Wolman, "The Urban Impact of Federal Policy during the Reagan Era: Evidence from Four Case Studies," Urban Institute Working Paper (Washington, D.C.: Urban Institute, 1984).

suburban counties. Richmond's political culture is dominated by traditional conservatism with a preference for low taxation and spending.

In each city and county we determined which agencies served each of the three selected populations. We interviewed managers and case workers from government agencies who were primarily responsible for the well-being of the populations. We also interviewed staff of private agencies and organizations serving the populations, and advocacy groups if they were available. We collected budget and caseload data for the years under study (1981 to 1983), and also gathered extensive impressions, anecdotes, and explanations of what was happening to agency clients.

The Plan of the Book

This volume is organized into three parts. Part I focuses on abused, neglected, and dependent children; part II, on the circumstances of the chronically mentally ill; and part III looks at the low-income elderly. Each part is further divided into three chapters. The first chapter in each part describes the population; the second chapter, the major federal programs affecting the population with details on the changes that have taken place in those programs at the federal level under the Reagan administration; and the third chapter, the impact of federal program changes on the population at the local level, using the data collected from our case studies in four cities. The concluding chapter of the book summarizes the findings and discusses them in light of administration goals and promises.

PART ONE

CHILDREN IN THE CHILD WELFARE SYSTEM

CHAPTER 1

WHO ARE THE ABUSED, NEGLECTED, AND DEPENDENT CHILDREN?

The past ten to fifteen years have seen tremendous strides in public, governmental, and professional concern for vulnerable children, yet the number of abused and neglected children has continued to grow, and children who need substitute care have placed heavy burdens on welfare agencies. Who are these children? What is being done to help them, and is it enough?

As commonly understood, *neglected children* are children whose parents show chronic and long-standing failure to provide them with the necessities of life, while *abused children* are children who are exposed to physical harm or endangerment. *Dependent children* are children who receive substitute care—that is, those living in foster homes, group homes, or institutions rather than with their families. In the parlance of child welfare agencies, children in substitute care are dependent on the state, not their parents.

This chapter describes these vulnerable children, looks at the size and composition of the populations of abused and neglected children and children in substitute care, examines characteristics of these populations such as family income and race, and identifies their special needs. Chapter 2 outlines the development of federal legislation and programs affecting these children and discusses changes proposed or enacted by the Reagan administration. Changes in actual services offered to these children are reviewed in chapter 3.

The Populations of Vulnerable Children Defined

Reliable figures on the total size of the population of vulnerable children are not available. Many but not all states report child abuse and neglect cases to the federal government, but until quite recently (1982 or later) states did not reliably record the numbers or status of children in foster care. The data we have come from special studies commissioned by the Department of Health and Human Services. These studies did not consistently cover every year, nor did they always report the same data in the same format. Even more important, they did not always report the reasons for placing children in substitute care, so the overlap in the abused and neglected population and the substitute care population can only be estimated. The remainder of this chapter contains the most precise estimates available, even though some figures are from the 1970s.

Annual estimates of the number of abused and neglected children in the United States in 1981 placed the number at more than 850,000, compared to about 416,000 in 1976—an increase of 104.5 percent over a five-year period. Between 1977 and 1982, children in substitute care dropped from 502,000 to 243,000—a decrease of 51.6 percent. The majority of this decrease occurred between 1977 and 1979. Even so, approximately a quarter of a million children were in substitute care each year between 1979 and 1982 (table 1).

TABLE 1

ESTIMATES OF THE NUMBERS OF ABUSED AND NEGLECTED CHILDREN AND
CHILDREN IN SUBSTITUTE CARE IN THE UNITED STATES, SELECTED YEARS, 1976–82

Reported Cases of Abuse and Neglect		Children in Substitute Care	
Year or Period	Number	Year or Period	Number
1976	416,033	1977	502,000
1977	516,142	1979	301,943
1978	614,291	1980	273,913
1979	711,142	1981	273,000
1980	788,000	1982	242,897
1981	850,980		
1976–81 (percent change)	104.5	1977–82 (percent change)	−51.6

SOURCES: The reported cases of abuse and neglect for all years except 1981 are from American Humane Association, "National Analysis of Official Child Neglect and Abuse Reporting" (Washington, D.C.: Department of Health and Human Services, 1979); the 1981 figure is from U.S. Department of Health and Human Services, National Center on Child Abuse and Neglect, *Guidelines for Policy and Programs* (Washington, D.C.: U.S. Government Printing Office, 1982). The national estimates of the substitute care population are from the following: 1977—Ann Shyne and Anita Schroeder, *National Study of Social Services to Children and Their Families* (Rockville, Maryland: Westat, Inc., 1978); 1979—Department of Health and Human Services, Office of Civil Rights, "Children and Youth Referral Survey of Public Welfare and Social Service Agencies" (Washington, D.C.: DHHS, 1980); 1980—Child Welfare League of America, Inc., "Foster Care Population for 1980: Final Estimate (New York: CWLA, 1983); 1981—Toshio Tatara, *Characteristics of Children in Substitute and Adoptive Care: A Statistical Summary of the VCIS National Child Welfare Data Base* (Washington, D.C.: American Public Welfare Association, 1983); and 1982— "Child Welfare Indicator Survey" (McLean, Virginia: Maximus, 1983).

These figures, chilling in their own right, are extremely sobering when one realizes that they are static, not cumulative, numbers. They represent the annual incidence of child abuse, neglect, and dependency. If one assumes that half of the cases seen by child welfare officials are new to the agency and half represent recurring or continuing problems, at present rates as many as one out of ten children would be neglected or abused and one out of thirty would be placed in substitute care at some point during childhood.

Abused and neglected children and children in substitute care represent only a subset of the vulnerable children receiving public social services in the United States. These children are at high risk of becoming statistics in abuse, neglect, or substitute care caseloads. In 1977 there were an estimated 1.8 million children whose families were receiving supportive services such as counseling or homemaker assistance, supplemental services such as day care, or substitute care services such as foster care or residential care (see table 2). The abused and neglected children and children in substitute care were the largest subgroups. In the same year there were 502,000 children receiving substitute care and more than 516,000 children receiving services following reports of neglect or abuse. These two figures represent somewhat overlapping populations, since about one-third of abuse and neglect cases are also in substitute care.[1]

We focus on abused, neglected, and dependent children because the quality and availability of services for these children stand as a barometer for services to all vulnerable children. These children have intensive service needs, and historical data indicate that they are likely to remain on the caseload rosters for years if aggressive actions are not taken by service providers soon after they enter the system. Services for these children have been singled out by both legislators and professionals during the Reagan administration as greatly in need of revision and expansion.

Characteristics of the Populations

Abused and Neglected Children

It is difficult to say whether the sharp increase in the number of reported cases of abuse and neglect between 1976 and 1981 reflects an actual rise in the incidence of abuse and neglect or changes in reporting rates. All sectors at all levels have focused both attention and funds on child abuse and neglect in recent years. As a result, the public has become more aware and more

---

1. Ann Shyne and Anita Schroeder, *National Study of Social Services to Children and Their Families* (Rockville, Maryland: Westat, Inc., 1978).

TABLE 2

CHILDREN AND THEIR FAMILIES RECEIVING SOCIAL SERVICES IN 1977
(*N* = *1.8 million*)

Type of Service	Percent Receiving Specific Children's Services of Those Receiving Any Service
Substitute services	
Adoption	5
Foster family care	25
Group homes	3
Institutional care	4
Residential care	3
Emergency shelter care	n.a.
Supplementary services	
Day care (for purposes other than employment or training)	16
Day treatment	2
Supportive services	
Protective	33
Health	26
Mental health	9
Counseling	19
Educational	10
Transportation	11
Legal	0
Financial or employment assistance	0

SOURCE: Ann Shyne and Anita Schroeder, *National Study of Social Services to Children and Their Families* (Rockville, Maryland: Westat, Inc., 1978), table 3.2. Figures are rounded.

n.a.   Not available.

willing to report abuse and neglect, state and local capabilities for processing reports have improved, and the definitions of abuse and neglect have been expanded to include emotional, sexual, moral, medical, and educational maltreatment in addition to physical harm or endangerment.

Reports striving to heighten public awareness of the problem repeatedly emphasize that every child is a potential victim; as noted in a recent report from Maine's Department of Human Services, "Child abuse and neglect occurs in urban, suburban, and rural areas, in all racial groups and in families

with a wide range of incomes. The incidence rate for overall maltreatment is almost identical for white children and black children."[2]
Patterns of Abuse and Neglect. Child abuse and neglect are often addressed as if they were a single phenomenon. Yet as Shyne and Schroeder note in their comprehensive study of social services to children, "the characteristics and circumstances of the children and the nature of the agency response in cases of neglect seem to differ sufficiently from those in cases of abuse to call for their separate consideration."[3]

Data collected in the late 1970s indicate that child neglect is twice as common as child abuse. Child abuse, however, transcends income levels. It is less closely linked with poverty (28 percent of abused children receiving services were from AFDC families, as opposed to 39 percent of neglected children; see table 3).

TABLE 3

COMPOSITION OF POPULATIONS OF ABUSED AND NEGLECTED CHILDREN,
1979 AND 1980
(*Percent*)

Category	All Children, 1980	Children Receiving Services, 1979	
		Neglected	Abused
Race			
White	79	63	67
Black	15	27	19
Other	7	11	14
Public assistance status			
AFDC recipient family[a]	6	39	28
Nonrecipient family	94	61	72

SOURCE: Data for all children in 1980 are from U.S. Bureau of the Census, *Statistical Abstracts: 1981* (Washington, D.C., U.S. Government Printing Office, 1980); Data for children receiving services in 1979 are from Shyne and Schroeder, *National Study of Social Services*. Figures are rounded.

  a.   Aid to Families with Dependent Children.

Abused children are more likely to be white than are neglected children. White children are underrepresented in both the abused and neglected populations, but they make up a slightly larger proportion of the abused population (table 3). Black children are only slightly more likely to be among the abused

---

2. Michael Petit and Donna Overcash, *America's Children: Powerless and in Need of Powerful Friends* (Augusta, Maine: Maine Department of Human Services, 1983), p. 64.
3. Shyne and Schroeder, *National Study of Social Services*.

population than their representation in the general population population would suggest, yet they are twice as likely to be part of the population of neglected children as their representation in the general population would indicate.
Incidence among Low-Income Families. Although abuse and neglect are universal threats to children, the incidence of child abuse and neglect is closely linked to poverty and to the stressful social, familial, and emotional problems that accompany it: "It is no accident that neglect, abuse, delinquency, and other definitions of social pathology are found in high proportions in neighborhoods where there is also an accompanying high level of infant mortality, poor educational achievement, low income, and inadequate health services. Also, there is the absence of viable social institutions that can provide the programs and resources that could help families cope with the day-to-day task of surviving in an urban environment."[4]

Data reported by the National Center on Child Abuse and Neglect indicate that the incidence of abuse and neglect is ten times higher among families with incomes below $7,000 than among families with incomes of $25,000 or more.[5] These figures probably overstate the actual differences in incidence rates because of the differential approach used in handling situations of suspected abuse and neglect in low-income as opposed to middle-income areas. Middle-income families are less likely than low-income families to appear as statistics in public reports because of their access to private sources of support (physicians, psychologists) and because of the reluctance of these private practitioners to comply with mandatory reporting laws.[6] Nonetheless, both statistics and research indicate an increased likelihood of neglect and abuse among low-income families. Families headed by a female single parent are at high risk for child abuse and neglect, contributing almost three times the number of cases that their frequency in the general population would suggest.[7]

---

4. George Silcott, "Institutionalized Social Bankruptcy Equals Child Abuse, Therefore Today's Challenge: Family Life Preservation," in Michael L. Lauderdale et al., eds., *Child Abuse and Neglect: Issues in Innovation and Implementation*, Proceedings of the Second National Conferences on Child Abuse and Neglect, vol. 1. (Washington, D.C.: U.S. Department of Health, Education, and Welfare 1978), p. 15.

5. U.S. Department of Health and Human Services, National Center on Child Abuse and Neglect, *Guidelines for Policy and Programs* (Washington, D.C.: U.S. Government Printing Office, 1982).

6. Private physicians in Westchester, New York, for example, reported only 6 of the 891 cases investigated by child protective services staff in 1976. Data are from Silcott, "Institutionalized Social Bankruptcy."

7. Based on data for families reported for child abuse and neglect from American Humane Association, "National Study on Child Neglect and Abuse Reporting," annual report (Denver: AHA, various years); and data for all families from U.S. Bureau of the Census, *Statistical Abstract of the United States* (Washington, D.C.: U.S. Government Printing Office, 1981), tables 61 and 62.

There is considerable overlap between these families and public welfare recipients, strongly suggesting the role of poverty rather than single parenthood per se as a backdrop for abusive or neglectful behavior. The 7 million to 8 million children receiving AFDC (Aid to Families with Dependent Children) and the 12 million to 13 million children living in families below the poverty line at any given time constitute a vast reservoir of high-vulnerability children, some significant proportion of whom will receive child protective services (services resulting from an abuse or neglect report) before reaching age eighteen.[8]

Children in Substitute Care

Although exact counts are not available, it is clear from estimates made by a variety of sources that the number of children in substitute care is declining. The number may not have dropped as precipitously as the estimates suggest (about 50 percent between 1977 and 1982), but it has decreased as a result of national, state, and local efforts to keep families together when solutions are possible and to move children who are in substitute care into permanent living arrangements as quickly as possible.

The use of substitute care, like the incidence of neglect and abuse, is related to poverty, race, and single parenthood. In 1980, 40 percent of the children in substitute care were minorities (32 percent were black); 1977 data show that 38 percent of the children were from families receiving AFDC payments.[9] A 1978 study reported that 60 to 80 percent of the children in foster care had been receiving some form of public assistance before they entered the system.

Abuse and neglect stand out as the foremost reasons why children receive substitute care. Indications are that, as reporting rates increase, abuse and neglect may account for as many as half of the substitute care cases.[10]

---

8. U.S. Congress, House, Select Committee on Children, Youth, and Families, *U.S. Children and Their Families: Current Conditions and Recent Trends*, 98th Cong., 1st sess. (Washington, D.C.: U.S. Government Printing Office, May 1983); and Jane Knitzer, Mary Lee Allen, and Brenda McGowan, *Children without Homes: An Examination of Public Responsibility to Children in Out-of-Home Care* (Washington, D.C.: Children's Defense Fund, 1978).

9. National estimates of the substitute care population are from the following: 1980 estimate from Child Welfare League of America, Inc., "U.S. Foster Care Populations for 1980: Final Estimate" (New York CWLA, 1983); 1977 estimate from Shyne and Schroeder, *National Study of Social Services*.

10. Administration for Children, Youth, and Families, "Child Welfare Research Notes no. 1: Characteristics of Children in Foster Care" (Washington, D.C.: U.S. Department of Health and Human Services, 1983).

The Special Needs of These Vulnerable Children

Reporting Abuse and Neglect, Community Efforts, and Agency Follow-up

Abused and neglected children stand out as truly needy even among other groups of vulnerable children because they need not only intensive services but widespread community awareness and cooperation in order to receive those services. Among the general population of children receiving all types of social services, about one-quarter of the cases were referred by parents.[11] The parents of abused and neglected children, however, rarely report themselves. Reports come frequently from nonprofessionals in the community— friends, neighbors, relatives. Medical, school, social service, and law enforcement personnel together account for about half of the reports.[12] Clearly, then, any efforts to help neglected and abused children must focus on the need for timely reporting and swift and thorough follow-up. The sharp increases in reporting rates during the past decade attest to the value of the general educational and organizational efforts to identify neglected and abused children and of the increased capability of agencies to follow up on reports. The National Center on Child Abuse and Neglect notes, however, that there is some evidence indicating an inverse relation between reports and resources; that evidence suggests "communities may respond by becoming less likely to report child maltreatment when they perceive that the response to the report will not be adequate."[13] Given the almost complete reliance of abused and neglected children on the voluntary efforts of community members for help, this perceived relation could be a serious problem.

Changing Attitudes: Deemphasis on Substitute Care

While the most distinctive changes in the nation's response to child abuse and neglect have been in community awareness of the problem, yielding higher reporting rates which begin the process that often culminates in substitute care placement, the most important changes in substitute care since the 1970s have been in the attitudes of those directly or indirectly involved in placement decisions. Legislators and professionals alike have begun to realize the importance of removing children from the substitute care system.

---

11. Ibid., p. 49.
12. American Humane Association, "Study on Child Neglect and Abuse Reporting," annual report (Denver: AHA, 1979 and 1983).
13. Richard Blume, "Foster Care in the United States: The State-of-the-Art" (Washington, D.C.: Social Services Research Institute, 1981).

The problem is that the number of actors involved in the child welfare system—from individual caseworkers to state legislators to officials who set federal policy and funding priorities—makes it difficult to implement this philosophical change.

In 1975 the Children's Defense Fund conducted an extremely comprehensive investigation of the U.S. foster care system. The major findings of that study, briefly outlined below, have since been confirmed by numerous other studies.[14]

1. Removing a child from the home in a situation of abuse or neglect is often the easiest course. Funds for removal are available; funds for alternative services (day care, homemaker services, alternative housing, and so on) are often unavailable or inadequate.

2. When a child is removed from the home, placement with relatives is often not actively pursued. In some states foster care payments cannot be made to relatives, thus many children who could maintain family ties are denied the opportunity if relatives cannot afford to take them in without financial assistance.

3. Once a child receives substitute care, parents are not explicitly encouraged to maintain contact with the child; sometimes they are actively discouraged by agency regulations. Parents wanting to maintain contact are not helped by the agency. Transportation funds are not provided even though the child may be placed at some distance from the parents. Parents are not routinely kept informed about their children's progress. Sometimes they are not even informed when their children are moved.

4. While the child is in substitute care, parents generally obtain little help in alleviating the problems that led to placement. Funds for services that would enable the family to be reunited are seldom available.

5. Even when parental ties with the child have been severed, either because of abandonment by the parents or the inaction of public agencies, parental rights are rarely terminated. Thus the child no longer has meaningful contact with the parents, but the parents retain legal control of the child.

6. For the child who has had (or should have) parental rights terminated, efforts to ensure adoptive homes are often inadequate. Adoption efforts are hampered by fiscal barriers, inadequate funds for subsidized adoptions or

---

14. See, for example, S. Vasaly, *Foster Care in Five States: A Synthesis and Analysis of Studies from Arizona, California, Iowa, Massachusetts, and Vermont* (Washington, D.C.: Office of Human Development, U.S. Department of Health and Human Services, 1976); Robert Mnookin, "Foster Care: In Whose Best Interest?" *Harvard Educational Review*, vol. 43 (1973); and David Fanshel and Eugene Shinn, *Children in Foster Care: A Longitudinal Investigation* (New York: Columbia University Press, 1978).

legal fees, and deeply embedded views that certain children—minority children, older children, and children with special medical needs—are "hard to place," and thus "unadoptable."

Although professional views on the treatment of child abuse and neglect cases have begun to deemphasize removing the child from the home and punishing the parents, substitute care may be necessary in instances in which a case-worker cannot satisfactorily guarantee that the child will be safe in the home while services are being provided. At least in theory, however, most child welfare agencies are now committed to using substitute care only as a last resort. While substitute care is the appropriate solution for some children with serious emotional, mental, or physical problems, a full three-fourths of the children in care are there not because of their problems but because of the problems of their caretakers.[15] This fact shapes the recommendations for the types of service perceived as preferable to substitute care.

Focus on Supportive and Supplementary Services

In place of substitute care the new perspective emphasizes a variety of supportive and supplementary services such as counseling, parent training, homemaker services, and day care, which combine to strengthen and stabilize the at-risk family. Professionals now realize the importance of focusing treatment efforts on *both* parents and children to break destructive family behavior patterns and provide all family members with new role models and coping skills. Among the specific services listed as possibilities for abused and neglected children by the National Center on Child Abuse and Neglect are early childhood programs; therapeutic day treatment for children with developmental delays, psychological problems, or both; special education for school-age children exhibiting emotional or learning problems; psychological counseling and therapy; and general community supports such as Big Brother programs and YMCA or YWCA activities.[16] For parents, parent education, family planning services, self-help groups, homemaker services, parent aides, crisis nurseries, and assistance with housing, transportation, and employment are just some of the possible supports suggested in addition to therapy. The emphasis is both on helping the parents change their behavior and on helping to remove some of the chaotic or stressful characteristics of their lives that provoke or exacerbate abusive or neglectful behavior.

---

15. Cynthia Ragan, Marsha Salus, and Gretchen Schultze, *Child Protection: Providing Ongoing Services* (Washington, D.C.: National Center on Child Abuse and Neglect, Department of Health and Human Services, 1977).

16. Shyne and Schroeder, *National Study of Social Services.*

Many of these services are seen as "soft" services by state and local legislatures and by agencies themselves. Their value has yet to be firmly established; their applicability in specific cases is often questionable; and they require more coordination and case management effort than their alternative, substitute care. Expenditures for preventive services have increased in recent years, but they still represent only a fraction of the dollars spent on substitute care.

The Push toward Permanency: Some Results

The most telling characteristic of the substitute care population is not a characteristic of either the children or their families, but of the system itself. Substitute care is supposed to be a short-term, emergency solution; it should not be accepted as a permanent solution except in rare cases. Several studies have found that the prospects of reuniting parents and children diminish rapidly after eighteen months to two years. This relatively short timespan for durability of the family bond makes intensive preventive and early reunification efforts essential. Yet in 1982 the average length of time in care was almost three years (thirty-five months). This period is an improvement over the average length of time in 1977 (forty-seven months), but it is still a long time. In 1981, about 50 percent of the children who left substitute care returned home, but 33 percent left because they had reached the age of majority.[17]

Preplacement Services are now viewed as both legitimate and effective, although their use is still hampered by the lack of funds and clear guidelines for matching families with services. Reunification and adoption services have also been intensified as a result of the push by the professional community (spearheaded by the Children's Bureau of the Department of Health and Human Services) to see every child as potentially placeable in a permanent home. By 1980, legislation (The Adoption Assistance and Child Welfare Act) authorized funding for subsidized adoptions and for upgraded preplacement and reunification efforts.

This recent push toward permanent homes for abused or neglected children has not benefited all subgroups of the substitute care population equally, however. For some groups of children who have been in substitute care for years, now appropriately called "special-needs children"—including the handicapped, minority, and older children—adoption is their only hope for

---

17. Toshio Tatara, *Characteristics of Children in Substitute and Adoptive Care: A Statistical Summary of the VCIS National Child Welfare Data Base* (Washington, D.C.: American Public Welfare Association, 1981). The age of majority is sixteen, eighteen, or twenty-one years of age, depending on state and sex of the child.

permanency.[18] Assisting these children requires intensive and often unconventional outreach methods; in many cases, child welfare personnel must be reoriented to understand that these cases are worth the effort. For these children, adoption is often largely dependent on adoption subsidies, either because of the child's entry characteristics, such as presence of a medical condition, or the adoptive family's income.

An example of one group of special-needs children is children with a minority background. The percentage of the substitute care population that is minority has increased steadily since the mid-1970s.[19] Several studies suggest that this increase is at least partially due to differences in the nature and amount of effort put forth by the child welfare agencies, not in the entry characteristics of the children.[20] Minority children tend to remain in substitute care longer. If these children are Hispanic, they are less likely to have had their ties to parents legally severed even though they have been in such care longer; and once parental rights have been terminated, they are less likely to find adoptive homes. Thus, although some results of the emphasis on permanency are positive, more effort rather than less needs to be exerted if all children in substitute care are to benefit.

Summary

Child abuse and neglect reporting have increased dramatically since the mid-1970s, at the same time that foster care placements and the number of children in foster care have dropped by about half. Abuse and neglect are major causes of placement in substitute care.

Poverty, often linked to race and single parenthood, appears as a major factor in neglect cases, and a less dominant but still significant factor in abuse cases. The increasing numbers of families and children living in poverty during the early 1980s may be an important precipitating condition of increases in child abuse and neglect reporting. Expanded public awareness of the issue is undoubtedly another contributing factor.

---

18. These children officially defined as having special needs are handicapped, minority, and older children, children with medical needs, and children who are members of a sibling group for whom placement together in a single foster home is deemed the preferred solution.

19. In 1977, 38 percent of this population was minority; in 1981–82, 46 percent. Figures are from, respectively, Shyne and Schroeder, *National Study of Social Services*; and from Tatara, *Characteristics of Children*, and "Child Welfare Indicator Survey" (McLean, Virginia: Maximus, Inc., 1983).

20. Arthur Emlen et al., "Overcoming Barriers to Planning for Children in Foster Care" (Portland, Oregon: Portland State University, U.S. Department of Health, Education, and Welfare, 1978); and Tatara, *Characteristics of Children*.

As the declining substitute care rates indicate, the child welfare system is responding to the need for prevention and permanency planning. The system, however, was not and still to a large extent is not designed to provide these services. Its strength is substitute care; it has a payment mechanism for substitute care; and inertia favors substitute care. Preference for substitute care was based first on the now outmoded belief that swift removal from an undesirable family setting was in the child's best interests. Now, by and large, continued reliance on substitute care responds to federal funding priorities that make such care the most financially attractive solution for local governments to use in resolving family problems (even though the costs of long-term substitute care far outweigh those of prevention, reunification, or adoption services). There is now a national child welfare policy that reflects current beliefs favoring active early intervention and prevention services, but child welfare services will be slow to respond to this legislation without the support of federal funds. The next chapter explores federal child welfare programs and policies.

CHAPTER 2

FEDERAL POLICIES AND PROGRAMS AFFECTING VULNERABLE CHILDREN

The 1960s and early 1970s saw a rapid growth in the federal financing of social services. Sparked by the Public Welfare Amendments of 1962, which legislated federal-state cost sharing for social services aimed at reducing or preventing dependency, federal expenditures soared. Between 1967 and 1972 federal expenditures grew from $281.6 million to $1.7 billion, a phenomenal increase even after allowing for inflation.

The federal role in financing children's services expanded concomitantly during these years. By the mid-1970s federal dollars accounted for about half of the total public spending on child welfare services. It was not until the enactment of P.L. 96-272, the Adoption Assistance and Child Welfare Act of 1980, however, that the federal government aggressively attempted to develop and implement a national child welfare policy.

The first and second sections of this chapter briefly outline the federal activities in child welfare before the 1980 act, summarize the changes created by the act, and discuss the effects of the law based on its first years of implementation. The third section details the changes and attempted changes in child welfare legislation and funding during President Reagan's first term.

Federal Involvement in Child Welfare, 1960–79

The Social Security Act of 1935 marked the first venture of the federal government into child welfare. Title IV(A), Aid to Dependent Children (later Aid to Families with Dependent Children, or AFDC), specifically addressed the financial needs of children in families deprived of parental support. Title IV(B), Child Welfare Services, encouraged states to develop, strengthen, or expand preventive and protective services for all vulnerable children, regard-

27

less of income, by providing limited federal funds to states through formula grants.

1960–69

In the 1960s legislation was enacted that substantially increased federal financial involvement in child welfare. As many excellent reports have made clear, however, these efforts served to encourage what in the late 1970s became widely publicized as a "national disgrace"—the rampant and often indiscriminate placement of children in foster care.[1]

1961—AFDC Foster Care, Title IV(A). In 1961 Congress passed legislation requiring states to provide foster care as part of their AFDC programs. Federal funds were available for room and board (maintenance) costs only, not for preventive, reunification, or even case-management services; these funds were available only when the child had been removed from the home as a result of a judicial determination, that is, not placed in care under a voluntary agreement with parents. By 1979, the total cost of caring for 104,000 of the estimated 300,000 children in foster care who were AFDC Foster Care recipients was more than $350 million, about half of which was federal funds.[2] The AFDC legislation significantly eased the burden of substitute care costs for states, but because few demands were placed on states to either justify or limit foster care, and limited federal effort was devoted to encouraging the use of alternative services, this open-ended source of funds reinforced the premature and often prolonged use of foster care as a solution to family problems.

1965—Medicaid, Title XIX. With the creation of Medicaid, medical assistance was extended to AFDC children in foster care. Again, while easing states' financial obligations and ensuring that children in care would receive adequate medical attention, this legislation inadvertently created an additional disincentive to permanency planning for AFDC Foster Care children—these children would now lose both maintenance reimbursements and medical coverage if adopted by families whose incomes were over the eligibility cutoffs for these programs.

---

1. Jane Knitzer et al., *Children without Homes: An Examination of Public Responsibility to Children in Out-of-Home Care* (Washington, D.C.: Children's Defense Fund, 1978); and Joseph Persico, *Who Knows? Who Cares? For Other Children in Foster Care* (New York: The National Commission on Children in Need of Parents, 1979).

2. The 1977 data cited in U.S. Congress, Senate, Committee on Finance, *Report on the Adoption Assistance and Child Welfare Act of 1979*, 96th Cong., 2d sess. (October 2, 1979), lists the federal share as 52 percent (table 1).

1968—Emergency Assistance Program. Title IV(A) of the Social Security Act was amended in 1968 to include an emergency assistance program that allowed states to provide services to families in crisis, including emergency shelter care and financial assistance. States could establish their own eligibility requirements. Federal matching funds were made available for emergency assistance provided for a maximum of thirty days in any twelve-month period. This program had the potential of keeping children out of long-term care by providing timely and targeted assistance. It was never fully implemented, however. Ten years after the legislation was enacted only half of the states were participating in the program (many states, however, used IV(B) monies for emergency shelter). Federal expenditures in 1978 were only $40 million.

1970–79

The 1970s saw a shift in federal involvement in child welfare. As research began consistently to document the substantial disparities among existing state and local programs, the federal government attempted to take a more active role in shaping the nature and quality of services provided to vulnerable children.

1972—Increased Authorization for Title IV(B). In 1972 Congress increased the authorization for funding child welfare services under Title IV(B) in an effort to encourage states to develop and expand supportive, protective, and preventive services, thereby decreasing reliance on foster care. Slightly less than $200 million was authorized for fiscal 1973, rising to $266 million in fiscal 1976 and thereafter. Appropriations did not come close to authorized levels, however, growing only from $45 million in 1970 to $56.5 million in fiscal 1979 (an actual decrease of 38 percent after adjusting for inflation). The language of Title IV(B) is progressive, encouraging states to "establish, extend and strengthen public social services which supplement parental care and keep families intact." But the low level of funding, combined with the lack of enforceable restrictions on the use of IV(B) funds, rendered the legislation ineffective as a control over state actions. Title IV(B) funds represent only 5 percent of total expenditures for child welfare. Without tight federal restrictions, the states have overwhelmingly used them to pay for substitute care. In fiscal 1976 less than 20 percent of federal Title IV(B) funds was spent on nonemployment-related day care, protective services, or adoption services.[3]

---

3. U.S. Department of Health, Education and Welfare, Public Service Administration, Social and Rehabilitation Service, "Child Welfare Expenditures by Type of Service, Fiscal Year 1976," (Washington, D.C.: DHEW, 1976).

1972—Cap on Social Services Expenditures. As noted at the outset of this chapter, the Public Welfare Amendments of 1962 created a major surge in federal social services spending. A doubling of expenditures between 1971 and 1972 ($741 million to $1,688 million) led Congress and the administration to place a $2.5 million cap on social services expenditures in 1972. This cap made it even more difficult for states to develop and use services that were alternatives to foster care.

1974—Child Abuse Prevention and Treatment Act (P.L. 93-247). This act established the National Center on Child Abuse and Neglect as the focal point for federal efforts to address the growing number of reports on abuse and neglect that, by the mid 1970s, had clearly evolved as a national problem. Authorized at $85 million for a four-year effort ($15 million in fiscal 1974; $20 million in fiscal 1975, $25 million in fiscal 1976 and in fiscal 1977), the act also provided funds to assist states, localities, and nonprofit organizations to develop preventive programs and services for abused and neglected children and their families. To be eligible for grants, states had to meet specific reporting and procedural requirements. This program, unlike IV(B), has been funded close to the authorization levels ($18.2 million in fiscal 1977).

The act has been quite effective in producing nationwide reform in public awareness of and states' responses to reports of abuse and neglect, as the increases in the number of reported cases described in chapter 1 suggest. The act does not, however, address services or procedures for children brought into the child welfare system as a result of these reports.

1975—Grants to States for Social Services, Title XX. Congress made a major effort in 1975 to improve state services to intact families, thereby hoping to reduce current and future dependency, through passage of another amendment to the Social Security Act, Title XX.[4] Although it did not focus specifically on children, Title XX was seen as a landmark step toward developing comprehensive and effective social services for neglected, abused, and dependent children and adults.

Under Title XX the states were given increased authority, responsibility, and flexibility in choosing and running programs and in defining the populations eligible for these programs. Title XX allowed a broad range of services (child care, protective services, foster care, homemaker services, transportation, training and employment services, nutrition and health-support services, family planning services), and opened up eligibility considerably. Service beneficiaries could be recipients of AFDC, Supplemental Security Income, or Medicaid and could also

---

4. Title XX combines the open-ended entitlement programs, which were part of Title IV(A) emergency assistance and services to AFDC families, and Title XVI services for the aged, blind, and disabled, and Supplemental Security Income recipients.

be any persons earning no more than 115 percent of the state median income (recipients earning between 80 and 115 percent of the median had to be charged for services, however, and 50 percent of the service recipients had to be on AFDC, Supplemental Security Income, or Medicaid rosters).

Title XX, like Title IV(B), had the potential of encouraging states to develop or strengthen prevention, protection, and permanency planning (reunification or adoption) services for children. The $2.5 billion cap on social service expenditures enacted in 1972, however, remained in effect under the new legislation, making Title XX more like a compromise that gave states flexibility than a new federal effort to lead states. By 1977 thirty of the fifty states had reached their spending ceiling—many had been at the ceiling for several years—and were effectively barred from developing new programs or expanding client eligibility using Title XX support unless they shifted money from some other services for that purpose.

Title XX, nonetheless, is a major source of social services funding for vulnerable children and their families. Title XX supplied approximately 30 percent of the budget for state child welfare services by 1982, compared to 52 percent from state, local, and private sources and 18 percent from other federal sources (Title IV(B), Title IV(E/A0, and other miscellaneous federal funds). On average about one-third of Title XX recipients are children; they receive about one-half of the Title XX dollars. Even though Title IV(B) has child welfare as its focus, Title XX has been the effective federal funding source for child welfare services since its enactment.

To summarize, by the end of the 1970s the federal government had enacted several pieces of legislation intended to encourage the development of preventive, protective, and reunification or adoption services, but that legislation provided few financial incentives or regulatory mechanisms for states to fully implement these alternatives to foster care. AFDC-Foster Care remained an open-ended entitlement program while Title IV(B) child welfare services and Title XX faced limited funding and could not adequately support the development of services for children in line with the legislative intent. When the decade closed, nearly three-fourths of all child welfare monies were devoted to foster care. Although some states were making significant strides in reducing their foster care loads through administrative reform and development of alternative services, there was no strong, unified push from the federal government for this to happen across the board.

The Adoption Assistance and Child Welfare Act of 1980

The most significant development in federal policy for child welfare occurred in 1980 when Congress approved the Adoption Assistance and Child

32   TESTING THE SOCIAL SAFETY NET

Welfare Act (P.L. 96-272). The act set forth a comprehensive set of standards for child welfare, stipulating improved casework practices and new protections and services for children in the system. As one official at the Department of Health and Human Services put it, "For the first time, the legislation reaches down and directly affects the experience of the individual child who comes in contact with the system."[5] By October 1983, state plans were supposed to demonstrate that reasonable preventive efforts had been made for each child prior to out-of-home placement and that reasonable efforts had been made to reunite family and child.

In addition to planning requirements aimed at ensuring more limited and appropriate use of out-of-home care, the 1980 legislation presented a set of fiscal incentives to help shift the service emphasis away from foster care. First, the act provided federal reimbursement for adoption subsidies for AFDC children with "special needs" (usually defined by states as older, minority, or handicapped children or children who are members of sibling groups and need to be kept together) and for continued Medicaid coverage after adoption (until age eighteen). While forty-five states already had some type of adoption subsidy program in place, this provision formally removed the financial barrier that kept many children in foster care.

Second, the act placed a conditional ceiling on federal support for foster care maintenance. Federal matching funds for AFDC foster care payments under Title IV(A) had been available to states on an open-ended, entitlement basis. The new legislation, which replaced Title IV(A) Foster Care with new Title IV(E) foster care and adoption assistance, sought to reduce the use of foster care in favor of preventive efforts by capping federal foster care funds when appropriations for Title IV(B) child welfare services reached specified amounts. For fiscal 1981 the trigger was $163 million; it was $220 million fiscal 1982, and $266 in fiscal years 1983 and 1984. In effect, the trade-off was more money for prevention, but less for foster care.

Third, the act allowed states to transfer unused foster care maintenance funds (funds below the state's ceiling) to child welfare services.

Fourth, the act ensured that increased Title IV(B) funds would go only to states conforming to the new state plan procedures and that these additional funds (above the states' pre-P.L. 96-272 share of $56.6 million, the 1980 allocation) would not be used for foster care maintenance, adoption assistance, or employment-related child care. Also, to be eligible to receive its share of the increased Title IV(B) appropriation, a state had to maintain its 1979

5. Margot Schenet "Federal Expectations for P.L. 96-272: Child Welfare Reform," Working Paper (Washington, D.C.: Urban Institute, October 1982).

spending level—it could not use the new federal dollars to replace state dollars.

Fifth, the act increased the federal matching rate for IV(B) funds to 75 percent. The rate had varied from 33 to 66 percent.

In 1981, the act's first funding year and the last year controlled by the Carter administration, Title IV(B) appropriations jumped from $56.5 million to $163.5 million—the level necessary to trigger the ceiling on federal foster care payments. The Title IV(E) ceiling was set at $349.2 million. Adoption assistance, an open-ended entitlement program, received an appropriation of $5 million, but only $442,000 was claimed by states that first year.

Many states had already begun to take legislative and administrative steps toward implementing the early intervention and permanency planning philosophy, as the drop in number of foster care cases before 1980 indicates. Thus, although no one would attribute all the changes in child welfare services since 1980 to the enactment of the Adoption Assistance and Child Welfare Act, the new legislation clearly made permanency planning a national goal and facilitated action at the state level. A comprehensive review of fiscal 1982 state child welfare program plans conducted by The Urban Institute found the requirements for receiving additional Title IV(B) monies to be a major influence on the long-range goals and objectives set by states.[6] For example, thirty-one states (60 percent) planned to develop or expand pre-placement preventive services; twenty-nine states (56 percent) listed initial implementation of a foster care tracking system or modification of an existing system; and seventeen states (33 percent) proposed to begin offering or to expand reunification services.

Federal Title IV(B) expenditures represent approximately 5 percent of the total child welfare services funding in most states, and cannot be considered a significant financial resource for states.[7] Similarly, the financial incentives it offers must be considered weak given its overall impact on child welfare spending. Yet, early indications are that change has occurred not only in goals but in services. Expenditures for foster care maintenance payments and services dropped from absorbing almost three-quarters of child welfare funds (from all sources) in fiscal 1979 to less than half in fiscal 1982. Pre-

---

6. In fiscal 1980, 34 percent of the primary recipients of Title XX were children (based on "Social Services U.S.A.," 1979–1980," table 11, statistical tables prepared by the Department of Health and Human Services, Office of Human Development Services, 1982). Budget data from state plans show that half of the states allocated more than 46 percent of their Title XX funds to children in 1982. See Madeleine H. Kimmich, "State Child Welfare Program Plans: Service Budgets and Expenditure Reports," Contract Report (Washington, D.C: Urban Institute, August 1983).

7. Ibid.

ventive and protective services concomitantly increased their share of child welfare funds from 8 percent to a little more than 23 percent.[8]

Again, the 1980 legislation was more the culmination of state efforts and earlier federal efforts (largely through the Children's Bureau) than it was the catalyst for new state initiatives. Its funding level, even when fully funded, was not sufficient to compel states to redirect their service emphases. The legislation nonetheless was seen as significant by child welfare administrators and advocates. For some, it reinforced strong claims that change was needed and made legislative battles easier when funds were difficult to procure. For many others, the act served as a guide for designing and implementing those changes. Thus it stood as the first major federal attempt to develop and implement a national child welfare policy.

Child Welfare during the Reagan Years, 1981–84

The states entered the 1980s with a renewed commitment to bringing child welfare services in line with the growing philosophy of early prevention and permanency planning. Title XX, the major federal funding source for child welfare services, was capped (1981 federal expenditures were $2.99 billion, up only $30 million from 1978). Title IV(B) was, for the first time, fully funded with appropriations at $163.5 million (the level necessary to trigger the cap on foster care funds), up $107 million from the previous year. Even with full funding, of course, Title IV(B) could supply only a fraction of the support available from Title XX. Adoption assistance funds were available for the first time, and grants to states for child abuse and neglect reporting were holding constant at about $7 million.

The Reagan administration sought to reverse the newly implemented trends in child welfare services. It met with only partial success as the figures in table 4 show, but its intent was clear—it proposed not only to reduce funding for child welfare services but, because of less federal involvement, to make irrelevant the complex balance of protections and fiscal incentives that were built into the 1980 legislation.

Reagan's proposals for child welfare legislation followed the general philosophy of his administration: they sought to reduce the federal role and turn responsibility back to states and localities. Funding reductions in this area, as in other human services, were based on assumptions that removing one layer of government would reduce costs through better management and greater efficiency, and therefore that programs and recipients would benefit,

---

8. Ibid.

TABLE 4

FEDERAL OUTLAYS FOR CHILD WELFARE SERVICES, FISCAL YEARS 1981–84
(*Millions of Dollars unless Otherwise Indicated*)

| | | | | | Percent Change, 1981–84 | |
| | | | | | Current Dollars | Constant Dollars[a] |
Legislation	*1981*	*1982*	*1983*	*1984*		
Title XX (social services)	2,813	2,536	2,684	2,693	−4.3	−17.6
Title IV(B) (child welfare services)	180	162	160	165	−8.3	−21.1
Title IV(E) (Foster care and adoption assistance)	328	261	410	435	32.6	14.2
Child abuse and neglect (state grants portion)	7	7	7	7	0	−13.9
Total	3,328	2,966	3,261	3,300	0.8	−14.6

SOURCE: Madeleine H. Kimmich, *America's Children: Who Cares? Growing Needs and Declining Assistance in the Reagan Era*, (Washington, D.C.: Urban Institute Press, 1985), table 3. Figures are rounded.

   a.   Real changes calculated by using deflator of the Office of Management and Budget (1972 base year).

or at least not suffer, from budget cuts. Reagan's budget documents retain all the pre-Reagan language describing program goals and objectives—even his proposal to convert child welfare funding to a block grant still adheres to goal statements paralleling those of the Adoption Assistance and Welfare Act of 1980. The administration made no apparent attempt to rethink or restructure child welfare services as such, other than to apply its basic strategy of defederalizing child welfare by proposing, unsuccessfully, a block grant for child welfare.

   Presumably, then, the Reagan administration espoused, or at least did not specifically change or repudiate, the intent of child welfare programs to ''strengthen families, prevent family break-up, and enable children to remain in their homes. In cases where children must be placed outside the home, the objective is to return these children home as soon as possible; or, when this is not possible, to secure suitable adoptive homes.''[9] It is appropriate, therefore, to evaluate the administration's actions by looking at the impact on prevention, reunification, and permanency planning.

---

   9. *Budget of the United States Government, FY 1983 Appendix* (Washington, D.C.: U.S. Government Printing Office, 1983), p. I-K59.

In both fiscal 1982 and fiscal 1983 the Reagan administration attempted to repeal the Adoption Assistance and Welfare Act. It proposed a block grant for child welfare that would combine funding for child welfare services, Title IV(B); foster care, Title IV(E); and adoption assistance, Title IV(E). Federal funds under this proposal would have been 20 percent below fiscal 1981 levels. If passed, this block grant would have removed both the financial incentives for developing alternative services to foster care and the requirements that states improve tracking, case planning, and case review capabilities in order to receive additional child welfare services funding. Also, given the 20 percent cut and the inevitable decision by states to fund crisis services first, the prevention, reunification, and adoption services would almost certainly have suffered as states attempted to meet increasing demands with fewer dollars.

Having just passed the 1980 Adoption Assistance and Welfare Act, Congress was unwilling to repeal it. The legislation remained intact, and the proposals to reduce funding by 20 percent were rejected. The foster care and adoption assistance programs were maintained as entitlements, ensuring funding for all eligible children. Child welfare Title IV(B) appropriations were cut back 4 percent from the fiscal 1981 level of $163.5 million—a significant cut given the expectation on the part of both Congress and the states that Title IV(B) appropriations would increase under the act. Authorization for fiscal 1982 was $220 million, up from $163 million in fiscal 1981.

In fiscal 1984 the administration sought to cap federal funds for foster care, Title IV(E), thereby eliminating the entitlement program that had been in effect since 1961 but without a compensatory increase in prevention, reunification, and adoption assistance. Congress rejected this proposal. The administration also sought to hold Title IV(B) at $156.3 million for the third year while eliminating $4 million available for training in fiscal 1983 through the Child Welfare Training Program. Congress raised Title IV(B) appropriations to $165 million.

As the Children's Defense Fund notes in its analysis of the 1984 budget, Congress was able to keep the legislation and most of the funding intact, but the administration was still able to undermine the 1980 act by delaying both issuance of final regulations and review of states that had self-certified that they were in compliance with the law in order to receive additional Title IV(B) funds.[10]

---

10. Children's Defense Fund, *A Children's Defense Budget: An Analysis of the President's FY 1984 Budget and Children* (Washington, D.C.: CDF, 1983).

Besides attempting to dismantle the 1980 act, the Reagan administration attempted to eliminate the Child Abuse Prevention and Treatment Act in fiscal 1982. Congress rejected the proposal, but funds for the program were reduced from $23 million to $16 million. State grants for responding to abuse and neglect reports were essentially held constant at a little below $7 million. In fiscal 1983 the administration proposed a 31 percent cut in the state grant portion of the program and further proposed to merge child abuse demonstration funds with other human services research and demonstration monies. Congress rejected these proposals. The state grants were maintained at $6.7 million, and child abuse research and demonstration programs were funded at $9.5 million.

The Reagan administration was more successful at cutting and altering Title XX. As described above, Title XX was in many ways already a block grant that allowed states considerable latitude in setting service priorities and funding levels. However, the shift to a block grant (the social services block grant) did bring with it some important changes: (1) previously separate appropriations for social services, training, and child care were merged; (2) states were no longer required to match federal funds (one state dollar for every three federal dollars); and, most important, (3) states were no longer required to commit 50 percent of their funds to welfare recipients. Presumably in exchange for these relaxed requirements, funding for fiscal 1982 was 21 percent lower than that for fiscal 1981.

An additional 17 percent cut in the social services block grant was proposed for fiscal 1983. Congress rejected this proposal and maintained the block grant at its fiscal 1983 authorized level, $2.45 billion. At the beginning of fiscal 1983 the administration reduced the funding level to $2.4 billion. Congress later appropriated $225 million for Title XX social services block grant services under the Emergency Job Bill. After receiving intensive lobbying by over eighty national organizations, Congress appropriated $2.68 million for the Title XX social services block grant in fiscal 1984.

Summary

What impact has the Reagan administration had on federal funding for services for vulnerable children? Congress has been particularly aggressive in rejecting the administration's proposals to cut child welfare funding and blunt the impact of the 1980 legislation. The effect has been that federal funds for services to vulnerable children have only decreased slightly in absolute terms during the Reagan years. These decreases have been exacerbated by inflation and, more important, by increased demand for services. A survey conducted by the National Committee for the Prevention of Child Abuse reported that thirty-nine states had seen an increase in abuse reports during 1982. Other states and localities reported that abandonment cases were up, as were requests for emergency shelter.[11] The number of children in foster care is rising across the country,[12] as the increased federal outlays for Title IV(E) foster care funds attest.

As we described in chapter 1, there is an undeniable relation between poverty and the vulnerability of children. The percentage of children living below poverty has been rising steadily since 1970 according to census data. In the single year from 1980 to 1981 this percentage jumped 1.6 percent; in the next year it rose an additional 1.8 percent, and in the following year, 0.4 percent.[13] In total there was an increase of 21 percent in children living in poverty during the first three years of the Reagan administration. Despite this trend, the administration proposed cuts not only in social services for children, but in almost every program that affects them. A separate Urban Institute book, *America's Children: Who Cares? Growing Needs and Declining Assistance in the Reagan Era*, shows this clearly.[14] Of the twenty federal programs that form the nucleus of federal support for children, only one program, Head Start, consistently received increased federal support between 1981 and 1984. Four other programs experienced net increases during that period, but their fortunes fluctuated from year to year. As we show in detail in the next chapter, these across-the-board cuts, especially in AFDC, increased the demand for all types of child welfare services at a time when states, recoiling from multilevel jolts to their budgets, could least afford to step up their response.

11. Cited in Children's Defense Fund, *A Children's Defense Budget*.
12. Madeleine H. Kimmich, *America's Children: Who Cares? Growing Needs and Declining Assistance in the Reagan Era* (Washington, D.C.: Urban Institute Press, 1985).
13. U.S. Bureau of the Census, *Current Population Reports*, series P-60, no. 138 (1981), table 17.
14. Madeleine H. Kimmich, *America's Children*.

CHAPTER 3

WHAT HAS HAPPENED TO ABUSED, NEGLECTED, AND DEPENDENT CHILDREN?

To investigate the impact of policy changes from 1981 to 1984 on local services and children involved in the child welfare system, we visited four local jurisdictions—San Diego, Detroit, Richmond, and Boston—and spoke with public officials and private providers (see the introduction to this book for selection criteria). In this chapter we review the budget data for the local governmental units responsible for child welfare, their caseloads for selected services, and the changes that have taken place in services since 1981.

Budget Changes

Budget data were available for three of the four selected jurisdictions. Funding for child welfare services has been reduced significantly during the period of study in both San Diego and Richmond and has been increased somewhat in Massachusetts (tables 5–7). San Diego's budget cuts came largely at the county level, although federal reimbursements for intake services (child protection referral and investigation) also fell by 12 percent after adjusting for inflation. The San Diego County budget is subject to extreme constraints, not only from Proposition 13 but also from the county's own version of tax relief, Proposition J. The county contribution to the welfare of its own abused, neglected, and dependent children fell 21 percent for intake services and 30 percent for placement and supervision services, respectively, after adjusting for inflation. These cuts reflect San Diego's priorities, which do not focus heavily on children who need protection.

Richmond's child welfare services budget was also reduced, significantly for foster care services, but dramatically for child protective services (down 14 percent and 65 percent, respectively, after adjusting for inflation). Other factors that limited children's access to protective services were the increased

TABLE 5

SAN DIEGO BUDGET FOR CHILD WELFARE SERVICES, FISCAL YEARS 1981–83

Type of Service	Budget for State Fiscal Year ($ Thousands)			Percent Change, 1982–83	
	1981	1982	1983	Current Dollars	Constant Dollars
Child intake services					
Federal	n.a.	3,206	2,955	−8	−12
Title XX social services block grant	n.a.	2,472	2,868	5	0
Title IV(B)	n.a.	200	0	−100	−100
Other	n.a.	264	87	−67	−68
County	2,746	2,664	2,406	−12[a]	−21[a]
Fees and other revenue	n.a.	25	138	452	430
Total	5,899	5,895	5,499	−7[a]	−16[a]
Child placement and supervision services					
Federal	n.a.	5,893	6,630	13	8
Title XX social services block grant	n.a.	3,068	3,783	23	18
Title IV(B)	n.a.	376	0	−100	−100
Other	n.a.	2,449	2,847	16	12
County	1,901	2,456	1,463	−23[a]	−30[a]
Fees and other revenue	n.a.	1,405	965	−31	−34
Total	9,817	9,754	9,058	−8[a]	−17[a]

SOURCE: San Diego Department of Social Services budget documents. Figures are rounded.

n.a.   Not available.

a.   Data are for 1981 to 1983.

number of cases (which almost tripled from six to sixteen cases per month), and the drastic reduction in the average grant for purchasing child protective services (from more than $2,000 per case to about $350 per case). Richmond's child protection staff is clearly faced with doing much more with much less.

Massachusetts averted reductions in child welfare services with major infusions of state resources. The state experienced a significant drop in federal Title XX social services block-grant funding available for child welfare, even though Massachusetts devoted its entire Title XX allocation to children's services. It also received significant increases in federal child welfare payments from Title IV(B), but the total dollar amounts did not compensate for Title XX losses. Service increases approximately matched the greater amount of resources available.

TABLE 6

RICHMOND BUDGET FOR CHILD WELFARE SERVICES,
FISCAL YEARS 1981–83

Type of Service	Budget for State Fiscal Year ($ Thousands)			Percent Change, 1981–83	
	1981	*1982*	*1983*	*Current Dollars*	*Constant Dollars*
Foster care					
State and federal reimbursememts	1,434	1,557	1,411	−2	−11
City	998	967	908	−9	−18
Total	2,432	2,524	2,319	−5	−14
Protective services					
State and federal reimbursements	10	6	4	−60	−64
Grants	13	8	5	−62	−65
City	3	2	1	−67	−70
Total	26	16	10	−62	−65

SOURCE: Richmond Department of Public Welfare budget data. These figures are for direct outlays for children receiving services but do not include staff salaries. Figures are rounded.

Detroit (Wayne County) could not provide budget data because, as a local office of a state agency (the Michigan Department of Social Services), it receives staffing equivalents instead of dollar figures from the state. The full-time-equivalent staffing levels in Detroit have remained relatively constant overall, although some specific services have lost heavily, as discussed below. At the same time, demand has skyrocketed for both child protection investigations and foster care placements, placing great strain on staff resources.

Caseloads

To fully appreciate the budget changes in the four jurisdictions, the dollar figures should be compared to caseload figures—what are the dollars being required to do, and do they begin to meet the need? Table 8 presents changes in child welfare caseloads between 1981 and 1983 to shed some light on this critical question. In San Diego and Richmond, the two jurisdictions with significant budget reductions for child welfare, the demand for services increased at the same time that the agencies responsible for care had fewer resources to meet the need. San Diego experienced an increase of 29 percent

TABLE 7

MASSACHUSETTS BUDGET FOR CHILD WELFARE SERVICES,
FISCAL YEARS 1981–83[a]

| | Budget for State Fiscal Year ($ Thousands) | | | Percent Change, 1981–83 | |
Type of Service	1981	1982	1983	Current Dollars	Constant Dollars
Federal	77,765	61,087	67,309	−13	−22
Title XX social services block grant	77,322	59,100	60,300	−22	−30
Title IV(B)	443	1,794	6,723	1,418	1,272
Other	...	193	286	48[b]	42[b]
State	94,935	129,413	136,691	44	30
Total	172,700	190,500	204,000	18	7

SOURCE: Massachusetts Department of Social Services. Local data for Boston were not available, but Boston receives a consistent proportional share of the state allocation. Figures are rounded.

a. Massachusetts allocated all of its social services block-grant funds to children's services beginning in 1982.

b. Data are for 1982 to 1983.

in requests for investigation of potential instances of child abuse, neglect, or dependency, in conjunction with a decrease of 16 percent in resources for the intake unit. Staff ability to respond to these requests worsened in both speed of response and numbers of cases receiving investigations. In addition, the county had to reduce slightly the number of children to whom they could offer protective supervision in their own homes (instead of removing them from their homes). It also reduced the number of children in substitute care. Overall, these figures indicate that, although the number of cases continued to grow, services did not keep pace with demand.

Richmond, like San Diego, experienced a significant increase in the number of cases receiving child protective services at the same time that staff resources and grant monies to deal with these cases were reduced.

Boston and Detroit also experienced increased demand for child welfare services, but only in Boston did the state provide the financial resources to meet the need (both states lost significant amounts of federal dollars for child welfare services). Alone among the sites, Michigan saw foster care caseloads increase despite the concerted nationwide effort to reduce the number of children in foster care, especially those receiving such care for prolonged periods. Ironically, Michigan was a leading state in promoting this nationwide effort. The increase in foster care levels in that state, therefore, attests to the

TABLE 8

CHANGES IN CHILD WELFARE CASELOADS, FISCAL YEARS 1981–83
(*Average Monthly Caseloads unless Otherwise Indicated*)

Jurisdiction and Service	*1981*	*1982*	*1983*	*Percent Change, 1981–83*
San Diego				
Child protective services				
requests	2,693	3,311	3,465	29
AFDC foster care	3,098	3,024	2,880	−7
Protective supervision				
in own home	1,980	2,016	1,920	−3
Detroit (Wayne County)				
Child protective services				
requests	7,158	8,285	12,242	71
AFDC foster care	2,265	2,934	2,867	27
Richmond				
Child protective services[a]	6	16	16	167
AFDC and non-AFDC foster				
care	563	563	550	−2
Boston (Region VI)[a,b]				
Child protective				
services	2,787	2,876	3,226	12
All foster and group				
care	1,877	1,630	1,601	−15
Protective supervision				
in own home	4,314	4,079	4,646	8

SOURCES: Department of Social Services data or personal communication from jurisdictions. Percentages are rounded.

a. Number of children, not number of requests or investigations.

b. In June of each year.

severe effects of unemployment, recession, and the accompanying strains on the ability of families to cope. Detroit has a significantly greater proportion of its children living below the poverty level than the other cities we visited— approximately 32 percent, compared to between 13 and 15 percent for the other cities. These poverty figures are for 1979, before the recession and unemployment hit other areas of the country (it was just beginning then in Detroit). In conjunction with a higher level of poverty than the other cities examined, the more extreme effects of the recession (unemployment hit 20 percent in Detroit in 1982) undoubtedly contributed to Detroit's increased need to use foster care placements.

Agency Service Structures and Populations Served[1]

In all four jurisdictions we visited, the department or division of social services has primary responsibility for child protective services and substitute care services. In two jurisdictions, Detroit and Richmond, income maintenance programs—aid to families with dependent children (AFDC), Medicaid, food stamps—operate through a separate division of the same department. In the other two cities, San Diego and Boston, a different department handles these programs. Regardless of structure, units handling the social services aspects of substitute care must coordinate with units administering AFDC, since the majority of foster care placements receive support from the AFDC-Foster Care program.

San Diego's Department of Social Services handles all child protection, emergency placement, foster care placement, and adoptions for children in the public protection system. The department's children's services are organized into two divisions, Child Intake Services and Child Placement and Supervision Services. San Diego views children's services on a continuum from intake and emergency response through preventive work with families to potential placement or adoption. The department works with both voluntary and court-ordered cases.

According to the 1980 census, children under age eighteen made up 25 percent of San Diego County's population. About 15 percent of these children live in poverty, including 18 percent of children under age five and 13.5 percent of children aged five through seventeen. San Diego's Child Intake Services registered between 18,000 and 19,000 reports of suspected child abuse, neglect, or exploitation in 1981. The data for 1982 show an increase in these reports of about 16 percent over the previous year. If we assume that each of these calls represents a different child (which probably overestimates the actual number of children by some undeterminable amount), this would mean that 4.5 percent of San Diego's 461,000 children are suspected victims of abuse, neglect, or exploitation every year. Tensions associated with economic difficulties usually exacerbate child abuse, and these figures reflect the effects of the recession on San Diego's children.

Michigan's Department of Social Services and its Wayne County office handle child welfare services similar to San Diego. In Wayne County these services are organized into three divisions: Child Protective Services, Adult and Family Services, and Foster Care and Adoption. Child Protective Services

---

1. Readers who are not concerned with the detailed service structures in the four jurisdictions might want to skip to the next section.

receives child abuse and neglect reports, makes investigations, and when appropriate, refers the case to the other two divisions. Adult and Family Services helps high-risk families reduce the probability of child abuse and neglect through an array of service options: in-home supportive services, day care, family counseling, employment or schooling-related counseling, and other preventive services. The Foster Care and Adoption unit receives referrals if investigation reveals that removing a child from its home is the best option for the child.

According to the 1980 census, children under age eighteen made up 30 percent of Detroit's population. About 32 percent of these children live in poverty, including 35 percent of children under age five and 30 percent of children aged five through seventeen. Making the same assumptions and calculations we did for San Diego, Detroit's 12,424 child protection investigations may affect approximately 3.5 percent of its 357,399 children under eighteen (in 1980). Since investigations (Detroit's figure) are a later stage in the process than initial requests (San Diego's figure), Detroit probably has a child abuse and neglect rate that is as high or higher than that of San Diego.

Services to children in Richmond are provided by the Department of Public Welfare through the Child Welfare Services and the Family Services divisions. Child Welfare Services includes foster care and adoptive placements, both of which receive specific federal appropriations under Title IV(E). Family Services covers a broad range of in-home supportive services for children and their families, including preventive and reunification services and day care. Federal funding comes primarily from the social services block grant; some funds also come through Title IV(B), specifically for in-home services.

The 1980 census indicates that Richmond is home to 163,793 children under eighteen, who make up 27 percent of the city's population. Approximately 14 percent of these children live in poverty, including 16 percent of children under age five and 14 percent of children aged five through seventeen. Richmond's statistics do not include the annual number of requests for child protective services, so we cannot calculate a rate for the city that would parallel the rate for San Diego and Detroit. We can, however, make some general assumptions that would permit an approximation of such a rate. Richmond has an average of sixteen child protection cases each month. If a case lasts approximately four months, one-fourth of the caseload is being replaced by new cases each month. Over twelve months, this would mean that Richmond helped an estimated sixty children in need of protective services in 1982 and 1983. If half the cases investigated result in protective services being given and half the referrals to protective services are forwarded for investigation, then the number of requests per year can be estimated at 240.

This would mean that an estimated rate of 1.5 percent of Richmond's children are becoming involved in child protective services each year—a rate far lower than that of either San Diego or Detroit.

The Massachusetts Department of Social Services delivers services to Boston's population primarily through its Region VI office. The department focuses its efforts on services to children and families. Its activities include all the child welfare services provided by our other three sites, through its Child Protection and Adoption Services units.

Census figures for 1980 indicate that Boston's 665,181 children under age eighteen make up 25 percent of its population. Thirteen percent of these children live in poverty. The rate for children under age five is 15 percent; that for children aged five through seventeen is 12 percent. Boston, like Richmond, reports only a child protective services census for a single month (June). Making the same assumptions we made for Richmond would yield an estimated 12,098 children receiving protective services each year, as a result of approximately 48,000 referrals, for an estimated rate of 7.2 percent per year involvement with child protective services in some way.

Impact of Budget and Program Changes

Child welfare services are a high priority in most states, and will usually have been protected as much as possible from absorbing the effects of federal policy changes (although some of this "protection" probably came at the expense of social services block-grant funding for employment-related child care). To some extent, however, services for abused, neglected, and dependent children felt the pinch in all four of the jurisdictions examined. Some of the strain comes from local rather than federal or state priorities, and some stems from federal policy changes in other programs (notably AFDC), which may indirectly affect the number of children in situations of high risk for abuse or neglect. In San Diego the failure to replace lost funding appears to be a combination of federal and local decisions, whereas all sources reduced spending in Richmond. In every jurisdiction except Boston, child welfare workers also cited the recession and unemployment as factors contributing to their growing numbers of abuse and neglect cases.

San Diego

Changes in funding patterns for child welfare services in San Diego, and the services themselves, have undergone great changes, but these are due at least as much to local fiscal decisions as to federal changes. Before Proposition 13 the counties paid 70 percent of foster care costs while state and federal sources paid the rest. The 1980-81 state bailout reduced the county share to 5 percent. This bailout was slated to revert to the old ratio in January 1984, which would have left San Diego $12 million in the red if they maintained their 1983 levels of service. Since the county could not legally raise taxes (and would not if it could), the situation was potentially disastrous. However, the state renewed the bailout provisions for at least two more years, so child welfare services will not be further curtailed. San Diego County's lack of commitment to maintaining child welfare services looms even larger when one realizes that for every dollar the county fails to spend it forgoes $19 of state matching funds, yet the county has significantly reduced its child welfare budget.

With the change from Title XX to the social services block grant, California also gave the counties control over their share of Title IV(B) money for child welfare services. This has helped provide more money to San Diego because previous spending rules made it almost impossible for San Diego to spend the Title IV(B) money it nominally had available. Earlier state requirements had constrained Title IV(B) funding for use only with county recipients who were not eligible for Title XX. In San Diego there was almost no one in this category.

Child Intake Services screens potential cases; provides emergency response, short-term counseling, crisis intervention, and emergency shelter care; and has a volunteer service. This unit experienced funding reductions of 7 percent and staff reductions of 8 percent between 1981–82 and 1982–83. At the same time, initial requests for services rose 16 percent. The percentage of initial requests referred for intake screening has been dropping steadily since 1979–80. In that year 72 percent of initial calls were referred, whereas only 54 percent were referred in 1982–83. The percentage of referrals acted upon within forty-eight hours has held steady at about 30 percent, but the net effect is an approximate one-third reduction in the number of initial requests for service that receive an investigation within forty-eight hours.

Caseworkers in San Diego report having to ignore all but the most severe and immediately life-threatening situations. All over the country, child protection and mental health services staff have reported increases in battering, neglect, and other mental health consequences that they attribute to the recession and unemployment. San Diego is no exception. In addition, San Diego has worked successfully to encourage people to report child sexual abuse. Reports have jumped from 400 in 1977 to over 3,000 in 1982, but now workers have no services to offer in these cases.

Child Placement and Supervision Services, which handles foster care, adoptions, protective supervision in own homes, and licensing of out-of-home care facilities, has experienced a 17 percent drop in its budget, a 9 percent drop in staffing, and a 5 percent drop in the average number of active cases per month. The noncounty share of this unit's budget actually increased by 4 percent between fiscal 1982 and fiscal 1983, but the county's contribution dropped by 40 percent. During 1982 and 1983, staffing levels dropped a total of 17 percent while the workload stayed approximately the same.

San Diego has reorganized both its child welfare services programs and its concept of what it is trying to do for children, largely in response to budgetary pressures. In 1982–83 San Diego put maximum effort into intensive early intervention, trying to prevent out-of-home placement where possible. During the first quarter of fiscal 1982 San Diego reduced placements by 10 percent; the staff anticipated using the $850,000 saved on placements to give intensive services to children who had only recently been removed from their homes. In this way the staff hoped to help those already removed from their homes to get back to their families. Their theory was (and is) that short-run intensive services save long-run foster care costs. It is unfortunate that the county's fiscal situation is so bad and its priorities are so different from child welfare that the county took back the $850,000 and reassigned it to public safety uses. This left the child welfare staff completely demoralized.

In addition to San Diego's child welfare services budget of $14,557,000, the AFDC foster care program supported children in foster care at a cost of $17,949,813 in fiscal 1982.

The staff voiced numerous complaints about the irrationality of some recent changes in their service and reporting obligations. One of these was due to the Adoption Assistance and Child Welfare Act of 1980, compounded by state actions. The California legislature complied with this legislation by ordering reviews of children in placement every six months. At the same time it reduced required reviews of adult cases from every six months to annual reviews. Reasoning that one change offset the other, the state legislature failed to appropriate any more money for the paperwork required in case reviews for children. The San Diego Social Services Department staff does not find these changes an even trade. Child welfare caseworkers are spending significantly more time on paperwork and less on casework, according to their perceptions. All felt the federal legislation makes sense but cannot be translated into the services intended if it is seriously underfunded.

Finally, caps on funding available to provide child care for children in potentially abusive families, instituted by new regulations for Title IV(A), social services block grants, and AFDC, are viewed as counterproductive for families who become child protection cases. Resources in these families are so low that children are often left alone. The staff believes there is more neglect and abuse as more pressures are loaded on parents whose performance is already marginal. More child care funding would enable parents to leave their children under adequate supervision while working, looking for work, or receiving employment training. In these matters the San Diego staff's feelings mirror perceptions nationwide, that the array of federal resources withdrawn from poor and near-poor families, coupled with the pressures of the recession, increase the likelihood of child abuse and neglect.

Detroit

Child welfare services have long been a high priority in Michigan. When Michigan began experiencing recession in 1978 and the Department of Social Services faced reductions in services and staff positions, children's services were cut only 8 percent while all other programs lost 20 percent of their support. The federal cutbacks exacerbated the already existing strains on the state budget. In fiscal 1982 the department made large layoffs in assistance payments workers and services workers. Child Protective Services was perhaps the hardest hit because many of the workers were new (due to high turnover and some new positions) and they had little seniority. Adult and Family Services workers were also initially slated for cuts, but the department redefined family services to be preventive services for high-risk clients and hence was able to cover personnel costs with the new Title IV(B) monies.

As unemployment rises and AFDC, Medicaid, and general assistance benefits decline, families are known to be under greater stress and the incidence of child abuse and neglect appears to increase. As table 8 shows, protective services requests for Wayne County rose markedly between fiscal years 1981 and 1982. However, substantiations dropped, both absolutely (down 9 percent) and as a proportion of requests (down from 86 percent to 67 percent). Detroit child welfare officials offer several possible explanations: public awareness has grown, hence they receive more requests for less serious problems; or the staff is overworked and takes less time to thoroughly investigate the cases. The Department of Social Services staff suspects the latter is closer to the truth; protective services in Wayne County has lost staff and gained cases to the point that the staff acknowledges they do less intense follow-through across the board. Improvements were presumably at hand—protective services statewide was slated to receive 100 staff positions and $2 million from a 1983 tax increase. However, state-level protective services staff reports that it has not received staff increases to date, even though the tax increase passed. The staff reports that it continues to have far too few staff members for the ever-growing number of cases.

With the loss of Title XX funds in fiscal 1981, the Department of Social Services transformed the Family Support Services program into the Preventive Child Abuse and Neglect Services program, which could then be supported with Title IV(B) monies under the Adoption Assistance and Child Welfare Act. The shift nonetheless meant a major reduction in staffing statewide. Wayne County services remained fairly stable, but far below the level needed to implement any new service programs (as originally planned under the act). Preventive Services receives its cases by referral from Protective Services; thus the primary focus is on families at high risk of child abuse or neglect.

In fiscal 1982 the state took several actions affecting foster care. First, it froze rates for foster care providers. Second, the state legislature passed a law requiring the Department of Social Services to reduce from 24 percent to 18 percent the proportion of its nonadoptive preadolescent child population that was in residential care. The burden of this reduction fell on Wayne County, where all but ten of the ninety-seven children in residential institutions live. Third, Michigan capped the amount it would spend for AFDC-eligible foster care children, thus passing the financial burden on to the counties.

Between fiscal years 1981 and 1982 the Department of Social Services lost substantial funding for foster care services, which exacerbated the effects of its funding cutbacks in the social services block grant, Title XX. Title IV(B) fell from $6.2 million to $5.9 million, and the new Title IV(E) foster care reimbursements fell from $21.7 million to $15.2 million. AFDC-Foster Care placements rose by about 30 percent during this time (see table 8), adding greater demands on both county budgets (to match the federal AFDC-Foster Care payments) and on local staff to find suitable placements. Reductions in Medicaid coverage added another complication to the difficulties of recruiting foster homes. Foster families' unhappiness with the frozen rates was increased because they had to pay for children's eyeglasses and prescriptions.

Group homes face a different problem. Reductions in coverage for mental health services have led to diagnosing more children with "character disorders" as victims of abuse or neglect so that Title IV(B) can be used to pay for the services they need. These children are being placed in group homes, which are not equipped to handle the problems the children present. Placement of these children in group homes puts unnecessary strain on staff and, equally important, fills foster care slots that are needed for other children.

Michigan has a strong adoption subsidy program. Statewide, the number of adoptive placements has been increasing, as has the number of special needs placements. Adoptive placements rose 32 percent between fiscal years 1979 and 1982. Placement of minority children and handicapped children rose 59 percent and 32 percent, respectively, during the same period. Subsidized adoptions, an important emphasis of the Adoption Assistance and Child Welfare Act, rose 122 percent. Nonetheless, Wayne County faces a serious problem of understaffing that restricts its ability to proceed with adoption plans for all appropriate children. At public hearings held in Detroit in May 1983, participants testified that in Wayne County alone 250 children await adoptive placement.

The overall picture in Detroit is one of increasing demand for services, staff and service cuts, and less optimal care for children in need.

Richmond

The significant changes made by the Reagan administration in many human service programs directly or indirectly affect children served by the Richmond Department of Public Welfare. The program area with the most easily identifiable impact on children is social services, which is primarily funded by the social services block grant. Title IV(B) and Title IV(E) of the Social Security Act also support child welfare services, although funding levels are low compared to social services block-grant dollars going for the same services. The city absorbed a decrease of 19 percent in social services block-grant monies between fiscal years 1981 and 1982; for child welfare services, this has meant both drastic cutbacks in the purchase of services and increased caseloads for direct service staff.

The Child Welfare Services division has maintained fairly steady budget and staffing levels since 1980–81, largely because of open-ended federal support. Title IV(E)and Title IV(A) foster care had a federal ceiling in 1981, but Virginia was not affected. Foster care caseloads have been decreasing, from an average of 563 cases per month in 1980–81 to 520 currently. There were 1,153 children in foster care on December 31, 1980; two years later, there were 942, a drop of 18 percent. The average age of children in care has decreased, from age seven to age five, and the average length of stay is also shorter. Nearly half of all foster care children are returned home within ninety days (perhaps partly due to the state's ninety-day limit on entrustment, or voluntary, placements). These reductions in foster care cases reflect the nationwide push to reduce the number of children in foster care.

Adoption services similarly have fared well in recent years. With the start of open-ended federal adoption assistance in 1981, Richmond benefited from federal sharing in what was previously a state-local subsidy program. In 1980, the Child Welfare Services division placed thirty-four children in adoptive homes; in 1981, thirty-seven children; and in 1982, twenty-eight children. Of adoptive homes, 40–60 percent receive adoption subsidies.

While out-of-home services to children in Richmond were largely untouched by federal cutbacks because of new Title IV(E) funds, the situation is dramatically different for in-home services. The Family Services division had a staff of 157 in January 1982; one year later, the staff numbered 70. The budget similarly dropped drastically, from over $1 million in fiscal 1982 to $374,000 in fiscal 1983. The cuts came chiefly at the expense of the non-AFDC population; all the day care and education and training services were eliminated for income eligibles (those whose income qualified them for services but who did not receive AFDC). More recently, day care has been additionally cut back to exclude all former AFDC recipients.

The impact on both recipients and service providers has been substantial. Day care is now available only for AFDC families in which the parent is working or in training (but those training and placement services have been drastically reduced). The staff providing services reports many former AFDC recipients returning to the rolls. The combination of day care cuts, Medicaid changes, and food stamp reductions have posed critical problems for many families. Families are entering with more serious problems than previously. Family Services currently has three protective services units, handling 260 cases. In addition, two intensive services units work with 144 cases in which there is a high risk of child maltreatment or other crisis. Family Services is also pioneering a project in structured family therapy, aimed at returning foster children to their natural families.

As the demand for crisis intervention has increased, Family Services workers have become less able to deliver noncrisis preventive and supportive services to intact families. It is paradoxical that the Adoptive Assistance and Child Welfare Act encourages preventive service to children at the same time that cutbacks in general social service funds force states to focus on crisis intervention. Social services department managers and supervisors express much frustration with state and federal "prevention policy" that is not backed up by adequate funds to enable agencies to move beyond the emergency needs of families. Prevention remains largely a luxury.

Boston

The budget for the Massachusetts Department of Social Services has grown slightly in recent years, which is surprising in light of the cutback in social services block-grant funds. Children and family services are a high priority in Massachusetts. When the Department of Social Services faced a loss of nearly $20 million in federal social services funds, the legislature was prepared to fill the gap. The governor objected to a short-term solution that would heavily tax other state activities, so the Department of Social Services, the legislature, and the governor together worked out a compromise whereby the department would absorb half the cuts ($10 million) in state fiscal 1982, but would not have to absorb cuts in subsequent years. At the same time, Massachusetts received increased funding from Title IV(B), legislated by the Adoption Assistance and Child Welfare Act, so the social services budget actually increased from its 1981 level. This pattern is projected to continue throughout state fiscal 1984.

State officials say the $10 million loss in social services block-grant funds was absorbed through reductions in out-of-home care, both foster family and group care. Statewide caseloads dropped 10 percent between June 1981 and June 1982, and another 3 percent the following year (see table 12). The decline was even greater in the Boston region—15 percent over the two-year period. The social services staff there reports that the focus was on reducing the number of children in group care, but the figures belie that assertion. Foster family care in Boston decreased at four times the rate of group care.

While substitute care caseloads did drop during fiscal years 1982 and 1983, state officials now feel that the projected cutbacks were overly optimistic. Placements are reportedly rising again, especially for group care. Funds are becoming tight because the anticipated decrease in placements was budgeted into state fiscal 1984. There may have been programmatic side effects as well. To achieve the cost savings, it became more difficult to get children into substitute care, perhaps putting added stress on many families and increasing the likelihood of abuse.

Massachusetts apparently has not significantly increased its subsidized adoptions since 1981. Data are incomplete, but the state as a whole had forty-one subsidized adoptions in 1982 and only twenty-four in 1983. No data are available for the state or for the Boston area on unsubsidized adoptions. This rate of subsidized adoptions is extremely low. Michigan, with approximately 65 percent of Massachusetts' population, placed sixteen times the number of children in subsidized adoptions in 1982 (663 versus 41). Given the low level of Massachusetts' adoption activity, it seems unwarranted to place too much emphasis on fluctuating numbers.

The staffs at both state and local levels note a significant increase in abuse and neglect referrals. This may be due to the cutbacks in income assistance and service programs or due to the greater visibility of the Department of Social Services (it is a fairly new agency, previously part of the Department of Public Welfare).

Whatever the cause, staff members are facing increasing demand for services in this area. Neighborhood Health Centers staff also see increased need for child protective services and mental health counseling; they note greater difficulty in making referrals to the local Department of Social Services agency, presumably because that agency's staff is overloaded.

Summary

Assessing the impact of federal changes on child welfare services is complicated by the contradictory thrusts of the Adoption Assistance and Child

Welfare Act (pre-Reagan administration) and the Reagan administration's underfunding of its provisions. The act emphasizes preventive, supportive, and reunification services and permanency planning, and the Reagan administration continues to endorse these program goals. Several of the states and jurisdictions visited during the preparation of this study were moving in these directions even before this legislation passed in the last days of the Carter administration. With full funding for its provisions, one would have expected to see reduced foster care placements, reductions of average time in foster care; increased permanency planning, adoptions, and subsidized adoptions; and increased in-home supportive services for high-risk families. The preventive, reunification and adoption assistance services that would have increased with appropriate funding levels would have helped families avoid removal of a child, helped children return to their natural families, or increased adoptions. All these activities either remove children from foster care or prevent their initial entry into the system, hence the projected reductions in the foster care rolls.

Foster care cases have indeed been reduced in three of the four jurisdictions included in this study at the same time that child protection requests, referrals, investigations, and services increased, often dramatically, in all jurisdictions. It is impossible to sort out how much of the foster care reductions stem from a concerted programmatic effort to reduce this type of care and how much they have occurred because reduced staff have been overwhelmed by the increased child protection work. If a clear pattern could be documented showing an increase in in-home protective services, coupled with a reduction in foster care placements, the progammatic explanation would be strengthened. The available data do not allow us to make this case, however. In San Diego both foster care services and in-home protective services show decreases during the years under investigation, while Boston's figures indicate that in-home protective services rose as foster care caseloads fell (see table 7). The other two jurisdictions do not report their service data in a way that permits a comparison to be made.

All these factors lead one to think that reductions in foster care rates reflect jurisdictions' efforts to implement the philosophy of the Adoption Assistance and Child Welfare Act, complicated by their budgetary and staffing difficulties. In all jurisdictions the staffs commented that they agreed with the federal emphasis on reducing substitute care placements, doing more permanency planning, and making greater efforts to strengthen families so that children did not have to be removed from their homes. Many also commented that budget cutbacks had made it very difficult for them to implement this approach and that the federal incentive system (the combination of mandates of the Adoption Assistance and Child Welfare Act and Reagan administration funding patterns) was self-contradictory. Cutting funds for child welfare services (prevention, reunification, and adoption assistance) and child protective services covered by the reduced social services block grant could only lead, in their opinion, to more foster care placements, longer lengths of stay for children placed in substitute care, and more children at risk who receive no services. When money is available for foster care but not for prevention, in the long run more cases will be resolved by out-of-home placement than by family support services.

The significant increases in child protective services in all jurisdictions very possibly reflect additional contradictions in and ramifications of the patterns of federal cutbacks. In all jurisdictions many families have lost AFDC benefits as a result of federal program changes. All jurisdictions have experienced significant cutbacks in funding for day care through (1) the social services block grant (Title XX) cuts, (2) changed priorities for spending the remaining dollars, (3) reduced per-person allowable costs, and (4) switching from Title XX to a Title IV(A) disregard as a source of day care funding (which means much less money available for each day of child care).[2]

It is also likely that the change in foster care policy itself increased child protection cases. Decisions to leave children at "less severe" risk of abuse in their homes, when they would previously have been removed, probably expose these children to continued and possibly increased risk. Child protective services staff in all jurisdictions mentioned these changes and viewed them as putting increased pressures on families whose economic and interpersonal or parental viability was marginal. The social services staff believes these pressures and strains are probably responsible, along with general economic hard times in most of the jurisdictions, for the increased amount of child abuse and neglect being reported in all the cities studied here.

By reducing funding for all child welfare services beyond the capacity or willingness of many jurisdictions to compensate, federal changes during the Reagan administration have increased the risk of severe harm to children through parental abuse or neglect. Pressures on local agencies to avoid removing children from their homes, coupled with increased abuse and neglect reporting and decreased agency resources for intervention, appear to have left more children in high-risk situations without the protection of preventive or ameliorative services. As a result of budget cuts, staff reductions, or increased service demand, the remaining staff members report doing less thorough investigations of reports and selecting only the life-threatening cases for in-

---

2. Specifically, this disregard is a provision that allows AFDC recipients to spend some earned money on day care without having it reduce their AFDC eligibility or grant amount.

vestigation and services where previously they would have intervened in less severe (but still harmful) cases. There is little doubt that federal changes have reduced the ability of child protection workers in local jurisdictions to serve children at levels prevailing before the cuts in the social services block grant and other changes occurred in federal policy.

PART TWO

THE CHRONICALLY MENTALLY ILL

CHAPTER 4

WHO ARE THE CHRONICALLY MENTALLY ILL?

Changes in federal programs and benefits have significantly affected the structure of services for the chronically mentally ill during the last two decades. Beginning in 1963, the federal government undertook financing for the development of community mental health centers. The impetus behind developing these centers was an intention to prevent admissions and re-admissions to public mental hospitals and reduce long-term stays by providing more mental health services in the community.

In 1965, Medicaid (Title XIX of the Social Security Act) began to pay for long-term nursing home care for indigents, and many states transferred geriatric and other patients from mental hospitals into nursing homes to shift the cost burden at least partially to the federal government. Supplemental Security Income (Title XVI of the Social Security Act) became available in 1974, providing cash income at a minimum living standard to persons unable to work. Many chronically mentally ill qualified for this assistance but could only receive it if they resided in the community, not in a mental hospital. Supplemental Security Income (SSI) payments made it even more attractive for states to discharge patients from mental hospitals and thereby increase the numbers of chronically mentally ill living in the community.

By 1980 Congress and the Carter administration had taken a long look at federal involvement with the chronically mentally ill. It appeared that community mental health centers, the federal program initially intended to focus directly on the chronically mentally ill, were not doing enough for this population. The Mental Health Systems Act, passed in October 1980, refocused efforts specifically on the chronically mentally ill.

Legislative and adminstrative changes under President Reagan came swiftly. The Omnibus Budget Reconciliation Act of 1981 repealed all important programmatic changes of the Mental Health Systems Act and appropriated a reduced amount of federal funding for mental health into a block grant to the states (the alcohol, drug abuse, and mental health block grant). At the same time the Social Security Administration began more frequent and more stringent reviews of applications from new and continuing recipients of SSI payments, with serious results for many chronically mentally ill SSI recipients.

The history of federal policy addressing this population and the changes that have occurred under the Reagan administration, as well as the clearly vulnerable nature of the chronically mentally ill, led us to select this group as one of the three needy populations in this study.

The Chronically Mentally Ill Population Defined

One of the hallmarks of a vulnerable group is the inability of its members to take care of their own most basic needs. The stereotypical image of the chronically mentally ill is of people so out of touch with other people, and so incapable of functioning in the world of work and family, that they must be hospitalized for their own protection, usually for a long time. The actual state of these chronically mentally ill people has changed somewhat over the last quarter century, both in their place of residence and in the ability of some of them to function. A large proportion of chronically mentally ill persons who once resided in state and county mental hospitals now live in the community, where they may receive supportive services. However, many thousands do not receive such services.

Chronically mentally ill persons, by reason of their mental disorder, usually need help with very basic things: taking medications regularly, grooming and dressing, feeding themselves regularly and nutritiously, and finding adequate and safe housing. Very often they have no family on which to rely, no friends, and no associations with other community members. Typically they have poor job histories or have never worked, have few skills, and lack the concentration necessary to do even the simplest jobs in most work settings. Finally, they may lose their mental or emotional stability in response to stress in their lives, and behave in ways that disturb others enough to become hospitalized, sometimes for long periods of time.

Despite the potential functional limitations of the chronically mentally ill, most practitioners now recognize that many of these persons can be helped to achieve a range of functional abilities, including living in the community, partially supporting themselves, and relying less on repeated hospitalizations. Social supports and services provided from a rehabilitative perspective can assist members of this population to live more independent lives, as evidence cited below indicates.

The National Institute of Mental Health uses three components in its definition of chronic mental illness: diagnosis, disability, and duration.

Diagnosis—To be considered chronically mentally ill, a person must first meet the criterion of diagnosis—does the person have a severe mental condition? Diagnoses most common among the chronically mentally ill are the psychoses (schizophrenia, depression and manic-depressive disorders, paranoid and other psychoses, and organic brain syndrome). Other diagnoses include some severe personality disorders (for example, "borderline disorders") and nonpsychotic organic brain syndrome (senility without psychosis). Current estimates indicate that approximately 3 million adults meet the diagnosis criterion at any given time in the United States.[1]

Disability—Not everyone with a diagnosis of severe mental disorder suffers a significant amount of disability. Disability refers to functional impairment—that is, the inability to carry on major life activities. Inability to work, to keep house, and to look after children are obvious functional impairments arising from mental illness. Other impairments include self-care, communication with others, learning, ability to get around by oneself, and the ability to make daily and more long-term decisions. Although functional impairment may be difficult to measure precisely, disability remains a necessary component of the definition of chronic mental illness. The National Institute of Mental Health estimates that of the 3 million people with diagnoses of severe mental disorder, 2.4 million, or 80 percent, suffer moderate to severe disability caused or exacerbated by their mental condition.

Duration—The final criterion in defining the chronically mentally ill is duration. Usually twelve months is the shortest period of disability that justifies the designation of "chronic." The National Institute of Mental Health estimates that of the 2.4 million people experiencing moderate to severe disability arising from severe mental disorder, 1.7 million maintain this condition for at least one year. This is 57 percent of those with severe disability due to a mental disorder. It also represents approximately 1 percent of the U.S. adult population.

Combining the definitional components of diagnosis, disability, and duration, the National Institute of Mental Health developed the following definition of the chronically mentally ill population.[2]

---

1. The estimates of the chronically mentally ill in this section are based on U.S. Department of Health and Human Services, Steering Committee on the Chronically Mentally Ill, *Toward a National Plan for the Chronically Mentally Ill*, Report to the Secretary, publication (ADM) 81–1077 (Washington, D.C.: U.S. Department of Health and Human Services, December 1980), pp. 2–1, 2–17 to 2–20.

2. Ibid., p. 2–11.

The chronically mentally ill population encompasses persons who suffer certain mental or emotional disorders (organic brain syndrome, schizophrenia, recurrent depressive and manic-depressive disorders, paranoid and other psychoses, plus other disorders that may become chronic) that erode or prevent the development of their functional capacities in relation to (three or more of) such primary aspects of daily life as personal hygiene and self-care, self-direction, interpersonal relationships, social transactions, learning, and recreation, and that erode or prevent the development of their economic self-sufficiency. Most such individuals have required institutional care of extended duration, including intermediate-term hospitalization (ninety days to one year in a single year), long-term hospitalization (one year or longer in the preceding five years), or nursing home placement on account of a diagnosed mental condition or a diagnosis of senility without psychosis. Some such individuals have required repeated short-term hospitalization (less than ninety days), have received treatment from a medical or mental health professional solely on an outpatient basis, or—despite their needs—have received no treatment in the professional-care service system. Thus, included in the population are persons who are or were formerly "residents" of institutions (public and private psychiatric hospitals and nursing homes), and persons who are at high risk of institutionalization because of persistent mental disability.

Characteristics of the Population

The standard demographic characteristics of the chronically mentally ill differ substantially from those of the nondisabled population of the United States. Estimates come from the 1978 Survey of Disability and Work, conducted by the U.S. Bureau of the Census, and from data collected on clients of a special program designed to serve the chronically mentally ill—the Community Support Program. The demographic data from the Survey of Disability and Work for the chronically mentally ill describe only those persons residing in households, either with family members or by themselves. The majority of persons described in the data from the Community Support Program also reside in the community (91 percent). These statistics for the chronically mentally ill do not include patients under long-term residential care, either in mental health facilities or nursing homes. Table 9 presents data by sex, age, marital status, race, and earnings for persons aged eighteen to sixty-four in 1978 who were residing in households (not institutions or other group living quarters) and data on the chronically mentally ill who participated in the Community Support Program in 1980.

The chronically mentally ill residing in U.S. households are more often female, middle aged or older, and less often married than their nondisabled counterparts. They are also more often female, older, and married than Community Support Program participants. The biggest difference observable in table 10 lies in the earnings data. Persons participating in Community Support Programs had median incomes of $3,900 in 1980, compared to the median

TABLE 9

DEMOGRAPHIC CHARACTERISTICS OF THE CHRONICALLY MENTALLY ILL AND
PERSONS WITHOUT DISABILITIES, 1978 AND 1980
(*Percent unless Otherwise Indicated*)

Characteristic	Persons Aged 18 to 64 Residing in Households, 1978		Percent of Participants in Community Support Programs, 1980, Who Are:[b]
	Percent of Persons with No Mental or Other Disabilities Who Are:	Percent of Persons with Chronic Mental Illness Who Are:[a]	
Male	50	37	47
Female	50	63	53
Age 20 to 34	47	21	43
Age 35 to 64	53	79	57
Married	72	59	11
Separated, divorced, or widowed	10	27	33
Never married	18	13	56
White	90	87	91
Black	10	13	9
Median income (dollars)	17,710	...	3,900
Unable to work	7	50[c]	75

SOURCES: Persons aged 18 to 64—John W. Ashbaugh et al., "Estimates of the Size and Selected Characteristics of the Adult Chronically Mentally Ill Population Living in U.S. Households," *Research in Community and Mental Health*, vol. 3 (1984), pp. 3–24; percent participating in community support programs—Ingrid D. Goldstrom and Ronald W. Manderscheid, "The Chronically Mentally Ill: A Descriptive Analysis from the Uniform Client Data Instrument" (Rockville, Maryland: National Institute of Mental Health, Division of Biometry and Epidemiology, 1981); median income of persons without mental or other disabilities—median household income for 1980, based on U.S. Bureau of the Census, *Statistical Abstract of the United States* (U.S. Government Printing Office, 1984), table 755; unemployment data for persons aged 18 to 64—ibid., table 755, rate for 1980. Figures are rounded.

a. Totally or partially disabled for at least twelve months.

b. Many states offer a Community Support Program to enable the chronically mentally ill to remain in the community.

c. See text for explanation.

income of U.S. households of $17,710. Seventy-five percent of those in a Community Support Program were not in the work force due to disability and 50 percent of them received income from government income support programs (Supplemental Security Income). These figures can be compared to a national unemployment rate in 1980 of 7 percent among nondisabled persons, and an estimated 16 percent in 1978[3] for persons aged eighteen to sixty-four residing in households who were unable to work due to disabling conditions other than chronic mental illness. Persons identified in the Survey of Disability and Work as "disabled due to chronic mental illness" had, by definition, either total or partial work disability. Other research (see table 10) suggests that approximately half are severely disabled (unable to work at all) and half are partially or moderately disabled (able to work less and at less demanding tasks). This would put the "unable to work" rate in the second column of table 10 at 50 percent or higher. These data on earnings and nonparticipation in the labor force for the chronically mentally ill clearly indicate their disabled and vulnerable status and their need for assistance.

Changes in Living Arrangements

Over the past three decades the most dramatic change in the situation of the chronically mentally ill has been in place of residence. In 1955 almost 80 percent of the chronically mentally ill occupied beds on a long-term basis in state and county mental hospitals. Such inpatient status accounted for 559,000 beds in that year, virtually all of which were occupied by long-term residents. The years have seen an accelerating shift away from inpatient care, to 504,000 in 1963, 216,000 in 1974, and 150,000 beds in 1980.[4] A shift toward shorter and more frequent hospitalizations has also occurred. Although the daily census in inpatient mental health facilities averaged 150,000 in 1980, there were more than 650,000 readmissions to such facilities in the course of a year.[5]

Institutions

While mental health facilities (state and county hospitals, Veterans' Administration inpatient facilities, private psychiatric hospitals, residential treatment centers, and community mental health centers' inpatient facilities) have

---

3. John W. Ashbaugh, et al., "Estimates of the Size and Selected Characteristics of the Adult Chronically Mentally Ill Population Living in U.S. Households," *Research in Community and Mental Health*, vol. 3 (1984), pp. 3–24.
    4. Ibid., p. 1–2.
    5. Ibid., pp. 2–12.

TABLE 10

LIVING ARRANGEMENTS OF THE CHRONICALLY MENTALLY ILL, LATE 1970s

Type of care	Number (Thousands)[a]
Community	
Board and care facilities	300–400
Persons aged 18–64 residing in households	
Severe disability	530
Moderate and severe disability	1,000
Subtotal	830–1,400
Institutions	
Mental health facilities	150
Nursing homes	
Severe mental disorders	350
Senility but no psychosis	400
Subtotal	900
Total	1,730–2,300

SOURCES: For persons in institutions, mental health facilities—includes residents for 1 year or more in state and county hospitals, Veterans' Administration inpatient facilities, private psychiatric hospitals, residential treatment centers, and community mental health centers, based on estimates provided by the Division of Biometry and Epidemiology, National Institute of Mental Health, 1975; nursing homes—based on 1.3 million residents of skilled nursing and intermediate care facilities sampled by the National Center for Health Statistics, National Nursing Home Survey, 1977; residents with mental disorders—persons with a diagnosis (primary or nonprimary) from Section V of the International Classification of Diseases-9, National Nursing Home Survey, 1977; and residents with senility but without psychosis—persons with a diagnosed condition (primary or nonprimary) coded 797 in the International Classification of Diseases-9, National Nursing Home Survey, 1977. Figures are rounded.

For persons in communities, board and care facilities—based on Department of Health and Human Services, Public Health Services, Steering Committee on the Chronically Mentally Ill, *Toward a National Plan for the Chronically Mentally Ill*, Report to the Secretary, publication (ADM) 81–1077 (Washington, D.C.: DHHS-PHS, December 1980), p. 2–20; households, persons aged 18–64—based on John W. Ashbaugh et al., "Estimates of the Size and Selected Characteristics of the Adult Chronically Ill Population Living in Households," *Research in Community and Mental Health*, vol. 3 (1983), pp. 3–24; severe disability—includes persons with a mental disorder who are unable to work for one year and those who could work only occasionally or irregularly, estimates of proportions derived from proportion severely disabled and proportion partially disabled as reported in Ashbaugh et al., ibid., multiplied by the respective proportions found in The Urban Institute, Comprehensive Needs Survey, 1973; and moderate disability—includes so-called "partially disabled" persons whose work, including housework, was limited by a mental disorder, estimates of proportions derived from The Urban Institute, Comprehensive Needs Survey, 1973, and applied to Ashbaugh et al., "Estimates of the Size and Selected Characteristics."

a. For community population, upper and lower bounds of estimates; for institutional population, number of occupied beds.

registered a dramatic drop in daily census in recent years, many of the chronically mentally ill who once resided in such facilities have not returned to community living. Rather, many of them have simply been moved from one institution to another. The nursing home population expanded greatly during the same years that the mental health facility census dropped, and a large number of nursing home beds are now occupied by people who would earlier have been placed in mental health facilities.

Table 10 shows the current best estimates of the residential location of the chronically mentally ill. In 1977 a total of 1.3 million people lived in skilled nursing and intermediate care facilities. Of these, 350,000 (27 percent) had a diagnosis of severe mental disorder and an additional 400,000 (31 percent) had a diagnosis of senility without psychosis (these people are included in our calculations because they were once housed in mental health facility geriatric units). For all practical purposes, nursing home residents with mental illness diagnoses can be considered just as "institutionalized" as if they were in state or county mental hospitals. In fact, they often receive fewer or no services directly relevant to their mental disorder in nursing homes than they would in mental health facilities, and they are otherwise equally regimented. They are therefore grouped under the category "Institutions" in table 10.

The Community

Since the number of chronically mentally ill persons, as a proportion of the adult population, has remained quite constant during the time that mental health facilities were reducing their inpatient capacity, the number of chronically mentally ill living in residential arrangements other than mental health facilities increased as the hospitalized population shrank. Estimates of the chronically mentally ill population living in a variety of community residential settings indicate that this population equals or exceeds the population in institutions, both in hospitals and in nursing homes (table 10).

Between 300,000 and 400,000 persons with chronic mental illness live in board and care facilities. These facilities have many names—board and care, foster care, group foster care, domiciliary care, residential care, personal care homes, group homes, and congregate facilities. Many such facilities offer only room and board as required services. Some, known as SROs (for single-room-occupancy hotels) offer only lodging. Some, but by no means the majority, offer residents some personal supervision, possibly in the areas of managing their medications or finances.[6]

---

6. Kenneth J. Reichstein and Linda Bergofsky, *Summary and Report of the National Survey of State Administered Domociliary Care Programs in the Fifty States and the District of Columbia* (Dedham, Massachusetts: Horizon House Institute, December 1980).

A study published in 1983 has produced estimates of the number of chronically mentally ill in households—that is, persons who live with family members or by themselves but do not live in group quarters or institutions—based on national samples of U.S. households and not on samples of service agency clients.[7] These estimates offer a more accurate reading of the total chronically mentally ill population than has previously been available. As table 10 indicates, approximately one million adults between the ages of eighteen and sixty-four are chronically mentally ill and living in households at any given time. This figure includes people who are severely disabled and those who are moderately or partially disabled.

Since the data in table 10 come from different sources and cover different components of the population, adding the numbers to obtain a total figure is risky. Nevertheless, the number of chronically mentally ill in the community appears to be between 800,000 and 900,000 individuals with severe disability, and 1.3 to 1.4 million with severe and moderate disability. When these numbers are combined with the 900,000 in institutions, the estimates yield numbers that quite closely approximate those in estimates of the U.S. Department of Health and Human Services.[8]

The Special Needs of the Chronically Mentally Ill

The shift in the location of the chronically mentally ill population, from the back wards of state mental hospitals to other residential settings, has evolved as a consequence of several factors acting concurrently. First, the availability of psychotropic drugs, which appeared in the early 1950s, made it possible to reduce disturbing psychiatric symptoms to the level of community acceptance for many chronically mentally ill persons. Second, a therapeutic ideology and social movement developed within the mental health community that condemned the dehumanizing effects of long-term institutionalization. This movement emphasized treatment and rehabilitation for people with mental illness rather than custodial care. It also argued that with appropriate supportive services, most mental patients did not have to live in large institutional settings. Instead, they could be more appropriately and more humanely cared for in the community.

Although therapeutic innovations and arguments did play important roles in promoting deinstitutionalization, an even stronger impetus was financial. States could save considerable amounts of money by closing state hospital

---

7. Ashbaugh et al., "Estimates of the Size and Selected Characteristics of the Adult Chronically Mentally Ill Population Living in Households," pp. 3–24.
8. U.S. Department of Health and Human Services, *Toward a National Plan*.

wards and returning mental patients "to the community." Some of these savings came about because the burden of financial support could be shifted from state to federal programs, but some of the savings occurred for the very simple reason that the former patients received less care and support in the community than they had in the hospital. According to numerous research studies, in many instances released patients received no care or supportive services once they left the hospital.

Bachrach, summarizing and analyzing twenty years of research on deinstitutionalization, attributes many of the flaws in the concept to the failure to recognize the many different functions once performed by state mental hospitals.[9] State mental hospitals served largely custodial functions, but they did successfully fulfill these functions, whereas many of them go unfulfilled when mental patients are released to or remain in the community. Housing, food, clothing, hygiene, and physical health needs were all attended to, the hospital provided a continuum of wards to shelter patients with more and less extreme symptoms, and the hospital could serve as a retreat for persons who had trouble coping with daily life. No coordination among agencies or services was needed because the hospital staff oversaw all activities that occurred on the hospital grounds. Patients did not need to know how to manage their money, how to use the public transportation system, or how to contact government agencies because none of these were relevant to their lives as patients. They did not receive much, if any, treatment in a mental health sense, nor were they "rehabilitated" to enable them to return to productive community lives. But they usually did receive the maintenance or custodial aspects of care.

The greatest criticism of the deinstitutionalization movement is that it has left too many former patients with no system of care at all. Elderly patients, and many nonelderly as well, have been shifted or diverted from state hospitals to nursing homes. In nursing homes they continue to receive the custodial aspects of care, but receive no more and usually less therapeutic intervention for their mental illness than they did in state hospitals. For states, the big benefit of nursing home care is that the federal government picks up a good share of the cost through Medicaid.

Many people who would formerly have entered state hospitals now reside in board and care facilities or single-room occupancy hotels. These facilities are often referred to in the literature as "psychiatric ghettos" because their residents are largely former mental patients who receive little or nothing

---

9. Leona L. Bachrach, *Deinstitutionalization: An Analytical Review and Sociological Perspective*, U.S. Department of Health, Education, and Welfare publication (ADM) 76–361, (Washington, D.C.: U.S. Government Printing Office, 1976).

besides a roof over their heads. Because several such residential facilities often exist close together in the same neighborhood, these areas can quickly become stereotyped and isolated from the larger community. As Bachrach notes, "most reports indicate that on a widespread basis alternative living arrangements usually have fallen short of the desired goal of providing a humane environment."[10]

Another significant segment of the chronically mentally ill population can be found among the homeless (people without regular, reliable shelter). Few studies have been done of homeless populations, and those that exist cover only single cities or counties, but the evidence to date indicates that half or more of the samples in these studies are of people with diagnosable mental illness, most of whom have spent some time in public mental hospitals.[11]

The evidence from numerous studies strongly suggests that many basic needs of chronically mentally ill persons lie not in therapy or treatment for a mental condition, but in shelter, food, clothing, medical care, and provision of structure to their days, delivered within a rehabilitation framework. Traditional mental health programs have focused more on treatment or therapy and have not done enough to help former patients cope with the actual circumstances of maintaining a life in the community. Interactions between mental health agencies and other agencies have not been as extensive as needed, with the consequence that former patients do not obtain what they need from other agencies, even when they may be eligible for benefits. The exploration of federal programs in mental health in the next chapter describes services available for people with chronic mental illness, funded at least partially with federal dollars, and shows ways in which these programs have changed over the years as a result of changes in federal goals and favored strategies to meet them.

Summary

In this chapter we have defined chronic mental illness, described important ways that chronically mentally ill persons differ from the rest of the population, and looked at trends and issues affecting their well-being. At any

---

10. Ibid., p. 16.
11. Colleen Cordes, "The Plight of the Homeless Mentally Ill," *APA Monitor*, vol. 15, no. 2 (February 1984), pp. 1–13. Dr. Ronald Manderscheid, Director of the Division of Biometry and Epidemiology, National Institute of Mental Health, summarized his reading of the existing studies as justifying an estimate in the range of 30 to 60 percent of the homeless who are chronically mentally ill. No greater precision is possible at this time, according to Manderscheid, because no adequate data exist at the national level (personal communication, 1985).

given time, approximately 1.7 million adults in the United States suffer from debilitating chronic mental illness. The chronically mentally ill experience varying degrees of disability over periods of one year or more—many have lifetime histories of impairment and inability to function in normal life. State and county mental hospitals once housed large numbers of the chronically mentally ill, but deinstitutionalization has removed from these facilities almost three-fourths of the population who lived in these facilities in 1955. The major shift came after 1965, with the advent of Medicaid.

Deinstitutionalization has left increasing numbers of chronically mentally ill persons dependent on the resources of local communities. These resources have usually proved less than adequate and often are completely nonexistent. Several federal programs have provided either direct support for the chronically mentally ill or have stimulated local services intended to provide care for these people. Changes during the Reagan administration have affected most of the programs. Chapter 5 describes the history of these programs and their current status.

CHAPTER 5

FEDERAL POLICIES AND PROGRAMS FOR THE CHRONICALLY MENTALLY ILL

Before 1963, when President Kennedy proposed and Congress passed the Community Mental Health Centers Construction Act, the federal government played a minimal role in providing care or support for the chronically mentally ill. State and local governments had almost exclusive responsibility for this population, which they exercised by maintaining state and county mental hospitals. A few chronically mentally ill persons received some benefits from federal programs, largely through the disability provisions of the Social Security Act and the Veterans' Administration. Veterans' Administration hospitals were the principal form of federal responsibility.

Since 1963 the federal government's involvement with programs and services for the chronically mentally ill has expanded, both directly and indirectly. Community mental health centers were supposed to provide direct services to this population. More important sources of financial support have been the Medicaid and Supplemental Security Income programs (Titles XIX and XVI of the Social Security Act, effective in 1965 and 1974, respectively). While neither of these programs was primarily intended to benefit the chronically mentally ill, both have provided significant resources for nursing home care and community living. Their availability has encouraged states to reduce the number of inpatients at mental hospitals by almost 75 percent between 1955 and 1980, with almost 90 percent of the reduction since 1963.

A historical frame of reference for mental health services and federal involvement with the chronically mentally ill is important because the Reagan administration inherited a state of affairs that was by no means ideal. Deinstitutionalization practices had left many chronically mentally ill "out in the cold" without adequate community services to compensate for the loss of state hospital residence. Federal policy, articulated through community mental health center legislation, repeatedly tried to focus services and attention on

71

the chronically mentally ill, but simultaneously expanded the mandate of the community mental health centers to include more and more populations and services. Since populations that are not chronically mental ill are easier to serve than chronically mental ill patients, these centers often took the path of least resistance (thus creating the need for federal policy to reiterate with each legislative reauthorization an interest in the chronically mentally ill). Policy decisions at the state and local level often rested more on fiscal considerations than on commitment to good services. In short, the mental health field was ripe for reorganization and improved targeting on the chronically mentally ill when Reagan assumed the presidency, and Congress had recently passed legislation to that end. The following review of federal actions briefly summarizes some important milestones affecting the chronically mentally ill from 1963 through 1983.

Community Mental Health Centers

In 1955 the Joint Commission on Mental Illness and Health was established to examine the circumstances and needs of persons with mental health problems. The commission, in its 1961 report to President Kennedy entitled "Action for Mental Health," detailed the deteriorated condition of most public mental hospitals and the largely custodial types of care they provided. At this time approximately 80 percent of patient contacts with the mental health system were inpatient episodes, mostly in public mental hospitals. The plight of long-term residents of mental hospitals appeared especially unacceptable, yet there was little expectation that state and county mental hospitals would be significantly upgraded through the funding provided by local resources.

The mental health movement in the early 1960s pushed for community-based care and rejected the notion that most mentally ill persons need hospitalization—especially long-term hospitalization—if adequate services exist to care for them in the community. Although based more on theory than on the presence of widespread community-based services, this philosophy become strongly embedded in the rhetoric behind the community mental health center concept. Implicit in the federal decision to finance these centers was an assumption that federal dollars would be needed in any case because the substantial improvement needed to make public mental hospitals into humane and therapeutic environments was very unlikely to come from state and local efforts.

Federal involvement thus arose from a sense of national responsibility for the chronically mentally ill population, articulated in the commission's report. This sense of responsibility was coupled with the idea that federal investment would stimulate equal or greater state and local commitments, which would eventually replace federal support. Although by 1978 another study group, the President's Commission on Mental Health, reported that each federal dollar invested in community mental health centers had generated an estimated three dollars from nonfederal sources, the federal role in funding the centers never phased out as originally planned. Instead, during the two decades following enactment of the Community Mental Health Centers Construction Act (P.L. 88-164) in 1963, the act that authorized federal funding for the construction of such centers, Congress found itself routinely reassessing and extending the federal role in funding center development.

Amendments to the act in 1965 (P.L. 89-105) recognized that community mental health centers would need federal assistance with initial staffing requirements and authorized the use of federal funds for this purpose. Legislation in 1966 (P.L. 90-31) extended through 1970 the authorizations for construction and staffing of the centers. In 1968 more responsibilities for alcohol and drug abuse treatment were added to the centers' mission; children's facilities and services were added in 1970. Additional legislation in 1970 (P.L. 91-211) extended the basic community mental health centers' programs with an acknowledgment that local financing likely could not replace federal support as originally scheduled. Further, this law recognized that some high-poverty areas could not generate the matching funds required to begin developing a community mental health center and established special requirements for such locations (federal funds made up a greater percentage of total funds for these places). Further extensions and revisions of the 1963 act occurred in 1973, 1975, and 1978. The 1975 amendments in particular (P.L. 94-63) completely rewrote the act and expanded the centers' services and structures. Federal funding grew from a startup outlay of $30 million in fiscal 1965 to a high of $298 million in fiscal 1979. In fiscal 1981 the federal outlay was $270 million. About 20 percent of these funds served the chronically mentally ill.[1]

Between 1963 and 1978 the mission of community mental health centers expanded to include many populations in addition to the chronically mentally ill, so that by the end of the 1970s it was becoming increasingly clear that this population, for whom the centers were initially created, still did not receive the attention it needed. Both the President's Commission on Mental Health and the Department of Health and Human Services' Steering Com-

---

1. Based on data provided by the National Institute of Mental Health, Office of State and Community Liaison, from an unpublished document entitled "Total Federal Obligations for CHMCs, by State," n.d.

mittee on the Chronically Mentally Ill[2] recognized the continuing lack of services for the chronically mentally ill. For instance, the commission concludes:

> For many years, deinstitutionalization has meant being "dumped" into a community, to live in an inadequate boarding home or single room occupancy hotel. Former mental hospital patients were, thus, left without adequate food, clothing, recreation, or social services. . . .
> CMHCs have inadequately planned for and developed the community services required by the chronically mentally ill. . . .
> There is a lack in many communities of effective follow-up, outreach, and case management for the residents discharged from state mental hospitals.[3]

The Mental Health Systems Act of 1980 (P.L. 96-398) sought to refocus the efforts of community mental health centers to reach harder-to-serve persons, including the chronically mentally ill. The Carter administration used many of the recommendations in the report by the President's Commission on Mental Health to draft the provisions of the Mental Health Systems Act, which substantially revised the programming and structure of federal support for the centers. The act was signed into law in October 1980, just before the change from the Carter to the Reagan presidency. Most of its provisions were repealed by the Omnibus Budget Reconciliation Act of 1981, which created the alcohol, drug abuse, and mental health block grant to replace direct funding for the community mental health centers.

The Alcohol, Drug Abuse, and Mental Health Block Grant

The alcohol, drug abuse, and mental health block grant eliminated most of the provisions of the Mental Health Systems Act that created funding for specific populations, including the chronically mentally ill. It also significantly reduced the funding available from federal sources for mental health services.

Nothing in the wording of President Reagan's budget request or justification of the alcohol, drug abuse, and mental health block grant indicates that his administration wanted to abandon or change the basic program goals and objectives of federal mental health funding. Here, as with proposed budgetary and program structure changes for child welfare programs, the

---

2. President's Commission on Mental Health, *Report to the President from the President's Commission on Mental Health* (Washington, DC: U.S. Government Printing Office, 1978); and U.S. Department of Health and Human Services, Steering Committee on the Chronically Mentally Ill, *Toward a National Plan for the Chronically Mentally Ill*, Report to the Secretary, publication (ADM) 81-1077 (Washington, D.C.: U.S. Department of Health and Human Services, Public Health Service, December 1980).

3. Presidents' Commission on Mental Health, *Report to the President.*

Reagan administration retained a stated interest in pursuing program goals as expressed by earlier administrations. Rather, the administration simply applied its basic philosophy of government—its preference for reducing federal involvement and increasing state and local responsibility—to mental health funding along with funding for many other programs. In the process it repealed those aspects of the Mental Health Systems Act that were designed to encourage more attention to the chronically mentally ill without repudiating those goals, but also without retaining any mechanism that would assure local adherence to those goals. (Actually, as reported below, the state administrators who acquired new authority to control federal funds through the alcohol, drug abuse, and mental health block grant have been more committed to using those funds for the chronically mentally ill than the staff of the community mental health centers had been).

Table 11 gives the actual spending levels for the mental health component of community mental health center activities from 1978 through 1984, the federal budget requests for the first four years of the Reagan administration, and the spending levels adjusted for inflation. Except for the first year of the alcohol, drug abuse, and mental health block grant, 1982, Congress has consistently appropriated somewhat more money for mental health than the administration requested. These amounts have still fallen far short of the funding levels before the block grant, especially when one looks at the inflation-adjusted figures. Mental health programs have lost one-fourth of their purchasing power under the Reagan administration, as shown in the last column of table 11.

From the viewpoint of the states, mental health funding in the block grant is considerably less restricted than it was before 1982. Under the Community Mental Health Centers Act, federal funding went directly to community mental health centers, bypassing state mental health agencies and state priorities for mental health spending. The alcohol, drug abuse, and mental health block grant reduced the overall amount of federal money available within a state but increased state control over where that money was spent. The result, as reported in an Urban Institute study by Durman, Davis, and Bovbjerg,[4] is that mental health block grant funds are now being spent more in line with state priorities. This has some importance for the chronically mentally ill because state priorities have always been somewhat more directed toward this population than have federal priorities. For mental health, Durman et al. states "the federal ADM programs [alcohol, drug abuse, and mental

---

4. Eugene C. Durman, Barbara A. Davis, and Randall R. Bovbjerg, "Block Grants and the New Federalism: The Second Year Experience," Research Paper 3076-01 (Washington, D.C.: Urban Institute, April 1984), pp. 119–21.

TABLE 11

FEDERAL SPENDING FOR MENTAL HEALTH THROUGH COMMUNITY MENTAL HEALTH
CENTERS OR ALCOHOL, DRUG ABUSE, AND MENTAL HEALTH BLOCK GRANT,
FISCAL YEARS 1978–85
(*Millions of Dollars*)

Federal Fiscal Year	Administration Request	Percent Reduction from 1981 Spending Level		Actual Spending	Percent Reduction from 1981 Spending Level	
		Current Dollars	Constant Dollars[a]		Current Dollars	Constant Dollars[a]
1978	...	...	...	267	...	...
1979	...	...	...	298	...	...
1980	...	...	...	252	...	...
1981	...	...	...	270	...	...
1982	216[b]	−20	−25	214[b]	−21	−25
1983	216[b]	−20	−28	234[b]	−13	−22
1984	220[b]	−19	−30	231[b,c]	−14	−26
1985	236[b]	−13	−28	...	...	...

SOURCES: Data for 1978 to 1981 were taken from unpublished budget documents provided by the National Institute of Mental Health, Office of State and Community Liaison. Figures for 1982 to 1985 were taken from Office of Management and Budget, *Budget of the United States Government* (Washington, D.C.: U.S. Government Printing Office, various fiscal years), appendixes. Actual spending figures for a given year appear in the budget document of two years later (for example, actual spending in 1982 was taken from the 1984 *Budget* appendix). Figures are rounded.

a. Using deflator calculated from unpublished document provided by Office of Management and Budget, "Federal Government Expenses, 1985 Budget Data," February 1984, tables 11 and 12.

b. Based on a formula for distribution of block grant funds among services for alcoholism, drug abuse, and mental health. Mental health receives approximately 50 percent of the total block grant funds.

c. Based on spending estimates given in appendix to the 1985 federal budget.

health] previously supplemented or paralleled state grant systems. . . . All of [the states] preside over community mental health budgets that dwarf the federal CMHC program."[5] Two states in the Durman et al. sample of eighteen states are described as requiring:

CMHCs to serve chronically ill patients as their top service priority. The states' goal is to further their policy of deinstitutionalization by assuring services to former inpatients. Many states enforce such a policy for their state grantees;

5. Ibid., p. 106.

what is new since the block is its vigorous application to newer CMHCs once receiving only federal funds.[6]

Because of priority shifts, the history of state and federal funding patterns before the block grant and the phased nature of funding reductions, resources for mental health services supporting the chronically mentally ill have probably not suffered greatly from federal reductions, despite cuts in federal funding for the alcohol, drug abuse, and mental health block grant.

The Community Support Program

The Community Support Program of the National Institute of Mental Health began in 1977 as a federal initiative to stimulate states to do more for adults with chronic mental illness. The program is quite small in terms of federal dollars—states conducting demonstration projects under the program have received $20.5 million over a four-year period.[7] These projects involved states in efforts to develop systems of support for the chronically mentally ill in local communities. This federal initiative responded to many of the failings of the community mental health centers to provide such community support systems. Nowhere in the federal legislation or regulations were these centers required to provide posthospital planning services or after-care services to the chronically mentally ill once they left the hospital environment. Nor were the centers held responsible for coordinating care or services with non-mental-health agencies, despite the fact that housing, employment, recreation, and social services were often at least as important as mental health services to the success of a chronic mental patient in the community.

Contracts and grants from the Community Support Program to states support largely coordinating and development activities designed to increase state capacity to promote and maintain local community support systems. Very little of the money is spent on direct services. The program uses a rehabilitation framework in its approach to services to the chronically mentally ill. It assumes that people suffering from chronic mental illness nevertheless have a capacity for some degree of independent living. Services are structured to help these people achieve as much independence as is consonant with their maintaining a stable community living situation. The program goals are to reduce the "revolving door" phenomenon of repeated crisis hospitalizations, and to replace that pattern with stable community supports.

---

6. Ibid., p. 121.
7. "The Community Support Program of the National Institute of Mental Health," unpublished document, Office of State and Community Liaison, National Institute of Mental Health, February 1984.

Evaluations of program projects indicate that community support systems can be quite successful at keeping chronically mentally ill individuals in the community and reducing the number of costly inpatient days they use each year. One of the premises behind the Community Support Program is that resources already exist in the community that can be coordinated to the benefit of the chronically mentally ill. The program's projects have tapped and organized those resources, including, most important, other federal funding mechanisms benefiting the chronically mentally ill. Chief among these have been Supplemental Security Income and Medicaid. The chronically mentally ill appear to be losing ground in both programs, however, due to administrative and regulatory changes made by the Reagan administration.

Supplemental Security Income

The Supplemental Security Income (SSI) program began in 1974. It is an entitlement program—all persons who meet its eligibility criteria may apply for benefits. Its purpose is to provide an income supplement to aged, blind, and disabled individuals whose Social Security or other income is insufficient to provide a minimum standard of living. Its placement in the Social Security Administration rather than a more welfare-oriented federal agency was intended to avoid welfare connotations and to make it possible for people to receive SSI payments with the same dignity associated with Social Security.

At least some congressional supporters of the initial legislation perceived it as focused on the elderly, or at least on persons who had substantial work histories before becoming disabled.[8] In 1981, 50 percent of SSI recipients had such work histories, as indicated by their also receiving Social Security benefits. However, individuals in the three SSI eligibility categories have quite different patterns of participation in both programs—70 percent of the aged but only 38 percent of the blind and 36 percent of the disabled receive both SSI and Social Security benefits.[9] Disabled SSI recipients, of which the chronically mentally ill constituted approximately 18 percent in 1977,[10] are

---

8. U.S. Congress, Senate, Committee on Finance, *The Supplemental Security Income Program*, 95th Cong., 1st sess. (Washington, D.C.: U.S. Government Printing Office, 1977).

9. U.S. Department of Health and Human Services, Social Security Administration, *Social Security Bulletin, Annual Statistical Supplement, 1981*, (Washington, D.C.: U.S. Government Printing Office, 1981), table 169.

10. Ibid., table 178. Reported data are for 1977, the last year available. They indicate the chronically mentally ill comprise 17.7 percent of the disabled SSI recipients at the time of initial eligibility determination.

thus much less likely than aged SSI recipients to have participated in the work force long enough to qualify for Social Security benefits.

SSI Recipients

Table 12 summarizes participation in SSI from 1980 through 1983, with estimates included for 1984 and 1985. The table also includes information from January 1974, the first month of SSI operation. All figures except those for 1974 and those for the chronically mentally ill are taken from presidential budget documents prepared by the Reagan administration. Figures for the chronically mentally ill were calculated as a fixed percentage of the "blind and disabled" category, based on the only available estimate of this percentage

TABLE 12

NUMBER OF PERSONS RECEIVING FEDERAL SUPPLEMENTAL SECURITY INCOME,
SELECTED YEARS, 1974–85
(Thousands unless Otherwise Indicated)

Category	1974	1980	1981	1982	1983	1984 (Estimate)	1985 (Estimate)
Aged	1,690	1,584	1,506	1,452	1,333	1,400	1,387
Blind and disabled[a]	1,265	2,116	2,157	2,157	2,176	2,267	2,327
Chronically mentally ill[b]	217	363	370	370	374	389	400
Blind and disabled (percent of total)	42	57	59	61	62	59	63
Total	2,955	3,700	3,663	3,562	3,509	3,667	3,714

SOURCES: Data for 1974 are from U.S. Department of Health and Human Services, Social Security Administration, *Social Security Bulletin: Annual Statistical Supplement, 1981* (Washington, D.C., U.S. Government Printing Office, 1981) table 157; these data represent recipients at the beginning of the SSI program, January 1974. Figures for 1980 are from Office of Management and Budget, *Budget of the United States Government, Fiscal Year 1982* (Washington, D.C.: U.S. Government Printing Office, 1982), appendix (hereafter referred to as the *Budget*); for 1981, *Budget, Fiscal Year 1983*, appendix; for 1982, *Budget, Fiscal Year 1984*, appendix; and 1983–85, *Budget, Fiscal Year 1985*, appendix. Figures are rounded.

a. Approximately 3 percent of the "blind and disabled" are blind. Approximately 20 percent of the "blind and disabled" are 65 and older.

b. The "blind and disabled" category × 0.97 = disabled × 0.177 = percentage chronically mentally ill. These figures assume that the proportion of the disabled who are chronically mentally ill has remained constant at 17.7 percent since 1977, the last year for which diagnosis data are available (*Social Security Bulletin, Annual Statistical Supplement, 1981*, table 178). However, the contention of many service providers is that the chronically mentally ill are being disproportionately dropped from the SSI rolls or rejected at application.

by the Social Security Administration.[11] It should be noted that this method does *not* yield the true number of chronically mentally ill individuals receiving SSI in the years after 1977; these figures are nowhere available. The evidence for disproportionate reductions in chronically mentally ill persons from the SSI rolls will of necessity take the form of publications and testimony by agencies that determine SSI eligibility or provide services to the chronically mentally ill.

The data in table 13 indicate that a relatively stable proportion of between 57 and 63 percent of SSI recipients between 1980 and 1985 are eligible by reason of blindness or disability. This represents approximately a 15 to 20 percent increase over the initial distribution of recipients in 1974. To place this increase in perspective, the rate of disability per 1,000 U.S. population increased 13 to 19 percent (depending on the source of estimates) between 1972 and 1978.[12] The disabled individuals exceeded 50 percent of the SSI rolls for the first time in 1976, just two years after the program began. The table shows a steady decrease in the absolute numbers of aged recipients between 1980 and 1983, and there was a slight decline in their proportional representation (not shown). This pattern has held since 1976. The number of blind persons receiving SSI has remained relatively constant and the number of disabled recipients has increased in absolute numbers as well as proportionally. Our estimate, based on 1977 data, is that approximately 370,000 to 375,000 chronically mentally ill persons a year receive SSI benefits. This represents between 20 and 25 percent of the estimated 1.7 million persons with chronic mental illness in the U.S. population.

Federal Support for SSI

SSI and the Medicaid eligibility it entails reflect far greater federal investment in support for the chronically mentally ill than any investment in community mental health centers. Table 13 presents the federal outlays (excluding state supplements) for SSI payments to all recipients, to the blind and disabled, and estimates for the chronically mentally ill, for the years 1980 through 1983. It also includes estimates for 1984 and 1985, and 1974 data for historical comparison.

As can be seen from the table, estimates of SSI payments for the chronically mentally ill indicate federal expenditures of $632 million in 1980, increasing to slightly more than $1 billion projected for 1985; this is an

---

11. Ibid.
12. John W. Ashbaugh et al., "Estimates of the Size and Selected Characteristics of the Adult Chronically Ill Population Living in Households," *Research in Community and Mental Health*, vol. 3 (1983), pp. 3–24.

TABLE 13

FEDERAL SSI PAYMENTS TO THE CHRONICALLY MENTALLY ILL, SELECTED FISCAL
YEARS, 1974–85
(*Millions of Dollars unless Otherwise Indicated*)

Payment Category	1974	1980	1981	1982	1983	1984 (Estimate)	1985 (Estimate)
Total payments	3,833	6,434	7,170	7,604	8,683	8,471	9,346
Blind and disabled[a]	2,050	3,680	4,223	4,605	5,384	5,237	5,856
Chronically mentally ill[b]							
Current dollars	352	632	725	791	924	899	1,005
Constant 1972 dollars	313	355	374	383	429	396	426
Maximum allowable monthly payment (dollars)[c]							
Current dollars	146	208	238	265	284	314	325
Constant dollars	130	117	123	128	132	140	136

SOURCES: Data for 1974 are from *Social Security Bulletin, Annual Statistical Supplement, 1981*, tables 158 and 159; data for 1980 are from *Budget, Fiscal year 1982*, appendix; for 1981, *Budget, Fiscal Year 1983*, appendix; for 1982, *Budget, Fiscal Year 1984*, appendix; for 1983–85, *Budget, Fiscal Year 1985*, appendix.

a.   Proportional to the ratio of blind and disabled to all recipients, as given in appendices to the federal budget for 1982–85.

b.   The "blind and disabled" category × 0.97 = disabled × 0.177 = percentage chronically mentally ill. These figures assume that the proportion of the disabled who are chronically mentally ill has remained constant at 17.7 percent since 1977, the last year for which diagnosis data are available (*Social Security Bulletin, Annual Statistical Supplement, 1981*, table 178). However, the contention of many service providers is that the chronically mentally ill are being disproportionately dropped from the SSI rolls or rejected at application.

c.   Payment for a single person living alone or in a community residential facility. See *Social Security Bulletin, Annual Statistical Supplement, 1983*, p. 42. Benefits increase by same percentage and at the same time as Old Age, Survivors, Disability, and Health Insurance (OASDI).

apparent increase of almost 60 percent. In constant 1972 dollars the increase is 36 percent, which is still a substantial real increase. As one can infer from table 14, by looking at the last two rows for average monthly payments, most of these increases are attributable to inflation or to increasing numbers of persons on the rolls. Persons who continuously received SSI payments during the period shown in the table would maintain their position with respect to inflation, but would not experience any significant increase in their overall ability to purchase goods and services. In fact, in 1980, 1981, and 1982, SSI recipients would have received fewer inflation-adjusted dollars than they got in 1974. The increase in real spending power between 1974 and 1985 is just 4.6 percent.

Note the contrast between SSI support and community mental health center funding. Of the $214 million to $298 million spent for community mental health center services annually between 1980 and 1984, a high estimate of the proportion devoted to services for the chronically mentally ill is 20 percent, or $43 to $60 million per year.[13] SSI expenditures thus equal ten to twenty times as much money as specifically targeted mental health services.

The Importance of SSI for the Chronically Mentally Ill

SSI provides major federal support for the chronically mentally ill but its importance is not measured in terms of the magnitude of dollars alone. Rather, SSI payments, because they go directly to the recipients to dispose of according to their own needs, provide essential goods and services not available through community mental health centers or other mental health services.

As expressed in congressional testimony by a deputy commissioner of the New York State Office of Mental Health, which operates thirty-two psychiatric centers serving 46,000 inpatients and 77,000 outpatients and licenses or funds an additional 900 mental health programs,

> We are experiencing the effects of the changes in the disability determination process as we submit applications for the patients served in the programs we operate, as we admit patients who have decompensated when their disability payments have been threatened or ceased, and as we are called upon to provide additional funding and support to the programs we regulate because of the reduction in disability payments.
>
> The significance of the [Social Security Disability Income, SSDI] and SSI programs in providing basic income support to the mentally ill living in the community is, too often, not fully recognized. I would, therefore, like to provide some data to put this into perspective:
>
> Of a total 2.3 million SSI recipients nationally, approximately 750,000 are mentally ill. For New York State, this means that approximately 75,000 mentally ill individuals receive $310 million in income support.
>
> Of a total of 4.4 million [SSDI] recipients nationally, 485,000 are mentally ill. Again, for New York State this means approximately 48,500 mentally ill individuals and $165 million in income support.
>
> Moreover, many of the community based residential programs established to support the most seriously mentally ill individuals in the community are

---

13. In its attempt to refocus community mental health centers efforts on underserved populations, the Mental Health Systems Act of 1980 stipulated that approximately 20 percent of funding for these centers should be devoted to the chronically mentally ill. The act recognized that this would constitute an *increased* level of effort for services for this population.

dependent upon the residents' receipt of disability payments. In New York State there are two such programs:

The community residence program provides shelter and supervision for individuals in apartments or freestanding housing. Of approximately 2,000 residents, 1,300 are on SSI or [SSDI].

The family care program supports one to six individuals living with a family. Of 2,700 participants, 2,400 are on SSI or [SSDI].

In addition, SSI and [SSDI] entitlement carries with it entitlement for coverage of health and mental health services through the Medicaid or Medicare program. Loss of entitlement jeopardizes eligibility for these programs as well.[14]

Much discussion of deinstitutionalization has made clear that chronically mentally ill individuals in the community need services that replace the custodial or maintenance aspects of mental hospitals.[15] Equally clear is the fact that often they do not receive these services. Finding and paying for housing is an overwhelming problem, but so are obtaining adequate food, clothing, transportation, human contact and daily activities, medical and dental care, and management of medications necessary to maintain psychological equilibrium. Mental health programs, including community mental health centers, have not traditionally provided most or all of these services, nor have they offered the case management assistance often necessary to assemble an adequate array of supports for normal living. When experts speak of "dumping" deinstitutionalized chronically mentally ill people on the community, they mean that people have been released from public mental hospitals without having either a plan for how to obtain the services they need or the resources to purchase them. Therapy, the traditional "stock in trade" of community mental health centers and other mental health agencies, is a much lower priority for the chronically mentally ill than finding a stable source of shelter and food. SSI payments to chronically mentally ill persons provide the financial resources to purchase what they need.

SSI and the state supplemental payments that often accompany it enable the chronically mentally ill without families to pay for board and lodging in community residential facilities. These facilities sometimes include other services, such as managing medications or finances. Recipients' payments usually cover the cost of such care, with a little left over for incidental expenses,

14. Joanne K. Hilferty, Deputy Commissioner for Quality Assurance and Finance of the New York State Office of Mental Health, prepared statement in *Social Security Disability Benefits Terminations: New York*, Hearing before the Subcommittee on Retirement Income and Employment of the House Select Committee on Aging, 97th Cong., 2d sess., committee publication 97-353 (Washington, D.C.: U.S. Government Printing Office, July 1982), p. 34.

15. Leona L. Bachrach, *Deinstitutionalization: An Analytical Review and Sociological Perspective*, U.S. Department of Health, Education, and Welfare, publication (ADM) 76-361 (Washington, D.C.: U.S. Government Printing Office, 1976).

because the size of state supplements is usually geared to prevailing rates in community residential facilities. In addition, SSI carries with it another critical source of support—recipients are categorically eligible for Medicaid.

Medicaid eligibility means that chronically mentally ill SSI recipients can obtain psychotropic medications that enable them to remain in the community, medical and dental care for general physical ailments not related to their mental illness, and periodic inpatient care when necessary. Table 14 provides estimates for the federal share of medical assistance payments for the chronically mentally ill from 1980 through 1984. As with SSI payments, Medicaid financing for the chronically mentally ill greatly exceeds federal financing for special mental health programs—in this case by a factor of seven or more. Estimates are based on the assumption that the disabled in general, and the chronically ill in particular, absorb a simple proportional

TABLE 14

MEDICAL ASSISTANCE (TITLE XIX) PAYMENTS FOR THE CHRONICALLY MENTALLY
ILL, FISCAL YEARS 1980–84
(Millions of Dollars)

Year	Total Outlays under Title XIX (All Recipients)	Federal Share (All Recipients)	Federal outlays		Total outlays	
			Disabled[a]	Chronically Mentally Ill[b]	Chronically Mentally Ill	Constant 1972 Dollars
1980	24,557	13,826	1,956	346	615	312
1981	28,828	16,153	2,015	357	637	298
1982	30,879	16,589	2,150	381	708	311
1983	33,700	18,245	2,379	421	778	328
1984	36,575	19,616	2,580	457	775	312

SOURCES: Data for 1980 are from *Budget, Fiscal Year 1982*, appendix, actual expenditures; for 1981, *Budget, Fiscal Year 1982*, appendix, actual expenditures; for 1982–84, *Budget, Fiscal Year 1984*, appendix, actual expenditures. Data for 1983 and 1984 are estimates. The appendix to *Budget, Fiscal Year 1985* does not give this information. Figures are rounded.

a. The federal share (second column) multiplied by number of disabled recipients divided by number of total recipients. AFDC adults and children, poor elderly, blind and disabled individuals, SSI recipients, and other eligibles receive Medicaid. AFDC recipients use less than their proportional share of Medicaid dollars, whereas the aged use proportionately more. The disabled fall in between, but because their disabling condition almost always entails significant ongoing medical expenses, they resemble the elderly more than the AFDC population in their use of Medicaid.

b. Federal outlays for the disabled (third column) multiplied by 17.7 percent (the proportion of SSI disabled recipients who are chronically mentally ill).

share of Medicaid expenditures.[16] Because Medicaid coverage entails state and local matching funds almost equivalent to federal expenditures, the total public outlay for medical care for the chronically mentally ill can be estimated at between $600 million and $800 million annually from 1980 to 1984.

Changes in Social Security Administration Procedures

The expenditures just detailed, which contribute the lion's share of federal investment in services and support for the chronically mentally ill, are obviously critically important to the well-being of many persons affected by mental illness. However, new procedures pursued by the Social Security Administration during Reagan's presidency have made it more difficult to establish eligibility for SSI. Equally important, new redetermination procedures that review the continuing eligibility of people already receiving SSI have terminated SSI benefits for many long-term recipients.'

During the last year of the Carter administration, the Social Security Disability Amendments of 1980 (P.L. 96-265) mandated several administrative changes. These included periodic review at least once every three years of many disability cases that previously had not been reviewed. Congress established January 1982 as the date for beginning these reviews, but the Reagan administration accelerated the process and began in March 1981, just two months after taking office. These reviews covered persons receiving Social Security Disability Income only and persons receiving both this income and SSI.

A report compiled by the state of Michigan relates the following:[17]

> the SSI disability program grew beginning with its enactment in 1974, and appeared to continue this growth until January 1982. By taking into account the SSA practice of categorizing SSI recipients over age 65 as "disabled" rather than "elderly," it becomes clear that SSI disabled caseloads have dropped to their 1976 levels (i.e., the number of disabled SSI recipients *under* 65 years of age equalled 1.8 million in both 1976 and 1982).

---

16. AFDC children and adults, who comprise two-thirds of medicaid recipients, absorb much less than their proportional share of medicaid payments. The elderly, who make up 17 to 18 percent, absorb much more than their proportional share, due largely to nursing home costs. The disabled comprise 14 to 15 percent of Medicaid recipients and have regular medical expenses associated with their condition plus periodic inpatient or nursing home stays. Assigning them a proportional share of Medicaid expenses thus seemed both reasonable and the simplest way to estimate their share of federal Medicaid outlays.

17. This and the other quotation in this paragraph are from Philip Michel, *The SSI/SSDI Controversy: How and Why the Social Security Administration has Reduced the Number of SSI/ SSDI Beneficiaries* (Ann Arbor, Michigan: State of Michigan, Interagency Task Force on Disability, April 1983).

> The decline in caseload was preceded by a decline in approvals which began in 1976 and has continued to the present . . . approvals for SSI have reached the lowest level in the program's history. (p. 24)

The Social Security Administration began large-scale reviews of all current recipients in March 1981, immediately after the Reagan administration assumed office.

> [These] large scale increases in the number of reviews, termed "Continuing Disability Investigations (CDIs)" caused multiple thousands of clients to be reevaluated under more rigid procedures which had, by 1981, become standard. These periodic reviews using narrower standards caused nearly half of the beneficiaries examined to be declared ineligible for further benefits . . . many of the recipients terminated as a result of CDIs remained "disabled" under almost any definition of that word. (p. 3)

The chronically mentally ill have been among the hardest hit by these terminations. In specific reference to people with mental disorders, the report quotes a December 1981 letter to the federal Region V assistant regional commissioner from the director of Wisconsin's Disability Determination Bureau, stating that "the current adjudicative climate involving mental impairments seems to be one of deny, deny, deny" (p. 16). This opinion is echoed in testimony before the U.S. Congress in 1982. One report from New York City summarizes a study of accelerated continuing disability investigations:

> Over 160,000 people receive Social Security Disability (SSD) and Supplemental Security Income (SSI) benefits each month in New York State as a result of being mentally disabled and unable to work. Many of these people are state psychiatric hospital dischargees, living in single room occupancy hotels, adult homes, and community residences. They are dependent on federal disability benefits to buy food and pay the rent.
> Thousands of these chronically ill, mentally disturbed men and women will lose these benefits due to a federal initiative to reexamine the eligibility of all disabled Social Security beneficiaries. While the publicly stated intent of this action is to eliminate improper payments to employable people, the harsh reality is that many "truly" mentally disabled are being terminated as well. The fact that they still suffer from recurring and debilitating mental illness is apparently being routinely ignored.
> An estimated 5,500 mentally disabled beneficiaries in New York State (including 2,300 in New York City) will lose benefits in federal fiscal year 1982 alone. This federal initiative is yet another way in which the Reagan administration is removing the federal safety net for helpless people dependent on government benefits for survival.
> The outcome of this process is all too predictable. After losing federal disability benefits, some people will apply for the public assistance program of last resort, Home Relief, further increasing state and local welfare costs. The

less fortunate will end up destitute on the streets, causing yet another surge in the number of homeless people in New York City.[18]

At the same congressional hearing, the deputy commissioner of the New York State Department of Social Services testified, based on a study of 451 terminated cases:

> The Department of Social Services has initiated a study of claimants whose benefits have been terminated to identify their characteristics and needs. The preliminary results of this study support our impressions regarding the vulnerable nature of this population. The data suggest that the typical individual losing benefits is a single male aged forty-one with no other source of income and a limited residual functioning capacity. He is most likely to be suffering from a mental illness, particularly schizophrenia, or from a musculoskeletal disorder such as a back problem. The questionable prospects for employment for such individuals is supported by the finding that nearly a quarter of those who have lost benefits have made a new application for public assistance. This percentage will grow with time.[19]

Administrative Changes in Disability Definitions

In addition to reviews of continuing eligibility, the Social Security Administration began enforcing a more stringent definition of disability for both initial and continuing eligibility. This was done through changes in the policy manual governing disability determinations, but was never submitted to public scrutiny or acceptance through either legislative or rule-making procedures. Indeed, Congress has declined since 1977 to change the definition of disability through several sessions in which it explicitly addressed the issue.[20]

Three categories exist for determining eligibility. The first of these is made up of a number of disabling conditions specified by the Social Security Administration. Applicants qualify as "meets level of severity" if they have one of these conditions. The second category, known as "equals level of severity," allows the worker determining eligibility to assess the applicant's condition and make the judgment that that person's level of disability equals that of other people who qualify because they have the specific conditions

18. Office of the City Council President, New York City, "Passing the Buck: Federal Efforts to Abandon the Mentally Disabled," reproduced in *Social Security Disability Benefits Terminations: New York*, pp. 136–75.

19. Nelson Weinstock, Deputy Commissioner, Division of Operations, New York State Department of Social Services, prepared statement in *Social Security Disability Benefits Terminations: New York*, p. 18. The study to which Weinstock refers also appears in the hearing record, "Accelerated Continuing Disability Investigation Cessations: A Characteristics Profile of Affected Persons," pp. 176–267.

20. Philip Michel, *The SSI/SSDI Controversy*.

allowed in the first category. The third category, "medical and vocational consideration," includes persons whose level of functioning does not quite qualify them as severely disabled, but whose age, previous work experience, or other mitigating factors make it extremely unlikely that they could find and maintain a job.

The Social Security Administration has reduced state agencies' flexibility in determining disability by making it extremely difficult to qualify anyone for benefits unless they fall into the first category—that is, the applicant must have one of the disabling conditions specified by the policy manual. Table 15 shows why this approach has been particularly hard on chronically mentally ill applicants and beneficiaries.

The table gives the distribution for the three categories of eligibility for chronically mentally ill recipients of SSI, for all other recipients, and for all recipients. These data come from eligibility determinations in 1977, the most recent year available. The chronically mentally ill are significantly overrepresented in the second category, "equals level of severity," and underrepresented in the first category. New Social Security Administration procedures greatly favor the first category over the second and third. Thus, any group with a lower probability of qualifying due to a specific disabling condition acceptable to the Social Security Administration will suffer disproportionately under the new qualifying and review procedures. This has been true for the chronically mentally ill. (It has also been true for those with musculoskeletal problems, the most populous condition in the third category.) As the New York State deputy commissioner for the Office of Mental Health summarizes:

> The changes in the review process are difficult for all the disabled, but are particularly so for the mentally ill. The cycle of chronic mental illness is such

TABLE 15

ELIGIBILITY CHARACTERISTICS OF ADULT SSI RECIPIENTS, 1981

Item	Mentally Ill Recipients	All Other Recipients	Total Recipients
Total number of recipients	51,136	237,768	288,904
Percent of total	17.7	82.3	100.0
Social Security category (percent)			
"Meets level of severity"	35.0	41.0	40.0
"Equals level of severity"	54.0	34.0	38.0
"Medical and vocational consideration"	11.0	25.0	22.0
Total	100.0	100.0	100.0

SOURCE: *Social Security Bulletin, Annual Statistical Supplement, 1981*, table 178. Percentages are rounded.

that an individual may, under low stress and with the right supports, be able to live in the community. We've made tremendous strides in New York in sup- porting people in the community. But, if the federal government pulls their basic income support out from under them, there is no easy way to provide a stable living environment. For the chronically mentally ill, a stable living environment is essential to permit them to maintain themselves in the community.[21]

Pressures on the Social Security Administration from Congress and else- where resulted in a suspension of continuing disability investigations in mid- 1984. In addition, Congress is considering legislation to clarify that the Social Security Disability Amendments of 1980 were never intended to authorize more severe standards resulting in widespread findings of ineligibility for recipients of SSDI and SSI payments. It remains to be seen what effects these legal and administrative changes will have on the ability of the average chronically mentally ill person to obtain and retain eligibility status.

Summary

When President Reagan took office in 1980, the mental health system's ability to support the needs of the chronically mentally ill was open to question. The Mental Health Systems Act had just been passed after long congressional consideration of how to restructure the federal role in that system. The new administration had the opportunity to increase federal focus on the chronically mentally ill and promote greater concentration of federal effort than had previously existed. Nowhere did the administration reject long-standing fed- eral policy to benefit this population.

This chapter has reviewed the history, from 1963 to the present, of the federal programs most relevant to the chronically mentally ill. The initial federal support for community mental health centers in 1963 was based on an intent to improve the well-being of the chronically mentally ill, then residing almost entirely in state and county mental hospitals. Yet community mental health centers never fulfilled that intent, despite repeated federal efforts to focus their efforts on the chronically mentally ill.

The shift of community mental health center support to block grant funding in 1982 put more resources directly in the hands of state mental health agencies, whose priorities have always focused on the chronically mentally ill. As a result, services provided for the chronically mentally ill using block- grant funding do not appear to have suffered greatly, despite an inflation- adjusted cut of approximately 25 percent in overall funds available. Admin-

---

21. Hilferty, prepared statement in *Social Security Disability Benefits Terminations: New York*, p. 31.

istrative changes in initial and continuing eligibility for Supplemental Security Income, also affecting Medicaid eligibility, have much more seriously affected the well-being of the chronically mentally ill. These two programs contribute ten to twenty times more federal resources for the chronically mentally ill than does funding for community mental health centers. The effects of severely tightened eligibility criteria for mental disabilities has been felt throughout the country, as we detail in chapter 6.

Enabling the chronically mentally ill to maintain themselves in the community through coordinated systems of services (promoted by the Community Support Program) and financial resources (SSI) is cost-effective in the long run, but only if one adopts the perspective of the whole public.

CHAPTER 6

WHAT HAS HAPPENED TO THE CHRONICALLY MENTALLY ILL?

This chapter explores the ways in which changes in federal programs affect the lives of chronically mentally ill service recipients at the local level. Our basic approach has been to look at service patterns and recipients of those services at the local level through visits and data collection in four cities.[1] We report on San Diego City and County, Detroit (Wayne County), Richmond (which is its own county-equivalent jurisdiction) and Massachusetts State Region VI, which includes Boston.

We look first at the overall change in state funding patterns for the services covered in the alcohol, drug abuse, and mental health block grant. We then look at budget changes for mental health services in each of the cities we visited. Then, to put flesh on the budgetary skeleton, we describe the structure of services for the chronically mentally ill in each city, the size and other characteristics of the chronically mentally ill client population, and changes in service patterns. To the extent possible, we also describe the reasons for changes, such as direct fiscal or policy responses to federal changes, independent state or local fiscal or policy changes, or the recession. The chapter concludes with an assessment of the overall impact of federal policy on the chronically mentally ill between 1981 and 1983.

State Funding Patterns

Of the four states (California, Michigan, Virginia, and Massachusetts) in which the selected cities are located, two experienced real growth in their alcohol, drug abuse, and mental health financing between 1981 and 1983, and two

---

1. The criteria and methods for selecting the cities are explained in the introduction to this book.

experienced real funding losses. Table 16 displays the funding patterns in these four states, with details on funding sources and on both the nominal dollar change (current dollars) and the real change after inflation (constant dollars).[2] The data in the table do not report funding for mental health separately; rather, all funding is combined that is relevant to alcohol, drug abuse, and mental health block-grant activities, regardless of target population.

In all four states the real losses associated with this block grant funding are substantial and would have been greater if the respective states did not have carry-over funding available. California also reported significant reductions in funding from Title XIX (Medicaid) and Title XX for alcohol, drug abuse, and mental health functions. Michigan and California increased their use of other federal funds, but the total amount of money involved was very small. In three of the four states spending at the state level increased in nominal terms, but in two of the four the state resources devoted to alcohol, drug abuse, and mental health decreased in real purchasing power. California experienced the biggest loss in state support for these activities. However, community mental health programs in Massachusetts suffered disproportionally, despite overall increases in state revenues.

According to Department of Mental Health staff in Massachusetts, funding for community mental health centers was reduced because the governor rejected a former state policy of picking up this funding when federal support expired. The Department of Mental Health was unable to win replacement funds from the Massachusetts legislature in large part because governor King refused to supplement federally funded programs without a previous written agreement. Written contracts between community mental health centers and the state turned out to be virtually nonexistent. The reduction in state monies reflects a statewide austerity and denotes a lack of state support for the expansion of community services for the mentally ill. Because the Department of Mental Health decided against supporting the centers with other departmental monies when federal cutbacks occurred, the burden of reduced funds fell almost totally on the centers. The average community mental health center program absorbed cuts ranging from 30 to 34 percent, according to a study on block-grant implementation and federal cutbacks by the Massachusetts Human Services Coalition.[3]

---

2. Constant dollars were calculated using deflators derived from Office of Management and Budget, "Federal Government Expenses, 1985 Budget Data" unpublished document (Washington, D.C.: February 1984), tables 11 and 12. Except for SSI, the deflators used were for "all other grants and contracts" the deflators for payments to individuals were used for SSI.

3. Massachusetts Human Services Coalition, *Analysis of Human Services Block Grants in Massachusetts* (Boston, Massachusetts: MHSC, 1983).

TABLE 16

CHANGES IN FUNDING SOURCES FOR ALCOHOL, DRUG ABUSE, AND MENTAL
HEALTH SPENDING, STATE FISCAL YEARS 1981–83
(*Millions of Dollars*)

State and Funding Source	1981	1982	1983	Percent Change, 1981–83 Current Dollars	Percent Change, 1981–83 Constant Dollars
California					
Block grant and carry-over	57.3	49.0	41.4	− 27.7	− 34.7
Other federal	0.3	0.5	0.8	166.7	141.0
State	417.9	417.1	411.8	− 1.5	− 10.9
Titles XIX and XX	48.8	47.2	43.3	− 11.3	− 19.8
Local and other	16.0	36.9	51.2	220.0	289.1
Total	540.3	550.7	548.5	1.5	− 8.3
Massachusetts[a]					
Block grant and carry-over	22.4	20.5	18.5	− 17.4	− 25.4
Other federal	0.6	1.0	0.8	33.3	12.1
State	46.6	53.5	61.9	32.8	20.0
Titles XIX and XX	0.0	0.0	0.0	. . .	. . .
Local and other	2.9	3.7	1.6	− 44.8	− 50.1
Total	72.5	78.7	82.8	14.2	3.2
Michigan[a]					
Block grant and carry-over	11.5	11.0	11.2	− 2.6	− 12.0
Other federal	0.3	1.2	1.0	233.3	201.3
State	497.8	529.8	537.7	8.7	− 1.8
Titles XIX and XX	0.5	0.4	1.4	180.0	153.1
Local and other	19.4	22.7	25.7	32.5	12.0
Total	529.5	565.1	577.0	9.0	− 1.0
Virginia					
Block grant and carry-over	8.5	10.4	7.7	− 9.4	− 19.1
Other federal	0.7	0.6	0.7	0.0	0.0
State	6.5	8.3	10.1	55.4	40.4
Titles XIX and XX[b]	. . .	. . .	. . .	. . .	. . .
Local and other	7.3	7.7	8.1	11.0	0.3
Total	23.0	27.0	26.6	15.7	4.5

SOURCE: Data provided by states and taken from Eugene C. Durman, Barbara A. Davis, and
Randall R. Bovbjerg, "Block Grants and the New Federalism: The Second Year
Experience," Research Paper 3076–01 (Washington, D.C.: The Urban Institute, April
1984), table 23. Data for Michigan state mental health expenditures are from Michigan
Department of Mental Health, *Impact of Budget Reductions—1983* (Lansing, MI.:
MDMH, 1983).

a. Data based on federal fiscal years.
b. Included in "Other federal."

A special report by the Michigan Department of Mental Health details the actual and anticipated budget reductions for mental health in that state from fiscal 1979 to fiscal 1983.[4] In fiscal 1980 the Michigan legislature appropriated $494.7 million for mental health programs; in fiscal 1983 the appropriations totaled $537.7, a small increase in actual dollars but a significant decrease in real dollars.

To partially compensate for loss of state and federal revenues, local sources of funding increased greatly in California. However, this increase was insufficient to maintain statewide alcohol, drug abuse, and mental health services at the 1981 level. Only in Massachusetts did local revenues drop substantially. Michigan experienced a modest increase in local funding, while Virginia's local funding support remained relatively constant.

City and County Funding Patterns

The relatively benign picture painted by the state data in table 16 does not hold for the local data in the four cities we visited for intensive data collection. Tables 17 through 20 present the information on funding patterns for these cities and counties equivalent to that given for the state level in table 16, except that the city and county data pertain only to mental health programs rather than to all alcohol, drug abuse, and mental health functions.

Two cities, Richmond and Boston, show both nominal and real (after inflation) budget cuts, as tables 19 and 20 indicate. Richmond's mental health funding levels in 1983 were 18 percent lower in real terms than in 1981. Boston's funding declined 23 percent after inflation. In neither case did federal cuts have much effect on budget reduction. In Richmond mental health services did not rely on federal money at all, while federal funding in Boston amounted to less than 5 percent of the overall mental health budget for the years under study. State reductions brought most of the losses in the Boston area. Richmond lost funding from almost all sources; there the state alone increased its contribution to mental health services.

On the surface, table 17 suggests that San Diego's mental health budget showed no real dollar change between 1981 and 1983. However, totals for 1983 include $2.7 million transferred from the state to the county to cover mental health care for medically indigent adults.[5] MediCal (California's Med-

---

4. Michigan Department of Mental Health, *Impact of Budget Reductions—1983* (Lansing, Michigan: MDMH, 1983).

5. A medically indigent adult is any person who needs but cannot pay for medical care and does not qualify for federal medical assistance. The category includes, but is not limited to, people with chronic mental illness.

TABLE 17

SAN DIEGO BUDGET FOR MENTAL HEALTH PROGRAMS,
STATE FISCAL YEARS 1981–83
(*Thousands of Dollars*)

| | | | | Percent Change, 1981–83 | |
| | | | | Current Dollars | Constant Dollars |
Item	*1981*	*1982*	*1983*[a]		
Services					
Adult inpatient	7,477	7,264	7,794	4	−6
Adult partial day	3,363	4,686	4,107	22	10
Adult community services	2,764	3,396	3,851	39	26
Adult outpatient	6,403	7,015	6,338	−1	−11
Funding[b]					
State	13,758	13,994	14,014	2	−8
			(11,314)	(−18)	(−26)
County	1,715	3,696	2,717	60	45
Charges[c]	4,533	4,672	5,330	18	6
Total	20,006	22,360	22,091	10	0
			(19,291)	(−4)	(−13)

SOURCE: San Diego County, Department of Health Services budget documents.

    a. Includes $2.7 million in state payments for medically indigent adults (see text for description) that was not handled through the county system in 1982 or earlier. New recipients came with the new money.

    b. The numbers in parentheses were calculated without the $2.7 million for medically indigent adults.

    c. Includes MediCal payments, patient fees, and insurance payments. MediCal accounts for approximately half of this category.

icaid program) previously provided care for these persons, but with 100 percent state funding.

Before 1983, San Diego County had no financial or case-management responsibility for people in this category. Further, the $2.7 million set aside for the medically indigent in 1983 represents about 70 percent of what the state had spent on these people in past years. Thus the county received both more money and more recipients but insufficient additional funds to support what those additional recipients traditionally absorbed. The numbers in parentheses in table 17 describe the level of state funding in 1983 that equals the county's 1982 program responsibility. According to the numbers, state support for mental health programs in San Diego fell 26 percent in real terms between 1981 and 1983. County financial outlays increased 45 percent after inflation, bringing the real decrease in overall funding to 13 percent.

TABLE 18

DETROIT (WAYNE COUNTY) BUDGET FOR MENTAL HEALTH PROGRAMS,
STATE FISCAL YEARS 1981–83
(*Thousands of Dollars*)

| | | | | Percent Change, 1981–83 | |
| | | | | Current | Constant |
Item	1981	1982	1983	Dollars	Dollars
Medicaid					
Federal	668	904	1,137	70	54
State	668	904	1,208	81	63
State Department of Mental Health	26,415	27,575	31,649	20	8
County	3,009	3,164	3,643	21	9
SSI from recipients	2,533	2,434	1,386	44	30
Recipient fees and insurance			2,266		
Other[a]	13,314	14,763	12,188	−8	−17
Total	46,607	49,744	53,477	15	4

SOURCE: Data supplied by Detroit (Wayne County) Community Mental Health Board. Actual expenditures. Figures are rounded.

a. Includes miscellaneous grants and grantee or contractor income from numerous sources.

TABLE 19

RICHMOND BUDGET FOR MENTAL HEALTH PROGRAMS,
STATE FISCAL YEARS 1981–83
(*Thousands of Dollars*)

| | | | Percent Change, 1981–83 | |
| | | | Current | Constant |
Item	1981	1983	Dollars	Dollars
Federal	...	...	...	...
State	1,044	1,285	23	11
City	1,423	1,274	−10	−19
Other and local	210	40	−81	−83
Fees	408	237	−42	−48
Total	3,084	2,837	−8	−17

SOURCE: Richmond Department of Mental Health and Mental Retardation budget documents. Figures are rounded.

Only Detroit (Wayne County) experienced an after-inflation increase in funding for mental health programs. Table 18 shows that this increase came partly from increased fee and insurance income, partly from switching charges for services to Medicaid where possible, and largely from increased levels of state support.

TABLE 20

BOSTON (REGION VI) BUDGET FOR MENTAL HEALTH PROGRAMS,
STATE FISCAL YEARS 1981–83
(*Thousands of Dollars*)

| | | | | Percent Change 1981–83 | |
| | | | | Current Dollars | Constant Dollars |
Item	*1981*	*1982*	*1983*		
Federal	1,188	1,185	1,219	3	−7
State	28,901	32,384	24,347	−16	−24
Total	30,089	33,569	25,566	−15	−23

SOURCE: Massachusetts Department of Mental Health budget documents. Figures are rounded.

TABLE 21

CHRONICALLY MENTALLY ILL CASELOADS OF PRIMARY MENTAL HEALTH AGENCIES
IN SAN DIEGO, DETROIT, AND RICHMOND, STATE FISCAL YEARS 1981–83[a]

Site	*1981*	*1982*	*1983*	Percent Change, *1981 83*
San Diego	148,857	153,334	158,107	6
Detroit				
(Wayne County)	15,280	15,934	20,138	32
Richmond	550	550	650	18

SOURCES: Agency records from respective sites. San Diego data are based on units of service (*not* counts of recipients) for all adult patients. Services include all twenty-four-hour residential care, all partial day, and extended care program outpatient recipients. They exclude outpatient clinic hours, which few chronic patients use. An unknown portion of these service units went to acute rather than chronic patients. The Detroit (Wayne County) data are based on a formula whereby number of adults equals 0.67 of the total direct caseload, and chronically mentally ill equals 0.75 of the adult caseload. The figure for 1981 is derived from an earlier and less detailed data system. Data for Richmond are from verbal estimates of the administrator of the Day Treatment Center. The program there has no reliable data on unduplicated recipient counts for the years of interest. Figures are rounded.

    a. Data for unduplicated counts or units of service are not available for Boston.

Caseloads

Informative as these budget figures are about what has happened in the four selected cities, the picture is not complete without a description of what happened to agency caseloads during the period studied.

Table 21 presents the best available data on caseloads in three of the four cities. San Diego was able to provide units of services but not unduplicated recipient counts. Detroit (Wayne County) provided unduplicated recipient counts. Richmond had only the agency director's estimate of persons served before and after a reorganization of the agency in 1983. Boston had no reliable data on either units of service or unduplicated recipients.

All three cities reporting caseload data show increases in services and recipients between 1981 and 1983; in two cities these increases are substantial. Detroit's 32 percent increase in recipient caseload more than offsets the 4 percent real growth in its budget. Richmond's 18 percent client increase in recipients accompanies a 17 percent decrease in purchasing power. San Diego's service unit counts are up 6 percent, and this figure includes services to persons who once received care under California's now-defunct state program for medically indigent adults.

Agency Service Structures and Populations Served[6]

In each county visited a single agency had primary responsibility for programs and services for the chronically mentally ill. This agency provided direct services in three counties and purchased many services from a variety of private providers in all counties. In every county the primary agency also helped people obtain financial assistance and other services for which they were eligible from other government agencies.

San Diego

San Diego County's Department of Health Services operates or contracts for a full range of mental health services. The county has its own ninety-two-bed psychiatric hospital. It operates an Extended Care Program that oversees approximately 2,400 chronically mentally ill clients. It operates and also contracts for partial day programs, twenty-four-hour crisis care, twenty-four-hour long-term care, and case-management services. Under contract to the Department of Health Services, the state Office of Mental Health and Social Services provides case management for about 500 voluntary (chronically mentally ill) clients. The conservatorship program of the County Department of Social Services oversees another 1,800 people with mental health problems, and a contract agency has case-management responsibility for another 900 people a year who are primarily elderly and experiencing confusion and other mental problems associated with aging. Most of this group (85 percent) have never had a psychiatric hospitalization. In addition to services for the chron-

---

6. Readers who are not concerned with the detailed service structures in the four jurisdictions might want to skip to the next section.

ically mentally ill, San Diego's Department of Health Services purchased outpatient therapy services for adults at the rate of about 66,000 hours in fiscal 1983 and provides another 30,000 hours in its own clinics. Almost no chronically mentally ill use these therapy services. The agencies with major responsibility for the chronically mentally ill seem to communicate with each other regularly and to understand the services each provides.

About half the people participating in San Diego's Extended Care Program live in board and lodging homes, as do a significant number of persons served by the state Office of Mental Health and Social Services. Some extended care recipients and many conservatorship recipients live in nursing homes.

The Income Maintenance Division of the Department of Public Welfare makes SSI and Medicaid eligibility determinations. All persons served by the state Office of Mental Health and Social Services are SSI recipients; the same is true for about half of extended care patients. Almost none of the contract agency's elderly clients with mental complications receive SSI, although many receive Social Security payments and Medicare. Conservatorship recipients have mixed sources of income. Of clients not receiving SSI, many obtain general relief from the county and get medical care from programs for the medically needy or medically indigent adults, also administered by the Department of Public Welfare. Relations between the Income Maintenance Division and the mental health agencies are more adversarial than cooperative. Many of the mental health agencies assist in their recipients' appeals for the Income Maintenance Division's decisions on SSI eligibility.

Detroit (Wayne County)

The Detroit-Wayne County Community Mental Health Board (DWCCMHB; hereafter DWB), administered jointly by the city and county, funds over forty mental health agencies throughout Wayne County, seven of which are comprehensive community mental health centers. The Detroit-Wayne County Board uses state funds from the Michigan Department of Mental Health to purchase all direct services by contract. Seventy percent of the services are provided in the city of Detroit.

The DWB agencies provide three basic categories of services for the adult chronically mentally ill: outpatient services and aftercare, day hospitalization, and placement in residential care programs and follow-up case management. Among the DWB agencies are the county's seven comprehensive community mental health centers. The centers provide outpatient services, aftercare, and day hospitalization, as well as inpatient care, consultation and education, and crisis and emergency services.

In Detroit virtually every state-supported mental health agency in the county is under contract to the centralized DWB, so we can estimate the size of the population that receives some type of community-based mental health services. According to DWB, their forty-four agencies gave direct services to approximately 30,000 clients in fiscal 1980, 32,000 in fiscal 1981, and 40,000 in fiscal 1982. Two-thirds are mentally ill adults. The remaining recipients are mentally retarded adults and children or mentally ill children.

Of the mentally ill adults, about 75 percent are chronically mentally ill, and 25 percent are nonchronic—that is, either first episodes or emergency crisis cases involving drinking, battering, attempted suicides, police referrals, and so on. This latter category is said to be growing, a trend that is widely attributed to unemployment and layoffs. Almost all chronically mentally ill adults who receive community mental health support services show up in these figures; the only exception is the chronically mentally ill who seek care only through private physicians, psychologists, or social workers.

The DWB total recipient population is approximately half female and half male, and is made up of 46 percent white and 48 percent black recipients. Most are persons with low income and many receive Social Security payments or other forms of public assistance. Many of the chronically mentally ill adults have been deinstitutionalized after long stays in Northville, a large state psychiatric facility in Wayne County, and others have been in and out of Northville and other nearby state institutions (part of the often-described "revolving door phenomenon"). According to the DWB staff, the chronically mentally ill who have *never* been institutionalized, including a number of "street people," are least likely to be in the board's population because most placements in community support services occur at the time of discharge from hospitals. Approximately 70 percent of the people served by DWB agencies are solely outpatient and aftercare patients. Another 25 percent are enrolled in day hospitals, and 5 percent live in over 400 community-based residential care facilities where they are placed and supervised by two contract agencies.

The Michigan Department of Social Services, Wayne County Area Office, administers the SSI and Medicaid programs for Wayne County residents.

Richmond

The Department of Mental Health and Mental Retardation is the city agency responsible for providing community support services to deinstitutionalized mentally ill adults. Community services and case management are provided through agencies under contract with or managed by the Richmond Community Services Board. Established in 1968 by state statute, the board has responsibilities for planning, implementing, and reviewing all public mental health, mental retardation, and substance abuse services and facilities in the city. Private services and facilities that receive state or federal funds also come under jurisdiction of the board, and the board appoints and supervises the director of the Department of Mental Health and Mental Retardation.

The department funds a mental health center that serves deinstitutionalized chronically mentally ill adults primarily through day support, case management, and medication maintenance programs. It is also the agency's responsibility to provide predischarge planning for city residents leaving state institutions. Chronically mentally ill services are housed in a day treatment center. Approximately one-third of the chronically mentally ill recipient population is involved in socialization or rehabilitation programs, day hospital, and stabilization. Some of these persons and others are in group therapy (approximately one-half of the total caseload of 600 to 650). Others are maintained in their homes through medication maintenance services.

There are no specific residential programs in Richmond for the chronically mentally ill. Most live in licensed adult homes. Those unable to qualify or requalify for SSI live in rooming houses. Few live with their own families.

Eligibility determinations for SSI are made by the Department of Rehabilitation Services. There is consensus and considerable dismay among staff and administrators of mental health services that eligibility criteria are being tightened at the expense of the chronically mentally ill.

Boston (Region VI)

Services for Boston's chronically mentally ill population are administered through the State Department of Mental Health. Massachusetts is divided into forty-one mental health catchment areas within seven geographical regions. Region VI, which includes the Boston area, has six community mental health centers serving various communities in greater Boston. Each of these community centers is associated with a medical center and also subcontracts or provides outreach activities and community programs to local agencies. In each region there are also state hospitals that provide inpatient backup facilities for acute and long-term care.

Boston area community mental health centers provide a broad range of services for chronically mentall ill adults, including nonresidental and outpatient treatment programs (emergency services, day hospitalization, day activities, day treatment) and residential treatment programs (inpatient care, group homes and apartments, foster care, and emergency shelters).

Each of these centers is responsible for providing or arranging for all the care its patients receive. Their programs are different, because each has been relatively autonomous in developing programs and services. Some have had a good deal of federal funding in the past, whereas at least one had just applied for a federal initial operations grant in 1980 and never received it. Although Region VI is an official Massachusetts Department of Mental Health designation, in effect, each community mental health center operates as a separate, independent entity within its own geographical boundaries. There is little or no crossover of clients or services. Because of this situation, statistics for the entire Boston area are difficult to obtain and one cannot get a clear picture of mental health services in Boston. To determine the service delivery system in Boston, we therefore selected two of the six community mental health centers for more detailed interviews and data collection. These two centers are the Massachusetts Mental Health Center, which serves a catchment area approximately twice the size of the other Boston centers, and the Dorchester Mental Health Clinic.

Housing options for the chronically mentally ill in Boston depend to some extent on which center serves them. Some centers have developed quite elaborate community residential programs, including boarding homes, adult foster care, and apartment living. Individuals in these living situations receive case management and supervision from the respective center staff and participate in coordinated day programming at the center. Other centers do considerably less to assist their patients with life in the community.

At Massachusetts Mental Health Center, one of the two Boston community mental health centers whose staff we interviewed, they estimate they have approximately 600 admissions to inpatient care each year, representing 300 to 400 individual clients. They also estimate they have 38,000 outpatient visits a year, probably to no more than 1,500 persons, many of whom are the same persons admitted periodically to the inpatient services. Their population is approximately half female and half male, and is made up of 75 percent white and 25 percent nonwhite recipients. The majority are of low socioeconomic background; about 65 percent have incomes of $5,200 or less, and most have very little formal schooling.

The Dorchester Mental Health Clinic did not have equivalent data on its patients. However, staff there indicate the patients are of two primary types: middle-age or older white clients who were institutionalized at a nearby mental hospital and who have remained in the area, and younger patients in their twenties who are members of ethnic minorities. Dorchester is a federally designated poverty area with a high rate of unemployment and poor services.

The Department of Public Welfare administers the SSI and Medicaid programs. SSI eligibility determination and redetermination actions have put the community mental health centers into an adversarial relationship with the department in many instances.

Impact of Budget and Program Changes

Budget and caseload numbers can provide only a small amount of information about what has really happened to services in a community. It is even more difficult to capture a sense of what has happened to patients in the face of numerous changes in different programs. For each community visited, we summarize our findings below based on interviews with case managers, service providers, funders, and advocacy groups.

San Diego

The chronically mentally ill in San Diego have suffered significant cutbacks in care and financial support due to both federal changes and to state financial difficulties. The changes having the greatest effects are SSI eligibility determinations and MediCal rule changes, which appear to be motivated by the need to reduce costs as much as possible in the short run.

Community mental health services in California are funded largely by state and federal money. State money is authorized under the Lanterman-Perris-Short Act of 1968. (This act replaced the earlier Short-Doyle Act of 1957; the money is still referred to as Short-Doyle funding.) The county match for this funding is only 10 percent. MediCal, Medicare, and Supplemental Security Income (SSI) augment community mental health dollars for many chronic adult patients.

For the 4,700 clients in San Diego's Extended Care Program, the state Office of Mental Health and Social Services program, and the conservatorship program, SSI efforts to purge the rolls have greatly affected their well-being. One way to prove one's disability to SSI workers is to be rehospitalized, and many have taken this route, if only because the tension associated with uncertainty is enough to destabilize them. Many chronically mentally ill persons have not understood the notices they receive from SSI, and so have let appeal dates and hearing dates pass by. Only when the checks stop coming do they realize what has happened. Once without SSI, former recipients can only turn to general relief or the streets. The general relief fund in San Diego pays only $310 per month; SSI plus the State Supplemental pays $452 per month plus $50 spending money if the recipient lives in a board-and-care facility. (Most states supplement federal SSI payments up to an amount that will provide room and board in a board-and-care facility.) Board-and-care rates are geared to SSI payments; thus the decrease to general relief rates often means the recipient cannot continue to live in the boarding house. The frequent alternative is the street, and caseworkers report that more and more of their chronically mentally ill clients are forced to take this alternative.

For those who still retain their SSI eligibility, MediCal has begun to use a new method to calculate income available for medical care, using the general relief fund payment of $310 as the base rather than the SSI payment of $452. This means that recipients who once were expected to pay for medical care with only the $50 discretionary money they receive every month are now assumed to have $192 per month available for medical expenses (the difference between $452 and $310, plus the extra $50). In fact recipients do not have this money, since their residential care (board-and-care homes) costs $452 per month. Their choice comes down to housing or medical care.

The 900 or more mostly elderly clients receiving case management from a contract agency have other problems due to changes in federal regulations. These people largely suffer from confusion and other mental problems associated with aging. The majority do not receive SSI. The picture for them is complicated by changes in MediCal and Medicare regulations that spell the difference between chronically mentally ill clients receiving medical care or not.

Until 1982 MediCal picked up the copayment that Medicare required of elderly recipients. It no longer does so. For hospitalization the copayment is $304. Many chronically mentally ill elderly recipients do not have this money and hence forgo medical care they received under the old regulations. The $75 copayment requirement for outpatient care has the same effect.

If the patient does receive the care, outpatient or inpatient, and then cannot pay, Medicare is aggressively using promisory notes and liens on property and estates; such actions tend to frighten patients and prevent them from seeking the care they need. This point and the copayment requirement affect the near-poor who do not receive SSI. They also affect all the low-income elderly discussed in subsequent chapters.[7]

Poor, mentally ill people seeking MediCal assistance for the first time are affected by the changes. Because of new MediCal ways of counting assets (nonliquid assets like burial plots and life insurance policies that were previously disregarded are now counted), there is no guarantee that patients will qualify for MediCal even if they spend all their available money on health care before they apply.

Pressures from MediCal also threaten the Extended Care Program. This program supervises approximately 2,400 chronically mentally ill clients, as mentioned above. Teams made up of a psychiatrist, a nurse, and a clerk visit clients in 28 clinic sites for medication management and supervision. Many of these clinics are held in the board-and-care homes where the clients live.

---

7. See chapters 7 through 9 of this volume.

San Diego previously certified these clinics as part of MediCal and billed MediCal in a lump sum for the care delivered. MediCal is now increasing the certification requirements in such a way that San Diego may have to close down a large part of this very efficient operation. The care that MediCal will pay for hereafter will be more expensive and there will be less of it.

San Diego's spending for the chronically mentally ill remained the same from fiscal 1981 to fiscal 1983, but this includes a $2.7 million increase because of changes in the medically indigent adult program. During the last two fiscal years San Diego has cut $2.74 million worth of programming, closing or reducing 14 outpatient, partial-day, and socialization services, all but one for adults. The total community mental health budget is around $22 million, of which approximately 75 percent is spent on adults for all types of care. The chronically mentally ill have thus been hard hit by federal changes, especially regulatory changes, and will not receive compensatory services or support from San Diego.

Detroit

According to staff at the Detroit-Wayne County Community Mental Health Board (DWB), the mental health services the the board funds have not been substantially reduced over the past three years. In fiscal 1981 the state cut the board's funds by 10 percent, a cut that was absorbed by reducing salaries and benefits to employees. Since then, the state funds to the board have remained constant. By and large, the chronically mentally ill in the Detroit area have not been hit with substantial cutbacks, since the DWB has managed to keep its funding relatively constant to the agencies with which it forms contracts. (Most of these forty-four agencies receive the vast majority of their funds from the board, although they are required to raise at least a 10 percent match on their own). The only noticeable change that the DWB has implemented is a shift in funding away from some recreational ("non-therapeutic") facilities into emergency services and more therapeutic, professional services, such as day hospitalization. The DWB terminated a few purely recreational day activities programs; and the staff do not know whether these facilities replaced the lost funding or closed their doors.

Staff from the statewide Mental Health Association in Michigan—a private nonprofit United Way agency that advocates, organizes, and lobbies on mental health issues—painted a markedly less optimistic picture than did the DWB staff. State funds and caseloads in the past few years in the Detroit area have been relatively constant, but the demand for services has escalated greatly. As a result, the number of unserved people has risen sharply. The large influx of people seeking services is a function of stressful times—

extremely high unemployment and layoffs due to the recession. The result is an increase in requests for mental health services from a nonchronic population, many of whom need emergency intervention. Federal cuts in dollars to community mental health centers exacerbate the problem.

Increasing nonchronic cases are also noticeable at Northville, the state-run inpatient facility in Wayne County with a current population of 1,100, where the number of admissions has actually grown despite the statewide deinstitutionalization policy. Many informants in the Detroit-Wayne County area mentioned their perception that the rising demand for a whole range of services has resulted in *less* care for chronically disabled clients in order to meet the crises experienced by those who do not traditionally use the mental health system. The less immediately disabled recipients (people who have no immediate, pressing need, although they have chronic problems, including many chronically ill) are being displaced by those experiencing acute psychotic episodes. As a result, community-based services are even further taxed by the increased severity of their patients' conditions. Furthermore, prevention programs are being tightened to free funds for more direct services such as aftercare programs.

Local agency staff confirm this pattern. At Community Case Managers, a contract agency that places the chronically mentally ill in adult foster care, the staff sees few of the new type of patient (the crisis patient who is troubled by layoff or unemployment) because such clients rarely use adult foster care. However, because of the continuing deinstitutionalization of the chronically mentally ill from all hospitals in Michigan, this agency has had a three-fold rise in caseload, from 400 in 1980 to 1100 in 1982, with more than 1,200 expected in 1983. The rise in caseload has been coupled with a slight decrease in funds from the DWB. The decrease has been absorbed by freezing salaries and benefits; by shifting staff from case management to placement, thereby reducing the intensity of the service each patient receives; and by eliminating the aftercare program for patients who leave adult foster care for independent living. The staff believes this has led to higher rates of rehospitalization.

Providers of foster care for adults have also absorbed recent cutbacks. Many patients have lost their SSI and have switched to general assistance. As a result, they can no longer pay as much for room and board. Although the providers are expressing dissatisfaction, patients are rarely turned out when they lose their SSI. Adult foster care facilities have maintained their numbers, but many have closed and have been replaced by new providers with less experience dealing with the chronically mentally ill.

The situation at the state level is similar to that in Detroit. In 1979 the Department of Mental Health developed a comprehensive written plan to use case managers across a broad continuum of care, from inpatient hospital settings to independent living. This whole plan was abandoned in the early 1980s and now virtually no outreach exists anywhere to those living independently.

The State Department of Mental Health staff estimates that, in Michigan due to the statewide pressures on the mental health system, 36,000 people seeking mental health services were turned away in 1983. In contrast, almost every person in the state who sought care three years before was served. Now in most areas only the most severely in need actually receive services.

Richmond

The Department of Mental Health and Mental Retardation, which has primary responsibility for Richmond's chronically mentally ill, has not been directly affected by federal retrenchments and changes. It has been faced with cutbacks closer to home, particularly at the local level. Hardest hit by these cuts was the Mental Health Services Division, which went through a major consolidation effort in order to avoid staff reduction. Administrators feel confident that the consolidation effort actually improved services to city residents with mental health needs. According to the staff and the administration, the deinstitutionalized chronically mentally ill are receiving higher quality services than before reorganization. These same staff members and administrators both are quick to note, however, that deinstitutionalized adults are feeling the effects of changes in income maintenance, Medicaid, and other secondary support services that enable them to remain in the community.

Mental health services underwent major changes in fiscal 1983. As of July 1982 the acute care inpatient unit housed in a local hospital was closed and six neighborhood clinics (four outpatient, one day treatment, one acute care) were consolidated into one downtown facility. These actions were taken in response to an anticipated fiscal 1983 loss of $361,000 in city funds compared to fiscal 1982 levels. Even maintenance of fiscal 1982 funding, according to mental health administration calculations, would have resulted in a $73,000 deficit if staffing and services had been kept constant.

In addition to this expected revenue loss of 20 percent of the personnel and operating budget for fiscal 1982, mental health services faced further reductions in the following fiscal year because of changes in pay scale for city employees. Personnel costs jumped from $1,200,000 in fiscal 1982 to $1,865,000 in fiscal 1983—a 54 percent increase. Concomitantly, operations money fell from $918,000 to $704,000—a 23 percent drop.

The above-mentioned consolidation into one downtown facility occurred at this time because the agency anticipated reduced city funds. However, plans to consolidate had "been on the back burner" for several years. The existing system was always supported solely with state and city funds. Staff and administrators say that because of poor staffing patterns, the previous decentralized system was ineffective and inefficient. Caseloads were high (75 to 100 per staff member), specialized staff had to be generalists, outreach was impossible. By all reports, the reduction in city funds was a blessing in disguise because it finally forced the Mental Health Committee to act.

Maintaining chronically mentally ill adults in the community requires an array of support services. In addition to special programs that develop social skills or prepare these adults for some form of employment, deinstitutionalized adults require a variety of community-living support—income, housing, food, personal care, and transportation assistance. In Richmond it is this second category of services and support that has been directly affected by federal program changes.

The effects of SSI changes have already been mentioned. With respect to housing, Richmond has no special residential programs or housing supplements for chronically mentally ill adults. These adults live primarily in licensed adult homes; those who are unable to qualify or requalify for SSI live in rooming houses. Chronically mentally ill adults are much less likely than mentally retarded adults to be living with families. They are a much more transient population.

One of the supports that caseworkers once relied on to meet emergency housing needs for the chronically mentally ill—church assistance—is now difficult to obtain, according to the Mental Health Center's chief caseworker. Churches that once offered food and housing assistance to chronically mentally ill clients are low on funds. Many have earmarked their remaining dollars for church members because of increasing demands.

The number of licensed foster homes for adults in Richmond appears to grow to meet demand. The quality of these homes, however, is suspect. The director of the Virginia Mental Health Association said that one of the main goals of the association is to "clean up these places." A bill is being introduced in the state legislature that will define the rights of residents of these licensed homes. The chronically mentally ill, for the most part, are in homes where bed space has not been filled with elderly persons. The chronically mentally ill are not the preferred residents.

Boston

According to the staff of the State Department of Mental Health, the mental health budget for Massachusetts has not been greatly affected by federal funding cutbacks. This is because in most of the affected community mental health centers in the state had completed the cycle of their eight-year federal grants by fiscal 1982. In anticipation of this event, the state had replaced most of the expiring federal funds through appropriations.

However, the block-grant legislation brought about a significant shift of power in community-based mental health services. Before the block grant, community mental health centers functioned as semiautonomous agencies and received funding directly from the federal government. Block-grant funds now go instead to the Department of Mental Health's area offices for distribution. In fiscal years 1982 and 1983 all the funds were distributed to center programs that had held operations grants and would have received the money directly under previous federal procedures. In the future, however, it is possible that a third of block-grant monies will go to area offices to be distributed through a proposal mechanism to those bidders deemed most responsive to area service needs and priorities. This means that the centers might absorb an additional cut in block-grant funds, which would result in a further reduction in the provision of community mental health services through the centers.

According to the Massachusetts Human Services Coalition:

> Although it is generally acknowledged that the cuts resulted in lost services, there seems to be some disagreement about the degree of hardship. On one hand, it is argued that the planning process will be enhanced by combining state and federal funds, that community services can be more fully integrated into the area-wide planning process, and that Community Mental Health Centers can be held accountable for delivering services to the most severely disturbed clients. On the other hand, it is claimed that the shift from federal prospective payments to state retrospective payments (resulting in a funding gap of up to three months), the state's cumbersome voucher system and the potential loss of eligibility as Community Mental Health Center result in program inefficiencies that compound lost federal revenue.[8]

The impact of federal changes on specific community mental health agencies serving the chronically mentally ill, can best be seen by first taking a close look at the Massachusetts Mental Health Center, one of six community mental health centers serving the Boston area. Chronically mentally ill adults enrolled in this center's residential treatment programs appear to be the ones most affected by recent federal program changes. These deinstitutionalized adults require long-term care. Many who are dependent on SSI have been hit hardest and have been most vulnerable to changes in available support services. Between 1981 and 1983 there has been a dramatic increase in the number of chronically mentally ill clients who have been denied SSI benefits or have had their benefits reduced. Eligibility has been tightened by a more

---

8. Massachusetts Human Services Coalition, *Analysis*, p. 21.

rigorous criterion to qualify as chronically mentally ill. The criterion calls for extensive medical documentation that is highly specific about prognosis, the time frame of the illness, and the degree of impairment. The Massachusetts Mental Health Center has introduced training sessions for staff doctors to teach them how to write medical histories that will satisfy SSI requirements. The center's staff explained that while it has been generally successful in appealing the SSI denials, the process is a lengthy one and causes undue stress on chronically mentally ill patients.

The center staff reported they have stopped sending new applicants to the SSI office, since experience has shown that it is a waste of time for their chronically mentally ill clients to apply. (Caseworkers in other cities reported equal levels of frustration.) The staff also reported that state monies for general assistance have simultaneously been tightened and that consequently less emergency income-maintenance funding is available for the chronically mentally ill. Because of this and the prevalence of area unemployment, increasing numbers of chronically mentally ill are unable to pay $200 a month for room and board in group residences.

The Massachusetts Mental Health Center is part of a state mental hospital as well as being a community mental health center, so it has two different organizational systems and funding sources. As a psychiatric teaching hospital for fifty years, this center has always had a steady source of funding through which it offers an extensive, comprehensive program for chronically mentally ill adults. Federal grant requirements for community mental health center activities have been met by adding services through federal community mental health center funding, while basic continuing-care services have remained the same. However, block-grant implementation and declining state funding have increasingly forced the center to serve only the "sickest" or the most severely disturbed clients. Outreach, consultation and education, prevention, and community activities and services have been cut or deemphasized. Now people who are not severely disabled are less likely to receive services.

Federal changes to the alcohol, drug abuse, and mental health block grant have had a more direct effect at the Dorchester Mental Health Clinic than they have at the Massachusetts Mental Health Center. Dorchester has been in the unique position of experiencing the full impact of the alcohol, drug abuse, and mental health block-grant implementation and federal cutbacks. The Dorchester clinic applied in 1980 for a categorical initial operations grant as a community mental health center. The request was rescinded, converted into a block-grant request, and the money was subsequently allocated through the state rather than given directly to the clinic by the federal government. The Dorchester clinic's block-grant allocation was one-fifth to one-sixth of what it originally requested. The block-grant legislation affected *anticipated* services, which had a high probability of receiving federal support before the Reagan administration created the state-administered block grant. To develop residential programs, Dorchester had applied for funds to develop half-way houses and cooperative apartments to provide transitional, independent living situations for chronically mentally ill adults in its catchment area. Without federal funds, Dorchester could not implement this program.

The Dorchester clinic had planned a major expansion in emergency services that would have created fifteen staff positions and increased programs to minimize hospitalization. This expansion of emergency services was canceled due to funding cutbacks. Finally, to meet community needs, Dorchester had planned to expand services to include alcohol and drug abuse and senior services components; these plans were also canceled because of insufficient funds.

Summary

Federal changes in funding specifically earmarked for community mental health centers do not appear to have made a great deal of difference for agencies serving the chronically mentally ill. In most cases local or state changes in funding levels have had the biggest influence. In two states, California and Massachusetts, these local and state changes have been driven by relatively more conservative government philosophies than in previous years, backed up by referenda constraining public revenue activities. Proposition 13 in California, Proposition $2\frac{1}{2}$ in Massachusetts, and Proposition J in San Diego all constrain revenue-raising actions (the two state propositions) or total budget growth (San Diego's Proposition J). Michigan's budget problems at the state and local level are overwhelmingly due to the troubled automobile industry and its effects on the economy and employment in Detroit and elsewhere in the state. These conditions have also exacerbated mental health problems at a time when the state does not have the financial resources to meet them in a manner consonant with its generally liberal philosophy of government. All jurisdictions in this study except Boston also reported funding difficulties as a result of the recession—a recession that brought both reduced revenue and more need for services in the mental health area (and in many other areas).

In all jurisdictions the federal changes most seriously affecting the chronically mentally ill were the changes in SSI operating procedures. The precise nature of these changes was neither legislatively mandated nor subjected to normal rule-making procedures. Rather, the Social Security Administration issued detailed changes in its policy manual that affected SSI eligibility decisions for both new applicants and continuing recipients, as discussed in chapter 5.

The Social Security Administration maintains that continuing disability reviews pertain only to recipients of Social Security Disability Income (SSDI) and to people who receive both SSDI and SSI. Those who receive only SSI should not be affected by these reviews of cases. However, somewhere between the Social Security Administration's official intent and the local disability determination offices these restraints appear to have been lost. In every city we visited there were many instances of people who received only SSI, whose cases were called up for redetermination hearings, and who were dropped from the SSI rolls as a result.

No one in any of the cities we visited had concrete numbers for the magnitude of the SSI problem, yet everyone felt it was the most significant change in federal policy affecting the people who use SSI services. We can make some estimates of the numbers of chronically mentally ill adults affected by SSI changes if we are willing to make some assumptions. In chapter 5 we estimated that there are 1.7 million chronically mentally ill adults in the United States. Assume first that approximately half of these people receive services from some mental health agency at any given time. Then assume that approximately half of these persons also receive SSI (this assumption is derived from our local interviews). Assume further that approximately half of the SSI recipients are called for a redetermination hearing, and that approximately half of those hearings result in termination of SSI benefits (this assumption is based on local perceptions and on research).[9]

According to these assumptions, approximately 106,000 chronically mentally ill former SSI recipients will lose their benefits, at least temporarily, as a result of redetermination hearings under new federal procedures. This figure represents approximately 12 percent of chronically mentally ill SSI recipients. We add the proviso, "at least temporarily," because many of these recipients of SSI who have caseworkers in mental health or other service agencies have filed appeals of these redetermination decisions. Initial negative eligibility determinations are being reversed about 65 to 67 percent of the time if they are appealed. State and county officials perceive the importance of helping SSI recipients with appeals both because they see the human cost involved in lost SSI benefits and because they know that state and local welfare dollars will eventually have to assist the chronically mental ill when

---

9. See P. Michel, *The SSI/SSDI Disability Controversy* and *Social Security Disability Benefits Terminations: New York*, Hearing before the Subcommittee on Retirement Income and Employment of the House Select Committee on Aging, 97th Cong., 2d sess. (Washington, D.C.: U.S. Government Printing Office, July 1982), committee publication 97-353.

they (and other recipients of SSI) lose those SSI benefits.[10] All officials with whom we spoke expressed concern for people on SSI who do *not* have caseworkers to help them with the appeals process. Undoubtedly, many of the failures to appeal SSI decisions arise not because of the merits of the case, but because the paperwork and bureaucratic expertise one must have to prevail and win an appeal are enormous and often are well beyond the coping ability of the chronically mentally ill.

To conclude, the major impact of the Reagan administration on the lives of the chronically mentally ill has come about through regulatory or procedural changes, not through budget cuts or changes in administrative structure from categorical to block grants. These changes, particularly those in SSI and the Medicaid eligibility that goes along with it, have not been as highly published as the budget cuts. Nevertheless, their influence has been felt in every part of the system that serves the chronically mentally ill, all of whom report that losing SSI benefits is devastating to the well-being of these recipients.

---

10. Ibid.

PART THREE

THE LOW-INCOME ELDERLY

CHAPTER 7

WHO ARE THE LOW-INCOME ELDERLY?

The economic situation of the elderly has improved dramatically in the past two decades and has continued to improve during the Reagan administration. As late as the 1960s, poverty among older Americans was seen as a very serious concern. Data prepared for the delegates to the 1961 White House Conference on Aging showed that 6 million elderly (more than one-third of the population over age sixty-five) had inadequate income. Between 1960 and 1970 this number decreased to 5.7 million; the 1980s have seen it drop to under 4.0 million. Given that the number of persons over age sixty-five has increased 54 percent from 16.6 million in 1960 to 25.6 million in 1980, this decline in the number of elderly living below poverty is impressive.

The economic situation of the elderly has improved not only in absolute terms but in relative terms in recent years. In 1959, 22.4 percent of America's total population lived below the poverty line; more than one-third of those aged sixty-five and older, however, (35.2 percent) were among the impoverished (see table 22). As late as 1970 America's domestic policies were much more successful at reducing poverty overall than they were at addressing poverty among the elderly; the poverty rate for the entire population had fallen to 12.6 percent by this time, but poverty among the elderly was still quite common, with one out of four persons falling below the line (24.5 percent).

Federal actions during the 1970s (most specifically the indexing of Social Security to the consumer price index) significantly closed this gap. In 1981 the poverty rates for the total population and for the elderly were within two percentage points of each other: 14 percent and 15.3 percent, respectively. By 1983 this situation was almost exactly reversed. For the first time, older Americans were marginally less poor than those under age sixty-five.

The overall portrait of the elderly in the 1980s, then, is very different from that painted for the White House Conference on Aging twenty years

TABLE 22

POVERTY RATES AMONG THE ELDERLY, SELECTED YEARS, 1959–83
(*Percent*)

Year	Total Population	Under Age 65	Age 65 and Older
1959	22.4	21.1	35.2
1970	12.6	12.6	24.5
1980	13.0	12.6	15.7
1981	14.0	13.8	15.3
1983	15.2	15.3	14.1

SOURCE: U.S. Bureau of the Census, advance data later published in "Money Income and Poverty Status of Families and Persons in the United States: 1983," *Current Population Reports*, series P-60, no. 145 (Washington, D.C.: U.S. Government Printing Office, 1984).

earlier. Tremendous strides, mainly at the federal level, have been made in improving the economic conditions of the elderly. Consideration of these gains, in conjunction with recent deficit increases, inflation, and shrinking rather than expanding budgets for domestic programs has led some critics to argue that most of the elderly do not need more federal assistance. Rather, they contend that the time has come for a move away from *age-based* policies and legislation to *need-based* ones. Bernice Neugarten, a well-known scholar on aging, has become a very vocal advocate of need-based policies:

> Age-based legislation may have the eventual effect of denying services to those older persons who are most in need. By most estimates about 15 to 20 percent of people over sixty-five require some form of special health or social services. In a period of inflation and shrinking economic resources, when the public clamors for a curb on government spending, the worry is that this 15 percent may not be served adequately because it is being obscured by the other 85 percent in the age category.[1]

This concern—that services to the elderly who are heavily dependent on them may decline because of a perhaps misplaced desire to provide services to all elderly—coincides with the Reagan administration's general policy stance of trimming domestic spending by targeting resources more effectively to the "truly needy."

In this and the following two chapters we explore characteristics of the low-income elderly population, the history of federal involvement in efforts to reduce poverty among the elderly, and the effects of federal changes in the early 1980s. The chapter begins with a description of the low-income

1. Bernice Neurgarten, "Age or Need?" *National Forum* (Fall 1982), pp. 25-27.

elderly population, a population that in many ways is becoming very different demographically from the general elderly population. We then examine the special needs of the low-income elderly, both in comparison with the general U.S. population and with more economically advantaged elderly.

The Population of the Low-Income Elderly Defined

In 1980 an income of $3,949 for an older American living alone and $4,983 for an elderly couple placed them at the poverty line.[2] Almost 4 million persons aged sixty-five and older (15.7 percent of this age group) fell below this line. These low-income elderly were disproportionately women, minorities, the very old (age seventy-five and older, often referred to as the frail elderly), and elderly living alone or with unrelated individuals.

Table 23 shows the recent poverty rates among these subgroups. The poverty rates for these "vulnerable" individuals are higher than the general rate for all those aged sixty-five and older in every instance. When compared with their more affluent counterparts, these vulnerable subgroups present poverty rates that are 50 percent to more than 300 percent higher. Although only 8 out of 100 elderly persons residing with relatives experienced poverty in 1980 and 1981, 30 out of 100 of those living alone or with nonrelatives found themselves below the poverty line. Women were almost twice as likely as men to have inadequate income in 1981 and 1983. In 1983 black elderly persons were three times and Hispanic elderly about twice as likely as white elderly persons to live below the poverty line. The incidence of poverty was 50 percent greater among elderly persons aged seventy-two and older than among those aged sixty-five to seventy-one.

These disparities between vulnerable subgroups and the more well-off subgroups are disturbingly large, and it appears that they have grown over the past two decades. As the last column in table 23 shows, poverty among elderly whites, men, and family members has decreased 60 to 70 percent since 1959. Gains among the other subgroups, particularly the black elderly, are less impressive. Federal policies and legislation have improved the economic status of all older people, but the subgroups have not shared equally in the gains. As we discuss in detail in chapter 8, most of the income gains can be attributed to changes in Social Security payments (the Old Age and Survivors' Insurance provisions of the Social Security Act). Women, minorities, and, to a certain extent, single elderly tend to have had less permanent and less profitable attachments to the labor force during their preretirement

---

2. The poverty index is based solely on money income and does not reflect noncash benefits such as food stamps, Medicaid, and public housing.

TABLE 23

CHARACTERISTICS OF THE ELDERLY IN POVERTY, SELECTED YEARS, 1959–83
(Percent of Elderly U.S. Population)

Category	1959	1970	1980	1981	1983	Percent Change, 1959–81
All elderly (age 65 and older)	35.2	24.5	15.7	15.3	14.1	−60.0
White	33.1	22.5	13.6	13.1	12.0	−63.7
Black	62.5	48.0	38.1	39.0	36.3	−41.9
Hispanic	n.a.	n.a.	30.8	25.7	23.1	...
Women	35.6	27.5	18.5	18.6	17.0	−52.2
Men	34.7	20.2	11.1	10.5	10.0	−71.2
Residing with relatives	26.9	14.8	8.5	8.4	a	−68.8[b]
Residing alone or with nonrelatives	61.9	47.2	30.6	29.8	a	−51.9[b]

SOURCES: U.S. Bureau of the Census, *Statistical Abstracts of the United States, 1984* (Washington, D.C.: U.S. Government Printing Office, 1985), table 781. Note that in estimates of poverty for women, female heads of household and other female family members were combined to obtain the total number of women in families. Data for 1983 are from Bureau of the Census, "Money Income and Poverty Status" (Washington, D.C.: U.S. Government Printing Office, 1985).

n.a. Not available.
a. Not available by age.
b. Data are for 1959–81.

years. These groups, consequently, have benefited less from Social Security payment increases than have whites, males, and the elderly residing with relatives.

Characteristics of the Population: Trends

It is important to note that the elderly subpopulations most at risk of having low income are those segments of the total elderly population that are growing most rapidly. The number of Americans between ages sixty-five and seventy-four has doubled since 1950, rising from 8 million to 16 million in 1980. The number of frail elderly (aged seventy-five and older) has risen 150 percent during the same period, from 4 million to 10 million. Women and men were approximately equal proportions of the elderly population in 1950. By 1980 there were three elderly women for every two elderly men. The life expectancies for black Americans and Hispanics have begun to increase, although the numbers of people in these groups over age sixty-five are still small in comparison with the number below age sixty-five. Between 1983 and 2030 the number of black elderly is estimated to increase by 329 percent, boosting the number of blacks in the elderly population from one in twelve to one in eight. The elderly population as a whole is expected to increase during the same period by 212 percent, and the percentage of elderly persons in the United States is expected to shift from 11.6 percent to 21.2 percent of the entire U.S. population.[3]

One of the most striking changes to occur during the past thirty years is in the living arrangements of the elderly. The situation for elderly men has changed little: in 1979, 83 percent lived with relatives (most with their wives); in 1950, the figure was 89 percent. Fewer elderly men are living with spouses now than in earlier years, but this decline has been offset by an increase in elderly men living with their grown children. Older women, on the other hand, are now much more likely to live alone than they were thirty years ago. In 1950, 19 percent of elderly women lived alone or with nonrelatives. By 1979 this figure had increased to 42 percent. In contrast with elderly men, older women are not being taken in by their children when faced with living alone. The percentage of elderly women living with spouses has remained stable since 1960, but the proportion living with children or other relatives has dropped from 23 percent to 11 percent.

Changes in labor force participation, pension plans, and general economic circumstances for women and minorities suggest that in future years these populations may be somewhat less "at risk" of being in poverty in their later years than they are now. Nonetheless, it is important to note that the subpopulations of elderly who have benefited least from the federal efforts occurring in 1980 or earlier are expected to make up an increasingly large proportion of the elderly population. Without major policy changes, it is quite likely that these subgroups at risk will constitute an even larger proportion of the low-income elderly population.

The Special Needs of the Low-Income Elderly

Older Americans in general face the dilemma of increasing health needs and decreasing income.

---

3. U.S. Bureau of the Census, "Projections of the Population of the United States by Age, Sex and Race: 1983-2080," *Current Population Reports*, series P-25, no. 952 (May 1984).

Health-Related Needs

In 1979 the costs of health care for Americans aged sixty-five and older accounted for 29 percent of the country's health care expenditures even though the elderly made up only 11 percent of the population. Per capita expenditures for health among the elderly were almost three times higher than those of nonelderly adults during that year. At a little over $2,000, these expenditures represented over one-fourth of the average elderly person's income.[4]

Obviously the low-income elderly have no means of meeting these kinds of health care costs without assistance. If medical insurance or subsidized medical care are pressing needs for the majority of the elderly population, they are vital for the low-income elderly. Women, minorities, people living alone, and the frail elderly—the subgroups disproportinately represented in the below-poverty elderly population—have greater health care needs, as described below. In conjunction with their poverty status, these needs make them vulnerable and reliant on public help to obtain adequate medical care.

Women. Longevity, poor health, and lack of relatives to provide care have led elderly women to enter nursing homes in large numbers. In 1977 more than 70 percent of nursing home residents were women. The overrepresentation of women in the nursing home population is due mainly to the fact that there are more women in the upper-age brackets, the ages when health care needs are more acute.

Minorities. Minorities are underutilizers of health care services both before and after retirement age. As a consequence, they enter old age with more severe health problems and move through old age in relatively poorer health. A 1979 survey by the National Center for Health Statistics found that 31 percent of white elderly persons reported fair or poor health but 46 percent of the black elderly made similar assessments.[5]

Elderly Persons Living Alone. According to this 1979 survey, about one in six older Americans needs some assistance in getting around their house or neighborhood and about one out of eleven needs help with daily self-

---

4. The costs of nursing home care make up more than one-quarter of the per capita average for health care costs. Projections suggest that nursing home utilization and costs will be the fastest rising segment of the health care system in the next two decades, increasing about 49 percent, with 89 percent of the users being over age sixty-five. Nursing home costs tend to be concentrated among a small segment of the elderly population (only about 5 percent are nursing home residents) and thus should be used cautiously when estimating average health care expenditures. Factoring these costs out completely, however, still leaves the average American over age sixty-five with health care costs amounting to more than one-sixth of their income. See Carole Allen and Herman Brotman, eds., *White House Conference on Aging: 1981 Chartbook on Aging in America* (Washington, D.C.: 1981), pp. 92–93.

5. Ibid., p. 74.

care tasks (eating, bathing, dressing). Many of the elderly who live alone undoubtedly receive regular help from family and friends, but some must rely on help from public or private agencies or live in nursing homes in order to receive adequate care.

The Frail Elderly. Mobility impairment increases with age, as does the accompanying need for in-home assistance, nursing home stays, and hospital care. Three out of ten elderly persons between ages sixty-five and seventy-four were hospitalized in 1978, compared to five out of ten elderly over age seventy-four who received in-patient treatment during that year. In addition, hospital stays were usually longer among the frail elderly than among persons aged sixty-five to seventy-four.

Income Needs

The low-income elderly by definition have a greater need for income assistance than do other older Americans. It is useful at this point to discuss why. The low-income elderly differ not only in the amount of income they have at their disposal, but also in the sources of income. Low-income elderly are less likely to have earnings to augment retirement or SSI benefits than are higher-income elderly (0.9 percent versus 18.0. percent, respectively). They are also much less likely to receive income from dividends, interest, or rent (32.6 percent versus 73.6 percent). The low-income elderly are also less likely to have private or government pensions than are elderly at higher income levels (6.1 percent versus 32.6 percent).[6]

These differences in income sources between the moderate- and low-income elderly populations, when combined with the demographic differences outlined earlier (more women, elderly residing alone or with nonrelated persons, and so on), mean that the quality of life for low-income elderly is very much dependent on the availability and cost of a full spectrum of services and supports—from affordable housing and transportation to home-delivered meals, chore and homemaker services, and personal care. Lack of income makes fulfilling basic needs more difficult. Obtaining physically adequate housing in safe neighborhoods, food in sufficient quantities and of good nutritional value, heat and other utilities, and personal services if disabled are all made less likely by severe financial constraints. Rent increases, reductions in the availability of discounts for senior citizens on public transportation, bottlenecks in demand for public housing, increases in minimum charges for meals in senior citizen food programs, and similar changes in

---

6. Data in this paragraph are from U.S. Bureau of the Census, *Current Population Reports*, series P-60, no. 138 (1981) table 15.

other support services all erode the quality of life of low-income older Americans. Collectively, such reductions may jeopardize their ability to remain living independently. This group is both much more reliant on public support for income and much more sensitive to small changes in the quantity or costs of public supports and services than are more affluent older Americans.

Summary

Government action beginning in the 1970s substantially eased the poverty situation of many elderly Americans. Nevertheless, significant subgroups of the elderly—especially minorities, women, and people living alone—still suffer disproportionate levels of poverty. They have important, and often unmet, health, housing, nutrition, social service, and other needs that government programs have addressed to greater or lesser degrees. Chapter 8 describes the major federal initiatives to alleviate poverty and their effects on the elderly. It also reviews what has happened to those programs since 1981 when the Reagan administration took office and looks at how the income of elderly households has fared from 1980 to 1984. Changes in actual services for the low-income elderly are reviewed in chapter 9.

CHAPTER 8

FEDERAL POLICIES AND PROGRAMS FOR THE LOW-INCOME ELDERLY

The past two decades have seen dramatically increasing social welfare expenditures in the public sector. Federal expenditures have grown the fastest, rising from a third of the budget in 1965 to more than half of the budget in 1976. The greatest increases have been in health and income security expenditures—Social Security, Supplemental Security Income (SSI), Medicare, and Medicaid—programs that greatly benefit the aged. While a 1975 study by the General Accounting Office estimated that more than 130 federal programs affect the elderly, these four programs capture most of the federal activity on aging and account for virtually all the improvements that have been made in the economic conditions of the elderly in recent years.[1]

The first two sections of this chapter briefly review the development and effects of these four programs and four others that benefit proportionately large numbers of low-income older Americans—food stamps, housing assistance, Older Americans Act programs, and social services block-grant programs). The remainder of the chapter discusses federal outlays and changes under the Reagan administration and summarizes the network of programs benefiting the elderly.

Development of Policy for the Aging

It is important to note that public response to the elderly, while impressive, was slow to come. The first part of the century found the United States

---

1. U.S. Congress, House, *Government's Response to the Elderly*, Hearings before the House Select Committee on Aging, 94th Cong., 1st sess. (Washington, D.C.: U.S. Government Printing Office, November 20, 1975), p. 8.

well behind many other industrial nations in developing a policy for the aging. As Lammers in a recent book, *Public Policy and the Aging*, notes:

> When the delegates to the 1961 White House Conference on Aging met to review existing policies and propose new initiatives they had good reason to feel that their nation had given short shrift to the problems of the aging. A system of Social Security benefits was not established in the United States until 1935— much later than in other countries with a comparable level of socioeconomic development. In 1961 health costs still were not covered for the aging (or any other group) as a matter of right, and the expanding nursing home industry was receiving very little effective regulation. Social services for the aging existed only to a limited extent even in the most progressive states.[2]

In 1960 only 62 percent of retired workers were receiving Social Security benefits. At their maximum, these benefits were barely adequate for individuals relying on them as their sole, or even primary, source of income. The poverty threshold for a single person aged sixty-five or older was $1,397 in 1960. The *maximum* monthly Social Security benefit, $119, placed a retired worker just above this threshold with an annual income of $1,428. Retired workers receiving the minimum monthly benefit of $33 were obviously well below the poverty threshold if they were relying on Social Security as their primary income source. When one bears in mind that health care coverage was not generally available to the elderly and that social services were still in their infancy at this time, it is clear that many older Americans lived their lives on the brink of physical and economic disaster.

The 1960s and early 1970s—the heyday for America's social programs— saw a rapid expansion of interest and commitment to the elderly, most of which came about through amendments to the Social Security Act of 1935.

The 1965 Amendments to the Social Security Act

Medicare, Title XVIII. Building on the Kerr-Mills Medical Assistance Act of 1960 that utilized federal matching grants to expand medical assistance to the needy, Medicare (Title XVIII) was established in 1965 to make possible a national system of health insurance for the elderly. The legislation provided partial coverage of the costs of hospital and related care for Social Security beneficiaries aged sixty-five or older (Part A) and offered a voluntary contributory program, that is, paid for through monthly premiums, to help with the costs of physician services (Part B). By 1981, 96 percent of the population aged sixty-five and older had Medicare coverage. Virtually all these persons were insured under both the hospital (Part A) and supplemental (Part B) plans.

---

2. William Lammers, "Public Policy and the Aging," *Congressional Quarterly*, vol. 40 (1983), p. 33.

The minimum cash outlay for persons paying their own premiums, deductions, and copayments was $132 in 1981.[3] This jumped to $336 for those hospitalized under sixty days during the year.

Medicaid, Title XIX. Medicaid, also established by the 1965 amendments, is a program of medical assistance for the needy administered by each state within broad federal guidelines. The federal, state, and local governments share the costs of assistance; the federal government pays approximately half. States must cover the "categorically needy," that is, persons receiving SSI or Aid to Families with Dependent Children (AFDC) and may also cover "medically needy" persons whose incomes are not sufficient to cover living expenses and medical costs. Under Medicaid, full or partial payment for inpatient and outpatient hospital services, laboratory services, skilled nursing services, and physician services must be made on behalf of all eligible beneficiaries. States may also opt to cover a wide variety of other services, including prescription drugs, eyeglasses, private day care, nursing, intermediate care facility services, physical therapy, and dental care. For the elderly, Medicaid essentially supplements Medicare coverage; at the state's discretion, Medicaid pays Medicare premiums, copayments, and deductibles and provides inpatient services that are not fully covered under Medicare (such as skilled nursing care and prescription drugs). In 1981, 12 percent of the elderly population (33 percent of those below the poverty threshold) received Medicaid coverage.

The Older Americans Act of 1965

In addition to these amendments to the 1935 Social Security Act, Congress in 1965 passed the Older Americans Act, which created a central administrative office, the Administration on Aging, within the U.S. Department of Health, Education, and Welfare. The purpose of this act was to make a comprehensive range of social services available to the elderly through the cooperation and partnership of community agencies and state and local governments. As it currently stands, the act authorizes funds for establishing state and substate agencies to plan and coordinate services, for professional training and research on aging, for developing work opportunities for the elderly through community service employment, and for delivering social and nu-

---

3. Beyond the monthly premium for supplementary medical insurance, Medicare recipients are required to pay a deductible for inpatient hospital care ($204 in 1981) and to copay for hospital stays beyond sixty days and for nursing home stays beyond twenty days. In 1981, 12 percent of the elderly had some or all of these expenditures paid by Medicaid. Many of those ineligible for Medicaid had private insurance policies to provide supplementary coverage.

trition services. Programs and services under the act are available to all elderly persons aged sixty years and older, without regard for income.

The 1972 Amendments to the Social Security Act

Supplemental Security Income, Title XVI. This amendment redirected primary responsibility for the aged, blind, and disabled from the states to the federal government, guaranteeing a minimum income level for all eligible persons. Eligibility is based on both a categorical requirement and an income test. Categorically, applicants must be age sixty-five or older or blind or disabled as defined by the Social Security Administration. Income limits have generally been set below the poverty threshold. In 1981 the income limit for an individual was $3,176, 73 percent of the poverty threshold of $4,360.[4]

States are required to supplement the federal SSI payments if the federal payment does not maintain the 1973 income level of recipients who were transferred from the federal-state old age assistance programs to SSI in 1974 when SSI payments began. In addition, states have the option of supplementing the SSI minimum level for all or selected categories of persons. In 1981 all states except Texas provided some supplementary assistance. Of the 1.7 million aged receiving SSI, in that year 650,000 (39 percent) received state supplements; 250,000 additional persons received state supplements even though they received no federal SSI payments.[5] Approximately 20 percent of SSI recipients classified as disabled are also elderly (age sixty-five and older). They receive state supplements in roughly the same ratios as those who qualify on the basis of age.

Indexing Social Security and Increases in Benefit Levels. Effective June 1975, Social Security payments (including SSI) were automatically indexed to the consumer price index, rising by the percentage of increase in this index whenever this increase is 3 percent or more. At the same time, Congress passed a 20 percent rise in benefits for current Social Security recipients. As of July 1980, over 90 percent of the elderly were receiving Social Security payments. The average monthly benefit was $330 for a retired worker, $538 for a retired couple, and $305 for an elderly widow or widower.

4. A person's countable monthly income in 1981 excluded the first $20 of any unearned income (for example, Social Security benefits), the first $65 of any earned income, plus half of any earnings over $65. Resources needed to be under $1,500 for any single person, but excluded the value of a home, a car valued at under $4,500, and life insurance with a face value of $1,500 or less, plus reasonable household and personal possessions.

5. U.S. Department of Health and Human Services, Social Security Administration, *Social Security Bulletin, Annual Statistical Supplement, 1981* (Washington, D.C.: U.S. Government Printing Office, 1981), tables 154 and 156.

Benefits for 1980 were 140 percent more than 1970 levels, an increase that outstripped price increases, which rose 106 percent over the decade.

The 1975 Amendment to the Social Security Act

Social Services, Title XX. With the passage of Title XX, states were given increased authority, responsibility, and flexibility in choosing and running social services programs for neglected, abused, and dependent children and adults. Under the legislation, beneficiaries of Title XX services could be AFDC, SSI, or Medicaid recipients, but could also be residents earning up to 115 percent of the state median income. This condition allowed states to provide in-home services for elderly persons who were not covered under Medicaid. The services prevented or delayed nursing home placement for many elderly unable to live independently without some external support.

The Effects of Federal Programs by 1981

By the mid-1970s, the legislation had authorized a set of programs designed to meet the income and health needs of most elderly. What impact did this legislation have on the low-income elderly by the end of the Carter administration? This is a difficult question to answer. We begin by noting that the policy expansion of the 1960s and 1970s did not produce any legislation directed exclusively toward the low-income elderly. Social Security and Medicare—programs from which large numbers of low-income elderly undoubtedly benefit—*are age-entitlement programs*, as are those provided under the Older Americans Act. These programs benefit all elderly, regardless of their other sources or their level of income. SSI and Medicaid are *means-tested programs* for which the elderly must qualify as must other low-income groups, by demonstrating that their income falls below the eligibility threshold.

Changes Introduced by Amendments to the Social Security Act

The major strides toward improving the economic status of the elderly have come through changes in and expansion of Social Security benefits. The 1972 amendments increased the average benefit level and tied future benefit increases to inflation. The two years from 1979 to 1981 alone saw federal outlays for Social Security rise from $69 billion to $97 billion, largely as a result of increases in monthly benefits. (Average monthly benefits for retired workers rose from $294 to $386 over this two-year period.)

As noted earlier, the improvements in Social Security have brought many elderly out of poverty, but they have done relatively little to ameliorate conditions for those who had tenuous or unprofitable attachments to the labor force during their preretirement years. Congress has been reluctant to increase minimum benefits for these people. The minimum benefit approach to reducing poverty among the elderly has, as Lammers notes, a serious flaw:

> To increase the income of those who qualify for Social Security benefits and have no other income, substantial sums are spent on individuals who have qualified for the minimum under Social Security but actually use this income to supplement other pensions and income sources. In 1977 Congress moved to create a special minimum benefit based on the needs of those who had worked for a longer period of time at low wages. . . . The use of special minimum benefits did not develop sufficiently to alleviate the basic problem, however, so that by 1981 the pattern of minimum benefit allocations going to those with substantial alternative revenue sources remained.[6]

In 1981, 87 percent of the elderly living below the poverty threshold were receiving some Social Security benefits. One-third of this population was living on Social Security benefits alone. With average monthly payments to retired workers placing recipients just above the poverty line, it is clear that those receiving minimum or reduced benefits needed additional financial assistance to avoid serious economic hardships.

As can be seen in table 24, persons receiving only the minimum Social Security benefit in 1981 would have incomes 53 percent below the poverty threshold for that year. This is an improvement of only 6 percent over 1970 levels. Average monthly benefits have, in contrast, increased substantially relative to the poverty threshold. In 1970 the average individual payment was 24 percent below the poverty level. By 1981 the average payment was slightly above the threshold. Similarly, a retired worker and spouse receiving average monthly Social Security payments that placed them at the poverty level in 1970 were 34 percent above the threshold in 1981. The data in the table make clear the fact that Social Security increases have benefited many elderly, but not all.

Supplemental Security Income was originally designed for both those ineligible for Social Security and those receiving low Social Security benefits. This program was to be the answer to the dilemma of trying to provide a guaranteed minimum for the low-income elderly (and other categorically eligible populations) while not benefiting those with other significant income sources. However, the program has not grown as expected for the elderly population. Between 1975 and 1981, for example, increases in Social Security

---

6. Lammers, "Public Policy," p. 112.

TABLE 24

MONTHLY AVERAGE SOCIAL SECURITY BENEFITS FOR THE ELDERLY AND
THEIR FAMILIES, COMPARED TO POVERTY THRESHOLD, 1970 AND 1981
(Dollars per month unless otherwise indicated)

Measure	Persons Aged 65 or Older (Workers and Widows or Widowers)		Families Headed by Recipient Aged 65 or Older	
	1970	*1981*	*1970*	*1981*
Poverty-level income	155.08	363.33	195.67	458.33[a]
Minimum Social Security benefits	64.00	170.30	96.00	255.50[b]
Percent of poverty-level income	41.3	46.9	49.1	55.7
Average Social Security benefits	118.10	385.97	198.90	488.60[c]
Percentage of poverty-level income	76.2	106.2	101.7	133.7

SOURCE: U.S. Department of Health and Human Services, Social Security Administration, *Social Security Bulletin, Annual Statistical Supplement, 1981,* (Washington, D.C.: Government Printing Office, 1982), table 6 (monthly poverty level), table 32 (minimum monthly benefits), table 16 (individual average monthly benefits), and table 47 (family average monthly benefits).

a. Poverty level for a two-person family with head of household age sixty-five or older.

b. Family benefit given for any family structure—worker and spouse; worker, spouse, and child; widow or widower (age sixty-five or older) and one or more children.

c. Average monthly payment to worker and spouse; a widow and child receive $532.90. Data (and percentage of poverty) are for 1979.

benefits and beneficiaries far outstripped those in SSI. Average Social Security benefits increased 19 percent in inflation-adjusted terms while average SSI benefits for the elderly dropped 4 percent in real terms. The number of elderly SSI recipients qualifying first as ''aged'' dropped 22 percent while the number of Social Security recipients increased by an almost equal amount. One could argue that the decline in the number of elderly receiving SSI is in line with the increases in Social Security benefits were it not for the fact that 87 percent of the elderly living below the poverty threshold in 1981 were Social Security recipients.

SSI, like Social Security, is means-tested and is indexed to inflation. However, the federal SSI income floor (the guaranteed minimum income and therefore the maximum income a person can earn, after adjustments, without becoming ineligible for SSI) is about 27 percent below the poverty level.

This gap between the programs means that with each cost-of-living increase some Social Security recipients become ineligible for SSI payments (it was estimated that with the 1975 cost-of-living adjustment, 66,241 elderly became ineligible for SSI benefits).[7]

More important, the low eligibility cutoffs for SSI mean that a significant number of elderly receive Social Security benefits that are too high to allow them to collect SSI but too low to allow them to provide for themselves adequately. In 1981 only 26 percent of the elderly below poverty (about 1 million persons) were receiving SSI payments. It was originally estimated that about one-fifth of all elderly Social Security recipients, 4.6 million people in 1981, would receive both SSI and Social Security benefits once the SSI program became fully operational.[8] The total number of SSI recipients in 1981 was 1.7 million, less than half of the predicted number.[9] State supplements to the federal payments lifted about 700,000 of these recipients above the official poverty line.

The low federal SSI income limit means more than a loss of needed supplementary income to many elderly Americans; it means a possible loss of medical coverage through Medicaid when they lose their categorical eligibility as SSI recipients. Losing Medicaid eligibility also entails a loss of resources to pay the recipient's share of Medicare. Medicare deductibles and copayments rose 122 percent between 1975 and 1981, while average Social Security benefits for an individual retired worker rose only 86 percent (minimum benefits rose only 72 percent). These increases mean that elderly persons requiring hospitalization in 1981 paid a minimum of $336 in deductibles and premiums—7 percent of the average Social Security recipient's total annual benefits and 18 percent of the total annual benefits of the elderly person receiving minimum payments. If these elderly were eligible, Medicaid picked up the hospital charges. However, the elderly who require prescription drugs, in-home care, or long-term nursing home care, who are not SSI recipients, and who are not able to afford private supplementary coverage face serious financial trouble.

States can provide Medicaid coverage, at their option, to residents deemed medically needy. The fact that 33 percent of the below-poverty elderly received Medicaid coverage in 1981 while only 26 percent were SSI recipients

7. U.S. Department of Health, Education, and Welfare, SSI Study Group, *Report to the Commissioner of Social Security and the Secretary of Health, Education, and Welfare on the Supplemental Security Income Program* (n.p.: January 1976), p. 71.

8. Joseph A. Pechman, ed., *Setting National Priorities: The 1974 Budget* (Washington, D.C.: Brookings Institution, 1983), p. 113.

9. U.S. Census, *Current Population Reports*, series P-60, no. 138 (1981), table 15.

suggests that states use this option. Nonetheless, it is an option and not a requirement. States facing tight fiscal times may curtail their program for the medically needy under Medicaid.

Changes in Nutrition, Housing, and Other Noncash Benefits

Although the SSI program has not been as effective as envisioned in removing more elderly from poverty status, other programs do supplement the income of the low-income elderly. In 1981 almost 1 million elderly lived in federally assisted housing, and more than 1 million received food stamps. These supplementary programs are also means-tested—to be eligible for them an applicant must not have income above the levels specified by the program. As shown in table 25, not all these recipients were below the official poverty level, although all met the income requirements of the programs from which they benefited. For example, while only half of the elderly households living in publicly owned or subsidized rental housing were officially below poverty, 83 percent had incomes below $7,500. Those with incomes slightly above the poverty threshold receive a proportionately smaller subsidy.

In addition to the means-tested programs shown in table 25, other programs serve the low-income elderly. Most notable of these are congregate and home-delivered meals, the nutrition programs offered under the Older Americans Act. These programs served about 3 million elderly in 1981. Federal mass transit assistance also helps the low-income elderly because it

TABLE 25

ELDERLY HOUSEHOLDS RECEIVING MEANS-TESTED BENEFITS,
SELECTED PROGRAMS, 1981

Benefit Received	All Elderly Households (N = 17.3 Million)		Below-Poverty Elderly Households (N = 3.2 Million)	
	Number (thousands)	Percent	Number (thousands)	Percent
Food stamps	1,143	6.6	815	25.5
Medicaid	2,505	14.5	1,134	35.3
Subsidized housing	949	5.5	433	13.5
Supplemental Security Income	1,499	8.7	894	27.9
All benefits	104	0.6	97	3.0
No benefits	13,698	79.1	1,561	49.0

SOURCE: Derived from data in U.S. Bureau of the Census, *Current Population Reports*, series P-60, no. 136 (Washington, D.C.: U.S. Government Printing Office, 1983), table 10.

enables cities to keep public transportation costs down for all residents and to provide reduced-fare transportation to the elderly and handicapped.

It is difficult to assess the cumulative influence of multiple benefits (for example, Social Security, SSI, Medicaid, Medicare, and food stamps) on the incidence of poverty in the elderly population simply because of the complexities involved in tracking recipients through multiple programs. A Congressional Budget Office report issued in 1977 estimated that the number of elderly living below the poverty threshold would have been almost ten times its 1977 level had the elderly not been able to benefit from the various social insurance (such as Social Security), money transfer (SSI, for instance), and in-kind transfer (like Medicaid and food stamps) programs now in existence.[10] The effect of the non-health-related, in-kind transfer programs (housing subsidies and food stamps) is small compared to the other programs. Even so, these general means-tested programs reduced the poverty rolls an estimated 15.5 percent in 1977. Medicaid, Medicare, food stamps, housing assistance, and SSI—the major programs that extend the income security provided to most elderly through Social Security—reduced the number of elderly living in poverty by 72 percent, a significant reduction by any reckoning. Yet in 1981 half the elderly living below the poverty threshold were not receiving SSI, food stamps, Medicaid, or housing assistance, as can be seen in the last row of table 26. By 1981 the array of federal programs that were developed during the 1960s and 1970s had certainly increased the financial security of

TABLE 26

GROWTH OF FEDERAL BENEFITS FOR THE ELDERLY BY PROGRAM,
SELECTED PERIODS, 1979–83

Program	1979 Total Outlays ($ Billions)	Percent Change	
		1979–81	1981–83
Food stamps	0.5	80.0	−22.2
Medicaid	4.3	39.5	11.7
Medicare	24.6	52.9	19.2
Social Security	69.0	48.9	25.3
Subsidized public housing	1.6	43.8	60.9
Supplemental Security Income	1.7	40.7	25.8

SOURCE: U.S. Bureau of the Census, *Statistical Abstract of the United States: 1984* (Washington, D.C.: U.S. Government Printing Office, 1983), table 616.

10. Congressional Budget Office, *Poverty Status of Families under Alternative Definitions of Income*, unpublished background paper 17 (Washington, D.C.: CBO, 1977).

the low-income elderly, but these programs did not guarantee an existence above the poverty level for many elderly households.

Federal Legislation and Policy Changes Affecting the Low-Income Elderly, 1981–84

The Reagan administration's initial position on assisting the elderly has been described as follows:

> The Reagan administration came to Washington in 1981 placing a high priority on its economic policy agenda and a plan to shrink the federal government's role in most domestic areas. While it hoped that economic growth would benefit everyone, and a pledge was made to preserve the "social safety net," it did not have a social agenda that addressed specifically those issues of particular concern to the elderly. Thus, there have been no initiatives by the administration to increase the incomes of the needy aged through transfer payments, improve directly medical or institution care, protect the elderly against crime, improve employment opportunities for older workers, or construct more housing for the elderly.[11]

The administration did, however, have a general approach to assisting the elderly population in meeting its financial needs that went along with its broad economic policies. Reasoning that inflation was the principal drain on households with fixed incomes, the administration maintained that its policies designed to reduce inflation and promote economic growth were the best social insurance the government could provide. Furthermore, since elderly voters make up an important part of the electorate, programs benefiting them have not been the target of major retrenchment efforts.

In fact, at every income level the elderly experienced income growth under the current administration, suggesting that they have benefited in some respects from administration policies and the economic conditions prevailing between 1980 and 1984. Thus one study found "Over the 1980-1984 period, the disposable incomes of families headed by someone sixty-five or older rose by 9.5 percent—nearly three times the increase . . . for all families. Older individuals living alone had even greater gains—their incomes rose about 15 percent. . . . Even the bottom quintile enjoyed income increases of about 6 percent."[12]

---

11. James Storey, *Older Americans in the Reagan Era: Impacts of Federal Policy Changes* (Washington, D.C: Urban Institute Press, 1983), p. 22.

12. Marilyn Moon and Isabel V. Sawhill, "Family Incomes," in John L. Palmer and Isabel V. Sawhill, eds., *The Reagan Record: An Assessment of America's Changing Domestic Priorities* (Cambridge, Massachusetts: Ballinger, 1984), pp. 317–46.

Elderly households benefited during the early 1980s from low inflation and high interest rates and were not appreciably affected by the high unemployment experienced by the nation as a whole.[13] Although Social Security outlays slowed during these years, as shown in table 26, lower inflation (and hence lower cost-of-living adjustments) accounts for these changes; real Social Security benefits rose 7 percent during the period.[14]

Table 26 also shows that growth in federal outlays for the other major programs serving the elderly was generally slower between 1981 and 1983 than between 1979 and 1981. In only one program, food stamps, was there an actual reduction in funding from 1981 to 1983. To the extent that the low-income elderly have been affected by budget cuts and policy changes, they have been hurt because of the cumulative buildup of small reductions in benefits and services. These losses are difficult to document and are best identified at the local level (see chapter 9). The legislative changes made by the Reagan administration are outlined below.

Social Security and SSI

The major change in Social Security outlays under the Reagan administration was a six-month delay in the cost-of-living increase. Under the new law, these increases are paid in January instead of the preceding July. The delay, enacted in the Social Security Amendments of 1983, is projected to save about $9.7 billion in Social Security outlays between 1983 and 1985. Most significant are the administration's proposals for changes in Social Security that were not enacted. Reagan had proposed eliminating the minimum benefit for all current recipients, but Congress rejected this proposal. The minimum benefit was eliminated only for new beneficiaries under the 1981 Omnibus Budget Reconciliation Act.

Built into the 1983 legislation was income protection for low-income beneficiaries who receive SSI: these persons were given benefit increases (up to $20 monthly for single persons and $30 monthly for married couples) to offset the six-month delay in cost-of-living increases. The 1983 legislation may work to decrease the percentage of elderly who are below the poverty line and receive SSI—it requires the Social Security Administration to notify certain Social Security recipients of their possible eligibility for SSI.

It remains to be seen whether future retirees will be able to utilize SSI to compensate for the loss of Social Security minimum benefit payments: "There appear to have been approximately 2 million persons among the 3.1

---

13. Ibid.
14. Ibid.

million individuals receiving the minimum benefit who would not be eligible for SSI either because their incomes were too high (from other sources such as government pensions), or they were between the age of sixty-two and sixty-five."[15]

Some of these persons are the "double-dippers" at whom the legislative change was aimed. Others, however, may find themselves joining the ranks of the low-income elderly who are caught in the gap between the two income security programs.

As discussed in chapter 5, the Reagan administration did not make any major legislative changes in the SSI program except, as mentioned above, the increase to offset the delay in the cost-of-living allowance. The main administrative change—tightened eligibility requirements and more frequent case reviews—did not affect the elderly, whose age-based claims to SSI are indisputable.

Food Stamps

Benefits from the food stamp program, redeemable food coupons to low-income families and individuals, are federally funded and do not vary by state. These benefits are based on the "Thrifty Food Plan" index, which was developed by the Department of Agriculture. Benefits received equal 100 percent of the Thrifty Food Plan amount appropriate for the household size, minus thirty cents for each dollar of countable income. Under the Omnibus Budget Reconciliation Act of 1981 the inflation adjustment for 1982 benefits was eliminated and certain later inflation adjustments were postponed. First-month benefits were prorated based on date of application, and households with gross monthly incomes of over 130 percent of the official federal poverty index were declared ineligible *unless they had elderly or disabled members.*

The elderly thus escaped the income-related cuts in 1981 but were affected by further across-the-board reductions enacted in 1982. The basic benefit amount was reduced from 100 percent to 99 percent of the Thrifty Food Plan amount for fiscal years 1983 to 1982 and benefits were rounded down to the next lowest dollar.

Housing Assistance

Housing assistance is provided to low-income families through three major programs—public housing, federally subsidized, newly constructed or rehabilitated units built by the private sector (Section 8 and Section 202

---

15. Lammers, "Public Policy," p. 112–13.

housing), and direct rent subsidies to individuals and families living in existing private market housing. In 1980 about 3.1 million households were being served under these programs, 40 percent of which were headed by elderly persons. The Section 202 housing construction program in that year included the highest percentage of elderly (about 80 percent), because this program provides direct federal construction loans for the development of housing projects to serve elderly and handicapped individuals.

The system of housing programs grew in both budgetary commitments and the number of households assisted until the advent of the Reagan administration.[16] Since then the policy for housing assistance has essentially been to reduce spending by eliminating funding for additional subsidized units and by decisively moving away from new construction and rehabilitation toward more cost-efficient rental subsidies.

In 1981 Congress moved to ensure an even mix of existing, new, and rehabilitated housing, reversing a pattern of HUD-promoted reductions in the role of subsidies for existing housing. The current administration, however, has moved far beyond this adjustment to an almost sole reliance on existing housing. Total new commitments for public housing and Section 8 housing fell from 206,000 units in 1980 to 100,000 units for 1984. The Congressional Budget Office reports total housing assistance outlays were reduced by $1.8 billion for 1982-85 compared to previous policy, largely due to reduced new commitments.[17] Because housing commitments are long-term, the effects of the decreased outlays will continue far into the future. Reductions in units subsidized by the U.S. Department of Housing and Urban Development would have been greater if Congress had passed the additional recisions proposed by President Reagan in 1983.

In addition to reducing the number of subsidized units available, the administration changed the eligibility requirements and the expected contribution of those placed in subsidized units. The maximum percentage of occupants of HUD-subsidized housing with incomes between 50 and 80 percent of the median income (that is, the near poor) was lowered from 20 percent to 10 percent. In addition to this change, the required rent in subsidized units will rise from 25 to 30 percent of countable income between 1982 and 1986. It has been estimated that this new requirement will reduce the eligible pool of elderly households by one-third.[18] Of those elderly households actually

---

16. James P. Zais, Raymond J. Struyk, and Thomas G. Thibodeau, *Housing Assistance for Older Americans: The Reagan Prescription* (Washington, D.C.: Urban Institute Press, 1982).

17. Congressional Budget Office, "Major Legislation Changes in Human Resources Programs Since January 1981," staff memorandum, August 1983.

18. Zais, Struyk, and Thibodeau, *Housing Assistance*.

residing in assisted housing, about one-fifth will be ineligible under the new rule. The provision increasing rents to 30 percent of countable income will make one in nine participating elderly households ineligible. All changes combined eliminate eligibility for about one-fourth of participating elderly households.

Health Care

Medicare. The major change made in Medicare in 1981 was an increase in deductibles for hospital payments and medical costs. In 1980 the deductible for Medicare hospital insurance stood at $180. It rose to $204 in 1981, to $260 in 1982 and to $304 in 1983—a 69 percent increase in a three-year period. In addition, copayments for daily hospital costs for the sixty-first through the ninetieth day of hospitalization increased over the same period from $45 to $76 per day; for the ninety-first and subsequent days from $90 to $152 per day; and for the twenty-first and subsequent days of skilled nursing facility care from $22.50 to $38.00 per day. All of these are 69 percent increases between 1980 and 1983.

In 1982 Congress raised the premiums that the elderly must pay for supplementary medical insurance. These premiums rose from $9.60 in 1980 to $12.20 in 1983, for a 27 percent increase in three years. In addition, deductibles went from $60, which they had been since 1973, to $75—a 25 percent increase, but a reasonable one in light of inflation during that ten-year period. Medicare beneficiaries must also pay their own physicians if their doctors' fees exceed the maximum allowable under Medicare. Only about half of all nonhospital physician visits are fully reimbursed by Medicare. In chapter 9 we explore the meaning of these federal program changes for elderly persons at the local level.

Congress also acted in 1982 to limit the level of Medicare reimbursement to hospitals, and in 1983 established payment mechanisms based on the average cost to treat a condition with a particular diagnosis rather than reimbursing for actual costs. It remains to be seen whether hospitals respond to these constraints by lowering their actual costs or by adopting cost-cutting—and potentially harmful—practices such as reducing the quality of care, discharging patients who have no appropriate place to go, or avoiding expensive but necessary treatments.

Medicaid. Congress also acted in 1981 to lower the federal share of Medicaid costs. Federal matching contributions were reduced by 3.0 percent in 1982, 4.0 percent in 1983, and 4.5 percent in 1984. In exchange for this reduced support, states were given more freedom to shape their own Medicaid programs. New approaches to population and service coverage and new reimbursement mechanisms were permitted, and new delivery methods were encouraged. States have used this increased latitude to revamp their programs, that is, increase their efficiency. There have been service cutbacks, however, particularly in the optional services (for example, dental care, podiatry, optometry, prescription drugs) that states were required to provide as a condition of participation in the program. These services appear to be particularly relevant to older people. Loss of Medicaid coverage frequently means that the poor elderly go without these sources.

Social Services

Because of its flexibility, the social services block grant, formerly Title XX, is used to provide a variety of in-home, supportive, and protective services to the elderly. Funding for these services also bore serious cutbacks under the current administration. Grants funded under the Older Americans Act to Area Agencies on Aging for nutritional and other supportive services also lost funding under President Reagan. Congress appropriated $673 million in fiscal 1981; funding dropped to $636 million in fiscal 1982 but by fiscal 1984 it had been restored at its fiscal 1981 level—a loss of 14 percent in program dollars when adjusted for inflation.

Summary

During the 1960s and 1970s several administrations, both Republican and Democratic, contributed to the development of a network of social programs benefiting the elderly. These programs dramatically reduced the proportion of the elderly population living in poverty. More than 90 percent of the elderly receive Social Security, and their income from this source has more than kept pace with inflation since mid-1975 when benefits were indexed to the consumer price index. Medicare and Medicaid provide significant amounts of medical care, and other programs supply an array of noncash benefits including food, housing, and social services.

The major federal programs benefiting the elderly do not differentiate among elderly households on the basis of their financial or human resources. As the data in chapter 7 indicate, the elderly have quite heterogeneous characteristics, and many are fully able to support themselves without government assistance. Even before Reagan assumed the presidency, many critics believed programs serving the elderly needed restructuring to target most public resources on that small segment of older Americans in greatest need.

When the Reagan administration took office in 1981, it made no promises to protect the elderly beyond its general pledge to preserve the ''social safety net,'' its commitment to maintain Social Security, and its philosophy that economic policies to reduce inflation were the best way to assure the well-being of elderly citizens. Low inflation and high interest rates have indeed benefited elderly households at all income levels, with real disposable income rising an average of 9.5 percent between 1980 and 1984. But no restructuring has occurred that focuses on more precise targeting of resources away from the well-off and toward the needy.

The numerous changes in income security, health, housing, and social services programs that the administration pushed through Congress did not specifically protect or exempt elderly recipients from cuts, with the exception of the 1981 food stamps legislation. As a small but highly vulnerable subset of older Americans, the low-income elderly have undoubtedly been affected, although the extent of the impact is difficult to assess. Each change or cutback has not been dramatic, but the cumulative effects may be large for the elderly who rely on multiple public benefits with few or no other sources of income. The 1981 cuts in food stamps and housing subsidies alone were estimated at $19 a month for an elderly couple receiving SSI payments and $13 a month for an unmarried person.[19] These sums represent 3.0 and 3.4 percent, respectively, of average monthly federal payments for Social Security or Social Security and SSI combined. For someone receiving only SSI, they represent 10-11 percent of their average federal cash payments.

In other words, the loss of these noncash benefits means that poor elderly persons must compensate with their available cash to make ends meet at the rate of 3-10 percent of their average monthly income from federal sources.[20] Most have no other source of income, so these changes can easily push strained budgets to the limit. In combination with increased deductibles and copayments for health insurance and health care, the poor elderly often face impossible choices among food, shelter, utilities, and health care. Against the backdrop of improved circumstances for most elderly households, such outcomes seem particularly incongruous.

The effects of these federal changes can only be guessed. In chapter 9, therefore, we move to the local level and to the impressions of service providers and advocates. Where federal programs have local administrative counterparts with budgetary discretion (the social services block grant that replaced Title XX and Area Agencies on Aging), we look at those local programs and

---

19. Estimated by the Congressional Budget Office in a report to Senator Edward Kennedy, September 28, 1981.

20. U.S. Department of Health and Human Services, Social Security Administration, *Social Security Bulletin: Annual Statistical Supplement, 1982* (Washington, D.C.: Government Printing Office, 1983), pp. I-II and Tables 167, 170, and 185.

budgets. For most of the programs described in this chapter, however, local offices simply administer federal eligibility and program requirements with little or no local discretion (food stamps, Medicare, Medicaid, and housing assistance). Local providers and advocates have much to say about how federal changes in these programs have affected their patients or members. These impressions are combined with the data from local social services departments and Area Agencies on Aging in chapter 9; we do not repeat the basic data on federal changes there.

WHAT HAS HAPPENED TO THE LOW-INCOME ELDERLY?

Local providers and advocates in the four cities investigated have much to say about the effects that changes in Social Security, SSI, food stamps, Medicare, and Medicaid programs have had on the low-income elderly in their jurisdictions. The federalized structure of these programs, however, has meant that the local offices administering them have little or no discretion in selecting eligible participants, deciding what types of payment these participants can receive, or determining what types of services the local staff can provide. Where local providers can give insights into how their low-income elderly have been affected by changes in Social Security, SSI, Medicare, Medicaid, food stamp and housing subsidy changes, we incorporate these comments in the discussion of local impact.

The focus of this chapter is on services funded through the social service block grant and the Older Americans Act. Although these funding sources account for a small part of the overall federal investment in the economic well-being of older Americans, they represent the major federal support for *direct services* to this population, and therefore the source of funding for programs that help the low-income elderly maintain their independence. They are also the programs over which local governments have the most control.

State Funding Patterns

Title XX (after 1982, the social services block grant) support was used to pay for a variety of services to low-income elderly people. The biggest service component for the elderly funded through this source was in-home services (chore, homemaker, personal care) to prevent or delay placement of the elderly in nursing homes. These services were frequently coordinated with home health services supported by Medicaid and Medicare. Other services receiving Title XX-social services block grant funding included case management, adult day care, and other miscellaneous services.

Funding provided by the Older Americans Act supported congregate and home-delivered meals (its biggest program), social services, some day care and transportation, community and legal services, and employment. Older Americans Act funding has remained relatively stable during the early 1980s at the federal level, experiencing slight increases in some service areas and substantial reductions in only one—senior employment. Thus state or local replacement of lost federal revenues is not an issue for Older Americans Act funding as it is for Title XX.

Table 27 shows the drop in Title XX-social services block-grant funding between fiscal years 1981 and 1983 in the states of the four cities we investigated and how these states adjusted to decreases in federal support. California and Massachusetts replaced more than the total amount of money lost from Title XX in the transition to the social services block grant. In Massachusetts, replacement and overreplacement used entirely state funds. In California, two-thirds of the change in nonblock spending came from the state budget, and one-third came from local government resources. Michigan was not able to replace 100 percent of lost Title XX revenues, but did replace 82 percent. Michigan's reassignment of social services block grant dollars caused a $12.7 million loss of other federal support for the same services, in addition to the funding cut from the Title XX-social services block-grant transition. Local and state resources compensated for both the social services block-grant cuts and the other federal losses, with local resources providing nearly four-fifths of the increase in nonblock spending. Of the four states, only Virginia did not replace lost Title XX revenues. In fact, state and local support for services previously funded through this source dropped slightly in Virginia.

City and County Funding Patterns

Title XX-Social Services Block Grant

State data on Title XX-social services block grant changes are interesting but do not give a very accurate picture of what happened to adult services at the local level in the four jurisdictions we studied. Table 28 presents sources of funding for adult social services in the four cities for fiscal years 1981 to 1983. The table shows that all cities experienced a drop in Title XX-social services block grant funding for adult services during this period, although the magnitude of that drop is quite different from the drop at the state level in all funding from this source. This occurred because the states shifted their funding patterns, often reducing the amount of block grant resources used for

TABLE 27

CHANGES IN SOCIAL SERVICES BLOCK GRANT FUNDS AND REPLACEMENT OF
FEDERAL DOLLARS, FISCAL YEARS 1981–83[a]
(*Millions of Dollars unless Otherwise Indicated*)

Item	California	Massa-chusetts	Michigan	Virginia
Title XX–social services block grant				
Funding, fiscal 1981 (Title XX, federal)	304.6	78.7	115.6	64.8
Total funding for social services[b]	732.3	134.8	580.4	85.4
Funding, fiscal 1983 (block grant)	257.4	61.7	108.0	57.3
Total funding for social services[b]	753.9	147.6	579.0	76.0
Percent change, 1981–83				
Block grant	− 15.5	− 21.6	− 6.6	− 11.5
Total	2.9	9.1	− 0.2	− 11.0
Percent nominal replacement of reduced block grant funds[c]	145.8	174.0	81.6	− 25.3
Change in nonblock spending				
Total change	68.8	29.6	6.1	− 1.9
Other federal change	20.7	− 0.3	− 12.7	0.0
State change	47.0	29.9	4.0	− 0.3
Local change	1.2	0.0	14.8	− 1.6

SOURCE: Eugene C. Durman, Barbara A. Davis, and Randall R. Bovbjerg, "Block Grants and the New Federalism: The Second Year Experience," Research Paper 3076-01 (Washington, D.C.: The Urban Institute, April 1984), tables 1 and 2.

a. Results between 0 and 100 reflect partial replacement. Numbers over 100 indicate states that have increased total spending by more than the loss of federal dollars. Negative numbers show instances in which total funding was reduced by more than the loss of federal block grant dollars. This table presents changes in nominal terms. If inflation of about 7 percent per year (the average inflation in state and local purchase of goods and services) is added, the magnitude of replacement would be less.

b. Total includes state, local, and other federal funds in addition to block grant or Title XX dollars.

c. The extent of replacement was measured as loss of federal block grant dollars minus loss of total social service dollars, all divided by loss of federal block grant dollars.

adult services and in one instance (Richmond) reducing the city's share of state funds. In some instances these shifts away from adult services were

TABLE 28

LOCAL CHANGES IN TITLE XX–SOCIAL SERVICES BLOCK GRANT AND OTHER
FUNDING FOR ADULT SOCIAL SERVICES, FISCAL YEARS 1981–83

| | Budget ($ Thousands) | | | Percent Change, 1981–83 | |
City and Type of Funding	1981	1982	1983	Current Dollars	Constant Dollars
San Diego					
Title XX–block grant[a]	n.a.	3,893	3,824	−2	−6
Refugee Resettlement[a]	n.a.	869	74	−91	−92
State[a,b]	n.a.	938	1,079	15	10
County	2,396	2,365	1,478	−38	−44
Total	7,711	7,355	6,455	−16	−24
Detroit[c]					
Title XX–block grant	44,536	31,576	31,371	−30	−36
Other	57,825	91,159	91,416	58	43
Total	102,361	122,735	122,787	20	8
Richmond					
Title XX–block grant	8,200	8,089	6,132	−25	−32
State	590	526	404	−31	−38
City	2,360	2,106	1,618	−31	−38
Total	11,150	10,721	8,154	−27	−34
Boston					
Title XX–block grant	4,746	0	0	−100	−100
State	8,875	15,181	16,118	82	64
Total	13,621	15,181	16,118	18	7

SOURCES: Local social services budget documents. Figures are rounded.

n.a.   Not available.

a.   Reflects 1982–83 change.

b.   Does not include $9.4 million in each year of state-administered payments to individual providers for in-home social services.

c.   Data are for Michigan as a whole. Detroit (Wayne County) accounts for approximately half of adult services expenditures in that state. "Other" includes both state and local resources, with local funding accounting for approximately 80 percent. See table 27.

compensated by state or local replacement, but in other instances they were not.

San Diego lost little of its Title XX funding with the shift to the social services block grant, and state replacement more than compensated for that drop. However, San Diego's county funding dropped almost 50 percent in real terms during the same period, reflecting county priorities for programs besides adult services. Overall San Diego's adult services program lost 24 percent of its funding between 1981 and 1983 (in constant dollars, after adjusting for inflation), and has had to cut services accordingly. Detroit lost approximately one-third of its Title XX funding for adult services with the shift to the block grant and local resources more than compensated for the loss. Massachusetts had been funding an increasing proportion of its adult services with state money, greatly exceeding the required 25 percent match for Title XX. With the advent of the social services block grant, Massachusetts decided to switch all its federal funding into children's services and to pick up in-home services for its elderly citizens with state funding. As in Detroit, funding for these services in Boston and in all of Massachusetts increased during the years under study because of the state's commitment to support them.

Richmond is the only one among the four cities in which adult services lost heavily from Title XX-social services block grant cuts and in which little occurred to compensate for the loss. Adult services cuts in Richmond during the first post-Reagan year due to the block grant cuts, but the cuts between fiscal years 1982 and 1983 occurred because the state changed its social services block grant allocation formula in a way that seriously hurt Richmond. These cuts followed others between fiscal 1980 and fiscal 1981 due to local circumstances, but the cumulative impact has been devastating. Adult services lost twenty-three positions from 1980 to 1983 and its purchase-of-services budget dropped 91 percent, from $1.4 million in fiscal 1980 to $0.1 million in fiscal 1983. Purchased services included in-home supportive services, adult day care, legal services, and adult protective services.

Area Agencies on Aging

Turning to the budgets for Area Agencies on Aging in the four cities, (table 29), we see that these agencies in three out of four cities lost ground in constant dollar terms between 1981 and 1983, despite relatively unchanged federal funding levels. In all four cities the agencies experienced inflation-adjusted losses in federal financial support. Local funding decreased in all four cities, but San Diego and Detroit had state funding increases to compensate for local cuts. This was not the case in Boston or Richmond.

Caseloads

Budget data do not tell the whole story, but must be matched with caseload figures to understand the actual pressures on local agency resources. Table 30 shows available caseload information in the four cities.

TABLE 29

BUDGETS FOR AREA AGENCIES ON AGING IN SAN DIEGO, DETROIT, RICHMOND, AND
BOSTON, STATE FISCAL YEARS 1981–83

| | Budget ($ Thousands) | | | Percent Change, 1981–83 | |
City and Funding Source	1981	1982	1983	Current Dollars	Constant Dollars
San Diego					
Older Americans Act	4,294	4,834	4,450	4	−6
Other federal	1,402	1,425	1,182	−16	−24
Total federal	5,696	6,259	5,632	−1	−11
State	479	818	1,450	203	174
County	663	365	378	−43	−48
Other	534	720	814	52	38
Total	7,372	8,162	8,274	12	1
Detroit[a]					
Older Americans Act	5,211	5,047	5,528	6	−4
Other federal	918	940	996	8	−2
Total federal	6,129	5,987	6,524	6	−4
State	702	1,043	1,039	48	34
City	76	76	26	−66	−69
Total	6,907	7,106	7,589	10	−1
Richmond[b]					
Older Americans Act	1,544	1,389	1,226	−21	−28
Other federal	109	105	356	227	195
Total federal	1,653	1,494	1,582	−4	−14
Boston[c]					
Older Americans Act	3,227	2,942	3,007	−7	−16
Other federal	54	332	415	669	595
Total federal	3,281	3,274	3,422	4	−6
State	0	15	90	*	*
City	2,065	1,791	1,901	−8	−17
Private grants and contributions	0	0	39	*	*
Total	5,346	5,080	5,452	2	−8

SOURCES: San Diego—Data derived from annual reports of the San Diego Area Agency on
Aging; Detroit—Detroit Area Agency on Aging; Richmond—Richmond Area Agency
on Aging; Boston—Boston Commission on Affairs of the Elderly. Figures are rounded.

   *   Lack of data precludes calculation.

   a.   In addition to the figures given, the budgets of the Detroit Area Agency on Aging for
each year include approximately $350,000 in program income, generated largely by the nutrition
programs.

   b.   State and local matching funds made up 14 percent of the total in 1981 and 1982 and
13 percent of the total in 1983. The agency did not construct its budget to show the state and
local shares.

   c.   In addition to the figures given, each year's budget includes approximately $215,000
in administrative costs.

TABLE 30

CASELOAD CHANGES FOR LOW-INCOME ELDERLY, FISCAL YEARS 1981–83

City and Type of Service	Number of Persons			Percent Change, 1981–83
	1981	*1982*	*1983*	
San Diego				
In-home social services	6,940	6,518	6,400	−8
Adult protective services	1,469	1,300	1,000	−32
Services of Area Agency on Aging[a]				
Nutrition	11,021	13,853	13,511	23
Social services	22,686	43,752	27,306	20
Detroit				
In-home social services[b]	9,367	9,804	10,055	7
Adult protective services	647	620	760	17
Services of Area Agency on Aging[a]	n.a.	15,831	15,282[d]	−3[c]
Richmond				
In-home social services (per month)	210	30	30	−85
Adult protective services[e]	262	345	376	44
Services of Area Agency on Aging[a,f]	n.a.	185,881	203,698	10[d]
Boston				
Home-care	7,673	7,842	8,243	7
Services of Area Agency on Aging[a]	12,593	28,501	26,726	112

SOURCE: Agency records of the respective cities.

   a.   Counts are unduplicated *within* services, but duplicated *across* services.

   b.   In fiscal 1981, 6,081 persons were served through Title XX and 9,367 clients were served with either Title XX or Title XIX (Medicaid) funding. In fiscal years 1982 and 1983 all services were paid for by Title XIX.

   c.   Reflects change from 1982 to 1983.

   d.   This figure for fiscal 1983 is comparable to the fiscal 1982 figure because it includes counts of persons only for those services for which counts were also available in fiscal 1982. If we included persons receiving services for which no comparable 1982 counts were available— information and referral, congregate meals, nutrition education, transportation, legal services and advocacy—the figure would be 45,791.

   e.   Data represent complaints per year, which equal *new*, not ongoing cases.

   f.   Service units, not recipient counts.

Agencies can take one of two different approaches to dealing with budget changes—especially budget cuts. They can either cut the number of persons they serve but maintain the level of services for any individual recipient or they can try to handle equal or greater numbers of persons but give them less intensive services. Comparing the budget data in table 29 with the caseload data in table 30 gives some insight into the ways the social service agencies in the four cities handled budget changes. Agencies handling adult social services in San Diego and Richmond took the former approach for in-home care, and San Diego did so also for adult protective services. These agencies lost staff because of budget cuts but elected to keep the workload approximately the same for the remaining staff, with the result that caseloads shrank for the agency as a whole.

Richmond's adult protective services staff was cut from ten to seven persons in fiscal 1983, and 100 ongoing cases were shifted to generic casework services. Yet the remaining staff still handled a caseload of complaints that represented a substantial increase over that served by the full staff complement the year before. Obviously workers had to reduce the amount of time they could devote to individual cases.

Detroit's social services agency experienced a postinflation growth of 8 percent and increased its caseload for in-home services by the same proportion. Boston also saw real growth in home care funding of 7 percent, and also passed it along in the form of increased caseload. In both San Diego and Richmond the changes and cuts beginning in 1981 followed equal or greater reductions in staff and services in previous years. There was no "fat" left in either agency after these earlier cuts, so the post-1981 changes had an especially severe impact.

The caseload data for Area Agencies on Aging, reported in table 30, are not as straightforward as those for social services agencies. The former deliver a greater range of services than the adult services units of social service agencies. Many of their services involve outreach, prevention, health checkups, and other activities that reach large numbers of people for an hour or two apiece. Alternatively, people participate repeatedly in other services, especially congregate and home-delivered meals, transportation, friendly visits, and telephone reassurance. Area Agencies on Aging can shift resources among their progams and can greatly increase their service population by increasing their outreach and educational activities relative to their more intensive services.

When the caseload data for Area Agencies on Aging are compared with the budget data for the same cities, no clear pattern emerges between funding and service levels. Two of these agencies, in San Diego and Detroit, had virtually flat funding patterns (no more than a 1 percent increase or decrease in inflation-adjusted funding), yet one city shows a jump in recipient caseload of approximately 21 percent and the other city appears to have a decrease of approximately 3 percent in those services for which comparisons can be made.

Boston and Richmond both report real drops in funding of 8 percent and 14 percent, respectively, yet each reports increased caseloads. In Boston's case, the increase is over 100 percent. This increase results from nearly doubling the number of recipients who use some services and adding some services that were not offered in 1981. Before we turn to the effects of federal changes on service recipients and caseloads, we must first describe the structure of those services and the characteristics of the low-income elderly in the four cities.

Agency Service Structures and Populations Served[1]

In each location visited, two county agencies had primary responsibility for the low-income elderly and several more local agencies controlled some program or resource of great importance to this population. These service structures for the low-income elderly are by far more complicated than the structures for other populations included in this book. The two primary agencies assisting the low-income elderly were the social services department, division, or bureau, and the Area Agency on Aging. The picture is a complex one because both types of agencies purchase services by contract from a wide range of community-based organizations and individuals. In addition, adult services units must help their recipients negotiate the maze of federal health and income maintenance programs, even when these programs are administered by another division or bureau in the "umbrella" agency that also houses adult services.

San Diego

In San Diego the Department of Social Services' Adult Social Services unit provides in-home supportive services, adult protective services, and conservatorship services.[2] The casework performed by Adult Social Services staff is supplemented by in-home services purchased from many individual providers who supply homemaker, chore, and personal care services. A large proportion of the agency's recipients are poor and elderly.

The San Diego Area Agency on Aging supports programs through ninety or more purchase-of-service contracts for nutrition, in-home supportive ser-

---

1. Readers who are not concerned with the detailed service structures in the four jurisdictions might want to skip to the next section.

2. Adult protective services are defined broadly as assistance to adults who are neglected, exploited, or in circumstances that may endanger their health and safety. This assistance may include legal, housing, in-home support, mental health, case management, and other services. Conservatorship services involve establishing legal control over and managing a mentally incompetent person's financial affairs to promote that person's welfare.

vices, legal services, information and referral, transportation, and outreach. It also directly provides information and referral, an ombudsman program, and a multipurpose senior center that gives case management to the frail elderly. Contractors include five adult day health centers, several senior employment programs, three information and referral agencies, seven home care agencies, a legal services agency, twenty-five nutrition contractors operating forty-six sites, and several senior citizens centers.

Before the pressure from budget cuts, the Department of Social Services and the Area Agency on Aging both provided social and in-home supportive services for the elderly, but without any interagency coordination. Budgetary pressure has resulted in more coordination. Persons applying to the Area Agency on Aging for in-home services are now sent first to Adult Social Services to determine if they are income-eligible for services supported by the social services block grant. Services funded by the Area Agency on Aging are reserved for those "marginal" people who have incomes just above the block-grant maximum but who cannot afford to pay for the care they need.

Medicare and Medicaid (MediCal in California), food stamps, housing, transportation assistance, mental health, and other services relevant to the elderly are each administered by a different agency. Caseworkers can help elderly persons gain access to these services, but coordination sometimes fails.

In 1980, persons aged sixty-five and older comprised 9.7 percent of San Diego County's population. Of these 181,477 people, about 7 percent are below the poverty line, or 12,862 people. About 31 percent of the elderly live alone and have a higher incidence of poverty; about 14 percent of the unrelated persons aged sixty-five and older are below the poverty line. Looked at another way, 62 percent of the poor elderly in San Diego live alone. These figures have implications for the types of services they may need and the types of help they can or cannot expect from other family members.

The average caseload each month for in-home services to the elderly provided through the Department of Social Services is projected to be 6,400 for fiscal 1982. Since there were 65,589 household units in San Diego County containing elderly (persons aged sixty-five or older) by the 1980 census, and since in-home services can be thought of as serving households rather than individual persons, these services reach approximately 10 percent of all elderly households with services intended to prevent or delay placement in nursing homes. All these households meet the income requirements that were in effect under Title XX and are therefore low-income.

Of the 40,000 to 50,000 people served by the San Diego Area Agency on Aging each year, approximately 65 percent are people of "greatest economic need,'' to use the agency's phrase. The agency does not record income levels for the elderly using its services, and the Older Americans Act explicitly rejects income as a basis for receiving services funded under the act.

Detroit

Public assistance and social services programs for Detroit residents, including those for the low-income elderly, are administered by the Michigan Department of Social Services through the Wayne County Area Office. Detroit constitutes approximately 50 percent of Wayne County's population but nearly 85 percent of its Department of Social Services recipients. As the designated Title XX-social services block grant agency, the department administers adult protective services, in-home services, and other case management and social services for adults. It manages the income maintenance and need-based assistance programs—Medicaid, Aid to Families with Dependent Children (AFDC), food stamps, the emergency needs program, and general assistance. It also operates a range of other services for AFDC, Medicaid, and SSI recipients and others who are eligible on the basis of low income.

The Detroit Area Agency on Aging is a nonprofit agency that funds, coordinates and monitors services for the elderly in the Detroit area. This agency serves the city of Detroit plus eight other areas: Hamtramck, Highland Park, Harper Woods, and the five Grosse Point communities. It administers a range of services including day care services, escort services, information and referral, health screening, in-home services (chore and homemaking), legal aid services, library services, minor home repair, nursing home monitoring, outreach services, senior center staffing, services for the visually impaired and hearing impaired, nutrition services (congregate and home-delivered meals), and transportation to nutrition programs. The agency also funds several other agencies in the city of Detroit: the Department of Health (nutrition and health screening services), the Public Library, the Recreation Department (day care), and the Senior Citizens Department (Information and Referral).

According to 1980 census figures, there are 230,823 elderly households above the poverty line. An additional 38,697 households that are below the poverty threshold in the area served by the Detroit Area Agency on Aging make up approximately 17 percent of the area's households. The 10,055 persons receiving adult services from the Department of Social Services thus constitute approximately one-fourth of the area's poor elderly households. Between 66 percent and 95 percent of the recipients of major services provided by the Detroit Area Agency on Aging (nutrition, in-home services, senior centers, information and referral) are low-income elderly.

Richmond

Richmond's Department of Public Welfare houses the Bureau of Social Services and the Bureau of Financial Assistance. Adult Services, including in-home supportive services, adult day care, and adult protective services, is a unit in the Bureau of Social Services. The Bureau of Financial Assistance includes the income maintenance programs—AFDC, aid to the aged, and aid to the disabled—and also handles eligibility for the related medicaid and food stamps programs. Approximately 55 percent of Adult Services recipients are elderly; 99 percent receive Medicaid and 75 to 85 percent, food stamps. The persons served are thus overwhelmingly low-income.

The Richmond Area Agency on Aging maintains purchase-of-service contracts with two agencies that provide transportation; two that provide outreach; twenty-five, congregate meal sites; and one agency each for in-home care, chore maintenance, telephone reassurance, legal, home-delivered meals, and employment services. The agency directly provides emergency support, some health services, and administrative and technical assistance for contractors.

According to the 1980 census, there were 43,693 households in the Richmond standard metropolitan statistical area (SMSA) with a household head sixty-five years old or older. These households represent 16 percent of all households in the Richmond SMSA. Of these, 42 percent (18,262) are single-person households. Those with incomes below the poverty level make up 28 percent of elderly households (12,234); similarly, 28 percent of all one-person elderly households were below poverty (5,094). Richmond's average in-home services caseload of 30 per month thus touches only a very small percentage of poor elderly, many more of whom are in need of assistance, judging from the city's 376 new cases of adult protective services complaints in 1983.

Boston

According to the 1980 census, there are 220,129 elderly households in the Boston metropolitan area—approximately 17 percent of the population. Of these, 25,232 households had incomes below the 1979 poverty level. The annual report of Boston's Commission on the Affairs of the Elderly, the local Area Agency on Aging, shows that in fiscal 1983 the commission reached 45,371 elderly clients with services, outreach, or information and referral. According to these figures, the commission had contact with approximately one-fifth of the area's elderly population. Program data on direct services provided by the commission in 1982 shows that 15 percent of the persons served lived below the poverty level and 11 percent had a minority background.

Boston's Commission on the Affairs of the Elderly has been the city's Area Agency on Aging since 1978. It offers the same range of direct and contracted services for the elderly as the similar Area Agencies on Aging in the three other cities included in this analysis. Services in the Title XX-social services block grant are provided in Massachusetts by a separate program—the home care program—run by the state's Department of Elder Affairs. In the Boston area, three Home Care Corporations funded by this program provide social casework services, in-home supportive services, adult protective services, and other miscellaneous services for low-income elderly persons. Those with incomes under $5,200 receive free services while elderly persons with incomes up to $8,464 receive services on a sliding-fee basis. The 8,243 elderly served during fiscal 1983 make up about one-third of the poor elderly households in the Boston area.

Relations between the commission and the home care corporations have become more complex as funding from the Older Americans Act has leveled off. The home care corporations now contribute approximately one-third of the revenues to the home-delivered meals program run by the commission.

Both the commission and the home care corporations are local extensions of state agencies serving the elderly. The same is true of a third agency important to the low-income elderly—the Department of Public Welfare. The department administers Medicaid, food stamps, SSI, and other means-tested programs. Case managers working for the commission and the home care corporations often help elderly persons negotiate the eligibility procedures they encounter at the Department of Public Welfare.

Impact of Budget and Program Changes

The interviews with service providers, funders, and advocacy groups in the four selected cities reveal more pressure on services and more difficulties for continuing and new recipients than the budget and caseload figures indicate. In many instances, state or local decisions about funding or priorities exacerbate federal actions. Regulatory or administrative changes in federal programs besides those administered by the adult social services agency or Area Agency on Aging also affect the low-income elderly—sometimes directly and sometimes only by the increased anxiety or uncertainty they create. In the remainder of this chapter we address the cumulative impact of changing programs and policies on the low-income elderly in each of the four cities.

San Diego

Looking first at the major programs serving the poor elderly, we note that San Diego's Adult Social Services unit of the Department of Social Services has experienced substantial cuts. Services consist of in-home support, adult protective services, and conservatorship. In-home support services help aged and disabled persons to remain safely in their own homes by providing cleaning, washing and shopping, food preparation services and cleanup, and help with dressing, bathing, walking, getting into and out of bed, and toileting. Adult protective services, as defined above, assist adults who are neglected, exploited, or who are in circumstances that may endanger their health and safety. Social workers assess the need for services, provide short-term problem solving, assist in finding appropriate out-of-home living arrangements, and provide for other services such as financial aid, medical help, transportation, and homemaker assistance. The objective of this program is to remove or alleviate abuse and danger as quickly as possible and then link the adult to other resources so that any ongoing needs for counseling, supervision, and support services are met.

The fiscal 1982 adopted budget is 5 percent smaller than the fiscal 1981 budget and dropped another 12 percent in fiscal 1983. These decreases followed budget cuts of 20 percent between fiscal years 1979 and 1981, and thus were particularly difficult to absorb. For in-home supportive services, paid for largely by the social services block grant, caseloads went from 34:1 in fiscal 1980 to 52:1 in fiscal 1983. In addition, staff dropped 25 percent between fiscal years 1981 and 1983. Caseload dropped 8 percent in the same interval. Caseload is expected to hit 120:1 in fiscal 1984 because of even more staff cutbacks. Services cut entirely include home visits to supervise impaired and home-bound elderly, noncritical medical transportation, and all protective services related to drug and alcohol abuse. With recipient counts of approximately 6,500 per year, San Diego's in-home supportive services appear to reach the equivalent of half the poor elderly individuals in San Diego. Some of this support goes to nonelderly people, of course, but the penetration of services is still impressive.

Since these services are aimed at preventing or delaying institutionalization, cutting back on them may be fiscally shortsighted. In-home services are much less expensive than nursing home care, yet persons cut off from in-home support may enter nursing homes sooner and cost both federal and state governments more in eventual Medicaid expenditures.

Eligibility for services provided by the social services block grant carries with it MediCal eligibility, but with a $140 per month copayment obligation. San Diego's Adult Services unit advises people to apply their copayment to homemaker services and receive MediCal coverage "for free." Actually, what happens is that for the same dollar outlay an elderly person receives both homemaker services and MediCal coverage, rather than just MediCal.

Adult Protective Services (with Title XX-social services block grant funding) lost 26 percent of its staff and reduced recipient load by 29 percent from 1982 to 1983. Thus the caseload size per staff person is stable, but significantly fewer people are served. Records are not kept of the number of referrals, so they it is not known whether the need for these services has increased or remained the same. The staff has cut caseloads by refusing all cases that appear to require more than six months to stabilize. (Adults in need of protective services are in emergency situations, which require intensive casework and which may take many months to resolve.) The staff refers long-term cases to other agencies but does not know if these elderly people actually receive care. This means that the county has stopped serving elderly people whose condition places them at continuing and long-term risk of illness or death through neglect, abuse, or inability to care for themselves.

San Diego's Adult Services unit also runs a conservatorship program for elderly and other disabled adults who are found to be incapable of taking care of themselves. Case numbers for the conservatorsip program have remained at around 1,900, but the staff has shrunk from thirty-eight to twenty-seven persons (a decline of 29 percent). State funds have replaced Title XX funds for this program at a reduced level. The unit has coped by dividing the cases into categories of persons assisted—"intensive," "minimal," or "stable." Thirty-six percent of the cases have been logged as persons having minimal need. These are "elderly in institutions with poor prognosis," people who will receive fewer social work services less often. Some elderly with minimal need and some stable ones in board-and-care homes will be moved from the conservatorship program to other units of the Department of Social Services or to state supervision.

Programs funded by the Older Americans Act are managed by the San Diego Area Agency on Aging. According to this agency's administrators, these programs have not suffered any significant cuts and some budget components have increased. (Their actual budget numbers, described below and in Table 30, tell a somewhat different story.) The agency anticipates being able to maintain its level of services to all senior citizens. The federal share of the agency's budget dropped 1 percent in nominal terms and 11 percent in real terms from fiscal years 1981 to 1983. In the same period the county share dropped 43 percent (48 percent after inflation), but the state share rose 174 percent after inflation. This latter increase was due largely to San Diego's three-year demonstration, the multipurpose senior center project. Although fiscal 1982 was the third (and presumably last) year of this project, the county budget planning showed the program as continuing and legislation was under consideration to extend the project concept statewide.

Specific federal programs operated by San Diego's Area Agency on Aging experienced significant changes from fiscal 1981 to fiscal 1983: Funding provided by the Comprehensive Employment and Training Act was completely eliminated; revenue sharing (used largely for nutrition) dropped 34 percent; social services Title III(B) decreased 26 percent; nutrition programs, Title III(C) and U.S. Department of Agriculture, rose 38 percent. The agency's drop in social services funding adds to the picture painted by the Adult Services unit of strained social services resources. With both major providers of in-home care, adult day care, chore, maintenance and personal care, and case management experiencing significant drops in service levels, the elderly who rely on them for services are sure to suffer.

Other goods and services affecting the elderly include transportation, housing, and energy assistance. The feeling in San Diego is that federal low-income energy assistance has not helped most low-income elderly since most do not own their homes. The public housing authority reports a stable allotment of approximately 2,700 Section 8 subsidy slots. The renter's share of the cost has increased from 25 percent to 30 percent of income for new renters (current recipients must pay increases of 1 percent each year up to 30 percent). With almost 13,000 elderly persons in poverty in San Diego county, available housing subsidies do little to fill the housing need. Transportation to meal sites and nonemergency medical care have been cut by several agencies, making it harder for the elderly to get to services even when they exist.

Changes in MediCal and Medicare have also affected the elderly. Caseworkers in San Diego report elderly persons forgoing hospital treatment because they cannot afford the $304 copayment required by Medicare. Outpatient treatment is also more frequently postponed or forgone because senior citizens cannot afford the $140 copayment obligation and are afraid of having liens placed on their property or income. MediCal once picked up this difference for some recipients but no longer does so. Recipients of SSI and Social Security Disability Insurance are also now being held to the $140 copayment obligation and usually cannot afford both board and care or other residential payments and medical bills. MediCal's utilization review process is also reported to be limiting hospital stays, so that people awaiting nursing home placement are now being discharged from hospitals whether or not they have a nursing home to which they can go. Often these elderly end up in completely inappropriate board-and-care facilities in the interim.

Since no single agency in San Diego is responsible for the low-income elderly, no one can make definitive statements about how many are affected by federal changes or how severely. The percentage differences in funding levels are small except for social services, but the general feeling is that there are serious difficulties.

Detroit

From fall 1979 until the time our data were collected, Detroit has had double-digit unemployment; in November 1982 it hit 20 percent. The demand for social services and health and welfare benefits has increased accordingly, while human services funding from both the federal and state levels is diminishing. Between fiscal years 1980 and 1983 Detroit lost $163.7 million in federal funds, a decrease of 45 percent. In the human services alone (AFDC, food stamps, Medicaid, health, nutrition, social services), the state of Michigan lost $421 million in fiscal 1982.

As a result of the structure of services in the Detroit area, it is difficult to isolate services utilized specifically by the low-income elderly. While we do have some caseload data for the major social service programs for low-income persons such as Medicaid and food stamps, which the elderly are likely to use, we do not have the recipient figures by age bracket. Furthermore, all publicly funded services designed specifically for the elderly in the Detroit area are administered by the Detroit Area Agency on Aging—including those operated by the city government. Although the majority of the agency's services are utilized by elderly persons of all income levels, most service recipients have low incomes.

According to the Detroit Area Agency on Aging staff, there have not been substantial changes in the agency's services during the past few years. Service funding levels have not been altered except for a few minor changes. Beginning October 1983, the funding for a few services, such as small home repairs, was cut, and the money was shifted to homemaker, chore, and other in-home support services. Although more funds for services for the aged could easily be used, what they had seemed to be relatively stable.

Budget data provided by the Detroit Area Agencies on Aging show that cuts have occurred or will occur in home repairs, escort services, library, recreation, information and referral, and a few other services; increased funding is available for in-home services, day care, and all nutrition programs. Recipient populations remained constant or increased slightly in nearly every service category during fiscal years 1982 and 1983.

The recent experiences of two services funded by the agency shed some additional light on funding issues and demand for services to the elderly in Detroit. The staffs of these services—the home-delivered meals program, based in the Detroit Health Department, and the general information and referral program, based in the city's Senior Citizens Department—were asked to describe service changes that they have implemented and to comment on general changes in services and on the effects of those changes on recipients in the community.

The home-delivered meals program is funded almost entirely with a grant from the Detroit Area Agency on Aging; the city contributes the space and a secretary. The elderly are eligible for the service only if they have a condition so disabling (temporarily or permanently) that they are unable to go to a congregate meal site. The program has enjoyed the agency's consistent funding during the past few years, although the staff plans to begin some fundraising efforts in the private sector.

In 1979 the home-delivered meals program served approximately 1,600 persons. In 1980, in response to declining funds, the program staff reduced the caseload to 1,300, mainly by attrition; when recipients died or left the program, the staff did not replace them with people on the waiting list. Between 1981 and 1983 the caseload slowly rose again to 1,600. In fiscal 1984 the program planned to serve 1,600 persons out of public funds, plus an additional 200 persons who could pay. The waiting list remains very long— nearly 1,000 people—and the staff believes that this is a serious problem. Demand is definitely growing for home-delivered meals. As a result, the program has tightened eligibility requirements (for example, requiring more careful review of medical documentation) and has also begun a periodic reinvestigation process. If a person's condition improves, the program staff may determine that the person is no longer eligible for meals, something that was virtually never done until recently.

The home-delivered meals program staff believed that money for meals was relatively stable but that there was not enough. Money for services to the low-income elderly is tight throughout the community, and demand for services is rising. Recipients of the home-delivered meals program are isolated, frail, and vulnerable—very old and very poor. For some, their only contact with the outside world is the person who brings the meals. As the program budget has been tightened, the staff has made a greater effort to put unserved persons in touch with the general information and referral program so that even if they cannot receive meals, they may be able to obtain some other in-home services such as homemaker or chore assistance.

The general information and referral program, in the Senior Citizens Department of the city, is funded by the Area Agency on Aging with a city match. The information and referral program provides information, referral, telephone assistance, advocacy, community organizing, and some casework. Half the agency's calls concern housing problems and the other half are a combination of problems related to health care, social security, nutrition, and transportation. While numbers of people served have remained approximately constant in recent years, the program has been hard pressed to deliver services. The staff has been reduced from twenty-seven to eighteen persons. In addition, people now come to the agency with multiple needs and with problems that are more difficult to solve. Recipients of services need more casework now; merely providing phone numbers of other service providers is rarely sufficient.

Information and referral program staff were more pessimistic than the staff of the Detroit Area Agency on Aging about the recent changes in services and the general state of the elderly in Detroit. Housing is an "enormous problem." With new constraints on Section 8, the elderly in need of subsidized housing cannot receive help; waiting lists for senior citizen housing have been growing. Throughout the Detroit area rents are rising in units already occupied by the elderly. With a decrease in public funding for home repair services, the elderly are having difficulty paying their bills. One of the program's major advocacy efforts in 1983 was to persuade the gas company not to turn off elderly persons' utilities for nonpayment before April 15. The area's elderly are in "serious need" of assistance for energy bills. Cuts in recreation programs in the area have forced the aged to remain at home, increasing the demand for in-home services. In summary, the agency staff perceives that "basically, everything is getting tighter." Administrative changes in Medicaid, Medicare, and food stamps also contribute to the sense that there are insufficient resources to meet the need.

Richmond

Reductions in federal outlays for social services had the most direct impact on the low-income elderly in Richmond of all the Reagan domestic program changes. Cutbacks in Title XX-social services block grant funds at the state level translated into drastic reductions in chore and companion services and adult day care services in the city of Richmond because these services were nonmandated and relied on the purchase of service contracts. Many low-income elderly were forced to change their independent living situations in the absence of needed in-home supportive services. At the same time, the Capitol Area Agency on Aging received a moderate cutback in Older Americans Act funding between fiscal years 1982 and 1983, although overall funding for services remained steady.

In-home supportive services were the first and hardest hit by reductions in the social services block grant. The Adult Services Division's caseload for in-home services caseload dropped from an average of 343 recipients per month in fiscal 1981 to only 60 in fiscal 1982; the budget dropped from $615,000 to $162,000. Substantial cuts had come in fiscal 1979 also, when about 200 cases had to be dropped. The elderly were the population hit hardest, decreasing from 169 to 26 recipients per month between fiscal 1981 and fiscal 1982. These cutbacks affected not only the low-income elderly recipients but the in-home support providers, too, who often were themselves low-income.

The Department of Public Welfare was sufficiently concerned about the cutbacks in in-home supportive services that it surveyed the 282 cases that it closed in July 1981 to find out how the people were now coping. The majority, 166 people, still lived on their own, but they still needed in-home supportive services. Thirty-seven had moved from their independent residence: nineteen into nursing homes, three into licensed board-and-care homes, three into unlicensed homes, seven into relatives' homes, and five to unknown locations. Forty were still receiving in-home services, four through volunteers and thirty-six through Capitol Area Agency on Aging funds (at a reduced level of services). Twenty-five had died, and four no longer needed services. The department had systematically made the necessary program cutbacks, reducing or eliminating services for those people judged most able to do without in-home help. The survey results clearly suggest that these "best off" people still need the service. The net result has been to shift the responsibility for these people to the private sector and to families. As the director of the Department of Public Welfare lamented: "The agency is now out of touch with the community's need for in-home services."

Funding for in-home supportive services is presently on the upswing in Richmond in response to the critical need brought out by Title XX reductions. The immediate response, in early 1982, came from the Capitol Area Agency on Aging and of United Way of Greater Richmond: the former directly paid $18,000 for in-home services for previous social services recipients; United Way made an emergency allocation to Family and Children's Services, a private provider of in-home services. Support from the private sector is expected to increase. In addition, the Department of Public Welfare is renewing efforts to meet the need for in-home services. It has secured $100,000 from the community services block grant and has received a share of additional state appropriations specifically for in-home services (funds transferred from Virginia's energy assistance program). There is also much debate about a state appropriation of $6 million to $11 million for in-home services earmarked in the state social services block grant budget. The legislature recently mandated in-home services on the condition that adequate funds were appropriated, so the state Board of Welfare recommended the earmark. Local welfare officials do not like this arrangement because it only aggravates their allocation problems: it increases the mandates but does not increase the funds available for all social services.

Adult day care services include maintenance or improvement of physical functioning, rehabilitation, social contact, occupational therapy, health monitoring, and other services. The respite that families receive from twenty-four-hour care of elderly family members during the hours of adult day services is also an important function. Although Title XX support for adult day care was never extensive in dollar terms, its elimination in 1981 in Richmond meant drastic changes for many elderly and for many adult day care centers. Day care in Virginia serves about 0.5 percent of the impaired elderly, approximately 400 people. In Richmond, there are facilities for 145 persons in four adult day care centers, three of which serve almost exclusively frail older people.

To compensate for the Department of Social Services' cutbacks in in-home supportive services and elimination of adult day care services, the Capitol Area Agency on Aging shifted funds to provide these two services between fiscal 1982 and fiscal 1984; simultaneously, Richmond's share of these services increased, especially in in-home services. The Capitol Area Agency on Aging dropped a homemaker program after fiscal 1982 because the private agency with which it had a contract to purchase personal care services was able to obtain Title XIX reimbursement after fiscal 1982. United Way also increased its support for adult day care programs.

Cutbacks in funds for Title XX-social services block grant and Older Americans Act services have had less but still noticeable impacts on several other services for the low-income elderly. Transportation has become more expensive for individuals because (1) Medicaid reimbursement for transportation is more limited; (2) federal grants to the local bus company decreased, so rider fees increased; and (3) the Social Services Bureau has been overwhelmed by requests for bus tokens (normally given for travel to agency appointments, to a doctor, and to day care) and is in the process of restricting usage.

In the health area, Medicaid changes have affected the low-income elderly in several ways. Medicaid no longer covers special wheel chairs, eye-glasses, certain dietary supplements, and prescriptions; it covers fewer transportation costs than previously. Medicaid restrictions are also indirectly affecting the health clinic services available to the elderly; the Health Department has stopped accepting new elderly persons at the clinics because it lacks sufficient staff to tend to the necessary home visits. Medicaid will not cover the needed nurse practitioners.

Virginia's Medicaid program has also discontinued podiatry and eye services coverage, except for eye examinations; instituted a deductible and copayment system for services delivered to the medically needy; restructured the program's pharmacy reimbursement system; and limited hospitalization to one day before nonemergency surgery unless there are medical reasons for longer stays. Medicare changes noted elsewhere in this book affect Richmond's elderly also. Increased copayment requirements are the most threatening to elderly persons whose incomes are barely adequate to meet daily expenses.

Housing is another area in which the low-income elderly in Richmond face increasing difficulty. Waiting lists have always been long for housing for the elderly, but there are indications that the situations is getting worse. The resource coordinators of the Capitol Area Agency on Aging, who work in local areas to help elderly persons obtain the services they need, see an increasing numbers of requests for housing assistance. Similarly, the Metro Alternatives Project identified housing services as one of three services in the most jeopardy: "Elderly, handicapped, and/or mentally retarded or emotionally disturbed individuals, as well as low-income people, may be forced to compete for already scarce low-cost, habitable shelter. The problem is further exacerbated by the lack of sufficient emergency housing services, the second highest emergency service request." In response to the growing need for housing, this agency and a consortium of Richmond churches are separately working to set up home-sharing programs for the elderly.

Nutrition is a significant service need of low-income elderly people in Richmond. Congregate meal sites are extensively supported by the Capitol Area Agency on Aging; primarily using Older Americans Act-Title III funds, the agency provides meals at twenty-three sites, including transportation to bring the elderly to the sites. The agency also arranges by contract for the home delivery of 175 meals per day in the Richmond area, and the meals-on-wheels program serves an even greater number; as more people of limited mobility try to stay in their own homes, the demand for home-delivered meals increases.

Two other service programs that underwent changes in response to the needs of the low-income elderly are transportation and emergency services. Transportation funding has remained fairly constant but demands on it have markedly increased, consistent with other reports of transportation needs in the city. Richmond has also experienced a sharp rise in requests for emergency services, testifying to the critical needs facing elderly residents.

Simultaneous changes in these various services can have a substantial impact on an elderly person. The Richmond Adult Services staff estimates that 99 percent of the elderly served receive Medicaid and 75 to 85 percent receive food stamps. An example commonly used locally of the effects of federal changes is an elderly female SSI recipient in Richmond who is eligible for care in an intermediate-level nursing home but chooses to stay in the community. Medicaid will pay up to $7 per hour for in-home supportive services, but the recipient must contribute all but $208 of her SSI income and Medicaid will limit the number of hours of services she may receive.

Because the woman is eligible for nursing home care, SSI will pay approximately $450 per month; at that level, the woman is no longer eligible for subsidized housing, so she loses her Section 8 rent-subsidized apartment. She not only has to move, but because of what she must pay for Medicaid services, she does not have most of her SSI check to use for housing costs. Since she now has to pay more for housing (although she does not have the money), her net income is less and she becomes eligible for food stamps. She will probably also request home-delivered meals from the Capitol Area Agency on Aging. The living costs for this elderly person may be lower overall, but the costs to her and to the private sector have increased while public costs have decreased. The woman has also been put through a series of bureaucratic "Catch 22s" that are likely to leave her confused, anxious, and fearful about her future resources and ability to cope. If the net result is that she gives up and enters a nursing home (paid for by Medicaid), both she and the taxpayers will be ultimate losers in this eligibility maze.

Boston

In-home supportive services for the elderly in Boston were not adversely affected by cutbacks in Title XX-social services block grant funding, as was the case in the other three cities. This was because in 1972 Massachusetts instituted a home care program, which has become one of the most highly funded social services programs for the elderly in the country. When faced with Title XX-social services block grant cuts, Massachusetts decided to fund the home care program entirely with state money, at a level well above the 1981 funding level.

Created by state mandate, the program is geared toward encouraging the elderly to maintain themselves in independent living situations by providing needed in-home supportive services. This experiment has been highly successful. The program relies on local private nonprofit agencies to deliver services to the elderly.

Three community-based home care corporations in the Boston area act as case managers and purchasers of social services for the elderly. The program staff's primary responsibility is case management. The staff evaluates elderly persons by means of a comprehensive needs assessment and then draws up an individualized social services plan that includes companion, homemaker, choremaker, and transportation services. The actual service provision is subcontracted to local provider agencies. Homemaker services make up 80 percent of total expenditures for the home care program.

That the program is totally state funded and has received increased appropriations during the past two years may eventually have an effect on the program's eligibility standards. In the past people aged sixty and older and who were SSI recipients or whose income was within the state's Title XX income limits were financially eligible for home care services. The basic program provided free services for elderly people whose gross income was $5,200 or less. The program also had a sliding fee schedule, which allowed the elderly with incomes between $5,200 and $8,464 to receive homemaker services, based on their ability to pay. The past practice has been that the elderly could not be denied services if they claimed inability to pay. Recently, however, the state legislature, concerned about the escalating costs of the program, has proposed more strict enforcement of eligibility standards in an effort to generate revenue.

According to the staff of the senior home care program, cutbacks and policy changes in other federal programs have had a number of indirect effects on the program. The staff explained that as the Title III(C)-Older Americans Act nutrition monies have stabilized and leveled off, the home care program has picked up some of the cost for home-delivered meal services. For example, in 1983 the program paid $200,000 to nutrition service vendors in the Boston area. This amount represented 31 percent of the budget allocated by the Boston Commission on the Affairs of the Elderly for home-delivered meals. The staff also mentioned that as the Medicaid standards for duration of care have become stricter, the program has received more referrals and has increasingly picked up social services functions previously provided by Medicaid.

The Boston Commission on the Affairs of the Elderly also manages all programs funded by the Older Americans Act. According to the commission's staff, services have undergone some significant changes in the past few years. The Omnibus Budget Reconciliation Act of 1981 eliminated funding for support services under the Older Americans Act, Title III(C) Nutrition Services. These funds had been used for site management and transportation. The responsibility for such activities was shifted to Title III(B) Social Services, but without providing additional funding. In order to continue nutrition transportation services, the agency decided to deemphasize recreational activities and services previously provided by Title III(B) Social Services monies. The commission instead allocated more money to what it considers essential services, such as health and legal services. From fiscal years 1981 to 1983 the commission increased funding for in-home services by 17 percent and funding for legal services by 15 percent.

Commission-supported agencies serving the elderly experienced a complex set of shifting priorities and funding losses at federal, state, and local levels (see table 29). In fiscal 1982 the reduction of the commission's available funds had as much to do with lack of state support and a 13.3 percent reduction in city matching funds as with federal funding cutbacks. It is true, however, that in fiscal 1983 the rise in the commission's available funds was largely due to increased state and private funding.

We spoke to commission staff involved in the administration of nutrition services and to the staff at one of the local legal services agencies. They described changes they had implemented in their own services and commented on the general changes in services and the effects on recipients across the Boston area.

According to the commission's administrative staff, funding from Older Americans Act-Title III(C) has provided from $1.7 million to $1.8 million annually for the past three years, constituting about half of the nutrition services budget. Other funding sources include the surplus food and cash payment program, funded by the U.S. Department of Agriculture, and the elderly lunch program, funded by the State Department of Education. The six nutrition sites in Boston are autonomous and operate on a direct reimbursement basis. The program also receives funding from Medicaid reimbursement, and some staff is provided by existing on-site agencies such as the Salvation Army.

When support services funds were removed from Title III(C) in 1981, the response of the program staff was one of panic. The program has fared better than the staff expected, although it was necessary to drastically reduce the social and recreational services previously available at the nutrition sites. In response to this, program staff chose as new nutrition sites locations at which existing social services agencies were already on site and providing these services.

The commission's nutrition services staff explained that the elderly population it serves has changed significantly over the past five to ten years. Today, the typical participant is more than seventy-five years old. Service needs have changed, consequently, for with increased age there are fewer well elderly and more elderly with health impairments; the demand for home-delivered meals goes up accordingly. The number of elderly people receiving home-delivered meals increased from 1,281 in 1982 to 2,300 in 1983; an increase of 80 percent.

The commission's perceived need for increased funding to support legal services is due in large part to federal cutbacks borne by the Legal Services Corporation. The overall reduction has adversely affected the agency's service delivery. The staff has been reduced from seven to three full-time attorneys, making it necessary to rank services and to become more restrictive in the kinds of cases acccepted. For example, the program no longer handles consumer cases nor offers financial management advice or counseling. The staff now gives more legal advice than actual representation.

According to the legal services program staff, there has been a sharp increase in the number of SSI eligibility redetermination cases. The staff explained that the regulations regarding SSI eligibility had changed little, but the interpretation and administration of the regulations had changed due to the Omnibus Budget Reconciliation Act. Typical cases involved tighter eligibility requirements, which required stricter medical documentation and narrower income limits with back payment penalties. Current enforcement of an elaborate appeals process means that it now takes a longer time to appeal SSI eligibility redetermination cases and it is more difficult to resolve these cases. In the meantime, the affected low-income elderly are in need.

The Reagan administration's domestic program changes and subsequent funding cutbacks have had an impact on several other services for the low-income elderly in the Boston area. Boston's programs funded by the Department of Transportation have been severely reduced since fiscal 1981. In that year the city received approximately $11 million; by 1983 funding had dropped to $6.1 million, a 45 percent decrease. This large reduction in the mass transit operation assistance program has forced an increase in rider's fees. With public transportation becoming more expensive, there has been a greater need for subsidized transportation for the elderly. Use of the the commission-supported transportation service has increased more than 400 percent—from 79,373 trips in fiscal 1981 to 405,455 trips in 1983.

One of the service areas in which the low-income elderly in Boston have been hardest hit has been housing. With the virtual elimination of Section 8 rent subsidies and cutbacks in Section 202 construction loans, the commission estimates that approximately 12,200 low-income elderly are on waiting lists for subsidized housing in the Boston area. This means that a large proportion of the area's total elderly population is in need of rent assistance (Section 8) and low-rent public housing (Section 202/8) that includes special recreational and health care facilities.

Health needs have also been severely affected by federal changes. The commission estimates that health expenditures for the elderly in Boston are as follows: 38 percent of health care costs are paid by Medicaid, 20 to 30 percent are funded by Medicare, and 30 percent are out-of-pocket expenses for the elderly. The commission staff commented that out-of-pocket costs were taxing for many low-income elderly. With the massive program changes in Medicaid and Medicare, many elderly are troubled by the possibility of being unable to pay medical expenses.

Summary

Although real disposable income has risen for all elderly households between 1980 and 1984, changes made during the Reagan administration in federal programs and policies specifically affecting the low-income elderly

have not made life any easier for this segment of the elderly population. It is impossible to determine exactly how much harder it is for the low-income elderly to maintain a minimum standard of living and sense of security.

According to Moon and Sawhill, the real disposable income of elderly families and unrelated persons in the bottom two income quintiles rose between 5.9 and 9.2 percent from 1980 to 1984, but only 0.1 to 0.8 percent of this change is attributable to Reagan administration policies. Elderly households represent an anomaly in these lower quintiles, since all other family types lost real disposable income during the same years.[3] These authors go on to explain that the direct policy impacts on poor households reflected the loss of federal government benefits to households with incomes under $10,000. All low-income elderly would be included in this category. The average household with less than $10,000 income lost $217 in cash benefits and $158 in in-kind benefits, representing 4.3 and 3.2 percent of their income.[4] Thus policy changes in the Reagan administration policy changes have been estimated to have reduced the available resources of the poorest families, including elderly families, by 7.5 percent.

The sense of many service providers is that service cuts necessitated by less funding plus the tighter requirements and changed rules for a wide variety of federal transfer and insurance programs have placed the low-income elderly in a position of greater stress and uncertainty. If the intent of federal policy has been to protect the "truly needy," changes in federal programs have not reflected that intent, either with respect to single programs or collectively. State and local resources have in some instances compensated for federal losses, and this pattern could be said to be in keeping with the administration's preference for nonfederal determination of priorities for local services. However, the promise of *federal* protection for the truly needy and maintenance of *federal* effort on their behalf has not been met with respect to the low-income elderly.

Consistent findings in the four cities investigated indicate that changes in the major federal programs of Medicare, Medicaid, food stamps, housing, and transportation assistance have affected the low-income elderly in negative ways. Required copayments for Medicare tax the ability of these persons to live within meager budgets, with the result that in many instances they go without needed medical care. Changes in Medicaid rules governing eligibility raise the specter that even after an elderly person has spent all available cash,

---

3. Marilyn Moon and Isabel V. Sawhill, "Family Incomes: Gainers and Losers," in John L. Palmer and Isabel V. Sawhill, eds. *The Reagan Record: An Assessment of America's Changing Domestic Priorities* (Cambridge, Massachusetts: Ballinger, 1984), table 10.6 and figure 10.1.
4. Ibid.

that person will still not be eligible for Medicaid due to the presence of some fixed asset previously disregarded by eligibility determination procedures. Other Medicaid changes have increased the degree of disability or illness necessary before one is eligible for Medicaid-covered nursing home care (in Virginia) or decreased the time allowed for hospital stays (in California). Both changes mean that the low-income elderly must turn to community resources at a time when other federal changes have strained these resources to the breaking point.

Affordable housing is scarce, and many low-income elderly are on hopelessly long waiting lists for subsidized housing (as many as 13 percent of Boston's low-income elderly—12,000 people—are waiting for senior citizen housing). Cuts in transportation budgets and specialized transportation services for the elderly curtail daily activities and in effect confine many of these elderly people to their homes.

Social services for the elderly, particularly in-home supportive services such as homemaker, chore, home maintenance, companion, and personal care services, have suffered the largest direct cuts with the transition from Title XX to reduced funds under the social services block grant. Two of the cities studied cut these services significantly, and in both these post-1981 cuts followed a year or more of staff and service reductions due to state and local reductions. These agencies had no "fat" left to trim by the time federal funding reductions hit. A third city switched these services from Title XX to Title XIX (Medicaid) funding and increased the number of people receiving services, resulting in questionable net savings to the federal government.

In the four cities we studied, all programs have felt the pinch of the Reagan administration's approach to social programs. The Older Americans Act has been the most stable of the locally administered programs, protected as it is by the considerable political power of large numbers of older Americans of all income levels. Even within this program, funding for social services Title III(B) has declined in three of the four cities. Area Agency on Aging budget components deriving from the Older American Act have fallen between 4 and 11 percent in inflation-adjusted dollars. Some of these services, frequently social services, have suffered accordingly. Thus all sources of support and services for the low-income elderly have experienced cutbacks, largely because of federal changes, and agencies providing social services to the elderly continue to report pressures and strains on their capacity to meet the need.

CONCLUSIONS

We use the debate surrounding the issue of federal versus local control—that is, which level of government has the responsibility for protecting and supporting the truly needy—as the context in which we draw our conclusions. This book addresses the question, is the social safety net intact for some of the nation's most vulnerable people? More specifically, we investigate in four local jurisdictions the welfare of three needy populations—abused, neglected, and dependent children; the chronically mentally ill; and the low-income elderly. We ask whether states and localities have been able, and willing, to protect the well-being of these populations in the face of federal program and budget changes made during the early 1980s.

When President Reagan took office in 1981 he asserted the philosophy that his administration intended to use with respect to social welfare programs and the people who rely on them. He acknowledged that some people live in circumstances that leave them without the basic necessities of life. He said that the federal government would not desert the truly needy and asserted his commitment to the goals, if not to the means, of most social welfare programs. He espoused the position that except for the truly needy, social welfare programs and the populations served by them were better left to states and localities than to the federal government. Further, he promised to reduce federal government spending for social welfare programs. Finally, he asserted that a strong economy was the best form of social insurance, and committed his administration's efforts to improving U.S. economic performance and reducing inflation.

The Role of the Federal Government

In taking the positions just described, President Reagan placed himself firmly on the "local" side of a recurring policy debate about the relative

171

value of central versus local control over social welfare programs. This debate is decades old, as are the pendulum swings in policy and practice that accompany it. The issue of central versus local control is debated at all levels of government—between state and local governments as well as between the federal government and all other levels of government. Practical realities render the argument unresolvable, except perhaps as a philosophical preference.

A brief description of both central and local positions in the debate will set the stage for our findings regarding the effects of Reagan administration changes on the three vulnerable populations we studied. On the side of greater local control of resources and services, advocates advance the practical argument that social welfare is best provided at the local level because only local people know the needs of their area intimately and can make appropriate priority decisions for distributing resources to many potential recipients with different needs. They add the philosophical argument that social welfare began as a family and community function and ought to continue to be the responsibility of the people closest to those in need.

Arguments for local control have their greatest appeal when one considers the inflexibility and excessive bureaucratization that often accompany central control, and the frequently counterproductive incentives that federal funding categories create for local decision makers. Exceptional circumstances occur in individual cases, and situations develop that are reasonable but not allowable according to the rules. These cannot be accommodated in a rigid centralized system that must be administered similarly in all jurisdictions. Central control mechanisms, rules, and eligibility criteria begin to drive the local planning process, so that at the local level governments, providers, and interest groups begin to think only of federally fundable approaches and solutions rather than the most appropriate ones. Central control can also create uneven service coverage. Needy persons not covered by some federal program receive very few services. At the same time, there are children who receive foster care and elderly who receive nursing home care—not necessarily because they badly need that care or because placing them in those settings is good for them, but because federal or state dollars pay most of the cost of that care and the county or locality making the actual placement decision can thereby keep its own investment as low as possible. Supporters of local control state that if counties received the same dollar amount of federal and state input but were not tied to using it in specified ways, they could probably make the same dollars go a lot further and provide more optimum services for needy populations.

On the side of greater central control (federal or state, but in the present instance, federal), advocates point to inconsistencies of support and protection for the needy across jurisdictions. Spokespersons for particular disadvantaged or disabled groups argue that the nation as a whole has some moral obligation to maintain minimum standards of living, health, and other services for members of these groups—abused children, the elderly, the mentally ill, or any other group of vulnerable people. Because support and assistance for these groups by local jurisdictions and states is documentably uneven, such that a person with a given disadvantage or disability may receive twice or three times as much assistance in one state or locality as in another, the federal government must become the protector of last resort. It must set minimum standards of assistance and provide the resources to meet these standards so that the nation as a whole can meet its obligations to care for the neediest citizens wherever they may live.

The arguments for central control appear strongest when one examines the very real inequities across jurisdictions experienced by persons with essentially identical needs. Both the ability and the commitment to help the truly needy vary across jurisdictions, as does the definition of the level of need itself. Communities differ greatly in their resource base and hence in their ability to raise tax revenues earmarked for assistance programs. Communities also hold quite different values regarding who needs and deserves help. Often these values parallel the interests of strong voting blocks; equally often, the truly needy are neither well-organized politically nor part of the political process at all (for instance, abused children, chronically mentally ill adults). Such issues as public safety and public roads have been the focus of county boards for much longer than social welfare programs, and these issues continue to exercise strong budgetary pulls in many communities, to the detriment of programs to assist disadvantaged or disabled people.

What Has Happened?

The ultimate questions on which we focus the findings of our study are, is the social safety net intact, and does it function equally well to protect the truly needy in all local jurisdictions? Are people who are without resources and who cannot help themselves at least as well off, in every jurisdiction, as they were before the Reagan administration instituted its many changes in federal social welfare activities? In particular, are the three populations we investigated, who appear to be truly needy by almost anyone's definition— abused, neglected and dependent children; the chronically mental ill; and the low-income elderly—suffering in significant ways from Reagan administration cuts or changes in social welfare programs?

In the introduction to this book we outlined seven possible ways that the circumstances of needy people could have remained stable despite many federal changes. Now we return to these seven possibilities and assess the extent to which they have occurred, thereby yielding continued protection for vulnerable individuals. The possibilities are (1) programs serving these populations remained intact, but programs serving other populations were cut or changed at the federal level; (2) programs serving these populations underwent significant restructuring at the federal level to more effectively serve the populations with less revenue; (3) action at the state or local level cushioned federal changes by increasing administrative efficiency; (4) local action protected these populations by shifting as many people as possible to federal programs less affected by cuts and changes; (5) the non-profit sector filled the gap at the local level; (6) local action protected these populations by making them high priority and shifting scarce resources to cover their needs; and (7) state and local governments raised revenues to compensate for federal cuts.

The first two possibilities are ways that the federal government might have fulfilled its commitment to protect the truly needy, thereby retaining some federal (central) role in providing the social safety net. The remaining five possibilities are ways that local jurisdictions might have acted to compensate for federal changes and maintain the social safety net. The discussion that follows assesses the extent to which each possibility became a reality. Taken as a whole, this assessment will reveal whether the shift to greater local control has benefited the needy people in the three populations studied.

Programs Affecting These Populations Did Change at the Federal Level

We have seen that, for each of our three populations, significant programs affecting their well-being *were* changed at the federal level. While maintaining written commitments to program goals, the Reagan administration cut funding for many programs and sought to repeal statutory authority for still others. With respect to abused, neglected, and dependent children, the administration sought unsuccessfully to repeal the Child Welfare and Adoption Assistance Act of 1980, and has consistently underfunded its provisions for preventive, supportive, reunification, and permanency planning services. With respect to the chronically mentally ill, the administration was successful in its efforts to repeal the Mental Health Systems Act of 1980, to cut funding for its services by approximately 25 percent, and to transform its structure into a block grant. It also significantly changed the eligibility criteria for Supplemental Security Income (SSI), which greatly affected the fortunes of many chronically mentally ill.

The administration has done least to directly affect the low-income elderly, although reductions in the availability of in-home services (funded through the social services block grant), increases in Medicare copayments, restrictions in Medicaid, and reduced availability of housing, transportation, nutrition, and others subsidies have all affected the well-being of this population.

Programs Were Not Significantly Restructured at the Federal Level

Programs serving the three populations we studied were far from perfect when President Reagan took office. Dissatisfaction with the quality and types of care available to abused, neglected, and dependent children and to the chronically mentally ill led Congress in 1980 to pass the Child Welfare and Adoption Assistance Act and the Mental Health Systems Act. Both legislative mandates were the result of extensive study of existing support programs and their deficiencies. Both were designed to remedy some of the more dysfunctional aspects of service delivery for the respective populations and promote their welfare. President Reagan's policies could have built on these reforms, or could have proposed even more extensive changes in system structures to more effectively and efficiently assist these needy populations.

Incentive structures arising from federal policies in existence before 1980 often promoted more expensive and less appropriate care for all three selected populations. Much more money was available to provide foster care for children in need than for preventive efforts to keep natural families together; similarly, greater funds were at hand to provide hospital-based care for the chronically mentally ill rather than supportive community-based services and to make possible nursing home placement for frail elderly people rather than in-home supportive services. The easiest and least expensive type of care from the county's viewpoint was usually the most expensive type of care overall and the most costly for the federal government—thus the needy were removed from their homes and placed in institutions. These actions often proved disadvantageous in human terms as well because they disrupted the lives of the needy and their connections with people, places, and communities. States had been using an even less expensive strategy for the chronically mentally ill—releasing them from state mental hospitals and providing no alternative care.

Clearly the incentive structures underlying service decisions for all three populations needed a thorough rethinking. Underlying the legislation and provisions of the Child Welfare and Adoption Assistance Act of 1980 was the intent to alter the incentive structure for child welfare services—to discourage foster care and promote prevention and permanency planning. The Mental Health Systems Act contained provisions directing approximately 20 percent of its federal assistance toward services for the chronically mentally ill in the community. Medicaid and Medicare expenses were rising astronomically but ironically the programs would not pay for less expensive and more humane community-based care. Also, many programs for the elderly served all persons above a certain age, regardless of financial need, when some greater focus on poor or frail elderly persons might have been a more judicious use of public resources.

When President Reagan took office, his administration had ample opportunity to tackle malfunctioning incentive structures and make them both more rational and more humane. Other aspects of program structure might also have been addressed and redesigned. The evidence of this study indicates that little program restructuring took place. Rather, the administration simply provided less money for essentially unchanged programs, whether those programs remained under federal control or shifted to a block-grant format. Thus the opportunities for continued protection of needy populations through continued federal (central) control were not taken.

Some Local Agency Management Did Become More Efficient

Turning now to the possible ways that local action might have protected the well-being of needy people, we look first at efficiency—whether agencies simply became better, more streamlined, more efficient at providing appropriate services. The Reagan administration placed great faith in the ability of state and local operations to achieve efficiency gains and justified funding cuts with the reasoning that bureaucratic inefficiencies were absorbing large proportions of federal funding. Eliminating the federal role, so the argument went, would result in efficiency gains to offset budget reductions.

In two instances, confirmed by the providers themselves, greater efficiency did indeed occur. San Diego's child welfare services reorganized to place more emphasis on preventing placement in substitute care, and Richmond's mental health services reorganized into a clinic structure that serves more people better, according to all the people we interviewed. In addition, agencies serving the elderly in both San Diego and Boston improved interagency coordination by processing applications so that eligible persons could be better matched with different programs; other gains were seen in purchasing services through the agency that could deliver them most efficiently.

However, in none of these examples did changed operating structures fully compensate for dollar losses. In addition, these cases are exceptions to the more basic finding, that seriously reduced funding occurred at a time when the demand for services rose, when agencies began to see more people and families with multiple problems, and when all types of resources for helping vulnerable people were shrinking. Agencies responded by cutting caseloads as much as they dared, although most did not cut in proportion to their reduced funding levels. Alternatively, agencies tried to serve more persons with limited resources, and each recipient got less from the agency. "Less" might mean less time spent on an investigation of child abuse, less time spent assisting families to resolve their difficulties so that children would not have to be removed from their homes, less time in a day program for mentally ill clients, less attention to the eligibility difficulties of the mentally ill when applying for assistance from entitlement programs, fewer social services for older people, or less help given to adults in life-threatening situations if their plight was not readily resolvable.

Many Local Agencies Did Shift the Financial Burden to Other Federal Programs

To increase their available resources as much as possible, most jurisdictions actively pursued the option of shifting people they served to federal entitlement programs whenever their characteristics matched relevant eligibility criteria. Of course, these actions thwarted rather than furthered the federal effort to increase local and state financing for social welfare programs. States and localities varied in the degree to which they switched recipients entitled to in-home services from Title XX to Medicaid (Title XIX) funding. Of the states we examined, Michigan pursued this course with greatest zeal, resulting in an increase of almost 50 percent in people served. States with Medicaid waivers for community-based services to prevent nursing home placement were more able to make this shift than others.

A number of states, including California and Michigan, shifted federal low-income energy assistance funds into social services, as permitted in the block-grant legislation. States and localities replaced Title XX day-care funding with income disregards authorized under AFDC (Title IV(A)). Finally, at least one state (California) interpreted new federal funding available for emergency services for children as applying to crises involving child abuse and neglect. They charged their regular crisis intervention services heavily to this program until federal officials rejected the state's interpretation and refused to pay.

Despite all these efforts to shift the financial burden back to the federal government, states and localities shouldered most of the burden of replacing lost federal dollars. The budget and caseload figures given throughout this book include increases from other federal funding sources (if the jurisdictions examined were able to find such resources), yet the fact remains that agencies faced greater need with fewer resources.

The Nonprofit Sector Filled Some, but Not All, of the Gap

Many services for the three populations are delivered by nonprofit agencies. Payment structures are such that local government supplies the funds and nonprofit agencies deliver the services under contract to county or city agencies. In the four jurisdictions under investigation in this study, the nonprofit agencies hit by cuts in government contracts tried to compensate largely by increasing fees—shifting to a population that could pay for services. In only one instance did private philanthropy clearly step in to compensate for some (but not all) lost government revenue—that was the case of the Richmond local United Way shifting support into more in-home services for the low-income elderly.

Nationally, nonprofit agencies as a group behaved much as those in the four jurisdictions. Another Urban Institute study reports that nonprofit agencies that did manage to offset losses of government funding did so by increasing commercial sources of income (fees and product sales). Nonprofit agencies serving the neediest were least able to do this, ending up with the largest overall revenue losses. The net result appears to be a shift away from nonprofit agencies' service to the neediest people.[1]

Local Government Responses: Priorities Shifted and Revenues Increased, but Not Enough

We have just seen that five of the seven possible ways to protect the truly needy while cutting federal programs have not been consistently put into effect, nor have they been able to fill the gap left by decreased federal support. The remaining options are the most important in the context of policy debate on the relative merits of local versus central control of social welfare policy. Did state and local governments compensate for cuts and changes made at the federal level, either by shifting priorities among service recipients or by raising revenues to replace lost federal funds, so that services for these three needy populations were maintained?

To summarize our findings on this issue, we compiled the budget changes from fiscal years 1981 to 1983, adjusted for inflation, for agencies serving

---

1. Lester M. Salamon, "Nonprofits: The Results are Coming In," *Foundation News* (July-August 1984), pp. 16–23.

Conclusions

the three selected populations in our four local jurisdictions. These figures appear in table 31, along with caseload changes during the same period. Looking first at the "Total" column in the table, we see that two jurisdictions, San Diego and Richmond, show consistent and rather sizable re-

TABLE 31

SUMMARY OF BUDGET CHANGES AFTER INFLATION AND THE CASELOAD CHANGES FOR VULNERABLE CHILDREN, THE CHRONICALLY MENTALLY ILL, AND THE LOW-INCOME ELDERLY IN THE FOUR SELECTED CITIES, FISCAL YEARS 1981–83
(Percent Change)

City and Type of Service	Budget Change					Caseload Change
	Federal	State	Local	Fees and so on	Total	
San Diego						
Adult social services	− 6	10	− 44	*	− 24	− 13
Area Agency on Aging	− 11	174	− 48	38	1	21
Child intake services	− 12	*	− 21	430	− 16	29
Placement and supervision	8	*	− 30	− 34	− 17	− 5
Mental health	*	− 26	45	6	− 13	6
Detroit						
Adult social services	− 36	43	*	*	8	8
Area Agency on Aging	− 4	34	− 69	*	− 1	− 3
Children's services	n.a.	n.a.	n.a.	n.a.	n.a.	60
Mental health	− 29	10	9	− 17	4	32
Richmond						
Adult social services	− 32	− 38	− 38	*	− 34	− 15
Area Agency on Aging	n.a.	n.a.	n.a.	*	− 14	10
Foster care	− 11	*	− 18	*	− 14	− 2
Protective services	− 64	*	− 70	*	− 65	167
Mental health	*	11	− 19	− 60	− 17	18
Boston						
Adult social services	− 100	64	*	*	7	7
Area Agency on Aging	− 6	*	− 17	*	− 8	112
Child welfare	− 22	30	*	*	7	6
Mental health	− 7	− 24	*	*	− 23	n.a.

SOURCE: Tables 5–8, 16–21, and 28–31.

n.a. Not available.

* No money from this source.

ductions in funding for all services. Service funding in Detroit held steady or increased slightly, and Boston shows a mixed pattern of increases and decreases. Data in the "Federal" column indicate that federal funding for all services in all cities decreased. The next three columns show the source of replacement resources. The most obvious pattern in these columns is that state governments provided the lion's share of replacement funding while the local governments were more likely to cut their own investment in these services than to increase it.

Before commenting in detail on the budget picture revealed in the table, it is necessary to complete the analysis by examining caseload changes. It is possible, after all, that funding reductions followed from reduced need and that they do not reflect a reduced commitment to serve needy populations at all. As can be seen from the last column in table 31, in only one instance did caseload size shrink in proportion to funding cuts (Detroit's Area Agency on Aging). In three cases (adult social services of Detroit and Boston and Boston's child welfare services), caseload increased in proportion to funding increases. In all remaining cases (thirteen of the seventeen services examined in the four cities for which data are available), agencies emerged from budget changes with increased ratios of people served per dollar available. Sometimes these ratios are extremely skewed, such as San Diego's child intake service, which suffered a total budget reduction of 16 percent but faced an increased recipient load of 29 percent, or Detroit's mental health services, which served 32 percent more people with a budget increase of only 4 percent.

Based on the caseload data summarized in table 31, it is reasonable to conclude that budget reductions occurred despite continued or increased need for services, not because demand slackened. The anecdotal data presented in chapters 3, 6, and 9 on waiting lists and unserved needy persons in each of the four jurisdictions further reinforce the conclusion that the need for service still exists or has increased. In addition, where agencies have conducted follow-up studies to assess continued need among those for whom services were reduced or eliminated, they have found that the need has remained at the same level or has increased. Richmond's Adult Services unit interviewed almost 300 of its "least needy" cases, for whom in-home supportive services had been terminated due to reduced program funding. Most were found to still need services, and many had been forced to enter more expensive levels of residential care because they no longer received in-home services. New York State's follow-up study of individuals removed from the SSDI/SSI roles revealed that virtually all such people, declared by the Social Security Administration to be employable, remained unemployed and without income, and that many had applied for state and local welfare.

Resources and Commitment

If we view state or local action to replace lost federal revenues as a result of two factors, resources and a sense of values or commitment, we have a final basis for assessing the results of the current movement to local responsibility. Michigan, the state in our sample with the worst economic circumstances and the least favorable revenue situation during the period under consideration, did the most to protect all three of the vulnerable populations of interest in this study. Michigan has a long history of liberal social welfare spending, and the state's values and commitments clearly directed its attempt to find the resources, even under constrained economic conditions.

California and Massachusetts, both states with legislation inspired by taxpayer dissatisfaction, behaved very differently. Both protected the elderly; Massachusetts compensated for lost child welfare funding; and both reduced spending for mental health even further than federal cuts. The state of California and San Diego County together did not fully compensate for federal losses for any of the three needy populations. In this matter, San Diego County was the chief source of revenue loss. This jurisdiction, pursuing the same philosophy that the Reagan administration espouses with respect to individual responsibility, not only did not replace federal funds but cut its support for social welfare services even further. In both these states, and in San Diego as a local jurisdiction, values and commitments overshadowed ability to pay. Neither state, nor San Diego, suffered badly from the recession or unemployment; both states are traditionally liberal supporters of social welfare programs. Massachusetts protected two out of three of the populations we studied. This was possible because Massachusetts administers its social welfare programs from the state level, so state action was all that was required. In California local jurisdictions have a considerable amount of control over their social welfare programs. San Diego County, on the strength of its own values, acted to cut social programs even though it had the resource base to do otherwise.

In Richmond cuts came from both the state and local levels, reflecting philosophy more than resource base. Virginia did nothing to compensate for federal cuts in most of the services we investigated. As a consequence, Richmond sustained all the federal cuts, and the city added proportional reductions of its own.

Central versus Local Control for the Three Needy Populations

Our final assessment of whether the social safety net was intact during the 1980s, made in the context of the central versus local debate, is that the three vulnerable populations in this research representing the truly needy have *not* been uniformly protected by state and local decision making in response to federal program reductions. We have presented evidence from four jurisdictions showing that these populations received less service, from agencies under more stress and struggling to meet increased need, than they did before federal changes went into effect. States and localities have responded more on the basis of values and philosophy than on the basis of resources—when they thought the services were important, they found the resources; but when they did not place a high priority on the public's responsibility to protect and support fellow citizens in need, they withdrew resources from those functions even when the resources could have been made available. We conclude on the basis of this evidence that federal involvement is still critical to assure equitable treatment of these vulnerable people who cannot protect themselves. Federal withdrawal from that involvement has resulted in poorer services to fewer people and made the availability of those services contingent on the values and priorities of a jurisdiction.

The Reagan administration for the most part has not restructured federal programs in ways that increase achievement of program goals in comparison to pre-Reagan achievement. Rather, these programs have simply received less money to do the same job in the same way. The administration repealed key provisions of the Mental Health Systems Act. It has repeatedly sought repeal of the incentive restructuring aspects of the Child Welfare and Adoption Assistance Act, and has underfunded components of the act in ways that hinder the restructuring it was designed to accomplish. Among the programs we examined for our three populations, only community-based care for the frail elderly has seen significant innovation at the federal level. The Omnibus Budget Reconciliation Act of 1981 established opportunities within Medicaid for states to use this funding to provide community-based care in order to delay or prevent nursing home placement. One of the selected jurisdictions used this mechanism to protect some persons whose ability to remain in their own home would otherwise have been jeopardized by cuts in the social services block grant.

The administration's basic position on redressing the federal-local balance in favor of state and local emphasis has been its only "restructuring" effort. It has not conducted detailed program reviews for federal programs serving the three populations that resulted in substantial rethinking of program structures or incentive systems. To the extent that the administration has failed to take advantage of its opportunity to restructure, it has failed to make programs more responsive to the needs of the people they are designed to serve. Coupled with reduced resources for program services, this lack of program responsiveness and restructuring has translated into a lower likelihood of assistance to needy people at the local level, and a higher likelihood that people with similar needs will receive different levels of assistance, depending on where they live. We conclude that the needy people in the three populations we studied have suffered as a result of federal changes and local response.

The
California Column
in New Mexico

Darlis A. Miller

Published in cooperation
with the Historical Society
of New Mexico

University of New Mexico Press
Albuquerque

Library of Congress Cataloging in Publication Data

Miller, Darlis A., 1939–
   The California Column in New Mexico.

   Originally presented as the author's thesis (Ph. D.—
University of New Mexico)
   Bibliography: p.
   Includes index.
   1. New Mexico—History—1848–   —Biography.
2. New Mexico—Biography. 3. United States. Army.
California Column—Biography. 4. Soldiers—New Mexico—
Biography. 5. United States. Army. California Column—
History. I. Historical Society of New Mexico. II. Title.
F801.M47 1982   978.9′04   82–10943
ISBN 0–8263–0637–3
ISBN 0–8263–0638–1 (pbk.)

A version of chapter four appeared as "Carleton's California Column:
A Chapter in New Mexico's Mining History," *New Mexico
Historical Review* 53 (January 1978):5–38.

To Ira G. Clark
Scholar, Teacher, Friend

Contents

Illustrations

Foreword

The Historical Society of New Mexico has sponsored two publications on the California Column—one done in 1908 by George H. Pettis, a soldier in the Column, and this volume by Darlis A. Miller, a historian of the military in the Southwest. The Pettis work was part of a series of titles the Society issued in the early years of this century; Miller's book is the third volume in a joint-publication program between the Society and the University of New Mexico Press.

The books in this series are works on New Mexico, in particular on areas and topics not dealt with previously or ones needing updating. This volume on the California Column is in the category of revising and expanding the limited literature on a topic. This account of the California Column takes up where all the other works have ended—with a history of the impressive contributions some 340 of the ex-Volunteers made to New Mexico's development in the several decades following their discharge in 1865. The decisive impact these men had on the social, political, and economic development of southern New Mexico is recounted here for the first time.

That some of the ex-soldiers became active and prominent in business and politics is only part of their collective history. Many of the ex-Volunteers were men whose lives are little remembered today, yet the re-creation of how they went about starting up in New Mexico is a fascinating glimpse of life a century ago. Whether

on farms or ranches, in mining camps, or in towns, the ex-
Volunteers were hardy, determined settlers who faced and endured
numerous challenges in the Territory. Darlis A. Miller has told
their story with sympathy and deep understanding of the time and
place in which they lived.

The publication program of the Historical Society enables it
and the University of New Mexico Press to achieve important
goals: for the Society, to increase the research and writing of New
Mexico history; for the Press, to contribute to the development
and enjoyment of our regional culture.

The 1982 officers and directors are: *Officers:* Albert H. Schroeder, President; John P. Conron, Vice President; Austin Hoover,
2nd Vice President; Mrs. Hedy M. Dunn, Secretary; and Charles
Bennett, Treasurer. *Directors:* Thomas E. Chavez, Timothy Corn-
ish, Hobart Durham, Octavia Fellin, Dr. Myra Ellen Jenkins,
Loraine Lavender, William Lock, Luther L. Lyon, Morgan Nelson, Mrs. George G. Otero, Mrs. Gordon Robertson, Joe W.
Stein, Dr. Spencer Wilson, and Stephen Zimmer.

John P. Conron, Chairman
Publications Committee
Historical Society of New Mexico

Preface

At the start of the Civil War, California volunteers—known as the California Column—marched overland across the Southwest desert to help expel Confederates from New Mexico. Before this force of some 2,350 men reached the Rio Grande in 1862, the Confederates had been driven from the territory. Consequently the California soldiers spent most of their enlistments guarding against a possible Confederate reinvasion of the Southwest and fighting hostile Indians.

A number of writers have recorded the military services performed by the Column, but none have described the importance of California veterans to the territory's development in post-bellum decades. In fact, the vast majority of the more than three hundred forty California soldiers who settled in New Mexico after the war heretofore have remained unidentified. The reason for this neglect is not difficult to discover. Most California soldiers were common, hard-working Americans, who were more interested in improving their personal fortunes than in recording their deeds for posterity. For the most part, their collective history must be gleaned from military service records, territorial newspapers, county courthouse records, census and tax returns, and an assortment of related materials scattered in a variety of repositories.

My purpose is to tell the story of the men from California, who, motivated by patriotism or adventure, traveled to New Mexico during the war and remained to seek their fortunes in the territo-

ry. California veterans represented the first significant influx of
Anglo settlers into New Mexico after the Mexican War, and in
the post-Civil War era ex-California soldiers played important roles
in the economic development of New Mexico. They were responsible for opening five leading mineral districts, including Elizabethtown, Silver City, Hillsboro, Magdalena, and White Oaks, and
they compiled impressive records in farming and pastoral enterprises, opening new lands to cultivation, experimenting with new
crops and farming machinery, and improving local breeds of cattle and sheep. In addition, California veterans operated a wide
assortment of business establishments, offering their services in
exchange for profit and social standing. They were among the
territory's most enthusiastic boomers, expending money and energy
to attract outside capital for the railroads that so completely altered
New Mexican society in the 1880s. Some became government
employees, providing the civilian work force necessary for federal
agencies to operate in western territories, while others signed supply contracts with those same agencies to ensure their own economic success at the expense of the federal government.

California veterans became avid politicians and entered territorial politics, especially at the grass roots level, in impressive
numbers. They were for the most part conservative politicians
intent upon developing the territory's resources, and many had
close ties with the powerful Santa Fe Ring. On the other hand,
they labored to improve social conditions within local communities; this generally meant that they worked to reconstruct in New
Mexico institutions resembling those found in the more settled
"American" states. Nonetheless, many veterans married Hispanic
women, thereby helping to bridge cultural differences between
Anglo and Hispanic residents.

There were lawbreakers and criminals among California veterans, but for the most part they were law-and-order men who labored to establish stable communities. Still, violence touched the
lives of numerous California veterans in the two decades following the war's end. Indeed, a significant number died from an assassin's bullet, a mob's vengeance, or an Indian's well-aimed arrow.

The history of California veterans in New Mexico is in reality the story of that territory's development in post-Civil War America. The collective lives of these volunteers help document the rich and varied social history of a western territory isolated from the nation's mainstream and beset by problems of law and order, expansion and growth, and accommodation within a pluralist society. They provided the labor and ingenuity that helped modernize New Mexico during an era when expansion was the key element in the nation's history. They formed a cross-section of American males who streamed into the western states and territories after the war in search of new opportunities for social and economic advancement.

The story of the California volunteers in New Mexico is in one sense nearly unique. These men were permitted to muster out of the service in the territory where they had served their enlistments, although it was the general policy of the War Department to return volunteer units to the location of their enrollment. Volunteer soldiers from mid-western states who were stationed in Colorado, Idaho, Dakota, and other western territories invariably returned east for final severance from the military. Only in Utah were conditions similar to those in New Mexico. Seven hundred California volunteers under Col. Patrick Edward Connor occupied that territory during the war years. At the end of their enlistments, many stayed in Utah to develop mining claims they had located in previous months.

Yet in numbers involved, New Mexico's experience was unique. The fact that nearly 2,000 soldiers were discharged far from their native homes, in a land ripe for exploitation and development, accounts for the large number of California veterans who took up residence in New Mexico at the war's end. They were experienced soldiers, toughened by the rigors of Indian campaigns and familiar with the territory and its resources. Had these men been transported to the Pacific Coast for final discharge, it is unlikely that many would have returned in subsequent years. Their talents and expertise would have been lost to the territory.

These soldiers arrived in New Mexico as an identifiable group and retained their distinction as "Column men" or "California boys" for the rest of their lives. During their productive careers, they united in business partnerships, held reunions, and corresponded with one another. In their twilight years, afflicted with the infirmities of old age, the Californians relied upon each other for notarized affidavits supporting claims for federal pensions. And with death, the California label followed the former soldiers into the grave, for repeatedly they were identified in obituaries as "old Column men" or "old California veterans." This continued group identity adds to the experience of the California volunteers and elevates their life-stories into a vital chapter in New Mexico's history.

A book of this nature—one that attempts to identify all former volunteers who settled in New Mexico—can never be complete. Men with common names proved impossible to label as California men. Then too a number of men enlisted in the California volunteers using aliases. Owen J. McCabe served throughout the war as John M. Adams, stating in his pension claim that he changed his name and joined the army to avoid marriage to a woman who deceived him.[1] Despite the difficulty of identifying all the men in the California Column, with extensive research the central patterns of the Californians' experiences have emerged in surprising vitality.

The terminal date for this work—1885—reflects changing conditions within the territory. During the 1880s New Mexico, like other western states and territories, experienced boom conditions and rapid growth. Expansion of the railroad network provided relatively cheap and rapid transportation for a multitude of immigrants seeking a new start. The population of New Mexico jumped from approximately 92,000 in 1870 to 160,000 in 1890.[2] As new settlers filled the land, the impact of the California men became progressively weakened. By 1885 a sizable number of the old soldiers had either died or migrated out of the territory, and the names of those who remained appeared less frequently in territorial newspapers.

Still, in the twenty years following the war's end, the California veterans mingled their destinies with that of their adopted land and contributed enormously to its growth. The public announcement in 1910 of the death of one old Column man, Lawrence Lapoint, reflects the admiration and praise accorded these men by a later generation.

Lawrence Lapoint, a member of the famous California Column which marched across the Great American desert during the civil war, editor of one of the pioneer papers of the southwest and a leading citizen of New Mexico, died Sunday morning at 1 o'clock, after a brief illness. The biography of Lawrence Lapoint is the history of southern New Mexico since the civil war.[3]

Acknowledgments

I would like to thank Ira G. Clark of New Mexico State University who provided the original impetus for this study and whose enthusiasm for western American history inspired my own commitment to the field. I am also deeply grateful to Richard N. Ellis of the University of New Mexico for professional encouragement and for directing this study in its original form as a doctoral dissertation. Special thanks are due to Myra Ellen Jenkins, formerly of the State Records Center and Archives, Santa Fe, New Mexico, for courtesies extended over several years and to Sara D. Jackson, National Historical Publications Commission, who helped a neophyte feel at home in the National Archives.

I wish also to thank personnel of Colfax, Doña Ana, Grant, Lincoln, Otero, and Socorro county courthouses for their kindly assistance and also staff members at the University of New Mexico Library, New Mexico State University Library, Library of Congress, National Archives, Denver Federal Records Center, Bancroft Library, and Henry E. Huntington Library for beneficial aid. I am deeply indebted to Ann M. Cullen who read the complete manuscript, offering invaluable editorial suggestions. I extend special thanks to August Miller for unending support.

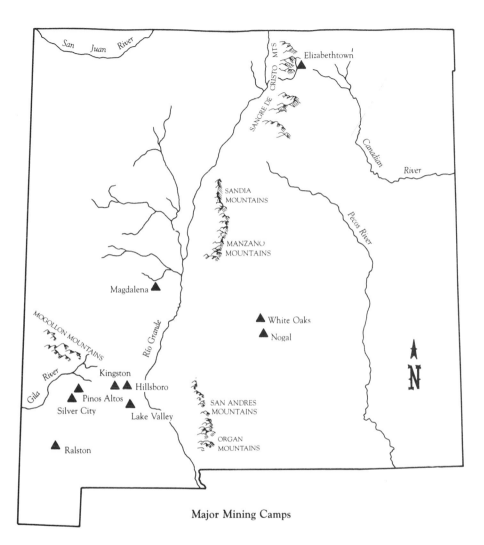

San Juan River

Elizabethtown

SANGRE DE CRISTO MTS

Canadian River

SANDIA MOUNTAINS

Pecos River

MANZANO MOUNTAINS

Magdalena

White Oaks

Nogal

MOGOLLON MOUNTAINS

Río Grande

Gila River

Kingston

Hillsboro

Pinos Altos

Silver City

Lake Valley

SAN ANDRES MOUNTAINS

Ralston

ORGAN MOUNTAINS

N

Major Mining Camps

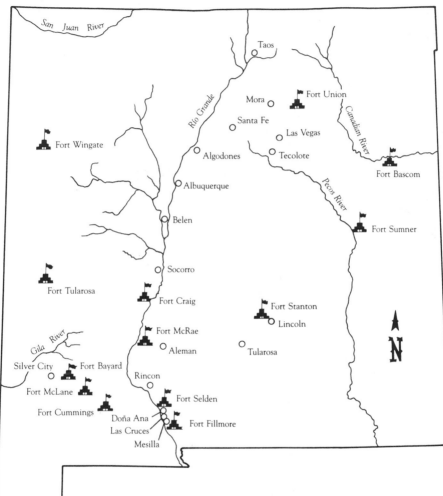

New Mexico Forts and Settlements

The
California Column
in
New Mexico

1

The Call to Arms

On April 15, 1861—after receiving news of Fort Sumter's surrender—President Lincoln called upon loyal Americans to defend their nation's honor and to crush the southern rebellion. That summer, Secretary of War Simon Cameron called for volunteer troops from California, and the young men from that state eagerly responded. The new recruits—eventually numbering over 17,000—wanted to be sent east to help defeat the Confederate forces, but the majority remained in California or served in adjacent western territories. Their destinies, nonetheless, were affected by Confederate strategy, and over two thousand Californians marched to Arizona and New Mexico to prevent those lands from falling into Confederate hands.[1]

In the early stages of the Civil War, it was clear to leaders of the Confederate States of America that New Mexico would have to be seized by force to ensure economic outlets on the West Coast. This territory was viewed as the key to Pacific expansion. The Confederate invasion of the Southwest was launched July 23, 1861 when Lt. Col. John R. Baylor led some three hundred volunteers across the Texas border into New Mexico. Within days they had forced Union troops stationed at Fort Fillmore on the Rio Grande to surrender, and on August 1 Baylor by proclamation established the Confederate territory of Arizona comprising all New Mexico territory south of the thirty-fourth parallel.[2]

Most Anglo-Americans in the area greeted Baylor's arrival with

3

enthusiasm. Residents of Mesilla and Tucson, the two major population centers in southern New Mexico, were bitterly dissatisfied with the federal government's indifference to local problems. Consequently, after the southern states seceded, these disgruntled westerners chose to end their allegiance to the Union. During the month of March, townspeople in both Mesilla and Tucson had voted to join the Southern cause.[3]

The Confederacy commissioned Brig. Gen. Henry Hopkins Sibley to complete the subjugation of New Mexico. In mid-December 1861 he established his command at Fort Bliss, Texas, and during the first week of the new year he advanced up the Rio Grande with approximately twenty-five hundred men. In addition, Sibley ordered Capt. Sherod Hunter, with a company of cavalry, to occupy Tucson, three hundred miles west of the Rio Grande.[4]

A DESERT EXPEDITION

Union officials quickly moved to counter the Confederate invasion. By December 1861 Gen. George C. Wright, commander of the Department of the Pacific, was aware that Confederate troops had occupied southern New Mexico and that California might be subject to invasion by way of Tucson and Fort Yuma. To guard against this possibility, Wright ordered Col. James H. Carleton to organize an expedition to march east across the desert to expel the rebels. This force—the California Column—was made up by five companies of the First California Cavalry under Col. Edward E. Eyre, ten companies of the First California Infantry under Lt. Col. Joseph R. West, five companies of the Fifth California Infantry commanded by Col. George W. Bowie, Company B, Second California Cavalry commanded by Capt. John C. Cremony, and Company A, Third U.S. Artillery under Lt. John B. Shinn. A total of some 2,350 men marched to New Mexico as members of the Column; but by the time they reached the Rio Grande, Union soldiers under Lt. Col. Edward R. S. Canby, Commander of the Department of New Mexico, had successfully repulsed the Confederate invasion. For the remainder of the war, California volunteers spent their time on garrison and escort duty, fighting Indians, and guarding against a Confederate reinvasion.[5]

THE CALIFORNIA COLUMN

The men who marched east from California under Carleton's command had a variety of backgrounds. They ranged in age from eighteen to forty-five and practiced diverse occupations prior to enlistment. While the men most frequently listed their occupations as farmer or miner, other enlistees classified themselves as laborers, mechanics, carpenters, cooks, teamsters, saddlers, merchants, and printers.[6] And several who settled in landlocked New Mexico after the war had earlier careers sailing the seas. John Ayers and David N. Catanach, both of whom became well-known public figures, each went to sea at age thirteen, the former spending nine and the latter three years before the mast.[7] Samuel Creevey, who later settled in Socorro County, was wounded in a fight with Chinese pirates in 1851; a decade later his ship docked at San Francisco in time for him to enlist in Company G, First California Infantry.[8]

California volunteers came from virtually every state in the Union and every European nation. Distant Maine contributed at least nine future New Mexico residents, while New York, Ohio, and Pennsylvania together accounted for over seventy-five. The New Yorkers were a resourceful and versatile group and included Carleton's Assistant Adjutant General Benjamin C. Cutler, Indian agent John Ayers of Santa Fe, hotel owner Chauncy N. Story of Elizabethtown, surveyor William McMullen of Santa Fe, Mesilla saloon keeper Bernard McCall, rancher John D. Slocum of Doña Ana County, the "King of the Jornada" John Martin, lawyer Albert J. Fountain of Mesilla, and businessman-politician Joseph F. Bennett of Silver City.[9]

Natives of both the border and southern states enrolled in the Union army, and among California veterans who settled in New Mexico were eight Kentuckians, five Virginians, and a smattering of men from Maryland, North and South Carolina, Mississippi, Alabama, Louisiana, and Tennessee. England, Ireland, and Germany accounted for over twenty-five veterans who remained in New Mexico, while Holland contributed Grant County pioneer Linklain Butin, and Poland contributed Lyon Phillipouski of Lincoln County. Westy Peterson of Norway marched to New Mexico as a private and stayed to prospect in Kingston and Hillsboro, and Samuel Zimmerly of Switzerland arrived a corporal and subsequently became owner of a flour and grist mill in the town of Socorro. One or two future New Mexicans recorded on their enlistment papers that they had been "born at sea."[10]

LIVES IN MOTION

A prominent characteristic shared by California volunteers was physical mobility. For some men, migration to the California gold fields was the second or third major relocation of their young lives. Their subsequent removal to New Mexico merely continued this pattern of mobility. Richard D. Russell, born in Canada, ran away from his Illinois home at the age of sixteen and joined an immigrant train headed for California. When mining proved unprofitable, he worked on a cattle ranch and then homesteaded lands adjacent to the Sacramento River.[11]

Several future New Mexicans—like Russell—had turned from mining in California to more lucrative pursuits. Barney W. Connelly became a manufacturer and merchant in Nevada City, California, while John D. Barncastle labored two years as a clerk at a Grass Valley store and one year in a similar job in Marysville. William L. Rynerson, one of the leading southern New Mexico politicians in the 1870s and 1880s, migrated to California in 1852 and spent one year prospecting throughout the state. He subsequently studied law, became a captain in the state militia, and served as deputy clerk of Amador County.[12]

What motivated these eager young men to rush to arms 3,000 miles from their nation's capital? Certainly deeply engrained prejudices and loyalties precluded apathy on the part of Pacific Coast residents. It is difficult to ascribe motives to individuals who left so few written records, yet a sampling of extant letters portrays the California soldiers as idealistic patriots. An officer in Carleton's command, in writing to a friend, stated "I am determined to stick by the dear old flag, and contribute what little I can to the honor and welfare of our beloved country. In doing this I sacrifice much of my happiness."[13]

A young private summarized the patriotism of his comrades when he asserted that they were "willing to lay down their lives to uphold this glorious Government and Union. Only give us a chance, and California will find her soldiers true as steel."[14] Similar sentiments were expressed by Joseph F. Bennett, who urged his brother to seek a commission in the army and help crush "this infernal Rebellion." Bennett's own "faith in the power of the government to strike down the infamous hand of rebellion" was strong.[15]

Few California soldiers revealed any real interest in emancipation or the welfare of black people during the war. Among the minority moved by idealism for the slave was John Ayers, who was known as the "Little Abolitionist" of his regiment. His captain, on the other hand, threatened to resign his commission if his actions helped free a single "nigger."[16]

Like volunteers throughout the North, Californians enlisted for mixed reasons—patriotism, excitement, lure of new places, example of friends, soldier's pay, and bounties.[17] Tested by the harsh realities of camp life, however, scores wavered in their commitment to the Union cause and either deserted or were court martialed for angry remarks voiced against the federal government. Andrew J. Callahan of Ohio deserted fifteen months after enlisting at San Francisco for not being "treated well by our Major [Edwin A.] Rigg." He subsequently enlisted in the First Texas Cavalry at New Orleans under the name John Callahan.[18] Former New Orleans resident Thomas Martin was charged with expressing disloyal sentiments. Specifically, he was quoted as saying that "he wished to God he was where the Secession flag floated" and was accused of calling the men of his regiment "damned black Abolition Sons of bitches." Martin escaped custody before his court martial was completed and no verdict was issued.[19]

SEASONING THE RAW RECRUITS

The vast majority of California volunteers had no previous military experience, a fact bemoaned by Colonel Carleton who worked feverishly to mold his men into seasoned troopers before leaving the California coast. He ordered all boot camp commanders to drill the men eight hours a day when necessary and ordered officers to recite tactics every evening and to read the Articles of War to their men every Sunday after inspection. He would leave nothing undone to "insure efficiency and discipline and the most perfect subordination" among enlistees.[20]

But Carleton could not work miracles, and the inexperience of the new recruits is graphically described in the wartime reminiscences of Edward E. Ayer. At age eighteen young Ayer left his job as night clerk in his father's hotel in Harvard, Illinois, and traveled overland by wagon train to California, stopping enroute to work in the Nevada mines. Once in California, he worked sawing wood and then at a planing mill until war broke out. A handful of the boys employed at the mill immediately joined a cavalry unit, and Ayer was made corporal, though he readily admitted that he knew nothing of drilling or military affairs. He observed that "our experience [in camp] undoubtedly was about the same as all new camps, almost everybody being as ignorant as could be of the duties and everything military."[21]

One Sunday morning Ayer's commanding officer ordered the first full-scale mounted inspection. The enlistees proved eager but sadly inept. Encumbered by revolver, saber, Sharp's carbine, saddlebags, overcoat, and bedroll, a soldier needed training to mount on command in a formation of three hundred men. At this particular inspection, only seventy-five or eighty of the 300 men succeeded in mounting their horses on command. At least one hundred horses began to buck violently and ran into each other. Ayer comments that "the whole thing was one of the most awful and comical mixups imaginable. When the thing cleared up there were at least one hundred of these horses running on the prairie. . . . It was an hour before we could get them together."[22]

Most units, nonetheless, had men in their ranks with some prior military experience who could give direction to training and help acculturate newcomers to military life. Several California volunteers were also veterans of the Mexican War, including Oscar M. Brown, John Martin, John S. Powers, Linklain Butin, and Jason Covey.[23]

Whether seasoned veteran or raw recruit, all suffered during the winter of 1861–62 when unusually heavy rains flooded California and delayed the Column's departure for New Mexico. Wagons mired in mud-clogged roads had to be unloaded and then hauled forward with ropes. At least one California veteran later based his pension claim on the fact that he had ruptured himself trying to pull wagons out of the mud. And Corporal Ayer recalled that wagons in his command traveled only two and a half miles a day because of poor road conditions.[24]

MARCH TO THE RIO GRANDE

In late February and early March 1862, however, several detachments of the 2,000 man column started the long, grueling, 800 mile march to the Rio Grande. At his headquarters in Los Angeles, Colonel Carleton untangled problems and issued a fascinating assortment of directives to keep his column moving. Troopers were ordered to practice saber exercises one hour a day while they marched and to gather, cook, and eat nettles and mustard to "freshen" their blood.[25]

The march from Fort Yuma to Tucson was particularly fatiguing. Corporal Ayer recalled it as a hot, dirty, and dusty trip. An army correspondent described the region through which the Column passed as barren and worthless.[26] Carleton later wrote to department headquarters at San Francisco that "the intolerable heat and the alkali dust of the Gila desert makes the transportation of supplies from Fort Yuma to Tucson a matter of great difficulty. The teamsters suffer greatly with inflamed eyes and with coughs."[27] At least one private later claimed that marching over the sands in Arizona had caused his eyes to become diseased and that he had become almost totally blind after his discharge.[28]

The march east, nonetheless, kindled enthusiasm among the former California miners, and one soldier-correspondent wrote that the entire route to Tucson had been prospected by the volunteers. He and his comrades spent two to three feverish hours prospecting with tin pans and buckets while encamped at Cañada del Oro, twenty-eight miles north from Tucson. Everyone found traces of gold and concluded that rich diggings could be located. This correspondent expressed the widely held belief that the "marching of this expedition, composed for the most part of old Californians and experienced miners, over this country, will eventually be the means of developing it."[29]

Confederates under Sherod Hunter had occupied Tucson in late February, but they evacuated the town to rejoin Sibley on the Rio Grande just sixteen days before the arrival of an advanced detachment of the California Column on May 20, 1862. When Carleton received this information, he announced to California headquarters that Tucson had been taken without firing a shot and that all the secessionists were in flight.[30] The Colonel himself arrived in Tucson early in June and was compelled to remain there with the major portion of his troops until supply wagons could be repaired and summer rains refilled water holes in the desert.

Finally, on July 17 Carleton issued orders to move the main body of his command to the Rio Grande. The Californians undoubtedly were eager to reach their destination, but at least eleven men died on the overland trip from California to New Mexico. And their deaths undoubtedly sobered the high spirits of their marching comrades. Privates James F. Keith, Peter Maloney, and Albert Schmidt were killed by Apache Indians while watering their horses at Apache Pass. A sorrowful funeral was held over their mutilated bodies, and their graves and those of others killed at the pass were pointed out to soldiers who later moved through that dreaded region.[31]

Newly commissioned Brig. Gen. Carleton arrived at the Rio

Grande on August 7, and three days later he established his command at Las Cruces. He was disappointed that the Column had arrived too late to engage the enemy in combat, but he paid highest tribute to the men who formed his command. He extolled their discipline, perseverance, and cheerful endurance of hardship. With zeal and alacrity they had overcome seemingly insurmountable obstacles, and Carleton told his superiors in California that he would have failed with troops other than those from California.[32]

CHAMPAGNE IN MESILLA

Civilians in southern New Mexico enthusiastically welcomed the arrival of the California soldiers. The retreating Confederates had ravaged the countryside, driving off cattle and horses, robbing hens' roosts, and confiscating supplies. Some local residents of Mesilla had cached personal property and various supplies in their yards to keep them from being taken by the Texans. When the Union army arrived, the Mesillans greeted the soldiers with champagne, unearthed their wares, and reopened their stores.[33]

New Mexicans initially were delighted by the behavior of the California troops and invited the young men into their homes. Joseph F. Bennett, who after the war served three years as probate clerk for Doña Ana County, informed his brother in Red Wing, Minnesota, that "we had many public and private demonstrations of good feeling when we entered the Dept. Balls and dinners were all the rage."[34] One newspaper correspondent wrote that it was necessary only to be known as a member of the California Column to be assured universal respect, confidence, and affection by the local citizens.[35]

2

The War Years

———

Gen. James H. Carleton officially assumed command of the Department of New Mexico in September 1862. During the next four and one-half years, his primary objectives were to guard against possible Confederate invasions and to subdue hostile Indian tribes so that New Mexico could be opened for economic development. The responsibility for achieving these goals primarily fell to units of the California Column and New Mexico volunteers.

One of Carleton's first acts as commander was to reissue his predecessor's order establishing martial law in New Mexico. Civilians found that military jurisdiction in wartime impinged heavily upon their own lives, although interference in civilian affairs occurred most frequently in the southern part of New Mexico which had attempted to unite with the Confederacy. Moreover, any attempted Confederate reinvasion would probably be initiated in southern New Mexico, and Carleton appeared undisturbed when military actions instituted to meet that threat fell heavily upon the civilian population.[1]

In early November 1862 it was rumored that Baylor was in San Antonio raising a force of 6,000 men to reinvade the territory. Carleton's plan for resisting a Confederate offensive was fairly simple. He would strip the Mesilla Valley of all excess food so that the invading forces could not replenish their dwindling supplies. All suspected southern sympathizers were to be rounded up and sent to Fort Craig where they could help build fortifications. As the enemy advanced, houses and stores owned by secessionists in Las Cruces and Mesilla would be burned to the ground. Mexican residents were to be reminded that the Texans were ready to plunder and rob; they were to be encouraged to harass the enemy from every cover.[2]

CARLETON'S PROTECTION AGAINST SPIES

The Controversial "Grain Order"

On December 2, Col. Joseph R. West ordered the people of the Mesilla Valley to turn in surplus corn and wheat to military authorities; any person found after December 17 with over a two-months' supply of food for his family and animals would be treated as an enemy to the United States. This order was detested by civilians, and numerous valley residents abandoned their lands and migrated into Mexico to avoid compliance. It was later charged in the Santa Fe *New Mexican* that Carleton ordered this grain to be seized at three dollars a *fanega*, but that at a later date it was sold to citizens at fourteen dollars a *fanega*.[3]

Passports Required

The Confederates failed to launch a second invasion of the territory, although southern spies were active in the Franklin-El Paso area throughout most of the war, and rumors of a Confederate invasion periodically swept the countryside. To counteract southern espionage, Carleton devised a passport system to identify loyal citizens. All persons not native to Arizona or New Mexico were required to carry military passes whenever they traveled through the territory. Travelers who failed to present their passes to the provost marshal upon entering towns were subject to arrest and imprisonment.[4]

Holding court in Mesilla was District Court Judge Joseph G. Knapp. He argued that such orders were inapplicable to civil officers commissioned by the President of the United States. And in protest, he refused to carry a military pass. After suffering arrest and imprisonment, he became increasingly critical of Carleton's administration, calling it an oppressive military despotism. The judge failed to find support in Washington in his fight against military oppression and was removed from office in August 1864. His defense of civil liberties, nonetheless, won the admiration of many New Mexican residents, including several disgruntled California volunteers who were mustering out of the service.[5]

ENCOUNTERING HOSTILE INDIANS

As the threat of a Confederate invasion vanished, the most pressing problem facing Carleton and the men in blue was subduing hostile Indians. Raids by Indian bands had always made life in the Southwest hazardous, and their frequency increased with the outbreak of the Civil War. The worst offenders were the Navajos in northwestern New Mexico and the Mescalero Apaches in the southeast.

Upon taking command in Santa Fe, Carleton ordered Col. Christopher Carson with five companies of New Mexico volunteers to reopen Fort Stanton, in the heart of Mescalero country. They were soon joined by two units of the California Column who operated independently of Carson's command, although all commanders in the field were issued similar orders:

You will make war upon the Mescaleros and upon all other Indians you may find in the Mescalero country, until further orders. All Indian men of that tribe are to be killed whenever and wherever you can find them; the women and children will not be harmed, but you will take them prisoners and feed them at Fort Stanton until you receive other instructions about them.[6]

The troopers' relentless pursuit of the Mescaleros produced the effect Carleton wanted. By the end of the first week in November 1862 some one hundred Mescaleros were camped at Fort Stanton awaiting the return of their chiefs, who had gone to Santa Fe to seek peace with Carleton. The general now ordered the Mescaleros to settle at Fort Sumner on the Pecos River, some 160 miles southeast of Santa Fe. By February 1, 1863, 350 members of that tribe were gathered at Fort Sumner, and Carleton informed his superiors in Washington that the Mescalero Apaches were entirely subdued.[7]

In this small mountainous region, a pattern, characterizing the entire western movement of the American people, was repeated. By forcibly removing native inhabitants, the military opened coveted lands to economic development and protected the pioneers who ventured into the new environment. Once the Mescaleros had been driven north, settlers from all parts of the territory began moving into the Fort Stanton region. By late December 1862, fifty or sixty former residents of Mesilla had begun farming on the Tularosa River, where Capt. William McCleave and the California volunteers established a permanent camp.[8]

Throughout the American West, military personnel served as advance agents of Western civilization and quickly publicized new areas opened to settlement as a result of their campaigns. Kit Carson, in a letter published in the Santa Fe *Gazette,* described the Fort Stanton region as the best grazing and most productive area in the territory.[9] A California trooper wrote that the rolling hills and tree-covered mountains surrounding Fort Stanton were a veritable paradise, filled with all varieties of wild game.[10] And a number of soldiers from California would spend their most productive years toiling and laboring in these verdant mountain valleys after the war.

Carleton's next move was against the Gila Apaches, who terrorized the Pinos Altos gold region near the headwaters of the Gila River. Gold had first been discovered at Pinos Altos in 1860, but brutal raids by the Apaches had nearly depopulated the region. Carleton believed it a rich mineral district, and he was determined to reopen the region. The campaign began in earnest in January 1863 when New Mexico and California volunteers commanded by Gen. Joseph R. West took to the field with orders to slay all Indian men wherever they could be found.

The Unexplained Death of Mangas Coloradas

Capt. Edward D. Shirland, with twenty California volunteers, specifically was ordered to find Mangas Coloradas, noted warrior chief of the Gila Apaches. Shirland located the chief in the neighborhood of Pinos Altos and persuaded him to accompany the soldiers to Fort McLane, four miles south of what is now Hurley, New Mexico. Sometime during the night of January 18, the Apache chief was killed.[11]

The circumstances of the death of Mangas Coloradas have never been satisfactorily explained. General West officially reported that he was killed while trying to escape his guard, consisting of a sergeant and three privates of Company A, Fifth California Infantry.[12] Fifteen years later California men residing in New Mexico offered accounts of the death of Mangas Coloradas that contradicted the official report.

Two veterans, John S. Crouch and John Martin, the latter apparently at Fort McLane when the chief was killed, agreed that after Mangas Coloradas had fallen asleep, adobes had been thrown at him, causing him to awaken and rise, whereupon he was immediately shot and killed.[13] A third veteran, John Townsend, recounted that Mangas Coloradas had been tied to a soldier on each side before lying down to sleep. Hot coals were then thrown upon him, causing him to rise, whereupon he was shot.[14]

Two of the guards responsible for the chief's death have been identified as James Collyer and John V. Mead, the latter in turn killed by Indians in April 1868.[15] The unofficial historian of the California Column, Lt. George H. Pettis, undoubtedly expressed an attitude widely held among the soldiers when he wrote that "[Mangas Coloradas] had committed so many murders and outrages that the question of whether or not he really attempted to escape, [sic] was never satisfactorily settled—probably on the score that 'the only good Indian is a dead one'."[16]

Base camp for the Gila campaign was established on a bluff overlooking the Gila River and was named Fort West in honor of the commander. On March 22, 1863 Apaches stampeded the horse herd grazing near the fort, leaving the California Cavalry poorly mounted. Seventy-six enlisted men and officers doggedly pursued the Apaches and, after overtaking them, succeeded in killing twenty-eight Indians and recovering the stolen horses.[17]

The return to Fort West was difficult. Food supplies gave out and the men subsisted on horse flesh. Apaches attacked the command as it rode through a narrow canyon, wounding Lt. Albert H. French and killing two horses. The actions of Corporal Charles E. Ellis, a principal actor in the later El Paso Salt War, merited official recognition:

The superiority of the Californians over the Apaches at their own style of fighting was shown in the case of Corporal Charles E. Ellis, of Company A, who crawled unseen to a rock behind which was an Indian, and giving a short cough the Indian raised his head to discover its cause when a bullet from Ellis' rifle dashed through his brain.[18]

While their comrades were in the field chasing Apaches, Capt. Joseph Smith's Company A, Fifth California Infantry, was stationed at Pinos Altos to protect the miners. Smith and his men had worked in the placer and quartz mines in California and now at Pinos Altos they resumed their quest for gold. But their reports were pessimistic; the placers at Pinos Altos had all been worked out and quartz mining required more water than was available.[19]

By mid-summer the volunteers had cleared the Indians from the headwaters of the Gila, though various bands of Apaches continued to plague the area for years. Nonetheless, the presence of the military inspired confidence, and citizens began both farming and mining in the vicinity of Fort West. The Californians stationed at the fort were themselves ordered to plant corn and cultivate a garden for the greater efficiency and economy of their post.[20]

War Against the Navajos

Following the Mescalero and Gila campaigns, Carleton ordered his men to wage war against the Navajos. Small army units were sent guerrilla style throughout Navajo land to kill Indians and to destroy crops. By August 23, 1863 nearly all of Carleton's soldiers were in the field harassing Navajos. The constant probing by Carleton's guerrilla units caused many Navajos to disperse westward and southward; some traveled as far as the Grand Canyon to avoid contact. Still, Carleton's scorched-earth strategy worked sooner than he expected; early in the new year Navajos surrendered in such large numbers that the army lacked facilities to handle them. More than five thousand Navajos had surrendered by March and were sent to the reservation at Bosque Redondo on the Pecos River.[21]

As the Navajo campaign neared its end, observers in New Mexico were optimistic. One correspondent to the Albuquerque newspaper predicted that farming and grazing lands within a radius of 150 miles of Fort Canby—the army's supply depot during the campaign—would rapidly be settled now that the Indian problem had been solved.[22] Expressing the gratitude of many citizens, the Santa Fe *New Mexican* heaped praise upon the California soldiers:

The California Volunteers have shown a ready zeal and energy to perform any duty which might fall to their lot. The soldierly, orderly and patriotic behavior of officers and men . . . have commanded the confidence and good-will of the inhabitants of this country.[23]

Carleton had already committed the bulk of his command to the Navajo campaign when he learned in June 1863 that gold had been discovered in the San Francisco Mountains northwest of Tucson. Nonetheless, he quickly dispatched Capt. Nathaniel J. Pishon with twenty-seven California volunteers to escort Surveyor General John A. Clark to the new mines. In addition, Pishon and his men were instructed to prospect for gold once they reached the diggings so that Carleton could evaluate their worth. The general wrote his superiors that the new Arizona gold fields not only would pay the expense of the current war but would attract settlers to develop that desert area and bring the railroad over the thirty-fifth parallel to unite the country.[24]

When Surveyor General Clark returned to Santa Fe, he reported that an industrious man could expect to make no more than ordinary wages in the Arizona gold fields, but this sobering report was partially countered by the more optimistic one submitted by Captain Pishon. The captain's men—all former California miners—were convinced that California never produced any claims richer than these. Carleton's faith in the Arizona mines thereafter remained strong, and in October he ordered Maj. Edward B. Willis, commanding a small detachment of California volunteers, to establish a new military post, Fort Whipple, at the site of the diggings and to protect miners and preserve order in the mining region.[25]

Rigors of the Indian Campaign

Most California veterans who remained in New Mexico after the war had experienced the fatigue and danger associated with Carleton's Indian campaigns. A number had received serious wounds and some men simply collapsed on the long grueling marches into Indian territory. During the last three months in 1863, California volunteers were ordered to proceed to the headwaters of the Gila River to aid in the war on the Gila Apaches. The men experienced much hardship on this 1,000 mile trip: nights were cold and the river had to be crossed several times, resulting in the death from exposure of five or six soldiers. Several men had to be hauled in wagons on the last leg of the expedition.[26]

Twelve months later Col. Oscar M. Brown commanded an expedition to eliminate all Apaches between Fort Craig, New Mexico, and Fort Goodwin, Arizona. He had in his command fifty New Mexico infantrymen and fifty California cavalry, the latter under the command of Lt. Lewis F. Sanburn, who after the war prospected in the Magdalena Mountains west of Socorro. During the two-month trip, the men traveled through rain, mud, and snow, often on reduced rations. Though five soldiers deserted, Brown at the conclusion of the campaign praised his command in official reports for their cheerfulness under hardship.[27] He also eulogized the California volunteers in poetry published in the Santa Fe *Gazette*. Included in his six stanza verse are the following lines:

We came from California
With hopes bright and strong
To struggle for the nation
Be she right or wrong.

We'll whip the Apache
We'll exterminate the race
Of thieves and assassins
Who the human form disgrace;
We'll travel over mountain
All through the valley deep
We'll travel without eating
We'll travel without sleep.[28]

Other soldiers experienced similar hardships during the fall of 1864 when units of New Mexico and California volunteers concentrated at Fort Bascom in eastern New Mexico to chastize Plains Indians who had attacked supply trains on the Santa Fe Trail. Under the command of Col. Kit Carson, 335 Union soldiers marched some two hundred miles down the Canadian River to Adobe Walls, an abandoned trading post in the Panhandle of Texas. After attacking a Kiowa village of 150 lodges, Carson's troops were surrounded by a large force of about one thousand Indians. Only the firing of two howitzers kept the Indians at bay.[29] Privates John H. O'Donnell and John Sullivan, California volunteers, were killed in the engagement and ten to twenty other soldiers were injured. Theodore Briggs, who later worked as a carpenter in San Miguel County, was shot through the right shoulder and the right lung and lanced under the right arm. Private Briggs was loaded with other wounded men in a wagon and survived the rough, fifteen-day return trip to Fort Bascom. One future Lamy, New Mexico, resident, Patrick Brady, escaped injury at the hands of the Comanches at Adobe Walls but was hurt when he fell into a prairie dog hole while marching in the dark. His comrade Samuel Eckstein, known in the 1870s as one of Silver City's most hospitable saloon keepers, similarly avoided Indian arrows but was severely injured when he was run over by one of the two guncarriages in the heat of the battle.[30]

In letters to family and friends and in reminiscenses published years later, the California soldiers recorded in vivid detail the privations they had endured during the Indian campaigns. An unknown California volunteer described the horrendous ordeal suffered by seven men who had left Fort McRae on the Rio Grande to pursue Indians and to capture their sheep. After four days on the trail, their rations of jerked beef and hard bread gave out; henceforth they lived on occasional Indian sheep that had fallen by the wayside—consumed raw because the soldiers had no matches. On the eighth day the men caught up with the Indians, killed their chief, and captured 150 sheep. Since the soldiers had consumed their supply of water, they killed two sheep and drank blood to quench their thirst. Private Ben Argust went "raving mad" before the men returned to camp. The young soldier wrote that "it was horrible to hear Ben raving for water. God spare me from such another trip and sight again. . . . Many a man shed tears at the sight of poor Ben Argust raving for water." The Californians returned to camp, dirty, ragged, resembling skeletons having lost so much weight.[31]

One Californian who gloried in combat was Lt. Albert J. Fountain. Never a modest man, Fountain dramatically recounted fourteen years after the event in the pages of his own newspaper an Indian adventure that had taken place on the Jornada del Muerto during the war years. In June 1863 Fountain and his comrades in Company G, First California Infantry, established a new post, Fort McRae, to protect travelers and wagons crossing the Jornada, ninety miles of waterless desert between Roblero to the south and San Marcial to the north. Minutes after receiving word that a mail coach had been attacked by Apaches, thirty California soldiers were in the saddle in hot pursuit.[32]

During the chase, Lieutenant Fountain galloped through a narrow canyon leading four men in advance of the main command. Emerging from the canyon, the soldiers unexpectedly found themselves in full view of 150 Indians, their retreat cut off by a score of the enemy who had been stationed on the canyon walls. Fountain and his men dashed forward yelling at the tops of their voices, praying that a surprise attack would stampede the Indians. The remainder of the command, hearing their shouts, galloped through the canyon and joined the fight.

Soon there was a churning mass of soldiers and Indians locked in hand-to-hand combat. The troopers routed the Indians, but not without the loss of twenty-one-year-old Private George S. Dickey, shot while crawling through thick underbrush looking for hidden Indians. His assailant was immediately fired upon and killed by Fountain and a half-dozen other men. Reporting this incident years later, Fountain wrote:

Dickey was avenged. We carried our wounded comrade to a shady place, and as his blue eyes grew dim with approaching dissolution, the fair haired boy spoke of mother and sister in their Ohio home. "They'll be sorry" he said "that I didn't have a chance to fight for the old Flag at the front, but there's better men than me there, its sure, to come out all right." And so he died. We carried his body to Fort McRae, and gave it a soldiers burial. There his bones lie, but not alone; on the stone that marks his last resting place is carved the names of three of his comrades who died as he had died.[33]

ESCORT DUTY AND CAMP LIFE

California soldiers performed a multitude of services during the war, in addition to attacking Indians and defending the frontier against secessionists. They were called upon to carry dispatches to distant parts of the territory, escort trains and stages, patrol selected areas of the Rio Grande, transport captured Navajos to the Pecos reservation, repair buildings, stables, and corrals at the military posts, and tend company gardens. Escort duty was fatiguing and required persistent energy. Lt. Edward E. Ayer went on escorts of 600 to 800 miles, returning to Santa Fe only to start on another trip the following morning. Neither he nor his comrades carried tents, which meant sleeping in snow and sleet in the winter.[34]

Soldiers universally found camp life dull and monotonous and preferred being out on scouts and escort duties. A frequent notation in their letters and diaries is the statement that nothing new had occurred, often accompanied by the lament, "I have the blues." Letters from home and the arrival of eastern newspapers relieved the tedium of garrison duty, and soldiers frequently complained when families and friends were slow in sending news of the outside world. One officer stationed at the isolated post of Fort Sumner avowed that only vigorous Indian scouts relieved "the insufferable dullness and stupidity of the place."[35] Andrew Ryan, stationed at Fort Craig, wrote to his sister that he was tired of soldiering and discouraged by the news from the eastern battlefields. "The time passes off very slowly at this post," he wrote, "I get the blues most horably [sic] sometimes."[36]

Food was a major item for complaint. Although some posts planted company gardens, Lieutenant Ayer recorded that he had gone an entire year without vegetables, while at Fort Craig the men were issued a meager dinner consisting of bread, bacon, greens, and water. To protest the quality of the beef they received as ration, California soldiers stationed at Fort Craig attached a rope to the beef and hauled it to the post parade grounds where it was left exposed to the elements. Their first sergeant subsequently received a dishonorable discharge for his role in this so-called mutinous conduct.[37]

Officers also became targets for criticism. Sergeant George O. Hand, who became an Arizona saloon keeper and a politician after the war, complained that the officers at Mesilla set a poor example for the enlisted men when on a drunken spree.[38] A similar charge of drunkenness was leveled against Lt. Edward A. Descourtis by thirty-three-year-old Private John W. Teal. This same private complained that officers at Fort Sumner exploited enlisted men, ordering them to clean up the filth that had collected around officers' quarters. He felt that if private citizens knew how soldiers were treated in the army there would be no stigma attached to desertion.[39]

One California officer stationed at Fort Sumner, though complaining of its monotony and dullness, described his rather comfortable life at that post. His men had built for him a one-room adobe house measuring 18 by 16 feet with two windows and a fine stone chimney. It was warm in winter and cool in summer. He had access to an excellent bakery and a smokehouse to cure wild meat and had ordered a company garden planted with corn, cabbages, lettuce, onions, and other vegetables. He also was supplied with his own corrals, in which he kept six tamed antelope and a flock of goats and sheep.[40]

Many California soldiers missed the companionship of Anglo-American women. Twenty-nine-year-old Andrew Ryan, writing to his sister in September 1863, expressed the fear that he would not know how to act when he returned to civilization where "women" existed. Astonishingly, he noted that he had spoken only once or twice to an "American woman" since leaving California and that was to his colonel's wife. He expressed distaste for "Mexican" women, whom he described as being of the lowest class and "as black as the ace of spades and ugly as sin."[41]

Other Californians, though, disagreed with Ryan's harsh assessment of New Mexican women. One soldier-correspondent listed the pleasures that he and his comrades enjoyed at Mesilla: hunting, fishing, swimming in the Rio Grande, and "basking in the sunny smiles of the 'Castilian beauties' of Mesilla."[42] Dances were held frequently and the volunteers welcomed the gaiety of the señoritas. Large numbers of the California veterans eventually married Hispanic women. During the war many entered into casual relationships with local women. María Baca worked during the war as a laundress for a company of California volunteers. When an order was issued requiring that only married women be employed at such work, she entered into a written contract with a soldier named Webber that they would live together as man and wife, though they were not officially married. Upon being discharged three years later, Webber tore up the contract, left his "wife," and went off to Texas.[43]

Prostitutes of all races frequented New Mexico's military posts. Some entered the territory as laundresses attached to the California Column. It was common practice for such women to claim marriage to a soldier because that was the only way they could receive transportation and rations. One laundress for Company G, First California Infantry, trekked across the desert in the company of Private Lycurgus Demosthenes Fuller and politely was referred to as his wife. Called "Adobe Mary," she was known to be a common prostitute. Fuller's comrades later reported that when the two argued, he would be replaced in her tent by some other soldier.[44]

Some California volunteers found wives among the few Anglo-American women residing in New Mexico and adjacent areas during the war. Within four months of entering the territory, Lt. Col. Edwin A. Rigg married the seventeen-year-old daughter of H. H. Cooper, engineer and superintendent of Hart's Mill located near El Paso. Lt. William V. B. Wardwell, a government contractor and sutler at Fort Craig after the war, soldiered in New Mexico less than one and one-half years before he married nineteen-year-old Mary Watts, the daughter of New Mexico's wartime delegate to Congress, John S. Watts. Love at first sight united Marian Sloan and Lt. Richard D. Russell in marriage less than six months after their first meeting at Fort Union. Theirs was a happy union, although their first child—born thirteen months after the wedding—died within its first year and was buried at Fort Bascom.[45]

California soldiers sought release from the tedium of camp life in various leisure activities. Horse racing, musicals, and dances were all favorite forms of entertainment. The California volunteers stationed at Albuquerque presented nightly minstrel performances billed as "Charley Chicken's California Minstrels," while the citizens of Santa Fe during certain summer months were regaled with music performed nightly by the California military band. Christmas, Washington's Birthday, and the Fourth of July were welcome holidays, generally accompanied by an increased flow of liquor and spritely dances. Christmas at Fort Craig 1864 found officers and friends comfortably gathered in front of a roaring fire sharing champagne, eggnog, and whiskey.[46]

Company payday generated its own festivities as soldiers quickly exchanged cash for whiskey and dances increased in frequency.

Whiskey was also a key ingredient in the festivities staged to celebrate Union victories at Gettysburg and Vicksburg. Soldiers at Fort Union, for example, were given a holiday, and each company was issued two gallons of whiskey. In Santa Fe, the artillery shot off rockets, civilians built bonfires, and a civil and military dress ball was held for the town's elite.[47]

The more sober among the California volunteers were disturbed by their comrades' immoderate use of whiskey and organized lodges of the International Order of Good Templars to reduce its consumption. The first such lodge in New Mexico originated with Company K, First California Cavalry—a unit once known as the "Drunken K's." These soldiers pledged themselves to temperance before leaving California and then organized three lodges of Good Templars after arriving in New Mexico. The lodge established at Fort Union was particularly strong and took credit for the decline in whiskey drinking at that post. Corporal William S. Lackey, who homesteaded in San Miguel County in the 1880s, was praised by members of the Fort Union lodge for his zeal in the cause of temperance and his faithful discharge of duties as their Worthy Chief Templar.[48]

California volunteers also engaged in a wide variety of civic activities, from contributing funds for the relief of Socorro residents who had suffered devastating floods and Indian raids to providing music for the inauguration of Gov. Robert B. Mitchell.[49] And with sorrow in their hearts, they joined with civilians to pay funeral honors to the assassinated President Lincoln. On the official day of mourning, the battery at Fort Marcy, commanded by Lt. John Ayers, fired thirteen guns at dawn, a single gun at intervals of thirty minutes between sunrise and sunset, and thirty-six guns at the close of day. Two California officers who later became prominent residents of the territory, Capt. Benjamin C. Cutler and Col. Oscar M. Brown, joined six Santa Fe civilians and one regular military officer in drafting resolutions expressing the town's profound grief and sorrow. On May 1, 1865 a large concourse of people gathered in front of the Governors' Palace to pay tribute to the fallen president and to listen to memorial addresses by Gov.

Henry Connelly, Col. Oscar M. Brown, Major José D. Sena, and four other Santa Fe luminaries.[50]

Poisoned from Vines

Violence and death are constant companions of soldiers, and many young men who left the California diggings to fight in the war died before completing their enlistments—some before their units left California, others on the overland march, and still others in the desert wastes of New Mexico. California state officials in the adjutant general's office recorded over two hundred deaths among the California units assigned to Carleton's command. Ninety-nine men were listed as having died in a hospital or at a particular military post with cause of death unrecorded. Thirty-one volunteers died from named diseases, while only thirty-two were recorded as having been killed by Indians. During their enlistments, five California volunteers were murdered, one committed suicide, two were executed by order of military authorities, one was shot and killed while resisting arrest by a provost marshal, ten died from miscellaneous gunshot wounds, and fourteen drowned.[51]

Among the most unusual deaths is that of Private William Lunn, who died at Camp Stanford, California, "poisoned from vines while bathing."[52] Among the most tragic deaths was that of Capt. Daniel B. Haskell, who, along with eight New Mexico volunteers and two civilians, drowned when the boat used at Fort Craig to cross the Rio Grande capsized. Haskell had a wife and small children in Marblehead, Massachusetts, and had reenlisted in the Veteran Batallion of the California volunteers nine months before his death. He was a popular officer, and the post at Fort Craig went into mourning after the tragedy.[53]

Two California soldiers, Private Robert Kerr and Corporal Charles Smith, were executed by military firing squads, the former for having killed his first lieutenant, Samuel H. Allyne, and the latter at Mesilla, New Mexico, for conduct deemed mutinous by his commanding officer, Col. Joseph R. West. Smith's execution occurred November 26, 1862 shortly after his company had

arrived in the territory. There had been many escapes from the
guard house by soldiers incarcerated for attempting to desert and
by civilians suspected of being Texas spies. A stern disciplinari-
an, West suspected that the sergeant of the guard and three senti-
nels—all of K Company, First California Infantry—aided in these
escapes, and hence he ordered them placed in irons. The privates
in K Company, with Corporal Smith as their spokesman, protested
by refusing to perform any further services, and, when Smith repeatedly refused to return to duty, West ordered him shot. Though
he regretted the necessity for taking the life of one of his own
men, West felt that discipline had to be enforced, particularly
since his command had "become somewhat demoralized by desertion, and remaining in a town [Mesilla] where whisky, gambling
and women were plentiful."[54]

Several California volunteers, in addition to Samuel H. Allyne,
suffered bodily injury at the hands of their comrades. Two privates,
for example, fought a duel at Las Vegas on horseback, one severely
wounding the other; a few months later a private shot and killed
his sergeant at a "fandango" in Leasburg shortly before both were
to be mustered out of the service.[55] Samuel Creevey, employed
as a cook both in civilian and military life, was stabbed in the
back at Fort Wingate while on duty as corporal of the kitchen.
And Sergeant John G. Atkinson was shot in El Paso by two
drunken noncommissioned officers who mistook him for their
major.[56]

Not all Californians who died in New Mexico were left undisturbed in their desert graves. On occasion sorrowing families had
their remains shipped east for reinterment in family burial plots.
An interesting case is that of Samuel Whitney of Company G,
Fifth California Infantry, who was buried near Ft. Craig in 1863.
His remains were subsequently removed to the national military
cemetery in Santa Fe, and after a search of twenty years, his
mother and sister received permission to ship his remains to Os-
wego, New York.[57]

Volunteer soldiers had all the weaknesses and virtues of their
society, and it was inevitable that some would violate military

law and stand before court martials to be judged by their superiors. Frequent charges were drunk while on guard duty, absent without leave, selling government property, burglary, and conduct subversive of good order and military discipline. Punishments varied with the seriousness of the crime but frequently entailed confinement at hard labor wearing a twenty-four pound ball attached to the leg by a three-foot chain. Marian Russell, who lived with her soldier-husband at Fort Bascom, recalled that for trivial offenses soldiers at that post were suspended by their thumbs for several hours or sometimes sentenced to sixty days of the "California Walk," in which the soldier had to carry a heavy four-foot log on his shoulders and march around a flag pole from sunrise to sunset, alternating one hour of march with one hour of rest.[58]

The overwhelming majority of the Californians, however, were conscientious soldiers who loved their country and performed their duties well, meriting praise and respect from both civil and military officials. These blue-clad soldiers had left the Pacific Coast to engage the enemy in combat but spent their enlistments instead chasing Indians, protecting civilians, and fighting the boredom of garrison duty. A brief but tragic interlude in the Republic's history, the war dramatically touched the lives of many California men. As enlistments ended, critical decisions were made that affected the destinies of these volunteers over the next half-century. But the skills acquired and the lessons learned under Carleton's command while fighting Southwest Indians would not be forgotten in civilian life.

3

Mustering Out

The three-year enlistments of many of the California volunteers ended during the fall of 1864, but prior to that date efforts were made to recruit new volunteers on the West Coast and to encourage those already in the service to reenlist. Disgusted with desert garrison duty, however, a number of officers already had resigned their commissions to accept posts in eastern units.[1] Moreover, General Carleton feared that the majority of men serving in Arizona and New Mexico had tired of soldiering and that few would reenlist unless they were offered large bounties. He believed that it was essential to continue the services of the California men who had "learned this country" and were "worth three times their numbers of any strangers who might be sent to take their places."[2] Although reenlistments from the First and Fifth California Infantry were sufficient to form a battalion consisting of seven companies, Carleton was disappointed because the vast majority of these "well-disciplined and splendid troops" chose to be discharged.[3]

As the war progressed, the state of California attempted to encourage enlistments by offering bounties and salary increases to volunteers. During most of the war privates were paid thirteen dollars a month from the federal government, a sum considerably below the average take-home pay of three to four dollars a day that miners received. To compensate for the low pay, the California legislature in April 1863 voted five dollars a month additional pay to every enlisted man, and twelve months later it authorized a bounty of $160 to every soldier enlisting for three years or for the duration of the war and a bounty of $140 to every veteran reenlisting. The federal government similarly provided a fifty dollar bounty for men reenlisting for one year and a one-hundred dollar bounty for those reenlisting for two years.[4]

The *Daily Alta California* reported in September 1864 that the number of recruits mustered into service every week in San Francisco was "quite large."[5] Vacancies in the First California Cavalry, stationed for the most part in New Mexico and Arizona, were filled by new recruits as well as by seasoned troopers. As men enrolled on the Pacific Coast, opinions varied as to whether the California volunteers stationed in Arizona and New Mexico should be discharged in those territories or returned to California. Rumors sped through the posts that the men were to be marched across the desert to the West Coast, but on the request of numerous volunteers the secretary of war ordered that the Californians be discharged in the territories. This order pleased those men eager to exploit the mineral resources of Arizona and New Mexico, not to mention General Carleton, who believed that these experienced miner-soldiers were needed to develop the economy of the two territories.[6]

Veterans who wished to return to California, however, found this order extremely irritating. Although all soldiers were paid mileage and rations in cash from the place of discharge to the place of enrollment, the homeward-bound soldiers had to provide their own subsistence and their own transportation. Typically the veterans banded together in small groups to make the wearisome march across the desert. Lt. Edgar Pomeroy, for example, led seventeen men who had been discharged at Fort Whipple, Arizona, to Los Angeles, covering 500 miles in seventeen days. Some men traveled on foot and most were without firearms.[7]

Several volunteers left the service highly critical of their commanding general. By fall 1864 the civilian population of New Mexico was divided into two factions, supporting and opposing General Carleton's military administration. Recently-discharged soldiers, adding their voices to the controversy, met in Mesilla on September 15, 1864, and issued a lengthy indictment against Carleton that they later sent to newspapers throughout New Mexico, California, and the East. The soldiers charged that Carleton was not only incompetent and derelict in his duty, but also that he had allowed the enemy to escape the territory without active pursuit and that he had established repressive and tyrannical control over civilians and soldiers alike.[8]

INADEQUATE TRAVELING EXPENSES

Some discharged volunteers complained loudly to Gov. Frederick F. Low and Sen. John Conness of California because they had been discharged in New Mexico rather than in California and had not been paid proper traveling expenses. Twenty-two veterans claimed that they had received $75 to $125 to finance their return trip to the West Coast but had incurred expenses amounting to $350 or $400. Indeed, Paymaster Samuel C. Staples admitted that pay had been incorrectly computed but that corrections had been made before most soldiers had left the territories; others would receive just compensation upon making formal application.[9]

The last California volunteers to be mustered out of the service in the fall of 1866 were granted by the War Department the opportunity to be discharged in New Mexico or to march under officers for discharge in California. Those returning to the coast were organized into two companies, one of cavalry commanded by Capt. Thomas A. Stombs, and one of infantry commanded by Capt. William F. Ffrench. The men of this return column left Los Lunas October 15, 1866, and on December 31 were discharged at the Presidio.[10] Large numbers of the volunteers, however, elected to muster out in New Mexico rather than California, a decision enthusiastically praised by the editor of the Santa Fe *Gazette,* who predicted that many of the men would settle permanently in the territory, where they would become "a powerful element in developing the latent resources of the country."[11]

RELOCATION AND CAREER CHOICES

Regardless of whenever and wherever the mustering out occurred, California volunteers who had served in New Mexico and
Arizona scattered widely. Some men, eager to join the fighting
still raging in the East, requested the War Department to transfer
their units to eastern battlefields; however, the government refused
citing the expense in transporting troops half-way across the continent. Seventy men from the First California Infantry, nonetheless, crossed the Plains to Kansas City where they arrived in time
to participate in the fighting against the forces of Confederate
Gen. Sterling Price. Only forty-three of these California veterans
survived.[12]

Three days after Capt. John C. Cremony's Company B, Second California Cavalry, mustered out of the service in San Francisco, the *Daily Alta California* announced that forty of the men
were leaving that morning on the steamship *Constitution* to volunteer in the Army of the Potomac.[13] Other California veterans
sought military excitement across the border in Mexico where the
Republican army was hard pressed by French forces. Resigning
his commission on February 28, 1865, Capt. Robert S. Johnson
left New Mexico with about 250 discharged soldiers purportedly
to colonize in northern Sonora. Since Johnson went highly recommended to Gov. Ignacio Pesqueria by an officer in the Mexican Army, it is likely that the former Union soldiers anticipated
fighting for the Mexican forces. Indeed, the following year numerous officers in the volunteers left California, traveling through
Tucson and El Paso, to offer their services to the Republican government of Mexico.[14]

A number of California men at the end of their first term of
service accepted commissions in the New Mexico volunteers.
Among those commissioned second lieutenants in New Mexico
units, for example, were Thomas Coghlan, Edward E. Ayer,
Thomas W. Smith, Joseph Felmer, John Ayers, and Thomas V.
Keam.[15] Still others continued their military careers in the regu-

lar army, serving at various frontier posts after the war. John L. Viven, who arrived in New Mexico as a sergeant in the First California Cavalry and subsequently married Victoriana Connelly, the daughter of New Mexico's wartime governor, enrolled as a second lieutenant in the Twelfth Infantry at the war's end and later commanded the post at Fort Yuma.[16]

Among the most talented of the California officers to pursue a military career was Irishman William McCleave, who had served ten years under Carleton in the First Dragoons before the outbreak of the war. Carleton believed that there was no finer soldier in the Department of New Mexico and stated that McCleave possessed "all the elements of which heroes and patriots are made."[17] After mustering out of the California volunteers, McCleave was commissioned a second lieutenant in the Eighth Cavalry and subsequently served at a variety of posts scattered throughout the Southwest where he campaigned against Apaches for the next fourteen years. Retiring from active service in 1879 because of a back injury, McCleave settled in Berkeley, California, where he died at age eighty-two in 1904. Nine years prior to his death, a fellow officer told a gathering of California veterans in San Francisco that "no braver soldier, or truer patriot ever drew a sabre or straddled a horse than Major Wm. McCleave, the pride of the Column from California!"[18]

Many Californians who had served under Carleton remained in the Southwest after mustering out of the service; in so doing they repeated the experiences of hundreds of military men who had settled in the very frontier regions where they had served as soldiers.[19] Numerous Anglo-Americans residing in New Mexico before the Civil War had arrived as soldiers during the War with Mexico; Grant County, for example, listed in 1875 five veterans of the Mexican War who had lived in the territory since the close of that conflict.[20] Additional soldier-residents arrived in the interim between the two wars, including the feisty Louis Hommell of Germany, editor of the Las Vegas *Gazette,* and William McGuiness of Ireland, editor of the Albuquerque *Republican Review.*[21]

More than three hundred forty California volunteers spent some portion of their future careers in New Mexico. Had this total been present in the territory in 1870, they would have been about 8 percent of the Anglo-American population, estimated for that year at about 4,500 men, women, and children. Through death and migration out of the territory, however, only 196 of the veterans are listed in the 1870 census, making up about 4 percent of the Anglo population.[22]

SUICIDE AND VIOLENT DEATH

Many veterans died in New Mexico shortly after mustering out of the service. At least two committed suicide. In September 1865 William Hofedank, late lieutenant in the California volunteers but then employed as a quartermaster's clerk at Fort Selden, shot himself a few weeks after an investigation had been launched into the illegal sale of commissary supplies in the towns of Las Cruces and Mesilla. The following month William Kline of Mesilla shot himself less than one week after he had been discharged from the service.[23]

Several of the former California soldiers died violently at the hands either of their fellow territorial residents or hostile Indians. Two veterans were murdered by Hispanos in September 1865 at the Cottonwoods, nineteen miles south of Las Cruces; another veteran, employed as a constable at Roblero, was killed the following July trying to make an arrest in Mesilla.[24] Three months later, Christian Foster, a former private in the California volunteers, was brutally murdered in a Santa Fe alley.[25] In November 1867 Thomas Baxter, an employee in the quartermaster's department at Fort Union, was shot and killed at a dance in nearby Loma Parda; two days later his murderer was hanged by a band of armed men.[26] In the same month, John Slater and Charles Young, both mail carriers, were killed by Indians, the former in the vicinity of Apache Pass and the latter nine miles west of Fort Cummings.[27] Patrick Quigley was killed by Indians less than two years after mustering out of the service while working in his own corn-field in the vicinity of Fort Bayard. John V. Mead, who was impli-cated in the murder of Mangas Coloradas, was himself killed in a terrible Indian massacre in March 1868 when eleven men and two women, including Mead's wife, were slaughtered near George W. Nesmith's mill (later known as Blazer's mill) within a period of forty-eight hours.[28]

At least one California veteran was hanged in New Mexico prior to 1870. Described in the territorial press as "one of the most reckless and dangerous men that has disgraced New Mexi-co," Dan Diamond was tried, convicted, and hanged by a com-mittee of miners in 1867 for having killed George B. Schwartz, the butcher at Pinos Altos. Rumor claimed that young Diamond had killed at least four men in New Mexico and had shot Schwartz in a jealous rage over a Mexican woman.[29]

Among the more talented California volunteers whose lives were cut short by death was Benjamin C. Cutler, who had served as General Carleton's adjutant-general. He died on October 18, 1868, at the age of thirty-four, after a six-day illness and only two months after having been appointed surveyor-general for the ter-ritory. His death was mourned in Santa Fe by officials and friends who gathered in a public meeting, presided over by Gov. Robert B. Mitchell, to express grief that the territory had lost "one of her most useful and honest public officers."[30]

Smallpox carried off at least two potentially valuable territo-rial residents when an epidemic raged through the Mesilla Valley in November 1868, killing Alonzo D. Winship and William D. Tallman, both former corporals in the California volunteers.[31] Other veterans who lingered in the territory simply disappeared. Julius A. Hulburd, for example, was discharged at Las Cruces in November 1864 and spent the following months in that vicinity. Thereafter his former friends lost contact with him, and three years later a sister living in Whitewater, Wisconsin, advertised in the pages of the Santa Fe *New Mexican* for information con-cerning his whereabouts.[32]

TEMPORARY RESIDENTS

Several men established businesses at the close of the war but for a variety of reasons—both known and unknown—departed the territory prior to 1870. Simon Leavick became part-owner of the Socorro Flouring Mill in 1865. In Santa Fe James A. Jeremiah opened the California Restaurant in 1866, and George W. Dement operated a barber shop in 1867. These commercial enterprises lasted less than a year, and all three men apparently had left the territory by the end of the decade.[33]

At least one former soldier of the California Column, William W. Beman, fled the territory in disgrace. A lawyer and clerk of the district court at Mesilla, Beman was accused of stealing letters from the United States mail. Although acquitted on the charge of mail theft, he was driven from the town by outraged Mesilla residents who felt that he was "so morally lost as to be no longer fit or safe to live in the community."[34]

Among the more successful California veterans who lingered in New Mexico for just a short time after the war were Otto Mears and George H. Pettis. Born in Russia, Mears became a store clerk in Santa Fe after his military term expired in August 1864. The following year he went into the merchandising business at Conejos, Colorado, and in later years became one of Colorado's leading railroad builders.[35] Pettis, born in Rhode Island, followed the occupation of printer in that state prior to his sojourn to the California gold fields in 1854. He mined for four years and then took positions on various California newspapers, including the *Alta California.* After mustering out of the service in September 1866, Pettis opened the Railroad House in Algodones, where he offered "a good table, good stabling, and good prices." He served as postmaster in the little community and was recognized in the press as a genial gentleman and worthy citizen. Shortly after flood waters of the Rio Grande severely damaged his property in 1868, Pettis decided to return to Rhode Island, where he was elected to the state legislature in 1876.[36]

Numerous California soldiers who left the territory at the war's end returned in later years to make New Mexico their home. Andrew Stewart of Germany, for example, was discharged from the California volunteers in 1865 and journeyed to Missouri, where he remained until 1881. He thereupon sold his property and removed to Grant County, New Mexico, where he engaged in mining and ranching for a number of years.[37] A similar pattern was followed by miner George Bendle, who, after mustering out of the service, resided at Georgetown, Colorado, until 1879, at which time he moved to Albuquerque, where he labored as a carpenter.[38] Old soldiers who returned to New Mexico after a lengthy absence were greeted warmly by their former comrades.

Scores of men who migrated to New Mexico after 1865 were veterans of Union and Confederate regiments who had seen service in various parts of the United States. Among these were several California volunteers whose regiments had been stationed in territories other than New Mexico. At least three members of the Fourth California Infantry—Isaac N. Misener, Richard W. Pease, and John Oaks—eventually settled in New Mexico, the former two individuals in Santa Fe County and the latter in Bernalillo County.[39] After serving in the Second California Infantry, Palle F. Herlow of Denmark journeyed to New Mexico from California and subsequently established a meat market and a hotel in Santa Fe, where he became one of the town's leading citizens. A second member of that regiment, John W. Honsinger, resided in the 1880s in the small mining town of Kingston.[40]

California veterans who remained in New Mexico at the end of the war scattered throughout the territory searching for economic opportunities, either in well-established frontier towns or in isolated ranching districts and raw mining camps. Well over half of the 196 California veterans whose names appear in the 1870 census resided in the four southern New Mexico counties. The county having the largest number of California veterans in 1870 was Grant, the leading mineral region occupying the southwest corner of the territory. Forty-four of the veterans lived in that county, while twenty-three resided in Lincoln County, twenty-three in Doña Ana County, and seventeen in Socorro County.[41]

Colfax County, an important mining and ranching region located in the northeast corner of the territory, had the second
largest population of California soldiers. Twenty-seven former
volunteers lived there in 1870, while sixty-two were dispersed
among the remaining northern counties: seventeen in Santa Fe,
fourteen in San Miguel, twelve in Mora, thirteen in Valencia,
three in Rio Arriba, and three in Bernalillo. No California veteran was located in the 1870 census for either Taos or Santa Ana
counties.[42]

Collectively, these men had arrived in New Mexico with a wide
assortment of talents; individually, they differed radically in terms
of their educational background and ability to amass riches. At
least one individual, William L. Rynerson, had studied at a university; several were partially illiterate, signing official documents
with their mark—X—rather than with their signature.[43]

The economic worth of the California soldiers at the time that
they enrolled in the service is not known, although the editor of
the *Daily New Mexican* believed that most were practically penniless at the time of their discharge. Louis Clark, for example,
began his civilian life with "almost nothing" but established a
dry goods store in the small town of Plaza Alcalde in Rio Arriba
County after his discharge. He estimated the value of his personal
property and real estate in 1870 as $9,000, and his establishment
was described as one of the best stocked stores in the territory.[44]
Less than half the California veterans whose names appear in the
1870 census reported their net worth to the census taker. Figures
ranged from a low of $50 declared by Henry Ostrander, a farmer
in northern Mora County, to $65,000 by William V. B. Ward-
well, sutler at Fort Craig.[45]

At the close of the war, the former soldiers scattered throughout the territory intent upon making new lives for themselves.
As they aged, the old veterans nostalgically recalled their Civil
War adventures and accomplishments with pride. In writing of
his wartime experiences, John Ayers reflected more clearly than
any other writer the inherent pride and chauvinism of the California soldiers who served in New Mexico. He believed that

the war and the presence of American troops helped elevate the native New Mexicans, stating emphatically that "the general progression of New Mexico commenced from the war of the rebellion. . . . a curse to many but a blessing to the Mexican people."[46] And Lawrence G. Murphy, the future economic magnate of Lincoln County, believed that "the right class of men" settled in New Mexico at the war's end—men like the California volunteers who were not afraid to work and who would help develop the territory's economic resources.[47]

4

At the Mines

As Americans turned from military to civilian pursuits, the nation experienced a surge of activity that radically transformed its rural-agrarian economy. Everywhere citizens were seeking to exploit natural resources, and important advances were made in agriculture, mining, manufacturing, transportation, and communications. Expansion was the order of the day as a new, modern, industrialized nation emerged from the wartime chaos. In postwar New Mexico, economic growth was slow but steady prior to the arrival of the railroads in the late 1870s. A large sector of the economy was based on government expenditures for military and Indian supplies, while big mercantile establishments dominated the business life of the territory, providing investment capital for mining, cattle, and other enterprises. With the coming of the railroads and cheap transportation, all of these enterprises expanded, property values rose, towns were modernized, and the territory prospered. Railroads also brought immigrants into the territory so that the Anglo-American population grew from a small fraction to more than one-third of the total population by the end of the century.

IN SEARCH OF EL DORADO

For many California soldiers, New Mexico was a land of opportunity. And in postwar decades they competed with other entrepreneurs—both Hispanic and Anglo-American—in practically every economic endeavor imaginable. Not surprisingly, scores of California veterans resumed former occupations as prospectors and miners and scoured New Mexico's hills for traces of precious metals. In doing so, these ex-California volunteers, usually working with partners, were responsible for the initial discovery of precious minerals in at least five major mining districts in post-Civil War New Mexico: Elizabethtown, Silver City, Hillsboro, Magdalena, and White Oaks. In addition, ex-volunteers staked claims in practically all areas where mining was attempted between 1865 and 1885.

Elizabethtown

One of the most spectacular gold rushes in the territory's history occurred in the Moreno Valley country of northern New Mexico. Gold was discovered on Willow Creek in October 1866 by Peter W. Kinsinger and his two partners, Larry Bronson and a man named Kelley. Kinsinger had worked as a miner in California before the war and while stationed at Fort Craig in 1863, he discovered silver ore at Pueblo Springs about five miles north of Magdalena in Socorro County.[1]

Private Kinsinger was mustered out of the service at Fort Union in November 1864. Two years later, after having discovered gold on Willow Creek, he and his two partners returned to Fort Union to spend the winter. Although they agreed to say nothing about their strike, news of the discovery became common knowledge during the long winter months. As spring approached, swarms of miners descended upon Willow Creek to initiate one of the nation's more colorful gold rushes.[2]

The population of the region quickly mushroomed, and California miners, who had crossed the desert with Carleton, contributed both to its organization and exploitation.

Kinsinger joined Tom Lowthian and Col. Edward J. Bergman, a former officer in the New Mexico volunteers, to work the famed Spanish Bar on the banks of the Moreno River. Kinsinger and his brother Joseph, who also had marched under Carleton's command, became incorporators with Nicholas S. Davis and Lucien B. Maxwell in the Copper Mining Company, organized to exploit copper deposits on Baldy Mountain and to work placer claims on Cimarron Creek.[3]

By mid-May 1867 miners in Moreno Valley had adopted a constitution and bylaws for the gold region, which they named Cimarron Mining District. During the summer George Buck, a former private in the California volunteers, along with John Moore and other miners organized a town named after Moore's daughter— Elizabethtown. It quickly became a prosperous mining center, which in 1868 boasted a population of over 2,000 people, fifty or sixty houses, several stores, two restaurants, two saloons, a drug store, a billiard table, a barber shop, and gambling houses.[4]

One of the most colorful saloon keepers in the town's history was Joseph W. Stinson, who arrived in the territory in 1862 as a private with the California Column. After his discharge he joined the rush to Elizabethtown where he apparently assumed that he could acquire more gold by selling whiskey and beer to miners than by digging and panning for the mineral himself. Brawls and shootings were common occurrences in western saloons, and Stinston's establishment witnessed its share. It was there that Stinson shot and killed the notorious Wall Henderson on October 26, 1871 after the latter threatened to burn down the premises.[5]

The major problem facing miners at the Moreno placer fields, however, was not violence but water. A solution was offered by Capt. Nicholas S. Davis, an engineer and former officer in the California volunteers, who proposed constructing a ditch to tap water from Red River, eleven miles west of Elizabethtown, for use by miners in Moreno Valley. Completed in July 1869 under Davis's supervision, the "Big Ditch" was a system of canals and flumes that circled hills and bridged ravines, extending over forty-one miles in length. The ditch has been called "one of the most remarkable engineering feats in the West," but it failed to provide the volume of water anticipated by its backers because of leaks and breaks.[6]

Pinos Altos-Silver City

One of the most productive mineral regions to be prospected by California veterans was the Pinos Altos-Silver City area, situated in the hills and mountains of southwestern New Mexico. Gold had been discovered at Pinos Altos in 1860, but Apaches forced most of the miners to abandon the area, despite Carleton's Indian campaigns. A few brave men found their way to Pinos Altos in 1865, including Albert H. French, who had mustered out of the California volunteers the preceding year. Together with four partners, he located three copper mines in the vicinity of the famous Santa Rita and Hanover mines and four gold claims, including the Santa Juliana, near the town of Pinos Altos. French and his partners organized the Bay State Pinos Altos Mining Company and diplomatically deeded two hundred shares of the company to Carleton for the nominal sum of one dollar.[7]

In 1866 hordes of miners descended upon Pinos Altos, and a second gold rush to the region began. Soldiers formerly stationed at military posts in southern New Mexico were among those who rushed to the scene. Five months before their enlistments expired, Captains John D. Slocum and Charles P. Nichols of the California volunteers joined former comrade Robert V. Newsham and two other men in locating a claim one-half mile north of Pinos Altos. On the same date and in the same locality 1st Lt. John K. Houston, together with Nichols, Newsham, and two other men, staked a claim on Turkey Creek Lode. Indeed, California soldiers ranging in rank from private to lieutenant-colonel located several claims in the district before severing their connections with the military.[8]

Pinos Altos quickly became a mining camp of sizable proportions. Carleton, visiting the mines in June 1867, estimated that eight hundred to one thousand miners inhabited the camp. The following year the Santa Fe *New Mexican* reported that over six hundred quartz leads had been discovered within six miles of Pinos Altos, a town that now boasted eight good stores to handle miners' needs.[9]

Large numbers of former California soldiers searched surrounding hills and gulches for traces of valuable minerals; at least twenty-seven acquired mining property in the Pinos Altos district, several holding more than one claim.[10] William L. Rynerson was owner or coowner of at least nine Pinos Altos mines, including the Amberg, located October 15, 1866. The company organized to develop this mine involved these leading civil and military officers in the territory: Chief Justice John P. Slough, Gov. Robert B. Mitchell, Col. Herbert M. Enos, Gen. James H. Carleton, and Lt. Col. William L. Rynerson. During the summer 1867, Rynerson brought a quartz mill from California to operate at Pinos Altos and subsequently sold one-fifth interest in it to Carleton for $3,000. While commander of the Department of New Mexico, the general had acquired extensive mining property, particularly in the territory's southern mountains. Before leaving in 1867, Carleton appointed Lt. Col. David L. Huntington, who was assistant surgeon at Fort Bayard, as his attorney to oversee his mining interests. Huntington received one-fourth of Carleton's mineral claims in return for his services.[11]

Many California soldiers who staked claims near Pinos Altos subsequently became prominent in the political and social life of southern New Mexico. Rynerson, for example, served three terms in the territorial legislature, while Richard Hudson, who located at least four mines in the district, became Grant County's first sheriff. James Crittenden, who held joint interest with Hudson in the Humboldt and John Billings mines, served three years as sheriff of Grant County, and John K. Houston, who was part owner of the Independence, the Alpha, and the Omega mines, was Grant County's first probate judge.[12] The political careers of these ambitious miners are explored further in chapter nine.

Placer and lode mining prospered at Pinos Altos well into the seventies, but the opening of new mining camps drew miners away and the camp declined from its earlier brilliance. In 1877 the population of Pinos Altos had declined to one hundred, of whom it was estimated eighteen were "American."[13] Typical of the miners who drifted from one mining camp to another was Barney W.

Connelly, who mined in Pinos Altos in 1872 with his younger brother Patrick. Together the two men had enlisted in the California volunteers at Nevada City, California, in 1861, serving in the same unit while stationed in New Mexico.

From pension records, Barney's movements can be traced in some detail. Mustered out of the service at Fort Craig in August 1864, Barney Connelly moved to Mesilla, where he kept a hotel called the Fonda House until he reenlisted in January 1865. After his discharge the following year, he resided at Fort Union where he had charge of the saddler's shop. He subsequently moved to Colorado, living at Georgetown, Blackhawk, and other mining camps, staying at each place but a short time.[14]

Connelly returned to New Mexico in 1868 and resided in mining camps in the southwestern part of the territory until 1872. During this time he and his brother ran a shoe shop in Silver City and acquired mining properties in Silver Flat, Lone Mountain, Virginia, and Pinos Altos mining districts.

From New Mexico, Barney drifted to San Francisco and then to Arizona, where he resided for several years in Pinal County with his brother. In 1877 the New Mexico press reported that Barney Connelly had made a rich strike in Arizona, his ore assaying about $5,000 per ton. Two years after this alleged bonanza, the forty-seven-year-old miner married Mary A. Shannon at San Jose, California. In subsequent years, he returned to Arizona apparently to continue mining operations with his brother Patrick, but on January 6, 1889 the latter was killed in the Silver King Mine in Pinal County, leaving Barney to mourn at his graveside.[15]

Documents in the pension files of the two Connelly brothers indicate that neither became wealthy from their mining enterprises nor did their reputations receive favorable comment from agents investigating their applications for pensions. One investigator reported a year prior to Patrick's death that the latter was "almost an imbecile from the effects of drink," and that among the miners Barney was "considered a moderate drinker—among respectable people, a common drunkard." On September 6, 1889 Barney W. Connelly died in San Francisco—eight months to the day after the death of his brother. Thus the Connelly brothers passed unheralded from the scene, two immigrants from Ireland who had struggled to find fortunes among barren and dusty hills in the American Southwest.[16]

Others who came west with Carleton fared better than the Connellys, especially after 1870. When silver was discovered in the Pyramid Mountains south of modern Lordsburg, veterans of the California Column as well as other miners rushed to the site to stake out claims and to build the town of Ralston. One hundred seventy-five miners located claims in the Virginia District, which centered on Ralston in 1870. In this and subsequent years, at least twenty-three California veterans acquired mining property in the district, including Sidney R. DeLong, pioneer Arizona newspaper editor and one of six Anglo participants in the infamous Camp Grant Massacre.[17] Another was one of New Mexico's most prominent pioneers, John S. Crouch, frontier lawyer, newspaper editor, politician, mine speculator, and former officer in the California volunteers.

The chief significance of the Ralston strike was that it led to the discovery of silver in San Vicente Valley where Silver City blossomed as a roaring mining camp later in 1870. In the spring of that year, California veteran Richard Yeamans, John Bullard, and six others left their farms in San Vicente Valley to join the silver rush to Ralston. Upon examining ore at Ralston, Bullard reportedly remarked, "Well if that is silver ore, I know where there is lots of it."[18]

The men returned to San Vicente Valley, picked up samples of ore from a hill west of their farms, and had the samples assayed at Pinos Altos. The ore was sufficiently promising to lead to a stampede once news of the strike spread to surrounding mining camps. The eight partners organized the Silver Flat Mining Company and staked the first three claims in the district on May 27, 1870, including the famous Legal Tender Mine.[19] Miners from the entire adjacent country poured into San Vicente Valley so maddened by the silver craze that candles were used so prospecting could continue at night. Eventually two districts emerged: Silver Flat and the far richer Chloride Flat, which became the first major silver-producing district in the territory.[20]

At least eighteen California veterans located or purchased mines in the Silver Flat District, several of whom were among the first to locate in the district. The most famous of the Silver Flat mines was the Legal Tender. Richard Yeamans, the former private in the California volunteers who had helped initiate the stampede to San Vicente Valley, sold ten feet in that mine in August 1870 to Robert V. Newsham for one hundred dollars and subsequently published a notice in the *Borderer* that he would sell his one-eighth interest in the mine for two thousand dollars. Whether Yeamans truly enjoyed the fruits of his labor is unknown. He was brutally beaten to death in 1875. His estate showed assets of less than two hundred dollars.[21]

The first discoveries in Chloride Flat District were made in September 1870, and among individuals acquiring mining property in this district were no less than twelve former California volunteers, a number of whom came to own some of the principal mines in the area. Joseph F. Bennett became part owner of the valuable Providencia Mine in 1872; in the following year ore from the mine paid over one hundred dollars a ton.[22]

Among the most publicized mines in Chloride District was the Dexter, purchased in 1872 for $5,200 by two former officers of the California volunteers, George W. Arnold and Sidney M. Webb, and their partner Frank M. Wilburn. During one week in June the threesome extracted five and one-half tons of ore from the mine, yielding $532; however, the mine was shut down in August because of a controversy over ownership. A lawsuit was initiated by Martin W. Bremen, owner of the neighboring Seneca Mine, who claimed title to the Dexter property. The attorneys employed in the case included two former California officers, William L. Rynerson for the plaintiff (Bremen) and James A. Zabriskie for the defendants. During the litigation, Wilburn and Webb transferred their shares in the Dexter and other mines to Arnold for $2,000 and $3,000, respectively, although Webb continued to be associated with the mine's management.[23]

The impasse was partially resolved in November when Judge

Warren Bristol threw out Bremen's claim to the entire mine, limiting the area in dispute to a small strip of land lying between the two mines. This allowed the defendants to resume work on the mine, and by the end of the year they were again extracting large quantities of rich ore. In the spring of 1873 the disputants agreed to new boundaries separating their properties, and the case was eventually dropped from the court docket. Although the press continued to eulogize the richness of the Dexter, Arnold apparently was finished with mining; on July 1, 1873 he sold the mine for $4,000 to Cornelius Bennett, brother of the owner of the Providencia mine.[24]

Arnold and Webb spent the next several years in the vicinity of Silver City, their wanderings and activities occasionally being described in the local press. In 1876 Arnold was growing vegetables at his farm on the banks of the Gila River. These he delivered in Silver City to his friend Webb, who had opened a vegetable store on Broadway Street. The two men subsequently moved to Globe, Arizona, where Webb opened a commercial establishment. Violent death was close at hand, however, and the two partners who had labored so hard to extract wealth from the hills of Chloride Flat met similar fates across the border in the dry, barren deserts of Chihuahua. On May 14, 1878, George W. Arnold was shot to death while on a trip south of the border to purchase cattle. Six months later, the *Grant County Herald* reported that Sidney M. Webb and his entire family were murdered while traveling in Chihuahua.[25]

A frustrating problem faced by the first miners in Silver City was lack of equipment to reduce extracted ore. The first bullion produced at Chloride Flat was smelted in crude adobe furnaces constructed in the spring of 1871, but three years later six mills and four furnaces existed in camp, including the Tennessee Mill, owned in part by Richard Hudson and said to be the largest and most complete mill in New Mexico. Two of the mills, however, the old Rynerson, which had been transported from Pinos Altos to Silver City, and the Cibola Reduction Works, had been out of commission for some time.[26]

The Cibola Reduction Works had been plagued with problems

since its construction in the fall of 1872. The company defaulted
on its indebtedness, its machinery was attached by the courts,
and all work stopped on the mill, casting "a gloom over the
buoyant spirit" of the mining camp. To bolster the company, Joseph F. Bennett and his two partners, Cornelius Bennett and
Henry Lesinsky, doing business under the name of Bennett Brothers and Company in Silver City, advanced the Cibola Reduction
Works $5,000 in October 1872 and $4,000 the following March,
taking a mortgage on the property in return. When the Cibola
Reduction Works again defaulted, Bennett Brothers and Company
instituted a suit in the courts, and in October 1873 the Cibola
Reduction Works was sold at public auction to meet its indebtedness. The highest bidder was Bennett Brothers and Company,
who purchased the mill for a mere $3,000.[27]

The company—consisting of the two brothers and Lesinsky—
was a powerful commercial enterprise in Silver City during the
seventies. Operating out of a two-story building described as the
finest building in New Mexico, Bennett Brothers and Company
employed a buyer in New York but also purchased goods from H.
Lesinsky and Company in Las Cruces and agricultural produce
from Casas Grandes, Chihuahua. Not only was it one of the largest
mercantile establishments in town but it also frequently served as
a banking house, extending loans to local miners and other commercial men. The company also acquired ownership—at least for
a time—to the Pope Mill, erected in 1874 by Nathaniel Pope,
former superintendent of Indian Affairs for New Mexico.[28]

Hillsboro

One of the most illustrious mining camps to emerge in the seventies in southern New Mexico was Hillsboro, located near the
south end of the Black Range Mountains, where gold was discovered in the spring of 1877 by David Stitzel, a former private in
the California volunteers, and his partner Dan Dugan. When news
of the strike filtered through New Mexico's mining community,
prospectors rushed to the scene, turning Hillsboro into a thriving

town by the end of the year. The territorial press reported that one hundred men, mostly "American," were at the mines during the first winter and that miners were confident that they had rich strikes.[29] The North Extension of the King Mine, owned by Stitzel, Joseph Yankie and Company, was considered one of the most productive in the district; in 1879 it was producing ten tons of ore a day and employed twenty men, ten working on the day and ten on the night shift. The El Dorado Mine, owned by Westy Peterson—a California veteran—also was considered to have good prospects.[30]

David Stitzel made one of New Mexico's most important gold strikes, yet it does not appear that he grew wealthy from this celebrated strike. Nor did he manage to live a quiet and peaceful life on his homestead near the town of San Lorenzo in Grant County.[31] In 1884 he shot and killed Charles Ramm, a former tenant, in an argument over ownership of a plow. Stitzel was tried, found guilty of murder in the fifth degree, and sentenced to eighteen months confinement in the new territorial prison. There is no record that Stitzel served his sentence, but it is known that he lived the last thirty years of his life in Sierra County. His Hispanic wife, Juana, died at Hillsboro in 1902, and, twelve years later, at the age of seventy-five, Stitzel married Margarita Martínez. He died at Hillsboro on June 8, 1914, four months after the wedding ceremony.[32]

The Las Animas Mining District, which Stitzel helped found, underwent considerable expansion during the eighties and nineties, producing in a twenty-year period an estimated $6,750,000 in bullion. The population of Hillsboro rapidly expanded and by 1884 the town sported five stores, a good hotel, a lumber yard, a soda water factory, two saloons, one restaurant, two butcher shops, two blacksmiths, a drug store, and a livery stable.[33]

Among Hillsboro's leading citizens was George O. Perrault, an ex-California trooper of Canadian birth, who engaged in mining and retailing and was part owner of a saloon. This gentleman located mines with tremendous energy; in a three-month period he staked twenty-two claims in the mining districts surrounding Hillsboro, including one in the appropriately named Fraud Gulch, one and one-half miles southeast of Animas Peak. He immediately sold eighteen of these claims for $1,000 to a capitalist from Greenfield, Massachusetts, and in the same year, 1881, Perrault and two partners sold a half interest in two mines in the Lake Valley District for $600 to an investor from Washington, D.C.[34]

A handful of other California veterans labored in the Hillsboro region, men like Jacob Laycock, Richard M. Johnson, Westy Peterson, and Charles Brakebill. These men left few written records, though, and consequently failed to attract historial attention.

Organ Mountains

Seemingly no ravine, gulch, or mountain slope in southern New Mexico escaped scrutiny from miners struck with gold fever. One of the least productive mineral districts proved to be the San Andres Mountains in Doña Ana County, where, in the fall of 1866, at least eight California veterans, as well as Gen. Carleton, joined other prospectors in locating gold and silver claims thirty-five miles northeast of the town of Doña Ana.[35]

The real center for mining activity in Doña Ana County was the Organ Mountains, seventeen miles east from Las Cruces, where in the 1850s Hugh Stephenson of El Paso worked the famed Stephenson Mine, which became the most productive mine in the region. The tangled, complex history of this mine has never been completely recounted but the Stephenson touched the lives of several men from the California Column.

It began in 1848 or 1849 when Hugh Stephenson acquired part interest in the mine and worked the claim for ten years, smelting ore in an adobe furnace located near Fort Fillmore south of Las Cruces. Originally known as the Santo Domingo de la Calzada, the mine had several owners during the fifties,[36] but in 1858 Stephenson sold his three-fourths interest to Josiah F. Crosby of El Paso and John T. Sprague, United States Army commander at Fort Fillmore, for $8,000. The two men subsequently deeded their three-fourths interest to Chauncey Bush of New York City. The remaining one-fourth interest, owned by Welcome B. Sayles of

Providence, Rhode Island, was also transferred to Bush, who, in August 1859, deeded the Santo Domingo de la Calzada Mine to the Stephenson Silver Mining Company, organized to develop the "richest mine" in the Organ Mountains.[37]

Two officers in the California Column, Col. George W. Bowie and Capt. Charles A. Smith, together with El Paso politician William W. Mills gained possession of the Stephenson Mine during the Civil War through the courts, charging that it had been abandoned by its owners. Several California soldiers, in fact, believed that the Organ Mountains contained vast deposits of untapped mineral wealth.

In August 1864 Capt. William McCleave and Surgeon William H. McKee, both officers in the California volunteers, joined Bowie, Smith, Mills, and Nepomuceno Carrasco in organizing the Carrasco Mining Company to work three mines located in the Organs—the Dolores, the Santa Susana, and the Santo Domingo de la Calzada. McKee was chosen director of the company while Carrasco was appointed superintendent. By November, fifteen men were working under Carrasco's direction in the Calzada mine.[38] In 1867 the Carrasco Mining Company purchased several claims that had been staked on the Calzada and Dolores lodes in earlier months, including those of three former California soldiers: Albert H. French, who became a member and shareholder in the company, Benjamin F. Harrover, and Joseph F. Bennett.[39]

For several years the Stephenson Silver Mining Company and the Carrasco Mining Company engaged in litigation concerning ownership of the old Stephenson Mine, but in November 1872 the Las Cruces *Borderer* announced that the two companies had consolidated and would soon begin active mining. Possibly as a result of this consolidation, the San Augustin Mining Company received a patent from the Interior Department to the Stephenson Mine on May 15, 1874, but for several years the company failed to develop the mine. Occasionally the press announced that work on the mine was about to begin, but it remained idle as late as 1882, apparently because of disagreements among stockholders.[40]

Despite inactivity at the Stephenson Mine, the Organ Moun-

tains continued to excite imaginations of residents living in the
southern portion of the territory. At least a dozen California veterans staked claims in the Organs in the two decades following
their discharge from the army, including William L. Rynerson
and Joseph F. Bennett, who located or became associated with
mines that developed into valuable mining properties. Among
the better known mines in the Organ Mountains was the Modoc,
situated on the western slope about five miles south of the Stephenson and on the same mother lode as the Stephenson.

The Modoc was located December 16, 1879 by John H. Rynerson, brother of William L. Rynerson who, on the same date,
staked the Backbone Mine adjoining the Modoc. The two brothers
and Nestor Armijo subsequently located The Great Republic
Mine, also adjoining the Modoc. Additional mines staked by the
Rynerson brothers included the Little Giant, the Valley Rose,
and the Lebanon. In 1882 the two brothers and John A. Miller,
a former post trader at Fort Bayard, incorporated the Modoc Mining and Reduction Company to work the Modoc and nearby
mines. Although the *Rio Grande Republican* predicted a lucrative
future for the Modoc, lack of capital hampered its development.[41]

Joseph F. Bennett located the Bennett Mine in the Organ Mountains on November 16, 1880—a mine which adjoined the Old
Stephenson Mine and which later became part of the famed Stephenson-Bennett Consolidated Mine. Bennett staked two additional
claims adjacent to the Stephenson on the same date, the Trinity
and the Patton mines. He subsequently sold to William O. Cory
of the United States Army one-half interest in the Trinity and
Patton for $500 and one-half interest in the Bennett for $50. Bennett then sold one-fourth interest in the Trinity, Bennett, and
Patton to John Dougher and William H. Skidmore for $300 and
one-fourth interest in the Bennett to Anne M. Dougher, John's
wife, for $350, thus ending in 1884 his ownership in the Bennett.
Skidmore, who was superintendent of the Organ Mountain Mining Association of Philadelphia, purchased Cory's one-half interest
in the Bennett in May 1886 for $200.[42]

The Bennett and the Stephenson were valuable mines, and efforts were made in the eighties to combine the two properties. Controlling interest in the San Augustin Company was held in the East, although in 1884 New Mexicans Joseph F. Bennett, Singleton Ashenfelter, and Henry Lesinsky held one-third of the company's stock. Lesser shareholders included former California soldier Benjamin E. Davies, whose ranching property lay east of the Stephenson Mine in the Organ Mountains. To prevent litigation against the Bennett Mine by creditors and to enhance the value of each, the two famous mines were eventually combined as the Stephenson-Bennett Consolidated Mine. The president of the new company in 1891 was William T. Thornton, future governor of New Mexico, and its secretary was former California soldier Albert J. Fountain.[43]

Magdalena

One of the earliest discoveries of silver ore in New Mexico was made by California volunteer Peter W. Kinsinger at Pueblo Springs in Socorro County in 1863. Numerous prospectors worked that area in the later sixties, including a number of Kinsinger's former comrades, George F. Brown, Hugh D. Bullard, Emerson L. Smart, and John J. Shellhorn. It was Brown who located the famed Ace of Spades Mine in this district in 1868.[44]

Kinsinger's discovery at Pueblo Springs ultimately led to establishment of the Magdalena District near the north end of the Magdalena range of mountains, twenty-six miles west of Socorro. Col. J. S. Hutchason had traveled to the Pueblo Springs region in 1866 seeking the source of Kinsinger's silver ore. Failing to find it, he turned toward the Magdalena Mountains, where he discovered rich lead ore.[45] Other prospectors soon swarmed to the area and initially were interested in gold and silver to the exclusion of lead. By mid-1868 several former soldiers in the California Column were staking claims on the western slope of the Magdalena Mountains. George F. Brown and Hugh D. Bullard joined six other men, one of whom was Stephen B. Elkins, in locating 1500 feet of silver ore on the President Juarez Lode, while William V. B. Wardwell,

David T. Harshaw, and five others located a silver claim on the Buena Vista Lode in the same locality.[46]

The early seventies witnessed increased activity in the Magdalena Mountains, and the Albuquerque *Republican Review* boasted that Socorro's mines were the richest in New Mexico. Listed among the leading mines in this region were several located by California veterans: Powell Bingham's Poney and Alpine mines; Henry S. Hays's Grand Tower; and Lewis F. Sanburn's Succor. By December 1874, a mixed population of some two-hundred-fifty Anglos and Hispanos had settled at Magdalena, and by the following year the camp had numerous primitive houses, two stores, two saloons, one hotel, several boarding houses, and two or three fandango halls.[47]

The true bonanza period of the Magdalena mines, however, came in the 1880s with arrival of the railroad and the increased flow of eastern capital into the region. Prior to 1900 the Magdalena District was one of the most productive mineral regions in the territory, and it was sturdy miners, like the ex-soldiers from California, who had paved the way for this development.[48]

Contemporary with discoveries made in the Magdalena District was the discovery of gold in Water Canyon on the northeast slope of the Magdalena Mountains sixteen miles west of Socorro. Miners were at work in Cañon de Agua as early as January 1867, but a California veteran, Patrick Higgins, is credited with establishing the first mineral claims there in 1868.[49] The following year Higgins and a partner located preemption claims of 320 acres on the west side of the Magdalena Mountains, two miles from Ojo Arreta where they had land under cultivation. Other miners continued to work in Water Canyon for several years but with little success.[50]

In the early seventies, Emerson L. Smart and others began prospecting the Cat Mountain District, twelve miles southwest of Magdalena. Although they failed to uncover significant leads, Smart continued prospecting in the region and staked at least five new claims in the early eighties. The district, though never a major producer of mineral wealth, was actively mined into the twentieth century.[51]

Far to the west of Socorro, James C. Cooney, a soldier stationed at Fort Bayard, discovered silver in the Mogollon Mountains in 1875. Hostile Apaches prevented miners from working the area effectively, and during a raid on the district in 1880 Cooney was killed by Victorio and his warriors. The area's spectacular development dates from the mid-eighties after the Apaches had been driven from the region.[52] Still, at least two California veterans, William L. Rynerson and Robert V. Newsham, staked claims in Cooney District prior to the quieting of the Indian frontier. On July 5, 1878 Rynerson located—with James C. Cooney serving as witness—the North Extension Number 3 Copper Queen Mine, seven miles from the San Francisco River on the northwestern slope of Mogollon Mountains. The following year Newsham located his Vault Mine in the same general area, and three months before Cooney's death Newsham located the Alta Mine.[53]

California veterans searched for gold and silver throughout most of the territory, prowling the mountains and ravines in present-day Lincoln County. East of Sierra Blanca a few miles west of the village of Nogal, placer gold was found in Dry Gulch in 1865. Prospectors swarmed over the area, and in 1868 William Gill, a California veteran, made the first discovery of gold quartz in the Nogal District. Although the region produced only small amounts of gold, Gill sold his famed American Mine and two other claims in 1885 to Dr. W. G. Hunter of Kentucky for $25,000.[54]

North of Nogal District in the Jicarilla Mountains, placer gold was worked intermittently during the sixties and seventies; however, scarcity of water hindered development. Col. Emil Fritz, a California veteran and one of Lincoln County's most illustrious pioneers, located several claims in the district, and with his partner Lawrence G. Murphy backed a major effort to sink artesian wells.[55] About three hundred "American" and forty "Mexican" miners were at work in the Jicarilla District in 1877. Small mountain streams and a few wells supplied water for the operation of several "dry washers." For the most part, however, the Jicarilla placers remained undeveloped, although territorial boomers kept their enthusiasm for Jicarilla's mineral potential.[56]

White Oaks

John V. Winters, a former saddler in the First California Cavalry, was a member of the small group of prospectors whose discovery of gold ore in 1879 led to the establishment of White Oaks, one of New Mexico's most celebrated mining camps and center of mining activity in Lincoln County. Winters and John E. Wilson staked a claim in the fall of that year to 1,500 feet on a gold lode they named the Homestake, the first quartz mine to be located in the Jicarilla Mountains. The two partners shortly thereafter split the claim, with Wilson taking the south section and Winters the north. The customary stampede to the new location soon followed; by April 1880, over two hundred men were in camp, with fresh prospectors arriving daily.[57]

Wilson sold the South Homestake to the Homestake Gold Mining Company for $300,000, although he retained stock in the company.[58] On December 23, 1879 Jack Winters deeded to Caroline Dolan, the wife of James J. Dolan of Lincoln County War fame, 350 feet of the North Homestake, and on the same date Dolan and wife conveyed half their interest to Joseph A. LaRue. LaRue and Marcus Brunswick, a silent partner in the proceedings, then advanced several thousand dollars to work the mine. Everyone estimated that the North Homestake was worth millions, and in succeeding years it did indeed become the leading producer of gold in the district. With his share of the proceeds, Winters bought a "wagon load of whisky and made the whole town drunk."[59]

Winters died March 21, 1881 at the age of sixty-four, so it is not likely that he enjoyed the benefits of his early discovery. As he had died intestate and without a known wife or relatives living in New Mexico, a notice of his death was published in the Pennsylvania press since it was thought that he had relatives living in western Pennsylvania. Several "pretender" brothers, sisters, and widows subsequently turned up to claim Winters's estate, but, after a lengthy court battle, his legitimate heirs were granted ownership to the Homestake Mine, which they then sold for $40,000 to W. G. Hunter, the mining investor.[60]

THE DIAMOND FRAUD OF 1872

Very few former California soldiers struck it rich in New Mexico's mining districts, but the fantasy of instant wealth kept large numbers combing isolated mountain valleys and barren hill slopes for signs of color. Men holding such visions quickly succumbed to one of the most celebrated mining frauds perpetrated in the American West—the diamond hoax of 1872.

Two prospectors, Philip Arnold and John Slack, took uncut diamonds to San Francisco in the early part of that year and let it be known to interested investors that the diamonds had been found at some undisclosed site in the West. Word of this discovery soon leaked to the rest of the world, and by autumn men with acquisitive instincts diligently were seeking the new diamond fields. Many speculated that these fields would be found in Arizona; consequently Santa Fe became a staging area for easterners seeking their fortune among the newly discovered gems.[61]

New Mexico residents contributed to, and were affected by, the diamond hysteria. Former California cavalryman John Ayers was given credit by the Santa Fe press as being the first New Mexican to interest himself in the Arizona gems and was thereafter called "their discoverer."[62] Ayers led a party to Navajo country in September to investigate the fields at close hand, returning with what he labeled a true diamond, along with reports that Navajo agent and former California volunteer Thomas V. Keam had discovered several others larger in size. And in October Joseph F. Bennett journeyed to the diamond fields, where even strong-willed investors like Bennett went wild with excitement. It was difficult not to succumb to diamond fever after hearing such fantastic stories as the one told by an old regular army man, Michael

Cronin. He reported that some sixteen years earlier "Navajo diamonds were then so numerous and cheap with the men of the old rifle regiment, that, a canteen of sutler's whiskey could at any time command a haversack full."[63]

In November Clarence King, director of the Fortieth Parallel Survey, revealed that the diamond field, which he located in northwestern Colorado close to the Wyoming border, was a gigantic fraud. The New Mexico press carried articles exposing the hoax, but such reports failed to dampen the enthusiasm of fortune seekers such as Thomas V. Keam, who continued to profess that precious gems could be found near Fort Defiance.[64]

Hundreds of Anglo and Hispanic men combed New Mexico's hills and mountains after the close of the Civil War seeking easy wealth and fortune. Americans everywhere were intent upon exploiting the nation's resources, and mountainous regions throughout the West were painstakingly searched. The rigors of living in primitive camps and rough surroundings were readily accepted by these fortune seekers.

The men of the old California Column represented only a small percentage of pioneers who prospected and mined in New Mexico's rugged terrain, but their contributions were significant. Peter W. Kinsinger, Richard Yeamans, David Stitzel, and John V. Winters were responsible for opening at least five of the territory's leading mineral districts. Dozens of other California men who prospected the hills and who opened mines in isolated regions created jobs for other New Mexicans, helped establish several new towns, and worked to attract eastern and foreign capital that was necessary to develop New Mexico's mining potential. The California veterans helped prepare the groundwork in the sixties and seventies that allowed New Mexico's mining industry to grow to the importance it finally achieved in the last two decades of the century.

5

Cattlemen
and Cattle Thieves

At the close of the Civil War, prospectors and cattlemen alike envisioned quick and easy wealth by making only limited investments in new economic enterprises. To stock their ranges, ranchers would purchase Texas cattle at low rates and then allow them to roam over the public domain eating free grass. Fabulous profits seemed assured. The first important Texas herds were trailed into New Mexico in 1866 by Oliver Loving and Charles Goodnight, who sold their beeves at mining camps and frontier military posts. Other cattlemen followed, and slowly New Mexico's range land became stocked with Texas cattle. In 1870 an estimated 57,000 head of cattle grazed in the territory; by 1880 that figure had jumped to 348,000. The boom period came in the eighties, and by 1890 an estimated 1,632,000 cattle were in New Mexico.[1]

Ex-California soldiers who raised cattle in New Mexico ranched on a relatively modest scale, but they nonetheless made an impact. Only three California veterans listed their occupation in the 1870 census as "stock raiser": Thaddeus W. Roberts and John H. Scott, living at Tortugas in Doña Ana County, and George W. Arnold, residing at Gallinas Crossing in San Miguel County.[2] Men who farmed in the territory's river valleys ordinarily owned a few Texas cattle in addition to their milk cows, but they were primarily engaged in agriculture.

But additional California veterans turned their attention to the cattle industry in the 1870s and 1880s. Among the more interesting partnerships formed in northern New Mexico was that be-tween James T. McNamara and William S. Lackey, who ran cattle on the ranges of San Miguel County in the early eighties. Each had served as a corporal in the California volunteers, and after the war McNamara married the eighteen-year-old daughter of Lackey at Fort Union. The younger partner, McNamara, became well-known among territorial stockmen and played an active role in New Mexico's stockmen's association. [3]

Typical of the small ranches located in Colfax County was that of Mathias Heck. Heck came to the United States from Germany in 1844 at the age of fifteen and peddled jewelry in the southern states before joining the gold rush to California. In 1863 he crossed the desert with the First California Cavalry, mustering out of the service three years later in Santa Fe. He then rushed to Baldy Mountain with other discharged soldiers, searching for gold and staking claims near Elizabethtown. Heck subsequently relocated some eighteen miles south of Cimarron at Sweetwater, where he managed a government supply station and operated a store. Around 1876 the former soldier established a ranch on the banks of the Cimarroncito where he ran a small but respected cattle herd, raised corn and beans, and cut hay on twenty acres of grassland. Heck became a well-known rancher and farmer and continued ranch-ing in the area with his sons until 1909, the year of his death. [4]

One of the early pioneers in the western section of Socorro County was Richard C. Patterson, who came to New Mexico in 1862 with the First California Infantry. At the end of his enlist-ment, he settled in Cañada Alamosa where he and comrades Jo-seph D. Emerson and Samuel Creevey began farming. Southern Apaches raided extensively through this canyon, and Patterson acquired a reputation as an Indian fighter. [5] In the early 1870s, Patterson joined several ex-volunteers in searching the Magdalena Mountains for gold and built a small smelter in Patterson Can-yon. By mid-decade he had turned his full attention to farming and stock raising on Patterson Ranch, which he located on the western border of San Augustin Plains where numerous stockmen grazed cattle during the hey-day of the open-range cattle indus-

try. In 1880 Patterson claimed ownership to 160 acres and estimated the value of his farm, livestock, and farm products at
$3,845. He worked his family-sized enterprise until 1903, when
he moved to Polvadera, New Mexico.[6]

Patterson's ranch was somewhat less successful than the one
established by Patrick Higgins near old Fort Tularosa in western
Socorro County. Higgins had been born in Ireland and spent four
years at sea before landing on the Pacific Coast during the great
California gold rush. He accompanied the California Column to
New Mexico and then settled in Socorro County at the close of
the war, serving as deputy sheriff for fourteen years. In 1874 he
registered a preemption claim to 160 acres in Tularosa Valley,
120 miles west of the Rio Grande, where he engaged in the cattle
business and ran a few sheep. In 1880 Higgins claimed ownership
to about six-hundred-twenty acres of land. Six years later the assessed value of his property was listed as $6,500 and Patterson's
as $2,739. Higgins retained this property until 1897, at which
time he moved to a ranch on the Frisco River. Although Patterson
and Higgins engaged in the cattle business on a relatively small
scale, each is remembered as a pioneer rancher in western Socorro
County.[7]

Several California veterans engaged in ranching on a larger
scale, but none approached the stature of John Chisum, who reportedly had sixty to seventy thousand head of cattle on the banks
of the Pecos. In Grant County, Richard Hudson grazed around
six hundred head in the late 1870s near his famous Hot Springs
resort, twenty-five miles southeast of Silver City.[8] In 1874 Robert V. Newsham, pioneer merchant at Rio Mimbres, had about
1,500 head of cattle in the Mimbres Valley, "one of the best herd-
ing grounds in New Mexico," making him one of the largest
stockmen in Grant County. In 1881 Newsham sold his ranch and
entire herd of cattle for $12,000 and devoted his attention to his
considerable mining claims.[9]

One of the best known ranches in southern New Mexico was
owned by John D. Slocum, twenty-six miles west of Mesilla on
the road to Silver City. Slocum's Ranch was advertised as "the

only watering place between the Rio Grande and Fort Cummings," offering water for stock, good stabling, clean beds, and well-supplied tables.[10] His property consisted of a "good" house, two large corrals, stables to accommodate thirty animals, and several large water tanks. In times of scarce rainfall, Slocum was compelled to haul water from the Rio Grande—a distance of twenty-two miles—to fill his tanks. In addition to his problems with water, Slocum had to contend with hostile Apaches who frequently raided the ranch and ran off his stock.[11]

In 1875 Slocum rented his property to Richard S. Mason for seventy-five dollars a month and went first to Silver City and then to Mesilla. Following the death of his wife in 1876, he lodged his two daughters in the Las Cruces convent school and traveled to Carisal, Mexico, where he engaged in ranching, grazing at one time about two thousand head of cattle.[12]

Three California veterans became notable stockmen in Doña Ana County—David Wood, Benjamin E. Davies, and William L. Rynerson. Wood and his partner, D. M. Reede, both of Las Cruces, ran over one thousand cattle in the mid-seventies on the slopes of the Organ Mountains. They attempted to improve their herd in the early eighties by placing about "forty Missouri thoroughbred and high grade animals" on their ranges. The two partners also owned a ranch—the Carisalillo—in Grant County.[13]

THE CATTLE KING OF DONA ANA COUNTY

Benjamin E. Davies built up a small herd in the 1870s, procuring six Durham heifers in 1877. These were said to be the first blooded and pedigreed cattle brought into Doña Ana County.[14] At this time, however, his interests focused primarily on sheep. A former private in the California volunteers, Davies became one of the most knowledgeable sheepmen in New Mexico.[15] In the early seventies, he became post trader at Fort Selden and then entered into partnership with Morris Lesinsky in the San Augustin Ranch on the east side of the Organ Mountains in Doña Ana County. Davies began sheep raising around 1873 and within two years had 7,500 sheep grazing on the eastern slopes of the Organs. He took great pride in improving the local breed of sheep by crossing native ewes with Leicester or Merino bucks and frequently offered advice on the care of sheep in the pages of the territorial press. In 1882 he had 10,000 sheep and local newspaper editors applauded his success, attributing it to hard work, pluck, and close attention to business. By 1885, however, Davies was out of the sheep business and devoted all his attention to his expanding cattle enterprise.[16]

Davies and Lesinsky had purchased in 1882 1,000 head of cattle from Wood & Reede at twenty dollars a head and thereafter phased out their investment in sheep. The range on which these cattle grazed was in Soledad Canyon on the east side of the Organ Mountains, where Soledad Springs fed water to the animals. To improve their herd, Davies and Lesinsky purchased blooded herefords from famous Colorado stockman John W. Prowers of West Las Animas and acquired additional cattle from the Carlos Armijo ranch in the Three Rivers area. By the close of 1882 Davies, who had made two trips east that year to procure blooded cattle, was heralded in the press as "The Cattle King of Doña Ana County."[17]

A mania to invest in western cattle hit the nation in the 1880s and soon spread to Europe, but Davies differed from the typical outside investor because he had started on a small scale, learned the industry from scratch, and pragmatically assessed his chances for success. Yet Davies, like other experienced cattlemen, ran into financial difficulties which were compounded by inclement winter weather. The winter of 1886–87 took a frightful toll of cattle on the Northern Plains but was felt less severely in New Mexico. Davies's problems came in the winter of 1890–91, when severe winter weather seriously weakened his cattle. To save himself financially, Davies opened a meat market in El Paso and began butchering his cattle. He died there of pneumonia on a Sunday morning in 1891, leaving his widow a $5,000 life insurance policy, bills to pay, and bitterness for the Lesinksys—Morris, Charles, and Henry—whom she charged "had swindled her out of nearly everything," including a half interest in the San Augustin Ranch.[18]

RYNERSON AT RANCHING

The success of New Mexico's cattlemen in the good years, however, encouraged William L. Rynerson—"the Tall Sycamore of
the Rio Grande"—to invest in ranching. Rynerson clearly was
one of the dominant personalities among the ex-soldiers who settled in New Mexico. Born February 22, 1828 in Mercer County,
Kentucky, Rynerson studied at Franklin College, Indiana, before
the excitement of the California gold fields enticed him to leave
school and head west. In 1861 he enlisted as a first sergeant in
Company C, First California Infantry. Mustered out of the service in Mesilla in November 1866 with the brevet rank of lieutenant colonel, Rynerson settled briefly in. Mesilla before taking
up residence in Las Cruces. Rynerson had purchased property adjacent to the town of Las Cruces prior to his discharge, and in
the next several years—while he established himself as one of the
territory's leading lawyer-politicans—he acquired additional choice
farming and ranching property. [19]

In 1880 Rynerson owned 160 acres of good agricultural land
between Las Cruces and Mesilla. The value of his farm was an
estimated $10,000, while his farm machinery was valued at $200,
his livestock at $1,200, and his farm production for 1879 at $2,000.
In the previous twelve months, he had produced on this farm 20
tons of hay, 15 bushels of clover seed, 50 bushels of barley, 200
bushels of Indian corn, 250 bushels of wheat, 10 bushels of beans,
and 10 bushels of sweet potatoes. He also cared for apple trees,
peach trees, and a vineyard from which he manufactured 200 gallons of wine. By 1884 Rynerson had acquired a smaller ranch of
about sixty acres in the same vicinity. There he raised alfalfa,
corn, cabbages, and swine. The local press reported that Rynerson
was "probably more extensively engaged in the hog business than
any man west of the Mississippi." He was also among the first in
the Mesilla Valley to employ new farm equipment; in 1878 he
invested in a corn planter and three years later he was using a hay
baling machine to prepare his alfalfa for market. [20]

Rynerson's grazing land was located primarily in Lincoln County.

By the summer of 1884 he was associated with John H. Riley in the Membrillo cattle ranch and had joined Numa Reymond, James J. Dolan, and John Lemon in establishing a ranch of some twelve to fifteen hundred head of cattle on the Rio Felix, land said to be part of the old Tunstall property. Occasionally Rynerson made trips east to purchase purebred bulls for his own and neighboring ranches.[21]

In 1885 Rynerson, John H. Riley, and Pantaleon Sandoval became partners in a cattle venture to run stock on the banks of the Tularosa River. Thomas B. Catron joined and Sandoval left the partnership in December 1889, and the following spring Rynerson, Riley, Catron, Albert L. Christy, and Henry J. Cuniffe incorporated the venture as the Tularosa Land and Cattle Company, with ranges located west of the Mescalero Indian Reservation along the Tularosa River. In 1891 Hinman Rhodes—the Mescalero Indian agent and father of Eugene Manlove Rhodes—estimated that Riley and Rynerson ran 10,000 head of cattle on lands adjacent to the agency.[22]

ORGANIZING THE STOCK GROWERS

While few former California soldiers invested in the cattle industry, among those who did were men such as Benjamin E. Davies, Richard Hudson, James T. McNamara, Robert V. Newsham, William L. Rynerson, and David Wood, who were known as successful cattlemen throughout the territory and took the lead in organizing county and territorial stock growers' associations. For the most part, western ranchers such as these were rugged individualists, yet they knew that cooperation was essential to lobby effectively for laws beneficial to the industry and to protect their property from outside interlopers. When rustlers moved onto the ranges to share the prosperity of an expanded cattle market, stockmen in the several western states and territories organized to protect themselves.

Probably the first cattlemen's association in New Mexico was the Southwestern Stockmen's Association formed on January 15,

1881 at Silver City. Robert V. Newsham, "a well-known ranch man" who chaired the meeting, stated that the principal object of the association was to protect members' stock, to bring horse and cattle thieves to justice, and to secure legislation beneficial to cattlemen. The meeting attracted stockmen from eastern Arizona and southwestern New Mexico, including Richard Hudson who served as its secretary. Members of the association agreed to hold meetings four times a year and to appoint a hide inspector. An entrance fee of five dollars and quarterly fees of six dollars were established for all members.[23]

The association's first president, William W. Wines, disappeared in April, causing some members to speculate that he had met foul play. Others suspected he had skipped the country to avoid arrest for the theft of $5,000 from his mother-in-law. The association survived its shaky beginnings, nevertheless, and in December 1883 it claimed twenty-six members, with Richard Hudson serving as its president.[24]

The Doña Ana County Stock Association was organized by the principal stock owners of the Mesilla Valley on March 31, 1883. George Lynch was elected as president of the organization, Albert J. Fountain as vice-president, John H. Riley as secretary, and Evangelisto Chavez as treasurer. Fountain, William L. Rynerson, and Benjamin E. Davies were appointed to draft bylaws for the organization. Among the thirty men elected to membership were California veterans Davies, Fountain, Rynerson, David Wood, and John D. Barncastle.[25]

In March 1884 delegates from all New Mexico's stock associations met in Santa Fe and organized a territorial stockgrowers association, with Joseph W. Dwyer elected as president, Rynerson as vice-president, and Max Frost, a prominent member of the Santa Fe Ring, as secretary. Official delegates to the territorial meeting included four California veterans: James T. McNamara of San Miguel County, Richard Hudson of Grant County, and Davies and Rynerson from Doña Ana County. McNamara and Hudson became members of the executive committee, with Hudson being chosen its chairman.[26] The following year territorial stockmen reorganized under a new name, The Cattle and Horse Growers Association of New Mexico, and reelected Dwyer as president and Rynerson as vice-president. Rynerson was also chosen as one of three men from the association to represent New Mexico at the national cattle convention held in St. Louis in November 1885.[27]

Apaches, Rustlers and Gunmen

These pioneer cattlemen faced countless hazards. Rustlers and Apaches alike, for example, preyed upon the area's expanding cattle herds. When Victorio's Warm Spring Apaches went on the war path in 1879, Gov. Lionel A. Sheldon called out companies of volunteers to protect lives and property. With frightening ferocity, Victorio plundered settlements, ranches, and mining camps in southern New Mexico and Arizona. By March 1, 1882 fifteen companies of militia were organized in the territory ready to move against either hostile Indians or renegade white men. The First Regiment was commanded by Col. Richard Hudson, with Albert J. Fountain serving as major, and John Townsend of Santa Fe serving as regimental quartermaster and first lieutenant. All three men had military experience in the California volunteers. In subsequent months, the men in Fountain's command rendered valuable service as scouts and guides to the regular army as it waged war against the Apaches.[28] Governor Sheldon also utilized Fountain's command to rid the southern counties of rustlers and gunmen who terrorized that region.

Fountain's "Fair Warning"

Fountain himself, as a crusading editor of the *Mesilla Valley Independent*, had launched a newspaper war against cattle and horse thieves in 1877. His articles were highly inflammatory, and he apparently intended them to galvanize law-abiding citizens into action and to bully the lawless into leaving the country. On July 14 Fountain published "A Fair Warning" in his paper stating:

There is, and has been for the past two years an organized band of horse and cattle thieves in this county. Some of this band do the stealing, others receive and dispose of the stolen property. The thieves are known, the receivers, some of whom pretend to be honest men—are also known. . . . There are twelve of you; and if room cannot be found for you in the county jail, twelve ropes and twelve cottonwood limbs *can* be found. You cannot escape the swift retribution of an outraged community. WE WARN YOU TO BEWARE!

In the following week's edition, Fountain asked the citizens of Doña Ana County how long they would permit "thieves and murderers . . . to commit crimes with impunity." He urged the people to enforce the laws, but if there were flaws in the legal system, the guilty had to be dealt with accordingly.[29]

On July 18 Fountain telegraphed his coeditor, John S. Crouch, who was attending district court in Silver City, that a band of thieves had threatened to clean out Mesilla and to kill Fountain on sight. District Attorney William L. Rynerson wired the governor on the same date asking for authority to call out the militia to protect the lives of prominent citizens threatened by these thugs.[30]

Fountain's law-and-order campaign slowly came to a halt. His critics publicly stated that his articles had been sensationalism at its worst, intended to sell papers and to create a reputation for his newspaper. His accusations and fiery prose had kindled violent and brutal emotions among his enemies, and when that violence endangered his own family Fountain terminated his association with the newspaper.[31]

A man of physical courage, Fountain relished the glory and excitement of the martial life. When Governor Sheldon authorized Fountain and his militia units in 1882 and 1883 to break up bands of cattle thieves operating in the southern counties, the former California trooper responded with alacrity. In May 1882 Fountain and his men chased thieves who had raided the R. S. Mason ranch (Slocum's old ranch) into Mexico where they were apprehended by Mexican police. For his prompt action and "zeal and wisdom," he was generously praised by Governor Sheldon and Edward L. Bartlett, the territory's adjutant general.[32]

Kinney's Gang

Another series of stock thefts swept Lincoln, Grant, and Doña Ana counties at the start of the new year. Led by John Kinney, a gang of thirty to forty thieves rustled cattle from New Mexico's ranges, driving them into El Paso and Mexico for quick sale. The entire town herd of Doña Ana was run off in January, and angry citizens and stockmen appealed to the governor for action.[33] In February Fountain's militia captured three of Kinney's gang at La Mesa, a small community about twelve miles south of Mesilla, and killed another who tried to escape. Within days, one of Kinney's most blood-thirsty lieutenants, Doroteo Sains, was shot to death by Major Fountain as Sains attempted to escape from custody.[34]

When John Kinney was captured March 7 by Fountain's men, the territory was ecstatic and bestowed upon Fountain and his citizen-soldiers endless tributes and accolades.[35] Later that month, Fountain led his militia to Lake Valley and to Kingston where members of the Kinney gang were reported to be in hiding. At Lake Valley, John Watts and William ("Butch") Leland were arrested for cattle stealing and then shot to death when they tried to escape. Fountain's command pushed on to Kingston where two more men were arrested, although the main body of rustlers had fled the vicinity. The militia continued to search the surrounding countryside, and John Shannon, who was attempting to arouse the people in Lake Valley to attack the militia, was taken into custody and killed when he attempted an escape. When Fountain learned that the remaining rustlers had headed toward Mexico, he reported that "his campaign had broken the back-bone of the most dangerous if not the most extensive combination of thieves in the Territory."[36]

The Lake Valley raid involved Fountain in further controversy. No one in Kingston believed that Watts and Leland had been trying to escape when shot and killed; rather they were thought to have been senselessly executed by Fountain's men at close range. On April 16 the governor called for a court of inquiry into Fountain's conduct, but this order was canceled when it was learned that a Doña Ana County grand jury had fully investigated the Lake Valley raid and had completely exonerated Fountain. The old soldier's critics remained unconvinced.[37]

Once the militia had departed, rustlers quickly reestablished their headquarters in Kingston, and in June Governor Sheldon ordered Fountain to investigate reports that a new reign of terror existed in that mining community. This expedition was a total fiasco, with the militia and the civil authorities working at cross-purposes. Fountain blamed his failure to round up rustlers on the two deputy sheriffs who were sent along with the warrants, while the deputy sheriffs implied that Fountain and his militia were merely lusting after glory. Charges and recriminations published in the territorial press embittered relations between Fountain and the civil officers for several months.[38]

FOUNTAIN'S ASCENDANCY

But Fountain was clearly the man of the hour. Governor Sheldon had supported and praised him throughout the militia campaign, and Doña Ana County residents believed his efforts on behalf of law and order had benefited the community. In July Fountain's admirers presented him with a bronze clock and a silver tea service of eleven pieces, including a silver salver on which was engraved: "Presented to Major Albert J. Fountain, by the citizens of Doña Ana County, in recognition of his services in suppressing lawlessness in Southern New Mexico 1883."[39]

A lawyer by profession, Fountain entered the courtroom to conclude his crusade against Kinney and his gang. The Doña Ana grand jury that had investigated Fountain's Lake Valley raid returned some 132 indictments against the rustler band, including 14 against Kinney. The territory's case against John Kinney was presented in court April 12 by District Attorney S. B. Newcomb and Major Fountain. After listening most of one day to arguments presented by the defense and by the prosecution, the jury deliberated eight minutes before finding Kinney guilty of cattle rustling.[40]

Fountain's fame and prestige among cattlemen increased as a result of his campaign against rustlers. In February 1883 he was retained by the Doña Ana County Stock Association to assist in prosecuting Charles Ray, alias Pony Diehl, charged with stealing cattle from a member of the association, and to prosecute other individuals similarly charged. Receiving a fee of one hundred dollars, Fountain performed "admirably" and soon secured Ray's conviction.[41] Several months later, Fountain was paid five hundred dollars by the association to assist in the prosecution of the Toppy Johnson gang, which operated in Sierra County. When Johnson and his cohorts were convicted, the Doña Ana County Stock Association tendered a vote of thanks to Fountain and retained him to prosecute future cases of cattle theft.[42]

A gentleman of considerable talents, Fountain was also ambitious and vain, acquiring as many enemies as friends. In 1896 he and his son were murdered somewhere on the edge of the White Sands, and the mystery that enshrouds his fate largely accounts for his continued notoriety.[43] A fellow California Column man, George W. Nesmith, met a similar fate in 1882, and his story, though less well-known than Fountain's, ensures his continued memory among Tularosa Basin residents. The assassination of each man reportedly was linked to cattle rustlers or those accused of stealing stock, although in neither case could this charge be upheld in a court of law.

NESMITH'S MYSTERIOUS DEMISE AND PAT COGHLAN'S TRIAL

George Nesmith, a sergeant with Company A, Fifth California Infantry, mustered out of the service at Mesilla on November 30, 1864. On December 8 of that same year he and two Company A comrades, George M. Kenyon and Elias D. Ryan, paid James Patterson of Socorro County $3,200 for a saw mill and buildings located thirty-seven and a half miles south from Fort Stanton below the Upper Forks of the Tularosa River. Kenyon sold his interest in the mill to Nesmith and Ryan in 1865, and for the next several years the property was referred to as Nesmith's Mill. In 1869 Joseph H. Blazer, a Union veteran from Iowa, purchased one-third interest in the mill from Nesmith and in 1876 owned the mill in partnership with George A. Abbott. Thus the mill once owned by Nesmith became immortalized in Lincoln County history as Blazer's Mill.[44]

Nesmith and Blazer jointly ran the sawmill in 1870, but by 1876 Nesmith was living north of Blazer's Mill on the Tularosa where he owned a log cabin and other improvements in partnership with Robert Dickson, an old comrade from Company A. Their property, located within the Mescalero Indian Reservation, was purchased by the Mescalero agent in February 1876 for $1,000.[45]

Nesmith subsequently became caretaker on Pat Coghlan's ranch at Three Rivers where his wife, Lucy Newcomb Nesmith, managed the cooking, gardening, milking, and similar chores. Coghlan had the contract to supply beef to the military post at Fort Stanton where George W. Peppin, a former private in Nesmith's old company, had charge of Coghlan's herds. Known as the "King of Tularosa," Coghlan was suspected of purchasing stolen cattle from William Bonney and other notorious lawbreakers.[46]

In 1881 the famous cowboy detective, Charlie Siringo, while on a mission to recover cattle stolen from the LX Ranch in the Texas Panhandle, discovered fresh hides with the LX brand in Coghlan's slaughter pens at Fort Stanton.[47] At Mesilla in April 1882, Coghlan was forced to stand trial under eleven indictments for purchasing stolen cattle. He was defended in court by William L. Rynerson. The prosecution was headed by S. B. Newcomb, the district attorney, assisted by Albert J. Fountain, who had been employed by the Texas Cattle Association. Prior to the trial, the Rio Grande Republican, a newspaper in which Rynerson had a financial interest, assured its readers that Coghlan, "one of the wealthiest and best known citizens of our Territory," would be found innocent of all charges.[48]

Although Lucy Nesmith had a premonition before the trial that something terrible would happen, she and her husband agreed to appear as witnesses. Her testimony in court has not survived, but

Charlie Siringo later said that it was Lucy who had overheard Coghlan reach an agreement with Billy the Kid to buy all the stolen cattle that the Kid could supply. In spite of this damaging testimony, Coghlan got off lightly. After an unsuccessful attempt by his lawyer to quash the initial indictment, Coghlan entered a plea of guilty to one count of illegally purchasing cattle and was fined $150. The remaining indictments were dismissed. The Nesmiths were paid $38 each for their twenty-seven days attendance at court and proceeded home to Three Rivers.[49]

Sometime in mid-August, Nesmith, Lucy, and a small adopted daughter were murdered near St. Nicolas Springs, about eighteen miles from San Augustin, while traveling to Las Cruces. Their bodies were so badly decomposed when discovered that it took several weeks before they were positively identified. Friends in Lincoln County, including J. H. Blazer and Pat F. Garrett, pledged sums ranging from $25 to $50 and Governor Sheldon put up $500 for the arrest and conviction of their murderers. Pat Coghlan added his name to the list of subscribers to the reward fund, saying that he was "just as anxious for the apprehension of the murderer, as any one of his neighbors."[50]

The Nesmith murders remained an impenetrable mystery for nearly three years, although suspicion was directed at Pat Coghlan because of difficulties between him and Nesmith over land titles. In March 1885, however, the law caught up with the murderers, Maximo Apodaca and Ruperto Lara, who were traced through the recovery of a coat stolen from Nesmith at the time of his death. Apodaca confessed that he and Lara, a Pueblo Indian, had killed the Nesmith family for their team of horses. At their trial, Albert J. Fountain, William L. Rynerson, and S. B. Newcomb assisted District Attorney E. C. Wade for the prosecution—"an array of legal talent seldom seen on one side of a criminal case in this Territory." Apodaca turned state's evidence and received a life sentence; Lara was convicted of first degree murder by a jury composed of eleven Hispanos and one Anglo and was hanged April 30 at Las Cruces.[51]

Three days before the execution, Lara made the startling announcement that Pat Coghlan had offered him $1,000 to kill the former soldier. According to Lara, Coghlan complained that Nesmith was trying to jump Coghlan's spread at Three Rivers. News of Lara's confession was immediately relayed to Coghlan at Tularosa, who, making a rapid trip to Las Cruces to confront his accuser, arrived the morning of the execution. Four hours before he was to be hanged, Lara failed to identify Coghlan from a line-up of twenty-five men. Lara was escorted to the scaffold later that afternoon by Fountain and two companies of militia and executed before a crowd of about 1,200 people. His partner, Maximo Apodaca, later jumped from the fourth tier of cells in the Santa Fe penitentiary, a suicide. "The murder of Nesmith," wrote the editor of the local Las Cruces paper, "is now avenged."[52]

Although cattlemen were few in numbers among California veterans, their contributions to the development of the cattle industry in New Mexico were indeed significant. They labored hard to protect their herds and expended large sums of money to import blooded stock to improve local breeds. Men such as Robert V. Newsham, Richard Hudson, Benjamin E. Davies, and William L. Rynerson took the lead in establishing stockmen's associations and were known during their own era as substantial cattlemen. Other men, such as George W. Nesmith and Albert J. Fountain, whose lives ended tragically, contributed their experiences of violence and cattle rustling to the lore of the western cattle industry. And in implementing the postwar law-and-order campaign, Fountain and his "legalized" band of vigilantes fell back on lessons and techniques learned in the army while fighting Navajos and Apaches, the most important being that "might makes right."

Above left: Gen. James H. Carleton, c. 1866, commander of the California Column. (Courtesy Museum of New Mexico.)

Above right: William L. Rynerson, prominent southern New Mexico lawyer and politician. (Courtesy Rio Grande Historical Collections, New Mexico State University Library.)

Left: Albert J. Fountain in his militia uniform. (Courtesy Rio Grande Historical Collections, New Mexico State University Library.)

Capt. Emil Fritz, c. 1865–70,
sutler at Fort Stanton, N.M.,
and co-owner of the Lincoln
County mercantile firm of
Murphy and Company.
(Courtesy Museum of New
Mexico.)

Joseph F. Bennett, merchant,
politician, and civic leader in
Grant and Doña Ana counties.
(Courtesy Rio Grande Historical
Collections, New Mexico State
University Library.)

Above left: Robert V. Newsham, Grant County pioneer miner and merchant. (Courtesy Rio Grande Historical Collections, New Mexico State University Library.)

Above right: Benjamin E. Davies, Doña Ana County rancher and sheep man. (Courtesy Rio Grande Historical Collections, New Mexico State University Library.)

Left: William R. McCormick, former sergeant in the California volunteers and Las Cruces resident. (Courtesy Rio Grande Historical Collections, New Mexico State University Library.)

Camp Reamembers March 4th 1864
Dear mother Brother & Sisters I once more
attempt to write a few Lines to you I
received a Letter from Silas & Syntha
on the 20 of Last month I was pleased to
hear that you was all well my health
is very good at present our Company is
Doing videt Duty at Present Caring the
Government mail through arizona, wee are
Stationed 10 & 20 men at a Station about
75 miles apart, wee have to carry it boath
ways on the 5 & 20 of each month. wee are
in hopes of being Beleived in the coars
of this month. wee have ben in the Servis
30 months and have never ben in quarters
to exceed one month our inlistment is out
on the 16 of august next their is but 3 of
our company that has reinlisted in the
vetrons Some companys have nearly all
Reinlisted if wee have aforen war every
man in the california Colume is ready to
march in to mexico or any other Place if they

Letter written by Private William Chamberlin, First California Cavalry, while
on vedette duty in Arizona six months before mustering out of the service. (Courtesy Rio Grande Historical Collections, New Mexico State University Library.)

can get to fight the enemy of the U
united States whether rebels or foriners
the most of them think of going east
before they reinlist their has ben sow
much humbug with the california troops
in new mexico & arizona they are very much
Dissatisfide theis is talk of the troops being
Discharged in the teritory the majority
of them wants to be taken back to Cal
by the Goverment as their milage would
not Pay one fourth of their expences back
if I am Discharged here I think I Shall
try my fortune in the mines of arizona
I think in time they will equal California
or nevado Tritory in Gold Silver copper
if the indians are Subdued this Sum
mer Sow that Small Parties can travel
their will be acomdabble Prospecting
Don next winter in our Last winter Scouts
after the indians wee Discoverd Gold Silver
and Copper Leads that have the apperance
of being very rich and extensive the indians
are Still very troublesom wee had afight
with them on the 26 of Last month which

Lasted for nearly one hour wee killed
13 and captured a mexican woman that
the indians have had a prisone for 15 years
wee Get Some good information from his
conscerning the apachees Shee Says they intend
to attack this camp with a force of 300 warriors
they think that they can Soon kill all the
white men that is in their country they are
Detirmind to fight as Long as they have one
man Left. wee have had very Little nuse
from the east for the Last 3 months I Suppose
their has ben but Little Don this winter
~~in the way of crushing the rebellion~~
it Seems that the northern traitors and cowards
at home are worse than the rebbels in arms
I Shall be Pleasid to Say ~~that~~ I have served
my contry for 3 years that I am willing to Serve
for 3 years more or untill every traitor to this
goverment is exterminated what has St
Lawrence County Dan in the way of furnish
troops to Protect the goverment I have never
Seen any acount of any troops from their
it Seems that N Y is far behind in
Raising his quota of troops is it because

84

they are traitors or cowards the State of
New York Should be the first to uphold
and protect the government every man
that is for the union Should uphold
the administration and the war as Long as
their is an armed fo against the union
Now more this time Pleas excuse all mistaks
From Wm C
Direct to Lascruses ..N..M
Co.. C.. 1st Cav Cal vol

Lincoln, N.M., c. 1885, was the principal settlement in the Lincoln County War. (Courtesy Museum of New Mexico.)

Facing page, top: Fort Union, c. 1870, where many ex-soldiers worked as artisans and laborers. (Courtesy Museum of New Mexico)

Facing page, bottom: Fort Stanton, c. 1885. California veterans stationed here later returned to ranch and farm in the vicinity. (Courtesy Museum of New Mexico.)

East side of Hudson's Hot Springs, 1888, with Mary and Richard Hudson second and third from the left. (Courtesy John Harlan Collection, Silver City Museum.)

Thomas V. Keam's Trading Post, Arizona. (Courtesy School of American Research Collections in the Museum of New Mexico.)

Las Cruces, N.M., c. 1900, became the residence of many California volunteers after the Civil War. (Courtesy Rio Grande Historical Collections, New Mexico State University Library.)

Next three pages: William Chamberlin in this letter to his family complains of being discharged in New Mexico rather than in California. He subsequently settled in Grant County, became one of its leading citizens, and died there in 1890. (Courtesy Rio Grande Historical Collections, New Mexico State University Library.)

Lascrusus N M Sept 21th 1864

Dear Mother I once more take the Pleasure
of writin a few Lines to you, it has ben
Some time Since I have weate to you
and nearly as Long Since I have reveived
a Letter from any one, I have good health
at Peerent the only thing I can beag of is good health
when I Last weate I Supposed the troops
would be taken back to california to be
Dischaiged, but in Stid of being ordeeb
back to california wee was kep in the feal
untill the 20 of August when wee was
ordeeb to this Plase to be Dischaeged
having Served our contey for 3 years
faithfuly in time of need, wee have ben
Dischaeged here without transpotation
and without rations our transpotation and
rations money would not by Provision
a nough to tak a monhaf way back to
california, this is rather haed usage to Serve
men that have Given 3 years for their
contey General Carlton the commander
of this Department isueb an ordee to all
of the quaetemastees Prohibiting them from
isuing or Selling rations to any Dischaeged
Soldier he Says his reason is to have them

Reinlist all of the men that could
By a horse to get out of the contey with
has Left, Some Bought oxen and Some
Jacks all of which they had to Pay three
times what they war worth I have ben trying
to By a team but cant find any to By
it has ben my intintion to Soldier as
Long as this Rebllion Lasted but I have got
a nough of this out fit if I Soldier any
more it must be whare a man is thought
as much of as a Beute at Least, I am for the
union as Strong as ever but if it is all Like
this Department She will have to Stand a
hard old Racky the first of Last august the
Rebbels commenced coming to this tritory
from teas, they ware fed from our comisaus
and had escorts furnished and treated Like
Lords by our officers and get imploynent
when our own Discharged Soldiers cant
I intend to Stop here untill Spring as the
winter is low clost at hand, and pe haps Longe
every thing out Side of the goverment
is very Scarce flour is worth 15 cts pr Pound
Sugar 75 coffe 125 tea 400 as for Butter their
is non this Letter must Do for all this
time I want all to write and Let mee know
all a bout times and who is in the war

I received a St Lawrence Republican Some
time ago from Amanda or caroline I
have forgaton which I Should Like to
have it aftn I am for old Abe for
four yeaes more Silas how are you
on that question

write mee all the news you now of
my Love to all
I will try to Do better in writing to you
after this, aftr this Direct your Lettes

to Laseruses New Mexico
omit the Soldier adress

From Wm C

Mesilla, N.M., c. 1890, which was the site of the Mesilla riot in 1871. (Courtesy Rio Grande Historical Collections, New Mexico State University Library.)

White Oaks, N.M. c. 1892, and it was here that California veteran John V. Winters discovered gold in 1879 leading to a gold rush. (Courtesy Rio Grande Historical Collections, New Mexico State University Library.)

Elizabethtown, N.M., 1899, which was site of a gold rush in 1867. (Courtesy Museum of New Mexico.)

Silver City, N.M., 1883, was the mining and commercial center for southwestern New Mexico. (Courtesy John Harlan Collection, Silver City Museum.)

American Mine, Nogal, N.M., owned in the 1880s by California veteran William Gill. (Courtesy Rio Grande Historical Collections, New Mexico State University Library.)

Stephenson-Bennett mine and mill, Organ Mountains, N.M., near the turn of the century. (Courtesy Rio Grande Historical Collections, New Mexico State University Library.)

Modoc mine and mill, Organ Mountains, N.M., near the turn of the century. (Courtesy Rio Grande Historical Collections, New Mexico State University Library.)

6

Land, Water, and Violence

In his famous 1893 essay, historian Frederick Jackson Turner postulated that free land on the western edge of settlement served as a magnet to draw American pioneers westward across the face of the continent. But expansion into the Far West was not an orderly movement from east to west. Miners who rushed West to extract mineral wealth from the California Sierras in 1849 and the early 1850s moved eastward once again in subsequent years to populate raw mining camps in the Colorado Rockies, the Montana and Idaho high country, and the hills and mountains of Arizona. Moreover, California volunteers, under military orders and to prevent national disunity, traveled from west to east adding their numbers to the growing Anglo population in a predominantly Hispanic society. It was not "free land" they were seeking, but once in the territory the practiced eyes of farmers-turned-soldiers discerned fertile valleys and rich soil. When their enlistments were up, many stayed to farm the land.

Farmers and farm laborers made up the largest single category of California veterans who remained in the territory in 1870. Yet men who listed their occupations as merchant, lawyer, or artisan also took up farming, filing for agricultural land under one of several land laws operating in post-Civil War America. Like other westerners, California veterans struggled to acquire and to hold land and water rights, and in doing so they precipitated violent encounters with men who contested their holdings.

Several ex-soldiers conformed to Jefferson's ideal of the small farmer who labors on a plot of land with wife and children to produce a satisfactory living. Others barely eked out an income from the soil, while still others lived in relative affluence, speculating in land and supplementing incomes from other sources.

HOMESTEADING THE FARMS

Few California veterans between 1865 and 1885 applied for homesteads under the act of 1862, which allowed adult citizens and individuals seeking citizenship to acquire title to 160 acres of public domain. Fifteen volunteers applied for homesteads in Lincoln County, six in Grant, four in Doña Ana, three in Socorro, two in Santa Fe, and two in San Miguel counties. Of the thirty-two applications for homesteads, thirteen were canceled or relinquished, and nineteen were patented (two being acquired under the commutation clause). The 59 percent of homesteads actually patented by the veterans about equals the New Mexico average of 55 percent for patented homesteads of all entries.[1] Not a single California veteran among the five who filed in the southern counties under the Timber Culture Act and the seven who filed under the Desert Land Act received a final patent.[2] Land could be acquired, of course, by outright purchase, and the deed books are filled with land transactions of individuals seeking either to build up their holdings or to dispose of property for speculative or other purposes.

The largest number of homesteads entered by California veterans was located in Lincoln County, but several ex-soldiers in Grant County tilled the soil without acquiring homesteads. The Rio Mimbres Valley, with its rich soil and life-giving water, was farmed extensively in the 1870s. Extolled as the principal agricultural region in the county, farmers planted corn, wheat, barley, and potatoes; the corn and potato crops produced in 1875 were described as superior to any grown in New Mexico.[3]

Rio Mimbres, located where the highway crossed the river, had existed since the Overland Mail was established in 1857. In 1870 at least fourteen California veterans resided in or near the town. John D. Gibbins was the town's blacksmith, Wilson G. Holman the butcher, James G. Crittenden the sheriff, and Benjamin F. Harrover and Reece Bulger were carpenters. The town's three mercantile establishments were operated by former California soldiers: Robert V. Newsham, Marshall St. John, and Sydney M. Webb, who was also the town's postmaster. William B. Morgan, justice of the peace for the community, clerked in Webb's store, while John E. Oliphant performed duties as a deputy collector of customs. Three were farmers—Richard Mawson, Leonidas V. Steele, and Andrew M. Herron—and one, Jason Covey, a farm laborer.[4]

None of the above three farmers entered homestead applications, although in 1870 forty-six-year-old Andrew Herron claimed ownership to 160 acres of land, estimating the value of his farm at $1,000. His household consisted of his wife Manuela and four Hispanic farm laborers, three of whom were teen-agers. In September 1870 Herron mortgaged his corn crop to the merchant Webb as security on a loan for $500.[5]

By 1876 the town of Rio Mimbres had been abandoned, reportedly because its water supply increasingly was being diverted to irrigate neighboring farms. At the same time, San Lorenzo on the Upper Mimbres witnessed steady growth as an agricultural area; by 1876 its population numbered about five hundred people, including two California veterans, George O. Perrault and David Stitzel, who farmed on lands adjacent to the town.[6] Each claimed 160 acres under the Homestead Act, but Perrault was the more productive farmer. He valued his farm in 1880 at $3,000, his livestock at $600, and the value of all farm production in 1879 at $6,445. Perrault subsequently moved to Hillsboro, where he became a well-known merchant, but he continued to own land in the San Lorenzo district. His property remained in Perrault's family long after his death in 1898.[7] Many California veterans, such as Perrault, became successful farmers, but agriculture in New Mexico made few advances until the twentieth century when new irrigation projects were initiated and dry farming techniques perfected.

HOT SPRINGS RANCH AND HOTEL—
A HAVEN FOR PLEASURE SEEKERS

One of the most elaborate economic enterprises managed by a California veteran in Grant County was the Hot Springs Ranch and Hotel, operated by Richard Hudson, twenty-five miles southeast of Silver City. An Englishman by birth, Hudson acquired extensive real estate and mining properties in the county and became one of its most respected citizens.

In the early seventies Hudson lived with his wife Mary in Silver City, where he was proprietor of the Legal Tender Livery Stable and held the government forage contract for Fort Bayard. In 1872 Hudson and his father-in-law, Isaac N. Stevens, purchased half interest in the 160-acre Hot Springs Ranch from D. B. Lacy for $1,500. That same year, Hudson filed a homestead claim on lands adjacent to the ranch. By 1874 Hudson and Stevens had bought Lacy's remaining half interest in the old resort for $4,000, and in April Hudson temporarily moved his family to the Springs to make needed repairs on the buildings. He moved there permanently in 1876 to take over its management.[8]

The hotel catered to invalids and pleasure seekers. A prospectus issued by Hudson and Stevens in 1874 stated that invalids had long known the healing power of the resort's waters, which cured all chronic diseases, mercurial affections of the throat, skin or bones, blotches, debility, dizziness, nervousness, coughs, and indisposition.[9] In August 1877 Hudson acquired Stevens's one-half interest in the resort at public auction for $1,530 and in succeeding years undertook major additions to the resort. By 1885 the Hot Springs Hotel was a haven for pleasure seekers, offering elegant rooms for bathing and sleeping, in addition to a first-class bar and billiard room. Tall shade trees, well-kept gardens, sparkling fountains, and fragrant flowers provided a relaxing atmosphere for vacationers.[10] Hudson expanded his land holdings around the resort by claiming 160 acres under the Timber Culture Act in 1879 and 320 acres under the Desert Land Act in 1883, but neither claim was patented. He had planned to run water to his desert claim from the Hot Springs through pipes, though the claim was six miles from the springs.[11]

Hudson's cattle grazed on the surrounding countryside, and farm crops were raised on five acres of improved land near the hotel. In 1880 he valued his farm land at $5,000, his farm machinery at $600, and the total value of farm products raised in the preceding twelve months, including fruit and garden produce, at $2,200. By 1885 Hudson was the largest taxpayer among the California veterans living in Grant County.[12]

LINCOLN COUNTY

In the two decades following the Civil War, numerous farmers and homesteaders looked for promising agricultural land in gigantic Lincoln County, which sprawled in the southeast corner of the territory. Among the twenty-three California veterans who lived in Lincoln County in 1870, eight listed their occupations as farmer. Five of these eight had served at Fort Stanton in A Company, Fifth California Infantry, during the war.[13] Several other veterans listed their occupations as something other than farmer, yet settled and farmed lands along river banks in Lincoln County's fertile valleys.

A handful of ex-soldiers in Lincoln County, including Andrew Wilson, Wesley Fields, and John Walters, lived on homesteads in Tularosa Canyon and became embroiled in disputes over water allocation with the predominantly Hispanic townspeople of Tularosa. Ohio-born Andrew Wilson and his wife Natividad Durán farmed eighty acres of improved land, on which they raised corn and wheat. In 1880 the Wilsons estimated the value of their farm at $6,000 and of all farm production the preceding year at $2,000. In 1875 Wilson discovered copper on his ranch and worked the mine for several years. The Wilsons lived on this property with their four children until 1905. During these years, Andrew took an active role in county affairs. He was elected county commissioner on at least one occasion and frequently served on jury duty. In 1905 the Wilsons left the canyon and moved to the town of Tularosa.[14]

The estimated value of the 160-acre farm of John and Alvina Walters on the Tularosa, including farm machinery, livestock, and farm produce in 1880 was $1,390. In addition, John ran some four hundred head of cattle at Seven Rivers.[15] His neighbor in the valley, Indiana-born Wesley Fields, claimed 160 acres of land in 1875. His improvements were two log cabins, one slab shed, 15 fruit trees, 2,000 yards of irrigating ditches, and 45 acres under cultivation. Although Fields retained ownership to this land until 1890, he and his young wife Macaria García, along with his three children, were listed in the 1880 census as living in Precinct 3, which centered on Dowlin's Mill on the Ruidoso. The estimated value of his ranch, farm machinery, livestock, and farm production was $5,240 in 1880.[16]

Wesley Fields and Henry C. Brown had served together—both as privates—in Company A, and after the war they became neighbors, residing in the valleys of the Tularosa and Ruidoso rivers. In 1867 Brown, known as "Crooks" to his friends, worked as a cook for Emil Fritz and Lawrence G. Murphy, post traders at Fort Stanton. He married Juana Gurule the following year, and by 1875 "Crooks" and his wife were living on a farm a few miles east of Blazer's Mill close to the South Fork on the Tularosa, where they had thirty-five acres under cultivation.[17]

Because the Brown property was included within the Mescalero Reservation when its boundaries were expanded in 1875, the Mescalero agent purchased Henry and Juana Brown's farm and improvements in 1876 to $731.50, causing them to enter a new homestead on the Ruidoso near Dowlin's Mill.[18] In 1880 he valued his farm, farm machinery, and livestock at $1,175 and his farm produce for the preceding year at $750.[19] Juana died in 1878 or 1879, and shortly thereafter Brown was married by a justice of the peace to Margarita Estrada at the house of a former comrade, William "Billy" Gill.

Brown had no children by either of his wives, but he and Margarita adopted a ten-year-old boy. The former California soldier lived most of his adulthood in New Mexico, but late in life he returned to the West Coast, where he died in 1908 at the Old Soldiers' Home in Los Angeles.[20]

According to the agricultural census for Lincoln County, several California veterans made reasonably good livings from tilling the soil and raising livestock. In 1870 the largest agricultural producer among the veterans in that county was thirty-six-year-old Frederick A. Smith, who on eighty acres of improved land raised 40 bushels of wheat, 650 bushels of corn, 100 bushels of barley, and 100 bushels of oats, for an estimated value of $1,200. The value of all farm production for the veterans ranged from Smith's $1,200 to $230 recorded for George W. Peppin, who on twenty acres of improved land raised twenty bushels of oats.[21] In 1880 the average value per farm in New Mexico was $1,091, although two Lincoln County veterans, Andrew Wilson and Wesley Fields, owned farms in that year valued at $6,000 and $4,000, respectively, values not reached by the majority of New Mexico's farms until the twentieth century.[22]

THE TULAROSA DITCH WAR

Quarrels over control of water and irrigation systems in Lincoln County led to the Tularosa Ditch War, which erupted in the 1870s and periodically flared anew in subsequent years. The village of Tularosa, situated at the mouth of Tularosa Canyon, had been settled by Hispanos from Doña Ana County in 1862. The colonists used water from the Tularosa River, originating from large springs far up the canyon, to irrigate small farms adjacent to the village. The river provided sufficient water until Anglo settlers established ranches up the canyon and diverted water for their crops.[23]

The California veterans who homesteaded in the canyon— Andrew Wilson, Wesley Fields, and John Walters—contributed to the friction between villagers and canyon dwellers. Serious trouble flared in May 1873 when Tularosa residents quickly destroyed dams built across the river by Andrew Wilson and other farmers. The villagers mounted a second attack on the canyon dwellers after Wilson and his neighbors repaired the dams.

Upon receiving a request for aid, Capt. C. H. McKibbin, commander at Fort Stanton, sent a detachment of five men to the canyon. The soldiers, in dispersing the dam-breakers, became embroiled in the confrontation. Violence erupted, and one Hispano was killed. The small detachment was forced to retreat to Blazer's Mill where, joined by twelve or fourteen Anglos, they were surrounded and fired upon by an angry Hispanic crowd. When McKibbin arrived with reinforcements, the Hispanos dispersed. In June of the following year, the Doña Ana grand jury issued a number of indictments as a result of quarrels over Tularosa water, but the troubles continued.[24]

In the spring of 1877 residents of Tularosa and settlers in the canyon reached an agreement allowing the Hispanos to build a ditch from the head spring of Tularosa River to the village plaza. The ditch was to be constructed in a manner that would not impede or reduce volume in the ditches maintained by canyon dwellers, who, in addition, were ensured use of water in the new ditch to irrigate their lands. If canyon dwellers expected that this accord would solve the villagers' water problems without decreasing their own supply of water, they were sadly disappointed.[25] When John S. Crouch, editor of the *Mesilla Valley Independent*, visited Tularosa in July 1877, he found that crops were light because of scarcity of water. He noted that "if reservoirs were erected at some of the many convenient places that can be found for such works along the stream, and in the vicinity of the town of Tulerosa [sic], most of the water that is now wasted could be saved, and it would be sufficient to irrigate and make crops on four times the amount of land now under cultivation."[26]

Two years later the problem remained the same; insufficient water was reaching the town of Tularosa to irrigate crops. The *Mesilla Valley Independent* continued to argue that there was plenty of water in the river if people would observe economy and build a system of reservoirs; such comments failed to comfort Tularosa residents who found themselves without drinking water during parts of May.[27] Violence erupted the following year in May 1880 when canyon residents again interrupted the flow of water. This caused village officers to arrest two men, sentencing them to work fifteen days on the town *acequia*. Canyon dwellers retaliated by securing the arrest of the constable and posse making the first arrests.[28]

The heightened tensions made for inevitable bloodshed, which occurred in 1881 on the James West ranch, five miles above Tularosa. A posse from Tularosa was sent to the ranch to arrest West's employees for increasing the volume of water taken from the river. Led by Deputy Sheriff Cruz Padilla, the four-man posse met resistance, and in the ensuing gun battle all four were killed.

The next day a party of forty to fifty Hispanos approached Blazer's Mill, demanding the surrender of the participants. When they learned that the men had already surrendered to Lincoln County authorities, the Hispanos contented themselves with destroying West's flood gates and robbing his house. Over 220 court cases resulted from this encounter, though most, if not all, were eventually dismissed. The water problem, though, was not solved, and litigation over allocation of Tularosa River water continued into the twentieth century.[29]

THE RICH MESILLA VALLEY

One of the richest agricultural regions in the territory was Mesilla Valley—located in Doña Ana County and noted for its orchards, vineyards, and production of wheat, corn, and barley. Four veterans of the California Column who lived in Doña Ana County listed their occupations in 1870 as farmers: David Wood of Las Cruces, Robert Taylor of Tortugas, Henry C. Haring of Doña Ana, and Felix Leibold of Rio Palomas. Their farms were small affairs in 1870. Wood and Taylor each worked twenty acres of improved land, and Haring worked forty acres. Census records show that the cash value of the Wood farm was $225, of the Taylor farm $500, and of the Haring farm $600. Leibold simply listed the value of his real estate at $200. John D. Barncastle, merchant in the town of Doña Ana, also farmed on a small scale in 1870, valuing his fifteen acres of improved land at $1,000.[30]

BARNCASTLE'S VINEYARDS

The Barncastle name has been prominent in Doña Ana County since John D. Barncastle first settled in the small town of Doña Ana after mustering out of the service as sergeant in Company E, Fifth California Infantry. In time he became one of the prominent agriculturalists in the territory, one of the largest taxpayers in the county, and the principal merchant in the town of Doña Ana. His commercial enterprises were extensive: a merchandising store, a flouring mill, and a well-developed farm. By 1880 he owned 700 acres of land and valued his farm at $5,000, farm machinery at $100, and livestock at $400. He had spent $550 on fencing in 1879 and had produced farm crops valued at $6,500.[31]

Barncastle's vineyards were heralded in the press as being among the finest in the territory. Occasionally he shipped barrels of wine to Santa Fe, but for the most part his wine was eagerly consumed by the local populace. Profits for the wine maker were high; in an interview Barncastle reported that the vintage of 1876, amounting to ninety barrels, had been sold for $45 per barrel with the purchaser returning the barrel. Expenses amounted to a mere $258, which left him with a net profit of $3,792 on ten acres of vineyards. Like other pioneer farmers, Barncastle believed in experimenting with new crops, and he was among the first in the valley to plant pecan and pomegranate trees and to experiment with raising tea.[32]

Adjacent to Barncastle's farm was a tract of land he rented to soldiers at Fort Selden for a company garden. In addition, Barncastle sold a large section of his land in the fall of 1884 to representatives of the Shalam Colony to help them launch their experiment in communal living.[33] Barncastle was clearly Doña Ana's "leading citizen." One correspondent provided the following picture of Barncastle's commercial enterprise:

The outbuildings surrounding the Barncastle residence are models of neatness and adaptability to their several purposes. A steam flouring mill, driven by a fifteen horse power engine, wine presses, stills, and the most improved farming implements, are seen on every side; while in a quiet corner modestly hides a new hay-bailer, the invention of the proprietor himself.[34]

DISPUTES OVER TITLES

Although several California veterans established successful farms in New Mexico at the end of the Civil War, the real invasion of the territory by Anglo farmers came after the railroads linked New Mexico with eastern farming states between 1879 and 1882. In 1870, however, much developed agricultural land lay in the northern counties of Santa Fe, San Miguel, Mora, Colfax, Santa Ana, Rio Arriba, and Taos, but few of the former California soldiers elected to farm in these northern regions. Mathias Heck was the only California veteran in the 1870 census for Colfax County whose occupation was listed as farmer. The census for that year indicated only that six veterans labored on other men's farms in San Miguel County. In general, settlement patterns for California veterans support the contention that confusion over titles to Spanish and Mexican land grants adversely affected economic enterprise and immigration into the territory. The California soldiers, at least, established their farms in regions generally unencumbered by such grants.[35]

Certainly dissension over land and water rights has been a persistent theme in New Mexico's history, and violence frequently erupted when peaceful means failed to satisfy disputants. Not surprisingly, several men from the old California Column—in addition to the Tularosa Canyon dwellers—were involved in bitter disputes over titles to land and water. John Townsend, for example, owned a plot of land near Tesuque in Santa Fe County that was also claimed by a Hispano, who began to plow and work the land despite Townsend's objections. Although Townsend had a reputation for being a quiet man and a good citizen, working at various times as cashier, teacher, Indian interpreter, and bookkeeper, he was hauled into court after ordering the Hispano off his property and forced to give bonds to keep the peace.[36]

A more serious dispute, because it involved an entire community, occurred in Doña Ana County between the residents of Mesilla and William L. Rynerson. Prior to American occupation of the Southwest, the Mexican government had granted to the town of Mesilla some two leagues of land to be used for pasture and woodlands. Following the War with Mexico, the United States Congress established the office of surveyor general to investigate the validity of all lands granted to individuals and to communities by the Spanish and Mexican governments. These investigations were often lengthy affairs complicated by grasping lawyers who found lucrative practices in helping clients establish title to their lands. The community land grant to the town of Mesilla was still unconfirmed in 1874, although Surveyor-General James K. Proudfit had investigated the claim and had forwarded a favorable report to Washington.[37]

Like other territorial lawyers, Rynerson saw an opportunity for personal gain in the confusion surrounding land titles. In February 1874 he staked out 160 acres as a preemptor, declaring that the community grant had been defective. Several days later the enraged residents of Mesilla physically ejected Rynerson when he refused to vacate their land. Rynerson then entered suit in district court to establish his title and to collect damages from his assailants.[38]

Rynerson's suit against the citizens of Mesilla was tried in Grant County in December 1874. Acting as his own attorney, he testified that after making improvements and residing on the claim for twenty days he had been ejected by the defendants. He demanded clear title to the land in addition to damages. The defendants, represented by attorney Albert J. Fountain, had cause to rejoice when after ten minutes of deliberation the jury rendered a verdict in their favor.[39]

As an attorney, Rynerson occasionally defended in court a

client's title to land while continuing to defend his own holdings against outside challengers. His desert land entry made in 1884 upon lands in Tularosa Canyon was challenged the following year by California veteran Henry C. Brown, who was joined by William S. Lewis and Almira Tucker. They claimed that the land had been farmed without irrigation for the previous twelve years and consequently could not be classified as desert land. Brown claimed that he had a house on this land, was living there with his family, and had improved a portion of it while preparing an entry under the Homestead Act. When he admitted in a public hearing that he had taken up other parcels of land in different places, disposing of them for money, officials questioned the sincerity of his intentions. Further evidence presented at the hearing supported Rynerson's contention that crops could not be raised profitably without irrigation, and the land office decided the case in Rynerson's favor.[40]

THE MAXWELL LAND GRANT

The most celebrated and prolonged land dispute in post-Civil War New Mexico was the Maxwell Land Grant controversy, which periodically erupted into violence between 1875 and 1893. The English-Dutch combine that had acquired the nearly two million acre grant in the early seventies met with resistance when it attempted to eject farmers, ranchers, and miners who claimed title to the land by possession. The giant grant extended across New Mexico's northern border, and in 1888 violence rocked Stonewall Valley in the Colorado portion of the grant, leaving dead ex-California soldier Richard D. Russell.[41]

Russell and his friend, Joseph A. DeHague, had mustered out of the California volunteers at Fort Union at the close of the war. Many of the discharged soldiers settled and farmed in the fertile valleys surrounding Fort Union, finding a ready market for grain and forage at the post. Russell and DeHague, though, went to Tecolote, a resting spot on the Santa Fe Trail about ten miles south of Las Vegas, where they established a trading post, purchasing anything that neighboring Indians had to sell and trading corn bought cheaply from Hispanos to the Indians for cattle. When DeHague absconded with the firm's profits, Russell and his wife sold the trading post and migrated to Colorado in 1871, where they became the first to settle in Stonewall Valley.[42]

Other pioneers quickly joined Marian and Richard Russell in Stonewall Valley, where he established a store, sawmill, and planing mill, and served as the local postmaster. In later years the Maxwell Land Company attempted to come to terms with the ranchers and farmers who had settled on company property, and in 1888 the company paid Russell $1,500 for the improvements that he and his wife had made on their land as well as twenty dollars a head for their cattle.[43] Apparently, however, Russell reconsidered his decision to leave the valley, siding with those settlers who resisted eviction. Russell was mortally wounded on August 24, 1888, in a confrontation with Maxwell agents, and died at age forty-nine—truly one of the best and most gallant of the California Column, still young in body and spirit—leaving behind a strong-willed wife, three daughters, and four sons.[44]

THE BRAZITO GRANT

The Spanish and Mexican land grant problem, which complicated land ownership and ensnarled titles in decades of litigation, affected the lives of most California veterans only indirectly. However, two of the ex-troopers, Lt. James A. Zabriskie and Capt. Albert H. French, were intimately linked with the history of one grant, the famed Brazito Land Grant located in Doña Ana County south of Las Cruces. The two soldiers had been stationed in the vicinity of El Paso, Texas, during the Civil War, where they met and later married daughters of Hugh Stephenson, the lieutenant to Adelaide and the captain to Benancia.[45]

Their father-in-law had acquired ownership to the northern two-thirds of the Brazito Grant in 1851, and it was on his property that the military subsequently constructed Fort Fillmore. When the Civil War broke out, Stephenson left his 920-acre

Concordia Ranch (east of the Rio Grande, where present-day El Paso is located) and went to live across the river in Mexico. He remained there throughout the war, refusing General Carleton's request to return to the United States. Consequently his considerable land holdings, including the Concordia Ranch and the 21,000-acre Brazito Grant, were confiscated by Union officials, who accused Stephenson of aiding and abetting the enemy.[46]

The two California officers, however, were instrumental in protecting the Stephenson property. Two libel cases were filed against their father-in-law's property in the Third Judicial District Court at Mesilla in 1865, one against the Concordia Ranch and the other against the Brazito Grant. At the November term of court, James A. and Adelaide Zabriskie, Albert H. and Benancia French, and other relatives of Stephenson contested the confiscation, denying that Stephenson had participated in the rebellion and introducing evidence to show that on July 22, 1859 Stephenson, "in consideration of love and affection," had deeded to his children, Albert, Hugh Jr., Margaret, Leonor, Nancy (Benancia), and Adelaide, the Concordia and Brazito properties.[47]

Like so many confiscation cases filed in the territory, the libels against Stephenson were dismissed in court, although the claimants were required to pay all court costs. James and Adelaide Zabriskie and Albert and Benancia French sold their interests in the Brazito Grant on May 20, 1868. The Zabriskies received $3,225.61 for their one-sixth interest and the Frenches $7,764.70 for their one-sixth interest. The two families stipulated in their deeds of conveyance that they preserved for themselves claims against the United States government for damages sustained on the Fort Fillmore property.[48]

A native of Massachusetts, Albert H. French settled in El Paso after the war where he became a government contractor and a member of the Texas State Police. In 1865 he received contracts to supply the military post at Franklin, Texas, with fresh beef and to supply Fort Stanton with 250,000 pounds of corn. In later months he signed corn and beef contracts for Forts Bayard, Selden, and Sumner. He also purchased at public auction James

Magoffin's property—old Fort Bliss—which had been seized by
Union officials during the war.[49] In later years, James A. Zabriskie,
on behalf of the Stephenson heirs, rented to the United States
government one hundred acres of the Concordia property on
which the new Fort Bliss was built.[50] Though heralded for his
military exploits, Albert H. French died in 1877 at age forty-one
in the State Hospital at Austin, Texas—a hospital for the insane.

James A. Zabriskie—a native of New Jersey—also settled in El
Paso and was appointed district attorney in June 1866. He served
until 1870 when he moved to Silver City, though he continued
to maintain a residence in El Paso. During the next several years,
Zabriskie practiced law in southern New Mexico and El Paso, and
was elected district attorney for the latter area in 1876. Surviving
the turmoil and bloodshed associated with El Paso's Salt War,
Zabriskie resigned as district attorney and moved to Tucson in
1878 to accept a position as a customs official. He was appointed
United States Attorney for Arizona in 1883 and remained a resident of Tucson until his death some years later.[51]

WATER FOR THE JORNADA DEL MUERTO

The arid Southwest lacked sufficient rainfall to support a large
agrarian population, and because of its scarcity, ranchers, farmers, and miners vigorously and sometimes violently competed to
acquire and then to hold their claims to water. Some ingenious
men, with physical strength to match their inventiveness, devised
local irrigation projects to bring water to relatively barren lands.
Such a man was Jack Swilling of Arizona, who gained long-lasting
fame for initiating an extensive irrigation project on the Salt River
in the vicinity of modern-day Phoenix.

Less well known in the annals of the Southwest is John Martin, who successfully sank a 164-foot well midway on the Jornada
del Muerto—thus providing much needed water to travelers on
the overland road between Santa Fe and Mesilla. Prior to Martin's success in locating water, travelers were compelled to carry
all necessary water for their animals and themselves when they

crossed the Jornada, a forbidding, waterless ninety mile stretch of road between Rincon and San Marcial.[52] Martin's accomplishments were extolled throughout the territory, and he became a widely-acclaimed, if short-lived, public figure.

"The King of the Jornada," as Martin was called in territorial newspapers, was born in Caledonia, New York, in 1829. After serving in the war against Mexico as a drummer boy, he went to California during the gold rush and enlisted in the California volunteers at the outbreak of the new war.[53] In a press interview, Martin said that he stayed in New Mexico at the war's end because he did not have enough money to return to California. Some suspected that his reason for staying was more a matter of the heart than of finances; shortly after leaving the service, he married Esther Catherine Wadsworth of Las Cruces. The couple then moved to Fort Selden, where Esther supervised the officers' meals and John built and managed a ferryboat to provide an easy means for crossing the Rio Grande.[54] He also became a government contractor, and in 1866 held contracts to supply fresh beef to Forts Cummings, McRae, and Selden.

In 1867 Martin went to Aleman, a resting spot midway on the Jornada. He found water there the following year. The army soon stationed a detachment of soldiers at Martin's place to protect the ranch and travelers from hostile Indians. At Aleman Jack and Esther operated a hotel, a stage station, a government forage agency, a post office, and a small cattle ranch, keeping about 200 head of cattle on nearby lands. Initially a hand pump was used to bring water to the surface of the famous well that Jack built, but in 1877 he hired two men to install a new-style windmill to provide power to operate the well. The windmill proved to be worthless, and Martin had to make do with the old hand pump.[55]

Territorial boosters, editors, politicians, and travelers who used Aleman's facilities believed that the Jornada Chief (Martin) deserved national recognition and suitable reward for having privately developed his desert oasis. Consequently in 1869 New Mexico's delegate to Congress introduced a bill to award Martin ten sections of land, but Congress turned a deaf ear. Nor did Congress respond to the request by area residents to purchase Martin's property so that the public could gain free access to water located there. Since Martin had expended considerable money and labor in sinking and maintaining his well, newspaper editors defended his right to charge for watering stock, but cattlemen and freight carriers disliked this extra expense.[56] The *Mesilla News*, however, stated that "if the California column [sic] had accomplished nothing more to benefit the territory, the fact that it brought Jack Martin to draw the sting from the Journey of Death would cause it to be held in grateful remembrance by every traveler in southern New Mexico."[57]

In 1876 Martin left Aleman to become proprietor of the Exchange Hotel in Santa Fe, though he retained ownership to his Jornada property. Less than eight months later, he died, apparently the victim of heart failure. Today Jack Martin's name is recalled with admiration among old-timers in the Mesilla Valley who speak in awe of his ability to sink a 164-foot well in the middle of the desert with primitive tools.[58]

7

Town Dwellers and Industries

In addition to work in farming and ranching, large numbers of California veterans settled and took jobs in towns. Collectively, the former soldiers exhibited such a wide range of talents that had they lived in a single community they would have provided most of the services needed for the town's survival. Several were dry goods merchants, liquor dealers, and retail grocers; others were butchers, blacksmiths, carpenters, stonemasons, clerks, and bookkeepers. Some built grist and flour mills, and still others operated hotels, saloons, stables, and stage services. There were a dozen or more teachers, attorneys, or journalists among the California veterans, as well as one physician and one man of the cloth.

Frontier merchants were among the most important members of the small communities that dotted New Mexico's countryside since they supplied residents with food, clothing, furniture, and luxuries that could not be produced locally. In 1870 eight California veterans recorded their occupations as dry goods or wholesale merchants and one—Richard Yeamans of Legal Tender fame—listed his as retail grocer.[1] Among the more industrious merchants in New Mexico was Louis Clark of Plaza Alcalde, a community of about one thousand inhabitants situated thirty-five miles north of Santa Fe in Rio Arriba County, located "in the midst of some of the finest farming and grazing lands in the territory."[2]

That the town prospered was attributed to the energies of one man, Louis Clark, a native of Poland who came to the village in

1865 as an impoverished discharged California volunteer. Through diligent labor, Clark amassed modest wealth, and by 1873 his premises contained four or five large granaries, some large storehouses, corrals, stables, cellars, ten or twelve well-furnished hotel rooms, and a well-stocked store. Clark gathered agricultural surplus from nearly forty miles around, dealing largely in grain, wool, and other products, receiving little money in exchange for the goods he provided from his store. He was also a government contractor, supplying Indian agencies at Abiquiu and Tierra Amarilla.[3] Early in Clark's mercantile career, he became active in political circles and in 1871 served on the Democratic territorial central committee. Four years later he switched loyalties and was elected Republican territorial senator from Rio Arriba County.[4]

Clark's life ended tragically in 1876, shortly after the adjournment of the legislature, when he was shot and killed by an assassin. A relative sitting on the Rio Arriba grand jury thwarted all attempts to have Miguel Maés, the alleged murderer, indicted and apparently Maés was never brought before a court of law. Administrators of the Clark estate, which included his wife Josefa Ortiz, continued to manage the hotel on the Clark property after his death.[5]

HOTELKEEPING AND THE BLOWUP
AT SAM ECKSTEIN'S SALOON

Hotels and boarding houses were also essential enterprises in frontier communities, offering travelers food and lodging as well as billiards and whiskey. Often they were located in isolated regions to fulfill needs peculiar to a given area or to capitalize on local assets. John D. Slocum at Slocum's Ranch and Jack Martin at Aleman each managed a hotel and forage agency mid-way on an overland highway where water was available for stock and travelers. The key to Richard Hudson's success as hotel owner was the natural hot springs on his property, which enticed invalid and pleasure-seeker alike to his premises. Numerous patrons also visited the bathing and hotel establishment at Las Vegas Hot Springs, six miles from the town of that name, operated for a short time in 1872 by California veteran Hugh D. Bullard.[6]

Among the best known hotels in southern New Mexico was the Corn Exchange in Mesilla, owned and operated in the 1870s by John and Augustina Castillo Davis. Born in Ireland, Davis came to the United States as a young lad and lived several years in Boston before making the trek to California in 1849. He came to New Mexico with the California Column in 1862 and engaged in stagecoaching after leaving the service. In 1874 he traded his property in Mesilla for Joseph F. Bennett's residence on the corner of the Mesilla plaza opposite the courthouse, where he subsequently opened the Corn Exchange Hotel. The premises included a bar and reading rooms, where the proprietor promised that "the strictest order will be enforced at all times, so that no gentleman shall be in any manner annoyed."[7]

The variety of food prepared for a Sunday dinner was sumptuous. The bill of fare for September 20, 1874 included the following:

Soups: Oyster, Ox-tail, vegetable
Fish: Catfish, mackeral, whitefish, boiled and broiled
Roasts: pig, beef, veal, lamb, ox-heart-stuffed
Boiled: mutton, beef, veal, beef ribs, venison
Side dishes: boned chicken, chicken pies, ham, boiled tongue, white sauce
Vegetables: green corn, cabbage, carrots, tomatoes, German rice, boiled onions, à la crème, string beans
Relishes: pickled tongue, cucumbers, sardines, pickled beets
Pastry: apple dumplings, custard pie, grape pie, peach pie, transparent pudding, tarts, cream puffs
Dessert: raisins, almonds, grapes, peaches, apples, filberts, melons

Occasionally Davis feasted his guests on fresh oysters, which came by stagecoach packed in ice.[8]

Christmas dinner, supervised by Augustina, was a feast for fifty invited bachelor-guests who had no families with whom to share the holiday. Chickens, turkeys, ducks, geese, rabbits, and pigs were the main bill of fare. After the guests had gorged themselves,

Augustina invited the unfortunates of Mesilla—men, women, and children too poor to celebrate Christmas—to partake of the abundance that remained. When John Davis died after a short illness in 1876, Augustina continued to manage the hotel.[9]

Far to the north in Colfax County, California veteran Chauncey N. Story became proprietor of the New National Hotel at Elizabethtown after the Moreno mining district had passed its peak period of production. He acquired a hotel license in May 1874 and apparently ran the Weinert Hotel, purchasing the National Hotel the following year and renaming it the New National Hotel. The advertisements that Story placed in the *Cimarron News* and *Press* assured sportsmen and tourists easy access to good hunting and fine trout fishing and offered health seekers a delightful climate and a "pleasant place to spend the summer months."[10]

Saloons were prominent in nearly all frontier communities, providing customers a place to relax, meet friends, play cards, enjoy a drink, and conduct business. Proprietors were well-known community figures who frequently ran for political office or participated in civic affairs. One of the most admired saloon keepers in the territory was Bavarian-born Samuel Eckstein, former corporal in the First California Infantry and well-known stage conductor. He opened a saloon and fresh fruit stand in Santa Fe in 1873 next door to Jacob Krummeck's Drug Store. Here he served English ale, porter, and other liquors as well as fresh fruits, fresh oysters, ham lunches, and rooms for card playing and reading.[11]

Eckstein closed his saloon in 1874 and returned as conductor for the southbound stage. He subsequently moved his family to Silver City, where in 1876 he leased the Bank Exchange Saloon in partnership with Charley Evans. Eckstein's establishment was shortly swept away by rampaging flood waters, which raced through Silver City's narrow streets, an event that frequently occurred following heavy summer rainfall in surrounding mountains.[12]

Eckstein opened a new saloon in Silver City in 1878, first door north of Wagner's Barber Shop, where he served "all kinds of Plain and Fancy Drinks." Calamity struck again four years later when fire destroyed a portion of the city's business district. Fire was a constant danger to frontier mining camps and few escaped at least partial destruction from this type of disaster. Civic leaders in Silver City had frequently discussed and occasionally implemented plans to organize a fire company, but at 2:00 A.M. on a Sunday in September the town was without a fire department. As flames spread rapidly and finally engulfed Wagner's barbershop, it was decided that the only means to check the fire was to blow up Eckstein's saloon with gunpowder.

After Sam removed his stock of liquor and other supplies, the old stand was "sent sky-high" and the fire was checked. While the fire was still blazing, angry residents hauled the old broken-down fire engine to the site of the conflagration and there denounced city fathers for failing to provide adequate fire protection. At the end of impromptu speeches, the engine was thrown into the flames.[13]

ROUGH TIMES FOR A PEACEFUL MAN

In Elizabethtown, Joseph W. Stinson had opened a saloon soon after mustering out of the California volunteers. By 1874 the thirty-six-year-old native of Maine had moved to Santa Fe where he leased the bar and billiard rooms of the Fonda Hotel on the southwest corner of the plaza. In later years Stinson opened saloons at various locations in the city, including the Broad Gauge Saloon on the east side of the plaza.[14] Though described as a peaceful man, Stinson—the son of a preacher—came close to losing his life in several shoot-outs similar to the affair with Wall Henderson. In June 1876 Stinson and Van Smith became embroiled in a drunken argument and in the duel which followed, Smith sustained two wounds and Stinson emerged unscathed. Three years later Stinson escaped unharmed after one Charley Henry fired six shots at him in Stinson's Santa Fe saloon.[15]

Stinson again was involved in near fatal gunplay on June 17, 1886. Future governor Miguel Otero later described the episode in his autobiography. Stinson, who had been drinking hard all night, exchanged angry words with a customer, William M. Mc-

Cann, around three o'clock on the morning of the shooting. Stinson ejected McCann from the saloon, but the latter returned thirty minutes later and the argument continued. In the course of their drunken conversation, Stinson reportedly asked McCann if he had not treated the younger man as a father, to which McCann answered that Stinson had always treated him decently. The next question kindled the violence. Otero reports the conversation as follows:

"Don't you think I would shoot any son of a bitch who would give me cause?" asked Stinson. "No," said McCann, "I think you a damn big coward."
"I'll just show you," exclaimed Stinson, and suiting his action to the word drew his revolver, raised it, and fired, the muzzle of the weapon being only about three feet from McCann's head. [McCann] fell backwards to the floor, and, as Stinson pocketed his smoking gun, said, "Joe, you damn son of a bitch, you have killed me. Come and shake hands!"[16]

Stinson shook hands and then fell asleep in a nearby chair. Fortunately McCann lived, but the ex-California soldier was indicted for assault and battery with intent to commit murder. The jury which returned a verdict of guilty and fined Stinson one hundred dollars received a scathing rebuke from the trial judge who felt that the punishment did not fit the crime.[17]

Violence was a near-universal characteristic of western saloons, and several California veterans in addition to Stinson owned saloons wherein violent encounters had ended in bloodshed. In 1875 Bernard McCall became proprietor of the Headquarter's Saloon in Mesilla. On the night of April 19, 1879 a gambler by the name of A. Lee Campbell was shot and killed there by Alexander Bull, son of Thomas J. Bull, one of the leaders in the local Democratic party. Under the influence of strong drink, Campbell and young Bull were playing poker when an argument ensued, resulting in the shooting that took Campbell's life. Bull was arrested but allowed to go free without bond. He was later indicted and tried in district court with District Attorney William L. Rynerson conducting the prosecution and Albert J. Fountain and three other lawyers maintaining the defense. Since no one witnessed the actual shooting, the jury acquitted Bull on a plea of self-defense.[18]

In the early 1880s former corporal Eli C. Priest established a popular saloon in the small railroad town of Rincon thirty miles north of Las Cruces. After his discharge from the volunteers, Priest had settled in Las Cruces, where in the space of five years he managed a hotel, meat market, saloon, brewery, and ferryboat. In 1869 he moved to Fort Quitman in Texas where he remained for the next four years. By September 1875, however, he was again running a meat market in Las Cruces and three years later was elected constable.[19]

Shortly after Priest moved to Rincon he was involved in a shooting fray that almost proved fatal to an innocent bystander as well as to one of the disputants. During a disturbance between an Anglo and some Hispanos outside the saloon, a heavy object was thrown through the door of Priest's establishment, hitting the proprietor on the head. Priest rushed outside; believing that he was about to be shot, he fired his revolver at one of the Hispanos. The bullet passed through the man's mouth and struck A. H. Cross, standing on the opposite side of the street.[20]

Priest was indicted for assault with intent to murder the Hispano, but in September 1882 a jury found him innocent of that charge, instead judging him guilty of simple assault and battery, for which he was fined $15 and costs. The former soldier lost little popularity as a result of this shoot-out; he was soon elected justice of the peace for his precinct and was described in the press as "a man of sterling worth . . . spoken well of by all his neighbors."[21]

Many of New Mexico's hotel and saloon proprietors violated territorial laws, particularly statutes that forbade gambling and which closed most businesses on Sunday. California veterans were no exception. In 1877 Joseph W. Stinson and John Martin each pleaded guilty to charges of permitting gaming; Sam Eckstein pleaded guilty to five counts of violating the Sunday law between 1878 and 1883. Richard Hudson, equally guilty, paid a ten dollar fine on five separate occasions between 1881 and 1883.[22]

NEW MEXICO'S PIONEER PRESS

Newspaper editors frequently spearheaded territorial improvement campaigns, such as the move to enact a Sunday law. Strong-willed and resilient, pioneer journalists were among the most influential men in a community. Most New Mexico editors combined newspaper editing with other occupations and went into journalism primarily for political advantages.[23] This was true for several California veterans who became editors and publishers in the two decades after the close of the war. Within the ranks of the California Column were men such as John F. Gould, Simon L. Snyder, William McMullen, George H. Pettis, and John C. Cremony, all of whom had worked on California or eastern newspapers prior to their enlistments. Although these men turned to occupations other than journalism after the war, five of their comrades played significant roles in the history of New Mexico's pioneer press.

The first to venture into the field was Henry W. Sherry, a native of Ireland, who moved to Tucson after his discharge and became associated with the *Arizonian*. By mid-July 1869 he was living in Las Cruces where he published the short-lived *Rio Grande Gazette*. He next worked for the *Las Vegas Gazette*, owned and edited by Louis Hommel, who had launched the paper in 1872.[24]

Sherry's journalistic career was as stormy and blustering as any frontier journalist's. In 1873 he was appointed acting editor of the *Las Vegas Gazette* while Hommel canvassed for subscriptions in southern counties. But Sherry had a falling out with Louis's wife, Trinidad Arias, who fired him. When Hommel returned to Las Vegas, he printed a warning to all employers "to look out and keep clear of that drunken vagabond and scoundrel, Henry W. Sherry, whom we can recommend as nothing else than a sot, a liar, and a thief, not worthy even of the appelations of human creatures."[25]

Sherry subsequently moved to Pinos Altos where he was elected justice of the peace and then to Silver City where he became school commissioner, city clerk, and member and officer in the

Good Templars, a society dedicated to sobriety and temperance. For a time he worked as foreman of the *Grant County Herald,* but in 1878 he purchased the press and materials of the old Las Cruces *Borderer,* which had suspended publication in 1875. Sherry published the first issue of the *Silver Record,* a twenty-four column weekly, on January 9, 1879, but four months later he retired from managing the paper to superintend Silver City's public school. When lack of funds forced the school to close, Sherry returned to journalism and began publishing in September 1880 the *Daily Telegram,* a small and short-lived newspaper.[26]

It appeared that Sherry labored under a multitude of problems, including the prolonged illness of his wife, which caused him to seek solace in liquor—despite his Good Templar membership. When his wife died in 1881, a fellow editor counseled him to "cast grief behind" and to start a new life. But Sherry's life remained troubled and turbulent; shortly thereafter he was brutally assaulted in the streets of Silver City by a school commissioner angered by a communication appearing in Sherry's *Telegram.* Penniless but not friendless, Sherry died of pneumonia in November 1882 and was buried by public subscription.[27]

Among important territorial newspapers in the seventies was the *Mesilla News,* launched by California veteran Lawrence Lapoint in September 1873. Ira M. Bond joined the firm as copublisher early in 1874 and in August of the same year the two partners started a Spanish weekly in Las Cruces, the *Eco del Rio Grande.* The firm of Bond and Lapoint was dissolved in 1875, although Bond continued as publisher and proprietor of the *Mesilla News* and Lapoint with the *Eco.* Lapoint was a journalist by choice, but like other members of his craft he discovered that income from his newspaper could not sustain a growing family. Consequently, Lapoint suspended publication of the *Eco* in 1878 and turned to other pursuits.[28]

In common with other California veterans, the career of Lawrence Lapoint was long and varied. Born in St. Louis of French and English-Canadian parents around 1837, he journeyed to California as a young man and enlisted as a musician in the California volunteers at the outbreak of war. He was discharged at Mesilla in November 1864, and the following year he and fellow comrade Milton D. Read jointly secured a license to manage a pawnbroker's shop in Doña Ana County. Although Read continued this enterprise, Lapoint soon began retailing liquor in Las Cruces, where he married Candelaria Lucero, the granddaughter of the poet Julian Tenorio, in October 1868. Three years later, Lapoint found employment on the *Borderer,* a pioneering paper launched in 1871 by Nehemiah V. Bennett in Las Cruces.[29]

Lapoint worked for Bennett for two years and then started his own newspaper. Under the editorship of Lapoint and Bond, the *Mesilla News* became a Republican paper, the chief rival and critic of the Democratic *Borderer.* Although Lapoint had been instrumental in organizing support for Horace Greeley in the 1872 presidential election, the territorial Republican establishment wooed him to their cause after he launched the *Mesilla News.* In September 1874 the press announced that Lawrence Lapoint had been appointed register and William L. Rynerson receiver of the new land office to be opened in Mesilla and implied that Stephen B. Elkins, New Mexico's delegate to Congress and a staunch Republican, had secured their appointments. Although Rynerson declined the appointment, Lapoint accepted; his tenure in office was brief and trouble-ridden. He had considerable difficulty securing proper materials from Santa Fe to carry on business of the land office, and he resigned as register late in 1875. It is possible that Lapoint's problems with the land office were politically induced by Republican leaders grown disenchanted with him after his refusal in the fall of 1875 to support Elkins's bid for reelection as delegate to Congress.[30]

Territorial newspapers rarely enjoyed large subscription lists in the seventies, and Lapoint struggled for approximately four years to increase circulation of the *Eco.* But the paper folded in 1878; the press was sold to A. H. Morehead of Silver City who planned to take it to Globe, Arizona. Lapoint then spent a short time as manager of a new bar opened by Augustina Davis in the Corn Exchange Hotel. When it was rumored that Lapoint was thinking of opening a brewery in Las Cruces, the editor of the *Mesilla Valley Independent*, with more than a bit of sarcasm, remarked that "Friend Lapoint is on the right track; men who cannot afford to subscribe for a newspaper can always find money to buy beer."[31]

In the spring of 1879, Lapoint opened a confectionary and bakery in Las Cruces and expanded his enterprise in later months to include the retailing of liquor and groceries. Lapoint's creditors, though, increased at a faster rate than his customers; he sold the store in the spring of 1882 and faced prosecution in the courts. Shortly after the district judge ordered Lapoint to pay his bills, amounting to over $850, the old soldier went prospecting in Doña Ana Mountains. There he helped locate—perhaps with tongue-in-cheek—the Ironical Mine.[32]

During the next several years, Lapoint worked in the stores of Aaron Schutz and Mariano Barela, staked a few claims in the Organ Mountains, began practicing law, and opened a new saloon in Las Cruces, which he said paid better than editing a newspaper. At age 65 Lapoint reentered the world of journalism, launching in 1902 the *Las Cruces Citizen*, which he managed until 1909, when his son Will took charge of the paper, though the senior Lapoint continued to write editorials until his death the next year.[33]

Although Lapoint used his newspapers to advance political causes, the best examples of California veterans entering journalism to promote their own careers are provided by John S. Crouch and Albert J. Fountain. These two gentlemen, together with local merchant Thomas Casad, launched the *Mesilla Valley Independent* in June 1877 in the town of Mesilla. The three partners shared editorial duties, while Crouch assumed responsibility as business manager. The first issue of the *Independent* informed readers that the object of the paper was to advance the interests of the southern counties, stimulate new industries, uphold good government, and elevate morals. It categorically denied that the journal was published "for the purpose of either advancing or retarding the political aspirations of any man or set of men."[34]

The political instincts of Crouch and Fountain, however, could not easily be submerged by weight of their own rhetoric. Each had served the Republican party in years prior to this journalistic venture, Fountain as Texas state senator from the El Paso district prior to his move to Mesilla in 1873, and Crouch as party organizer in the southern counties of Grant and Doña Ana. In 1871 Crouch received the Republican nomination for territorial senator from these two counties but lost the election to Democratic candidate Joseph F. Bennett. In the fall of 1876, while the three partners mulled over plans to open their journal, Crouch was elected senator to represent the three southern counties of Doña Ana, Grant, and Lincoln in the territorial legislature. When it was learned that Crouch proposed to edit a new journal, one observer speculated that its chief purpose would be to get Crouch elected to Congress.[35]

The newspaper failed to advance the political aspirations of either Crouch or Fountain, however, except in the sense of keeping their activities before the public eye. In his editorials, Fountain became embroiled in the movement to prevent Jesuits from teaching in public schools and in a campaign to end lawlessness in the southern counties. He lost Catholic support for his stand on the former issue and was bitterly criticized for his sensationalized reporting on the latter.[36]

Fountain retired from the editorial staff of the *Independent* in August 1878, following his sons' escape from a sniper's bullet in March and his own serious illness in the summer.[37] Crouch finally closed the office of the newspaper in July 1879 and turned to other pursuits, which included a position as deputy collector of customs at Silver City and as editor of the Silver City *Mining Chronicle*. In November 1882 Crouch was arrested on charges of embezzling over $900 in customs duties. The case was finally quashed in March 1885 following the death of the defendant on the last day of the old year.[38]

California veteran Joseph F. Bennett, while neither an editor nor a publisher, was indirectly responsible for the debut in Las Cruces of the *Borderer,* a journal clearly Democratic in its political affiliation. After leaving the service, Bennett settled in Mesilla where he became clerk of the district court, a position he held for three years. In 1867 Bennett encouraged his brother Nehemiah to come to New Mexico for his health, and by late the following year the latter was residing in Mesilla Valley.[39]

Nehemiah V. Bennett started publication of the *Borderer* in March 1871 and suspended operations in September 1875 because of failing health. During the intervening years, his paper served to revive the Democratic party in New Mexico and to champion his own political advancement as well as that of his brother Joseph.[40]

EXPRESS ROUTES AND STAGECOACHING

Joseph F. Bennett was a typical hard-working, independent frontier capitalist who invested funds in a variety of enterprises— mines, reduction works, cattle ranches, and mercantile stores. Like westerners elsewhere, Bennett's individualism was tempered by a pragmatic concern for profits; he accepted willingly and even courted government aid.

In the late 1860s and early 1870s, Bennett served the federal government as a mail contractor, initially running passenger coaches and carrying mail between Albuquerque and Mesilla but later extending his route to connect Santa Fe with El Paso and Tucson. Primarily he operated as a subcontractor for larger firms. For example, he and Henry Lesinsky ran the Southern United States Mail and Express Route late in 1868, under a subcontract from George W. Cook and J. M. Shaw, providing weekly service between Albuquerque and Mesilla.[41] Two years later Barlow, Sanderson and Company—a major western stagecoaching firm—sublet the mail contract from Mesilla to Tucson to J. F. Bennett and Company, a firm consisting of Bennett, Lesinsky, and Con Cosgrove.[42] Bennett and his partners dominated stagecoaching in New Mexico between Santa Fe and points south for the next several years. The advertisements for their Southern Overland Mail

and Express Line appeared frequently in the territorial press, offering accommodations to passengers traveling between Santa Fe,
Las Cruces, Silver City, El Paso, and Tucson.[43]

Marauding Indians caused stage proprietors like Joseph F. Bennett to suffer terrible losses both in men and property in the early
days of stagecoaching. John Slater and Charles Young, former
California troopers who served as mail carriers on the Tucson
route, were killed by Indians in November 1867. Two years later
three mail carriers were killed within a period of ten days by
Indians on the route between Mesilla and Tucson. In September
1869, mail carrier Ignacio Chavez was killed by Indians on the
Jornada eight miles south of Paraje, and another mail carrier was
attacked near the Point of Rocks.[44] Rampaging Apaches captured
the Tucson stage the following year, killing the conductor, stage
driver, and two soldiers. Late in January 1872 a mail carrier working for J. F. Bennett and Company and two other men were killed
by Apaches within three miles of Apache Pass in Arizona. As
the death toll mounted, one frontier editor marveled that men
still could be found to risk their lives to carry mail on the Tucson
route.[45]

In early 1873 stage proprietors and others were threatened by
an outbreak of disease known locally as the "epizootic." It affected
so many animals that stage companies either ceased operations
temporarily or drastically curtailed their services. Without railway
connections, Santa Fe was cut off from all communications to
the east, except by way of telegraph. With his usual energy, Joseph F. Bennett worked long hours to keep his teams on the road,
purchasing additional animals at exorbitant prices when his own
animals were too sick to be used. His diligence and vigorous action in the face of near disaster were highly praised in the territorial press.[46]

Bennett and John Davis (whose mail contract was secured by
Bennett in 1870) were the only California veterans who managed
stagecoach firms, yet a handful of old soldiers worked for similar
firms either as stage conductors or as drivers. Mention has been
made of Slater and Young, who carried the southern mail late in

the sixties, and of Samuel Eckstein, who was conductor on the southern stage in the seventies. Bavarian-born Philip Hantz lived at Fort Craig after his discharge, carrying mail along the Rio Grande; Tom Myers was conductor on the weekly coach between Fort Craig and Mesilla but died in December 1868 from injuries received in a gunfight.[47] Four veterans listed their occupations as stage drivers in the 1870 census: twenty-nine-year-old Oscar Monroe of San Miguel County, twenty-eight-year-old George Taylor of Mora County, forty-one-year-old Chapel Melton—an Irishman——who lived at Pajarito in Bernalillo County, and twenty-eight-year-old Allen Buchanan who lived at Los Lunas in Valencia County. Marcus V. Herring, who listed his occupation as teamster in the 1870 Doña Ana County census, served as conductor in the early seventies on the western coach to Tucson, while in the late seventies and early eighties Fountain "Fount" Williams drove a stage on the southern line.[48]

Like stagecoaching, freighting provided essential services to frontier communities, and although nine California veterans were listed in the 1870 census as freighters or teamsters, not one became a proprietor of a major freighting firm.[49] In related occupations, three veterans were listed as saddlers or harness makers—Walter Malcolm of Elizabethtown, Thomas Richards of Santa Fe, and Samuel Meek of Socorro—while seventeen men simply described themselves as general laborers. Only one California soldier, Richard Hudson, established a bonafide livery stable, although many hotel proprietors provided limited stable services for their customers.[50]

SMALL BUSINESS AND AN ABUNDANCE OF LAWYERS

Every frontier town had a blacksmith shop, and at least seven California veterans were listed as blacksmiths in the 1870 census, including Cyrus Bowie and Melvin Pool who established shops in lower Las Vegas.[51] There was one gunsmith listed among the veterans in the 1870 census, Albert F. Bruno, who for several years had been connected with the Ordnance Department at Fort

Union. However, Bruno and a partner in 1870 opened a black-smith shop in Santa Fe where the old soldier repaired small arms belonging to customers.[52]

Butcher shops were important to townspeople, and nine California veterans worked as butchers in the territory in 1870. Included were Oliver Butler and Patrick M. Kehoe, who were post butchers at Fort Union, and Albion K. Watts, post butcher at Fort Selden.[53] Forty-year-old Butler ended his life on June 12, 1875, when, "after imbibing strong drink," he shot himself in the temple and died instantly.[54]

"Strong drink" also led to the death of Irishman Nicholas Murphy, butcher at Ralston and former private in the First California Infantry. Murphy had been drinking heavily two weeks before Christmas, 1873, and had gone to a cabin six or seven miles north of Silver City to sober up. Nothing more was heard from him until his disfigured body was found—clad only in a shirt and a pair of drawers—in a canyon on the east side of Bear Mountain.[55]

A handful of former California soldiers opened small businesses in Santa Fe at the war's end, including George Dement who operated a barbershop, James A. Jeremiah who ran a restaurant, George Chase who opened a blacksmith shop, and Thomas Richards who had a saddlers shop on Main street. William Van Winkle, a scrivener, operated out of the City Drug Store, where he offered to make copies of "instruments in writing of every description."[56] Among the most interesting of the California craftsmen was J. Crocker Brown, a jeweler. Brown and a partner opened a shop in Santa Fe where they sold gold and silver watches, diamond pins, and the latest fashions in jewelry, including popular Mexican styles. In 1872 Brown married Jennie R. Taylor of Santa Fe and soon moved to his former home in Michigan.[57]

Among the less honorable California volunteers was George T. Martin, who opened the City Drug Store in Santa Fe opposite the Exchange Hotel and who also doubled as a book salesman and as deputy postmaster for Santa Fe. In 1872 Martin was indicted for embezzling government money while acting in the latter capacity. The former trooper took flight and was never brought to court.[58]

California soldiers who practiced their crafts in New Mexico included two stonemasons, fifteen carpenters, one painter, one machinist, one baker, and four cooks.[59] The baker, Charles Brakebill, offered his wares to miners at Ralston in 1870 but previously had operated the Gem Saloon in Santa Fe. The cooks were Irishmen John McKinn and Samuel Creevey of Colfax and Grant counties, respectively, the Frenchman John C. Sigwalt who cooked for the Lucien B. Maxwell household, and the Prussian August Gunzenhauser who worked at Richard Hudson's hotel in Pinos Altos.[60]

Professional men found that New Mexico's frontier communities sometimes offered opportunities to establish lucrative practices. Few Hispanos in the territory were physicians or attorneys prior to 1860, and their numbers did not increase significantly in later years. Several members of the medical profession arrived in New Mexico as military physicians, including George H. Oliver, an army surgeon stationed at Santa Fe during the Civil War. He resigned from the service in 1864 and continued to practice medicine first in El Paso, Texas, and then at Mesilla.[61]

But only one California veteran, Pennsylvania-born Henry S. Drinkhouse, listed his occupation in 1870 as a medical doctor, and he had arrived in the territory as a private rather than as an army physician. Drinkhouse mustered out of the service in 1864 and bought a house and lot in Las Cruces where he lived with his wife Guadalupe Chacon and small children. Little is known concerning the extent of his medical practice, but the records reveal that he was indicted in 1865 for practicing without a license and in 1871 for prescribing medicine while intoxicated. By mid-1877 Drinkhouse had moved to Mexico where he was "peddling pills" in the state of Chihuahua.[62]

The legal profession attracted more practitioners than any other in western communities. Certainly this was the case in New Mexico, which sported an abundance of frontier attorneys. At least seven California veterans practiced law in territorial courts, although Simon L. Snyder, a Santa Fe attorney, exchanged his Blackstone for a printer's manual, finding employment in offices of various Santa Fe newspapers.[63]

Among the more talented lawyers in the southern counties were
California veterans William L. Rynerson and Albert J. Fountain.
Their services were widely sought. Frequently they opposed each
other in court and occasionally they joined forces to defend a
client. In 1882, for example, they collaborated in defending Christian Moesner, indicted for the murder of Dr. Alex Kallenberg of
Lake Valley. Though observers felt that the defendant's case was
hopeless—he would either hang or receive a life sentence—the
jury, after listening to the impassioned arguments presented by
Rynerson and Fountain, convicted Moesner of murder in the fifth
degree, sentencing him to a mere three years in prison.[64]

The four remaining lawyers who arrived with the California
Column were John Ryan, Lawrence Lapoint, John S. Crouch,
and James A. Zabriskie, all of whom practiced in the southern
counties. Lapoint appeared in his first court case in 1884. The
opposing counsel was John Ryan, a resident of Mesilla who had
been admitted to the bar in 1876.[65] John S. Crouch was certified
to practice in New Mexico's courts in 1872, but with so many
other responsibilities, he gave but slight attention to his law practice, appearing more often in court as a district clerk than as an
attorney.[66]

Four ex-California soldiers ventured into the teaching profession—Henry W. Sherry, Englishmen John Townsend and Frederick DeFrouville, and German-born Otto Koernick. Koernick
died at Fort Wingate the summer of 1870 and little is known concerning his teaching career.[67] Townsend was hired in 1871 at $50
a month by Indian agent William F. M. Arny to teach the Indians at Tesuque Pueblo techniques of farming as well as English
and Spanish. Later Townsend opened a private school in Santa
Fe, charging three dollars a month for tuition, but the school did
not last long.[68] DeFrouville, a druggist by occupation, was employed from 1869 to 1872 as a school teacher by the Reverend J.
B. Fayet, parish priest at San Miguel. Several years later he was
still teaching school in San Miguel County.[69]

Although several ex-California soldiers were religious men, in
the sense that they supported established churches, only Albert

G. T. Jacobs dedicated his life to the ministry. He was discharged a private in April 1866 at Fort Sumner and shortly thereafter married Abrana Quintana at Fort Union. In 1870, twenty-five-year-old Jacobs and his wife were farming land in Lincoln County; in subsequent years, though, they moved to Colorado, living in various small communities in San Luis Valley. It was in Colorado that he became an itinerant minister for the Methodist church, preaching to congregations in Conejos and Costilla counties. A year before his death in 1898, he was transferred to Santa Fe, although his wife and children remained in Colorado to care for their 160-acre ranch at Terrace. Jacobs died in Santa Fe on March 21 while serving as missionary to the Hispanic population.[70]

On a more technical level, three veterans in 1870 listed their occupations as engineers or surveyors. Gilbert Haggert, a native of New York, was employed as an engineer at Fort Wingate in 1870 but little is known of his subsequent career. The two surveyors, John Lambert of Ireland and William McMullen of New York, resided in Elizabethtown and Santa Fe, respectively, in 1870 but surveyed land throughout the territory.[71] Lambert had been employed by the surveyor general's office as draftsman and produced the official territorial map that accompanied the surveyor general's report to the secretary of the Interior in 1867. Five years later he and J. Howe Watts were at Fort Bascom surveying the Montoya Grant.[72]

A veteran of the Mexican War, William McMullen journeyed to the California gold fields in 1849 by way of Cape Horn. He engaged in mining for a decade and then bought a printing office and established the Amador *Dispatch.* He mustered into the California volunteers in 1861 as captain and was discharged at Fort Union three years later as a lieutenant-colonel. The intervening years were stormy ones for McMullen. In December 1862 he became embroiled with Mexican authorities when he stationed pickets on the Mexican side of the Rio Grande opposite San Elizario without authorization. Although this action was subsequently approved by his commanding officer, McMullen later was reprimanded for inattention to duty while commanding the post at

Mesilla and again while in command at Fort Union. Despite this criticism, McMullen, after mustering out of the volunteers, was offered—but declined—a commission in the Mexican army under Benito Juárez. McMullen then sought employment as a surveyor and engineer, and in later years he frequently held contracts with New Mexico's surveyor-general to survey portions of the public domain. [73]

McMullen's surveying and engineering feats often were described in the territorial press, and none received more coverage than the bridges he constructed over the Santa Fe River in the seventies. Town officials awarded McMullen a contract in 1872 to construct one wagon and two footbridges across the river. Over five hundred wagonloads of rock were used in the piers and abutments of the wagon bridge, and when it was completed in September a grand ball was held to honor what was said to be the first wagon bridge ever to span the Santa Fe River. [74]

The editor of the *Daily New Mexican* praised McMullen for his professional skill and predicted that the bridge would stand for years against summer flood waters. In less than four months, however, the wagon bridge had fallen victim to vandals who wrenched out several of its banisters. And in less than two years, after a heavy summer rain, swift-running waters carrying rubble and debris from upriver slammed into McMullen's bridge, washing away the lower half of the north abutment and the first pier. [75]

A BRASS BAND FOR THE TELEGRAPH LINE

California veterans, along with most New Mexicans, eagerly awaited arrival of the telegraph and railroad to connect their towns with the outside world; many expended time, energy, and money to assure their arrival. The telegraph entered New Mexico in July 1868 when connections were established between Santa Fe and Denver. [76] Telegraph offices were located in Santa Fe and Las Vegas in rooms donated by hotel proprietors, who also agreed to board telegraph operators free of charge for one year. The two proprietors of the Las Vegas hotel, Charles Kitchen and popular California veteran Benjamin C. Cutler, joined two other leading citizens of Las Vegas to inaugurate the system on July 10 by sending a congratulatory message to the people of Santa Fe expressing hope that the telegraph would unite the two towns as closely in feelings as they were "now united by the electric wire."[77]

It was several years before the telegraph line was extended south from Santa Fe, and California veterans played significant roles in securing telegraphic communications for New Mexico's southern counties. Congress appropriated $30,000 in 1875 to build a military telegraph from Santa Fe, via Las Cruces, Mesilla, Fort Bayard, and Silver City, to connect with the Arizona line. After construction was underway, Lt. Philip Reade, in charge of building the route, appealed to citizens for contributions to supplement the niggardly amount set aside by Congress, and private citizens responded with undisguised enthusiasm, offering large subscriptions and rent-free office space. John Martin of Aleman, having submitted the lowest bid, received the contract to furnish telegraph poles between Santa Fe and Mesilla at $1.75 per pole. He apparently had made the low bid with an understanding that telegraph offices would be established both at Las Cruces and Mesilla. When the line was completed to these two southern communities in April 1876, residents in both towns celebrated, with the Mesilla brass band leading the celebration.[78]

Citizens of Silver City were as supportive as those in the Mesilla Valley. Joseph F. Bennett offered to provide a telegraph office and rooms for the accommodation of operators free of charge, while other men donated poles required for the line between Fort Bayard and Silver City. Bennett also held the contract to furnish 2,300 poles for the line between Ralston and Fort Bowie and in later years became one of six incorporators in a private firm, the Silver City Telegraph Company, which planned to construct a telegraph line between Silver City and Deming.[79]

FINALLY THE RAILROAD

While the telegraph line was being pushed to completion, visions of steel rails linking the territory with the rest of the nation generated enthusiasm—bordering on hysteria—among area capi-

talists. New Mexicans followed congressional railroad debates and
sent representatives to railroad conventions. They wooed and
pampered railroad companies to persuade them to build through
favored locations, and some dug deep into their own pockets to
finance railroad ventures.

The men of the California Column joined in promoting the
territory to the railroads and displayed exuberance when news
reached Ralston in 1871 that Congress approved the Texas Pacific railroad bill, providing for a transcontinental railroad along
the thirty-second parallel. Miners staged a giant celebration, il-
luminating the entire camp with massive bonfires. One hundred
guns were fired as a salute to commemorate the occasion. John S.
Crouch summarized the feelings of many miners when he stated
before an enthusiastic crowd that the railroad would inaugurate a
new order of affairs and "will do more to settle the Indian question than all the bayonets in the land, and fill our Territory with
men of enterprise and industry."[80]

When the National Southern Pacific executive committee proposed to stage a giant convention in St. Louis late in 1875 to
impress upon Congress the need for federal aid, several communities in New Mexico held meetings to elect delegates. Merchants,
mechanics, laborers, and professional men crowded into the Mesilla courthouse, where Judge Warren Bristol presided with Ira
M. Bond and John S. Crouch serving as secretaries. On the committee of five appointed to draw up resolutions to be presented at
the St. Louis convention were three California veterans—Albert
J. Fountain, William L. Rynerson, and John S. Crouch. The
resolutions called for a railroad to be built with government aid
from Fort Worth to the Pacific along the thirty-second parallel;
such a line "would develop beyond calculation the agricultural,
pastoral and mineral resources of Southern New Mexico" and
would allow consumptives to come to the Southwest for their
health.[81] Grant County citizens also met in a public meeting presided over by Richard Hudson to collect statistics and to elect
delegates to the St. Louis meeting. Joseph F. Bennett was elected
one of six to attend the convention, but apparently he was not
among the New Mexicans who actually traveled east to St. Louis.[82]

The enthusiasm for the railroad led to political maneuvering of questionable merit. California veteran John S. Crouch introduced a bill in the territorial legislature to exempt railroads from taxation during construction and for six years after completion. Enacted in 1878, this measure had almost unanimous support among New Mexico's legislators and received some praise in the press. The editor of the *Grant County Herald*, however, reported that the bill had been prepared by railroad men in their own interest and was foisted upon the people by ignorant legislators "too stupid to comprehend that they were throwing away a source of great future revenue without receiving a shadow of compensation therefor."[83]

The long-awaited arrival of steel rails occurred late in 1878 when the Atchison, Topeka and Santa Fe Railroad entered the territory through Raton Pass. Of major importance to New Mexican residents was the joining of that railroad with the Southern Pacific at Deming in 1881. With the coming of the railroads, property values rose, mining and cattle enterprises expanded, towns were modernized, and the territory prospered. Hoping to share this prosperity, William L. Rynerson and other Las Cruces capitalists purchased town land and deeded it to the railroad company to secure a railroad depot for their town. Rynerson's share of the purchase money was one thousand dollars.[84]

Whether railroad booster, lawyer, or merchant, the men from California were a remarkably diverse group and their versatility is readily apparent. Many led unspectacular lives as cooks or butchers or blacksmiths; several, especially merchants and professional men, became well-known public figures who rubbed shoulders with New Mexico's social and political elite. Many plied their trade in small rural communities, helping to hold the land for what they regarded as "white man's civilization." Discounting the crooks among them, each with his special talents contributed to the economic development of the territory.

8

Government Employees

New Mexico remained a territory for over half a century, and during those years Congress subsidized both its political and economic development. In fact, government expenditures for military and Indian supplies were essential to the territory's economy, and scores of New Mexicans found employment with a variety of federal agencies operating in the territory. Westerners may indeed have been self-reliant and independent, but their survival frequently depended upon the largesse of the national government.

Soldiers who mustered out of the service in New Mexico quickly saw the government as a source of continued income. Several found employment at military forts as laborers, clerks, butchers, blacksmiths, and post traders, while others received contracts to provision the posts with subsistence stores and other items needed to keep an army in the field. Several found similar employment at Indian agencies in New Mexico and received corresponding contracts to provide subsistence for reservation Indians.

Fort Union was the major supply depot for the military district of New Mexico. In 1863 it employed over four hundred civilians in a variety of jobs ranging from bookkeeper to cattle herder. Several California veterans found employment there after mustering out of the army, including gunsmith Albert F. Bruno, saddler Barney W. Connelly, kitchen employee James A. James, clerk James T. McNamara, quartermaster employee William S. Lackey, and butchers Oliver Butler and Patrick Kehoe.[1] Civilian employees at Fort Selden in Doña Ana County included post butcher Albion K. Watts and Seneca Ames, the latter a carpenter by trade who worked at the post from 1866 until 1870 or 1871, when he went with his family to reside permanently in Las Cruces.[2] Watts, a native of Maine, had been honorably discharged at that same post in 1866 and during the next ten years was a major competitor for beef contracts in the southern counties. His first contract was signed August 7, 1869 when he agreed to deliver to Fort Selden fresh beef at nine cents a pound and beef cattle at six cents a pound. In 1871 he held contracts to furnish beef cattle to Forts Selden, Bayard, and Cummings at ten, twelve, and fifteen cents a pound, respectively.[3]

In Santa Fe at least three California veterans were employed in 1870 as clerks in the quartermaster's department: thirty-one-year-old Lycurgus D. Fuller, thirty-four-year-old William B. Moores, and thirty-six-year-old Edward S. Merritt. Ex-California soldier David T. Harshaw, who in the 1870s became famous as the discoverer of silver ore near Harshaw, Arizona, worked as forage master at Fort Craig in the 1860s, while ex-private Samuel Meek was employed there as saddler.[4]

THE POST TRADERS

At least seven former California soldiers, ranging in rank from private to colonel, became post traders in the years immediately following their discharge. Post traders or sutlers operated stores on military reservations, where they sold goods and luxury items, including whiskey and beer, to soldiers and transients. Their establishments frequently served as post offices, canteens, and recreation centers.

Robert V. Newsham, a native of Illinois and former sergeant in the Fifth California Infantry, became post trader at Fort Cummings near Cooke's Canyon in Grant County in the late 1860s and employed a former private in his company, John A. Moore, as clerk. While post trader and later as merchant at Rio Mimbres, Newsham held government contracts to supply Fort Bayard and

Fort Cummings with a variety of commodities, including fresh beef, hay, bran, charcoal, corn, oats, and adobes.[5] Farther to the north on the Rio Grande, former lieutenant William V. B. Wardwell became civilian post trader at Fort Craig in 1865, representing the firm of C. S. Hinckley, C. H. Blake, and W. V. B. Wardwell—merchants and general dealers. Wardwell had been appointed United States assessor in 1864 and moved his office from Santa Fe to Fort Craig when he became post trader. He was among the most active competitors for military contracts among California veterans. Over a span of seven years, Wardwell submitted bids to supply beef, corn, hay, wood, and charcoal to Forts Bascom, Craig, McRae, Cummings, and Stanton. He signed his first contract in 1865, about one year after he mustered out of the service. In later years he held contracts to supply the army with corn, charcoal, mesquite wood, oak wood, beef cattle, lumber, adobes, and gypsum.[6]

In 1870 William V. B. Wardwell was thirty-two years old, married and the father of three children, with total assets listed in the census as $65,000—most of which was in real estate. In April 1873 Wardwell preempted 160 acres on the banks of the Rio Grande and located an additional 160 acres in his wife's name in the same vicinity. By September Wardwell had disposed of his dwelling house and other structures at Fort Craig; this property was eventually sold to Edwin A. Rigg of Buffalo, New York—former colonel in the California volunteers. The Wardwells subsequently left New Mexico for San Francisco where in 1884 the forty-seven-year-old veteran died, having been employed as a bookkeeper during the last years of his life.[7]

The new civilian trader at Fort Craig, Edwin A. Rigg, represented the firm of E. Montoya and Sons, which offered a "complete assortment of new goods" at "the lowest prices" in the territory. Rigg had been in command at Fort Craig as colonel in the California volunteers, and his daughter Sallie was born there on December 26, 1863. After mustering out of the volunteers, he joined the regular army as a first lieutenant in the 38th Infantry and was later assigned to the 25th Infantry, both black regiments serving in the West.[8]

Rigg left the army in 1871 and remained several years at Fort Craig, first as post trader and then as postmaster. Late in 1878 he opened the Telegraph House at Mesilla—a short-lived enterprise— and he soon left the territory owing the United States Post Office Department $147.07. Since the former colonel could not be located, Richard Hudson, who had signed as one of Rigg's sureties, was taken to court and eventually forced to pay the original debt plus court costs. Pension records indicate that Rigg had moved to Contention in Cochise County, Arizona, sometime in 1880 where he died two years later.[9]

MURPHY AND COMPANY

The sutler's store at Fort Stanton, located on the Rio Bonito in Lincoln County, was operated in the late 1860s by Lawrence G. Murphy and Emil Fritz, both former officers in the New Mexico and California volunteers, respectively. The two men had been stationed at Fort Sumner in 1865 where Murphy was military supervisor for the Mescalero Apaches. The following year, Murphy and Fritz were stationed at Fort Stanton, where the latter was in command. With ample opportunity to survey the surrounding countryside, Murphy predicted that it would become "*the* farming section of New Mexico," and it was in this vicinity along the banks of the Rio Bonito and the Ruidoso that the two partners spent the remainder of their productive careers.[10]

After mustering out of the army in 1866, Murphy and Fritz established a store, saloon, and brewery close to the fort and proved congenial hosts to troops garrisoned there. Col. August V. Kautz, in command at Fort Stanton in 1869, found the sutler's store to be the center of its social life, where officers gathered for conversation, beer and champagne, and billiards. On Christmas day, officers were treated to a late afternoon dinner of wild turkey and trimmings, while on New Year's day Fritz and Murphy staged a dance for the garrison, complete with three fiddlers, local women, and abundant wine and liquor.[11]

As government contractors for both Fort Stanton and the Mescalero Indian Agency, the two partners held economic power over neighboring farmers and ranchers, who of necessity had to sell their produce to the firm of Murphy and Company. Fritz and Murphy also exerted influence on men sent to staff the Mescalero Agency, partly because the agents had to depend on Murphy and Company for business and living quarters, but more importantly because the two traders were extremely knowledgeable in the ways of Indians. On more than one occasion their advice and personal influence were requested by officials of New Mexico's Indian superintendency.[12]

Murphy and Company were ordered to leave Fort Stanton in 1873 after complaints had been lodged against the firm with government officials. Colonel Kautz had tried to get the partners removed before he left command in 1872 because he believed that their saloon contributed to drunkenness among his young officers. Indian officials complained that the two partners interfered with agency policies and had virtual control over the Mescaleros. And finally it was believed that Murphy had kept his young friend, James J. Dolan, from going to jail after the latter had taken a shot at a Fort Stanton officer. In July the government purchased the trader's store for $8,000 and in early October the commander of Fort Stanton ordered Murphy, Fritz, and their employees to leave the post. Thereupon the two former soldiers moved their firm to the small town of Lincoln, nine miles to the east, where they erected one of the most imposing buildings in the county, known as "The House," and tightened their economic hold over the surrounding countryside.[13]

About one hundred miles northeast of Fort Stanton on the Pecos River stood Fort Sumner and the Bosque Redondo Indian reservation where Col. Oscar M. Brown, formerly of the California volunteers, was appointed sutler and licensed to trade with the Navajos at the war's end. A native of Petersburg, Virginia, Brown was joined in New Mexico by his brother John, who took charge of the store the summer of 1866 while Colonel Brown traveled to Washington on business. John Brown died at Fort Sumner late the following year and in June 1868 Annie Brown, wife of the colonel, also died after a long illness. Brown shortly thereafter closed his sutler's store and moved first to Texas and then to Globe, Arizona, where he practiced law.[14]

IN THE INDIAN SERVICES

California veterans made up part of the work force that federal agencies such as the War Department and the Indian Bureau required to operate in Western territories. Toughened by the rigors of military life and as experienced in dealing with New Mexico's Indians as any white men of their generation, their skills and labor were employed in a variety of jobs associated with the territory's Indian superintendency, ranging from such prosaic occupations as agency butcher and issue man to interpreter, teacher, office clerk, and Indian agent. Several veterans received licenses to trade among different tribes in New Mexico, and many were involved in some of the most important episodes associated with the history of Indian-white relations in the territory.

The various Indian agencies established in New Mexico simply could not function without a number of paid employees. During the second quarter in 1871, for example, the Navajo Indian agency at Fort Defiance was staffed by one agent, a clerk, Spanish interpreter, Navajo interpreter, carpenter, blacksmith, butcher, two issue men, two herders, one wagonmaster, one man in charge of grain, and one school teacher. Four of these positions were filled by California veterans: Thomas V. Keam as the Spanish interpreter, Anson C. Damon as butcher, Perry H. Williams as an issue man, and Robert Long as wagonmaster.[15]

At least seven California veterans were employed as interpreters by the Indian service after the Civil War. In addition to Keam, Ludwig Reventlow and John H. Van Order served as interpreters at the Navajo Agency, Frederick G. Hughes at the Southern Apache Agency, Henry W. Easton at Cimarron, Lyon Phillipouski, interpreter for the Mescalero Apaches, and John Townsend as special interpreter to the Utes.[16] Among other California veterans who worked at the agencies were George B. Duncan, a mail carrier for the Indian service and issue man for the Southern Apache Agency, Andrew Snyder and Charles Carter, who served as porter and teamster, respectively, for the superintendency, and George Chase who occasionaly did blacksmith work for the agencies.[17]

Of all ex-California soldiers who worked for the Indian Bureau, none gave more valuable service than John Ayers, Thomas V. Keam, and David N. Catanach, the former as Indian agent, Keam as interpreter and troubleshooter, and the latter as superintendency clerk. Something of a frontier philosopher, John Ayers believed that he held the key for solving New Mexico's Indian problems and said so in the pages of the territorial press. Born into a New York family of wealth and position, Ayers had gone to sea at the age of thirteen and after enlisting in the California volunteers as a private, proved an exemplary soldier, well-liked by officers and comrades, and eventually was promoted to first lieutenant in the New Mexico Cavalry.[18]

After his discharge Ayers became special agent for the Southern Apaches with an office at Santa Fe and thus began his lengthy but intermittent association with the Indian service. He was peculiarly suited for work with Indians, and his official communications reveal sincere interest in their welfare. Unfortunately, his tenure as Indian agent was continually interrupted by adverse bureaucratic decisions, often politically motivated. In 1869 he was appointed agent for the Capote and Wiminuche Utes at Abiquiu Agency in northern New Mexico, but after eight months his employment was terminated as a result of President Grant's decision to place military officers in charge of Indian agencies.[19]

During those eight months, however, Ayers became involved in the controversy surrounding the attempt to force New Mexico's Ute Indians to move to Colorado. The United States government alleged that the Utes had agreed by treaty in 1868 to be placed on a reservation in southern Colorado, but the Utes denied signing any such treaty and refused to go. As their agent, Ayers protested removal and urged that they and other tribes be allowed to remain on small reservations in their own homelands.[20]

Ayers was critical of most Indian agents serving the western tribes, calling them "a set of political hucksters," who came from the east with little knowledge of Indian character. He recommended that agents be hired who could identify with the tribes and look out for their interest.[21] Before Ayers was removed as Ute agent, a resident of Abiquiu, Antonio María Vigil, submitted a lengthy letter to the editors of the Santa Fe *New Mexican* expressing appreciation to Ayers "for the energetic and efficient manner and commendable deportment with which he manages and deals with the Indians of his agency."[22] Ayers also received commendation from both the superintendent and the military commander of the District of New Mexico, who recommended to the commissioner of Indian Affairs that he be retained as agent for the Utes.[23] Ayers accomplished the nearly impossible task of pleasing white residents, government officials, and his Indian charges.

Despite considerable success, Ayers was removed as a result of Grant's new policy, and in December 1869—out of work and low on funds—the ex-California volunteer applied for and subsequently received a license to trade with Navajos at Fort Defiance. Being a trader to the Navajos was not a lucrative position; Lehman Spiegelberg had obtained a license to trade at Fort Defiance in 1868 but had abandoned his tradership when expenses exceeded his income. Ayers, when he applied for the job, stated that he was willing to accept a meager living from the position.[24] He assumed his duties as Indian trader with apparent relish, occasionally writing letters to the editors of the *Daily New Mexican* describing conditions at the Navajo Agency. In June 1872 Ayers accompanied Navajo agent James H. Miller and two other men to the San Juan country about one hundred miles northwest of Defiance to look for new farming lands for the Navajos. On the morning of June 11 at about four o'clock they were attacked by a small party of Utes and Miller was killed.[25]

Later that summer, the ex-soldier expressed his distaste for Grant's Indian policy in the pages of the Las Cruces *Borderer*. The president had instituted a new program, later dubbed "Grant's

Quaker Policy." Complaints from eastern humanitarians had forced the president to end military control of Indian agencies, and, searching for a means to reform the Indian service, Grant subsequently allowed Quakers and other religious denominations to nominate candidates to fill the various agencies. Ayers reported in the press that about a year after his removal from the Abiquiu Agency, he had asked to be reinstated, but the Board of Presbytery that now controlled nominations to that agency refused because he was not a member of their church. Ayers cited this as an example of religious persecution, an opinion apparently widely held among westerners.[26]

JOHN AYERS AND THE GILA APACHES

In September 1872 Ayers was appointed temporary agent in charge of the Southern Apache Agency, then located on the banks of the Tularosa River in southwestern New Mexico. After years of conflict with settlers in the southern part of the territory, the Gila Apaches had been forced to leave their favorite camping place in the vicinity of Cañada Alamosa—present-day Monticello—and relocate at Tularosa, sufficiently remote from settlements to prevent further clashes.[27] Several California volunteers figured prominently in their forced removal.

In 1869 Indian depredations generated an outburst of public indignation against the Gila Apaches camped at Cañada Alamosa, apparently seeking peace and a permanent reservation. William L. Rynerson, then post trader at Bayard, requested Gov. William A. Pile in November to send additional troops to the region to prevent further raids. Citizens of Mesilla, Pinos Altos, and Mimbres passed resolutions supporting Rynerson's request and condemning the reservation system in New Mexico. On the five-member resolutions committee at Mimbres were three former comrades of Rynerson—Marshall St. John, Sydney M. Webb, and William B. Morgan—while California veteran Richard Hudson chaired the Pinos Altos meeting. The agent for the Southern Apaches, Lt. Charles E. Drew, while vigorously denying that Indians had left their camp at Cañada Alamosa, charged that certain parties opposed making peace with the Apaches because it was not to their economic benefit. Drew was supported by many local residents, including California veterans who lived near Cañada Alamosa. Richard C. Patterson, Joseph D. Emerson, and Frederick Sanburn were among several delegates who met at Alamosa and declared that the agent was an efficient and reliable officer and that Apaches had refrained from raiding while under his control.[28]

This assessment of Drew's reliability as Indian agent is open to question. His record for hard drinking was described in the diary of Col. August V. Kautz and criticized by Rynerson and other observers. Drew's career as an Indian agent, however, shortly ended as he died from exposure in June 1870 after wandering in the hills without water for forty hours searching for renegade Mescaleros.[29]

Gila Apaches camped at Cañada Alamosa continued to excite the hostility of residents in both Grant and Doña Ana counties. Early in 1871 John Bullard, one of the founders of Silver City, was killed while chasing Apaches who had raided the mining camps. The *Borderer* blamed the Indians at Cañada Alamosa for the raids and claimed that the reservation system in New Mexico was a failure, suggesting if the government insisted on operating reservations that they be established in Boston or Philadelphia where eastern humanitarians and Quaker enthusiasts could supervise the training of their unlettered brethren. With even more venom, the editor of the *Daily New Mexican* described the Gila Apaches as "the most murderous and utterly abandoned savages on the continent."[30]

Shortly after Bullard's death, miners at Silver City in a meeting chaired by ex-California soldier Richard Yeamans called upon Congress to end reservations and to use a recent appropriation for the Apaches to outfit volunteers to fight them. In addition, the miners appealed to all New Mexicans to contribute to a fund to pay for Indian scalps and to hire a scout who would remain permanently in the field hunting Apaches.[31]

Citizens of Doña Ana County quickly responded. Assembled at the courthouse in Mesilla, area residents listened to fiery speeches by William L. Rynerson, W. T. Jones, and others urging citizens to unite to protect the territory against "the scalping knife and tomahawk of these ruthless barbarians." Resolutions were adopted asserting that the Cañada Alamosa "reservation" was used only to deposit old men, women, and children while warriors raided the countryside, and pledges were made to support the miners in their war against Apaches. A committee of thirteen community leaders, including Rynerson and John D. Barncastle, formed to solicit contributions to support a full-time scout as suggested by the miners.[32]

With each new report of Indian depredations the wrath of New Mexicans mounted, reaching a dangerously explosive state in July. Richard Hudson, probate judge of Grant County, reported to the Indian agent at Cañada Alamosa, Orlando F. Piper, that several horses and mules reported stolen by Indians had been traced in the direction of his reservation. Hudson bluntly warned Piper that:

unless we have some reliable protection, furnished us soon from the thieving, murderous, villains, whom you are feeding, and have not the power to keep from robbing and plundering our people, I shall hereafter do nothing to prevent an armed body of true, bold, frontiersmen from leaving this County on one of the numerous trails that lead to Alamosa to find their stock and punish the robbers and murderers, wherever they may find them.[33]

On July 19 settlers at Rio Mimbres assembled at Robert V. Newsham's store to express outrage at the continuing Indian robberies. Three California veterans played key roles at this meeting: Newsham was elected as president, Henry Schwenker as interpreter and secretary, while Schwenker and Marshall St. John served on a committee of three to draft resolutions. These men were no less blunt than Hudson; they resolved to form a posse to retrieve their stock by force if necessary. Hudson forwarded the Rio Mimbres resolutions to the superintendent of Indian affairs in Santa Fe, who in turn warned Hudson and settlers in Grant

County that he would protect the Indians assembled at Cañada Alamosa against any civilian attack.[34]

In August Vincent Colyer arrived in New Mexico to promote President Grant's peace policy wherein western tribes were to be placed on reservations and there taught techniques of agriculture. Those Indians who refused to locate on reservations were to be subject to miliary action. Citizen protest was temporarily quieted when Colyer selected the valley of the Tularosa River, eighty miles west of Fort Craig, as a reservation for the Southern Apaches and requested superintendent Nathaniel Pope to supervise their removal from Cañada Alamosa to the new reservation. In the spring of 1872, the agency was transferred to the new site, and Gila Apaches were forced to move to the Tularosa.[35]

By September, however, the Apaches, dissatisfied with the Tularosa reservation, roamed freely over the countryside. In this atmosphere of discontent John Ayers assumed responsibilities as temporary agent of the Tularosa reservation. The Santa Fe *Daily New Mexican,* expressing pleasure with Ayers's selection, hoped that the former soldier, who "has been among Indians most of his life," would receive the position as permanent agent for the Gila Apaches.[36]

Ayers arrived at Tularosa on October 24, and he immediately requested clothing and other supplies for the Indians, reporting that his predecessor had left him with few provisions. Five hundred twenty-five Apaches were on the reservation, but some planned to leave to join Cochise in the Chiricahua Mountains, while the rest wanted their agency moved to Ojo Caliente—Hot Springs—about twenty-five miles from the town of Cañada Alamosa. In the interest of peace, Ayers appealed to his superior to allow the Apaches to move; he predicted they would all join Cochise if prevented from returning to their old camping grounds. Put the reservation where the Indians want it, he counseled; then they will be happy and contented. Critical of government inconsistency in treating with Indians, Ayers complained that "this vacillating policy as things are now is both ruinous to the Indians and detrimental to the government."[37]

In November Ayers issued rations to 603 Indians, including the famed Victorio, spokesman for the Gila Apaches, who warned the agent in a formal council that the Indians hated Tularosa and would not stay there. Ayers continued to request superintendent Pope to allow the Apaches to return to their own country; there they could be given sheep, taught to be self-supporting, and with assistance from the government and the proper agent settle into peaceful pursuits.[38]

Apparently satisfied with Ayers's performance, superintendent Pope wrote Indian Commissioner Francis A. Walker in Washington requesting that he be appointed permanent agent for the Tularosa Agency. Instead, on January 11, 1873, Ayers was relieved as acting agent by Dr. Benjamin M. Thomas, former farmer and medical attendant among the Navajos at Fort Defiance.[39] At first the Apaches refused to have anything to do with the new agent; they asked Capt. F. W. Coleman, commander at Fort Tularosa, to write to Washington that "all the old women, children, and men were crying and sad because Mr. Ayers was to go away." Coleman noted in his official report that Ayers "had acted firmly and faithfully" trying to convince the Indians that the change would do them no harm;[40] however, the new superintendent, L. Edwin Dudley, visited Tularosa in March 1873 and attributed Indian discontent to Ayers's lenient policy. Ayers was accused of encouraging their belief that they would one day return to Cañada Alamosa simply as a means to keep them happy.[41]

Nonetheless, the approach counseled by Ayers was eventually taken, and in April 1874 a reservation was established by executive order for the Southern Apaches at Ojo Caliente near the town of Cañada Alamosa.[42] Meanwhile, Ayers joined the surveying party led by Lt. George M. Wheeler and then moved to Fort McRae on the Rio Grande about fifty miles southeast of Ojo Caliente. There he became trader to the Indians and operated a ferryboat across the river. In November 1875 "Johnny" Ayers married Maggie C. Hackett, a niece of John Martin, in a ceremony at the Aleman ranch. Although the territorial press extended congratulatory messages and predicted years of wedded bliss for the

new couple, young Maggie Ayers left her forty-six-year-old husband for unknown reasons soon after their marriage, though the
isolation of Fort McRae was undoubtedly a contributing factor.
By mid-summer 1876 Ayers had filed suit in district court to dis-
solve the marriage. By May of the following year, when Apaches
at Ojo Caliente were moved to San Carlos reservation in Arizona, Ayers was living at Santa Fe and managing the Exchange
Hotel as an administrator for the John Martin estate.[43]

TROUBLED TIMES

Ayers's future career was as turbulent and rocky as that of the
Gila Apaches. A versatile individual, the former soldier apparently was proficient at no particular trade, taking jobs and pursuing opportunities as they arose. His true calling may have been
with the Indian service, for he was above all else an honest man
with sympathy for American Indians, an attitude that elevated him
above the average westerner. Meanwhile Ayers's former charges,
the Southern Apaches, began to desert the San Carlos reservation shortly after they had been driven to Arizona. Many sought
refuge on the Navajo reservation only to be escorted by the military back to Ojo Caliente. Other "Warm Spring" Apaches terrorized the settlers of Grant County, who reported that Apaches
were raiding on all sides of Silver City in September 1877. A party
attacked a coal camp near Clifton, Arizona, and then moved into
New Mexico where they raided Robert V. Newsham's ranch on
the Gila, killing one man, wounding another, and burning Newsham's house to the ground. After fourteen residents of Grant
County had lost their lives in this new Indian outbreak, a public
meeting, attended by over two hundred people, was held at Silver City to discuss what actions should be taken. Ex-California
trooper William Chamberlin was appointed to a committee of five
to procure arms from the military and to confer with Gen. Edward Hatch, in command of the District of New Mexico.[44]

Intermittent raiding continued, and Silver City organized scout-
ing parties to track marauding Indians. The raids intensified after

Apaches congregated at Ojo Caliente fled to the hills in the fall of 1878 rather than return to San Carlos as ordered by Washington officials. During the next two years, Victorio and his followers terrorized the small mining camps and settlements in southern New Mexico and Arizona. Citizen-led militia companies aided regular troops in tracking marauding Indians, with Albert J. Fountain and Richard Hudson commanding volunteer units in Doña Ana and Grant counties, respectively.[45]

In October 1879 residents in southern New Mexico were startled to learn that two hundred Apaches—identified as Mescaleros who had joined with Victorio—had attacked Lloyd's Ranch, located in an isolated region about nine miles from the settlement of Colorado in Doña Ana County. A small rescue party from the latter community was attacked a mile from the ranch and four men were killed. A second party of thirty-five men started for the scene to recover bodies, but they were forced to retreat after engaging in a furious two-day battle with the Apaches. When word reached Las Cruces, a party of seventeen went to assist the men already in the field, but ten or twelve miles from Lloyd's Ranch, the would-be rescuers were attacked by about one hundred Indians, who killed five area residents.[46]

William L. Rynerson then led a party of seventy-five men from Las Cruces, Doña Ana, Mesilla, and lower Rio Grande villages to recover the bodies of the dead. Rynerson was assisted by John S. Crouch, second in command, and David Wood, who with ten men protected one flank of the small mounted army. Four miles beyond Magdalena Canyon, the volunteers came upon a wagon train that had been hit by Apaches; cattle had been shot and ten bodies were found under the wagons and strewn among the cattle. After burying the dead, the command proceeded to the place where the local men had fallen and then on to Lloyd's Ranch, where the Indians had left five people dead, as well as the carcasses of a hundred slaughtered cattle and rotting bodies of all the chickens on the ranch.[47]

In the next several months, Victorio's warriors waged brutal and destructive war against isolated ranches and settlements, moving with lightning speed to elude United States forces sent to capture or to destroy them. California veterans in exposed areas faced constant danger, while those in larger communities, such as Silver City and Mesilla, spearheaded mass indignation meetings to protest mismanagement of the Indian campaign by Hatch and other officers. Charges of incompetence persisted, but the constant pressure from United States forces was having an effect. Victorio and his warriors retreated into Chihuahua where in October 1880 he and over eighty of his men were killed by Mexican troops.[48] Although Apache warriors occasionally raided the southern counties in succeeding years, none duplicated the fear and destruction generated by Victorio until Geronimo took to the warpath in 1885.

During the height of Victorio's War, John Ayers "for the sake of humanity" expressed his views in the territorial press. Having known Victorio and the Southern Apaches personally, he believed that the territory would have been spared its costly Indian war had the Apaches been allowed to remain on the Ojo Caliente reservation. In July 1879 and again early in 1880, the former Apache agent made contact with his former charges who assured him that they would die rather than return to San Carlos but would cease raiding if allowed to live at Ojo Caliente. Ayers subsequently offered to settle the whole Apache problem; he promised to bring in every Apache within four weeks if the government would pay his expenses and allow the Indians to live at Hot Springs. He blamed the government for the outbreak because it had broken faith with the Indians by driving them to San Carlos, violating a promise that they should live at Ojo Caliente. "How long will it be," Ayers asked, "before those who are in no danger . . . open their eyes and do justice to these Indians and save the lives of hundreds of our hardy pioneers by calling them in and fulfilling the honest treaty they chose to make with them." Hostilities could be ended quickly by giving the Apaches their promised home. "They have sworn to have their rights or die in fighting for them, and in this they are true-born Americans."[49]

In a letter dated April 12, 1880, Ayers referred to his own qualifications for serving as emissary to the Indians:

I do not speak as an egotist when I say I know more of Apache Indians than any man in New Mexico—having been their agent twice—and for some reasons they like me and have confidence in me. They also like Agent Jeffords, now in Tucson, Arizona. No other man in New Mexico can do what I can if clothed with authority.[50]

The editor of the *Albuquerque Review* supported Ayers's assessment of his own ability, noting that "his honesty coupled with a sense of true justice and aided by a genial disposition, has won for him, while dealing with the Apaches as their agent, their lasting esteem and friendship."[51] But Ayers was never given an opportunity to demonstrate his skills of diplomacy, and the Warm Springs Apaches met near annihilation in the mountains of Chihuahua.

Ayers remained in the Santa Fe region for the next several years. In the eighties he located a number of mines in Santa Fe District, opened a real estate firm in partnership with David N. Catanach, and laid plans to open public bathing facilities.[52] He fell onto hard times in the nineties, and in May 1892, suffering from deafness and unemployment, asked to be suspended from the Grand Army of the Republic until he could settle his debts. In the following year he had charge of the National Cemetery at Jefferson City, Missouri, and in 1901 supervised a similar establishment in Mexico City. Ayers had moved to the latter city at least by December 10, 1898 for on that date and in that city the seventy-one-year-old veteran married twenty-three-year-old Natalia P. Devrooman.[53]

A few other men besides Ayers in the California Column grew to respect and even to love the native inhabitants of the desert Southwest. Foremost among them was Thomas V. Keam, who became famous as an Indian trader to the Navajo Indians and bestowed his name on a colorful canyon in northeast Arizona. A native of England, Keam spent his early years in the English merchant marine. At the outbreak of the Civil War he was in San Francisco and enlisted in the California Cavalry. He mustered out in Santa Fe on January 22, 1865 and less than a month later

joined the First New Mexico Cavalry at Fort Bascom. He was
honorably discharged from the service in September 1866.[54]

In succeeding months, Keam became associated with a gentleman who became his nemesis, William F. M. Arny, secretary of
the territory during the Civil War and then Indian agent for the
United States government. In 1867 and 1868 Keam was present
at councils that Arny held with Jicarilla Apaches and Utes, serving as Spanish interpreter on at least one occasion. In partnership, the two men applied for commercial licenses in Rio Arriba
County in 1868, and Arny was listed as one of two sureties on a
bid that Keam submitted the previous year to supply wheat to
Abiquiu Agency.[55]

Shortly after the Navajos were released from Bosque Redondo,
Keam became Spanish interpreter at Fort Defiance at a salary of
$500 per annum. In 1871 he received a promotion to clerk and a
substantial increase in salary to $1,200 per year.[56] While employed
at Defiance, Keam was frequently sent on missions as peace emissary for the Navajos. Early in 1870, for example, he and one other
Indian official traveled to Cubero, Cebolleta, Albuquerque, and
Santa Fe to smooth differences that had long existed between that
tribe and Hispanos. Specifically, it was hoped that Hispanos could
be persuaded to return property stolen from Navajos, punish the
guilty parties, and release Navajo children held as peons. In mid-
summer, Keam and Defiance agent Frank T. Bennett made a similar trip but gained little cooperation from local Hispanos.[57]

During the summer of 1871, Keam was absent from the Navajo Agency on several assignments that brought him into frequent
contact with agent Arny. First, Keam and former comrade Henry
W. Easton served as Spanish interpreters at a council presided
over by Arny and Navajo agent James H. Miller to restore peace
between the Navajo and Zuñi tribes. Then, Arny, Easton, and
Keam traveled to Abiquiu to investigate thefts of stock belonging
to Navajo and Pueblo Indians allegedly committed by Ute Indians. Later they followed the Rio Grande south and attempted to
recover horses in the possession of Hispanos, which had been
stolen or obtained illegally from Navajos and Pueblos.[58]

KEAM AND THE MORALITY ISSUE

The death of agent James H. Miller in June 1872 elevated Keam to the position of acting Navajo agent, and on August 5 Gen. Oliver O. Howard, Special Indian Commissioner, appointed him as special agent for the Navajos, a position he held for about twelve months. During his short tenure, Keam organized the first Navajo police force at the agency and defended agency employees against charges of immorality leveled by Arny. By order of General Howard, Keam organized a force of 130 Navajo cavalry under war chief Manuelito to prevent depredations by tribesmen and to return stolen stock found on the reservation. After operating for less than one month, the Navajo patrol had succeeded in recapturing 56 horses, mules, and burros. Keam was convinced that an Indian police force was one of the best methods for recovering stolen stock; since Navajos were thoroughly acquainted with the reservation, they were more effective in trailing and gave better service than the United States Cavalry.[59]

Early in the seventies, Keam received favorable coverage in the territorial press. His visits to Santa Fe were frequently noted, and upon being promoted to special agent for the Navajos, the *Daily New Mexican* proclaimed that "Mr. Keams has the confidence of the Navajos, and his appointment cannot but be beneficial both to the government and the Indians. . . ." Navajos apparently trusted and respected him as well. When it was rumored that Keam would establish a subagency on the San Juan River, war chief Manuelito protested, expressing the desire that he remain among the Navajos at Defiance.[60]

Then, too, Keam had married a young Navajo woman in the formal Navajo Basket Ceremony sometime in 1869 as did his friend and ex-California trooper Anson C. Damon. A native of Maine, Damon had been appointed butcher for the Navajos at Fort Sumner after mustering out of the First California Cavalry in 1866. Two years later when the agency was moved to Fort Defiance, Damon, together with his California comrade and grain supervisor Perry H. Williams, accompanied the Navajos on their

Long Walk to Defiance where the two men continued their former occupations.[61]

Agency men who lived with Navajo women—squawmen—came under official displeasure soon after Keam was appointed special agent. General Howard had received information, undoubtedly from the hidebound Calvinist, William F. M. Arny, that employees at the agency had become addicted to gambling and profanity and were cohabiting with Navajo women. Although Keam was ordered to discharge all men guilty of moral offenses, he chose instead to defend agency employees against charges he considered unjust.[62]

In a letter to superintendent Pope, Keam—referring to himself and Damon—stated: "There are two Employees of this agency living with and married to Navajo women according to the customs of the Navajoes which in no way conflicts with their morals," and "these men have families and naturally look to the women as their wives, and treat them as such, they have been with the Navajoes and in the employ of the Government from five to seven years, are esteemed and respected by all the Indians." As for gambling and profanity, Keam knew of no one addicted to these vices. Keam concluded that he was using his "best endeavors to carry out the wishes of the Government, and look after the welfare of the Indians."[63]

The morality issue revived in mid-August 1873 when Arny arrived at Fort Defiance to become Navajo agent. As early as December of the previous year, the new superintendent at Santa Fe, L. Edwin Dudley, suggested to Commissioner Walker that Keam's services as special agent were no longer required since the projected agency in San Juan Valley had never been established. And his position with the agency finally was terminated shortly before Arny entered upon his new duties; in a letter dated July 22, 1873, superintendent Dudley ordered James L. Gould to "proceed at once to the Navajo Indian Agency at Fort Defiance and relieve sub-agent Keams, receipting to him all public property he may have."[64]

Once Arny assumed his position, he began to weed out employees deemed morally undesirable and to cripple Keam's influence on the reservation. Arny refused to grant Keam a license to trade with Navajos, although his bond for five thousand dollars was guaranteed by Lehman Spiegelberg and Herman Ilfeld, well-known Santa Fe merchants. Arny decided that Keam and his brother William were "not proper persons to be here, and that the Government, the Agent, and the Indians will be benefitted by their absence."[65]

On September 6, 1873 Arny submitted a report to superintendent Dudley requesting permission to discharge a number of employees he felt were unfit to live on the reservation. Specifically, he wished to purge Jesús Arviso, the Navajo interpreter, "an immoral man" who had one wife at Cubero but lived at Defiance with two Navajo sisters; W. W. Owens, employed as chief herder, charged with "improper intimacy with Indian women"; and Anson Damon and Perry H. Williams both guilty of living "with Indian Squaws."[66]

Apparently Damon and Arviso soon left the reservation, but Arny was not immediately successful in pushing the remaining "undesirables" off agency land. W. W. Owens remained for several months because Arny was unable "to obtain a better chief herder," and Perry H. Williams remained on the pay-roll until the last day of April 1874. In the final irony, Arny not only re-hired Arviso as interpreter in June 1874 after the latter promised "to set a good example to the Indians," but agreed to pay him extra compensation out of his own private funds because, Arny reported, it was necessary to have a good interpreter at the agency![67]

Shortly after his ouster as Navajo subagent, Thomas V. Keam left Santa Fe to visit his native England. He was absent from his wife and two sons for more than a year, and during his absence she remarried, believing that he planned not to return.[68]

It is not clear when Keam again touched American soil, but in December 1874 he was in the nation's capital making life miserable for his erstwhile colleague, William F. M. Arny. The agent had accompanied eleven Navajos on a trip to Washington in mid-November to arrange new boundaries for the reservation and

to impress the Indians with the power of white man's government.[69] California veteran Henry W. Easton and Bill Taylor traveled with Arny's party as interpreters and were viewed with as
much curiosity in the East as were the Indians, the former acquiring the sobriquet "Wild Hank" and the latter "Rocky Mountain
Bill."[70]

In Washington Keam made his appearance at the Arlington
Hotel where the Indians were staying before their scheduled meeting with President Grant. Arny was out of the hotel, and Keam
took several of his Navajo friends on a tour of the city's bars and
bordellos. Arny was furious when he returned to find Navajos stag-
gering and carousing through the Arlington Hotel. The meeting
with Grant had to be postponed.[71]

Upon his return to New Mexico in February 1875, Arny found
that his Navajo charges were growing restless. On May 28 the
principal chiefs and headmen met in council and signed a petition calling for his removal and requesting that Thomas V. Keam,
"knowing our wants and necessities," be appointed agent. Among
four Anglo witnesses who signed the petition were Anson C.
Damon and Perry H. Williams. Arny subsequently returned to
Washington to prevent his removal and to renew his project to
change the boundaries of the reservation. While he was absent
from the agency, the chiefs again met, this time at Fort Wingate
to sign a petition that repeated their appeal to remove Arny. Officers at the post sympathized with the Navajos and believed that the
only way to restore peace on the reservation was to appoint Keam,
a man with experience and who was trusted by the Indians.[72]

In August, while Arny was at Santa Fe preparing to return to
the agency, several Navajo chiefs rode into Defiance and seized
the agency. Although Arny had already submitted his resignation,
agreeing to leave at the end of the year, the Navajos forced his
immediate removal. Thomas V. Keam thereupon applied to the
Presbyterian Mission Board for appointment as agent but was
turned down by board members who believed that Keam was "not
the kind of man a mission board could nominate."[73]

Arny was convinced that "squawmen" were responsible for his removal, a stand supported by the editor of the *Daily New Mexican*.[74] Thereafter Arny lodged criminal charges against his detractors in the Second Judicial District Court at Albuquerque, and during its 1875 fall term the grand jury handed down indictments against William Keam, Daniel Dubois, and Anson C. Damon, but not against Thomas V. Keam, who appeared in court ten days prior to his brother's indictment to apply for American citizenship. It was granted October 6, 1875 after José Francisco Chavez and Benjamin Stevens testified that Keam had resided in the United States and in New Mexico the requisite number of years and was "a man of good moral character." William Keam was indicted on one charge of selling liquor to Indians and on two charges of sending a seditious message to Indians, while Dubois and Damon were indicted on the latter charge. These cases were continued until the spring of 1877, when the three men entered pleas of not guilty and eventually were cleared of all criminal charges.[75]

In subsequent years, Thomas V. Keam became a trader among the Navajos; in 1876 he operated a trading post one mile south of the agency and William Keam, living with a Navajo wife, operated a similar store for his brother in Keam's Canyon.[76] But clearly New Mexico's Indian officials continued to value his talents for treating with Indians. In September 1877 Keam was appointed Indian interpreter at Fort Wingate and supervisor of Southern Apache prisoners who had deserted the San Carlos reservation, and in November he was at Ojo Caliente serving with Jesús Arviso as interpreter.[77]

Keam left the Indian service in February 1878 to return to his trading post near Fort Defiance. He spent the remainder of his productive life as trader to Indians, operating various posts in the mesa lands of northeastern Arizona. Occasionally he was accused of exploiting Indians who traded at his stores, but more than most white men he had gained an intimate knowledge of American Indians and had come to respect and cherish their culture. Thomas

V. Keam finally sold his trading post to Lorenzo Hubbell in 1902 and returned to the land of his birth where he died two years later.[78]

Anson C. Damon established a trading post south of Fort Defiance and resided in that region for nearly the rest of his life. When Lt. John G. Bourke visited Defiance in 1881, Damon was employed as agency farmer and provided the lieutenant with considerable information on Navajos. In 1909, sixty-seven-year-old Damon was living at Charlotte, Maine, but later returned to Fort Defiance where he died in 1925. He and his wife, Ta-des-bah, were buried in adjoining graves in the family cemetery south of Fort Defiance.[79]

Henry W. Easton, the California veteran who accompanied Arny to Washington, lived until 1903 when he died in Santa Fe. He led an extremely mobile life, moving from place to place and never residing long in one locality. In most instances he performed minor chores among Indians in New Mexico, except for a decade working as a general laborer chiefly in Iowa and Nebraska. In 1884, he worked intermittently for the superintendent of public instruction, Amado Chaves, doing odd jobs and caring for his horses.[80]

A SANTA FE PIONEER

The hub of New Mexico's Indian superintendency was its central office in Santa Fe. Here the superintendent received reports and issued orders to agents serving in the field. His job was complex and frequently frustrating, but an efficient chief clerk supervising the office could make it less so. California veteran David N. Catanach filled this post most capably. Although his personal life was far from exemplary, he effectively discharged his occupational responsibilities. In addition to handling paper work, Catanach traveled on official business and was assigned tasks that brought him into direct contact with New Mexico's Indian tribes.[81]

The early history of Kentucky-born Catanach discloses a penchant to roam. At age thirteen he went to sea on a merchant ship and for three years sailed around the world. When the Civil War broke out, he enlisted at age sixteen in the Pennsylvania volunteers. Shortly thereafter he contracted typhoid and was sent home to die at his parents' house in Philadelphia. Instead his health improved, and in 1863 he boarded in New York a vessel bound for San Francisco. There he enlisted in the California volunteers and subsequently made the overland trip to New Mexico to help fill vacancies in the original California Column.[82]

After mustering out of the service in Santa Fe, Catanach married Rosario Donavant in 1867—the fifteen-year-old daughter of a Kentucky-born father and a Hispanic mother. Over the next fifteen years, Rosario gave birth to thirteen children. While in Santa Fe, they lived in a house three miles from the center of town, and David walked daily to his work at the Indian superintendency. Rosario experienced a mental breakdown after the premature birth of her last child during the spring of 1881. Their son James reported that David deserted his wife a few months after her illness and went to Lincoln County where he established a ranch. A second son John believed the cause of his parents' separation was his father's hard-drinking—"he would be drunk for a week at a time"—rather than his mother's breakdown. A third son Archibald felt that the separation was caused by his grandparents who simply took Rosario to their home after she became ill, claiming that David was not providing her proper care—an action that caused the latter to file charges against his father-in-law for abducting his wife. After Catanach moved from Santa Fe he filed for divorce in Doña Ana County, which was granted on May 12, 1885. Eight days later he deeded his Santa Fe house and flouring mill as well as additional tracts of land to Rosario and their children.[83]

Prior to his divorce, Catanach became involved in a bitter controversy over control of water in the Santa Fe River. In October 1880 Frank Sandoval, John P. Kennedy, and Palle F. Herlow incorporated the Santa Fe Water and Improvement Company to build a series of three reservoirs for the storage of water and to supply water to the capital by means of large pipes. By May 1881 sixty-five men were at work on the lower reservoir, and the contractor, Kennedy, predicted that the water works would be completed within four months.[84]

The company experienced numerous problems, however, which delayed the project several months. The most serious problem was posed by Santa Fe businessmen who feared that the company's plan to divert the channel of the river would deprive them of water power necessary to run their mills. On May 17, 1881 the *Daily New Mexican* published a notice signed by David N. Catanach and six other owners of land adjacent to the Santa Fe River stating that they would resist any encroachment upon their water rights. Catanach, who now operated a grist and flour mill, charged that the company had no legal right to divert the river's channel nor to sell its water to Santa Fe residents.[85]

Charles W. Greene, editor of the *Daily New Mexican,* publicly supported the water works project, believing it would benefit the entire community by doubling the amount of water available for use. Though he described Catanach as "one of the enterprising men of the city, interested in its growth and prosperity," he criticized the former soldier's opposition. Greene implied that Catanach undertook to block the project only after he and the company failed to agree on a settlement for any impairment that his property might suffer because of the water works. In following weeks, while more residents joined the opposition, financial difficulties delayed construction. Eventually, however, underground pipes were laid throughout the principal streets of Santa Fe, and on March 31, 1882 the water was turned on and flowed from the reservoir to the city.[86]

Occasionally in the seventies, Catanach had been employed as an issue clerk at the Mescalero Apache Agency in Lincoln County, and about the time of his divorce he was again working at that position. He journeyed to Philadelphia in 1886 to wed his childhood sweetheart and then returned to the Mescalero Agency with his new wife who taught in the Indian school while he was employed as agency farmer. Their sojourn in New Mexico lasted seven months as the new Mrs. Catanach suffered poor health.

They returned to Phildelphia where Catanach operated a real estate office almost to the day he died March 14, 1906.[87]

While it is impossible to trace all connections of California veterans with agencies of the federal government, examples provided in these pages indicate that they, like so many of their western compatriots, sought employment in the federal service or competed enthusiastically for military and Indian contracts. Independent, strong-willed, and self-reliant, they viewed the governmental machinery of the nation as a device for promoting their own economic fortunes. In seeking economic advancement, the former soldiers contributed to the work force that kept the machinery of government functioning in the territory of New Mexico.

9

Politics
and Politicans

The soldiers who arrived in New Mexico with Carleton's command proved as keen to invade the political arena as they were to carve economic niches for themselves upon their return to civilian life. Like other westerners, California veterans were practical opportunists and viewed political office as a means to acquire control over their immediate environment and to enhance their status within local communities.

The American frontier traditionally offered unusual opportunities for political advancement to men of modest wealth and social standing. Men who moved west, or east as was the case with the California Column, often were more aggressive and daring than those who remained behind, so it was not unusual for many of these citizens to throw their energies into politics and to be elected to political office, especially since there were numerous posts to be filled. But the California soldiers did not enter a political vacuum, though they moved to a thinly populated region.

New Mexico had an organized system of government, dominated at the local and territorial levels by Hispanic office holders, though the highest ranking officials, usually Anglos, were appointed by the president of the United States. Moving into a predominantly Hispanic society, California veterans learned to accommodate their political ambitions to those of Hispanic leaders and to devise power arrangements politically advantageous to each group. Yet ex-soldiers who pioneered settlement in the min-

ing districts (Grant County, for example) found themselves in a
different situation. Here Anglos predominated numerically and
politically, and it was in such districts that men from the old
California Column controlled an impressive number of political
offices.

As a group, California veterans took active interest in grass roots
politics, spearheading campaign rallies, serving as election judges,
signing petitions and protests, and adding their voices to the
cacophony of political rhetoric at election time. Many were elected
to local and county offices, a handful served in the territorial legislature, and one—William L. Rynerson—received major backing but failed to be elected as New Mexico's delegate to Congress.

Though Republicans controlled much of the political machinery in New Mexico in the twenty years following the close of the
Civil War, a substantial number of California veterans worked
ardently for the Democratic cause, particularly such men as Joseph F. Bennett and John D. Barncastle. And during these decades several veterans were involved in the most publicized political
imbroglios of the day. They campaigned for and against former
comrades, allied themselves with Hispanos of similar political per-
suasion, and formed political splinter groups to accomplish political ends. These men were steeped in the materialistic ethos and
political conservatism of the "Gilded Age," and there is little evidence that they supported the nascent populist movement that
emerged in the 1880s. Occasionally, violence, graft, and illegal
maneuvers served their cause, but the overall record of California
soldiers in New Mexico's political history is impressive.

While it is not possible to reconstruct the political involvement
for each former soldier, it is evident that California volunteers
who relocated in the southern counties of Grant and Doña Ana
after the war were more politically active than their comrades who
resided elsewhere in the territory. It is also true that extant territorial newspapers provide more extensive coverage for events and
elections in the southern counties than for similar events in, for
example, Colfax and Mora counties. Nevertheless the Santa Fe
newspapers, which covered political events throughout the terri-

tory, more frequently reported on political involvement of former soldiers living in the south than for those in the north. Moreover, the two southern counties of Grant and Doña Ana sent four ex-California soldiers to the territorial legislature between 1865 and 1885 while the northern counties sent only two. In addition, no county could equal the political record of California veterans who resided in Grant County, despite the fact that Colfax County attracted many soldier-miners to its borders.[1]

Grant County outdistanced all others in the number of political offices held by California veterans. Starting in 1868 California veterans filled the positions of county probate judge and county sheriff eight out of ten and five out of ten years, respectively. The leading politicians to emerge in Grant County among the ex-California soldiers were the four men elected to the above offices: John K. Houston, Richard Hudson, James G. Crittenden, and Joseph F. Bennett.[2] Several other veterans filled elective county offices ranging from justice of the peace to constable and county commissioner.

Although Doña Ana County could not equal its neighbor in the number of former California soldiers elected to political office, it produced a roster of California veterans who emerged as influential territorial politicians, including William L. Rynerson, Albert J. Fountain, John S. Crouch, and John D. Barncastle. The political actions of veterans who resided in Grant and Doña Ana counties were so intimately linked that it is appropriate to assess conjointly their impact on New Mexico's political history.

RYNERSON

The most influential politician to emerge in New Mexico from Carleton's old command was undoubtedly William L. Rynerson, Republican leader of Doña Ana County, a talented campaigner, and an effective vote-getter among both Hispanos and Anglos. Just eight months after leaving the service, he demonstrated his talent for galvanizing local political support at a political convention in Las Cruces on the last day of June in 1867. The meeting had been called to nominate candidates for territorial and county offices as well as to nominate a delegate to Congress.

From the time that New Mexico was incorporated into the United States, the biennial election of a congressional delegate had split the territory into two opposing factions that only loosely resembled modern political parties. In post-Civil War New Mexico, the two factions adopted or shed national party labels as a matter of political expediency; by the early 1870s, however, the major national parties had established some semblance of a formal party organization, including a territorial central executive committee.[3]

The two factions that emerged in 1867 rallied behind opposing nominees for delegate to Congress—the incumbent J. Francisco Chavez and the attorney Charles P. Clever. Chavez had been elected in 1865 by anti-Carleton forces supporting Radical Reconstructionists in Congress; his opponent, Francisco Perea, had the backing of pro-Carleton men who sympathized with the moderate reconstruction policies of President Andrew Johnson.[4] In 1867 Clever inherited the support of the old Johnson and pro-Carleton forces, which in later years emerged under the banner of the Democratic party, while the Chavez supporters later adopted the Republican label.

At the June convention held in Las Cruces, William L. Rynerson attempted to nominate J. Francisco Chavez as delegate, but the chairman of the meeting, Pinckney R. Tully, a Clever supporter and copartner in the freighting firm of Tully and Ochoa, refused to entertain his motion. Rynerson thereupon led Chavez supporters from the hall and presided over a separate meeting in the street. William R. McCormick, a former sergeant in the California volunteers, described the proceedings in a letter to the Santa Fe *New Mexican,* estimating that three hundred Chavez men rallied in the street while only a handful—he said seven—remained inside to support Clever. The street convention voted to back Chavez's nomination for Congress and then appointed a committee of one delegate from each precinct to nominate men for county offices. Nine Hispanos and four Anglos served on that committee, including California veterans John E. Oliphant and William R. McCormick. Six names were placed in nomination, four Hispanos and two Anglos: Rynerson received the nomination for senator to the territorial legislature, and John Davis was nominated as coroner.[5]

The campaign during the summer months was spirited as Carleton's reputation became a political issue. The Santa Fe *New Mexican* announced that "to vote for Clever is to vote for Carleton. Clever is pledged, if elected, to have Carleton returned as commander of New Mexico." In the same issue, the paper addressed a notice to California volunteers, stating that "Clever is Carleton's candidate. The California Volunteers should not forget this. Remember Carleton's outrageous treatment of you and vote accordingly."[6]

THE POET CANTERBURY

A former private in the California volunteers who took no active part in the campaign found that a poem composed at an earlier date entered the lively debate between Clever and Chavez forces. The poet, Rufus P. Canterbury, received an honorable discharge from the military December 25, 1864, although on that date he was in custody of civil authorities for murder. While in confinement in the guardhouse at Fort Selden or perhaps later when a prisoner at Lemitar in Socorro County awaiting trial, Canterbury composed "New Mexico and Arizona," described in the Santa Fe *Weekly Gazette* by Francisco Perea as "a scurrilous piece of poetry, defamatory of the people of New Mexico."[7]

Copies of the poem were printed in the office of the Santa Fe *New Mexican,* after some of the more vulgar verses were expurgated, under the title "New Mexico, by one who's been thar." Canterbury castigated New Mexico and New Mexicans in fifty verses of unadulterated doggerel. Among the least objectionable were those which dealt with New Mexico's flora and fauna:

> The dusty, long, hot, dreary way,
> Where 'neath a blazing sun you totter
> To reach a camp at close of day
> And find it destitute of water.

> The dying mule, the dried-up spring,
>   Which novel writers seldom notice;
> The song the blood mosquitoes sing,
>   And midnight howling of coyotes.

But the verses that caused so much commotion among the politicians were several that cast aspersion on Hispanic residents:

> These natives, in a Yankee's eyes,
>   Have neither virtue, brains nor vigor—
> A most unhappy compromise
>   Between the Ingin and the nigger.

> They tell a thousand barefaced lies,
>   To all the saints in heaven appealing
> Confess their sins with tearful eyes,
>   Devoutly pray—but keep on stealing.[8]

During the election of 1867 partisans of Francisco Chavez claimed that Canterbury's poem had been composed and published by friends of Mr. Clever, and it was to clear Clever's name that Perea published in the *Weekly Gazette* correspondence documenting the "true" history of the infamous poem. As for the alleged poet, Canterbury was cleared of the murder charge in 1866 and soon left the territory to return to Illinois, his native state.[9]

One of the more disreputable among Clever's backers was former California trooper William W. Beman, erstwhile clerk for the Third Judicial District Court, deputy sheriff, and jailer for Doña Ana County. Shortly after the 1867 election, the Santa Fe *New Mexican,* the voice of the Chavez party, asserting that Beman had been "Clever's right hand man and confidential adviser in Doña Ana County," smugly published a list of Beman's alleged misdemeanors: stealing money from the quartermaster's safe in Las Cruces as an enlisted man and stealing letters from the Mesilla post office as a civilian. Beman subsequently left New Mexico, allegedly driven from Mesilla Valley by angry residents.[10]

The Clever faction appeared victorious in the September election. With a slim majority of 97 votes, Clever was issued the certificate of election as congressional delegate by Gov. Robert B. Mitchell. Probate Judge John Lemon and Justice of the Peace Evangelisto Chaves counted votes in Doña Ana County and declared that Samuel J. Jones had won the election for territorial senator, receiving 432 votes to Rynerson's 423. For representatives, the leading vote-getters were George W. Nesmith and Cristobal Ascarate, both running on the Clever ticket against Chavez backers Ignacio Orrantia and Pablo Melendres. Loud and persistent were the charges of fraud during the election, and secretary of the territory Herman II. Heath issued certificates of election to Chavez and Rynerson because of alleged election improprieties. After a lengthy congressional investigation, Chavez was declared the rightful victor and was seated in Congress early in 1869, though Clever had served during the intervening months as New Mexico's delegate.[11]

Rynerson journeyed to Santa Fe to take his seat in the legislative council that convened December 2, 1867. Since Jones contested Rynerson's claim, the council conducted its own investigation and voted to seat Rynerson on December 5. Similarly, Ignacio Orrantia and Pablo Melendres received official recognition as representatives to the legislature from Doña Ana County rather than Nesmith and Ascarate.[12]

THE MURDER OF JUDGE SLOUGH

William L. Rynerson missed most meetings of the legislature that term because of his involvement in one of the most sensational killings of the decade. On Sunday, December 15, the former officer in the California volunteers was arrested and confined in the Fort Marcy guardhouse for killing Chief Justice John P. Slough, the Union colonel who had led Colorado troops in 1862 to expel the Confederates from New Mexico. While chief justice of New Mexico, Slough's caustic language and aggressive tactics created numerous enemies. Soon after the legislature began its sessions in 1867, Slough physically attacked William F. M. Arny

for allegedly persuading legislators to deny him—Slough—the traditional honor of administering oaths of office to members of
that body. [13]

Senator Rynerson thereupon introduced resolutions calling for
the chief justice's removal for unprofessional conduct. Rynerson
charged that Slough intimidated juries, made partisan decisions
on the bench, and frequently had been drunk in the streets of
Santa Fe. The Santa Fe *Weekly Gazette*, a voice for local Democrats, claimed that Secretary Herman H. Heath composed the
resolutions against Slough and that Rynerson, owing Heath a favor
for having issued him the certificate of election, agreed to intro-
duce them in Council. Nonetheless, both houses of the legislature approved these resolutions on December 14, and the next
day Rynerson and Slough confronted each other in La Fonda
Hotel, where after a verbal exchange Rynerson shot and killed
Judge Slough. [14]

A preliminary hearing was held before Judge Joab Houghton
on January 3, 1868 with Rynerson being represented by former
Chief Justice Kirby Benedict and United States District Attorney Stephen B. Elkins. Testifying for the defense, Samuel B.
Wheelock stated that on the night preceding the shooting Rynerson was playing billiards with Colonel Kinzie when Slough
entered the billiard room and remarked to a neighbor that they
were observing a strange combination, "a gentleman associating
with a damned thief; I allude to that damned seven-foot son of a
bitch playing billiards with Col. Kinzie." Slough added that Rynerson was a thief and a coward who had stolen both in and out
of the army, including his present seat in the legislature. Wheelock later repeated these statements to Rynerson. [15]

Rynerson the following day approached the chief justice in the
hotel demanding that he retract his statements. Slough refused
and Rynerson drew a gun. A witness to the tragedy testified that
Slough turned as if to draw a gun, saying something like "Shoot,
damn you!" Rynerson shot, and as Slough fell, a derringer clat-
tered to the floor, apparently from Slough's pocket. After hearing
the evidence, Judge Houghton remanded Rynerson to jail without
setting bond. [16]

Houghton's failure to grant bond evoked a storm of protest from Doña Ana County residents who at a meeting in Las Cruces on January 26 adopted resolutions signed by 195 men condemning the judge for perverting justice and lending himself to corrupt and partisan purposes.[17] Rynerson, meanwhile, demanded a writ of habeas corpus, and on January 23—three days prior to the Las Cruces meeting—Judge Perry Brocchus released him on a twenty-thousand-dollar bond. Rynerson was eventually tried in March for Slough's murder and was acquitted on a plea of self-defense.[18]

Rynerson served three successive terms in the territorial council, being reelected in 1868 and 1869. In each session he was the only Anglo serving in the council, although a handful were elected to the house. In 1869 he was joined in the legislature by a former California comrade, Hiram S. Russell, elected representative from Colfax County.[19] Rynerson's tenure was filled with controversy, and local Democrats staged at least one public meeting to protest his actions. Still, it was during his first term on January 30, 1868, that the legislature enacted a widely supported bill creating Grant County from the western portion of Doña Ana.[20] And for the following two years, Rynerson represented both counties in the territorial council.

ORGANIZING FOR POLITICS

The first political convention held in the new county of Grant occurred on April 4, 1868, at Pinos Altos, with at least three California volunteers serving as official delegates: Henry Barton, John S. Powers, and Leonidas V. Steele. The assembled delegates nominated miner John K. Houston, a former lieutenant in the California volunteers, for probate judge and three other Anglos for probate clerk, sheriff, and treasurer. These men, running on the so-called Republican Union Ticket, were opposed by candidates nominated by disgruntled delegates who bolted the April 4 convention. This opposition party ran Virgil Mastin for probate judge and former California lieutenant Richard Hudson for sheriff.[21]

Grant County voters went to the polls on April 28 to elect

justices of the peace for four precincts in addition to the above county offices. Five out of the eight men elected to office were former California troopers. Although they ran on opposing tickets, Houston and Hudson were each successful in their bids for public office and became, respectively, the first judge of probate and the first sheriff of Grant County.

Three of four justices of the peace were former California soldiers: Richard Yeamans, John S. Powers, and William B. Morgan. Sheriff Hudson subsequently relinquished his badge and was elected probate judge in 1869, serving in that capacity for four years. Both John K. Houston and Richard Hudson had long and distinguished political careers in southern New Mexico, and each became a loyal supporter of the Republican party.[22]

During the election of 1871 both Grant and Doña Ana counties were immersed in hard-fought campaigns that pitted former comrades against one another. Moreover, during the campaign the Democratic party emerged with renewed strength, thanks in part to the leadership and journalistic support of the Bennett brothers and to the creation of a new central executive committee. On April 19, 1871 over six hundred county residents met in Mesilla to organize the Democratic Club of Doña Ana County, said to be "the first Democratic Club in the Territory." Nehemiah V. Bennett, editor of the Las Cruces *Borderer*, was elected president of the club and sixteen men—including John D. Barncastle and George W. Nesmith—were named as vice-presidents.[23]

Leading Democrats from throughout the territory assembled in Santa Fe on April 29 to organize formally a territorial party and to establish a temporary central committee. R. H. Tompkins was named chairman of the central committee and former California officer Joseph F. Bennett of Grant County and Lawrence G. Murphy of Lincoln County were named two of its five vice-presidents. Appointed to the central committee were representatives from each county, including California veterans William McMullen of Santa Fe, Louis Clark of Rio Arriba, Hiram S. Russell from Colfax, Emil Fritz from Lincoln, and Robert V. Newsham and John S. Crouch from Grant counties.[24]

Two months later, Democrats convened in the House of Representatives at Santa Fe to nominate a candidate for delegate to Congress. Joseph F. Bennett was named one of four vice-presidents for the convention presided over by the Honorable Francisco Perea, while Thomas Coghlan served as cosecretary with Nicolas Quintana. Coghlan, an Irishman and ex-private in the First California Infantry, had served two years as deputy U.S. Marshall in Santa Fe. The party passed resolutions protesting the growth of big government, protective tariffs, control of territorial government by Republicans, and the political record of incumbent J. Francisco Chavez. Nehemiah Bennett placed in nomination for delegate to Congress the name of José Manuel Gallegos, the ex-padre who had served in that capacity in 1853.[25]

Democrats in Grant County subsequently staged an exuberant convention in Silver City on the Fourth of July. Two of the three men appointed to draft a Democratic ticket had been sergeants in the California Column: Henry M. Harshberger and Sydney M. Webb. Among those nominated by the convention were Joseph F. Bennett for territorial senator and William B. Morgan for probate clerk. Selected to serve for two years on the nine-man Democratic county committee were veterans Webb, George Perrault, and Robert V. Newsham.[26]

Territorial Republicans likewise staged conventions and nominated candidates. In Santa Fe Republicans renominated incumbent J. Francisco Chavez for congressional delegate and, among other appointments, selected Richard Hudson as Grant County's representative to the Republican central committee. In mid-June a respectable number of Grant County voters assembled at Central City to select candidates for county offices irrespective of party affiliation. The so-called People's Party nominated John S. Crouch as senator (representing Grant and Doña Ana counties), Richard Hudson for probate judge, James G. Crittenden for sheriff, Robert V. Newsham for county treasurer, and two other Anglos for probate clerk and representative to the legislature. The majority of the People's nominees were Republicans, but Newsham belonged to the opposing party, a fact that led at least one dis-

gruntled Democrat to charge that Newsham had "sold his princi-
ples for the petty office of Treasurer."[27]

Republicans in Doña Ana County also met in June, and nominated, among other candidates, John S. Crouch for senator and
John Lemon—a government contractor—for probate judge. William L. Rynerson, who served on both the resolutions and nomi-
nating committees at the meeting, closed the convention with a
rousing speech calling for party unity.[28]

THE VIOLENT CAMPAIGN OF 1871

Both political parties staged several rallies in Doña Ana County
during the course of a bitter campaign marred by acts of physical
violence and charges of graft and corruption. The most serious
accusations were made against Colonel Rynerson and his fellow
Republicans by incumbent probate judge Pablo Melendres, who
charged that Ignacio Orrantia, clerk of the probate court, had
asked Melendres to switch parties and join the Republicans. Then
Orrantia asked Melendres to allow him to perform the duties of
probate judge for six days following the election to assure a Republican victory. In return for these favors, Melendres was offered
Colonel Rynerson's office as customs inspector. According to
Melendres, Orrantia stated that the Republicans were determined
to win the election "whether they gained it by votes or use of bullets, clubs, rocks or blows." Several days later when unidentified
gunmen fired at two relatives of Democratic candidates for sheriff
and territorial legislator, the *Borderer* charged that the Republican
threat of violence had turned into attempted assassination.[29]

As pressures increased and tempers frayed, the possibility of serious violence between opposing factions mounted. Early in the
campaign, partisans for each faction gathered in the streets of Las
Cruces on a Sunday summer day shouting *vivas* for their respective parties. Liquor flowed, the band played, and one man was
struck on the head with a pistol. Serious violence was avoided
when political leaders arrived to calm matters. In a second incident several weeks later, the press reported that a riot was nar-

rowly averted in Mesilla after a group of Democrats had hurled "all sorts of insults" at a gathering of over three hundred Republicans.[30]

The tragic finale of this campaign occurred on August 27 when each party staged political meetings in Mesilla, with José Manuel Gallegos on hand to boost Democratic loyalty. Rynerson was probably the leading orator at the Republican conclave. After the speeches had ended, each party staged a parade through town, eventually meeting at the plaza. Emotions were high and when Apolonio Barela fired his gun in the air, indiscriminate shooting followed. Though an estimated forty or fifty men were wounded in what became known as the Mesilla Riot, nine were killed, including John Lemon whose skull had been fractured by a pickax.[31]

The Republicans were defeated in the September elections, not only in Doña Ana County, where election day passed very quietly, but also throughout the territory. The Republican vote for territorial delegate had been split between J. Francisco Chavez, the regular party candidate, and José D. Sena, who having bolted the party was running as an independent. Consequently Gallegos received a relatively easy victory. With Lemon's death, Rynerson's name went on the ballot as Republican candidate for probate judge, but he was defeated along with other Republicans.[32] California volunteers seeking office in Grant County on the People's Ticket were somewhat more fortunate. Hudson and Crittenden won their elections for probate judge and sheriff, while Newsham and Crouch lost to their Democratic opponents. The most important victory among California veterans was that of Joseph F. Bennett, elected territorial senator to represent Grant and Doña Ana counties.[33]

CONVENING THE NEW LEGISLATURE

The legislature that convened at Santa Fe on the first Monday in December 1871 was one of the most notorious in the territory's history. Two former California soldiers—Joseph F. Bennett and Hiram S. Russell—played significant roles in the tumult that subsequently enveloped the legislative chambers.

Trouble erupted shortly after the legislature enacted a measure moving Chief Justice Joseph G. Palen from the First Judicial District in Santa Fe to the Third District in Mesilla. It was a bold attempt to rid Santa Fe of a judge said to be an implacable foe to the moneyed interests entrenched in the capital city. After Gov. Marsh Giddings vetoed the bill, Democrats in the legislature initiated a power play to seize control of both houses. After a comic-opera sequence of intrigue and maneuvering, Democrats and Republicans each organized separate houses and proceeded to enact separate laws. Two days before adjournment, the Democrat-controlled council, eager to enact some important measures before the end of the session, agreed to recognize the "Republican House" after a compromise speaker was elected.[34]

One of the major leaders of the Democratic revolt in the house was Hiram S. Russell, former sergeant in the California volunteers. Born in Maine in 1831, Russell became a liquor dealer in Elizabethtown after mustering out of the service. He served two terms in the territorial legislature and while mayor of Elizabethtown married eighteen-year-old Racine McKay, twenty-one years his junior. In subsequent years his name occasionally appeared in the pages of the territorial press, and early in the spring of 1880 he became seriously ill while visiting Las Vegas Hot Springs and died there on April 12. Upon his passing, both the *Weekly New Mexican* and the *Cimarron News and Press* paid tribute to the old soldier, affectionately referred to as "Doc" and by all accounts a man of genial disposition, "a favorite with all who knew him, good hearted, open and generous to a fault."[35]

Joseph F. Bennett served only one term in the territorial legislature, but during the winter of 1871–72 he left his imprint upon the proceedings of that tumultuous body. It was Bennett who introduced the so-called alien bill, granting aliens who purchased real estate in New Mexico "all the rights and privileges in holding and disposing of the same as are now enjoyed by citizens." This bill, applauded by commercial men who believed it would entice foreign capital into the territory, was signed into law by Governor Giddings.[36] Second, Bennett introduced a resolution calling for inquiry into the stationing of soldiers in and about the legislative halls during the most turbulent days of the session. He subsequently chaired a special committee appointed to investigate this matter. Its report on January 24 concluded that, although Governor Giddings approved this action to preserve order, troops had in fact been dispatched to preserve the Republican faction in power.[37]

From Santa Fe the senator from Grant and Doña Ana counties returned to Silver City where he continued to labor long and hard for the Democratic party. He and three other veterans—John D. Barncastle, Lawrence Lapoint, and Henry C. Haring—were instrumental in organizing during the fall of 1872 the New Mexico Greeley and Brown Association, pledged to support the Democratic ticket in the forthcoming presidential election. One other veteran, William McMullen, also supported the Greeley-Brown ticket and spoke on its behalf at a Santa Fe rally—along with such well-known personalities as Charles C. Clever and Judge Kirby Benedict.[38]

The following autumn, the most important political campaign being waged in the territory was that between Stephen B. Elkins and Padre Gallegos for delegate to Congress. Elkins and his law partner, Thomas B. Catron, formed the nucleus of a Republican-dominated group of lawyers, judges, politicians, and businessmen known as the Santa Fe Ring. In 1873 the Republican party pictured Elkins as the candidate who would most advance territorial development by supporting "the introduction of railroads, the settlement of the land question, the encouragement of immigration." "Smooth Steve," as he was dubbed, won support from all parts of the territory.[39]

Joseph F. Bennett, and possibly his brother Nehemiah, crossed party lines with many Democrats to help secure Elkins's election.[40] This maneuver, however, failed to win support for Nehemiah's bid to succeed his brother in the legislature; he was defeated for senator in the September election by Republican John D. Bail.[41]

Similarly going down to defeat was James G. Crittenden, Grant County's Republican sheriff, seeking election as representative to the legislature. A native of Indiana, Crittenden was one of the county's principal miners and public officials. In subsequent years, the former soldier served as election judge, road supervisor, grand juror, justice of the peace, and member of the Republican county central committee. A former corporal in the Fifth California Infantry, Crittenden died July 13, 1882 in Silver City at the age of forty-eight.[42]

THE ELECTION OF 1875

As the territory girded itself for the biennial delegate election in 1875, Elkins's record was subjected to intense scrutiny by members of both political parties. In Grant County, Joseph F. Bennett was instrumental in organizing Democrats for the coming campaign. At the county convention held in June, he and four other men submitted several resolutions calling for an end to Elkins's tenure in office, since he had accomplished nothing in Washington. Bennett and one other gentleman were elected to represent Grant County at the Democratic territorial meeting.[43]

When the convention got underway in Santa Fe in June, both Joseph F. Bennett and Nehemiah were mentioned as possible nominees for delegate to Congress. The certain renomination of Elkins by the Republicans, however, helped undermine Democratic party loyalty. And the party's nominee, Mariano S. Otero, subsequently refused the nomination and threw his support to Elkins.[44] Meanwhile, Joseph F. Bennett was nominated by Grant County Democrats for probate judge while former comrades William Chamberlin—a miner from Silver City—and Henry Barton—a miner from Pinos Altos—received nominations for coroner and school commissioner, respectively. Dispensing with further conventions, Joseph F. Bennett and other members of the Democratic territorial central committee chose Pedro Valdez of San Miguel County as their party's nominee, replacing Otero. Notwithstanding Bennett's support for Valdez, the Republican *Mesilla News* reminded its readers that Bennett "some time ago" had written a letter endorsing Elkins.[45] In neighboring Doña Ana County, Democrats nominated Nehemiah V. Bennett for territorial senator and California veterans Henry C. Haring for sheriff and John Davis for coroner.[46]

Throughout the territory in 1875, Republican county conventions universally endorsed Elkins because he "could and did raise his voice and command a hearing for the rights of his constituents among the assembled wisdom of the nation."[47] In Doña Ana County, William L. Rynerson, as member of the territorial Republican executive committee, called for a meeting to select delegates to the territorial convention. Presided over by John D. Bail with Albert J. Fountain as one of four vice-presidents, the Doña Ana Republicans endorsed Elkins for Congress in May. Three months later, Fountain presided over a meeting of county residents—designated the People's Convention—to select candidates for local offices irrespective of party affiliation. John S. Crouch, John Davis, and three other men were appointed to the resolutions committee, which recommended unqualified support for Elkins's renomination. Jacinto Armijo was selected to oppose Nehemiah Bennett in the senatorial race, while John Davis received the nomination for coroner, thus becoming the nominee for each party. Republicans in Grant County endorsed Elkins at their county convention and proposed a ticket which included California veterans John K. Houston for probate judge, Richard Hudson for sheriff, and George O. Perrault for school commissioner.[48]

Although Elkins amassed a significant majority on election day throughout the territory, Republicans among California veterans running for office had mixed success. The most prestigious and powerful county office was that of probate judge, and in Grant County two California veterans were pitted against each other in the election: Joseph F. Bennett versus John K. Houston. In the highly sought after office of county sheriff, Richard Hudson was running against his brother-in-law Harvey H. Whitehill.

When the votes were tallied, it appeared that Bennett and Whitehill had barely squeezed through to victory, the former elected by a six-vote and the latter by a ten-vote margin. Their Republican opponents promptly contested the results of the election in district court and employed, among others, William L.

Rynerson and Albert J. Fountain to plead their case, but to no avail. By the close of the following year, both Houston and Hudson had withdrawn their protest and the case was dismissed.[49]

In other Grant County races, Republican George Perrault was elected a school commissioner while Democrat Henry Barton lost his bid for the school board. Democrats were successful in electing William Chamberlin as county coroner. And Republican James G. Crittenden was elected justice of the peace for precinct four while Joseph A. Moore, a former sergeant in the California volunteers, was elected constable for precinct two.[50]

In Doña Ana County, John Davis experienced no difficulty in winning his bid for county coroner, but Democrat Henry C. Haring was defeated for sheriff by Republican Mariano Barela. The only additional California veteran elected to office in Doña Ana County in 1875 was Robert Taylor, an Irishman and farmer, who won the post of justice of the peace for the village of Tortugas.[52]

BENNETT'S RISING STAR

Meanwhile Joseph F. Bennett's political star continued to rise, and in the autumn of 1876 a large number of Democrats and Independent Republicans in Grant County backed his nomination as Democratic candidate for delegate to Congress. Bennett possessed many of the attributes associated with successful politicians: he was well-educated and well-liked, relatively well-to-do, and commanded strong press support. Tragedies that befell his family, including the accidental shooting death of his eldest son Edward, undoubtedly garnered public sympathy and extended his image as a man of the people.[52]

Public support for Bennett's nomination appeared almost simultaneously with the emergence of a movement to annex Grant County to the territory of Arizona. To a considerable extent, proponents for annexation were the same individuals who supported Bennett.[53] Those wishing to sever political connections with New Mexico argued that Grant County was closer to the capital of Arizona than to Santa Fe and that laws enacted by the New Mexico legislature were ill-suited to the needs of Grant County. Moreover, New Mexico was ruled by an oligarchy, and many Grant County residents believed that Arizona, being an "American" territory as opposed to a "Mexican" territory, would provide government better suited to a progressive community such as Silver City.[54]

The annexation movement might have been nipped in the bud had Bennett received his party's nomination for delegate, since typically splinter groups emerged in southern counties in response to alleged neglect by Santa Fe politicians. But the Democratic party passed over Bennett and selected Pedro Valdez as its nominee. Consequently Grant County residents went to the polls November 2, 1876 and voted almost unanimously in favor of annexation. Although Arizona officials favored the addition of Grant County, Congress allowed a bill for annexation to die in committee, effectively ending the Grant County rebellion.[55]

Unable to exchange his Silver City residence for one in Washington, Bennett settled for election to the school board in the fall of 1876. Two years later he accepted employment with the Longfellow Mine in Clifton, Arizona, but subsequently returned to Silver City where he was elected to the city council in 1884. Bennett had labored long and hard for the Democratic party, a commitment seemingly inherited from his father who announced towards the end of his life that he had voted for seventeen Democratic presidential candidates.[56]

CROUCH AND HOUSTON

The 1876 territorial elections coincided with the presidential elections in the states, and each party in New Mexico chose either Rutherford B. Hayes or Samuel Tilden to head their tickets. In the southern counties, California veterans John S. Crouch and John K. Houston were elected to the territorial legislature as senator and representative, respectively, representing Grant, Lincoln, and Doña Ana counties.[57] Crouch, who chaired the judiciary and internal improvement committees, was the only Anglo in the upper house, while Houston, who chaired the judiciary, mines and waste lands committees, was one of three Anglos in the lower house.[58]

During the early weeks of the session, the Democratic editor of the *Grant County Herald*, Singleton M. Ashenfelter, criticized the composition of the legislature, stating that it was composed mainly of men whose "intelligence would hardly reach the average of scullions to a fifth-class restaurant." But among the most capable men in the legislature, he announced, were Republicans Crouch and Houston. The two former soldiers undoubtedly earned this praise by supporting Gov. Samuel B. Axtell's veto of an act incorporating the Society of Jesuits, one of the most controversial issues of the session.[59]

Senator Crouch and Representative Houston were each responsible for introducing at least one important bill into the legislature that was enacted into law. Houston's bill incorporated the town of Silver City, one of the first New Mexico towns to be incorporated, and Crouch's railroad bill exempted railroads from taxation. Houston's bill was welcomed by Silver City residents, who elected their first municipal officials on April 2, 1878. Robert Black, a Republican, became the first mayor of Silver City, while two of the four councilmen were former California soldiers William Chamberlin and Robert V. Newsham, both Democrats. After the close of the legislative session, Crouch's railroad bill was subjected to scrutiny by editor Ashenfelter, who now castigated the senator for gullibility. The bill had been prepared by railroad interests to advance their own cause, Ashenfelter editorialized, and mere enactment would not hasten construction of railroads.[60]

Houston's single term in the legislature apparently satisfied his political ambitions for there is no evidence that he again sought election to that body. Crouch's bid for reelection as senator in the fall of 1878 was singularly disappointing. He campaigned on a ticket that supported the Democratic nominee for Congress, but he met opposition from local Democrats, including Lawrence Lapoint, who believed that he was more a Republican than a Democrat. He was also accused as having "uniformly voted with

the Santa Fe ring" during his first term in the legislature. Consequently, he was defeated at the polls. Two years later Crouch and
his one-time business partner, Albert J. Fountain, supported the
Democrats in territorial elections, but the possibility of any political comeback by Crouch was ended by his death in 1884.[61]

For the most part the leading Republican in Doña Ana County,
William L. Rynerson, kept a low political profile throughout most
of the decade of the seventies, rarely seeking elective office. He
was a member of the territorial Republican central committee,
however, and in 1875 was mentioned as a possible candidate as
delegate if Elkins chose not to run.[62] He was appointed district
attorney for the Third Judicial District in 1876 by Governor Axtell
and was reappointed two years later. His second term in office
coincided with the outbreak of the so-called Lincoln County War
in which he played an official and highly publicized role.[63]

By the end of the decade Rynerson and Albert J. Fountain were
among Mesilla Valley's most distinguished citizens. Each had given
lengthy service to the Republican party. While the two men often
had worked together in social and civic affairs, during the violent
months of the Lincoln County War a rift developed, probably
initiated by Fountain's desertion to the Democratic party in 1878
and 1880.

The rift deepened when Rynerson and Judge Simon B. Newcomb persuaded the territorial legislature in January 1882 to change
the county seat from Mesilla to Las Cruces, thereby incensing
Mesilla residents. The *Mesilla News* claimed that Rynerson owned
the land where the new courthouse would be located. Denying
the charge, Rynerson stated that the land in question had been
deeded to the county by the New Mexico Town Company. Although Rynerson was the local agent for the company, he denied
owning any stock in it.[64] Certainly Rynerson and other town
boosters were working to establish Las Cruces as the political and
economic center of southern New Mexico, and it was with this
motive in mind that they also secured the railroad depot for Las
Cruces.

Passage of the courthouse bill transformed the 1882 elections

in Doña Ana County into a political war between Las Cruces and
Mesilla. Warren Bristol, the presiding judge of the Third Judicial
District Court and a resident of Mesilla, issued an injunction re-
straining county commissioners from issuing bonds to build a jail
and courthouse at the new county seat. Fountain, also a Mesilla
resident, supported Bristol's actions and exchanged insults with
Rynerson in the pages of the local press. Las Cruces residents nominated a bipartisan People's Ticket for the November elections,
while Mesilla supported opposing candidates. When the People's
Party won at the polls, the controversy ended and county commissioners soon began receiving bids for construction of the new
jail and courthouse.[65]

AGAINST THE SANTA FE RING

Shortly thereafter Rynerson and Fountain ended their feud and
embarked upon a joint effort in 1884 to challenge the political
power of Santa Fe politicians. At a spring meeting of county residents, the two former soldiers denounced the territorial legislature for enacting measures benefiting the capital city while
burdening the rest of the people with unfair taxes. Rynerson
pointed out that the legislature had voted $200,000 for capitol
buildings, $150,000 for a penitentiary, $5,000 for a Catholic
school in Santa Fe, and a large sum to construct a hospital in the
capital.[66]

As Republican leaders made plans for the coming November
elections, several men were mentioned as possible Republican
nominees for delegate to Congress, but the two leading contend-
ers were L. Bradford Prince and William L. Rynerson. It was Fountain who formally announced Rynerson's candidacy at an August
meeting of Doña Ana County Republicans, stating "the time has
arrived when we should select a strong candidate to represent
southern New Mexico in Congress."[67]

Delegates who assembled for the Republican convention in
Santa Fe later that month were divided between Rynerson and
Prince supporters, but a procedural dispute early in the conven-

tion caused Rynerson's backers to walk out of the convention, leaving the regular Republicans to nominate Prince. The splinter faction nominated Rynerson as an Independent Republican candidate for Congress, one who would drive the Santa Fe Ring from political power.[68] But William Breeden, the territorial Republican chairman from Santa Fe, in an open letter to the Republicans of southern New Mexico asserted that Rynerson had been in New Mexico politics for seventeen years, and

during that time he has never asked the Republicans of Santa Fe or the men known as the Santa Fe ring for any service or assistance that was not freely rendered him. They have done or tried to do everything that Col. Rynerson has ever desired to have done.[69]

Nonetheless, Rynerson won the backing of many former comrades, including Democrat John D. Barncastle and Republican Richard Hudson, the latter a long-time member of the Republican central committee and a member of the Grant County delegation to the Republican convention pledged to support Rynerson. Although several Democrats in southern counties endorsed Rynerson, Singleton M. Ashenfelter, Democrat and editor of the *Southwest-Sentinel,* wrote that he deserved defeat since the bolt by his supporters had been inspired by "the rule or ruin heresy"—desert the party if you can not rule it.[70]

As Ashenfelter suggested, the split in Republican ranks allowed Democrats to elect Antonio Joseph as New Mexico's delegate to Congress. Following the election, Rynerson dutifully thanked his supporters, implied that the antiring faction would eventually triumph, and then traveled east to attend a cattlemen's convention in St. Louis.[71]

In subsequent years, Albert J. Fountain and William L. Rynerson each compiled commendable political records. Fountain served one term in the territorial legislature, where as speaker of the house in 1889 he marshalled key support for the measure establishing a land-grant college at Las Cruces. Both Fountain and Rynerson attended the controversial Santa Fe constitutional convention in September 1889 and each worked long and hard for the statehood movement, though their immediate efforts were unsuccessful. [72] Prior to his death in 1896, Fountain carried on a political vendetta with the promising young Democratic politician, Albert Bacon Fall, and was appointed a United States district attorney for New Mexico at the same time Fall was serving as district judge. [73] Rynerson's voice remained strong in Republican circles despite effects of a stroke he suffered the autumn of 1889. In the early nineties, he was New Mexico's representative on the Republican national committee and attended several political conventions before his death in 1893. [74]

The two southern counties of Grant and Doña Ana produced a significant number of politically active politicians among ex-California soldiers. At least forty-seven California veterans from those two counties held office or attended political conventions between 1865 and 1885. Among the above veterans who can be identified with either of the two national parties, Democrats outnumbered Republicans almost two to one.

But throughout the territory, veterans from Carleton's old command were on the whole avid politicians, who in common with other settlers after the war supported either of the two national political parties, attended local rallies, and sought elective offices. For the most part, they were interested in developing the physical resources of the territory and little concerned with reforms that would become popular late in the century. They railed about "rings" which monopolized political and economic power in the territory, much as did residents in other western territories.

To the modern observer it appears that most territorial politicians, including California veterans, subscribed to the school of politics that decreed to the victor go the spoils. Political expediency, whether to build political careers or to advance local economic interests including community improvements, frequently dictated changes in political allegiances or formation of splinter groups. And demographic realities forced Anglo politicians to seek alliances with their Hispanic counterparts.

10

Frontier Society

California veterans, like most frontiersmen, carried with them into the sparsely settled West a firm determination to control the environment and to master their own destinies. Most pioneers moved West for economic advancement, but once rough edges were chiseled from the wilderness, they toiled to reestablish the social and cultural institutions they had known in more settled regions. With buoyant expectancy, settlers envisioned a new but familiar civilization rising on the frontier.

Although New Mexico in the 1860s was no longer a raw wilderness, California veterans who settled in the territory labored to recreate lifestyles that had existed in their former homes—complete with families, schools, literary societies, and fraternal organizations—despite the fact that they had moved into a predominantly Hispanic society. Most soldiers were bachelors when they arrived in the territory, although some had wives waiting for them in the states and a few officers had persuaded their wives to accompany them to New Mexico. A great number of veterans who remained in the territory after the war married Hispanic women, and together husband and wife created a stable family unit that frequently endured until the death of one partner. Many of their descendants reside within New Mexico today, and a number have assumed active roles in contemporary political and community affairs.

WEDDINGS AND MARRIAGES

California veterans who married Hispanic women came from
all walks of life, and such marriages were not restricted to any
one social class. Former soldiers who intermarried with Hispanos
were carpenters, butchers, farmers, laborers, lawyers, and merchants. Seneca G. Ames, for example, was a carpenter residing
in Las Cruces who married his wife Francisca less than two years
after mustering out of the service. At the time of their marriage
in 1868, Ames was thirty-four and his wife fifteen-years-old.[1]

Frank C. Arnett, who resided at Contadero in Socorro County
in 1870, listed his occupation as ferryman. Arnett was wed to a
Hispanic woman named Toribia, who died in 1874, leaving Arnett to care for their two children—nine-year-old Antonio and
seven-year-old Maria.[2] In 1869 butcher Wilson G. Holman of
Fort Bayard married Feliciania Montoya of Rio Mimbres in a ceremony witnessed by Richard Mawson, a former comrade, and his
Hispanic wife Martina. Holman was in his late thirties; his spouse
was about twenty-three years his junior.[3] These four men arrived
in the territory as privates and although neither Ames, Arnett,
nor Holman listed personal assets in the 1870 census, it is known
that Arnett died in destitute circumstances in 1923.[4] Mawson, a
small but industrious farmer residing in Grant County, listed his
assets in real and personal property as two thousand dollars.[5]

Among farmers who married Hispanic women were George
Krim and Joseph Franklin of Socorro County, Henry W. Easton
and George W. Lemon of Rio Arriba County, Wesley Fields, Albert Jacobs, and David C. Warner of Lincoln County, and David
Wood and Henry C. Haring of Doña Ana County. The estimated
value of their personal and real estate, as listed in the 1870 census, ranged from the $200 declared by Jacobs to Warner's decla-
ration of $2,100.[6] Among the laboring and artisan class who
married Hispanic women were Samuel Dean, a San Miguel County
farm laborer, carpenters Chester C. Little and Calvin Dotson from
Colfax and Lincoln counties, respectively, and Grant County

blacksmith John D. Gibbins. Gibbins and Dean each listed assets at $500, and Little recorded his at $200. Dotson failed to list any assets.[7]

Men of relative wealth and standing also married Hispanic women, including William L. Rynerson, Albert J. Fountain, Joseph F. Bennett, and John D. Barncastle. Rynerson listed his assets in the 1870 census at $20,000, Bennett at $10,000, Barncastle at $7,000, and Fountain at $2,000.[8]

Several veterans entered into common-law marriages with Hispanic women after their discharges. Alva Mason of Pinos Altos, a former private in the California volunteers, later stated in a deposition that after the war in New Mexico "it was very common for ex-soldiers and Mexican women to live together years before marriage and in many instances not marry until the law suggested. At that time there were very few white women in the country and most of the white men were discharged soldiers."[9]

His friend and former comrade, Linklain Butin of Pinos Altos, lived for seven years in such an arrangement with his wife Candelaria, who gave birth to two children during those years. When Butin became seriously ill in 1876, he and Candelaria were legally married. Butin died a few days after the marriage. Several years later, applying for a widow's pension, Candelaria testified that "we had all the time we were living together intended to get married but kept putting it off thinking to be married by a Catholic priest. But we seldom saw one and we never had any spare money to go to one until finally he was taken sick. So we were married while he was on his death bed by the justice of the peace so that our children might not suffer from our failure to do so."[10]

Henry Barton, a former sergeant in the California volunteers and, like Butin, a Pinos Altos miner, also apparently lived for several years with his wife Juana Pérez before they were legally married. Born in Mexico, Juana's first husband had died in Sonora, Mexico. In the 1870 census she was residing with Henry Barton, her occupation listed as "keeping house." Ten years later, in the 1880 census, Juana Pérez again is listed as residing in the Barton household, though not designated as his wife. Nonetheless, they were married at Silver City on December 11, 1880 and their marriage continued until Barton died ten years later.[11]

Similarly, Charles Brakebill, who worked as a baker in the mining community of Ralston, included in his household in the 1870 census twenty-one-year-old Clara Hill, a native of Mexico, and her two children. Grant County marriage records show that Brakebill married Clara Remudes in May 1877; it is likely that these two women are one and the same.[12] Characteristic of many marriages between veterans and Hispanic women was the disparity in ages: William L. Rynerson, for example, was thirteen years older than his wife; Joseph F. Bennett fifteen years older; Seneca Ames and Charles Brakebill each nineteen years older than their wives; Wilson G. Holman twenty-three years older; and Wesley Fields twenty-seven years older.[13]

A few of these marriages ended in divorce, though divorce was not common in the Spanish Southwest because of strong religious sanctions against it. Some divorces, such as that between Rosario and David Catanach, came after several years of marriage. Other veterans whose marriages ended in divorce include John Gibbins, who divorced his wife Josepha in 1876, and lawyer John T. B. Ryan, who was granted a divorce from his wife Juana Maria in 1878. In October 1880 Francisca Taylor received a divorce from her husband when the courts judged Robert Taylor guilty of "cruelty and abandonment."[14] Finally, although the records are not clear, it appears that Joseph Haskins of Lincoln County was granted a divorce from Benidito A. Haskins in November 1873, only a few months before he was killed in the Horrell War.[15]

Well over half the 196 California veterans listed in the 1870 census lived as single men or in households lacking women of marriageable age. Eighty-nine men lived in households that included their wives or women of marriageable age. Of this number, ten were married to Anglo women while seventy-nine were married to or living with Hispanic women.[16] These figures support an observation made by a Santa Fe resident that in the years immediately after the war "so few of the Americans were married

. . . that a married man was an exceptional man."[17] Yet the typical veteran who did marry, wed a Spanish-speaking woman.
Even in a county such as Grant, where residents prided themselves on living in an "American" county, the overwhelming majority of married California veterans had wives of Hispanic descent. Of the forty-four veterans listed in the 1870 census, only seventeen lived in households including women of marriageable age, but two, Benjamin F. Harrover and Reece R. Bulger, resided together in a household that also included John E. Sunders and twenty-year-old Susanna Chavez, whose occupation was listed as "keeping house." Of the remainder, fourteen were living with or married to women of Hispanic descent. Only one man, Sydney M. Webb, was married to an Anglo woman, Sarah, a native of Louisiana.[18] Several unmarried men took wives in later years. Richard Hudson, for example, married Mary E. Stevens in 1871, and Robert V. Newsham married Celestine Johnson, a native of Arkansas, in 1878.[19]

Whether married to Hispanic or Anglo women, many California veterans experienced a tragedy that befell so many pioneer families—the death of young children. For example, the adopted son of Bernard McCall, the proprietor of the Headquarters Saloon in Mesilla, was seriously burned while playing with coal oil. Although he appeared to be recovering from the burns, he later was stricken with fever and died.[20] A young daughter of John and Maria Townsend died of pneumonia in 1874, and two years later cholera claimed the infant daughter of Helen and Joseph H. Peacock.[21] The Rynersons and the Davies each lost a young daughter around 1880, with four-year-old Bertha Davies succumbing to the effects of a rattlesnake bite. Two years later the infant daughter of the Fountains died from pneumonia.[22]

Lola and Joseph F. Bennett lost their eldest son who was accidently shot in 1876, while the following year the infant son of Inistoria and James G. Crittenden died from unexplained causes.[23] Death made repeated visits to some pioneer families, including that of William and Martina Chamberlin of Grant County. Within the space of seven years they lost four of their children.

Chamberlin himself died in 1890 at about age fifty-seven, leaving as heirs his wife and four children, including an infant born
fifteen days after his death.[24]

SCHOOL

Family men among California veterans took the lead establishing and improving public education. Following American occupation of New Mexico in 1846, it was estimated that seven-eighths
of the population were illiterate.[25] Public education received little support from New Mexico politicians either prior to or after
1846. Gov. Robert B. Mitchell in his opening address to the legislature in December 1867 noted that there was not a single public school operating in the territory, and the situation had not
improved when Gov. Marsh Giddings delivered his address to the
legislature in December 1871.[26]

Focusing on the two southern counties of Grant and Doña Ana,
it is evident that Anglo veterans spearheaded the drive for public
education that emerged in the seventies and eighties. As a newly
elected senator, Joseph F. Bennett journeyed to Santa Fe late in
1871 determined to improve educational matters in the territory.
Backed by several hundred Grant County residents, he presented
a memorial to the legislature asking that Grant County be allowed
to assess a tax for building and maintaining free public schools.[27]

Two laws enacted during the 1871–72 session provided the legal
basis for tax-supported schools in the territory. One called for the
appointment of supervisors for public schools; the other called
for an ad valorem tax of one-fourth of one per cent on all real
and personal property to be used solely for educational purposes.
Sections in the revenue bill also required that a poll tax of one
dollar upon each adult male citizen and all county surplus funds
over $500 be paid into county school funds.[28]

The school laws remained ineffective for several years in most
sections of New Mexico, but Grant County residents soon elected
Robert Newsham, Cornelius Bennett, and John M. Ginn as the
county's first board of school commissioners and opened in a

rented hall on January 5, 1874 a public school free to all children five to fifteen-years-old.[29]

Although taxes were collected for public education, Grant County residents undertook a variety of fund-raising projects to augment school funds. Women in Silver City formed the Ladies Educational Society to raise money to build a schoolhouse. Appointed to the first building committee were William Chamberlin, Isaac N. Stevens, John R. Johnson, Mrs. Higgins, Mrs. Robert Florman, and Mrs. Richard Hudson. Local residents pledged almost $800 in cash and labor to the building fund.[30] Though the public schools of Grant County suffered from insufficient funds, a public school operated in Silver City throughout the seventies. Among California veterans elected to the school board during the first decade of its existence were Joseph F. Bennett, George O. Perrault, H. W. Sherry, and John K. Houston.[31]

The residents of Doña Ana County mounted a similar campaign to establish public schools, although parochial and private schools operated more frequently than did public schools. Late in 1877 a public school opened under the direction of Simeon H. Newman, but soon ran into financial difficulties and was closed.[32] With renewed zeal, local residents subscribed over one thousand dollars to a building fund by mid-1880; donors included William L. Rynerson, John D. Barncastle, and Lawrence Lapoint. By September the school building was completed and the school's three trustees, Rynerson, Martin Amador, and Jacob Schaublin, were accepting applications for a teacher, principal, and one assistant.[33] By 1883 the Las Cruces public school boasted a regular attendance of about sixty-eight students, among whom were the children of Rynerson, Lapoint, Seneca Ames, David Wood, and Marshall St. John, all California veterans.[34]

Rynerson and Fountain also played key roles in securing a college for Las Cruces. In 1888 Rynerson and a handful of other interested residents agreed to establish an institute of higher learning that would rival eastern colleges, and in September Las Cruces College opened with Hiram Hadley as president, although the institution initially was limited to elementary and college prepa-

ratory classes. In 1889 the territorial legislature authorized establishment of an agricultural land-grant college, and Rynerson was
among the group appointed to lobby for locating the college at
Las Cruces. As speaker of the House, Fountain marshalled support for a bill enacted February 28, 1889 naming Las Cruces as
the site for the college. In September Gov. L. Bradford Prince
appointed Rynerson to the school's first board of regents. He
served on the board as secretary-treasurer until his death. [35]

CULTURE

In addition to tax-supported education, many ex-soldiers supported public lyceums and organized musical and theatrical events
in response to their own twin needs for self-improvement and entertainment. The miners at Ralston, for example, established a
lyceum during the first winter of the camp's existence. It met twice
each week to entertain the men with discussions on a variety of
topics. [36] Miners at Silver City needed several more months to
organize, but in July 1872 permanent officers for the "Silver City
Lyceum" were elected, including California veterans James A.
Zabriskie as president, Henry M. Harshberger as vice-president,
and Richard Hudson as treasurer. The association soon established
a reading room for its members and provided entertainment for
"instruction and amusement" of local residents. The first lecture
sponsored by the organization was presented December 16, 1872
by Ben Stevens of Albuquerque who spoke on the Constitution.
Subsequent lectures were presented by Charles P. Clever, James
A. Zabriskie, and Richard Hudson. [37]

In Las Cruces, a Young Men's Social Club was organized, in
part to regale area residents with song and entertainment. Although William L. Rynerson took part in the choral presentations,
it was Albert J. Fountain who garnered praise for bringing to the
Mesilla Valley superb amateur theatrical entertainment. The first
performance of the Mesilla Amateur Dramatic Association, under
Fountain's direction, played to a capacity audience on November
9, 1874, opening night for the Mesilla Opera House. The pro-

duction was so successful that Fountain's troupe was asked to present a regular schedule of plays in subsequent years.[38]

LITERATURE

A handful of California veterans, in addition to those who were newspaper editors, possessed some talent for expository writing and subsequently had their materials published either as pamphlets or as full-length manuscripts. One of the earliest of the discharged soldiers to "break into print" was William H. McKee of the Carrasco Mining Company, who in 1866 produced a book entitled *The Territory of New Mexico and its Resources*. To a modern observer, McKee's manuscript is "full of romance, legend, and faulty geologic evidence," yet it did generate enthusiasm for mining in New Mexico after the war.[39] Although John C. Cremony left New Mexico before the war's end, in 1868 he published his now famous *Life Among the Apaches*, recounting his experiences with members of that tribe while serving as interpreter for the U.S. Boundary Commission and as a major in the California Cavalry.[40]

The unofficial historian of the California Column, George H. Pettis, remained in New Mexico but a short time after his discharge. From his home in Providence, Rhode Island, Pettis enjoyed discoursing on problems faced by western settlers and their conflicts with Indians. Many of his observations found their way into newspapers, but Pettis also produced more formal manuscripts. His short history of his own infantry company was published in 1885 by the Soldiers' and Sailors' Historical Society of Rhode Island, while two of his works, *Kit Carson's Fight with the Comanche and Kiowa Indians* and *The California Column*, were published in 1908 by the Historical Society of New Mexico.[41]

Albert J. Fountain published in his own newspaper romanticized accounts of his "hair-raising" adventures in the military, but he also wrote *New Mexico Bureau of Immigration Report on Doña Ana County*, published either in 1881 or 1882.[42] Several years later in 1905, former comrade Sidney R. DeLong published *The History of Arizona*, a survey of that territory from its earliest times to 1903.[43]

The member of the California Column who generated the greatest impact on the literary and intellectual world was former sergeant Edward E. Ayer, who left the Southwest after the war but who in later years returned on business trips. It was while serving in the California volunteers that Ayer read with amazement and delight *The Conquest of Mexico* by W. H. Prescott, an experience which he said opened "an absolutely new world to me." In subsequent years, Ayer became one of the notable book collectors in the world and the donor of the great Ayer Collection of Western Americana in the Newberry Library, Chicago.[44]

CITY SERVICES—FIRE PROTECTION

If optimism and a desire for self-improvement characterized westerners, so too did town-boosterism and concern for the physical well-being of residents. Businessmen were particularly interested in fire protection, but nowhere in New Mexico during the Gilded Age were adequate measures taken to fight major fires. Most towns established bucket and water brigades, or engine companies, but these proved totally inadequate. On the night of November 11, 1871, for example, a fire broke out in the town of Rio Mimbres in Grant County and destroyed most of the dwellings in the north end of town before the hook and ladder company, under the direction of California veteran Richard Mawson, could bring it under control.[45]

An early morning fire in Silver City four years later totally destroyed the town's major carpenter shop and threatened to envelop the nearby store of Bennett Brothers and Company. The latter establishment was saved when it was sprayed with water from a hose and pump system situated in the company's corral. After the fire had been contained, local residents subscribed funds to purchase a double action pump and three tall ladders for use in future crises. In addition Joseph F. Bennett chaired a citizen's meeting in which twenty-six men, including Bennett and California veteran Benjamin F. Harrover, were enrolled as members in a new fire company, with Harrover elected foreman of the company.[46]

Silver City, like other frontier towns, periodically suffered destructive fires, and, although residents protested inadequate protection, services remained primitive. The engine was frequently out of order, as was the case in June 1884 when fire destroyed Richard Hudson's brick building. Despite the local editor's warning that the city needed a new fire department, fire swept through the business district four months later, and, lacking any other means of checking its progress, Sam Eckstein's saloon was blown "sky high."[47]

CLUBS AND WAR MEMORIES

Fraternal lodges were popular among Anglo residents after the war, serving as vehicles for community and individual improvement as well as forums for political discussions. Lodge membership established important political links between distant sectors of the territory. The most popular of the lodges was undoubtedly the Masonic Order, and numerous California veterans, particularly those living in the southern counties, enrolled in local affiliates after their discharge. Among leading Masons in Doña Ana County were William L. Rynerson, Albert J. Fountain, Lawrence Lapoint, and John D. Barncastle. At least thirteen California veterans held office in Aztec Lodge, Las Cruces, in the years 1867 to 1884. And for the years 1876 and 1877, veterans held six of eight top posts.[48]

In August 1877, delegates from the territory's three lodges met in Santa Fe to form a Grand Lodge of New Mexico. Banker W. W. Griffin was elected Grand Master, while other elected officers included Rynerson as Deputy Grand Master, Thomas B. Catron as Grand Lecturer, and John S. Crouch as Grand Senior Deacon. In 1880, just four years before his campaign for Congressional delegate, Rynerson served as Grand Master, traveling throughout the territory on lodge business. The following year he again served as Deputy Grand Master, while former comrade Rufus C. Vose of Albuquerque served as one of two Grand Stewards. Clearly, Masonry brought California veterans into fraternal contact with some of the most powerful politicians in the territory.[49]

An organization that rivaled the Masonic Order in popularity was the Independent Order of Odd Fellows, whose Paradise Lodge No. 2 met in Santa Fe. Englishman John Townsend—former bugler in the California Cavalry—frequently served as an officer in the lodge and became its chief official in 1876. The lodge maintained a library, and, similar to Masonic lodges, presided over funerals for recently departed members. Upon the death of brother Louis Clark, for example, Paradise Lodge passed resolutions mourning his passing and decreed that badges of mourning be worn for thirty days.[50]

The Good Templar society continued to be popular after the war with those California veterans who thought temperance a worthy cause. By 1869 the Santa Fe Templar lodge boasted a membership of over forty men and women; among its officers was California veteran Lycurgus D. Fuller, clerk in the quartermaster's department. Santa Fe jeweler J. Crocker Brown, also a former bugler in the California volunteers, was elected to office the following year.[51] During August of 1877, a Templar lodge was organized at Silver City. Within twelve months it claimed a membership of eighty-four men and women, among whom were ex-soldiers Henry W. Sherry, Americus Hall, and Robert V. Newsham. Four years later both Newsham and his twenty-year-old wife Celestine served as officers in the association.[52]

Large numbers of military men joined patriotic and veterans organizations at the close of the war, and veterans of the California Column assumed leadership in these new associations. The Army of New Mexico was organized in Santa Fe on March 4, 1869 as a fraternal society "for mutual benefit and to perpetuate the memory of those who stood by our common country." Membership was open to men who had served honorably during the recent conflict in the Union Army. Former captain in the California volunteers William McMullen was elected president while former California private Thomas Coghlan served as corresponding secretary and treasurer. It was reported in the press that nearly one hundred men joined this organization.[53]

The Army of New Mexico soon dropped from sight, as its members were absorbed by the Grand Army of the Republic. The first G.A.R. post established in New Mexico was McRae Post No. 1, organized at Santa Fe in October 1867. Among the thirteen men who met to establish the post were Herman H. Heath, the influential Hispanic leader José D. Sena, and California veterans Thomas V. Keam and George T. Martin. By mid-1873 over one hundred men had joined McRae Post, including at least twenty-five former California soldiers. During the early seventies, it was the most active G.A.R. post operating in New Mexico, and men living in southern counties, such as John Davis of Mesilla, Emil Fritz of Lincoln, and Richard Hudson of Silver City, were enrolled in its ranks.[54]

McRae Post was active for six years, during which time it sponsored numerous educational, charitable, and patriotic projects. At a December meeting in 1869, for example, members called for a program of historical papers relating to the war to be presented periodically at meetings. A number of names were proposed for the papers—Kit Carson, James Carleton, Phil Kearney—but the lodge finally settled for the Grand Army Papers. Early the following year, a post charity fund was established and twenty-five dollars was appropriated to defray funeral expenses of the wife of comrade John A. Marvin, former private in the California volunteers. At subsequent meetings, the post petitioned Congress to provide a special pension for children of a departed comrade, collected money for a penniless Union soldier on his way to Philadelphia, and voted to pay medical bills for deceased comrade Thomas Richards, former sergeant in the California Cavalry.[55]

Decoration Day—the thirtieth of May—was one of two big patriotic events of the year. On that date G.A.R. members residing in Santa Fe decorated the Soldiers' Monument in the plaza and marched in procession to the cemetery to place sprigs of evergreens and flowers on graves of deceased comrades. In June 1873 McRae Post disbanded, apparently for lack of interest, and G.A.R. activities in the territory all but ceased. The *Daily New Mexican* noted on May 31, 1876 that Decoration Day went uncelebrated because the Grand Army of the Republic was no longer active.

The following year, however, G.A.R. members staged an elaborate ceremony in which Confederates joined Union soldiers in paying respect to former comrades.[56]

Among the most active members in McRae Post was Lycurgus D. Fuller—former private in the First California Infantry—who had joined the organization in February 1869. By August, Fuller was post adjutant responsible for keeping the association's records, and early the following year he was elected post quartermaster responsible for its funds. His successor as adjutant immediately proposed an investigation into discrepancies between quartermaster and adjutant reports concerning the number of comrades on the roster. A three-man committee, which included David N. Catanach, investigated Fuller's transactions, and as a result of their findings formal charges were brought against Fuller, who soon left the McRae Post. By May 1872, a second G.A.R. post had been established in Santa Fe—Dodd Post No. 3—and Fuller was serving as its adjutant general.[57] Certainly Fuller's apparent lapse in honesty or good judgement neither detracted from his popular standing in the Santa Fe community nor dampened his enthusiasm for civic projects. In subsequent years, he helped stage Santa Fe's Fourth of July celebrations, and with John P. Clum, later a famous Apache Indian agent, founded a gymnasium association in Santa Fe. He was active in the community life of Santa Fe until his death in the fall of 1875 after a protracted illness.[58]

Apparently the Grand Army of the Republic was moribund in New Mexico during the second half of the seventies, but, following a trend evident throughout the country, veterans began to reorganize in the eighties. Carleton Post No. 3 of the Grand Army was established in Santa Fe in 1883; among its nineteen charter members were Post Commander E. W. Wynkoop, Gov. Lionel A. Sheldon, and California veterans Erastus W. Wood, John Ayers, and John Townsend. That same year Slough Post No. 6 was established in Socorro with three California veterans—Samuel C. Meek, Joseph Kinsinger, and Joseph D. Emerson—assuming leadership roles in the association. Eventually the majority of

California soldiers who resided in Socorro County became members and like their counterparts in Santa Fe devoted themselves to charitable and community improvement projects.[59]

In Doña Ana County, the Phil Sheridan Post of the Grand Army was established at Las Cruces late in the eighties, and in 1891 that town also served as headquarters for the Grand Army's Department of New Mexico. Departmental officers during that year included Department Commander Albert J. Fountain, Assistant Adjutant General Joseph F. Bennett, Assistant Quartermaster General John D. Barncastle, Judge Advocate John Ryan, and assistant inspectors Samuel C. Meek and Richard Hudson.[60]

Veterans throughout the territory, Union and Confederate alike, helped commemorate the most important patriotic day of the year—Fourth of July. Ex-soldiers from the California command frequently played leading roles in organizing appropriate programs for the occasion. In 1870, for example, John S. Crouch presided over Fourth of July festivities at Ralston, while three years later James A. Zabriskie delivered the main oration at the Silver City celebration.[61] Lycurgus D. Fuller helped organize every Fourth of July celebration in Santa Fe from 1871 through 1875, the year that he died, serving as chairman of the committee on general arrangements in 1873 and again in 1875.[62]

Fourth of July in 1876 marked the one hundredth anniversary of the birth of the Republic, and New Mexico's residents prepared months in advance for the historical event. Five men, including Richard Hudson, Secretary William G. Ritch, and former Secretary W. F. M. Arny, were appointed as territorial centennial commissioners to coordinate plans for displaying New Mexico's agricultural and mineral products at the giant celebration in Philadelphia. Prominent citizens were named to advisory boards in each county to assist in securing exhibits for display; the seven member Doña Ana county board was dominated by California veterans Rynerson, Fountain, Barncastle, and Lapoint. Lincoln and Grant counties each had one California veteran on their boards, George W. Nesmith on the former and Joseph F. Bennett on the latter. Unfortunately the various county boards were slow to assemble their materials, and New Mexico's entry to the centennial exhibit arrived as the giant celebration was closing.[63]

Throughout New Mexico local communities staged their own celebrations to commemorate the birth of the United States. California veterans preceded the main Fourth of July festivities by staging a reunion on June 22, 1876 in the town of Mesilla. Heading the committee on arrangements were Doña Ana County residents John Martin, Marshall St. John, John D. Barncastle, William L. Rynerson, Henry C. Haring, and John Davis. The veterans planned a permanent organization, and during the reunion they selected Rynerson as their president, John Martin and John S. Crouch as vice-presidents, Barncastle as treasurer, and Albert J. Fountain as secretary. On the evening of June 22, some two hundred people attended the ball and supper held at "Re Union Hall," where dancing continued until daylight.[64]

In addition to Fourth of July festivities, several ex-soldiers assumed more somber responsibilities of organizing public displays of mourning following the deaths of the nation's great and near-great leaders. Although Gen. James H. Carleton was despised by many New Mexicans during the war, his death early in 1873 induced genuine expression of grief, especially by former soldiers who had served in his command. On the evening of February 4, for example, a large group of Santa Fe residents met in Senate chambers to express regret at Carleton's death. Lawrence G. Murphy was elected president of the meeting, while among eleven men selected as vice-presidents were former California soldiers Joseph F. Bennett and John Ayers. Four of five secretaries elected were California veterans: John Lambert, Edward S. Merritt, Lycurgus D. Fuller, and Thomas Coghlan. Louis Clark served on the committee that drew up resolutions honoring Carleton for his "zeal, honesty and ability with which he discharged the onerous duties of his high position." The highest praise for Carleton, however, came from Murphy, who stated in his opening address that although Carleton was "vested with the power of a despot he wielded it only to protect the rights of the citizen."[65]

When former commander and president Ulysses S. Grant died in 1885, public observances were held throughout the territory. At Silver City, veterans of the Mexican and Civil wars marched with citizens and the local militia in a mass procession that preceded public mourning ceremonies. Memorial services were also held in Las Cruces where houses and business establishments were draped in mourning. At courthouse ceremonies, Albert J. Fountain and William L. Rynerson spoke briefly on the virtues of the deceased president.[66]

CIVIC DUTIES

If self-improvement and community service characterized lives of the old California soldiers, so too did violence and personal tragedy. It was the rare veteran who failed to experience in the twenty years after his discharge some act of violence directed either against himself or the community in which he lived. Nevertheless, the vast majority of veterans were law abiding citizens, who relied upon courts to solve difficulties with neighbors. And it was the rare veteran who failed to appear in court, either as witness, juror, plaintiff, or defendant.

Court days were widely anticipated social events for most residents of county seats. Strangers crowded into town either to participate in the procedures or to witness the spectacle, much to the delight of merchants. Hotels did a lively business, and men such as John Davis and Joseph Kinsinger who operated such establishments in Mesilla and Socorro benefited from cluttered court calendars. In the late seventies, Kinsinger's hotel was the only one in Socorro, and while court was in session, guests were crowded two or three to a room to accommodate individuals in need of lodging.[67]

Male citizens frequently were called for jury duty, a civic responsibility entailing financial hardship for men living a great distance from court. California veteran Chauncey N. Story, for instance, failed to appear as a juror in Santa Fe during the summer of 1871 because he lacked funds to travel there from Elizabethtown.[68] Moreover, it was common for men to serve on juries during the same court term in which they appeared as litigants. James G. Crittenden, former sheriff of Grant County, on December 19, 1874 was found guilty of embezzlement and fined $500. Two days latter Crittenden sat on a jury that acquitted Americus Hall on a similar charge.[69]

Frequently, California veterans served together on grand or petite juries that issued indictments or verdicts against former comrades. Citing only one example, Richard Yeamans, Henry Barton, Linklain Butin, and Thomas Sunderland served on the Grant County grand jury in June 1870 which indicted Hugh L. Hinds, former captain in the California volunteers, for keeping a dram shop without a license.[70] And many of the old soldiers who went to court hired former California volunteers as their attorneys.

Several California veterans appeared in court to be naturalized as United States citizens, including Emil Fritz and Theodore Wendlandt, both natives of Germany, and Thomas V. Keam, a native of England. Frequently, former military comrades testified to the good character of those seeking citizenship. On June 18, 1873, for example, Richard Yeamans and Joseph A. Moore, both former California enlisted men, swore that George O. Perrault, a native of Canada, was a good citizen and had resided more than five years in the United States and more than one year in New Mexico. On the same date Moore and Perrault gave similar testimony for Peter Morris, a native of France and former private in the first California Cavalry.[71]

VIOLENCE AND TRAGEDY

Indictments handed down by juries against California veterans ranged from violations of Sunday law and licensing laws to assault and attempted murder. Among the more interesting murder trials was that of John E. Oliphant, who mustered out of the service at Albuquerque in September 1866 as a first lieutenant. Earlier in the year, Oliphant shot and killed David R. Knox at Fort Craig following an all night party on the post. The shooting was described in the Santa Fe *New Mexican* as "a most cowardly and cold blooded murder of an unarmed and defenseless man." Several military men from Fort Craig, including John S. Crouch and William McCleave, were subpoenaed to appear at Oliphant's trial held October 9, 1866. After entering a plea of not guilty, Oliphant was acquitted by a jury of twelve Hispanos. A native of New York, Oliphant then moved to the town of Rio Mimbres in Grant County, where in 1870 he resided with his Hispanic wife Elimita and three young children. The ex-soldier died in September of that year after a brief illness.[72]

Washington W. Hyde, a former private in the California volunteers, had the dubious distinction of being the only California veteran who listed his place of residence for the 1870 census as the Mesilla jail. This former trooper mustered out of the service at Santa Fe in 1866; two years later a grand jury convening at Mesilla handed down two indictments against Hyde for buying military arms from soldiers. Bond was set at $1,000, and former comrades John Davis and Milton D. Reed signed his bond as sureties. In 1869 Hyde was found guilty of one charge, acquitted of the other, and ordered to pay a $200 fine and to serve six months in county jail.[73] A musician by trade, Hyde moved to Central City in Grant County after serving his sentence. There he was shot to death early one June morning in 1871 after having played his fiddle at an all night dance.[74]

A significant number of old soldiers like Hyde died violent and tragic deaths. In addition to those previously noted, Calvin Dotson was killed in a saloon fight at Lincoln in 1872, Henry Schwenker accidently shot and killed himself at Tucson in 1876, and William R. McCormick and George M. Carpenter both committed suicide, the former in 1891 at Clifton, Arizona, and the latter in 1918 at the Old Soldiers' Home at Sawtelle, California. Moreover, in 1911 seventy-four-year-old Frederick G. Hughes was struck and killed by lightning in Arizona, while in 1923 Frank C. Arnett, in his late eighties, was robbed and killed in the town of Las Cruces.[75]

Among the more colorful veterans in Doña Ana County whose

life was marred by violence was John F. Gould, a former printer for the *Alta California* and a native of Boston. After his discharge, Gould married a Hispanic woman and became justice of the peace at Roblero. While serving in this capacity, Gould issued a warrant for the arrest of one John McGran, who had brutally assaulted a local rancher. The constable for Gould's precinct, John Rice—possibly the same John Rice who arrived in the territory as a private in Carleton's command—was killed attempting to arrest McGran in Mesilla. In the shoot-out, McGran—better known as Poker Jack—was also killed. Within four years of his discharge, Gould himself was indicted in the Third Judicial District Court for retailing merchandise without a license, selling liquor without paying a tax, and keeping a hotel without paying the proper fees. Gould eventually returned to California where he died in May 1876 from the effects of having been kicked in the stomach during a brawl.[76]

Lyon Phillipouski—former private in the Fifth California Infantry—lost his life in 1874 while serving as deputy sheriff in Lincoln County. Although Phillipouski was a Republican (he served as secretary to a Lincoln County Republican gathering in 1871), he had considerable business and personal connections with two staunch Lincoln County Democrats—Lawrence G. Murphy and Emil Fritz. Phillipouski served as county probate clerk while Murphy was probate judge; moreover, Emil Fritz and Paul Dowlin had signed Phillipouski's $2,000 bond as sureties. On March 27, seven months before his death, Phillipouski sold his ranch on the Ruidoso to Murphy and Fritz for $695.45. By reputation, Phillipouski was a mild-mannered man, but late one night in October he reportedly entered Murphy's store while intoxicated and threatened an employee—William Burns—in an argument over a bill. The two men moved outside and Phillipouski was killed in an exchange of gunfire.[77]

At least one California trooper, Robert Carr, died under such peculiar circumstances that a grand jury indicted his wife for murder. Carr died suddenly at Santa Rita in Grant County on Christmas day in 1875. The local press noted that he was forty-eight-years-old, a native of England, and a member of the Old First California Cavalry.[78] On July 18, 1877 Rachael Carr was indicted and brought to trial in December for the murder of her husband. The prosecutor was District Attorney William L. Rynerson, and on the jury sat three former California soldiers—Benjamin F. Harrover, Robert V. Newsham, and Joseph F. Bennett. The indictment alleged that Rachael had poisoned her husband while he was intoxicated. Witnesses testified that she had repeatedly threatened the deceased's life and had placed a "whitish drug" in his whiskey during his last spree. A search of the premises uncovered a vial of strychnine hidden in the fireplace. Other witnesses testified that the drug in Carr's whiskey was chloral and laudanum which he always took when on a drinking spree and that Carr had previously declared his intentions to kill himself by drinking whiskey. It was also noted that Carr had been drunk for twenty-eight days immediately preceding his death. After listening to contradictory testimony, the jury rendered a verdict of not guilty. Rachael continued to languish in jail, as she was also under an indictment for poisoning cattle.[79]

On occasion California veterans instituted court proceedings against former comrades, as in the highly publicized case involving two former sergeants, John D. Barncastle and Henry C. Haring. On the last day of the year in 1883, Barncastle was robbed of nearly five hundred dollars by two men entering his store to buy sardines and crackers. The merchant immediately offered a one hundred dollar reward for either of the two men—dead or alive— and residents of Las Cruces subscribed nearly one thousand dollars for their arrest and conviction. The man employed to track the robbers trailed them to Seven Rivers in Lincoln County, and Barncastle subsequently dispatched Haring with funds to proceed with the investigation. Word leaked back to Barncastle that Haring stopped in El Paso where he gambled away some of Barncastle's money and pawned the latter's overcoat and revolver. Barncastle then hired W. L. Jerrell—a "man of nerve, and brave as a lion"— to capture the robbers, but Jerrell was killed during an attempted hold-up of the stage in which he was riding. Residents of Doña

Ana County were shocked by this turn of events and blamed Haring for Jerrell's death.[80]

In April 1884, Haring was indicted for embezzlement and early the following year was sentenced to three months in the county jail. Haring's commission as a first lieutenant in the New Mexico militia was also revoked. The adjutant general in his official report noted that this was the first instance in which an officer had been judged guilty of conduct prejudicial to the service.[81]

Lawlessness seemed endemic on the western frontier, and New Mexico witnessed its share of killings, lynchings, and robberies in the years following the Civil War. Though California veterans labored to build stable communities, their history is punctuated by crimes against life and property. Three of the most notorious lawless episodes in the territory's history involved ex-soldiers: the Horrell War, the Lincoln County War, and the Socorro Vigilante action. And the infamous Salt War occurring on Texas soil also involved several troopers from Carleton's old command.

Two of the so-called wars took place in sprawling Lincoln County, where death by violence was common. Both the Horrell and Lincoln County wars erupted in the 1870s. Part of this lawlessness stemmed from the growth of the cattle industry; thieves proliferated as quickly as the herds. Then, too, the frontier attracted men of strong minds and narrow vision who connived and schemed to amass wealth and power. Arguments were settled all too frequently with revolvers and shotguns, though the territorial legislature enacted laws against carrying deadly weapons.[82]

DEATH IN LINCOLN COUNTY

The Horrell War, which blazed forth in late 1873 and 1874, derived its name from the five brothers who settled in Ruidoso Valley in 1873, having left Lampasas County, Texas, one step ahead of the law.[83] On December 1, 1873 Ben Horrell went into Lincoln on business accompanied by ex-sheriff of Lincoln County L. J. Gylam, California veteran David C. Warner, and two other men. All imbibed freely of whiskey and entered into a hot-tempered altercation with constable Juan Martínez. Warner subsequently shot and killed Martínez but was in turn killed by the constable's deputies. Shortly thereafter, Gylam and Horrell were taken into custody and allegedly shot in cold blood.[84]

The surviving brothers demanded an investigation into the killings, and when this was refused, the Horrells planned revenge. On December 20, the Texans raided a Hispanic wedding party in Lincoln, killing four men. Gov. Marsh Giddings subsequently offered a reward of $500 for apprehension of the Horrell brothers and their accomplices, while the citizens of Lincoln County held a mass meeting to discuss means of reestablishing law and order. Lyon Phillipouski reportedly was among those men who offered "eloquent and pertinent remarks" at the meeting.[85]

Rumors of war between "Texans and Mexicans" drifted through the countryside. Men deserted their ranches, fearing a general outbreak of lawlessness, and every man went armed. By the end of January 1874, the Horrell faction again raided Lincoln, dragging deputy sheriff Joseph Haskins from his bed and then killing him.[86] A stonemason by trade and a native of Michigan, ex-California soldier Haskins had married a Hispanic woman but probably was divorced by the time of his death. Shortly after this murder, the Horrells and their followers returned to Texas, killing a number of Hispanos as they left the territory.[87]

Despite the departure of the Horrells, shootings and killings continued until the onset of the infamous Lincoln County War in 1876. That conflict was between two opposing factions, each wanting to dominate the political and economic life of the county. Three California veterans played starring roles in the drama that unfolded in and around the town of Lincoln. William L. Rynerson, as district attorney for the Third Judicial District—which encompassed Doña Ana, Lincoln, and Grant counties—played a partisan role as public prosecutor. George W. Peppin, nominated by Rynerson as sheriff of Lincoln County, participated in some of the most violent episodes of the affray. And Emil Fritz, dead and buried in his native Germany at the onset of the war, unwittingly provided the tinder for this conflagration by purchasing a life insurance policy prior to his death in June 1874.[88]

The two factions that attempted to control Lincoln County

included Lawrence G. Murphy, James J. Dolan, and John H. Riley on the one hand and Alexander A. McSween, John H. Tunstall, and John S. Chisum on the other. In 1875, Murphy dominated business in the area as owner of the principal store in Lincoln County. Although a Democrat, Murphy apparently had amiable business relations with the newly arrived governor, Samuel B. Axtell. The *Daily New Mexican* remarked that several of the old "California Column" remembered Axtell "well and favorably" from the days of the gold rush, including, no doubt, William L. Rynerson, who accompanied the governor on a trip to Las Vegas soon after the latter's arrival in New Mexico.[89]

Although considered by observers as the kingpin of Lincoln County, Murphy, plagued by ill health, took Dolan and Riley into the firm as partners; by the time violence reached its peak, Murphy had retired from the company and was in Santa Fe seeking badly needed medical attention. McSween and Tunstall were newcomers, having arrived in the territory in 1875 and 1876, respectively. Tunstall entered the cattle business while McSween concentrated on building a law practice; together the two men ventured into the mercantile business to break Murphy's economic hold on the county. Chisum's role was primarily that of friend and counselor to the two men.[90]

The spark that started the violence concerned the collection of Fritz's insurance policy, which McSween had been hired to process. When he refused to turn the money over to Fritz's heirs, McSween was charged with embezzlement and his property was attached to satisfy claims on the insurance policy. McSween blamed Dolan and Riley for the court's actions, claiming that they wished to drive him and Tunstall out of business. Shortly thereafter an unsigned notice circulating in Lincoln County named Rynerson, Thomas B. Catron, and Sheriff William Brady as conspirators along with Dolan and Riley in a plot to crush economic competition in the county. Rynerson undoubtedly was partial to the Dolan-Riley faction. He and Dolan had cosigned a $1,600 attachment bond as sureties for the Fritz heirs when they initiated their suit against McSween, and Rynerson subsequently wrote to Dolan and Riley saying that matters had to be "made hot" for McSween and Tunstall, that the "McSween outfit" had to be driven from the territory. Rynerson concluded by assuring the two partners that "I shall help you all I can for I believe there was never found a more scoundrely set than that outfit."[91]

On February 18, 1878 a local posse shot and killed Tunstall while attempting to attach his property as the business partner of McSween. In retaliation, men said to be working for McSween killed Sheriff Brady, his deputy, and three members of the posse that killed Tunstall. It was at this point that Governor Axtell, on Rynerson's recommendation, appointed George W. Peppin as the new sheriff of Lincoln County. In July Sheriff Peppin attempted to arrest members of the McSween faction. They refused to surrender claiming the courts were controlled by the opposing faction. But on the night of July 19, McSween and three of his supporters were killed in a showdown with Peppin and his deputies.[92]

With McSween's death, the Lincoln County War reached a turning point. Violence continued but with the principal actors either dead or turning their interests elsewhere, the trouble slowly abated. Rynerson continued as district attorney, prosecuting a number of cases stemming from the Lincoln County violence until his second term in office ended in 1880. Peppin left his post as sheriff of Lincoln County to become post butcher at Fort Stanton.[93]

THE EL PASO SALT WAR

Two months prior to Tunstall's death, violence in the small community of San Elizario near El Paso, Texas, resulted in the death of two California veterans, Charles E. Ellis and John G. Atkinson. Referred to as the Salt War, this conflict was basically a matter of economics, although racial hatreds intensified hostilities. Involved was the control and use of the great salt deposits near Guadalupe Peak, one hundred miles east from San Elizario. Hispanos living on both sides of the Rio Grande since 1862 had gathered salt from these deposits to sell to residents in valley towns and in the interior of Mexico. Soon after the opening of the Guadalupe deposits Anglos started to preempt the best locations in the region.[94]

After Samuel Maverick successfully established his claim to two of the best sections at the deposits, a so-called Salt Ring was formed in 1868 to acquire remaining unclaimed portions. Ring members included California veterans Albert J. Fountain and Albert H. French, in addition to W. W. Mills, Frank Williams, Charles Conley, Ben Dowell, Gaylord Clarke, J. M. Lujan, Luis Cardis, and Father Antonio Borajo. When Fountain subsequently broke with Mills, the political boss of El Paso, he became the leader of the so-called Anti-Salt Ring, and promised to obtain title to the deposits for the citizens of El Paso County.[95]

In the election of 1869, Fountain defeated Mills in a race for the Texas senate; in later years Fountain claimed that the major issue in the campaign had been ownership of the Guadalupe salt deposits. At the end of Fountain's four year term, this issue remained unresolved, and Fountain, forced to stand trial on a number of charges brought by Mills, subsequently moved to Mesilla to remove himself and his family from possible harm by his El Paso opponents.[96]

Shortly after Fountain left El Paso, Charles H. Howard, a Missouri lawyer, filed on the unlocated portions of the Guadalupe Salt Lakes and also acquired the earlier claims of Samuel Maverick. Howard then posted notices that he was sole owner of the deposits and that intruders would be prosecuted. The stage was now set for a violent encounter between Howard and Hispanos who regarded the salt lakes as communal property. In the fall of 1877 Hispanos from both sides of the river went after salt, and Howard quickly pressed charges. Bitterness increased and in December a mob of about five hundred captured the town of San Elizario, killing four Anglos, including Howard and the two California veterans, Ellis and Atkinson.[97]

In the early 1870s, only about eighty residents in El Paso County were not of Hispanic descent. The "American" community in the town of El Paso itself included former California privates George W. Rand, Jonathan T. Evans, and John W. Hale, in addition to former officers James A. Zabriskie, Albert H. French, and Albert J. Fountain. Also listed in the 1870 census as a resident of El Paso was former California sergeant George O. Edgerton, but he frequently resided on the Mexican side of the border in his capacity as United States consul.[98]

Charles E. Ellis and John G. Atkinson settled in the small town of San Elizario after the war where they retailed merchandise and became inseparable friends. Ellis had served as sheriff and tax collector from 1871 to 1873, while Atkinson worked as his deputy. One observer noted that Ellis was "too good hearted" to enforce strictly his duties while Atkinson was too harsh, thereby generating enemies for both men. Ellis and Atkinson also served as school commissioners, backing compulsory school laws and working to remove Padre Borajo who forbade his Hispanic parishioners to send their children to public school. Although the school controversy occurred several years prior to the outbreak of the Salt War, it contributed to the violence which erupted in 1877.[99]

On the night of December 12, 1877 Ellis was stabbed to death and his body mutilated by a mob of Hispanos who apparently were looking for Howard. Later the mob ransacked Ellis's store and personal dwellings, carrying off at least $15,000 in merchandise and household property.[100] Atkinson met his death, along with Howard and one John McBride, on December 17 in front of a firing squad after Howard had surrendered to the Hispanic faction. Atkinson, who accompanied Howard as an interpreter, believed that he could help to arrange a peaceful settlement; instead he was executed by an angry mob that threatened death to all "gringos" in the valley. The *Mesilla Valley Independent* published an eyewitness account of the executions, noting that the three men had "faced their executioners with undaunted courage. . . . Atkinson stood with a contemptuous smile upon his lips." The first volley of bullets struck Atkinson in the stomach, whereupon he:

tore open his shirt so as to expose his breast and shouted 'Mas arriba' (higher) two shots were fired and two bullets pierced his breast, he fell, life was not yet extinct, and with the same smile of contempt on his lips he pointed to his head indicating that he desired to be shot there. He obtained his wish, a bullet pierced his brain, and John G. Atkinson died as he had lived, a brave man.[101]

Shortly after these murders, the Texas press noted that Ellis had married into a prominent Mexican family and had been highly esteemed by the Mexican population.[102] But the editor of the *Mesilla Valley Independent* more astutely noted that the mob considered Ellis a member of the "detested race of 'northern robbers'." Undoubtedly the fact that Ellis owned the gristmill at San Elizario contributed to his image as an exploiter of the people; the local populace was incensed by high tolls charged at the mill, although Ellis had promised to reduce charges when he acquired the mill in the fall of 1877.[103]

VIGILANTES IN SOCORRO COUNTY

The violence associated with the Socorro vigilantes similarly was preceded by local agitation over mill rates, and like the Salt War disturbances, racial bitterness split the Socorro community into armed camps. In February 1879, residents living on the Socorro community land grant demanded that proprietors of mills using the Socorro spring and stream grind ninety-three to ninety-eight pounds of flour for every fanega of wheat brought to their establishments for milling, which, according to the millers, was an impossible request. During the heat of the conflict, some residents wanted to destroy Samuel Zimmerly's mill, but calmer spirits prevailed. Zimmerly had taken possession of a tract of unoccupied land within the Socorro community grant on February 1, 1873; he subsequently erected a gristmill, dwelling house, and additional buildings. At the time of the disturbances, Zimmerly was married to a Hispanic woman named Paulita and had three children.[104]

Violence surfaced with the murder of A. M. Conklin, editor of the *Socorro Sun*, on Christmas Eve in 1880. Shot on the steps of the Methodist Church by three Baca brothers, Conklin was well-liked and respected among Anglo residents who immediately demanded that the Hispanic sheriff arrest his murderers. When the sheriff refused, Anglos gathered arms, seized the sheriff and eight other Hispanos as hostages, and demanded the surrender of the Baca brothers. The Las Vegas *Daily Optic* reported that Hispanos threatened to exterminate all the "Americanos" unless the hostages were released.[105]

Anglo residents quickly organized a Committee of Safety to bring law and order to the community and the murderers to justice. Practically all Anglos of any standing in the town were pressured to join the organization, including former California soldiers Emerson L. Smart, Joseph Kinsinger, and Samuel C. Meek. Soon after organizing, the Socorro vigilantes captured Antonio Baca, who was killed in an attempted jail break. Several weeks later a second brother was captured, jailed, and hanged by vigilantes from the gate frame in the Socorro courthouse plaza; the third brother lived to stand trial and win an acquittal from an all-Hispanic jury. The Socorro vigilantes continued their activities for about three years, lynching six men, only two of whom can be identified as Hispanos. Tension eventually lessened between Hispano and Anglo residents, but Socorro continued into the twentieth century as a town divided by racial prejudices.[106]

Contrasts within New Mexico's frontier society abounded and were readily apparent. In an environment fostering violence and lawlessness, residents established schools and stable communities. Entrepreneurs intent upon amassing wealth and fortune possessed civic consciousnesses, assisting their communities in enriching the lives of residents. New Mexicans violated local ordinances and yet at the same time served as municipal officers pledged to uphold the very laws that they broke. Throughout these tumultuous decades, towns and villages were beginning to modernize and expand, and men who came with the California Column, possessing all the virtues and vices of their age, helped to turn the territory into the most successful experiment in the nation of blending Anglo and Hispanic society and culture.

In Memoriam

"This humble tribute is to thee, Brave men of Company D, Who sleep the sleep that knows no wake. . . ."[1] So wrote former Captain Hugh A. Gorley in memory of comrades who had served with the First California Infantry. Long after volunteers had left the service and scattered, several old soldiers such as Gorley paid sentimental tribute to the California Column and its wartime record.

But the significance of the California soldiers goes beyond their wartime experiences. Over three hundred forty spent some portion of their productive careers in New Mexico after mustering out of the service. In two decades following the close of the Civil War, they participated in the remarkable transformation of New Mexico's society. During the late sixties and seventies, mining, farming, and grazing industries experienced steady growth, while federal funds flowed into territorial coffers. Anglo immigrants arrived in increasing numbers and placed new demands upon a conservative and tradition-bound Hispanic society.

When railroads entered the territory, the rate of change accelerated and the entire Southwest entered an era of rapid and inexpensive transportation. As eastern entrepreneurs journeyed west to survey opportunities, fresh capital poured into the territory for investment in mining, ranching, transportation, and irrigation projects. The westward flow of eastern immigrants significantly increased the Anglo portion of the population, contributing to the transformation of territorial life.

During these decades of expansion and growth, no one so in-fluenced New Mexico's history as did the men from Carleton's California Column. They were the first significant group of An-glos to settle in New Mexico since the Mexican War. They en-tered the territory in the prime of their lives. Optimism was high as military careers ended and opportunities beckoned to those who were willing to stay and grow with the land. They sank roots deep in the New Mexico soil, investing time, labor and money in the exploitation of its natural resources and in the development of its tiny, rural communities. Responsible for opening leading mineral districts, they helped lay the groundwork that allowed New Mex-ico's mining activities to prosper later on. They established ranch-es, experimented with crops, opened lands to cultivation, organized stockmen's associations, financed essential urban businesses, and supplied federal agencies with forage and subsistence stores as well as with civilian workers.

They became avid grass roots politicans and assumed major responsibilities for improving the quality of life in local commu-nities. Many married Hispanic women and sought to recreate in their adopted homeland the family life and institutions they had known in the "States." Nonetheless, as on other frontiers, vio-lence touched their lives, and a large number died senseless deaths. While several lived to witness the turn of the twentieth century, the attrition rate among them was high in the last years of the nineteenth century. Several left New Mexico late in life to spend their last days in various veterans' hospitals; others went for med-ical treatment but returned to die in New Mexico.

With advanced age, they reestablished contact with former comrades to verify claims for military pensions; it was a time to compare ailments and to jog memories of accidents and wounds sustained in the military. Few left their widows or heirs more than moderate inheritances; several ended their days in destitute cir-cumstances. One, Abner Frazier, was a veritable hermit at age sixty, living alone in a rough board shanty in Santa Fe County several miles from his nearest neighbor. A pension investigator reported that he was living in filth and squalor, "a more dirty and destitute human being could hardly be imagined."[2] Some were more fortunate and had families who mourned their deaths. But as the former troopers breathed their last, whether surrounded by sorrowing families or not, their deaths were routinely recorded in the nation's capital, where a minor functionary stamped two words on the outside cover of their pension files: "Dead" and "Dropped." Yet their twentieth-century descendants, scattered from Santa Cruz in the north to Mesilla in the south, form a living link to the distant past when over a hundred years ago the California Column entered New Mexico to preserve national unity.

Appendix 1

California Veterans Residing in New Mexico After Discharge

Name	County of Residence (1870 Census)[*]	Name	County of Residence (1870 Census)[*]
1. Seneca G. Ames	Doña Ana	21. William W. Bollinger	Colfax
2. Horace Arden	Grant	22. Cyrus Bowie	San Miguel
3. William Armstrong		23. Alexander Bowman	
4. Frank C. Arnett	Socorro	24. Patrick Brady	
5. George W. Arnold	San Miguel	25. Charles Brakebill	Grant
6. Grandville S. Arnold		26. Theodore Briggs	San Miguel
7. John W. Atwood	Colfax	27. Frederick G. Brill	San Miguel
8. John Ayers		28. George W. Bronson	
9. John D. Barncastle	Doña Ana	29. George H. Brooks	
10. Charles H. Bartlett	Lincoln	30. Crocker Brown	
11. Thomas T. Bartlett		31. George Brown	Socorro
12. Henry Barton	Grant	32. Henry C. Brown	Lincoln
13. Thomas Baxter		33. Oscar M. Brown	
14. Henry Beckham		34. Albert F. Bruno	Mora
15. William W. Beman		35. Allen Buchanan	Valencia
16. George H. Bendle		36. George H. Buck	Colfax
17. Joseph F. Bennett	Doña Ana	37. Reece R. Bulger	Grant
18. Powell Bingham		38. Hugh D. Bullard	Bernalillo
19. Charles W. Blake		39. George A. Burkett	
20. Robert Blair			

[*]Blanks indicate that the individual was not located in the 1870 New Mexico census.

Name	County of Residence (1870 Census)*		Name	County of Residence (1870 Census)*
40.	Linklain Butin	Grant	71.	Frederick DeFrouville	
41.	Oliver Butler	Mora	72.	George W. Dement	
42.	William P. Calloway		73.	Timothy Deneen	
43.	Rufus P. Canterbury		74.	Joseph Dennis	
44.	George M. Carpenter	Colfax	75.	James DeParty	San Miguel
45.	Robert Carr		76.	Daniel Diamond	
46.	Charles Carter	Santa Fe	77.	Thomas Dicken (alias John Humphrey)	Santa Fe
47.	David N. Catanach	Santa Fe	78.	William H. Dickerson	Colfax
48.	William Chamberlin	Grant	79.	Robert Dickson	Lincoln
49.	Thomas P. Chapman		80.	Philip Diemar	Valencia
50.	George Chase	Santa Fe	81.	Wallace Doan	
51.	Joseph B. Chichester	Colfax	82.	Robert R. Dorland	
52.	Louis Clark	Rio Arriba	83.	Calvin Dotson	Lincoln
53.	James A. Cochran		84.	Mannus Dougherty	
54.	Thomas Coghlan	Santa Fe	85.	Henry S. Drinkhouse	Doña Ana
55.	Barney W. Connelly	Grant	86.	George B. Duncan	Grant
56.	Patrick Connelly	Grant	87.	Henry W. Easton	Rio Arriba
57.	Theophilus Cooper	Grant	88.	Samuel Eckstein	Santa Fe
58.	William Cowden		89.	William F. Ellsworth	San Miguel
59.	Jason Covey	Grant	90.	Joseph D. Emerson	Socorro
60.	Samuel Creevey	Grant	91.	Gilbert Farnsworth	
61.	James G. Crittenden	Grant	92.	Henry Feldwick	
62.	John S. Crouch	Grant	93.	Benjamin F. Fergusson	Santa Fe
63.	Benjamin C. Cutler		94.	Wesley Fields	Lincoln
64.	Daniel Dameron	Valencia	95.	Charles Finn	
65.	Anson C. Damon		96.	Eley A. Fluke	
66.	Benjamin E. Davies	Doña Ana	97.	Eli B. Forbes	
67.	George Davis		98.	Charles W. Fortner	
68.	John Davis	Doña Ana	99.	Christian Foster	
69.	Nicholas S. Davis		100.	Albert J. Fountain	
70.	Samuel Dean	San Miguel	101.	Joseph Franklin	Socorro
			102.	Abner Frazier	San Miguel

Name	County of Residence (1870 Census)*	Name	County of Residence (1870 Census)*
103. Louis Fremont		138. John J. Hill	
104. Albert H. French		139. Hugh L. Hinds	
105. Emil Fritz	Lincoln	140. Frank Hodges	
106. Lycurgus D. Fuller	Santa Fe	141. William Hofedank	
107. Frank Garvey		142. Peter Hollenbeck	Socorro
108. John D. Gibbins	Grant	143. Wilson G. Holman	Grant
109. William Gill	Lincoln	144. John K. Houston	Grant
110. Samuel A. Gorham		145. Frank Howard	Doña Ana
111. Thomas H. Goshorn		146. John B. Hoyt	
112. John F. Gould		147. Richard Hudson	Grant
113. August Gunzenhauser	Grant	148. Frederick G. Hughes	Socorro
114. Charles Haberkorn		149. Josiah L. Hull	Doña Ana
115. Gilbert Haggert	Valencia	150. Washington W. Hyde	Doña Ana
116. Americus Hall	Grant	151. Albert G. T. Jacobs	Lincoln
117. Ansel Hammond			
118. Philip Hantz	Doña Ana	152. John A. James	
119. Addison P. Harden		153. Charles T. Jennings	
120. Henry C. Haring	Doña Ana	154. James A. Jeremiah	
121. Milton Harrison	Colfax	155. Richard M. Johnson	
122. Benjamin F. Harrover	Grant	156. William S. F. Johnson	Colfax
123. David T. Harshaw	Socorro	157. Peter Jones	Grant
124. Henry M. Harshberger	Grant	158. Elijah S. Junior	Grant
125. William R. Hart		159. Thomas Varker Keam	
126. Joseph E. Haskins	Lincoln	160. Patrick M. Keho	Mora
127. Thaddeus Hawes	Santa Fe	161. John H. Kemp	Colfax
128. Henry S. Hays	Socorro	162. George M. Kenyon	
129. Mathias Heck	Colfax	163. John M. Kerr	
130. William Henry		164. Asa J. Kimbrough	
131. Madison Hern	Colfax	165. Joseph Kinsinger	Colfax
132. Marcus F. Herring	Doña Ana	166. Peter W. Kinsinger	Colfax
133. Andrew M. Herron	Grant	167. William Kline	
134. Alvah O. Hicks		168. Otto Koernick	
135. Patrick Higgins		169. Andrew Knob	Bernalillo
136. Theodore M. Higgins		170. George Krim	Socorro
137. William Hightower		171. William S. Lackey	Mora

Name	County of Residence (1870 Census)*	Name	County of Residence (1870 Census)*
172. John Lambert	Colfax	207. John V. Mead	
173. Lawrence Lapoint	Doña Ana	208. Otto Mears	
174. Gustavus Lawson	Colfax	209. Samuel C. Meek	Socorro
175. Jacob Laycock	San Miguel	210. John Meister	San Miguel
176. Simon Leavick		211. Chapel Melton	Bernalillo
177. Felix Leibold	Doña Ana	212. Francis Mercer	Valencia
178. George W. Lemon	Rio Arriba	213. Edward S. Merritt	Santa Fe
179. Chester C. Little	Colfax	214. Charles Miller	
180. Robert Long		215. Oscar Monroe	San Miguel
181. Alvin B. Ludwig		216. John A. Moore	
182. George Luskey		217. Joseph A. Moore	Grant
183. Sandy Lynch	Colfax	218. William B. Moores	Santa Fe
184. Simon Madigan		219. John Moran	Colfax
185. Walter Malcolm	Colfax	220. William B. Morgan	Grant
186. Edgar Manley		221. Peter Morris	Grant
187. Lewis W. Mann		222. Nicholas Murphy	Grant
188. Thomas D. Marshall		223. Thomas Myers	
189. George T. Martin		224. William Neil	Mora
190. John Martin	Doña Ana	225. George W. Nesmith	Lincoln
191. Elias Marts	Colfax	226. Robert V. Newsham	Grant
192. John A. Marvin		227. Joseph B. Nickerson	Lincoln
193. Alva Mason	Grant	228. George John O'Connell	
194. Richard Mawson	Grant	229. John E. Oliphant	Grant
195. Bernard McCall		230. William Oliver	
196. William R. McCormick	Doña Ana	231. Edward W. Osgood	
197. Robert M. McCuistion	Valencia	232. Henry Ostrander	Mora
198. Thomas J. McCuistion		233. John Parquet	
199. Patrick McEneany	Mora	234. Richard C. Patterson	Socorro
200. Alden S. McIlvain	Grant	235. Joseph H. Peacock	Valencia
201. John McIntyre		236. George W. Peppin	Lincoln
202. William H. McKee		237. George O. Perrault	Grant
203. John McKinn	Colfax	238. Westy Peterson	
204. Patrick McLaughlin	Colfax	239. George H. Pettis	
205. William McMullen	Santa Fe	240. Richard Philipith	
206. James T. McNamara	Mora		

Name		County of Residence (1870 Census)*	Name		County of Residence (1870 Census)*
241.	Lyon Phillipouski	*Lincoln*	277.	William R. Sharp	
242.	Allen D. Pierce		278.	John J. Shellhorn	
243.	John S. Poisal		279.	John A. Shepherd	
244.	Melvin Pool	*San Miguel*	280.	Henry W. Sherry	*Doña Ana*
245.	John S. Powers	*Grant*	281.	Louis Shroyer	
246.	Eli C. Priest		282.	John C. Sigwalt	*Colfax*
247.	William W. Price		283.	Thomas B. Sitton	*Lincoln*
248.	Patrick Quigley		284.	Isaac H. Skillen	
249.	Augustus Y. Rand		285.	John Slater	
250.	Milton D. Read		286.	John D. Slocum	*Doña Ana*
251.	Myron C. Reid		287.	Emerson L. Smart	
252.	Ludwig Reventlow		288.	Frederick A. Smith	*Lincoln*
253.	Thomas Richards	*Santa Fe*	289.	Malcolm Smith	*Valencia*
254.	Edwin A. Rigg		290.	Nelson C. Smith	
255.	Thaddeus W. Roberts	*Doña Ana*	291.	Thomas W. Smith	
			292.	William M. Smith	
256.	Thomas L. Roberts		293.	Frederick C. Snyder	*Colfax*
257.	Gerbard Robin		294.	Jacob P. Snyder	*Valencia*
258.	Andrew Rodgers		295.	Simon L. Snyder	
259.	Henry L. Rubie	*Mora*	296.	John L. Spurr	*Socorro*
260.	Hiram S. Russell	*Colfax*	297.	Leonidas V. Steele	*Grant*
261.	Richard D. Russell	*San Miguel*	298.	Abram B. Stanton	*Valencia*
262.	Rufus C. Russell	*Socorro*	299.	Andrew Stewart	
263.	Elias D. Ryan		300.	Joseph W. Stinson	*Colfax*
264.	John Ryan	*Valencia*	301.	David Stitzel	
265.	William L. Rynerson	*Grant*	302.	Paul D. Stone	
			303.	Chauncey N. Story	*Colfax*
266.	Augustus E. St. John		304.	Thomas E. Sunderland	
267.	Marshall St. John	*Grant*	305.	William D. Tallman	
268.	Lewis F. Sanburn	*Socorro*	306.	George A. Taylor	*Mora*
269.	Frederick Sanders		307.	John Taylor	
270.	Richard N. Sarle		308.	Robert Taylor	*Doña Ana*
271.	William R. Savage		309.	Benjamin W. Tevalt	*Lincoln*
272.	Florence Scannell		310.	John Thayer	
273.	Andrew Schneider	*Santa Fe*	311.	Nelson Thayer	*Mora*
274.	Henry Schultz	*Santa Fe*	312.	John Townsend	*Santa Fe*
275.	Henry Schwenker		313.	Cyrus Tubbs	*San Miguel*
276.	John H. Scott	*Doña Ana*			

Name	County of Residence (1870 Census)*	Name	County of Residence (1870 Census)*
314. John H. Van Order	Valencia	329. Ira Wentworth	
315. Charles VanWagner	Socorro	330. Nicholas S. White	Lincoln
316. William Van Winkle		331. Thomas M. F. Whyte	
317. Rufus C. Vose	Lincoln	332. Fountain Williams	
318. Charles H. Walker	Grant	333. Mathew Williams	
319. James V. Walters	Lincoln	334. Perry H. Williams	
320. John Walters	Lincoln	335. Andrew Wilson	Lincoln
321. William V. B. Wardwell	Socorro	336. John Wilson	Grant
322. David C. Warner	Lincoln	337. Alonzo D. Winship	
323. William Warnick	Lincoln	338. John V. Winters	Santa Fe
324. Albion K. Watts	Doña Ana	339. William Witted	Valencia
325. William H. Watts		340. David Wood	Doña Ana
326. Sydney M. Webb	Grant	341. Erastus W. Wood	
327. Isaac T. Webber	Mora	342. Richard Yeamans	Grant
328. Theodore Wendlandt	Grant	343. Charles Young	
		344. James A. Zabriskie	
		345. Samuel Zimmerly	Socorro

Appendix 2

California Veterans Residing
in Arizona, Colorado and Texas After Discharge
(see note 19, Chapter 3.)

ARIZONA

1. Wales Arnold
2. John Baker
3. Joseph F. Bennett
4. George E. Berry
5. Charles Brakebill
6. William F. Bradley
7. George W. Bronson
8. John W. Campbell
9. William L. Campbell
10. Barney W. Connelly
11. Patrick Connelly
12. Theophilus Cooper
13. Robert M. Crandall
14. John W. Davis
15. Sidney R. DeLong
16. Joseph Felmer
17. Edwin B. Frink
18. Pleasant Gibson
19. George O. Hand
20. Joseph P. Hargrave
21. David T. Harshaw
22. John Harvey

23. William Henry
24. Hugh L. Hinds
25. Frederick G. Hughes
26. William B. Kennedy
27. Fritz Martin
28. James E. McCaffrey
29. William R. McCormick
30. James D. Monihon
31. Mahlon E. Moore
32. John C. Pugslay
33. Henry J. Pursell
34. Edwin A. Rigg
35. George K. Saunders
36. Gilbert Cole Smith
37. John T. Smith
38. Joseph Smith
39. Edward G. Taylor
40. John S. Thayer
41. Joseph H. Tuttle
42. Charles H. Walker
43. Thomas Wallace
44. Anthony Wright

COLORADO

1. John W. Atwood
2. Thomas T. Bartlett
3. George H. Bendle
4. Alexander Bowman
5. George M. Carpenter
6. Philip Hantz
7. William A. Hightower
8. James H. Holmes
9. Robert Kinney
10. Sandy Lynch
11. Otto Mears
12. Myron C. Reid
13. Richard D. Russell
14. David H. St. Clair
15. Rufus C. Vose
16. James White
17. John Wynkoop

EL PASO AND VICINITY

1. John G. Atkinson
2. Juan Mariany Baptiste
3. John P. Clark
4. Benjamin E. Davies
5. George O. Edgerton
6. Charles E. Ellis
7. Albert H. French
8. Albert J. Fountain
9. Hazard F. Gaskey
10. John W. Hale
11. Jacob Morrow
12. George W. Rand
13. Ruben Richards
14. Conrad Thoma
15. James A. Zabriskie

TEXAS

1. George H. Brooks
2. William A. Brown
3. John E. Calhoun
4. Andrew J. Callahan
5. Rufus P. Canterbury
6. David Doole
7. John B. Foster
8. John W. Green
9. Arthur Lockwood
10. Myron C. Reid
11. C. J. Theriott
12. Henry Warren

Notes

Preface

1. John M. Adams, Pension Application Files, Civil War Series, Records of the Veterans Administration, Record Group 15, National Archives, Washington, D.C. (hereafter cited as Pension Application Files).

2. U.S. Bureau of the Census, *Historical Statistics of the United States, Colonial Times to 1970, Bicentennial Edition* (Washington: Government Printing Office, 1975), pt. 1, p. 32 (hereafter cited as U.S. Bureau of the Census, *Historical Statistics*).

3. *Las Cruces Citizen*, March 12, 1910.

Chapter 1

1. Aurora Hunt, *The Army of the Pacific* (Glendale: The Arthur H. Clark Company, 1951), pp. 19–26.

2. Ray C. Colton, *The Civil War in the Western Territories* (Norman: University of Oklahoma Press, 1959), pp. 3, 13–19.

3. *Mesilla Times*, March 16, 30, July 27, 1861; Benjamin Sacks, *Be It Enacted: The Creation of the Territory of Arizona* (Phoenix: Arizona Historical Foundation, 1964), pp. 35–42.

4. Martin Hardwick Hall, *Sibley's New Mexico Campaign* (Austin: University of Texas Press, 1960), pp. 36, 45–53, 76–77.

5. Report of Surgeon James M. McNulty, October 1863, *The War of the*

Rebellion: A Compilation of the Official Records of the Union and Confederate Armies (Washington: Government Printing Office, 1880–1901), Series I, vol. IX, p. 595 (hereafter cited as Official Records); Richard H. Orton, comp., Records of California Men in the War of the Rebellion, 1861–1867 (Sacramento: Adjutant General's Office, 1890), p. 47; Colton, The Civil War, p. 101. For a general summary of the Civil War activities of the California volunteers in New Mexico see two books by Aurora Hunt, Major General James Henry Carleton (Glendale: The Arthur H. Clark Company, 1958) and The Army of the Pacific.

6. More than two hundred military service records and pension claims were consulted during the course of this study. See Compiled Military Service Records, Civil War, California Volunteers, Records of the Adjutant General's Office, Record Group 94, National Archives, Washington, D.C. (hereafter cited as Military Service Records), and Pension Application Files.

7. John Ayers, "A Soldier's Experience in New Mexico," New Mexico Historical Review, 24 (October 1949): 259; David N. Catanach, Pension Application Files.

8. Samuel Creevey, Pension Application Files.

9. Place of birth for California volunteers primarily was obtained from New Mexico census returns for 1870 and 1880, in addition to Pension Applications. See Population Schedules of the Ninth Census of the United States, 1870, New Mexico, Bureau of the Census, Record Group 29, National Archives, Microfilm Publication 593, rolls 893–897 (hereafter cited as New Mexico Census, 1870) and Population Schedules of the Tenth Census of the United States, 1880, New Mexico, Bureau of the Census, Record Group 29, National Archives, Microfilm Publication T 9, rolls 802–804 (hereafter cited as New Mexico Census, 1880).

10. Ibid.

11. Marian Russell, Land of Enchantment, Memoirs of Marian Russell Along the Santa Fe Trail As dictated to Mrs. Hal Russell (reprint; Albuquerque: University of New Mexico Press, 1981), p. 98.

12. Barney W. Connelly, John D. Barncastle, William L. Rynerson, Pension Application Files; Rynerson Profile in William Gillet Ritch Collection, MS no. 2009 (Huntington Library). (Hereafter cited as Ritch Collection.)

13. San Francisco Daily Alta California, October 12, 1863 (hereafter cited as Daily Alta California).

14. Ibid., February 4, 1864. This man was killed by Apaches near Fort Cummings several months before he was scheduled to be mustered out of the service. Orton, Records of California Men, p. 415.

15. Joseph F. Bennett to N. V. Bennett, September 30, 1862, E. F. Kellner

Papers, Special Collections, University of New Mexico (hereafter cited as Kellner Papers).

16. Ritch Collection, MS no. 1999.

17. Bell Irvin Wiley, *The Life of Billy Yank, The Common Soldier of the Union* (New York: Bobbs-Merrill Company, 1952), p. 37.

18. Andrew J. Callahan, Pension Application Files.

19. Proceedings of a General Court Martial Convened at Franklin, Texas, June 10, 1863, Trial of Thomas Martin, Records of the Office of the Judge Advocate General (Army), Record Group 153, National Archives, Washington, D.C. (hereafter cited as the Records of the Judge Advocate General).

20. Carleton to West, February 11, 1862, *Official Records*, Series I, vol. L, part 1, p. 859; Carleton to Dobbins, February 12, 1862, *ibid.*, p. 862.

21. Edward Everett Ayer, "Reminiscences of the Far West, and Other Trips, 1861–1918" (MS, Bancroft Library, University of California), pp. 1–16.

22. *Ibid.*, pp. 18–20.

23. Oscar M. Brown, Pension Application Files; George B. Anderson, *The History of New Mexico, Its Resources and People* (Los Angeles: Pacific States Publishing Co., 1907), vol. 2, p. 571; Silver City *Grant County Herald*, November 21, 1875 (hereafter cited as *Grant County Herald*).

24. John D. Barncastle, Pension Application Files; Ayer, "Reminiscences," p. 24.

25. Carleton to West, March 29, 1862, *Official Records*, Series I, vol. L, part 1, p. 961; Carleton to Shirland, April 17, 1862, *ibid.*, p. 1010; Carleton to Fergusson, April 21, 1862, *ibid.*, pp. 1018–19.

26. Ayer, "Reminiscences," p. 29; *Daily Alta California*, June 8, 1862.

27. Carleton to Drum, June 18, 1862, *Official Records*, Series I, vol. L, part 1, pp. 1146–47.

28. Benjamin Fergusson, Pension Application Files.

29. *Daily Alta California*, July 10, 1862.

30. Carleton to Drum, May 25, 1862, *Official Records*, Series I, vol. IX, p. 553.

31. *Daily Alta California*, August 10, 1862, February 14, 1863; Hunt, *The Army of the Pacific*, p. 123; Orton, *Records of California Men*, pp. 104, 107.

32. Carleton to Drum, September 20, 1862, *Official Records*, Series I, vol. IX, pp. 565–570; General Orders, No. 85, September 21, 1862, *ibid.*, Series I, vol. XV, pp. 574–75.

33. *Daily Alta California*, August 10, October 17, 1862.

34. Bennett to brother, September 30, 1862, Kellner Papers.

35. *Daily Alta California*, October 17, 21, 1862.

Chapter 2

1. See Darlis A. Miller, "General James Henry Carleton in New Mexico, 1862–1867" (Master's thesis, New Mexico State University, 1970), pp. 37–47 for military interference in civilian affairs in southern New Mexico.

2. Rigg to West, November 11, 1862, *Official Records*, Series I, vol. XV, pp. 598–99; Carleton to West, November 18, 1862, *ibid.*, pp. 599–601.

3. General Orders No. 24, December 2, 1862, *Official Records*, Series I, vol. L, part 2, pp. 239–40; General Orders No. 1, January 1, 1863, *ibid.*, p. 274; Santa Fe *New Mexican*, April 7, June 22, 1865. A *fanega* was equal to about two and one half bushels. West reported that citizens had left their lands because they feared a Confederate invasion. Captain William McMullen and Lieutenant Albert H. French, who played major roles in implementing the grain order, later became well-known figures in the Southwest. West was promoted to Brigadier General of Volunteers October 25, 1862. Francis B. Heitman, *Historical Register and Dictionary of the United States Army* (Urbana: University of Illinois Press, 1965), vol. 1, p. 1020.

4. General Orders No. 22, July 12, 1864, *Official Records*, Series I, vol. XLI, part 2, pp. 168–70.

5. Albuquerque *Rio Abajo Weekly Press*, April 12, 1864 (hereafter cited as *Rio Abajo Weekly Press*); Santa Fe *New Mexican*, November 4, 1864, January 13, 1865, February 23, 1867; Santa Fe *Weekly Gazette*, September 10, 1864, January 28, 1865; Knapp to Carleton, January 15, 1864, Records of the Secretary of State, Record Group 59, Territorial Papers, New Mexico, National Archives Microfilm Publication T-17, roll 2 (hereafter cited as Territorial Papers, State). After Judge Knapp's removal, discharged California volunteers met in Mesilla to condemn actions of General Carleton. Among charges leveled against the general was that he had "imprisoned and brutally treated" territorial judges. One month later on October 19, a convention composed of civilians and California veterans expressed thanks to Judge Knapp for having recently journeyed to the nation's capital on behalf "of the welfare of the people of this valley." Santa Fe *New Mexican*, November 4, 1864, July 14, 1866.

6. Carleton to West, October 11, 1862 and Carleton to Carson, October 12, 1862, *Official Records*, Series I, vol. XV, pp. 579–81.

7. Carleton to Carson, November 25, 1862, "Condition of the Indian Tribes," 39 Cong., 2d sess., *Senate Report No. 156* (Serial 1279), pp. 101–2; Carleton to Thomas, February 1, 1863, *Official Records*, Series I, vol. XV, pp. 669–70.

8. Carleton to Thomas, March 19, 1863, "Condition of the Indian Tribes," (Serial 1279), p. 106; Carleton to Halleck, May 10, 1863, *Official Records*, Series I, vol. XV, pp. 723–24; Santa Fe *Weekly Gazette*, December 27, 1862.

9. Santa Fe *Weekly Gazette*, December 27, 1862.

10. *Daily Alta California*, October 15, 1863.

11. West to Cutler, January 28, 1863, *Official Records*, Series I, vol. L, part 2, pp. 296–97.

12. *Ibid.*

13. Ritch Collection, MS no. 1735.

14. Ritch Collection, MS no. 1410.

15. Lee Myers, "The Enigma of Mangas Coloradas' Death," *New Mexico Historical Review*, 41 (October 1966): 299; Santa Fe *Weekly Gazette*, April 11, 1868. Myers presents additional versions for the killing of Mangas Coloradas but fails to mention the accounts of Crouch, Martin, and Townsend.

16. George H. Pettis, *The California Column*, Historical Society of New Mexico, No. 11 (Santa Fe: New Mexican Printing Company), 1908, p. 19.

17. William McCleave, "Recollections of a California Volunteer" (MS, Bancroft Library, University of California), pp. 10–11; General Orders No. 3, February 24, 1864, *Official Records*, Series I, vol. XV, p. 229.

18. General Orders No. 3, February 24, 1864, *Official Records*, Series I, vol. XV, p. 229.

19. Santa Fe *Weekly Gazette*, February 21, 1863; *Daily Alta California*, June 17, 1863.

20. West to McFerran, May 2, 1863, *Official Records*, Series I, vol. L, part 2, pp. 421–22; West to McCleave, March 5, 1863, *ibid.*, p. 339.

21. Carleton to Carson, August 18, 1863, "Condition of the Indian Tribes," (Serial 1279), p. 128; Carleton to Wallen, March 11, 1864, *ibid.*, p. 165; Carleton to Thomas, August 23, 1863, *ibid.*, p. 131.

22. *Rio Abajo Weekly Press*, December 1, 1863.

23. Santa Fe *New Mexican*, May 14, 1864.

24. Carleton to Pishon, June 22, 1863, "Condition of the Indian Tribes," (Serial 1279), p. 115; Carleton to Thomas, September 13, 1863, *ibid.*, pp. 135–36.

25. Santa Fe *Weekly Gazette*, September 26, October 3, 1863; General Orders, No. 27, October 23, 1863, *Official Records*, Series I, vol. L, part 2, pp. 653–54.

26. Alexander Bowman, Pension Application Files.

27. Brown to Cutler, December 1, 1864, *Official Records*, Series I, vol. XLI, part 1, pp. 867–78; Orton, *Records of California Men*, p. 145.

28. Santa Fe *Weekly Gazette*, December 17, 1864.

29. For an eyewitness account of the battle, see George H. Pettis, *Kit Carson's Fight With the Comanche and Kiowa Indians*, Historical Society of New Mexico, No. 12 (Santa Fe: New Mexican Printing Company, 1908).

30. General Orders, No. 4, February 18, 1865, *Official Records*, Series I, vol. XLVIII, part 1, p. 906; Theodore Briggs, Patrick Brady, Samuel Eckstein, Pension Application Files.

31. *Daily Alta California*, January 18, 1864. See General Orders, No. 3, February 24, 1864, *Official Records*, Series I, vol. XXVI, part 1, p. 30.

32. *Mesilla Valley Independent*, December 8, 1877.

33. *Ibid.* In December 1883, an unknown journalist traveling between Engle and Palomas in a buckboard driven by fourteen-year-old Eugene Manlove Rhodes visited the soldiers' graveyard at the old Fort McRae ruins, eight miles from Engle. There he saw the monument that had been erected in memory of the four dead California soldiers, the inscriptions nearly effaced by weather and barely decipherable. In addition to Private Dickey, the memorial was dedicated to privates Robert S. Johnson, age 29, killed by Apaches on July 20, 1863; Charles M. O'Brien, age 23, killed by Apaches on July 15, 1862; and William J. Rowlett, age 33, drowned in the Rio Grande on July 6, 1864. Las Cruces *Rio Grande Republican*, December 22, 1883 (hereafter cited as *Rio Grande Republican*); Orton, *Records of California Men*, pp. 364–66.

34. Ayer, "Reminiscences," p. 38.

35. *Daily Alta California*, October 12, 1863.

36. Ernest Marchand, ed., *News From Fort Craig, New Mexico, 1863, Civil War Letters of Andrew Ryan, With the First California Volunteers* (Santa Fe: Stagecoach Press, 1966), pp. 49–54.

37. Ayer, "Reminiscences," p. 36; Marchand, *News From Fort Craig*, p. 48; Henry P. Walker, ed., "Soldier in the California Column: The Diary of John W. Teal," *Arizona and the West*, 13 (Spring 1971): 56; General Orders, No. 14, District of New Mexico, July 22, 1866, Trial of Private David H. Sample, Records of the Judge Advocate General; Orton, *Records of California Men*, p. 408.

38. George O. Hand, Diary (MS, Arizona Historical Society, Tucson), entry for March 19, 1863.

39. Walker, "Soldier in the California Column," pp. 47, 56.

40. *Daily Alta California*, October 12, 1863.

41. Marchand, *News From Fort Craig*, p. 64.

42. San Francisco *Evening Bulletin*, December 6, 1862.

43. Henry Hays, Pension Application Files.

44. Lycurgus D. Fuller, Pension Application Files.

45. *Daily Alta California*, February 14, 1863; Santa Fe *Weekly Gazette*, March 26, 1864; Russell, *Land of Enchantment*, pp. 97–113.

46. *Rio Abajo Weekly Press*, March 31, 1863; Santa Fe *Weekly Gazette*, June 30, 1866; Darlis A. Miller, ed., *Across The Plains In 1864 With Additional Paymaster Samuel C. Staples* (Manhattan, Kansas: MA/AH Publishing, 1980), p. 65.

47. Miller, *Across The Plains In 1864*, p. 59; Walker, "Soldier in the California Column," p. 50; Santa Fe *Weekly Gazette*, August 1, 1863.

48. Santa Fe *Weekly Gazette*, December 31, 1864, July 14, 1866.

49. *Ibid.*, May 9, 1863, July 21, 1866.

50. John Ayers, Pension Application Files; Santa Fe *Weekly Gazette*, May 6, 1865.

51. Deaths of California volunteers are recorded in Orton, *Records of California Men*, pp. 87–167, 209–17, 335–80, 385–417, 676–719. Private James Jellings who is listed in Orton as having died at Los Pinos June 15, 1864 with cause not recorded was killed when the revolver being examined by another soldier, John Riley, accidentally discharged. See Marchand, *News From Fort Craig*, p. 72.

52. Orton, *Records of California Men*, p. 150.

53. *Ibid.*, p. 390; Santa Fe *Weekly Gazette*, May 20, 1865; Santa Fe *New Mexican*, May 26, 1865.

54. Orton, *Records of California Men*, pp. 94, 377; Charles Smith, Military Service Records; *Mesilla Valley Independent*, October 6, 1877; George H. Pettis, *Personal Narratives of Events in the War of the Rebellion, Frontier Service. . . . Or a History of Company K, First Infantry, California Volunteers* (Providence, Rhode Island: Soldiers' and Sailors' Historical Society of Rhode Island, 1885), pp. 34–38.

55. Santa Fe *New Mexican*, September 8, 1865, March 2, 1866.

56. Samuel Creevey, John G. Atkinson, Pension Application Files.

57. Silver City *Southwest-Sentinel*, August 23, 1884.

58. Russell, *Land of Enchantment*, p. 108.

Chapter 3

1. *Sonoma County Journal* (Petaluma, Calif.), August 1, 1862; Ritch Collection, MS no. 1522.

2. Carleton to Halleck, March 20, 1864, *Official Records*, Series I, vol. XXXIV, part 2, pp. 671–73.

3. Carleton to Low, July 18, 1865, "Relative to the discharge of certain California Volunteers stationed in the Territories," 39 Cong., 1 sess., *House Executive Document No. 138* (Serial 1267), p. 3.

4. Hunt, *The Army of the Pacific*, pp. 140–41, 356; Hunt, *Carleton*, p. 311; Don Rickey, Jr., *Forty Miles a Day on Beans and Hay, The Enlisted Soldier Fighting the Indian Wars* (Norman: University of Oklahoma Press, 1963), p. 127.

5. *Daily Alta California*, September 29, 1864.

6. *Daily Alta California*, October 10, 1863, January 12, August 6, 1864; Ritch Collection, MS no. 1534; Carleton to Nunn, September 24, 1865 and Carleton to Thomas, May 31, 1864, "Discharge of Certain California Volunteers," (Serial 1267), pp. 1–2, 8; Marchand, *News From Fort Craig*, pp. 63–64, 68.

7. Carleton to Nunn, September 24, 1865, "Discharge of Certain California Volunteers," (Serial 1267), pp. 1–2; *Daily Alta California*, September 21, 1864.

8. *Santa Fe New Mexican*, January 6, 1865.

9. Carleton to Nunn, September 24, 1865, Low to Carleton, May 22, 1865, Cutler to Staples, July 17, 1865, Staples to Cutler, July 17, 1865, "Discharge of Certain California Volunteers," (Serial 1267), pp. 1–2, 8, 9; *Daily Alta California*, December 15, 1864, December 21, 1865.

10. *Santa Fe Weekly Gazette*, September 1, 1866; *Daily Alta California*, December 29, 1866; Orton, *Records of California Men*, pp. 85–86.

11. *Santa Fe Weekly Gazette*, January 27, 1866.

12. *Ibid.*, December 31, 1864; *Daily Alta California*, December 25, 1864; Ritch Collection, MS nos. 1310, 1534.

13. *Daily Alta California*, October 13, 1864.

14. *Santa Fe New Mexican*, April 7, 1865; *Daily Alta California*, September 26, 1866; Orton, *Records of California Men*, p. 151.

15. Executive Records, November 2, 1863–October 29, 1864, and Executive Records, December 6, 1864–October 16, 1865, Territorial Papers, State, rolls 2–3.

16. *Santa Fe New Mexican*, June 8, 1866; *Daily New Mexican*, July 12, 1871; Heitman, *Historical Register*, vol. 1, p. 988.

17. Carleton to Halleck, November 14, 1862, *Official Records*, Series I, vol. L, part 2, pp. 222–23; Heitman, *Historical Register*, vol. 1, p. 655.

18. William McCleave, Papers (Bancroft Library, University of California).

19. No attempt has been made to identify all California veterans in regions other than New Mexico, but a cursory examination indicates that at least 44 former volunteers in Carleton's command settled in Arizona, 17 in Colorado, 15 in the El Paso area, and 12 in other Texas localities. Undoubtedly a more intensive search would inflate these figures. See Appendix 2.

20. *Grant County Herald*, October 31, 1875.

21. Ritch Collection, MS nos. 1948, 1949; Porter A. Stratton, *The Territo-*

rial Press of New Mexico, 1834–1912 (Albuquerque: University of New Mexico Press, 1969), p. 208.

22. See Appendix I. Hubert H. Bancroft states that in 1870 there were 2,760 people in New Mexico who were born in parts of the United States other than New Mexico and 1,717 people born in foreign countries other than Mexico. These figures have been used to estimate the so-called Anglo population of New Mexico. Hubert H. Bancroft, *History of Arizona and New Mexico, 1530–1888* (San Francisco: The History Company, 1889), p. 723.

23. Orton, *Records of California Men*, pp. 114, 335; Santa Fe *New Mexican*, June 22, September 29, November 24, 1865. Hofedank's name appears as Hopedank in the press.

24. Santa Fe *New Mexican*, September 29, 1865, July 28, 1866.

25. *Ibid.*, October 20, 1866; Santa Fe *Weekly Gazette*, October 20, 1866. Foster's given name appears as Christopher in the press.

26. Santa Fe *New Mexican*, December 3, 1867.

27. *Ibid.*, November 19, 26, 1867; Santa Fe *Weekly Gazette*, November 23, 30, 1867. A third mail carrier who may also have been a California veteran, Charles Williams, was killed by Indians near Fort Cummings in 1866. Santa Fe *Weekly Gazette*, November 23, 1867.

28. Santa Fe *New Mexican*, November 17, 1868; Santa Fe *Weekly Gazette*, April 11, 1868.

29. Santa Fe *New Mexican*, August 17, 1867; George B. Anderson, *The History of New Mexico, Its Resources and People* (Los Angeles: Pacific States Publishing Co., 1907), vol. 2, p. 727.

30. Santa Fe *New Mexican*, October 20, 27, November 3, 1868; Santa Fe *Weekly Gazette*, February 17, August 1, 1866, October 24, 1868.

31. Santa Fe *Weekly Gazette*, December 5, 1868, January 23, 1869.

32. Santa Fe *New Mexican*, December 31, 1867. This ex-soldier is listed as Julian A. Hubbard in Orton, *Records of California Men*, p. 696.

33. Santa Fe *New Mexican*, June 9, 1865, February 16, 1867; Santa Fe *Weekly Gazette*, April 14, October 20, 1866; License of Boss, Isaacs, and Leavick, Territorial Archives of New Mexico, Microfilm Edition, roll 52, State Records Center and Archives, Santa Fe, New Mexico (hereafter cited as Territorial Archives of New Mexico).

34. Santa Fe *New Mexican*, November 12, 1867, February 18, 1868; *Civil and Criminal Minute and Record Book* [1865–1870], Doña Ana County, (Doña Ana County Court House, Las Cruces, New Mexico), pp. 104, 121, 137, 175 (hereafter cited as *Civil and Criminal Minute and Record Book* [1865–1870], Doña Ana County).

35. Leroy R. Hafen, "Otto Mears, 'Pathfinder of the San Juan,' " *The Colorado Magazine,* 9 (March 1932): 72.

36. Santa Fe *Weekly Gazette,* September 29, 1866; Santa Fe *New Mexican,* September 29, 1866, March 2, July 20, December 24, 1867, July 7, October 20, 1868; Pettis, *California Column,* pp. 30–33; Robert Grieve, *Illustrated History of Pawtucket, Central Falls and Vicinity* (Pawtucket, R.I.: Pawtucket Gazette and Chronicle, 1897), pp. 414–15.

37. Andrew Stewart, New Mexico Dictations (Bancroft Library, University of California).

38. George Bendle, Pension Application Files.

39. Orton, *Records of California Men,* pp. 638, 648; Territorial Census of 1885, Schedule of Veterans of the Union Volunteer Forces and Regular Army (State Records Center and Archives, Santa Fe, New Mexico). (Hereafter cited as Census of Veterans, 1885).

40. Census of Veterans, 1885; Santa Fe *Daily New Mexican,* November 26, 1872, February 12, 1882; Santa Fe *Daily Herald,* September 12, 1888; John W. Honsinger, Pension Application Files.

41. See Appendix I.

42. *Ibid.*

43. Darlis A. Miller, "William Logan Rynerson in New Mexico, 1862–1893," *New Mexico Historical Review,* 48 (April 1973): 102.

44. Santa Fe *Daily New Mexican,* February 3, 1873; Lewis Clark, Rio Arriba County, New Mexico Census, 1870.

45. Henry Ostrander, Mora County, New Mexico Census, 1870; William V. B. Wardwell, Socorro County, New Mexico Census, 1870.

46. Ayers, "A Soldier's Experience," pp. 260, 266.

47. Santa Fe *Weekly Gazette,* June 9, 1866.

Chapter 4

1. Jim B. Pearson, *The Maxwell Land Grant* (Norman: University of Oklahoma Press, 1961), pp. 16–17; Paige W. Christiansen, *The Story of Mining in New Mexico* (Socorro: New Mexico Bureau of Mines and Mineral Resources, 1974), p. 35; Fayette Alexander Jones, *New Mexico Mines and Minerals* (Santa Fe: The New Mexico Printing Company, 1904), p. 123; Peter W. Kinsinger, Pension Application Files.

2. Orton, *Records of California Men,* p. 379; Pearson, *Maxwell Land Grant,* p. 17; Santa Fe *Weekly Gazette,* June 20, 1868.

3. Pearson, *Maxwell Land Grant*, p. 21; Jones, *New Mexico Mines and Minerals*, pp. 142–43.

4. Ralph Emerson Twitchell, *The Leading Facts of New Mexican History* (Cedar Rapids: The Torch Press, 1917), vol. 3, p. 67; Santa Fe *Weekly Gazette*, April 18, 1868; Santa Fe *Daily New Mexican*, July 14, 1868. For a description of Elizabethtown, see Pearson, *Maxwell Land Grant*, pp. 23–33.

5. Orton, *Records of California Men*, p. 362; Pearson, *Maxwell Land Grant*, pp. 30–33; Anderson, *History of New Mexico*, vol. 1, p. 235; Santa Fe *Daily New Mexican*, October 28, November 8, 1871. Anderson and Pearson are in error when they state that Wall Henderson shot and killed Stinson.

6. Pearson, *Maxwell Land Grant*, pp. 41–42; Twitchell, *Leading Facts*, vol. 3, p. 67; Santa Fe *Weekly Gazette*, June 20, 1868; Santa Fe *New Mexican*, November 24, 1868; Santa Fe *Daily New Mexican*, July 17, 1871. Captain Davis was hired in the 1870s as engineer for the Longfellow copper mine in Clifton, Arizona. He subsequently supervised the building of the first railroad in that territory, begun in 1878 and completed the following year, which ran between the mine and the smelter. After the Arizona Copper Company acquired the Longfellow Mine in 1882, Davis took charge of their mining department and in subsequent years directed building the railroad between Duncan and Clifton. Floyd S. Fierman, "Jewish Pioneering in the Southwest, A Record of the Freudenthal-Lesinsky-Solomon Families," *Arizona and the West*, 2 (Spring 1960): 62–63; Silver City *Southwest-Sentinel*, August 2, 1884 (hereafter cited as *Southwest-Sentinel*); *Rio Grande Republican*, August 2, 1884. Kinsinger died of pneumonia in April 1884 in the silver camp of Kingston in southern New Mexico.

7. *Mining Claims, Records, No. 2*, Doña Ana County (Doña Ana County Court House, Las Cruces, New Mexico), pp. 19–25, 36–47, 172–73 (hereafter cited as *Mining Claims No. 2*, Doña Ana County); Executive Records, October 6, 1865–November 5, 1866, Territorial Papers, State, roll 3.

8. *Mining Claims No. 2*, Doña Ana County, pp. 84–171. The soldiers included William R. Sharp, Henry Barton, Marcus F. Herring, George A. Burkett, Richard Hudson, and William L. Rynerson.

9. Santa Fe *Weekly Gazette*, June 27, 1867; Santa Fe *New Mexican*, February 25, March 17, 1868.

10. California men who owned mines in Pinos Altos District included John Ayers, Henry Barton, Linklain Butin, William Chamberlin, Barney W. Connelly, Patrick Connelly, Jason Covey, James G. Crittenden, George B. Duncan, Albert H. French, Marcus F. Herring, Wilson G. Holman, John K. Houston, Richard Hudson, Josiah L. Hull, Alva Mason, William R. McCormick, Joseph

A. Moore, Robert V. Newsham, George O. Perrault, John S. Powers, William L. Rynerson, William R. Sharp, John D. Slocum, Ira Wentworth, Theodore Wendlandt, and Richard Yeamans.

11. *Mining Claims No. 2*, Doña Ana County, pp. 190–92, 369–70, 427–35. For Carleton's gold and copper claims in the Pinos Altos District, see pp. 97–192.

12. Mineral holdings for Rynerson, Hudson, Crittenden, and Houston can be found in mining claims located in the courthouses for Doña Ana and Grant counties, but see specifically *Mining Locations No. 1*, Grant County (Grant County Court House, Silver City, New Mexico), pp. 18, 23, 220, 268 (hereafter cited as *Mining Locations No. 1*, Grant County); *Mining Claims No. 2*, Doña Ana County, p. 268.

13. Santa Fe *Daily New Mexican*, February 7, 1877; Christiansen, *Mining in New Mexico*, pp. 38, 48.

14. Barney W. Connelly, Pension Application Files; Orton, *Records of California Men*, pp. 112, 364, 395.

15. Barney W. Connelly, Pension Application Files; Santa Fe *Daily New Mexican*, July 19, 1872; Las Cruces *Borderer*, April 6, 1871, February 7, May 8, 1872 (hereafter cited as *Borderer*); *Mesilla Valley Independent*, December 8, 1877; *Mining Locations No. 1*, Grant County, p. 59; *Deeds No. 1*, Grant County (Grant County Court House, Silver City, New Mexico), pp. 208, 216, 307–8 (hereafter cited as *Deeds No. 1*, Grant County).

16. Barney W. Connelly, Patrick Connelly, Pension Application Files.

17. Rita and Janaloo Hill, "Alias Shakespeare, The Town Nobody Knew," *New Mexico Historical Review*, 42 (July 1967): 218. California veterans owning property at Ralston included Horace Arden, Joseph F. Bennett, William Chamberlin, Barney W. Connelly, Patrick Connelly, Theophilus Cooper, James G. Crittenden, John S. Crouch, John Davis, Sidney R. DeLong, John F. Gould, Benjamin F. Harrover, Henry M. Harshberger, Richard Hudson, Josiah L. Hull, Elijah S. Junior, William R. McCormick, Robert V. Newsham, John E. Oliphant, John S. Powers, William L. Rynerson, Henry Schwenker, and Fountain Williams.

18. Santa Fe *Daily New Mexican*, June 18, 1870; *Grant County Herald*, August 2, 1879; Conrad Keeler Naegle, "The History of Silver City, New Mexico, 1870–1886" (Master's thesis, University of New Mexico, 1943), p. 15.

19. Naegle, "Silver City," p. 18; Santa Fe *Daily New Mexican*, June 18, 1870; *Deed Record No. 18*, Grant County (Grant County Court House, Silver City, New Mexico), pp. 144–47 (hereafter cited as *Deed Record No. 18*, Grant County).

20. *Borderer*, March 16, 1871; Christiansen, *Mining in New Mexico*, p. 51.

21. *Borderer*, February 7, 1872; *Grant County Herald*, July 11, 1875; *Deed Record No. 18*, Grant County, p. 328; Richard Yeamans, Probate Files, Grant

County (Grant County Court House, Silver City, New Mexico, hereafter cited as Probate Files, Grant County). Among Californians who held claims in Silver Flat District were Henry Barton, Joseph F. Bennett, Linklain Butin, William Chamberlin, Barney W. Connelly, Theophilus Cooper, Albert H. French, Henry M. Harshberger, Andrew M. Herron, Richard Hudson, Alva Mason, Joseph A. Moore, Robert V. Newsham, William L. Rynerson, John D. Slocum, Sidney M. Webb, Richard Yeamans, and James A. Zabriskie.

22. Naegle, "Silver City," p. 22; *Deeds No. 1*, Grant County, pp. 65–68, 126–27, 133; *Borderer*, May 8, December 28, 1872; Santa Fe *Daily New Mexican*, April 5, 1873. Among Californians owning mines in Chloride Flat District were Horace Arden, George W. Arnold, Joseph F. Bennett, William Chamberlin, Albert H. French, John D. Gibbins, Josiah L. Hull, Richard Hudson, Alva Mason, Sidney M. Webb, Richard Yeamans, and James A. Zabriskie.

23. *Deeds No. 1*, Grant County, pp. 139–46, 189–91; *Borderer*, July 3, August 14, 24, September 14, November 30, 1872.

24. *Borderer*, December 7, 1872; Santa Fe *Daily New Mexican*, June 7, 1873; *Deeds No. 1*, Grant County, pp. 384–85, 415–16; *District Court Journal 1* [1868–1873], Grant County (Grant County Court House, Silver City, New Mexico), pp. 155, 163, 198 (hereafter cited as *District Court Journal 1*, Grant County); *Civil and Criminal Record* [1871–1874], Doña Ana County (Doña Ana County Court House, Las Cruces, New Mexico), p. 291 (hereafter cited as *Civil and Criminal Record* [1871–1874], Doña Ana County).

25. *Grant County Herald*, August 5, 12, 1876, September 22, 1877, May 4, June 1, November 16, 1878.

26. Naegle, "Silver City," pp. 121, 127; Santa Fe *Daily New Mexican*, June 6, 1874.

27. *Borderer*, September 14, 1872; *Deeds No. 1*, Grant County, pp. 198, 317–19, 493–95.

28. *Deeds No. 1*, Grant County, pp. 648–51; Santa Fe *Daily New Mexican*, June 6, 1874; Albuquerque *Republican Review*, February 20, 1875 (hereafter cited as *Republican Review*); *Borderer*, February 28, November 30, 1872; Silver City *Mining Life*, May 31, June 14, August 2, November 8, 1873, February 7, 1874 (hereafter cited as *Mining Life*); *Grant County Herald*, April 25, 1875.

29. *Records F* [1875–1879], Socorro County (Socorro County Court House, Socorro, New Mexico), pp. 296–326 (hereafter cited as *Records F*, Socorro County); Anderson, *History of New Mexico*, vol. 2, pp. 966–67; Twitchell, *Leading Facts*, vol. 4, p. 269; *Grant County Herald*, February 16, May 11, 1878.

30. *Grant County Herald*, May 11, 1878; Las Cruces *Thirty-Four*, March 5, August 20, 1879 (hereafter cited as *Thirty-Four*).

31. *Grant County Herald*, July 19, 1879. For Stitzel's land holdings and

wealth, see David Stitzel, Application No. 104, Homestead Declaratory State-
ments and Homesteads, Nos. 1 to 441, From October 3, 1872 to April 2, 1883,
Santa Fe, N.M. and La Mesilla, N.M., Records of the General Land Office,
Record Group 49, Federal Records Center, Denver Colorado (hereafter cited
as Homestead Declaratory Statements Nos. 1 to 441); David Stitzel, Grant
County, New Mexico Census, 1880; David Stitzel, Grant County, Agricultural
Schedules of the Tenth Census of the United States, 1880, State Records
Center and Archives, Santa Fe, New Mexico (hereafter cited as Agricultural
Schedules, 1880).

32. David Stitzel, Pension Application Files; *Southwest-Sentinel,* December
13, 20, 1884; *District Court Record 7 A* [1883–1885], Grant County (Grant
County Court House, Silver City, New Mexico), pp. 378–400, 475–76. Territorial law defined five degrees of murder, with the fifth being the lesser crime
and carrying the least penalty. It was defined as any murder not covered in degrees one through four.

33. Christiansen, *Mining in New Mexico,* p. 78; *Rio Grande Republican,* October 13, 1883; Santa Fe *Daily New Mexican,* February 14, 1882.

34. *Mining Claims No. 2,* Doña Ana County, pp. 592–612; *Mining Claims 3,*
Doña Ana County (Doña Ana County Court House, Las Cruces, New Mexi-
co), pp. 19–114, 255–56, 568–69 (hereafter cited as *Mining Claims 3,* Doña
Ana County).

35. *Mining Claims No. 2,* Doña Ana County, pp. 155–278. The eight veter-
ans were John D. Barncastle, William W. Beman, Joseph F. Bennett, John
Davis, William R. McCormick, William L. Rynerson, John Slater, and James
A. Zabriskie.

36. Jones, *New Mexico Mines and Minerals,* p. 73; Rex W. Strickland, *Six
Who Came to El Paso, Pioneers of the 1840's,* Southwestern Studies, vol. 1, No.
3 (El Paso: Texas Western College Press, 1963), pp. 35–36; *Records Vol. B,*
Doña Ana County (Doña Ana County Court House, Las Cruces, New Mexico), pp. 59, 175 (hereafter cited as *Records Vol. B,* Doña Ana County). The
definitive history of the Stephenson Mine has yet to be written.

37. *Records Vol. B,* Doña Ana County, pp. 325–26, 444–49. *Rio Grande
Republican* dated February 21, 1885 states that Hugh Stephenson became interested in the mine in 1852 and that he sold his three-fourths interest for $12,000.
Two other published works claim that officers at Fort Fillmore purchased the
mine for $12,500. Doña Ana County records show that Hugh Stephenson re-
ceived $8,000 for a three-fourths interest; they do not reveal how or for what
price Sayles received his one-fourth interest. In 1859 Horace Stephenson, Hugh's
son, sold to Sprague and Crosby for $5,000 the Stephenson Smelting House

and 160 acres near Fort Fillmore. Total receipt from the two sales may be the basis for writers stating that Stephenson received $12,000 or more for his mine.

38. *Probate Journal A*, Doña Ana County (Doña Ana County Court House, Las Cruces, New Mexico), entries for July 18, October 3, 5, 1864 (hereafter cited as *Probate Journal A*, Doña Ana County); *Deed Record 1*, Doña Ana County (Doña Ana County Court House, Las Cruces, New Mexico), p. 116 (hereafter cited as *Deed Record 1*, Doña Ana County).

39. *Mining Claims No. 2*, Doña Ana County, pp. 119–21, 286–94, 302–20, 326–47.

40. *Borderer*, November 9, 1872; *Rio Grande Republican*, January 21, 1882, April 21, May 12, 1883; *Mesilla Valley Independent*, January 11, 18, 1879.

41. Christiansen, *Mining in New Mexico*, p. 55; *Rio Grande Republican*, June 4, 1881, April 15, September 30, 1882, January 20, 1883; *Mining Claims No. 2*, Doña Ana County, pp. 502–4; *Mining Claims 3*, Doña Ana County, pp. 178–79, 195, 339, *Mining Deeds No. 1*, Doña Ana County (Doña Ana County Court House, Las Cruces, New Mexico), p. 54. In addition to Rynerson and Bennett, California volunteers who located claims in the Organs included Seneca Ames, Frank Arnett, John D. Barncastle, Benjamin E. Davies, John Davis, Albert J. Fountain, Albert H. French, Benjamin Harrover, Lawrence Lapoint, William Warnick, and Albion K. Watts.

42. *Mining Claims No. 2*, Doña Ana County, pp. 562–65; *Mining Claims 3*, Doña Ana County, pp. 539–40; *Mining Deeds No. 2*, Doña Ana County (Doña Ana County Court House, Las Cruces, New Mexico), pp. 140–41, 196, 198–200.

43. Bennett to Skidmore, August 24, 1884 and October 6, 1884, and contract dated October 24, 1888, W. H. Skidmore Collection, Rio Grande Historical Collections, New Mexico State University; *Rio Grande Republican*, March 20, 1891.

44. Jones, *New Mexico Mines and Minerals*, p. 123; *Book U*, Socorro County (State Records Center and Archives, Santa Fe, New Mexico), pp. 196, 198 (hereafter cited as *Book U*, Socorro County).

45. Jones, *New Mexico Mines and Minerals*, pp. 119–21.

46. *Book U*, Socorro County, pp. 200, 259.

47. *Republican Review*, October 5, November 23, 1872, December 4, 1875; Santa Fe *Daily New Mexican*, December 24, 1874. Other California ex-soldiers who staked claims in the Magdalenas were Joseph D. Emerson, Patrick Higgins, Peter Hollenbeck, Richard M. Johnson, and Richard C. Patterson.

48. Christiansen, *Mining in New Mexico*, pp. 52–53, 69.

49. Jones, *New Mexico Mines and Minerals*, p. 126; Santa Fe *New Mexican*, February 23, 1867.

50. *Book U*, Socorro County, p. 345.

51. Jones, *New Mexico Mines and Minerals*, p. 125; *Records J*, Socorro County (Socorro County Court House, Socorro, New Mexico), pp. 254, 258, 501, 647.

52. Twitchell, *Leading Facts*, vol. 4, p. 285; Christiansen, *Mining in New Mexico*, p. 70.

53. *Records F*, Socorro County (Socorro County Court House, Socorro, New Mexico), p. 462; *Records B*, Socorro County (Socorro County Court House, Socorro, New Mexico), pp. 106–7, 159–60.

54. Christiansen, *Mining in New Mexico*, p. 39; Anderson, *History of New Mexico*, vol. 2, p. 952; Morris B. Parker, *White Oaks, Life in a New Mexico Gold Camp, 1880–1900* (Tucson: University of Arizona Press, 1971), p. 4; *Deed Record G*, Lincoln County (Lincoln County Court House, Carrizozo, New Mexico), pp. 299–300.

55. *Mining Record Book A*, Lincoln County (Lincoln County Court House, Carrizozo, New Mexico), pp. 21–25 (hereafter cited as *Mining Record Book A*, Lincoln County); book marked *E-Misc.*, Lincoln County (Lincoln County Court House, Carrizozo, New Mexico), pp. 27–29; Santa Fe *Daily New Mexican*, August 26, 1870; *Borderer*, September 20, 1871; *Republican Review*, April 10, 1875.

56. Santa Fe *Daily New Mexican*, June 15, 1877.

57. Parker, *White Oaks*, p. 5; Anderson, *History of New Mexico*, vol. 2, p. 952; *Mining Record Book B*, Lincoln County (Lincoln County Court House, Carrizozo, New Mexico), p. 180 (hereafter cited as *Mining Record Book B*, Lincoln County); *Deed Record B*, Lincoln County (Lincoln County Court House, Carrizozo, New Mexico), pp. 46–47 (hereafter cited as *Deed Record B*, Lincoln County); Santa Fe *Weekly New Mexican*, April 26, 1880; *Cimarron News and Press*, February 26, April 15, 1880.

58. *Deed Record B*, Lincoln County, pp. 113–14; Las Vegas *Daily Optic*, February 22, 1881 (hereafter cited as *Daily Optic*).

59. *Deed Record B*, Lincoln County, pp. 44–45; *Brunswick v. Winters's Heirs*, 3 N.M., p. 241, 5 Pac., p. 706.

60. John V. Winters, Probate Files, Lincoln County (Lincoln County Court House, Carrizozo, New Mexico); *Brunswick v. Winters's Heirs*, 3 N.M., p. 241, 5 Pac., p. 706; *Deed Record H*, Lincoln County (Lincoln County Court House, Carrizozo, New Mexico), pp. 232–35.

61. William H. Goetzmann, *Exploration and Empire* (New York: Random House, 1966), pp. 452–57.

62. Santa Fe *Daily New Mexican*, August 24, 1872.

63. *Ibid.*, September 20, 1872; *Republican Review*, October 5, 1872; *Borderer*, October 5, 19, 1872.

64. Santa Fe *Daily New Mexican*, November 26, 27, December 4, 13, 16, 1872.

Chapter 5

1. Frank D. Reeve, *History of New Mexico* (New York: Lewis Historical Publishing Company, Inc., 1961), vol. 2, p. 210.

2. Thaddeus W. Roberts, John H. Scott, Doña Ana County, and George W. Arnold, San Miguel County, New Mexico Census, 1870. The extent of the cattle business of Roberts, Scott, and Arnold is unknown; the three men were not listed in the 1870 agricultural census nor were their ranching activities discussed in local newspapers. Arnold switched from raising cattle to mining when he moved to Grant County in the early 1870s; he may have re-entered the cattle industry when he later moved to Arizona. Records of the Grand Army of the Republic show that in 1888 Roberts was a rancher living at Tierra Amarilla in Rio Arriba County. During the seventies Scott homesteaded near the New Mexico-Texas border and for a time ran the Half-Way House offering accommodations to sojourners traveling between Mesilla and El Paso.

3. Orton, *Records of California Men*, pp. 115, 153, 354; Santa Fe *Daily New Mexican*, June 22, 1870; *Rio Grande Republican*, February 23, March 15, 1884; *Cimarron News and Press*, March 25, 1882.

4. Orton, *Records of California Men*, p. 153; Anderson, *History of New Mexico*, vol. 2, pp. 676–77; Lawrence R. Murphy, *Philmont, A History of New Mexico's Cimarron Country* (Albuquerque: University of New Mexico Press, 1972), p. 142; Charles C. Coan, *A History of New Mexico* (Chicago: The American Historical Society, Inc., 1925), vol. 2, pp. 505–6, vol. 3, p. 443; Mathias Heck, Colfax County, Agricultural Schedules, 1880.

5. Orton, *Records of California Men*, pp. 345, 363, 390; Anderson, *History of New Mexico*, vol. 2, p. 620; Santa Fe *Daily New Mexican*, January 29, 1870; Ritch Collection, MS no. 17.

6. Anderson, *History of New Mexico*, vol. 2, pp. 620–21; Ritch Collection, MS no. 17; Richard C. Patterson, Socorro County, Agricultural Schedules, 1880; Richard C. Patterson, Application No. 296, Homestead Declaratory Statements, Nos. 1 to 441.

7. Anderson, *History of New Mexico*, vol. 2, pp. 619–20; Patrick Higgins, Socorro County, Agricultural Schedules, 1880; Patrick Higgins, Richard C. Patterson, Socorro County, Assessment Roll, 1886 (State Records Center and

Archives, Santa Fe, New Mexico); *Records D* [1871–1875], Socorro County (Socorro County Court House, Socorro, New Mexico), p. 460 (hereafter cited as *Records D*, Socorro County).

8. *Grant County Herald*, August 2, 1879.

9. *Ibid.*, March 13, 1875, February 12, 1881; *Mining Life*, October 11, 1873; *Mesilla News*, May 23, 1874.

10. *Mining Life*, November 1, 1873.

11. *Grant County Herald*, August 22, 29, 1875, September 9, 1876; *Mining Life*, January 10, 1874; *Borderer*, May 15, 22, 1872; Santa Fe *Daily New Mexican*, October 9, 1874; *District Court Record 3* [1875–1876], Grant County (Grant County Court House, Silver City, New Mexico), p. 185 (hereafter cited as *District Court Record 3*, Grant County).

12. *Deed Record 5*, Doña Ana County (Doña Ana County Court House, Las Cruces, New Mexico), pp. 9–10 (hereafter cited as *Deed Record 5*, Doña Ana County); *Grant County Herald*, November 14, 1875, January 2, September 2, 1876, November 17, 1877, February 22, 1879; *Rio Grande Republican*, June 2, 1883. In the 1880 census, Slocum's two daughters are listed as scholars living in the household of Theodore Rouault, priest, in Las Cruces.

13. *Republican Review*, May 27, 1875; *Rio Grande Republican*, June 14, 1884, June 6, 1885.

14. *Mesilla Valley Independent*, October 20, 1877, February 8, 1879.

15. *Rio Grande Republican*, May 1, 1891.

16. Benjamin E. Davies, Pension Application Files; *Borderer*, July 19, 1871; *Mining Life*, May 31, 1873; *Republican Review*, April 17, 1875; *Grant County Herald*, April 28, 1877; *Mesilla Valley Independent*, August 4, 1877, February 8, 1879; *Rio Grande Republican*, May 6, 1882.

17. *Deed Record 5*, Doña Ana County, pp. 797–98; *Rio Grande Republican*, March 11, April 1, November 18, 1882.

18. Benjamin E. Davies, Pension Application Files; *Rio Grande Republican*, May 1, 1891. In a deposition made in 1910, David Wood estimated the value of the San Augustin Ranch owned by Morris Lesinsky and Benjamin E. Davies as being $40,000 to $75,000 at the time of Davies's death. He also stated that Davies was at that time heavily in debt to the amount of about $30,000. The ranch passed first into the hands of Numa Reymond who sold it to W. W. Cox. See Benjamin E. Davies, Pension Application Files.

19. Miller, "William Logan Rynerson," pp. 102–3.

20. William L. Rynerson, Doña Ana County, Agricultural Schedules, 1880; *Mesilla News*, May 18, June 1, 1878; *Mesilla Valley Independent*, March 9, 1878; *Rio Grande Republican*, May 21, September 3, October 29, 1881, September 23, 1882, July 26, 1884.

21. *Rio Grande Republican*, September 3, 1881, February 11, 1882, August
25, September 29, 1883, July 26, 1884; Robert N. Mullin, ed., *Maurice Garland Fulton's History of the Lincoln County War* (Tucson: University of Arizona
Press, 1968), p. 413. These are the same John H. Riley, James J. Dolan, and
John Henry Tunstall who were key participants in the Lincoln County War.
John Lemon was the son of the John Lemon who was killed in the 1871 Mesilla
Riot; his mother later married Rynerson.
22. Tularosa Land and Cattle Company, Articles of Incorporation, March
29, 1890, Thomas B. Catron Papers, File 608, Special Collections, University
of New Mexico; Victor Westphall, *Thomas Benton Catron and His Era* (Tucson:
University of Arizona Press, 1973), pp. 68–69; Stanley L. Crocchiola, *Fort Stanton*
(Pampa, Texas: Pampa Print Shop, 1964), pp. 178–83.
23. *Grant County Herald*, December 25, 1880; January 22, 1881.
24. *Ibid.*, March 12, April 16, 23, 1881; *Rio Grande Republican*, December
1, 1883.
25. *Rio Grande Republican*, February 24, April 7, 1883.
26. *Ibid.*, February 9, 23, March 15, 1884.
27. *Ibid.*, November 7, 14, 21, 1885.
28. Annual Report of the Adjutant General, 1882, Territorial Archives of
New Mexico, roll 84; Twitchell, *Leading Facts*, vol. 2, pp. 495, 496; Arrell M.
Gibson, *The Life and Death of Colonel Albert Jennings Fountain* (Norman: University of Oklahoma Press, 1965), pp. 105–8.
29. *Mesilla Valley Independent*, July 14, 21, 1877.
30. *Ibid.*, July 21, 1877; *Grant County Herald*, July 21, 1877.
31. *Grant County Herald*, July 28, 1877; Gibson, *Fountain*, p. 102. On March
1, 1878, while Fountain's two sons were working late at night in the *Independent's* composing room, gunmen fired into the building. The two boys escaped
uninjured. See *Mesilla Valley Independent*, March 2, 1878.
32. Gibson, *Fountain*, pp. 109–111; *Rio Grande Republican*, June 24, 1882;
Bartlett to Fountain, May 28, 1882 and Bartlett to Fountain, June 15, 1882, Letters sent by the Adjutant General, Territorial Archives of New Mexico, roll 78.
33. *Rio Grande Republican*, January 27, 1883; Annual Report of the Adjutant General, 1882–1884, Territorial Archives of New Mexico, roll 84, pp.
64–65.
34. *Rio Grande Republican*, February 24, 1883; Gibson, *Fountain*, pp. 118–19;
Bartlett to Fountain, March 4, 1883, Letters sent by the Adjutant General, Territorial Archives of New Mexico, roll 78.
35. Gibson, *Fountain*, pp. 120–21.
36. Annual Report of the Adjutant General, 1882–1884, Territorial Archives
of New Mexico, roll 84, pp. 66–75.

37. *Ibid.*, p. 75; *Southwest-Sentinel,* April 7, 21, 28, May 2, 1883; *Rio Grande Republican,* April 28, 1883.

38. Annual Report of the Adjutant General, 1882–1884, Territorial Archives of New Mexico, roll 84, pp. 76–84; *Rio Grande Republican,* June 30, July 7, 1883; *Southwest-Sentinel,* August 22, 29, 1883; Philip J. Rasch, "The Rustler War," *New Mexico Historical Review,* 39 (October 1964): 270–71.

39. *Rio Grande Republican,* July 7, 1883.

40. *Ibid.*, April 7, 14, 21, 1883; Gibson, *Fountain,* pp. 125–27. After the trial Fountain's friends descended upon his Mesilla home for a celebration party, and the editor of the *Rio Grande Republican* congratulated Newcomb and Fountain "for the able and energetic manner in which they prosecuted this case to a successful conclusion."

41. *Rio Grande Republican,* February 9, April 5, 1883.

42. *Ibid.*, August 23, 1884, April 11, 25, May 2, 1885.

43. For an account of Fountain's death, see Gibson, *Fountain,* pp. 212–55.

44. Orton, *Records of California Men,* p. 678; *Deed Record No. 11,* Doña Ana County Transcript (Otero County Court House, Alamogordo, New Mexico), pp. 2–3, 8–9, 11 (hereafter cited as *Deed Record No. 11* Doña Ana County Transcript); Lawrence L. Mehren, "A History of the Mescalero Apache Reservation, 1869–1881" (Master's thesis, University of Arizona, 1969), pp. 117, 133; C. L. Sonnichsen, *Tularosa* (reprint; University of New Mexico Press, 1981), p. 249.

45. Nesmith and Blazer, Lincoln County, Industrial Schedules of the Ninth Census of the United States, 1870 (State Records Center and Archives, Santa Fe, New Mexico); Mehren, "Mescalero Apache Reservation," pp. 118–21; Brooks to Russell, May 2, 1879, Records of the Mescalero Agency, Correspondence, Accounts, and Other Records, Undated and 1874–79, Records of the Bureau of Indian Affairs, Record Group 75, Federal Records Center, Denver, Colorado.

46. Sonnichsen, *Tularosa,* pp. 249, 251; Charles A. Siringo, *A Texas Cowboy* (New York: J. S. Ogilvie Publishing Co., 1946), p. 149; Orton, *Records of California Men,* p. 680; *Rio Grande Republican,* April 15, 1882.

47. Siringo, *Texas Cowboy,* pp. 150–52; Sonnichsen, *Tularosa,* pp. 251–53.

48. *Civil and Criminal Record* [1881–1883], Doña Ana County (Doña Ana County Court House, Las Cruces, New Mexico), pp. 137–38, 162–69 (hereafter cited as *Civil and Criminal Record* [1881–1883], Doña Ana County); *Rio Grande Republican,* April 15, 29, 1882; *Southwest-Sentinel,* April 25, 1883.

49. Sonnichsen, *Tularosa,* p. 254; Siringo, *Texas Cowboy,* p. 187; *Civil and Criminal Record* [1881–1883], Doña Ana County, pp. 141–42, 162–69, 197.

50. *Rio Grande Republican,* September 9, 16, 23, 30, 1882; March 10, 1883.

51. *Ibid.,* March 21, April 4, 25, May 2, November 7, 1885.

52. *Ibid.,* May 2, November 7, 1885.

Chapter 6

1. See the following registers: Register of Homestead Entries, 1 to 1358, Land Office, Santa Fe, From March 1, 1868-August 1882; Register of Homestead Entries, 1359–2497, Land Office, Santa Fe, From September 4, 1882 to December 31, 1885; Homestead Declaratory Statements and Homesteads, Nos. 1 to 441, From October 3, 1872 to April 2, 1883, Santa Fe, N.M. and La Mesilla, N.M.; Register of Entries, Homestead Act, Nos. 442 to 2950, From May 1, 1883 to November 28, 1898, Las Cruces, New Mexico, Records of the General Land Office, Record Group 49, Federal Records Center, Denver, Colorado; Victor Westphall, *The Public Domain in New Mexico, 1854–1891* (Albuquerque: University of New Mexico Press, 1965), pp. 47, 137–38.

2. See Register of Receipts, Timber Culture, Nos. 1 to 809, From November 16, 1878 to April 29, 1891, La Mesilla, Records of the General Land Office, Record Group 49, Federal Records Center, Denver, Colorado (hereafter cited as Timber Culture, Mesilla, Nos. 1 to 809); and the following registers: Abstract of Desert Land Entries, Nos. 254 to 837, December 13, 1883-December 31, 1892, Las Cruces, Records of the General Land Office, Record Group 49, Federal Records Center, Denver, Colorado (hereafter cited as Desert Land Entries, Las Cruces, Nos. 254 to 837); La Mesilla, Now Las Cruces, N.M., Desert Entries, 84–114, and 1883, Las Cruces, N.M., Desert Entries, 115–263, Records of the General Land Office, Record Group 49, Washington National Records Center, Suitland, Maryland.

3. Santa Fe *Daily New Mexican,* June 20, 1874; *Grant County Herald,* October 31, 1875.

4. *Grant County Herald,* July 22, 1876; Santa Fe *Daily New Mexican,* March 3, 1870; Grant County, New Mexico Census, 1870; Anderson, *History of New Mexico,* vol. 2, pp. 730–31. California veterans Richard A. Sarle and George W. Bronson resided at Rio Mimbres in the 1860s but apparently had left the county by 1870.

5. Andrew Herron, Grant County, Agricultural Schedules of the Ninth Census of the United States, 1870 (State Records Center and Archives, Santa Fe, New Mexico [hereafter cited as Agricultural Schedules, 1870]); Andrew Herron, Grant County, New Mexico Census, 1870; *Deed Record No. 18,* Grant County, p. 356. Herron died in 1888 at Afton, Kansas.

6. *Grant County Herald,* July 22, 1876; *Mining Life,* January 24, 1874.

7. George O. Perrault, David Stitzel, Grant County, New Mexico Census, 1870, and Agricultural Schedules, 1870; George O. Perrault, David Stitzel, Grant County, New Mexico Census, 1880; George O. Perrault, David Stitzel, Grant County, Agricultural Schedules, 1880.

8. *Deeds No. 1,* Grant County, pp. 143, 263–64; Richard Hudson, Application No. 174, Homestead Declaratory Statements, Nos. 1 to 441; *Mining Life,* April 25, 1874; *Grant County Herald,* September 9, 1876; Twitchell, *Leading Facts,* vol. 2, p. 435.

9. *Mining Life,* April 11, 1874; *Mesilla Valley Independent,* July 14, 1877.

10. *Deeds No. 3,* Grant County (Grant County Court House, Silver City, New Mexico), pp. 186–87; Silver City *New Southwest and Grant County Herald,* May 28, 1881 (hereafter cited as *New Southwest and Grant County Herald); Rio Grande Republican,* December 22, 1883, March 22, 1884.

11. Richard Hudson, Application No. 10, Timber Culture, Mesilla, Nos. 1 to 809, and Certificate No. 263, Desert Land Entries, Las Cruces, Nos. 254 to 837; *Southwest-Sentinel,* March 1, 1884.

12. Richard Hudson, Grant County, Agricultural Schedules, 1880; Richard Hudson, Grant County, Assessment Roll, 1885 (State Records Center and Archives, Santa Fe, New Mexico). In 1892 Hudson's hotel was destroyed by fire and he removed to Silver City where he ran the Timmer house. Hudson died in 1912. Hudson's Hot Springs later acquired the name of Faywood Hot Springs. Twitchell, *Leading Facts,* vol. 3, p. 310.

13. Those listing their occupation as farmer were Albert Jacobs, Joseph B. Nickerson, Frederick A. Smith, and the five men from Company A, Charles H. Bartlett, Wesley Fields, George W. Peppin, Thomas B. Sitton, and David C. Warner.

14. Andrew Wilson, Lincoln County, Agricultural Schedules, 1880; Anderson, *History of New Mexico,* vol. 2, pp. 832–33.

15. John Walters, Lincoln County, Agricultural Schedules, 1880; John Walters, Probate Files, Lincoln County (Lincoln County Court House, Carrizozo, New Mexico, hereafter cited as Probate Files, Lincoln County). John Walters died February 25, 1886.

16. Mehren, "Mescalero Apache Reservation," p. 119; *Deed Record No. 11,* Doña Ana County Transcript, pp. 396–98; Wesley Fields, Lincoln County, New Mexico Census, 1880, and Agricultural Schedules, 1880. Fields's first wife Dolores Baca died at Tularosa in 1877. He married Macaria García at Tularosa on November 18, 1878. Is is probable that the Fields were living in Precinct 3 in

1880 but continued to work the Tularosa homestead, as no record was uncovered of Fields owning 160 acres on the Ruidoso in 1880. Fields died August 14, 1904 at Alamogordo, New Mexico. Wesley Fields, Pension Application Files.
17. Henry C. Brown, Wesley Fields, Pension Application Files; Mehren, "Mescalero Apache Reservation," p. 107.
18. Mehren, "Mescalero Apache Reservation," pp. 105, 107, 121; Henry C. Brown, Application No. 70, Homestead Declaratory Statements, Nos. 1 to 441.
19. Henry C. Brown, Lincoln County, Agricultural Schedules, 1880.
20. Henry C. Brown, Pension Application Files.
21. See Lincoln County, Agricultural Schedules, 1870.
22. Andrew Wilson, Wesley Fields, Lincoln County, Agricultural Schedules, 1880; U.S. Bureau of the Census, *Historical Statistics*, pt. 1, p. 463.
23. William A. Keleher, *The Fabulous Frontier, Twelve New Mexico Items* (reprint, Albuquerque: University of New Mexico Press, 1982). p. 102; Philip J. Rasch, "The Tularosa Ditch War," *New Mexico Historical Review*, 43 (July 1968): 229; Santa Fe *Weekly New Mexican*, June 14, 1879.
24. Rasch, "Tularosa Ditch War," pp. 230–31; *Mesilla News*, June 27, 1874; Santa Fe *Daily New Mexican*, September 7, 1874.
25. *Deed Record 5*, Doña Ana County, pp. 19–20.
26. *Mesilla Valley Independent*, August 11, 1877.
27. *Ibid.*, June 21, 1879; Santa Fe *Weekly New Mexican*, June 14, 1879.
28. *Thirty-Four*, May 26, 1880.
29. Rasch, "Tularosa Ditch War," pp. 231–34; Santa Fe *Daily New Mexican*, April 24, 1881; *Rio Grande Republican*, April 8, 1882; Anderson, *History of New Mexico*, vol. 2, p. 1007; Mullin, *Lincoln County War*, p. 416.
30. Santa Fe *Daily New Mexican*, January 17, 1877. See Doña Ana County, New Mexico Census, 1870 and Agricultural Schedules, 1870. In 1870 the average value per farm in New Mexico was $404. U.S. Bureau of the Census, *Historical Statistics*, pt. 1, p. 463.
31. John D. Barncastle, Doña Ana County, Agricultural Schedules, 1880.
32. *Thirty-Four*, May 7, 1879; Santa Fe *Daily New Mexican*, January 15, 18, 1877; *Rio Grande Republican*, December 1, 1883, July 12, 1884, July 25, September 19, 1885.
33. *Rio Grande Republican*, July 12, October 11, 1884; K. D. Stoes, "The Land of Shalam," *New Mexico Historical Review*, 33 (January 1958): 16.
34. *Rio Grande Republican*, July 12, 1884.
35. Santa Fe *Daily New Mexican*, February 11, 1873; *Republican Review*, March

8, 1873. See Colfax, Santa Ana, Taos, and San Miguel counties, New Mexico Census, 1870. The six San Miguel men who listed their occupations as farm laborers were Frederick G. Brill and James DeParty of New York, Abner Frazier and Jacob Laycock of Ohio, Samuel Dean of Maine, and John Meister of Germany.

36. Santa Fe *Daily New Mexican*, May 4, 1882.

37. Howard R. Lamar, *The Far Southwest* (New York: W. W. Norton and Company, 1970), pp. 139–41; *Mesilla News*, June 6, December 26, 1874; U.S. Congress, 43 Cong., 1st sess., *Senate Executive Document No. 56*, 1874, "Reports . . . on Mesilla Colony Grant."

38. *Mesilla News*, June 6, 20, December 26, 1874, January 2, 1875.

39. *Ibid.*, December 26, 1874, January 2, 1875; *District Court Record 2* [1873–1875], Grant County (Grant County Court House, Silver City, New Mexico), pp. 209, 217–18 (hereafter cited as *District Court Record 2*, Grant County).

40. *Rio Grande Republican*, July 5, 12, 1884, March 7, September 19, 1885.

41. See Pearson, *Maxwell Land Grant*, for the history of this famous land controversy.

42. Russell, *Land of Enchantment*, pp. 115–30. DeHague mustered into the California volunteers in 1863 at Santa Fe and had not traveled overland from California.

43. Russell, *Land of Enchantment*, p. 134–36; Pearson, *Maxwell Land Grant*, p. 113.

44. Russell, *Land of Enchantment*, pp. 138–39; Pearson, *Maxwell Land Grant*, pp. 123–24; Santa Fe *Daily New Mexican*, September 3, 1888.

45. James Magoffin Dwyer, Jr., "Hugh Stephenson," *New Mexico Historical Review*, 29 (January 1954): 3–4. Benancia's name occasionally appears as Benacia.

46. J. J. Bowden, *Spanish and Mexican Land Grants in the Chihuahuan Acquisition* (El Paso: Texas Western Press, 1971), pp. 89–90; Santa Fe *Weekly Gazette*, September 2, 1865. The fate of Hugh Stephenson's property can best be followed in court records located in Records of the District Court of the United States, New Mexico Territory, Records of the Third Judicial District, Civil and Criminal Case Files, 1851–1865, Record Group 21, Federal Records Center, Denver, Colorado. (Hereafter cited as N.M., 3d Judicial District, Civil and Criminal Case Files, 1851–1865).

47. N.M., 3d Judicial District, Civil and Criminal Case Files, 1851–1865.

48. *Ibid.*; *Deed Record 3*, Doña Ana County (Doña Ana County Court House, Las Cruces, New Mexico), pp. 385–88, 389–91. Several authors have assumed that the Stephenson properties, Concordia and Brazito, were condemned in court

and subsequently sold at public auction, where French and others purchased and thus saved the property for the family. The property was not condemned in court; the records show that the libels were dismissed. It is possible, however, that one or both properties were ordered sold to pay for costs of court, though this is not documented in court records.

49. W. W. Mills, *Forty Years at El Paso, 1858–1898* (El Paso: Carl Hertzog, 1962), pp. 81, 135, 180; Entries for A. H. French, August 1, 1865, August 15, 1866, Register of Contracts for Fresh Beef and Beef Cattle, 1856 to 1869, pp. 64, 79, Records of the Office of Commissary General of Subsistence, Record Group 192, Washington National Records Center, Suitland, Maryland (hereafter cited as Register for Fresh Beef and Beef Cattle, 1856–1869); entries for A. H. French, October 31, 1865, October 25, 1866, Register of Contracts, vol. 16 (1864–1867), pp. 181, 183, Records of the Office of Quartermaster General, Record Group 92, National Archives, Washington, D.C.; Santa Fe *New Mexican,* April 20, 1866. The Santa Fe *New Mexican,* January 5, 1866 stated that French alone purchased the Fort Bliss property for $8,000. Mills claims, however, that Fort Bliss was sold for $6,000 to Henry J. Cuniffe, U.S. Consul at El Paso, Mexico, and Albert H. French.

50. Entries for J. A. Zabriskie, December 1, 1869, Register of Contracts, vol. 17 (1868–70), p. 109, Records of the Office of Quartermaster General, Record Group 92, National Archives, Washington, D.C. (hereafter cited as Register of Contracts, vol. 17), and July 1, 1872, July 1, 1874, Register of Contracts, vol. 1 (1871–1876), pp. 82, 114, Records of the Office of Quartermaster General, Record Group 92, National Archives, Washington, D.C. (hereafter cited as Register of Contracts, vol. 1).

51. Mills, *Forty Years,* p. 192; Jane Wayland Brewster, "The San Rafael Cattle Company, A Pennsylvania Enterprise in Arizona," *Arizona and the West,* 8 (Summer 1966): 143; *Mesilla News,* March 7, 1874, November 30, 1878; *Grant County Herald,* October 21, 1876; *Mesilla Valley Independent,* May 18, 1878. Zabriskie had been an attorney in California prior to the Civil War.

52. *Borderer,* April 20, 1871; T. M. Pearce, ed., *New Mexico Place Names* (Albuquerque: University of New Mexico Press, 1965), p. 77

53. Anderson, *History of New Mexico,* vol. 2, pp. 571–73; Twitchell, *Leading Facts,* vol. 2, p. 416.

54. Anderson, *History of New Mexico,* vol. 2, p. 572; *Mesilla News,* December 18, 1875.

55. Anderson, *History of New Mexico,* vol. 2, p. 572; Santa Fe *Weekly Gazette,* January 2, 1869; Santa Fe *New Mexican,* August 25, 1868, August 3,

1869; Santa Fe *Daily New Mexican*, June 18, 1875, January 12, February 15, March 16, 1877; *Borderer*, April 20, 1871; *Republican Review*, October 3, 1874; *Mesilla News*, December 12, 1874; *Daily Optic*, February 11, 1881.

56. Santa Fe *Daily New Mexican*, January 11, 1870; *Mesilla News*, December 12, 1874; Bancroft, *History of Arizona and New Mexico*, p. 768.

57. *Mesilla News* as quoted in the *Daily New Mexican*, September 22, 1874.

58. Santa Fe *Daily New Mexican*, September 27, 1876, March 10, 12, 1877. Mrs. Martin was described in 1881 as "probably the best known woman in New Mexico." *Daily New Mexican*, February 10, 1881.

Chapter 7

1. The eight merchants were Sydney M. Webb, Robert V. Newsham, and Marshall St. John at Rio Mimbres, John D. Barncastle of Doña Ana, Louis Clark at Plaza Alcalde, Emil Fritz at Fort Stanton, Rufus C. Vose of Precinct 3 in Lincoln County, and Richard D. Russell at Tecolote.

2. Santa Fe *Daily New Mexican*, August 13, 1872, February 3, 1873.

3. Ritch Collection, MS no. 1691; Santa Fe *Daily New Mexican*, February 3, April 2, 1873; Clark to Pope, October 21, 1871, Records of the New Mexico Superintendency, Miscellaneous Papers, 1871, Records of the Bureau of Indian Affairs, Record Group 75, National Archives, Micro-Copy T-21, roll 15 (hereafter cited as New Mexico Superintendency); Armstrong to Pope, January 10 and March 22, 1873, New Mexico Superintendency, Letters Received from Abiquiu Agency, 1873, roll 18.

4. *Borderer*, May 11, 1871; Santa Fe *Daily New Mexican*, May 26, June 1, 2, September 15, 1875.

5. Ritch Collection, MS no. 1690; Santa Fe *Daily New Mexican*, April 17, 1876, September 14, 1877.

6. Santa Fe *Daily New Mexican*, March 27, 1872. Richard Hudson also ran a hotel at Pinos Altos in 1870 prior to moving to Silver City.

7. Santa Fe *Daily New Mexican*, May 11, 1874, August 2, 1876; *Mesilla News*, May 30, June 13, 1874.

8. *Mesilla News*, September 19, 1874, December 4, 1875.

9. *Ibid.*, December 26, 1874; Santa Fe *Daily New Mexican*, August 2, 1876, May 11, 1877.

10. *Cimarron News and Press*, August 7, 1875, November 29, 1877, December 30, 1880; License of C.N. Story, May 1, 1874, Territorial Archives of New Mexico, roll 50.

11. Samuel Eckstein, Santa Fe County, New Mexico Census, 1870; Orton, *Records of California Men*, p. 376; Santa Fe *Daily New Mexican*, May 16, June 7, 10, 27, July 15, November 5, 1873.

12. Santa Fe *Daily New Mexican*, June 27, 1874; *Grant County Herald*, December 5, 1875, April 22, 29, August 19, 1876. By this date, Robert V. Newsham had sold his store at Rio Mimbres and had moved to Silver City. His new store erected on the corner of Broadway and Hudson streets also fell during the flood. *Grant County Herald*, September 2, 1876.

13. *Grant County Herald*, May 11, 1878; *Rio Grande Republican*, October 4, 1884.

14. Santa Fe *Daily New Mexican*, August 5, 12, 1874; Santa Fe *Weekly New Mexican*, June 14, 1879.

15. Santa Fe *Daily New Mexican*, June 21, 1876; Santa Fe *Weekly New Mexican*, October 4, 1879.

16. Miguel Antonio Otero, *My Life on the Frontier* (Albuquerque: University of New Mexico Press, 1939), vol. 2, pp. 149–50.

17. *Ibid.*; *Silver City Enterprise*, July 23, 1886. Stinson died September 6, 1902.

18. *Mesilla News*, July 17, 1875, April 8, 1876; *Mesilla Valley Independent*, November 16, 1878, April 26, June 28, 1879.

19. True Survey of the Western Boundary of the Hugh Stephenson Grant or Bracito Tract, The Bracito Grant #6, Records of the Surveyor General, State Records Center and Archives, Santa Fe, New Mexico, pp. 620–22; License of E. C. Priest, September 28, 1875, Territorial Archives of New Mexico, roll 50; *Mesilla Valley Independent*, July 14, 1877, November 16, 1878.

20. *Cimarron News and Press*, February 4, 1882; Santa Fe *Daily New Mexican*, February 4, 1882; *Rio Grande Republican*, February 4, 1882.

21. Cause No. 813, *The Territory v. Eli C. Priest*, 1882, Doña Ana County Court House, Las Cruces, New Mexico; *Civil and Criminal Record* [1881–1883], Doña Ana County, pp. 277–78; *Rio Grande Republican*, February 17, 1883.

22. Santa Fe *Daily New Mexican*, February 20, 1877. For court cases involving Eckstein and Hudson, see *District Court Record*, 4, 5, 6, 7, and 7A, Grant County Court House, Silver City, New Mexico.

23. Stratton, *Territorial Press*, p. 7.

24. Santa Fe *Weekly Gazette*, January 30, July 17, 1869; Santa Fe *Daily New Mexican*, April 14, 1873; Stratton *Territorial Press*, pp. 6, 273.

25. Santa Fe *Daily New Mexican*, April 14, 1873; *Republican Review*, May 5, 1873.

26. *Grant County Herald*, March 13, 1875, September 8, 1877, May 25, August 3, November 16, 23, 1878, May 3, 1879, August 28, September 11, 18,

November 13, 1880; *New Southwest and Grant County Herald*, June 25, 1881, November 18, 1882; *Thirty-Four*, January 15, April 9, May 7, 1879; *Mesilla News*, October 10, 1874; Stratton, *Territorial Press*, pp. 270, 290.

27. *New Southwest and Grant County Herald*, July 9, September 10, 1881, November 18, 1882.

28. *Mesilla News*, July 17, 1875; *Grant County Herald*, March 23, 1878; Stratton, *Territorial Press*, pp. 5–6.

29. Orton, *Records of California Men*, p. 677; *Las Cruces Citizen*, March 12, 1910; Santa Fe *New Mexican*, October 20, 1868; Santa Fe *Daily New Mexican*, October 3, 1873; Lawrence Lapoint, Doña Ana County, New Mexico Census, 1870; License of Read and Lapoint, August 1, 1865 and of Lapoint, January 1, 1866, April 7, July 7, October 7, 1868, July 8, 1870, Territorial Archives of New Mexico, roll 50.

30. *Borderer*, September 14, 1872; Santa Fe *Daily New Mexican*, October 3, 1873, October 1, 24, 1874, November 5, 1875; *Mesilla News*, September 26, 1874, September 25, 1875; *Republican Review*, July 3, 1875; *Grant County Herald*, August 29, 1875.

31. Stratton, *Territorial Press*, p. 16; *Grant County Herald*, March 16, 23, 1878; *Mesilla Valley Independent*, November 9, 1878; *Mesilla Valley Independent* as quoted in *Grant County Herald*, March 23, 1878.

32. *Mesilla Valley Independent*, March 15, 1879; *Thirty-Four*, May 19, 1880; *Rio Grande Republican*, May 6, September 30, 1882; *Civil and Criminal Record* [1881–1883], pp. 239, 255, 284, and *Civil and Criminal Record* [1883], Doña Ana County (Doña Ana County Court House, Las Cruces, New Mexico), p. 33.

33. *Rio Grande Republican*, June 3, 1882, May 19, 1883, March 1, 29, April 26, May 3, July 26, 1884; *Las Cruces Citizen*, March 12, 1910.

34. *Mesilla Valley Independent*, June 23, 1877.

35. Santa Fe *Daily New Mexican*, June 24, September 16, December 16, 1871, January 12, 1872, September 27, November 1, 1876; *Grant County Herald*, September 30, October 28, November 18, 1876, April 7, 1877; Gibson, *Fountain*, pp. 90, 96. For Fountain's political career in Texas, see Gibson pp. 45–88.

36. Gibson, *Fountain*, pp. 99–102; *Mesilla News*, June 8, 15, 1878; Santa Fe *Daily New Mexican*, August 18, September 4, October 18, 1877; *Grant County Herald*, June 8, 1878.

37. *Mesilla Valley Independent*, March 2, June 15, August 3, 17, 1878. In 1881 Fountain became a director of the Las Cruces Publishing Company which had purchased the Las Cruces *Rio Grande Republican* earlier in the fall. Incorporators of the company were listed as William L. Rynerson, Simon B. Newcomb,

William Dessauer, and Martin Lohman, with Newcomb serving as president and Rynerson as vice-president. The *Rio Grande Republican* became the voice of the Republican party in Mesilla Valley and in later years contributed to the rise of Rynerson and Fountain as leading territorial politicians. *Rio Grande Republican,* September 10, December 17, 1881; Records of Incorporation, Territorial Archives of New Mexico, roll 34.

38. *Mesilla News,* July 26, 1879; *Thirty-Four,* July 16, 1879; *New Southwest and Grant County Herald,* August 6, 1881, May 20, November 18, 1882; *Southwest-Sentinel,* January 10, 1885; *Record Book B, Third Judicial District,* 1880–1887, Records of the District Court of the United States, New Mexico Territory, Record Group 21, Federal Records Center, Denver, Colorado, p. 371; Stratton, *Territorial Press,* p. 289.

39. *Civil and Criminal Minute and Record Book* [1865–1870], Doña Ana County, pp. 126, 130, 181, 217, 295; J. F. Bennett to N. V. Bennett, March 22, 1867, Kellner Papers.

40. Stratton, *Territorial Press,* pp. 5, 8, 270. It should also be noted that an ex-California soldier by the name of William W. Bollinger helped establish the *Las Vegas Mail* in 1871 by contributing $175 to help cover initial expenses, thereby becoming one of its principal stock holders. Pennsylvania born, Bollinger was a printer by trade and in 1880 resided in Chauncey N. Story's hotel in Elizabethtown.

41. Santa Fe *New Mexican,* November 17, 1868; Albuquerque *Semi-Weekly Review,* December 22, 1868.

42. Morris F. Taylor, *First Mail West, Stagecoach Lines on the Santa Fe Trail* (Albuquerque: University of New Mexico Press, 1971), p. 126.

43. Santa Fe *Daily New Mexican,* August 28, 1871, March 8, 1873; *Mesilla News,* May 23, 1874; *Mining Life,* May 31, 1873; *Borderer,* December 14, 1872.

44. Santa Fe *New Mexican,* July 20, October 5, 1869.

45. Santa Fe *Daily New Mexican,* September 2, 3, 1870; *Borderer,* January 31, February 28, 1872.

46. Santa Fe *Daily New Mexican,* January 7–March 8, 1873.

47. Philip Hantz, Pension Application Files; Santa Fe *Weekly Gazette,* December 12, 1868, January 2, 1869.

48. New Mexico Census, 1870; Fountain Williams, Doña Ana County, New Mexico Census, 1880; *Grant County Herald,* June 24, 1876; *Mesilla Valley Independent,* January 11, 1879; *Borderer,* March 16, May 18, 1871; Santa Fe *Daily New Mexican,* May 22, 1871. It was reported in the press in 1867 that Fount Williams and Robert Dorland—a former lieutenant who had been cashiered out of the California volunteers—had stolen two mules from the Santa Fe and El

Paso Mail Company at Fort Selden trying to make their way to California. They were caught near Cooke's Canyon; Dorland subsequently escaped from jail, and his name ceased to appear in the territorial press. The records fail to reveal Williams's further activities in the sixties; he apparently reformed by the late seventies. Santa Fe *New Mexican*, April 13, May 11, 1867.

49. Freighters and teamsters included Charles Carter, William Chamberlin, George Chase, Philip Diemar, David T. Harshaw, Marcus F. Herring, Andrew Schneider, James V. Walters, Andrew Wilson, and William Witted.

50. Occupational information was compiled from New Mexico Census, 1870.

51. In addition to Bowie and Pool, the blacksmiths included William H. Dickerson, John D. Gibbons, William Gill, Frank Howard, and William Neil. Although not included in the 1870 New Mexico census, Powell Bingham of the Magdalena mines was listed as a blacksmith in the 1880 census.

52. Santa Fe *Daily New Mexican*, November 8, 1870.

53. The remaining butchers were Joseph D. Emerson of Alamosita in Socorro County, Wilson G. Holman of Rio Mimbres, Elias Marts of Elizabethtown, Nicholas Murphy of Ralston, John J. Spurr of Contadero in Socorro County, and William Warnick of Fort Stanton. In 1880 Felix Leibold was butcher at Hillsboro.

54. *Mesilla News*, June 26, 1875.

55. *Mining Life*, January 3, 1874.

56. Santa Fe *Weekly Gazette*, December 22, 1866; Santa Fe *Daily New Mexican*, October 8, 1870.

57. Santa Fe *New Mexican*, July 20, 1869; Santa Fe *Daily New Mexican*, January 22, April 9, 1872.

58. Santa Fe *Weekly Gazette*, February 3, December 8, 1866; Santa Fe *New Mexican*, February 25, March 24, 1868; Cause No. 472, *U.S.* v. *George T. Martin*, Civil and Criminal Case Files, 1870–1873, Records of the First Judicial District, *Record Book No. 2, First Judicial District* (1871–1874), pp. 205, 227, 344, and *Record Book No. 3, First Judicial District* (1874–1883), p. 303, Records of the District Court of the United States, New Mexico Territory, Record Group 21, Federal Records Center, Denver, Colorado.

59. The two stonemasons were Henry M. Harshberger of Ralston and Joseph E. Haskins of Fort Stanton. The fifteen carpenters were Andrew Knob of Bernalillo County, Chester C. Little and Sandy Lynch of Colfax County, Seneca G. Ames of Doña Ana County, Reece R. Bulger and Benjamin F. Harrover of Grant County, Calvin Dotson and Nicholas S. White of Lincoln County, Theodore Briggs of San Miguel County, Henry Schultz of Santa Fe County, Samuel Zimmerly of Socorro County, and Daniel Dameron, Joseph H. Peacock, Jacob

P. Snyder, and Abram B. Stanton of Valencia County. The one painter was Horace Arden of Ralston, and the one machinist was William S. Lackey of Fort Union.

60. Charles Brakebill, August Guzenhauser, Grant County, John C. Sigwalt, Colfax County, New Mexico Census, 1870; Santa Fe *Weekly Gazette*, December 8, 1866.

61. Heitman, *Historical Register*, p. 758; *Mesilla News*, August 8, 1874, March 11, 1876; Santa Fe *Daily New Mexican*, March 19, 1881.

62. Orton, *Records of California Men*, p. 126; Henry S. Drinkhouse, Doña Ana County, New Mexico Census, 1870; *Deed Record 1*, Doña Ana County, pp. 133–34; *Civil and Criminal Minute and Record Book* [1865–1870], Doña Ana County, pp. 14, 43; *Civil and Criminal Record* [1871–1874], Doña Ana County, p. 52; *Grant County Herald*, March 10, June 16, 1877. Both charges against Drinkhouse were eventually dropped. Drinkhouse was born June 6, 1835 in Pennsylvania and died June 27, 1891 at Tecoripa, Sonora, Mexico. Henry S. Drinkhouse, Pension Application Files.

63. Santa Fe *Weekly Gazette*, August 10, 1867; *Republican Review*, May 1, 1875. By 1877 "Judge" Snyder had left the territory and was working on the San Diego *World*. Santa Fe *Daily New Mexican*, January 13, 1877.

64. *Rio Grande Republican*, April 1, 8, 29, 1882; Gibson, *Fountain*, pp. 145–47.

65. *Rio Grande Republican*, March 1, 1884; *Civil and Criminal Record* [1875–1878], Doña Ana County (Doña Ana County Court House, Las Cruces, New Mexico), pp. 167–68.

66. *District Court Journal 1*, Grant County, pp. 168–69. Crouch served as district clerk from 1873 to 1878.

67. Records 1870 of McRae Post and Otto Koernick, Descriptive List, McRae Post, 1870, G.A.R. Collection (State Records Center and Archives, Santa Fe, New Mexico). (Hereafter cited as G.A.R. Collection).

68. Arny to Pope, August 18, 1871, New Mexico Superintendency, Letters Received from the Pueblo Agency, 1871, roll 14; Santa Fe *Daily New Mexican*, September 7, 16, November 4, 1874.

69. Frederick DeFrouville, Pension Application Files. In 1890 DeFrouville was living at Chaperito in San Miguel County and died August 14, 1894.

70. Albert G. T. Jacobs, Pension Application Files; Santa Fe *New Mexican*, March 21, 1898. Albert and Juana had thirteen children, seven of whom were living at the time of their father's death. Albert was buried at Taos where his daughter Emelia was buried.

71. Gilbert Haggert, Valencia County, John Lambert, Colfax County, William McMullen, Santa Fe County, New Mexico Census, 1870.

72. Santa Fe *New Mexican*, December 10, 1867; Santa Fe *Daily New Mexican*, April 17, 1872.

73. Orton, *Records of California Men*, pp. 335, 346; Ritch Collection, MS nos. 1232, 1233, 1411, 1523; C. L. Sonnichsen, "Major McMullen's Invasion of Mexico," *Password*, 2 (May 1957): 38–43; William McMullen, Record of Contracts, Office of Surveyor General, Santa Fe, Records of the General Land Office, Record Group 49, Federal Records Center, Denver, Colorado, pp. 6–14.

74. Santa Fe *Daily New Mexican*, July 10, 14, 29, 30, August 31, September 19, 21, 1872.

75. *Ibid.*, September 19, 1872, January 15, 1873, July 20, 1874. McMullen apparently never married; he died at Watrous in Mora County on October 23, 1880. Santa Fe *Daily New Mexican*, October 30, 1880.

76. Reeve, *History of New Mexico*, vol. 2, p. 261.

77. Santa Fe *New Mexican*, July 7, 1868; Santa Fe *Daily New Mexican*, July 10, 1868. Charles T. Jennings, former lieutenant in the California volunteers, worked as a clerk in the hotel owned by Cutler and Kitchen. Santa Fe *New Mexican*, December 22, 1868.

78. *Mesilla News*, October 2, 9, 1875, April 22, 1876; *Republican Review*, November 6, 13, 1875; Santa Fe *Daily New Mexican*, December 4, 1875.

79. *Grant County Herald*, September 26, 1875, March 3, 1877; *Mesilla News*, April 22, 1876; *New Southwest and Grant County Herald*, February 4, 1882; Records of Incorporation, Territorial Archives of New Mexico, roll 34.

80. *Borderer*, April 6, 1871.

81. *Mesilla News*, October 30, 1875.

82. *Grant County Herald*, October 24, November 7, December 12, 1875.

83. *Ibid.*, February 2, March 9, 1878.

84. *Rio Grande Republican*, October 14, 1882; *Deed Record 5*, Doña Ana County, pp. 233–38.

Chapter 8

1. Employment data come from Pension Application Files and New Mexico Census, 1870.

2. Albion K. Watts, Doña Ana County, New Mexico Census, 1870; Seneca Ames, Pension Application Files and Doña Ana County, New Mexico Census, 1870.

3. Entry for Albion K. Watts, August 7, 1869, Register of Fresh Beef Contracts, 1869–71, p. 156 and entry for Albion K. Watts, August 11, 1871, Register of Fresh Meat, 1871–94, p. 7, Records of the Office of Commissary General of Subsistence, Record Group 192, Washington National Records Center, Suitland, Maryland (hereafter cited as Register of Fresh Beef Contracts, 1869–71 and Register of Fresh Meat, 1871–94).

4. Lycurgus D. Fuller, William B. Moores, Edward S. Merritt, Santa Fe County, New Mexico Census, 1870; Hall to Clinton, June 25, 1870, New Mexico Superintendency, Letters Received from Headquarters, District of New Mexico (U.S. Army), 1870, roll 13; Report of Persons and Articles Employed and Hired at Fort Craig during the Month of November, 1867, Consolidated Correspondence File, Office of the Quartermaster General, Record Group 92, National Archives, Washington, D.C. For Harshaw's mining discoveries in Arizona, see Georgia Wehrman, "Harshaw: Mining Camp of the Patagonias," *Journal of Arizona History*, 6 (Spring 1965): 21–36.

5. Santa Fe *New Mexican*, January 7, 1868; Santa Fe *Weekly Gazette*, September 22, 1866. In December 1867 Moore was killed by Indians near old Fort McLane and Newsham became administrator for Moore's meager estate—one mule and a military draft for $100. Newsham, "the polite and courteous trader at Fort Cummings," sold his store late in 1869 and subsequently opened a retail store at Rio Mimbres. John A. Moore, Probate Files, Doña Ana County (Doña Ana County Court House, Las Cruces, New Mexico, hereafter cited as Probate Files, Doña Ana County); Santa Fe *New Mexican*, December 21, 1869.

6. Santa Fe *Weekly Gazette*, December 10, 1864, October 7, 1865, March 17, 1866; entries for William V. B. Wardwell, July 8, 1865, October 31, 1866, Abstract of Contracts, vol. B (1864–1865), pp. 311, 410, Records of the Office of Quartermaster General, Record Group 92, National Archives, Washington, D.C.; entries for Wardwell, January 1, June 18, December 16, 1868, April 8, 1869, September 30, 1870, Register of Contracts, vol. 17, pp. 11, 30, 64, 76, 142; entries for Wardwell, June 27, August 10, 1871, Register of Contracts, vol. 1, pp. 9, 24; entries for Wardwell, August 11, 1871, June 4, 1872, Register of Fresh Meat, 1871–94, p. 7.

7. William V. B. Wardwell, Socorro County, New Mexico Census, 1870; William V. B. Wardwell, Pension Application Files; *Records D*, Socorro County, pp. 124–25, 150.

8. Santa Fe *Weekly New Mexican*, September 30, 1873, June 9, September 8, 1874; Santa Fe *Daily New Mexican*, January 6, 1877; Heitman, *Historical Register*, vol. 1, p. 831.

9. Edwin A. Rigg, Pension Application Files; Cause No. 10, U.S. *v.* Edwin A. Rigg and Richard Hudson, Records of the District Court of the United States, New Mexico Territory, Records of the Third Judicial District, Civil and Criminal Case Files, 1871–1890, Record Group 21, Federal Records Center, Denver, Colorado. John Martin of the Aleman was the second surety on Rigg's bond but had died before the case was instituted in court.

10. "Condition of the Indian Tribes," (Serial 1279), pp. 244, 346–47, 350; Santa Fe *Weekly Gazette,* June 9, 1866.

11. Andrew Wallace, "Duty in the District of New Mexico: A Military Memoir," *New Mexico Historical Review,* 50 (July 1975): 243–46.

12. Frederick Nolan, *The Life and Death of John Henry Tunstall* (Albuquerque: University of New Mexico Press, 1965), p. 185; Mehren, "Mescalero Apache Reservation," p. 29.

13. Wallace, "Duty in the District of New Mexico," p. 254; Mehren, "Mescalero Apache Reservation," pp. 53–74; Nolan, *John Henry Tunstall,* pp. 185–87.

14. Oscar M. Brown, Pension Application Files; Santa Fe *Weekly Gazette,* June 30, 1866, November 2, 1867; Santa Fe *New Mexican,* May 11, June 29, 1866, January 26, 1867, June 16, August 25, 1868; *Grant County Herald,* April 7, 1877; Frank McNitt, *The Indian Traders* (Norman: University of Oklahoma Press, 1962), p. 46. Sometime later Brown returned to New Mexico and settled in East Las Vegas with his second wife Hattie. He died there in 1889. In addition to the above mentioned traders, William L. Rynerson was appointed post trader at Fort Bayard in 1869 and Benjamin E. Davies was post trader at Fort Selden early in the 1870s.

15. Report of Employees in the Navajo Indian Agency for the Second Quarter, 1871, New Mexico Superintendency, Letters Received from the Navajo Agency, 1871, roll 14.

16. Employment data come from New Mexico Superintendency, rolls 1–30; Santa Fe *Weekly New Mexican,* December 13, 1879.

17. Employment data come from New Mexico Superintendency, rolls 8–24.

18. Ritch Collection, MS no. 1999. Ayers's letters written as Indian agent are filled with grammatical errors and faulty sentence construction.

19. Ritch Collection, MS no. 1999. To verify the length of Ayers's service as Ute agent, see Gallegos to Ayers, January 23, 1869, Letterbook of Gallegos, New Mexico Superintendency, roll 28.

20. Twitchell, *Leading Facts,* vol. 2, p. 447; Ayers to Parker, August 16, 1869, *Annual Report of the Commissioner of Indian Affairs to the Secretary of the*

Interior, 1869, 41 Cong., 2d sess., *House Executive Document No. 1* (serial 1414), pp. 682–85 (hereafter cited as *Annual Report CIA*, 1869); Ayers to Gallegos, March 20, 1869, New Mexico Superintendency, Letters Received from the Abiquiu and Cimarron Agencies, roll 9.

21. Ayers to Parker, August 16, 1869, *Annual Report CIA*, 1869, pp. 682–85.

22. Santa Fe *Weekly New Mexican*, July 27, 1869.

23. Clinton to Parker, August 7, 1869, New Mexico Superintendency, roll 28.

24. McNitt, *Indian Traders*, pp. 47, 109; Clinton to Parker, December 27, 1869, January 24, 1870, New Mexico Superintendency, roll 28; Clum to Pope, December 12, 1870, New Mexico Superintendency, Letters Received from the Commissioners, 1870, roll 11.

25. McNitt, *Indian Traders*, pp. 132–35; Santa Fe *Daily New Mexican*, May 8, July 3, September 4, 1871, June 17, 27, 1872.

26. *Borderer*, August 31, 1872; *Republican Review*, October 12, 1872.

27. Santa Fe *Daily New Mexican*, October 2, December 31, 1872; Frank D. Reeve, "The Federal Indian Policy in New Mexico, 1858–1880," *New Mexico Historical Review*, 13 (July 1938): 292–304.

28. Rynerson to Pile, November 22, 1869, and Drew to Clinton, December 12, 1869, New Mexico Superintendency, Letters Received from the Southern Apache Agency, 1869, roll 9; Reeve *History of New Mexico*, vol. 2, pp. 193–95; Santa Fe *Daily New Mexican*, January 4, 17, 29, March, 3, 9, May 10, 1870.

29. Wallace, "Duty in the District of New Mexico," p. 237; Reeve, "Federal Indian Policy," p. 292; Santa Fe *Daily New Mexican*, June 9, 1870; cf., Dan L. Thrapp, *Victorio and the Mimbres Apaches* (Norman: University of Oklahoma Press, 1974), pp. 95–132.

30. *Borderer*, March 16, 30, 1871; Santa Fe *Daily New Mexican*, March 18, 1871.

31. *Borderer*, March 30, 1871.

32. *Ibid.*, April 6, 1871. Although area residents referred to Cañada Alamosa as a reservation, it never officially attained reservation status.

33. Hudson to Piper, July 18, 1871, New Mexico Superintendency, Letters Received from the Southern Apache Agency, 1871, roll 15.

34. Proceedings of a meeting of the citizens of the town of Rio Mimbres, New Mexico Superintendency, Miscellaneous Papers, 1871, roll 15; Pope to Hudson, August 3, 1871, New Mexico Superintendency, roll 29.

35. Reeve, "Federal Indian Policy," p. 296; Pope to Walker, October 10,

1872, *Annual Report CIA,* 1872, 42 Cong., 3d sess., *House Executive Document No. 1* (serial 1560), pp. 681–82 (hereafter cited as *Annual Report CIA,* 1872).

36. Pope to Walker, October 10, 1872, *Annual Report CIA,* 1872, pp. 681–82; Santa Fe *Daily New Mexican,* October 2, 1872.

37. Ayers to Pope, October 28, 31, November 3, 5, 1872, New Mexico Superintendency, Letters Received from the Southern Apache Agency, 1872, roll 17.

38. Ayers to Pope, November 14, 30, 1872, New Mexico Superintendency, Letters Received from the Southern Apache Agency, 1872, roll 17. Of five "Americans" present at this council, three were former California soldiers: Ayers, David P. Harshaw, and Albion K. Watts, the beef contractor for the agency.

39. Pope to Walker, November 8, 1872, New Mexico Superintendency, roll 30; Thomas to Dudley, January 13, 1873, New Mexico Superintendency, Letters Received from the Southern Apache Agency, 1873, roll 20; Santa Fe *Daily New Mexican,* December 31, 1872.

40. Thomas to Dudley, January 13, 1873, New Mexico Superintendency, Letters Received from the Southern Apache Agency, 1873, roll 20; Coleman to Acting Assistant Adjutant General, January 12, 1873, New Mexico Superintendency, Letters Received from the Headquarters, District of New Mexico (U.S. Army), roll 21.

41. Reeve, "Federal Indian Policy," p. 300. Thrapp dismisses Ayers as an incompetent agent. Thrapp, *Victorio,* pp. 151–58.

42. Reeve, "Federal Indian Policy," p. 303.

43. *Ibid.,* p. 307; Statement by John Ayers, March 13, 1874, New Mexico Superintendency, Letters Received from the Southern Apache Agency, 1874, roll 23; Santa Fe *Daily New Mexican,* June 19, November 15, 1873; August 12, 1874, June 2, 1876, May 18, 1877; *Republican Review,* November 27, 1875; *Mesilla News,* January 1, 1876.

44. *Mesilla Valley Independent,* September 15, 1877; *Grant County Herald,* September 15, 1877; Santa Fe *Daily New Mexican,* September 25, 1877.

45. *Grant County Herald,* August 17, 1878; Santa Fe *Weekly New Mexican,* January 17, 1880; Reeve, "Federal Indian Policy," pp. 308–9; Gibson, *Fountain,* p. 105.

46. *Thirty-Four,* October 15, 22, 1879; *Grant County Herald,* October 18, 1879.

47. *Ibid.*

48. *Thirty-Four,* March 31, June 23, 1880; *Grant County Herald,* May 15, June 12, July 24, 1880; Reeve, "Federal Indian Policy," p. 309.

49. Santa Fe *Weekly New Mexican*, April 5, 19, September 13, 1880.
50. *Ibid.*, April 19, 1880.
51. *Albuquerque Review*, April 3, 1880.
52. Santa Fe *Daily New Mexican*, February 9, 1881; *Book B, Records of Locations and Mining Deeds*, Santa Fe County (State Records Center and Archives, Santa Fe, New Mexico), pp. 331–32; *Deed Book O*, Santa Fe County (State Records Center and Archives, Santa Fe, New Mexico), pp. 312–13; *Deed Book S*, Santa Fe County (State Records Center and Archives, Santa Fe, New Mexico), pp. 358–59.
53. Ayers to Downs, May 18, 1892, G.A.R. Collection; John Ayers, Abner Frazier, Joseph F. Bennett, Pension Application Files.
54. Orton, *Records of California Men*, p. 114; Thomas V. Keam, Military Service Records; McNitt, *Indian Traders*, p. 125. In military records, Keam's name sometimes appears as Thomas V. Kearns.
55. For Keam's association with Arny, see New Mexico Superintendency, rolls 7–9; License of Thomas V. Keam and Arny, January 4, September 12, 1868, Territorial Archives of New Mexico, roll 51.
56. Report of Employees in the Navajo Indian Agency for the Second Quarter, 1871, New Mexico Superintendency, Letters Received from the Navajo Agency, 1871, roll 15; Walker to Pope, December 26, 1871, New Mexico Superintendency, Letters Received from the Commissioners, 1871, roll 13. Agents received $1,500 per year.
57. Bennett to Clinton, February 1, July 1, 1870, New Mexico Superintendency, Letters Received from the Navajo Agency, 1870, roll 12.
58. Santa Fe *Daily New Mexican*, June 14, August 1, 1871; Arny to Keam, July 31, 1871, New Mexico Superintendency, Letters Received from the Pueblo Agency, 1871, roll 14; McNitt, *Indian Traders*, pp. 126–27.
59. Keam to Pope, September 9, 1872 and Hall to Pope, September 9, 1872, *Annual Report CIA*, 1872, pp. 686–88; Keam to Pope, September 1, 1872, New Mexico Superintendency, Letters Received from the Navajo Agency, 1872, roll 16. For background on the founding of the Navajo police, see Oakah L. Jones, Jr., "The Origin of the Navajo Indian Police, 1872–73," *Arizona and the West*, 8 (Autumn 1966): 225–38.
60. Santa Fe *Daily New Mexican*, August 13, 15, 1872.
61. Lynn R. Bailey, "Thomas Varker Keam: Tusayan Trader," *Arizoniana*, 2 (Winter 1961): 17; McNitt, *Indian Traders*, p. 246; Report of Employees in the Navajo Indian Agency for the Second Quarter, 1871, New Mexico Superinten-

dency, Letters Received from the Navajo Agency, 1871, roll 14. Keam and Grey Woman had two children, Tom Jr. and Billy Keam; Damon and his wife produced nine children.

62. Pope to Keam, August 15, 1872, New Mexico Superintendency, roll 30; McNitt, *Indian Traders*, pp. 135–36.

63. Keam to Pope, August 15, 1872, New Mexico Superintendency, Letters Received from the Navajo Agency, 1872, roll 16.

64. Dudley to Walker, December 16, 1872, and Dudley to Gould, July 22, 1873, New Mexico Superintendency, roll 30.

65. Arny to Smith, September 15, 1873, New Mexico Superintendency, Letters Received from the Navajo Agency, 1873, roll 19.

66. Arny to Smith, September 6, 1873 and Arny to Lourie, September 23, 1873, New Mexico Superintendency, Letters Received from the Navajo Agency, 1873, roll 19.

67. Arny to Dudley, February 8, May 2, June 15, 1874 and Arny to the Superintendent, April 18, 1874, New Mexico Superintendency, Letters Received from the Navajo Agency, 1874, roll 22.

68. Santa Fe *Daily New Mexican*, September 16, 1873; Bailey, "Thomas Varker Keam," p. 17.

69. Lawrence R. Murphy, *Frontier Crusader: William F. M. Arny* (Tucson: University of Arizona Press, 1972), pp. 225–31.

70. Santa Fe *Daily New Mexican*, January 6, 1875. A frequently reproduced photo housed in the Smithsonian Institution showing the party of Navajos who journeyed to Washington with Arny in 1874 erroneously labels one of the two Anglo interpreters as Hank Sharp instead of Hank Easton. It also seems likely that the names of Jesús Arviso and Hank Easton should be interchanged in the caption. See Murphy, *Frontier Crusader*, pp. 228–29.

71. Murphy, *Frontier Crusader*, pp. 225–31; McNitt, *Indian Traders*, pp. 151–53. Murphy presents Arny in a favorable light and Keam as a villain, while McNitt does the reverse. By getting the Indians drunk, McNitt believes that Keam was able to convince them to refuse any change in reservation boundaries, thereby preventing Arny from defrauding the Navajos of land.

72. *Grant County Herald*, September 5, 1875; McNitt, *Indian Traders*, p. 156; Murphy, *Frontier Crusader*, pp. 235–36.

73. Murphy, *Frontier Crusader*, pp. 235–38.

74. Santa Fe *Daily New Mexican*, September 29, 1875.

75. *Record, Second Judicial District* (1872–1878), Records of the District Court of the United States, New Mexico Territory, Record Group 21, Federal Records

Center, Denver, Colorado, pp. 234–35, 267–68, 370–73; McNitt, *Indian Traders*, pp. 162–65.

76. McNitt, *Indian Traders*, p. 164.

77. Bailey, "Thomas Varker Keam," p. 17; Notice from A. E. Hooker, November 21, 1877, Camp Ojo Caliente, N. M., Post Records, Records of the War Department, U.S. Army Commands, Record Group 393, National Archives, Washington, D.C. (hereafter cited as Camp Ojo Caliente, Post Records).

78. Keam to Hooker, February 22, 1878, Camp Ojo Caliente, Post Records; Bailey, "Thomas Varker Keam," pp. 17–19. McNitt provides the best account of Keam's long years as trader in Arizona. See McNitt, *Indian Traders*, pp. 166–99. One of Thomas V. Keam's detractors was E. S. Merritt, a California veteran who in 1870 worked in the quartermaster's department in Santa Fe. He later became acting agent for the Hopi Indians and in 1883 was living in Winslow, Arizona, when he and other residents complained that Keam was guilty of robbing the Indians. Frank D. Reeve, "The Government and the Navaho," *New Mexico Historical Review*, 16 (July 1941): 299, and 18 (January 1943): p. 26.

79. Anson C. Damon, Pension Application Files; Bailey, "Thomas Varker Keam," p. 18; McNitt, *Indian Traders*, p. 246; Lansing B. Bloom, ed., "Bourke on the Southwest," *New Mexico Historical Review*, 11 (January-July, 1936): 85, 219–39.

80. Henry W. Easton, Pension Application Files. At the close of the war, Easton married Margarita Alcaria Martinez, widow of Nestor Quintana, one of the soldiers who was killed along with the wife of Captain Albert H. Pfeiffer when their party was attacked by Indians in 1863. Census records show that in 1870 Henry and Margarita had two sons, Abraham and Stephen; the latter became a soldier, like his father, serving as a Rough Rider under Theodore Roosevelt.

81. Santa Fe *Daily New Mexican*, November 7, 1871, February 23, 1872.

82. David N. Catanach, Pension Application Files; Orton, *Records of California Men*, p. 149.

83. David N. Catanach, Pension Application Files; Santa Fe *Daily New Mexican*, August 8, 1882; *Civil and Criminal Record* [1884–1885], Doña Ana County (Doña Ana County Court House, Las Cruces, New Mexico), p. 45; *Deed Book R*, Santa Fe County (State Records Center and Archives, Santa Fe, New Mexico), p. 410.

84. Santa Fe *Weekly New Mexican*, October 25, 1880; Santa Fe *Daily New Mexican*, May 6, 1881; Records of Incorporation, Territorial Archives of New Mexico, roll 33.

85. Santa Fe *Daily New Mexican*, May 17, 21, 1881.

86. *Ibid.*, May 19-June 23, 1881, April 1, 4, 1882. It was reported in the press that the first man in Santa Fe to receive water directly into his establishment was Joseph W. Stinson, who owned a saloon on San Francisco street.

87. *Rio Grande Republican*, September 12, December 5, 1885; David N. Catanach, Pension Application Files. Only three of the Catanach children—all sons—outlived their father, though they never saw David again after he left Santa Fe. The three sons were well respected in the Santa Fe community, where in the first decade of the twentieth century John and James were employed as electrical engineers for the Santa Fe Water and Light Company and Archibald labored as a miller.

Chapter 9

1. The six California veterans who were elected to the territorial legislature between 1865 and 1885 were Joseph F. Bennett, Lewis Clark, John S. Crouch, John K. Houston, Hiram S. Russell, and William L. Rynerson.

2. Anderson, *History of New Mexico*, vol. 2, p. 722; *Illustrated History of New Mexico* (Chicago: Lewis Publishing Co., 1895), p. 547.

3. Santa Fe *New Mexico*, July 13, 1867; Lamar, *Far Southwest*, pp. 134–35.

4. Lamar, *Far Southwest*, pp. 134–35.

5. Santa Fe *New Mexican*, July 13, 1867. Ignacio Orrantia and Pablo Melendres were nominated as representatives to the legislature, Nepomuceno Y. Ancheta received the nomination as probate judge, and Perfecto Armijo was nominated for sheriff.

6. Santa Fe *New Mexican*, August 24, 1867.

7. Rufus P. Canterbury, Pension Application Files; Orton, *Records of California Men*, p. 112; Santa Fe *Weekly Gazette*, June 1, 1867.

8. John Hanson Beadle, *The Undeveloped West: or, Five Years in the Territories* (reprint; New York: Arno Press, 1973), pp. 536–40. Canterbury probably did not realize that many of these verses would be preserved for later generations to sample in two of the bestknown travel journals of the American West—James F. Meline's *Two Thousand Miles on Horseback*, published in 1868, and Beadle's *The Undeveloped West*, published in 1873. Meline identified the author as George Canterbury and noted that he "was evidently in a bad humor when he wrote his poem." Beadle merely stated that the author was "a brave soldier who had spent three years of service in [New Mexico and Arizona]" and that the author "had to fly the country." Meline, *Two Thousand Miles on Horseback*, pp. 262–63; Beadle, *The Undeveloped West*, pp. 536–40.

9. Santa Fe *Weekly Gazette*, June 1, 1867; Rufus P. Canterbury, Pension Application Files. In 1883 Canterbury moved to Austin, Texas, where he resumed his occupation as a printer; he died in that town on July 30, 1907.

10. Santa Fe *New Mexican*, November 12, 1867, February 18, 1868. A general court martial was convened at Mesilla on January 28, 1864 presided over by Brig. Gen. Joseph R. West, Maj. William McCleave, and Capt. Charles A. Smith. William W. Beman, private in Company A, Fifth California Infantry, was charged with having stolen a package containing six hundred dollars of U.S. Treasury Notes and four certificates of stock of the Overland Mail Company valued at one hundred dollars each. The court found Beman guilty and sentenced him to confinement at hard labor at Fort Craig for two years and dishonorably discharged. However, a petition signed by a large number of officers and men of the Fifth Infantry persuaded the commanding general to issue special orders releasing Beman from confinement and returning him to duty. General Orders, No. 4, Department of New Mexico, February 29, 1864, Trial of Private W. W. Beman, and Special Orders No. 19, June 9, 1864, Department of New Mexico, Records of the Office of the Judge Advocate General.

11. Bancroft, *History of Arizona and New Mexico*, p. 716; Executive Proceedings, 1867, entry for September 20, Territorial Papers, State, roll 3; *Probate Journal A*, Doña Ana County, entry for September 7, 1867; Santa Fe *Weekly Gazette*, September 28, 1867; Santa Fe *New Mexican*, September 14, 21, October 12, 1867. See also Jane C. Sanchez, "Agitated, Personal, and Unsound. . . ," *New Mexico Historical Review*, 41 (July 1966): 217–30. At this September election, three California veterans were elected to offices in Doña Ana County: Richard Yeamans as constable of precinct 9, John Martin as justice of the peace for precinct 12, and John D. Gibbins as constable for precinct 12, *Probate Journal A*, Doña Ana County, entry for September 9, 1867.

12. Miller, "William Logan Rynerson," p. 103; Santa Fe *Weekly Gazette*, December 7, 1867; William G. Ritch, comp., *New Mexico Blue Book, 1882* (Albuquerque: University of New Mexico Press, 1968), p. 112.

13. Santa Fe *New Mexican*, December 3, 17, 1867, January 14, 1868.

14. *Ibid.*, January 28, 1868; Santa Fe *Weekly Gazette*, December 21, 1867, May 2, 1868; Sanchez, "Agitated, Personal, and Unsound," p. 220.

15. Santa Fe *New Mexican*, January 14, 1868.

16. *Ibid.*, December 17, 1867, January 7, 14, 1868; Santa Fe *Weekly Gazette*, December 21, 1867, January 11, 1868.

17. Santa Fe *New Mexican*, February 18, 1868.

18. *Ibid.*, January 28, March 24, 1868; Santa Fe *Weekly Gazette*, January 25, March 28, 1868.

19. Ritch, *New Mexico Blue Book, 1882*, pp. 112–13.
20. Santa Fe *Weekly Gazette*, February 6, 1869; Naegle, "Silver City," p. 2.
21. Santa Fe *New Mexican*, April 21, 28, 1868.
22. Executive Record for 1868, entry for May 9, Territorial Papers, State, roll 3; Santa Fe *Daily New Mexican*, December 29, 1869; *Illustrated History of New Mexico*, p. 547; Anderson, *History of New Mexico*, vol. 2, p. 722. Anderson seems to be in error in listing Houston as judge in 1870. It is important to note that in 1870 and again in 1872, two of the five justices of peace elected in Grant County were former California troopers: Reece R. Bulger and George O. Perrault in the former and Joseph A. Moore and William B. Morgan in the latter year.
23. *Borderer*, May 4, 1871.
24. *Ibid.*, May 11, 1871.
25. *Ibid.*, July 13, 1871. In 1871, Thomas Coghlan was also appointed to the finance committee of the newly organized Democratic territorial central committee. He soon fell upon hard times, however, and on March 20, 1874, Coghlan died at age of thirty-six. The press described him at the time of death as a man of "good character, honest and fair, [who] had but one bad habit," which—though left unidentified—led to his demise. Santa Fe *Daily New Mexican*, March 21, 1874.
26. *Borderer*, July 26, 1871.
27. Santa Fe *Daily New Mexican*, April 28, 29, July 25, 26, 1871; *Borderer*, July 26, 1871. Yet a second Democrat writing to the editors of the press supported Newsham and described him as "an honest, intelligent and upright gentlemen who is interested in the welfare of Grant County. . . ." Santa Fe *Daily New Mexican*, August 4, 1871.
28. *Borderer*, June 15, 1871.
29. *Ibid.*, July 19, August 2, 1871.
30. Santa Fe *Daily New Mexican*, July 8, 18, 1871.
31. *Borderer*, August 16, 30, September 6, 1871; Juan Donne, "Riots in Mesilla, Holes in Flica Horn Cause New Town of La Ascension to Rise in Chihuahua, Mexico," *The Southwesterner*, 2 (July 1962): 3, 5.
32. *Borderer*, September 6, 1871; Herbert T. Hoover, "History of the Republican Party in New Mexico, 1867–1952" (Ph.D. diss., University of Oklahoma, 1966), p. 54. In December 1872 Rynerson married Luciana Lemon, the widow of the unfortunate John Lemon.
33. Anderson, *History of New Mexico*, vol. 2, p. 722; Santa Fe *Daily New Mexican*, September 16, 21, 1871.
34. Robert W. Larson, *New Mexico's Quest for Statehood, 1846–1912* (Al-

buquerque: University of New Mexico Press, 1968), pp. 96–99; Calvin Horn, *New Mexico's Troubled Years, The Story of the Early Territorial Governors* (Albuquerque: Horn and Wallace, Publishers, 1963), pp. 153–64.

35. Hiram S. Russell, Pension Application Files; Hiram S. Russell, Colfax County, New Mexico Census, 1870; Santa Fe *Daily New Mexican,* January 11, April 14, 1870, October 9, 1873; Santa Fe *Weekly New Mexican,* March 29, April 12, 1880; *Cimarron News and Press,* April 15, 1880. For Russell's involvement in the legislative revolt see *Borderer,* January 24, 1872 and Copy of Journal of House of Representatives, Friday, January 5, 1872, Territorial Papers, State, roll 4.

36. Santa Fe *Daily New Mexican,* December 16, 1871, January 6, 1872; *Borderer,* December 20, 1871. Bennett was one of two Anglos elected to the Council in 1871.

37. *Borderer,* January 24, 1872; Report of the Committee of Investigation of the Council of the Legislative Assembly of the Territory of New Mexico, January 24, 1872, Territorial Papers, State, roll 4, pp. 9–12.

38. *Borderer,* September 14, 1872; Santa Fe *Daily New Mexican,* July 13, 17, 1872.

39. Santa Fe *Daily New Mexican,* August 5, 7, September 4, 1873.

40. *Ibid.,* August 7, 16, 1873.

41. *Ibid.,* September 27, 1873.

42. James G. Crittenden, Grant County, New Mexico Census, 1870; Santa Fe *Daily New Mexican,* August 18, 1873; *Mining Life,* November 22, 1873; *Grant County Herald,* August 8, October 10, 1875, October 20, 1877, October 19, 1878, August 14, 1880; *New Southwest and Grant County Herald,* July 15, 1882; Oath of James G. Crittenden, October 16, 1875, Oaths of County Officials, Grant County, Territorial Archives of New Mexico, roll 36.

43. *Grant County Herald,* June 6, 13, 1875. At the June Grant County Democratic convention, Henry Barton, a former sergeant in the California volunteers, served as vice president.

44. Santa Fe *Daily New Mexican,* June 25, 28, July 7, 1875.

45. *Grant County Herald,* August 8, 15, 1875; *Mesilla News,* August 28, 1875.

46. *Grant County Herald,* August 22, 1875.

47. Santa Fe *Daily New Mexican,* June 1, 1875.

48. *Mesilla News,* May 1, August 14, 28, 1875; Santa Fe *Daily New Mexican,* May 28, August 16, 1875.

49. *Grant County Herald,* September 12, 1875, January 16, February 6, 1876; Santa Fe *Daily New Mexican,* October 16, 1875; *District Court Record 3,* Grant County, pp. 76–77, 83, 268.

50. *Grant County Herald*, September 12, 1875; Oath of George Perrault, October 9, 1875, Oaths of County Officials, Grant County, Territorial Archives of New Mexico, roll 36; Executive Proceedings for 1875, entry for September 20, Records of the Secretary of the Interior, Record Group 48, Territorial Papers, New Mexico, National Archives, Microfilm Publication M 364, roll 1 (hereafter cited as Territorial Papers, Interior). In this election, California veterans were elected to five of seventeen elective offices of Grant County.

51. Executive Proceedings for 1875, entry for September 16, 1875, Territorial Papers, Interior, roll 1. This was Taylor's third term as justice of the peace for Tortugas precinct. Nehemiah V. Bennett was defeated in his second attempt to be elected senator by Republican Jacinto Armijo.

52. *Grant County Herald*, January 30, August 5, 1876; *Mesilla News*, January 29, 1876.

53. *Grant County Herald*, August 5, September 30, 1876.

54. *Ibid.*, September 16, October 7, 1876. For discussion of the annexation movement, see Naegle, "Silver City," pp. 31–48.

55. *Mesilla News*, September 16, 1876; Naegle, "Silver City," pp. 46, 48.

56. *Grant County Herald*, October 7, 1876, January 27, 1877, October 19, 1878; *Southwest-Sentinel*, April 5, August 16, November 29, 1884. Joseph F. Bennett became U.S. Consul in Mexico early in the twentieth century and died in Mexico City on June 8, 1904. Joseph F. Bennett, Pension Application Files; Ellis A. Davis, ed., *The Historical Encyclopedia of New Mexico* (Albuquerque: New Mexico Historical Association, 1945), vol. 2, p. 1502.

57. Ritch, *New Mexico Blue Book, 1882*, pp. 116–17.

58. *Ibid.*; *Grant County Herald*, January 12, 1878.

59. *Grant County Herald*, January 26, February 2, 1878; Lamar, *Far Southwest*, p. 168. Though passed over the governor's veto, the act to incorporate the Society of Jesuits was eventually annuled by Congress.

60. *Grant County Herald*, February 2, March 9, 1878; Naegle, "Silver City," pp. 5, 49–54. The remaining two councilmen elected, Charles P. Crawford and John B. Morrill, belonged to the Republican and Democratic parties, respectively.

61. *Grant County Herald*, October 26, November 2, 1878; Santa Fe *Weekly New Mexican*, December 7, 1878; *Thirty-Four*, October 6, 1880.

62. Santa Fe *Daily New Mexican*, July 16, 1873, April 22, 1875.

63. Rynerson's role in the Lincoln County War will be examined in the following chapter.

64. *Rio Grande Republican*, May 28, June 11, 1881, January 14, 21, June 3, October 14, 1882, February 24, March 31, 1883.

65. *Rio Grande Republican,* June 3, 24, July 15, 29, October 7, November 11, 1882, February 3, 1883; *Mesilla News,* July 22, 1882 (clipping in the L. Bradford Prince Papers, State Records Center and Archives, Santa Fe, New Mexico, hereafter cited as Prince Papers).

66. *Rio Grande Republican,* April 12, 1884.

67. Santa Fe *Weekly New Mexican Review and Livestock Journal,* July 17, 1884; *Rio Grande Republican,* August 23, 1884.

68. *Rio Grande Republican,* August 30, 1884.

69. Santa Fe *Weekly New Mexican Review and Live Stock Journal,* September 11, 1884.

70. *Rio Grande Republican,* October 4, 1884; *Southwest-Sentinel,* August 30, September 6, 1884.

71. Black to Prince, September 17, [1884], Crawford to Prince, September 21, 1884, Prince Papers; *Rio Grande Republican,* November 15, 1884.

72. Simon F. Kropp, "Hiram Hadley and the Founding of New Mexico State University," *Arizona and the West,* 9 (Spring 1967): 25–26; *Rio Grande Republican,* September 7, 1889; Gibson, *Fountain,* pp. 182–83. For the statehood movement in 1889, see Larson, *New Mexico's Quest for Statehood,* pp. 147–68.

73. Gibson, *Fountain,* pp. 192–211.

74. *Rio Grande Republican,* December 24, 1887, June 15, July 6, October 19, 26, 1889, June 14, 1890, April 8, June 3, 10, 1892, September 30, 1893; Santa Fe *Daily New Mexican,* June 3, September 6, 1886.

Chapter 10

1. Seneca G. Ames, Pension Application Files; Seneca G. Ames, Doña Ana County, New Mexico Census, 1870. Little research has been done on cross-cultural marriages in the Southwest, particularly, in the nineteenth century. Most sociologists have focused their studies on twentieth century intermarriages.

2. Frank C. Arnett, Pension Application Files; Frank C. Arnett, Socorro County, New Mexico Census, 1870.

3. Wilson G. Holman, Pension Applicatoin Files; Wilson G. Holman, Grant County, New Mexico Census, 1870; Wilson G. Holman, *Marriage Record,* Grant County (Grant County Court House, Silver City, New Mexico), hereafter cited as *Marriage Record,* Grant County.

4. Frank C. Arnett, Pension Application Files.

5. Richard Mawson, Grant County, New Mexico Census, 1870.

6. See appropriate entries in New Mexico Census, 1870.

7. *Ibid.*

8. William L. Rynerson, Joseph F. Bennett, John D. Barncastle, Doña Ana County, New Mexico Census, 1870; Albert J. Fountain, El Paso County, Population Schedules of the Ninth Census of the United States, 1870, Texas, Bureau of the Census, Record Group 29, National Archives, Microfilm Publication 593, roll 1583 (hereafter cited as Texas Census, 1870).

9. Linklain Butin, Pension Application Files.

10. *Ibid.* Punctuation added.

11. Henry Barton, Grant County, New Mexico Census, 1870; Henry Barton, Grant County, New Mexico Census, 1880; Henry Barton, *Marriage Record,* Grant County. Individuals are listed in the 1870 census according to household, but no relationship is recorded for people living in the same household. Women and children are listed beneath a male head of household, and where the surname for a woman has been deleted in preference for a straight line, it is assumed that she carried the same surname as the man and that they were husband and wife. It is not always possible, however, to claim a husband-wife relationship as some Spanish women apparently went by their own surnames even when married; hence Hispanic women living in a household with Anglo men may be married but carry different surnames. On the other hand, they may indeed have been employed as housekeepers by single men, but it seems more likely that they were living in some common law marriage arrangement. In the 1880 census, relationships among people living in the same household are generally given so that a woman is clearly designated as wife.

12. Charles Brakebill, Grant County, New Mexico Census, 1870; Charles Brakebill, *Marriage Record,* Grant County.

13. William L. Rynerson, Doña Ana County, New Mexico Census, 1880; Joseph F. Bennett, Seneca Ames, Doña Ana County, New Mexico Census, 1870; Charles Brakebill, Wilson G. Holman, Grant County, New Mexico Census, 1870; Wesley Fields, Lincoln County, New Mexico Census, 1870.

14. *District Court Record 3,* Grant County p. 234; *Civil and Criminal Record* [1878–1881], Doña Ana County (Doña Ana County Court House, Las Cruces, New Mexico), pp. 43, 339. Gibbins, Ryan, and Taylor married their wives sometime prior to the 1870 census. Ryan later married Margarita B. Barela of Silver City in December 1879. John T. B. Ryan, *Marriage Record,* Grant County.

15. *Civil and Criminal Record* [1871–1874], Doña Ana County, pp. 246, 307. The first entry lists the claimant as Joseph Haskins; a second entry lists the claimant as George W. Haskins.

16. Sixty-two Hispanic women carried the surname of their husbands, while

sixteen lived in the same household as California veterans but carried different surnames. One woman lived in a household that contained two veterans.

17. Lycurgus D. Fuller, Pension Application Files.

18. See appropriate entries in Grant County, New Mexico Census, 1870.

19. Richard Hudson, Robert V. Newsham, *Marriage Record*, Grant County.

20. *Mesilla Valley Independent*, July 6, September 7, 1878.

21. Santa Fe *Daily New Mexican*, March 4, 1874; *Grant County Herald*, September 16, 1876.

22. Santa Fe *Daily New Mexican*, December 17, 1880; *Rio Grande Republican*, March 25, May 13, 20, 1882.

23. *Mesilla News*, January 29, 1876; *Grant County Herald*, September 8, 1877.

24. *Grant County Herald*, August 15, December 5, 1875; *New Southwest and Grant County Herald*, October 7, 28, 1882; William Chamberlin, Probate Files, Grant County.

25. Horn, *New Mexico's Troubled Years*, p. 28.

26. *Ibid.*, pp. 121, 153.

27. *Borderer*, December 20, 1871, January 24, 1872.

28. Naegle, "Silver City," pp. 138–39.

29. *Mining Life*, August 9, 1873, January 3, 10, 1874. As probate judge, Richard Hudson served as president of the board of school commissioners. *Mining Life*, August 2, 1873.

30. *Mining LIfe*, November 22, 1873, January 17, 1874; Naegle, "Silver City," p. 141.

31. Santa Fe *Daily New Mexican*, January 16, 1877; *Grant County Herald*, November 16, 1878, November 8, 1880.

32. Simon F. Kropp, "Albert J. Fountain and the Fight for Public Education in New Mexico," *Arizona and the West*, 11 (Winter 1969): 344–46.

33. *Thirty-Four*, March 31, September 15, 1880. In later years, Lawrence Lapoint served as one of the school's three directors. *Rio Grande Republican*, November 8, 1884.

34. *Rio Grande Republican*, January 27, 1883. Although Joseph F. Bennett had been a strong supporter of the public school system in Grant County, he sent one daughter to Missouri and at least two of his sons to Atchison, Kansas, for schooling. *Mining Life*, August 2, 1873; *Southwest-Sentinel*, June 14, 1884.

35. *Rio Grande Republican*, April 28, May 5, 1886, March 15, 1890, September 30, 1893; Kropp, "Hiram Hadley," pp. 23–26; Simon F. Kropp, *That all May Learn, New Mexico State University, 1888–1964* (Las Cruces: New Mexico State University, 1972), pp. 11–17.

36. *Borderer*, March 16, 1871.

37. *Ibid.*, July 24, December 28, 1872; *Mining Life*, January 17, 1874. Among topics chosen for debate at weekly meetings were the questions of statehood and women's suffrage. A native of Ohio, Harshberger died of smallpox in Georgetown, Grant County, on February 20, 1877. After his discharge from the First California Infantry, Harshberger resided at Ft. Craig, Elizabethtown, Cimarron, and Fort Union before moving to southern New Mexico when the Ralston mines were discovered. He served two terms as Justice of the Peace in Silver City and at the time of his death was working a mine at Georgetown. The editor of the *Grant County Herald* described Harshberger as "a favorite with our citizens." *Grant County Herald*, February 24, 1877; Santa Fe *Daily New Mexican*, March 6, 1877.

38. *Mesilla News*, May 30, November 14, 1874; Gibson, *Fountain*, pp. 93–95.

39. Christiansen, *Mining in New Mexico*, p. 107.

40. John C. Cremony, *Life Among the Apaches* (Tucson: Arizona Silhouettes, 1951).

41. George H. Pettis, *Personal Narratives of Events in the War of the Rebellion, Frontier Service . . . Or a History of Company K, First Infantry, California Volunteers*, (Providence: Soldiers' and Sailors' Historical Society of Rhode Island, 1885); *The California Column*, Historical Society of New Mexico, No. 11 (Santa Fe: New Mexican Printing Company, 1908); *Kit Carson's Fight With the Comanche and Kiowa Indians*, Historical Society of New Mexico, No. 12 (Santa Fe: New Mexican Printing Company, 1908).

42. Bancroft, *History of Arizona and New Mexico*, p. 752.

43. Sidney DeLong, *The History of Arizona, From the Earliest Times Known to People of Europe to 1903* (San Francisco: Whitaker and Roy Company, 1905).

44. Frank C. Lockwood, *Pioneer Portraits, Selected Vignettes* (Tucson: University of Arizona Press, 1968), pp. 92–93, 103. It should also be noted that Richard H. Orton, compiler of *Records of California Men in the War of the Rebellion, 1862–1867* (Sacramento: Adjutant General's Office, 1890), served in New Mexico as a captain in the California volunteers.

45. *Borderer*, December 6, 1871.

46. *Grant County Herald*, June 6, August 29, 1875.

47. *Southwest-Sentinel*, July 5, 1884; *Rio Grande Republican*, October 4, 1884. Not one of the New Mexico fires equaled the Great Chicago Fire of 1871. When news of that disaster reached New Mexico, territorial residents—including several California veterans—quickly collected money to be sent east for the homeless and destitute. Santa Fe *Daily New Mexican*, October 11, 17, 21, 1871.

48. Louis E. Freudenthal, comp., *A Century of Freemasonry of Las Cruces, 1867–1967* (n.p.: 1967), p. 44. A copy of this publication is located in Special Collections, University of New Mexico.

49. Santa Fe *Daily New Mexican*, August 8, 1877, October 7, 1881; Santa Fe *Weekly New Mexican*, January 10, 1880. At the Grand Lodge meeting convened at Albuquerque in 1882, Albert J. Fountain was elected Deputy Grand Master, while Lawrence Lapoint served as one of two Grand Stewards. Santa Fe *Daily New Mexican*, December 30, 1882.

50. Santa Fe *Daily New Mexican*, July 2, 1875, January 7, April 25, 29, 1876, June 30, 1882. Townsend was typical of many westerners who accepted civic responsibilities without seeking political office. In the two decades following his discharge, Townsend served as judge of election for his precinct on at least two occasions and as grand juror at least twice. His most public political role occurred in 1882 when he served as a vice-president at the Republican meeting held in Santa Fe and nominated L. Bradford Prince to serve as president of the reorganized Santa Fe County Republican association. Santa Fe *Weekly New Mexican*, September 20, 1879; Santa Fe *Daily New Mexican*, April 4, July 7, August 1, 1882.

51. Santa Fe *Weekly Gazette*, January 30, 1869; Santa Fe *Daily New Mexican*, May 4, 1870.

52. *Grant County Herald*, September 8, 1877, February 2, 9, May 4, 1878; *New Southwest and Grant County Herald*, November 5, 1881.

53. Santa Fe *Weekly Gazette*, February 27, March 6, 1869; Santa Fe *New Mexican*, March 9, 1869.

54. Records 1870 of McRae Post, G.A.R. Collection; Descriptive List, McRae Post, 1870, G.A.R. Collection.

55. Records 1870 of McRae Post, G.A.R. Collection, pp. 111, 117–18, 126, 201, 252.

56. Santa Fe *Daily New Mexican*, May 28, 30, 1872, May 30, 1873, May 31, 1876, May 23, 24, 25, 31, 1877; Descriptive List, McRae Post, G.A.R. Collection.

57. Records 1870 of McRae Post, G.A.R. Collection, pp. 61, 98, 158 ff.; Santa Fe *Daily New Mexican*, January 10, 1870, May 9, 1872.

58. Santa Fe *Daily New Mexican*, September 22, 26, 1873, October 8, 9, 1875. Fuller married a Hispanic woman, Ursula Charmonate of Sonora, Mexico, on July 11, 1867. Apparently they had no children and she remarried after his death. Santa Fe *New Mexican*, August 10, 1867; Santa Fe *Daily New Mexican*, October 9, 1875; Lycurgus D. Fuller, Pension Application Files.

59. Mary R. Dearing, *Veterans in Politics, The Story of the G.A.R.* (Baton

Rouge: Louisiana State University Press, 1952), pp. 185, 218, 219–307; Rules, Regulations and By-Laws of Carleton Post No. 3, G.A.R. Collection; Slough Post No. 6, G.A.R. Collection.

60. Roster of the Department of New Mexico, March 1891, G.A.R. Collection; Gibson, *Fountain*, p. 166; *Rio Grande Republican*, August 14, 1891.

61. Santa Fe *Daily New Mexican*, July 20, 1870; *Mining Life*, June 28, 1873.

62. Santa Fe *Daily New Mexican*, June 5, 1871, June 5, 1872, July 3, 1873, June 20, 1874, June 26, 1875.

63. *Ibid.*, August 25, November 8, 13, 17, 30, 1875, November 13, 1876. See also *Grant County Herald*, February 24, April 28, 1877. California veteran Bernard McCall and wife were among New Mexicans who traveled to Philadelphia to "take in" the Centennial. *Mesilla News*, July 22, 1876.

64. *Mesilla News*, March 25, June 24, 1876.

65. Santa Fe *Daily New Mexican*, February 5, 6, 1873.

66. *Southwest-Sentinel*, August 15, 1885; *Rio Grande Republican*, August 15, 1885. California veterans also helped organize territorial fairs in the 1880s and the Tertio-Millennial—a giant festival held in Santa Fe the summer of 1883 to commemorate settlement of New Mexico by Spaniards.

67. *Borderer*, November 30, 1872; *Mesilla News*, June 20, 1874; *Thirty-Four*, November 12, 1879.

68. *Record Book No. 2, First Judicial District* (1871–1874), Records of the District Court of the United States, New Mexico Territory, Record Group 21, Federal Records Center, Denver, Colorado, p. 7 (hereafter cited as *Record Book No. 2, First Judicial District*); Cause 403—in the Matter of C.N. Story, Records of the District Court of the United States, New Mexico Territory, Records of the First Judicial District, Civil and Criminal Case Files, 1870–1873, Record Group 21, Federal Records Center, Denver, Colorado.

69. *District Court Record 2*, Grant County, pp. 228–29, 236–37. The judge set aside the guilty verdict in Crittenden's case, and eventually the case was dismissed. *Ibid.*, pp. 282–83, 289–90. Americus Hall died in Silver City in December 1879 apparently from an overdose of morphine. The local press stated that at the time of his death he was under indictment for the murder of "a Chinaman." *Grant County Herald*, December 27, 1879; Santa Fe *Weekly New Mexican*, January 24, 1880.

70. *District Court Journal 1*, Grant County, pp. 51, 60.

71. *Record Book No. 2, First Judicial District*, p. 99; *Record, Second Judicial District* (1872–1878), Records of the District Court of the United States, New Mexico Territory, Record Group 21, Federal Records Center, Denver, Colo-

rado, pp. 234–35 (hereafter cited as *Record, Second Judicial District*); *District Court Journal 1*, Grant County, pp. 207–8, 257–58, 258–59.

72. Orton, *Records of California Men*, pp. 142, 147, 162; Santa Fe *New Mexican*, March 16, 1866; *Journal, Second Judicial District, Record Book A1* (1865–1872), Records of the District Court of the United States, New Mexico Territory, Record Group 21, Federal Records Center, Denver, Colorado, pp. 24, 31, 60; Cause No. 15, The United States *v.* John E. Oliphant, Records of the District Court of the United States, New Mexico Territory, Records of the Second Judicial District, Civil and Criminal Case Files, 1866–1880, Record Group 21, Federal Records Center, Denver, Colorado; John E. Oliphant, Grant County, New Mexico Census, 1870; John E. Oliphant, Probate Files, Doña Ana County.

73. Washington W. Hyde, Doña Ana County, New Mexico Census, 1870; *Civil and Criminal Minute and Record Book* [1865–1870], Doña Ana County, pp. 203, 207, 224, 229, 287–88, 289, 293, 307, 319, 320.

74. Washington W. Hyde, Pension Application Files; Santa Fe *Daily New Mexican*, June 24, 1871. Hyde had married Elizabeth Van Matre in Wisconsin in 1848 and went to California in 1852. His wife remained in the east while Hyde was in New Mexico. When she applied for a widow's pension in 1891 she stated that she had heard nothing from her husband for more than twenty years but had heard that he had been killed in New Mexico. Washington W. Hyde, Pension Application Files.

75. Santa Fe *Daily New Mexican*, January 16, 1872; *Grant County Herald*, July 15, 1876; William R. McCormick, George M. Carpenter, Frederick G. Hughes, Frank C. Arnett, Pension Application Files.

76. Santa Fe *New Mexican*, July 28, August 18, 1866; *Grant County Herald*, June 17, 1876; *Civil and Criminal Record* [1865–1870], Doña Ana County, pp. 111, 154–58, 325.

77. Santa Fe *Daily New Mexican*, April 25, 1871, November 6, 1874; *Mining Record Book A*, Lincoln County, pp. 24–25; Oath of Lyon Phillipouski, September 17, 1870, Oaths of County Officials, Lincoln County, Territorial Archives of New Mexico, roll 36; *Deed Record E*, Lincoln County (Lincoln County Court House, Carrizozo, New Mexico), pp. 105–8; Emil Fritz, Probate Files, Lincoln County; Amelia Church, Transcript, Pioneer Foundation Tapes, No. 115, University of New Mexico.

78. *Grant County Herald*, January 2, 1876.

79. *District Court Record 4* [1877–1878], Grant County (Grant County Court House, Silver City, New Mexico), pp. 58, 124–26; *Mesilla Valley Independent*,

December 22, 1877. In July 1878 Rachael was acquitted of the cattle poisoning charge. See *District Court Record 4*, Grant County, pp. 128, 176–77.

80. *Rio Grande Republican*, January 5, 26, February 9, 1884.

81. Cause No. 1130, 1131, *The Territory* v. *Henry C. Haring*, 1884, Doña Ana County Court House, Las Cruces, New Mexico; *Rio Grande Republican*, February 14, March 7, 14, 1885; Annual Report of the Adjutant General, 1886, Territorial Archives of New Mexico, roll 84. Some ten years prior to Haring's indictment, the editor of the *Mesilla News* wrote that "Hank" Haring was "living at Doña Ana and the respect and esteem in which he is held by the good people of that town demonstrates the fact that they are able to distinguish and appreciate true merit." *Mesilla News*, June 20, 1874.

82. Santa Fe *Daily New Mexican*, November 7, 1872.

83. For a good summary of the Horrell War, see Phillip J. Rasch, "The Horrell War," *New Mexico Historical Review*, 31 (July 1956): 223–31.

84. *Ibid.*, pp. 226–27. A farmer by trade and a New Yorker by birth, David C. Warner was married to a Hispanic woman, Prudencia, who after her husband's death, "proved up" their homestead and received final title to the land in 1877. David C. Warner, Lincoln County, New Mexico Census, 1870; David C. Warner, Application No. 61, Homestead Declaratory Statements, Nos. 1 to 441.

85. Santa Fe *Daily New Mexican*, January 9, 20, 1874.

86. *Ibid.*, January 27, 30, 1874.

87. Joseph E. Haskins, Lincoln County, New Mexico Census, 1870; Rasch, "The Horrell War," pp. 229–30. Rasch states that Haskins was murdered "for no other reason than that he had a Mexican wife." (p. 229). Certainly the Horrell War had racial overtones in that the Horrells sought revenge for their brother's death against New Mexico's Hispanic population. David C. Warner, the former drinking companion of the Horrell brothers, however, also had a Hispanic wife; it would therefore be erroneous to assume that the Texans had started a vendetta not only against Hispanos but also against Anglo men who had married into the Hispanic community. Cf., Eve Ball, *Ma'am Jones of the Pecos* (Tucson: University of Arizona Press, 1969), p. 77.

88. The best accounts of the Lincoln County War are William A. Keleher, *Violence in Lincoln County, 1869–1881* (reprint; Albuquerque: University of New Mexico Press, 1982); Mullin, ed., *Lincoln County War*; Nolan, *John Henry Tunstall*.

89. Keleher, *Violence in Lincoln County*, pp. 22–75; Santa Fe *Daily New Mexican*, July 30, 31, August 11, 1875.

90. Keleher, *Violence in Lincoln County,* pp. 22–75.

91. Quote is from *ibid.,* p. 81, but see also pp. 31–108. On at least one occasion while Rynerson was district attorney, he successfully defended Dolan and Riley on charges of dispensing tobacco and liquor without proper licenses. *Record Book A, Third Judicial District* (1871–1879), Records of the District Court of the United States, New Mexico Territory, Record Group 21, Federal Records Center, Denver, Colorado, pp. 619, 621–22, 649–50.

92. Keleher, *Violence in Lincoln County,* pp. 82, 109–13, 124–27, 140–47.

93. *Ibid.,* pp. 134, 315, 316.

94. C. L. Sonnichsen, *Pass of the North, Four Centuries on the Rio Grande* (El Paso: Texas Western Press, 1968), p. 181; C. L. Sonnichsen, *The El Paso Salt War, 1877* (El Paso: Carl Hertzog and the Texas Western Press at the Pass of the North, 1961), pp. 7–8; "El Paso Troubles in Texas," 45 Cong., 2d sess., *House Executive Document No. 93* (Serial 1809), p. 3 (hereafter cited as "El Paso Troubles in Texas").

95. Sonnichsen, *Pass of the North,* p. 183 and *El Paso Salt War,* pp. 8, 11.

96. Sonnichsen, *Pass of the North,* pp. 183–92.

97. *Ibid.,* pp. 207–210; Sonnichsen, *El Paso Salt War,* pp. 18, 25, 43; Keleher, *Violence in Lincoln County,* p. 157.

98. See appropriate entries in El Paso County, Texas Census, 1870. Rand listed his occupation as blacksmith, Evans as member of the Texas state police, and Hale as general laborer.

99. Sonnichsen, *El Paso Salt War,* pp. 21–22; "El Paso Troubles in Texas," pp. 65–66.

100. Sonnichsen, *El Paso Salt War,* p. 48; *Grant County Herald,* December 22, 1877; "El Paso Troubles in Texas," pp. 30, 100–101.

101. Sonnichsen, *El Paso Salt War,* pp. 48–57; *Mesilla Valley Independent,* December 22, 1877. The *Independent's* account of Atkinson's death is found in the *Grant County Herald,* January 5, 1878. Atkinson had sold his store earlier in December, planning to leave the country. It was later estimated that he had nearly $11,000 in specie and notes hidden in his quarters which was confiscated by the mob after his death. "El Paso Troubles in Texas," pp. 31–33.

102. As quoted in the *Mesilla Valley Independent,* December 29, 1877.

103. *Mesilla Valley Independent,* August 18, December 22, 1877.

104. *Ibid.,* February 22, March 8, 1879; *Records D,* Socorro County, pp. 211–12; Samuel Zimmerly, Socorro County, New Mexico Census, 1880. A *fanega* is a hundred weight.

105. *Daily Optic,* December 27, 28, 29, 1880.

106. *Daily Optic,* December 29, 1880; Santa Fe *Daily New Mexican,* April 1, November 8, 1881; *Rio Grande Republican,* November 12, 1881; Chester D. Potter, "Reminiscences of the Socorro Vigilantes," ed. by Paige W. Christiansen, *New Mexico Historical Review,* 40 (January 1965): 25, 29–31.

In Memoriam

1. Hugh Alexander Gorley, *Selections from the Numerous Letters and Patriotic Speeches of my Husband, H. A. Gorley* (San Francisco: Bonnard and Daly, 1876), pp. 33–34.

2. Abner Frazier, Pension Application Files.

Bibliography

MANUSCRIPTS

1. National Archives, Washington, D.C.
    a. Records of the Veterans Administration, Record Group 15
        Pension Application Files, Civil War Series
    b. Records of the Bureau of the Census, Record Group 29
        Population Schedules of the Ninth Census of the United States, 1870, New Mexico and Texas, Microfilm Publication 593, rolls 893–897, 1583
        Population Schedules of the Tenth Census of the United States, 1880, New Mexico, Microfilm No. T 9, rolls 802–804
        Schedules Enumerating Union Veterans and Widows of Union Veterans of the Civil War, Eleventh Census, 1890, New Mexico, Micro Copy No. 123, roll 44
    c. Records of the Secretary of the Interior, Record Group 48
        Territorial Papers, New Mexico, Microfilm Publication M 364, rolls 1–9
    d. Records of the Department of Treasury, Record Group 56
        Letters Received by the Secretary of Treasury from Customs Officials and Relating to the Customs Service in New Mexico
    e. Records of the Secretary of State, Record Group 59
        Territorial Papers, New Mexico, Microfilm Publication T-17, rolls 1–4
        Despatches From United States Consuls in Ciudad Juárez (Paso del Norte), 1850–1906, Micro Copy M-184, rolls 1–3
    f. Records of the Bureau of Indian Affairs, Record Group 75

Records of the New Mexico Superintendency of Indian Affairs, Micro Copy T-21, rolls 6–30

g. Records of the Office of Quartermaster General, Record Group 92
    Consolidated Correspondence File
    Registers of Contracts, 1861–1880

h. Records of the Adjutant General's Office, Record Group 94
    Compiled Military Service Records, Civil War, California and New Mexico Volunteers
    Muster Roll of Light Co. A, of 3d Regiment of Artillery from August 31, 1862 to October 31, 1862

i. Records of the Office of the Judge Advocate General (Army), Record Group 153
    Court Martial Case Files
    General Courts Martial

j. Records of the War Department, U.S. Army Commands, Record Group 393
    Camp Ojo Caliente, N.M., Post Records
    Ft. Bayard, N.M., Letters Sent by the Post Quartermaster

2. Washington National Records Center, Suitland, Maryland
    a. Records of the General Land Office, Record Group 49
        Ledgers for Desert Entries, La Mesilla and Las Cruces, New Mexico, Entries 1–263
    b. Records of the Office of Commissary General of Subsistence, Record Group 192
        Registers of Fresh Beef and Beef Cattle Contracts, 1856–94
        Contracts

3. Federal Records Center, Denver, Colorado
    a. Records of the District Court of the United States, New Mexico Territory, Record Group 21
        Records of the First Judicial District, Record Books (1860–1888) and Civil and Criminal Case Files (1847–1886)
        Records of the Second Judicial District, Record Books (1861–1887) and Civil and Criminal Case Files (1866–1880)
        Records of the Third Judicial District, Record Books (1871–1892) and Civil and Criminal Case Files (1851–1890)
    b. Records of the General Land Office, Record Group 49
        Record of Contracts, Office of Surveyor General
        Registers of Homestad Entries, Land Office, Santa Fe (1868–1885)
        Homestead Declaratory Statements and Homesteads, Santa Fe, N.M. and La Mesilla, N.M. (1872–1883)
        Register of Homestead Entries, Las Cruces (1883–1898)

Register of Receipts, Timber Culture, La Mesilla (1878–1891)
Abstract of Desert Land Entries, Las Cruces (1883–1892)
  c. Records of the Bureau of Indian Affairs, Record Group 75
Records of the Mescalero Agency, Correspondence, Accounts, and other Records (1874–1891)
4. State Records Center and Archives, Santa Fe, New Mexico
  a. County Assessment Rolls
  b. G.A.R. Collection
  c. Industrial and Agricultural Schedules of the Ninth and Tenth Census of the United States, 1870 and 1880, New Mexico
  d. L. Bradford Prince Papers
  e. Records of the Surveyor General, Brazito Grant
  f. Santa Fe County Deed Books, Mining Claims, and Wills
  g. Socorro County Deed Books
  h. Territorial Archives of New Mexico, Microfilm Edition
  i. Territorial Census of 1885, Schedule of Veterans of the Union Volunteer Forces and Regular Army
5. County Records
  a. Bernalillo County Court House, Albuquerque. General Index to Deed Books
  b. Colfax County Court House, Raton. Deed Books, Mining Claims
  c. Doña Ana County Court House, Las Cruces. Court Records, Deed Books, Mining Claims, Marriage Record, Probate Files, Probate Journals
  d. Grant County Court House, Silver City. Court Records, Deed Books, Mining Claims, Marriage Record, Probate Files
  e. Lincoln County Court House, Carrizozo. Cash Book, Court Records, Deed Books, Mining Claims, Probate Files, Miscellaneous Book
  f. Otero County Court House, Alamogordo. Deed Books
  g. Socorro County Court House, Socorro. Deed Books, Mining Claims, Probate Files
6. Other Depositories
  a. Arizona Historical Society, Tucson, Arizona
George O. Hand Diary
  b. Bancroft Library, University of California, Berkeley, California
Edward Everett Ayer, Reminiscences of the Far West, and Other Trips, 1861–1918
William McCleave, Recollections of a California Volunteer
William McCleave, Papers
Andrew Stewart, New Mexico Dictations
  c. California State University, Fresno, California

Samuel C. Staples, Random Sketches or Trifles—Sights and Events
in my Western Border Campaigning

d.   Henry E. Huntington Library, San Marino, California
William G. Ritch Collection
J. B. Whittemore, comp., *Register of the Society of California Volunteers*
(San Francisco: C. W. Nevin and Co., January 1887).
Brevet Brig.- Gen'l G. W. Bowie, Late Colonel 5th California Infantry,
Address, Delivered Before the Society of California Volunteers at
the Second Annual Celebration at San Francisco, April 25, 1867.
Published by the Society, San Francisco: Edward Bosqui and Co.,
1867.

e.   New Mexico State University, Las Cruces, New Mexico
Freudenthal Papers
Skidmore Collection

f.   The University of New Mexico, Albuquerque, New Mexico
Joseph H. Blazer Business Records
Marcus Brunswick Business Records
Thomas B. Catron Papers
Ilfeld Company Business Records
E. F. Kellner Papers
Maxwell Land Grant Papers
Michael Steck Papers
Tularosa Mills Records

GOVERNMENT DOCUMENTS

1.   Congressional Documents
Annual Report of the Commissioner of Indian Affairs
39 Cong., 2d sess., *Senate Report No. 156,* "Condition of the Indian Tribes"
(Serial 1279).
43 Cong., 1st sess., *Senate Executive Document No. 56,* "Reports . . . on
Mesilla Colony Grant" (Serial 1581).
39 Cong., 1st sess., *House Executive Document No. 138,* "Relative to the
discharge of certain California Volunteers stationed in the Territories"
(Serial 1267).
45 Cong., 2d sess., *House Executive Document No. 93,* "El Paso Troubles
in Texas" (Serial 1809).

2. General Documents
   Brunswick v. Winters's Heirs, 3 N.M., 241, 5 Pac., 706 (1885).
   The War of the Rebellion: A Compilation of the Official Records of the Union and Confederate Armies. 128 vols. Washington: Government Printing Office, 1880–1901.
   U.S. Bureau of the Census. *Historical Statistics of the United States, Colonial Times to 1970, Bicentennial Edition.* 2 parts. Washington: Government Printing Office, 1975.
3. State Documents
   Orton, Richard H., comp. *Records of California Men in the War of the Rebellion, 1861–1867.* Sacramento: Adjutant General's Office, 1890.
   Prince, L. Bradford. *Report of the Governor of New Mexico to the Secretary of the Interior, 1889.* Washington: Government Printing Office, 1889.

ORAL COMMUNICATIONS

Bell, Ollie. Transcript. Pioneer Foundation Tapes, No. 20. University of New Mexico.
Church, Amelia. Transcript. Pioneer Foundation Tapes, No. 115. University of New Mexico.
Feather, Adali. Interview. Las Cruces, New Mexico, July 2, 1974.

NEWSPAPERS

Albuquerque Review, N.M.
Borderer, Las Cruces, N.M.
Cimarron News and Press, Cimarron, N.M.
Daily Alta California, San Francisco, Calif.
Daily Herald, Santa Fe, N.M.
Daily New Mexican, Santa Fe, N.M.
Daily Optic, Las Vegas, N.M.
El Paso Daily Times, Texas
Evening Bulletin, San Francisco, Calif.
Grant County Herald , Silver City, N.M.
Las Cruces Citizen, N.M.
Mesilla News, N.M.
Mesilla Times, N.M.
Mesilla Valley Independent, Mesilla, N.M.
Mining Life, Silver City, N.M.

Santa Fe *New Mexican*, N.M.
New Mexico Press, Albuquerque, N.M.
New Southwest and Grant County Herald, Silver City, N.M.
Republican Review, Albuquerque, N.M.
Rio Abajo Weekly Press, Albuquerque, N.M.
Rio Grande Republican, Las Cruces, N.M.
Semi-Weekly Review, Albuquerque, N.M.
Silver City Enterprise, N.M.
Sonoma County Journal, Petaluma, Calif.
Southwest-Sentinel, Silver City, N.M.
Thirty-Four, Las Cruces, N.M.
Santa Fe *Weekly Gazette*, N.M.
Santa Fe *Weekly New Mexican*, N.M.
Weekly New Mexican Review and Livestock Journal, Santa Fe, N.M.

DISSERTATIONS AND THESES

Bloom, Maude Elizabeth McFie. "A History of Mesilla Valley," Senior thesis, New Mexico College of Agriculture and Mechanic Arts, 1903.

Giese, Dale Frederick. "Soldiers at Play: A History of Social Life at Fort Union, New Mexico, 1851–1891," Ph.D. dissertation, University of New Mexico, 1969.

Hoover, Herbert T. "History of the Republican Party in New Mexico, 1867–1952," Ph.D. dissertation, University of Oklahoma, 1966.

Mehren, Lawrence L. "A History of the Mescalero Apache Reservation, 1869–1881," Master's thesis, University of Arizona, 1969.

Miller, Darlis A. "General James Henry Carleton in New Mexico, 1862–1867," Master's thesis, New Mexico State University, 1970.

Naegle, Conrad Keeler. "The History of Silver City, New Mexico, 1870–1886," Master's thesis, University of New Mexico, 1943.

Rogan, Francis E. "Military History of New Mexico Territory During the Civil War," Ph.D. dissertation, University of Utah, 1961.

BOOKS

Anderson, George B. *The History of New Mexico, Its Resources and People.* 2 vols. Los Angeles: Pacific States Publishing Co., 1907.

Atherton, Lewis E. *The Frontier Merchant in Mid-America.* Columbia: University of Missouri Press, 1971.

Bailey, Lynn R. *The Long Walk, A History of the Navajo Wars, 1846–68.* Los Angeles: Westernlore Press, 1964.

Ball, Eve. *Ma'am Jones of the Pecos.* Tucson: University of Arizona Press, 1969.

————. *Ruidoso, The Last Frontier.* San Antonio: The Naylor Company, 1963.

Ball, Larry D. *The United States Marshals of New Mexico and Arizona Territories, 1846–1912.* Albuquerque: University of New Mexico Press, 1978.

Bancroft, Hubert H. *History of Arizona and New Mexico, 1530–1888.* San Francisco: The History Company, 1889.

Bartlett, Richard A. *The New Country, A Social History of the American Frontier, 1776–1890.* New York: Oxford University Press, 1974.

Beadle, J. H. *The Undeveloped West; or, Five Years in the Territories.* Philadelphia: National Publishing Co., 1873.

Beck, Warren. *New Mexico: A History of Four Centuries.* Norman: University of Oklahoma Press, 1962.

Billington, Ray Allen. *Westward Expansion.* 4th ed. New York: MacMillen Publishing Co., Inc., 1974.

Bowden, J. J. *Spanish and Mexican Land Grants in the Chihuahuan Acquisition.* El Paso: Texas Western Press, 1971.

Browne, John Ross. *A Tour Through Arizona, 1864; or, Adventures in the Apache Country.* Reprint. Tucson: Arizona Silhouettes, 1950.

Bureau of Mines and Mineral Resources, New Mexico. Bulletin 11. *The Geology of the Organ Mountains.* Socorro: New Mexico School of Mines, 1935.

Charles, Mrs. Tom. *More Tales of the Tularosa.* Alamogordo, N.M.: Bennett Printing Company, 1961.

Chavez, Fray Angelico. *My Penitente Land.* Albuquerque: University of New Mexico Press, 1974.

Christiansen, Paige W. *The Story of Mining in New Mexico.* Socorro: New Mexico Bureau of Mines and Mineral Resources, 1974.

Coan, Charles C. *A History of New Mexico.* 3 vols. Chicago: The American Historical Society, Inc., 1925.

Colton, Ray C. *The Civil War in the Western Territories.* Norman: University of Oklahoma Press, 1959.

Conkling, Roscoe P. and Margaret B. *The Butterfield Overland Mail, 1857–1869.* 2 vols. Glendale, Calif.: The Arthur H. Clark Company, 1947.

Cremony, John C. *Life Among the Apaches.* Reprint. Tucson: Arizona Silhouettes, 1951.

Crocchiola, Stanley. *The Civil War in New Mexico.* Denver: The World Press, Inc., 1960.

————. *The Elizabethtown, New Mexico Story.* Dumas, Texas: F. Stanley, 1961.

————. *Fort Stanton.* Pampa, Texas: Pampa Print Shop, 1964.

————. *Fort Union.* Denver: The World Press, 1953.

Davis, Ellis A., ed. *The Historical Encyclopedia of New Mexico.* 2 vols. Albuquerque: New Mexico Historical Association, 1945.

Dearing, Mary R. *Veterans in Politics, The Story of the G.A.R.* Baton Rouge: Louisiana State University Press, 1952.

DeLong, Sidney. *The History of Arizona, From the Earliest Times Known to the People of Europe to 1903.* San Francisco: Whitaker and Roy Company, 1905.

Dick, Everett. *The Sod-House Frontier, 1854–1890.* Lincoln: Johnsen Publishing Company, 1954.

———. *The Lure of the Land.* Lincoln: University of Nebraska Press, 1970.

Emmett, Chris. *Fort Union and the Winning of the Southwest.* Norman:University of Oklahoma Press, 1965.

Freudenthal, Louis E., comp. *A Century of Freemasonry of Las Cruces, 1867–1967.* n.p.: 1967.

Gibson, Arrell M. *The Life and Death of Colonel Albert Jennings Fountain.* Norman: University of Oklahoma Press, 1965.

Giese, Dale F., ed. *My Life with the Army in the West, The Memoirs of James E. Farmer, 1858–1898.* Santa Fe: Stagecoach Press, 1967.

Goetzmann, William H. *Exploration and Empire.* New York: Random House, 1966.

Gorley, Hugh Alexander. *The Loyal Californians of 1861.* War Paper No. 12. San Francisco: Commandery of California, Military Order of the Loyal Legion of the United States, 1893.

———. *Selections from the Numerous Letters and Patriotic Speeches of my Husband, H. A. Gorley.* San Francisco: Bonnard and Daly, 1876.

Grant, Blanche Chloe. *When Old Trails Were New: The Story of Taos.* Chicago: The Rio Grande Press, Inc., 1963.

Gressley, Gene M. *West by East: The American West in the Gilded Age.* Charles Redd Monographs in Western History, No. 1. Provo, Utah: Brigham Young University Press, 1972.

Grieve, Robert. *Illustrated History of Pawtucket, Central Falls and Vicinity.* Pawtucket, R.I.: Pawtucket Gazette and Chronicle, 1897.

Grove, Pearce S.; Barnett, Becky J.; and Hansen, Sandra J.; eds. *New Mexico Newspapers, A Comprehensive Guide to Bibliographical Entries and Locations.* Albuquerque: University of New Mexico Press, 1975.

Hafen, LeRoy R. *The Overland Mail, 1849–1869.* Cleveland: The Arthur H. Clark Company, 1926.

Haley, J. Evetts. *Charles Goodnight, Cowman and Plainsman.* Norman: University of Oklahoma Press, 1949.

Hall, Martin Hardwick. *Sibley's New Mexico Campaign.* Austin: University of Texas Press, 1960.

Heitman, Francis B. *Historical Register and Dictionary of the United States Army.* Reprint. 2 vols. Urbana: University of Illinois Press, 1965.

Herndon, Richard, comp. *Men of Progress; Biographical Sketches and Portraits of Leaders in Business and Professional Life in the State of Rhode Island and Providence Plantations.* Boston: New England Magazine, 1896.

Hollister, Ovando J. *Colorado Volunteers in New Mexico, 1862.* Chicago: Lakeside Press, R. R. Donnelly and Sons Company, 1962.

Hollon, W. Eugene. *Frontier Violence: Another Look.* New York: Oxford University Press, 1974.

Holmes, Jack E. *Politics in New Mexico.* Albuquerque: University of New Mexico Press, 1967.

Horn, Calvin. *New Mexico's Troubled Years, The Story of the Early Territorial Governors.* Albuquerque: Horn and Wallace, Publishers, 1963.

Hunt, Aurora. *The Army of the Pacific.* Glendale: The Arthur H. Clark Company, 1950.

——. *Major General James Henry Carleton.* Glendale: The Arthur H. Clark Company, 1958.

Illustrated History of New Mexico. Chicago: Lewis Publishing Co., 1895.

Jones, Fayette Alexander. *New Mexico Mines and Minerals.* Santa Fe: The New Mexico Printing Company, 1904.

Keleher, William A. *The Fabulous Frontier, Twelve New Mexico Items.* Reprint. Albuquerque: University of New Mexico Press, 1982.

——. *Turmoil in New Mexico, 1846–1868.* Reprint. Albuquerque: University of New Mexico Press, 1982.

——. *Violence in Lincoln County, 1869–1881.* Reprint. Albuquerque: University of New Mexico Press, 1982.

Kropp, Simon F. *That All May Learn, New Mexico State University, 1888–1964.* Las Cruces, N.M.: New Mexico State University, 1972.

Lamar, Howard R. *The Far Southwest, 1846–1912, A Territorial History.* New York: W. W. Norton and Company, 1970.

Larson, Robert W. *New Mexico Populism, A Study of Radical Protest in a Western Territory.* Boulder: Colorado Associated University Press, 1974.

——. *New Mexico's Quest for Statehood, 1846–1912.* Albuquerque: University of New Mexico Press, 1968.

Lockwood, Frank C. *Pioneer Portraits, Selected Vignettes.* Tucson: University of Arizona Press, 1968.

Marchand, Ernest, ed. *News From Fort Craig, New Mexico, 1863, Civil War*

Letters of Andrew Ryan, With the First California Volunteers. Santa Fe: Stagecoach Press, 1966.

McNitt, Frank. *The Indian Traders.* Norman: University of Oklahoma Press, 1962.

Meline, James F. *Two Thousand Miles on Horseback.* Reprint. Albuquerque: Horn & Wallace, Publishers, 1966.

Miller, Darlis A., ed. *Across the Plains In 1864 with Additional Paymaster Samuel C. Staples.* Manhattan, Kansas: MA/AH Publishing, 1980.

Mills, William W. *Forty Years at El Paso, 1858–1898.* Edited by Rex W. Strickland. El Paso: Carl Hertzog, 1962.

Mullin, Robert N., ed. *Maurice Garland Fulton's History of the Lincoln County War.* Tucson: University of Arizona Press, 1968.

Murphy, Lawrence R. *Frontier Crusader: William F. M. Arny.* Tucson: University of Arizona Press, 1972.

———. *Philmont, A History of New Mexico's Cimarron Country.* Albuquerque: University of New Mexico Press, 1972.

Nolan, Frederick. *The Life and Death of John Henry Tunstall.* Albuquerque: University of New Mexico Press, 1965.

Otero, Miguel Antonio. *My Life on the Frontier.* 2 vols. New York: The Press of the Pioneers, 1935 and Albuquerque: University of New Mexico Press, 1939.

Parker, Morris B. *White Oaks, Life in a New Mexico Gold Camp, 1880–1900.* Tucson: University of Arizona Press, 1971.

Parker, William Thornton. *Annals of Old Fort Cummings, 1867–8.* Northampton, Mass.: By the Author, 1916.

Paul, Rodman W. *California Gold, The Beginning of Mining in the Far West.* Lincoln: University of Nebraska Press, 1947.

Pearce, T. M., ed. *New Mexico Place Names.* Albuquerque: University of New Mexico Press, 1965.

Pearson, Jim B. *The Maxwell Land Grant.* Norman: University of Oklahoma Press, 1961.

Pettis, George H. *The California Column.* Historical Society of New Mexico, No. 11. Santa Fe: New Mexican Printing Company, 1908.

———. *Kit Carson's Fight With the Comanche and Kiowa Indians.* Historical Society of New Mexico, No. 12, Santa Fe: New Mexican Printing Company, 1908.

———. *Personal Narratives of Events in the War of the Rebellion, Frontier Service . . . Or a History of Company K, First Infantry, California Volunteers.* Providence, Rhode Island: Soliders' and Sailors' Historical Society of Rhode Island, 1885.

Poldervaart, Arie W. *Black-Robed Justice: A History of the Administration of Justice in New Mexico from the American Occupation in 1846 Until Statehood in 1912.* Santa Fe: Historical Society of New Mexico, 1948.

Prince, L. Bradford. *A Concise History of New Mexico.* Cedar Rapids, Iowa: The Torch Press, 1912.

Reeve, Frank D. *History of New Mexico.* 3 vols. New York: Lewis Historical Publishing Company, Inc., 1961.

Rickey, Don, Jr. *Forty Miles a Day on Beans and Hay, The Enlisted Soldier Fighting the Indian Wars.* Norman: University of Oklahoma Press, 1963.

Ritch, William G. *A Complete Business Directory of New Mexico, and Gazetteer of the Territory for 1882.* Santa Fe: New Mexican Printing and Publishing Co., 1882.

———, comp. *New Mexico Blue Book, 1882.* Reprint. Albuquerque: University of New Mexico Press, 1968.

Russell, Marian. *Land of Enchantment, Memoirs of Marian Russell Along the Santa Fe Trail As dictated to Mrs. Hal Russell.* Reprint. Albuquerque: University of New Mexico Press, 1981.

Sacks, Benjamin. *Be it Enacted: The Creation of the Territory of Arizona.* Phoenix: Arizona Historical Foundation, 1964.

Schellie, Don. *Vast Domain of Blood, The Story of the Camp Grant Massacre.* Los Angeles: Westernlore Press, 1968.

Shinkle, James D. *Fifty Years of Roswell History—1867–1917.* Roswell, N.M.: Hall-Poorbaugh Press, Inc., 1964.

Siringo, Charles A. *A Texas Cowboy.* New York: J. S. Ogilvie Publishing Co., 1946.

Smith, Duane A. *Rocky Mountain Mining Camps, The Urban Frontier.* Lincoln: University of Nebraska Press, 1967.

Sonnichsen, C. L. *Colonel Greene and the Copper Skyrocket.* Tucson: University of Arizona Press, 1974.

———. *The El Paso Salt War, 1877.* El Paso: Carl Hertzog and the Texas Western Press at the Pass of the North, 1961.

———. *The Mescalero Apaches.* Norman: University of Oklahoma Press, 1958.

———. *Pass of the North, Four Centuries on the Rio Grande.* El Paso: Texas Western Press, University of Texas at El Paso, 1968.

———. *Tularosa, Last of the Frontier West.* Reprint. Albuquerque: University of New Mexico Press, 1981.

Speer, William S. *Encyclopedia of the New West.* Marshall, Texas: U.S. Biographical Publishing Co., 1881.

Spence, Clark C. "When Money Made the Mare Go: The Day of the Western Livery Stable," in *Essays on the American West, 1972–1973.* Ed. by Thomas

G. Alexander, Charles Redd Monographs in Western History, No. 3. Provo: Brigham Young University Press, 1974.

Stratton, Porter A. *The Territorial Press of New Mexico, 1834–1912*. Albuquerque: University of New Mexico Press, 1969.

Strickland, Rex W. *Six Who Came to El Paso, Pioneers of the 1840's*. Southwestern Studies, vol. 1, No. 3. El Paso: Texas Western College Press, 1963.

Taylor, Morris F. *First Mail West, Stagecoach Lines on the Santa Fe Trail*. Albuquerque: University of New Mexico Press, 1971.

————. *O. P. McMains and the Maxwell Land Grant Conflict*. Tucson: University of Arizona Press, 1979.

Thomlinson, M. H. *The Garrison of Fort Bliss, 1849–1916*. El Paso: Hertzog and Resler, 1945.

Thompson, Gerald. *The Army and the Navajo, The Bosque Redondo Reservation Experiment, 1863–1868*. Tucson: University of Arizona Press, 1976.

Thrapp, Dan L. *The Conquest of Apacheria*. Norman: University of Oklahoma Press, 1967.

————. *Victorio and the Mimbres Apaches*. Norman: University of Oklahoma Press, 1974.

Twitchell, Ralph Emerson. *The Leading Facts of New Mexican History*. 5 vols. Cedar Rapids: The Torch Press, 1911–1917.

————. *Old Santa Fe: The Story of New Mexico's Ancient Capital*. Chicago: Rio Grande Press, Inc., 1925.

Utley, Robert M. *Frontier Regulars: The United States Army and the Indian, 1866–1891*. New York: MacMillan Publishing Company, 1973.

————. *Frontiersmen in Blue: The United States Army and the Indian, 1848–1865*. New York: MacMillan Company, 1967.

Westphall, Victor. *The Public Domain in New Mexico, 1854–1891*. Albuquerque: University of New Mexico Press, 1965.

————. *Thomas Benton Catron and His Era*. Tucson: University of Arizona Press, 1973.

Wiley, Bell Irvin. *The Life of Billy Yank, The Common Soldier of the Union*. New York: Bobbs-Merrill Company, 1952.

PERIODICALS

Allen, R. S. "Pinos Altos, New Mexico," *New Mexico Historical Review*, 23 (October 1948): 302–32.

Ayers, John. "A Soldier's Experience in New Mexico," *New Mexico Historical Review*, 24 (October 1949): 259–66.

Bailey, Lynn R. "Thomas Varker Keam: Tusayan Trader," *Arizoniana*, 2 (Winter 1961): 15–19.

Blazer, A. N. "Blazer's Mill," *New Mexico*, 16 (January 1938): 20, 48–49.

Bloom, Lansing B., ed. "Bourke on the Southwest," *New Mexico Historical Review*, 11 (January-July 1936): 72–122, 188–207, 217–82.

Brewster, Jane Wayland. "The San Rafael Cattle Company, A Pennsylvania Enterprise in Arizona," *Arizona and the West*, 8 (Summer 1966): 133–56.

Carlson, Alvar Ward. "New Mexico's Sheep Industry, 1850–1900: Its Role in the History of the Territory," *New Mexico Historical Review*, 44 (January 1969): 25–49.

Clendenen, Clarence C. "General James Henry Carleton," *New Mexico Historical Review*, 30 (January 1955): 23–43.

Donne, Juan. "Riots in Mesilla, Holes in Flica Horn Cause New Town of La Ascencion to Rise in Chihuahua, Mexico," *The Southwesterner*, 2 (July 1962): 3, 5.

Dwyer, James Magoffin, Jr. "Hugh Stephenson," *New Mexico Historical Review*, 29 (January 1954): 1–7.

Fierman, Floyd S. "Jewish Pioneering in the Southwest, A Record of the Freudenthal-Lesinsky-Solomon Families," *Arizona and the West*, 2 (Spring 1960): 54–72.

Forrest, Earle R. "The Fabulous Sierra Bonita," *Journal of Arizona History*, 6 (Autumn 1965): 132–46.

Frazer, Robert W. "Perveyors of Flour to the Army: Department of New Mexico, 1849–1861," *New Mexico Historical Review*, 47 (July 1972): 213–38.

Greever, William S. "Railway Development in the Southwest," *New Mexico Historical Review*, 32 (April 1957): 151–203.

Hafen, LeRoy R. "Otto Mears, 'Pathfinder of the San Juan'," *The Colorado Magazine*, 9 (March 1932): 71–74.

Hagemann, E. R. "Scout Out from Camp McDowell," *Arizoniana*, 5 (Fall 1964): 29–47.

Hill, Rita and Janaloo. "Alias Shakespeare, The Town Nobody Knew," *New Mexico Historical Review*, 42 (July 1967): 211–27.

Hobbs, Marilyn. "What a Journey!" *Ash Tree Eco*, 9 (October 1974): 191–92.

Jones, Oakah L., Jr. "The Origin of the Navajo Indian Police, 1872–73," *Arizona and the West*, 8 (Autumn 1966): 225–238.

Kane, Randy. " 'An Honorable and Upright Man': Sidney R. DeLong as Post Trader at Fort Bowie," *Journal of Arizona History*, 19 (Autumn 1978): 297–314.

Kaplan, Michael, "Colorado's Big Little Man: The Early Career of Otto Mears,

1840–1881," *Western States Jewish Historical Quarterly*, 4 (April 1972): 117–45.

———. " 'The Joker in the Republican Deck': The Political Career of Otto Mears, 1881–1889," *Western States Jewish Historical Quarterly*, 7 (July 1975): 287–302.

———. "Otto Mears and the Silverton Northern Railroad," *The Colorado Magazine*, 48 (Summer 1971): 235–54.

———. "The Toll Road Building Career of Otto Mears, 1881–1887," *The Colorado Magazine*, 52 (Spring 1975): 153–70.

Kropp, Simon F. "Albert J. Fountain and the Fight for Public Education in New Mexico," *Arizona and the West*, 11 (Winter 1969): 341–58.

———. "Hiram Hadley and the Founding of New Mexico State University," *Arizona and the West*, 9 (Spring 1967): 21–40.

Mauson, Laura C. "Albert H. Pfeiffer," *The Colorado Magazine*, 10 (November 1933): 217–22.

Miller, Darlis A. "William Logan Rynerson in New Mexico, 1862–1893," *New Mexico Historical Review*, 48 (April 1973): 101–31.

———. "Carleton's California Column: A Chapter in New Mexico's Mining History," *New Mexico Historical Review*, 53 (January 1978): 5–38.

———. "Historian for the California Column: George H. Pettis of New Mexico and Rhode Island," *Red River Valley Historical Review*, 5 (Winter 1980): 74–92.

Myers, Lee. "The Enigma of Mangas Coloradas' Death," *New Mexico Historical Review*, 41 (October 1966): 287–304.

———. "Military Establishments in Southwestern New Mexico: Stepping Stones to Settlement," *New Mexico Historical Review*, 43 (January 1968): 5–48.

Newman, S. H. III. "The Las Vegas Weekly Mail," *New Mexico Historical Review*, 44 (April 1969): 155–66.

Potter, Chester D. "Reminiscences of the Socorro Vigilantes," ed. by Paige W. Christiansen, *New Mexico Historical Review*, 40 (January 1965): 23–54.

Rasch, P. J. "The Horrell War," *New Mexico Historical Review*, 31 (July 1956): 223–31.

———. "The Rustler War," *New Mexico Historical Review*, 39 (October 1964): 257–73.

———. "The Tularosa Ditch War," *New Mexico Historical Review*, 43 (July 1968): 229–35.

Reeve, Frank D., ed. "Albert Franklin Banta: Arizona Pioneer," *New Mexico Historical Review*, 27 (April-October 1952): 81–106, 200–252, 315–47 and vol. 28 (January-April 1953): 52–67, 133–47.

————. "The Federal Indian Policy in New Mexico, 1858–1880," *New Mexico Historical Review,* 12 (July 1937): 218–69, and 13 (January-July 1938): 14–62, 146–91, 261–313.

————. "The Government and the Navaho," *New Mexico Historical Review,* 16 (July 1941): 275–312 and vol. 18 (January 1943): 17–51.

Sanchez, Jane C. "Agitated, Personal, and Unsound. . . ," *New Mexico Historical Review,* 41 (July 1966): 217–30.

Schreier, Konrad F., Jr. "The California Column in the Civil War, Hazen's Civil War Diary," *The Journal of San Diego History,* 22 (Spring 1976): 31–48.

Sonnichsen, C. L. "Major McMullen's Invasion of Mexico," *Password,* 2 (May 1957): 38–43.

Spring, John A. "A March to Arizona from California in 1866," *Arizoniana,* 3 (Fall 1962): 1–6.

Stoes, K. D. "The Land of Shalam," *New Mexico Historical Review,* 33 (January-April 1958): 1–23, 103–27.

————. "Mutiny in Old Mesilla," *New Mexico Magazine,* 28 (February 1950): 16, 41–42.

Tittmann, Edward D. "The Exploitation of Treason," *New Mexico Historical Review,* 4 (April 1929): 128–45.

Waldrip, William I. "New Mexico During the Civil War," *New Mexico Historical Review,* 28 (July-October 1953): 163–82, 251–90.

Wallace, William S. "Stagecoaching in Territorial New Mexico," *New Mexico Historical Review,* 32 (April 1957): 204–11.

Walker, Henry P., ed. "Soldier in the California Column: The Diary of John W. Teal," *Arizona and the West,* 13 (Spring 1971): 33–82.

Wallace, Andrew. "Duty in the District of New Mexico: A Military Memoir," *New Mexico Historical Review,* 50 (July 1975): 231–62.

Wehrman, Georgia. "Harshaw: Mining Camp of the Patagonias," *Journal of Arizona History,* 6 (Spring 1965): 21–36.

Westphall, Victor. "Albuquerque in the 1870s," *New Mexico Historical Review,* 23 (October 1948): 253–68.

Wise, Clyde, Jr. "The Effects of the Railroads Upon El Paso," *Password,* 5 (July 1960): 91–100.

Index